Mastering Java

Mastering™ Java™

Laurence Vanhelsuwé

Ivan Phillips

Goang-Tay Hsu

Krishna Sankar

Eric Ries

Tim Rohaly

John Zukowski

SYBEX

San Francisco · Paris · Düsseldorf · Soest

Associate Publisher: Amy Romanoff
Acquisitions Manager: Kristine Plachy
Developmental Editor: Suzanne Rotondo
Editor: Bonnie Bills
Project Editor: Kim Wimpsett
Technical Editor: John Zukowski
Book Designer: Cătălin Dulfu
Graphic Designer/Illustrator: Patrick Dintino
Electronic Publishing Specialist: Deborah A. Bevilacqua
Production Coordinator: Alexa Riggs
Indexer: Ted Laux
Acquisitions Beta Coordinator: Jane Dalisay
CD-ROM Designer: Dale Wright
Cover Designer: Design Site
Cover Photographer: Mark Johann
Photo Art Direction: Ingalls + Associates

Screen reproductions produced with Collage Complete.

Collage Complete is a trademark of Inner Media Inc.

SYBEX is a registered trademark of SYBEX Inc.
Mastering is a trademark of SYBEX Inc.

TRADEMARKS: SYBEX has attempted throughout this book to distinguish proprietary trademarks from descriptive terms by following the capitalization style used by the manufacturer.

Netscape Communications, the Netscape Communications logo, Netscape, and Netscape Navigator are trademarks of Netscape Communications Corporation.

Every effort has been made to supply complete and accurate information. However, SYBEX assumes no responsibility for its use, nor for any infringement of the intellectual property rights of third parties which would result from such use.

Library of Congress Card Number: 96-69916
ISBN: 0-7821-1935-2

Manufactured in the United States of America

10 9 8 7 6 5 4 3 2 1

Software Support

The supplemental software and any offers associated with it may be supported by the specific Owners of that material but it is not supported by Sybex. Information regarding any available support may be obtained from the Owner using the information provided in the appropriate read.me files or listed elsewhere on the media.

Should the manufacturers or other Owners cease to offer support or decline to honor any offer, Sybex bears no responsibility. This notice concerning support for the software is provided for your information only. Sybex is not the agent or principal of the Owners, and Sybex is in no way responsible for providing any support for the Software, nor is it liable or responsible for any support provided, or not provided, by the Owners.

Warranty

Sybex warrants the enclosed CD to be free of physical defects for a period of ninety (90) days after purchase. If you discover a defect in the CD during this warranty period, you can obtain a replacement CD at no charge by sending the defective CD, postage prepaid, with proof of purchase to:
Sybex Inc.
Customer Service Department
1151 Marina Village Parkway
Alameda, CA 94501
(800) 227-2346
Fax: (510) 523-2373
After the 90-day period, you can obtain a replacement disk by sending us the defective CD, proof of purchase, and a check or money order for $10, payable to Sybex.

Disclaimer

Sybex makes no warranty or representation, either express or implied, with respect to this medium or its contents, its quality, performance, merchantability, or fitness for a particular purpose. In no event will Sybex, its distributors, or dealers be liable for direct, indirect, special, incidental, or consequential damages arising out of the use of or inability to use the medium or its contents even if advised of the possibility of such damage. The exclusion of implied warranties is not permitted by some states. Therefore, the above exclusion may not apply to you. This warranty provides you with specific legal rights; there may be other rights that you may have that vary from state to state.

Copy Protection

None of the files on the CD is copy-protected. However, in all cases, reselling or redistributing these files, except as specifically provided for by the copyright owners, is prohibited.

THE AUTHORS

Laurence Vanhelsuwé (`lva@telework.demon.co.uk`) is an independent software engineer. He is the typical self-taught wiz kid who, after dropping out of higher education, started his professional career writing arcade games. Soon after, he worked on such diverse technologies as X.25 WAN routers, Virtual Reality flight simulation, PostScript, and real-time digitized video-based traffic analysis. Laurence thinks Java will revolutionize computer science by leveling the computing landscape into one pan-Java playing field.

Ivan Phillips, Ph.D., is president of Pendragon Software Corporation, a software development and consulting firm specializing in Java programming and PDA applications. He is the author of the CaffeineMark applet, the industry standard Java benchmark.

Goang-Tay Hsu is a graduate of both Ohio State University and Carnegie Mellon University. He is now with Yahoo! Inc. Before that, he worked for Enterprise Integration Technologies Inc., Knight-Ridder Information Inc. (formerly Dialog), and Lexical Technologies Inc. His areas of interest include information retrieval, WWW service, user interface design, internationalization, and Java.

Krishna Sankar is the cofounder and president of US Systems & Services Inc., a San Francisco Java technology company. He has experience in designing and developing various systems ranging from real-time process control applications to client/server and groupware systems for companies like the U.S. Air Force and Navy, Hewlett Packard, AT&T, GM, Ford, Testek, Qantas Airways, and TRW. Currently you will find him evangelizing the "information re-engineering through components based on Java servlets and applets" paradigm. Occasionally you will also see him searching in vain for venture capitalists to expand his software company.

Eric Ries just graduated from San Diego High School and is on his way to Yale University. Currently he is employed as a Java developer by Pacific Communications Sciences Inc., where he enjoys using buzz words like *Intranet*. Eric writes in what spare time he has left after watching Star Trek and reading Ayn Rand.

Tim Rohaly, Ph.D., is an instructor of MageLang Institute's Java for C++ Programmers and a co-author of more than 70 peer-reviewed papers, with 15 years of experience developing large software projects in C and C++. He is a founder of ORC Incorporated, a company focused on research in visual computing. He is currently working on applying Java as a scripting language for distributed virtual reality.

John Zukowski (`j.zukowski@ieee.org`) is having fun with Java as he writes/edits books, speaks at conferences, and teaches Java around the country, all the while trying to find a real job that provides the same freedoms. In November 1995, John founded the Mid-Atlantic Java User Group (MAJUG) (+), which he coordinated until his move out of the DC area. Before Java, John was a C/X-Windows/Database/Network programmer for a Maryland-based consulting firm. He has a master's degree in computer science from Johns Hopkins University, with undergraduate degrees in math and computer science from Northeastern University. He is the author of his own Java book (*Java AWT Class Reference*) from O'Reilly.

ACKNOWLEDGMENTS

The reason there are no names on the front cover of *Mastering Java* is that listing every team member who worked on this book would obscure most of the cover artwork! It took a large group of people—working overtime and then some—to transform a mixed bag of material into a cohesive, in-depth exploration of Java technology.

In the frontline trenches, of course, were the authors:

Introduction: John Zukowski

Chapters 1–4 and Appendix A: Ivan Phillips

Chapters 5–8: Goang-Tay Hsu

Chapters 9–16: Laurence Vanhelsuwé, with help from Tim Rohaly

Chapters 17, 18, and 20: Krishna Sankar

Chapters 19 and 21: Eric Ries

At Sybex, many people processed the authors' less-than-perfect raw manuscript. Foremost were our Editors, Suzanne Rotondo, Bonnie Bills, Kim Wimpsett, and our technical editor, John Zukowski. And let's not forget Sybex's Patrick Dintino, who transformed Stone Age sketches into the quality illustrations and diagrams you see in the book; Electronic Publishing Specialist Debi Bevilacqua, who meticulously laid out every page of this big book; Production Coordinator Alexa Riggs, who worked to ensure these pages be error-free; and Associate Publisher Amy Romanoff and CD-ROM Producer Dale Wright, who created the high-quality, user-friendly CD that accompanies this book. Thanks also go to *Java Developers Journal* Editor-in-Chief Andrew Zolli for writing the foreword to this book.

Last but not least, we should acknowledge that without the Internet itself (the cauldron from which Java emerged glowing and hot), this book would have been much harder to produce. The authors of this book are scattered geographically over two continents. I, for example, live in a rather remote region of Scotland where transportation and communication means are not highly developed. But thanks to the Internet, the lines of communication among the team members were kept open. E-mail, World Wide Web, and IRC technologies were all exploited to meet the communication and organizational needs such a project requires.

While fascinating computer technology is both the raison d'être for and a key catalyst in creating the book you are holding, it is hoped that you—the reader and software developer—will use the knowledge presented herein to improve our world, and not just to make it smaller, faster, or cheaper.

—Laurence Vanhelsuwé

CONTENTS AT A GLANCE

TABLE OF CONTENTS

10 AWT: GUI Layout Management in Applets and Applications   317

11 AWT GUI Components   373

16 Network Programming   673

PART III Advanced Topics   719

17 Native Methods   721

Appendices

FOREWORD

```
import java.awt.Graphics;
public class HelloWorld extends java.applet.Applet {
        public void init() {
            resize(150,25);
        }
        public void paint(Graphics g) {
            g.drawString("Hello world!", 50, 25);
        }
    }
```

With these few lines of code, many programmers—experienced and novice alike—have begun their adventure with Java. In a flurry of well-deserved attention, Java has brought life to the Web, whipped the public and professional press into a frenzy, and is on the verge of challenging our assumptions of what networked computing is all about.

Paradoxically, in these few lines of code also lies great difficulty for the serious Java student, whether in school or in a professional context. For, while Java "resources" abound both on the Internet and in print, the carefully reasoned teaching tool, the concise and complete reference work, remains frustratingly elusive. What is available often contains material mechanically recycled from another medium.

This text, however, has taken a more considered, broader, and longer view of what Java represents, how it works, and what developers will need most in the future. As we look ahead to changes and developments in the language, those needs will almost certainly be as varied, as complex, and as extensive as the purposes to which Java will be put.

For example, the developers of Java at SunSoft and JavaSoft, along with an unprecedented array of industry leaders (from software and OS developers like Microsoft and Apple, to hardware vendors like

Fujitsu and Mitsubishi), have all announced plans to bring Java into every part of the "computer experience," while simultaneously extending that experience in profound new ways.

While some developers are currently hard at work on libraries of secure financial applets that communicate with your bank, others toil away on domestic, Java-based devices that help control the inventory of your refrigerator and save energy by turning off the lights when no one is home. Still others work to bring Java directly into the core of more traditional operating systems, heralding a new era in software distribution and network usage.

To understand this hotbed of developer activity, one must return again to the themes of this book: Java's scalability, portability, multi-threadedness, security, object orientation, and memory management. These are all elements in Java's widely discussed success, and as such, no serious Java developer can do work without a clear understanding of these core features of the language. (Incidentally, developers rarely get to see so clear a correlation between aspects of a computer language and its large impact: Java stands as an object lesson in the ripple-effects of good language design.)

While the features mentioned above make Java a natural fit for network-centric computing, they do not entirely explain Java's success, which has as much to do with timing as it does with elegant code. Java arrives at the birth of a new communications medium, with a public users community driving the demand for new forms of interactivity, entertainment, and commerce on the Internet. Java applets are quickly becoming a necessary part of every Web-designer's palette, and more and more clients are coming to expect them from interactive media firms.

Accordingly, this text spends time explaining the process of creating Java-based animation and multimedia in great detail, both at the simple (how to create basic animation) and advanced (how to synchronize multimedia threads) levels.

But if multimedia Web pages are the immediate cause of Java's success, they will not be what sustains it. Rather, it is Java's potential as a serious applications development framework (in both a stand-alone and networked context) that excites the professional development community. Highly robust, cross-platform software solutions are faster and cheaper to develop, simpler to maintain, and easier to deploy and manage than their platform-specific counterparts. With a unified underlying structure, these solutions become much easier to link into product suites, with a high degree of code reuse and extensibility, which satisfies users and developers alike.

When a network-centric view is added to this mixture, entirely new vistas open up in the computer experience: Imagine opening your word processor by pointing at it on the Internet, or being given the freedom to pick your own graphical user interface without sacrificing the availability of your favorite applications. These things (and much more) will be done with Java in the coming months—but not without a whole host of new extensions and APIs, which are only now just emerging from the draft stages. This text is designed to give you an overview, and, when possible, a working knowledge of these latest developments, which involve everything from Java database connectivity to online finance (see Chapters 20 and 21).

Finally, this text recognizes that no development process takes place in a vacuum. While the number has increased sharply, the quality of development tools has varied greatly as more and more professional vendors have begun to back Java in full force. This text cuts through much of the hype with no-nonsense reviews and tips on using the most common and cutting-edge Java development tools and IDEs. Additionally, throughout the text are numerous tips for building large-scale Java projects, covering everything from naming class libraries to hints on building intelligent object models. The authors have taken every care to include information that is valuable and salient for both the inexperienced and experienced developer.

The effort to provide a range of useful resources extends to the fully featured CD-ROM that is included with this book. On it, you will find tremendous resources, including relevant examples, source code, the latest and most stable versions of the Java Developers Kit, and a host of the most powerful authoring and development tools around. Using these tools will help students of Java at every level create libraries of code that are elegantly formatted, clear, properly segmented and documented, and highly reusable—in a nutshell, all of the support elements that go into successful programming projects. What's more, by including a wide variety of such tools, the authors of this book allow students to try out the ones that best meet their own particular learning and coding styles before making the step of purchasing commercially supported versions.

I know that you will find this text an invaluable resource in your adventures with Java—to consult when problems arise, to study as you acquire new skills, and to encourage you to learn more about this fascinating new language. Armed with this text, your imagination, and a determined will, the possibilities are endless.

—Andrew Zolli
Editor-in-Chief
Java Developers Journal

INTRODUCTION

Welcome to *Mastering Java*, a book that provides comprehensive coverage of the Java programming language. This book takes you through introductory, intermediate, and advanced topics to lead you on your way to becoming a proficient Java programmer.

A Road Map

Is this book for you? Although this book was designed with a logical sequence in mind, most readers will not pick it up and read it cover to cover. Depending upon your particular background, the following should help you figure out how to make this book suit your individual needs.

For Non-C/C++ Programmers

If you are new to Java and the C/C++ style of programming, you will pretty much need to go through the whole book. Some concepts will be similar to those of other languages, but in order to get a grasp on how Java does things, you will need to read through the entire book. To fully grasp the concepts presented, you should work each of the examples yourself. You might want to take a break of a few hours or days between sections to make sure the previous material sinks in.

For C/C++ Programmers

Due to the similarities between C/C++ and Java, C/C++ programmers can probably breeze through several chapters of this book. C programmers can skim through most of Chapters 4 and 6, while the

C++ programmer can additionally skim Chapter 3, the sections in Chapter 5 on classes, and Chapter 7 if you have dealt with exception handling. While these chapters are worth reviewing, they do not require the scrutiny that the completely new material in the remainder of the book requires.

For Java Programmers

If you have played with Java on your own and decided it was time to get a book to help you out, most of Part One will probably be review. Scan through it to see if there is anything you might have missed in your prior travels, paying special attention to Chapters 7 and 8, which cover exception handling and multithreading, respectively.

For Everyone

Once you have your bearings, use the table of contents to find the areas that interest you most in Parts Two and Three. Chapters 10, 11, and 12 go together somewhat—all deal with building and using Java forms—although some people might find reading Chapter 11 before Chapter 10 more natural. If you are really interested in Network Programming (Chapter 16), you need to have a grasp of I/O first (Chapter 15), since it builds upon input and output streams. The final chapters covering advanced topics can be read in almost any order.

The examples given in each chapter help support the concepts explained, and reviewing the code provides a better understanding of the topic. All the source code is on the enclosed CD, so you do not have to type the examples out.

Features and Structure of This Book

The goal of this book is simple: to make you productive with Java as quickly as possible. The following sections highlight the book's organization to help you find what you need in this information-packed guide to Java.

Table of Contents, Index

Like any useful book, this one has a table of contents in the front and an extensive index in the back to help you locate the information you need.

Part One: Foundations of Java

The first part of the book introduces you to Java—the history, the language, and the programming concepts. Chapter 1 starts off with a lesson on what Java is and where Java came from. Chapter 2 gets you started using the Java development environment. In Chapter 3, you are taught object-oriented programming basics. In Chapter 4, you learn about the Java language grammar. In Chapter 5, you start to build up your understanding of Java by learning about classes, interfaces, and packages. Chapter 6 explains how Java deals with arrays and flow-control statements. In Chapter 7, you learn about Java's exception-handling mechanisms. Finally, in Chapter 8, you learn how to create multithreaded programs in Java.

Part Two: Applying Standard Java Classes

The next part digs into the meat of the Java libraries (or packages, in Java-speak). Chapter 9 provides a brief overview of the different Java packages and their parts. Chapter 10 starts to dig into the windowing package to teach you how to position objects on the screen. In Chapter 11, you learn about the different objects a user interacts with. In Chapter 12 you learn to deal with those interactions, through events. Chapter 13 provides an overview of the graphics and animation capabilities of Java. In Chapter 14, techniques from the previous four chapters are put together to teach you advanced programming techniques. Chapter 15 introduces you to I/O programming through Java streams. Finally, Chapter 16 teaches you how to make your programs Internet savvy.

Part Three: Advanced Topics

The third part is designed for those who want to learn more about Java—those interested in taking their Java programs to the next level, and interested in looking under the covers to see how Java works from the inside. In Chapter 17, you learn how to hook C code into your Java programs to provide missing functionality, like interfacing to your local communication ports. Chapter 18 provides the behind-the-scenes details of the Java Virtual Machine. Chapter 19 provides an overview of the more popular third-party Java Tools. Chapter 20 introduces you to JDBC for access to SQL databases. Finally, Chapter 21 takes a look into the proverbial crystal ball to see what the future holds for Java. By the time you read this, some of the Java futures presented in Chapter 21 could be real.

Appendices

You will also find three appendices. Appendix A contains a list of the Java-enabled browsers. Although Netscape Navigator and Internet Explorer are popular Java-enabled browsers, they are not the only ones. Appendix B includes instructions on how to install the enclosed CD. Appendix C is a glossary that contains definitions of many Java-related terms found in this book.

What's on the CD?

The CD contains all the source code from the examples in the book, along with the appropriate HTML applet loaders. In addition, numerous third-party tools and class libraries are provided for many hours of enjoyment.

Conventions

This book uses various conventions to help you find the information you need quickly. Tips, Notes, and Warnings, shown here, are placed throughout the book to help you locate important highlights quickly.

TIP This is a tip. Tips contain information to help clarify the text and make you more productive with Java faster.

WARNING This is a note. Notes contain information that needs to be emphasized.

> **NOTE** This is a warning. Warnings contain information that flags potential trouble spots.

In addition, the book takes advantage of various font styles. **Bold font** in text indicates something that the user types (in a text field, for instance). A `monospaced program font` is used for program code, URLs, and file and directory names; `italic program font` is used for general forms the programmer will replace with actual code. Continuation marks (➡) are used where the program lines are broken.

Technical Support

When you need help, there are several places where you can look for more information.

FAQs

There is a plethora of Java-related Frequently Asked Questions lists (FAQs) available online. One of the most useful is maintained by Sun at `http://java.sun.com/sfaq/index.html`. It answers numerous security-related Java questions. Another two FAQs are at `http://kendaco.telebyte.com/~thekeep/javafaq.html` and `http://sunsite.unc.edu/javafaq/javafaq.html`. These tend to answer questions for people new to Java development. Some of the other FAQs are listed in the index at `http://www-net.com/java/faq/`.

Product Support

Depending upon the tools you are using, it may be prudent to go through the technical support channels available for a particular product. This could involve toll-free or 1-900 support (live or prerecorded), the World Wide Web, or online newsgroups, among other options. Check the documentation provided with the tool or Web-based source you are using to see what support is available. If you are using the Java Developers Kit from Sun, the first place to look is the bug list at `http://java.sun.com/java.sun.com/products/JDK/1.0.2/KnownBugs.html` to see if the problem you have encountered is a product bug. Symantec Café users should start at `http://cafe.symantec.com`. Most other products maintain similar sites.

Newsgroups

When the Java hype was just beginning, there were no newsgroups, and Sun was running a handful of mailing lists to keep everyone informed and provide a question-and-answer medium. Their mail server quickly got bogged down due to the popularity (and cross-mailing list postings), and the newsgroup `comp.lang.java` was born (along with `alt.www.hotjava`). Over time, `comp.lang.java` became so popular (thousands of messages per week) that the signal-to-noise ratio nearly made the group useless. After much debate, conflict, and a vote, the single group split into eight, `comp.lang.java.advocacy`, `comp.lang.java.announce` (moderated), `comp.lang.java.api`, `comp.lang.java.misc`, `comp.lang.java.programmer`, `comp.lang.java.security`, `comp.lang.java.setup`, and `comp.lang.java.tech`. Somewhere in one of those groups is either the answer to your unasked question or someone who can answer it. If the question has already been asked and answered, you can search the archives at either Digital Espresso (a digest version of the news groups), `http://www.io.org/~mentor/DigitalEspresso.html`, or DejaNews (a Usenet search utility) `http://dejanews.com`. For those who are inclined not to read the news, MageLang maintains a moderated mailing list (`http://www.MageLang.com/mailing_list.html`) that is monitored by some of the early development team.

User Groups

Another good source of information is area user groups. Focus tends to vary widely, but networking is almost always key. And there is usually someone in the group who can answer your question. For a list of area user groups look at JavaSoft's list at `http://java.sun.com/Mail/usrgrp.html` or the Java Special Interest Group (of the Sun User Group) list at `http://www.sug.org/java-groups.html` to find a group in your area. Most groups maintain a mailing list of some sort to send technical questions.

Books and Periodicals

Sybex offers many books at all levels of expertise. For more advanced questions, the forthcoming *Java Developer's Handbook* from Sybex (1997) may hold the key. Or if you encounter a problem that is not Java related, another Sybex offering may provide the answer. For the latest catalog, write to:

Sybex Inc.
1151 Marina Village Parkway
Alameda, CA 94501
Tel: (800) 227-2346
Fax: (510) 523-2373

Or visit their Web page at `http://www.sybex.com`, where you will find a searchable catalog and updates to this book.

On the Java side, there are also a handful of magazines: *JavaWorld* is an online publication at `http://www.javaworld.com`. *Java Report* is a print publication with information available from `http://www.sigs.com/java/authorgl.html`. Also, *Java Developers Journal* is a combined print-online publication at `http://www.JavaDevelopersJournal.com/java/`. There are others, and more are popping up all the time from the different magazine houses.

PART 1

Foundations
of JAVA

CHAPTER

ONE

1

Introducing Java

- Java and Its History

- Java and the World Wide Web

- The Java Architecture

- Using Java with Other Tools

What Is Java?

Java is a technology that makes it easy to build *distributed applications*, which are programs executed by multiple computers across a network. The state of the art in network programming, Java promises to expand the Internet's role from an arena for communications to a network on which full-fledged applications can be run. Its breakthrough technology will allow businesses to deploy full-scale transaction services and real-time, interactive information content on the Internet. Java also simplifies the construction of *software agents*, programs that move across a network and perform functions on remote computers on behalf of the user. In the near future, users may be able to send software agents from their PCs out onto the Internet to locate specific information or make time-critical transactions anywhere in the world.

Before Java, the Internet was primarily used for information-sharing. Though the Internet was created in the 1960s, it only started to realize its business potential in the 1990s, thanks to the World Wide Web. The Web is a technology that treats Internet resources as linked documents, and it has revolutionized the way we access information. The Web has enabled Internet users to access Internet services without learning cryptic commands, and has made it easy for businesses to create online corporate images, provide product information, and even sell merchandise directly through PCs. Java technology will take this a step further by making it possible to serve fully interactive applications via the Web. The reasons so much attention has been paid to Java are summarized in the following list of what Java allows the user to do:

- Write robust and reliable programs

- Build an application on almost any platform, and run that application on any other supported platform without recompiling your code

- Distribute your applications over a network in a secure fashion

In particular, Java programs can be embedded into Web documents, turning static pages into applications that run on the user's computer. No longer is online documentation limited to articles, like a printed book. With Java, the documentation can include simulations, working models, and even specialized tools. This means that Java has the potential to *change the function of the Internet*, much as the Web has changed the way we access the Internet. In other words, not only will the network provide us with information, it will also serve as our operating system.

In this chapter, you will learn about the history and evolution of Java, see how Java is enhancing the Web, and begin to understand how Java programming language features enable us to build robust Internet applications.

A Brief History of Java

In 1990, Sun Microsystems began a project called *Green* to develop software for use in consumer electronics. Sun is best known for its popular UNIX workstations, but has also engineered several popular software packages, including the Solaris operating system and the Network File System (NFS). James Gosling, a veteran of classic network software design, was assigned to the new project.

Gosling began writing software with C++ to embed into such things as toasters, VCRs, and Personal Digital Assistants (PDAs). The embedded software is used to make appliances more intelligent, typically by adding digital displays or by using artificial intelligence to better control the mechanisms. However, it soon became apparent to him that C++ was the wrong tool for the job. C++ is flexible enough to control embedded systems, but it is susceptible to bugs that can crash the system. In particular, C++ uses direct references to system resources and requires the programmer to keep track of how these resources are managed, which is a significant burden on programmers. This burden of resource management is a barrier to writing reliable, portable software, and was a serious problem for consumer electronics. After all, computer users have come to expect their software to have some bugs, but no one expects their toaster to crash.

Gosling's solution to this problem was a new language called Oak. Oak preserved the familiar syntax of C++, but omitted the potentially dangerous features like explicit resource references, and pointer arithmetic and operator overloading. Oak incorporated memory management directly into the language, freeing the programmer to concentrate on the tasks to be performed by the program. In order to be successful as an embedded systems programming language, Oak needed to be able to respond to real-world events within micro-seconds. It also needed to be portable—that is, it had to be able to run on a number of different microprocessor chips and environments. This hardware independence would allow a toaster manufacturer to change the chip used to run the toaster without changing the soft-ware. The manufacturer could also use some of the same code that runs the toaster to run, say, in a toaster oven. This would cut down on development and hardware costs, as well as increase reliability.

As Oak matured, the World Wide Web was in a period of dramatic growth, and the development team at Sun realized that Oak was per-fectly suited to Internet programming. In 1994, they completed work on a product known as WebRunner, an early Web viewer written in Oak. WebRunner was later renamed HotJava, and it demonstrated the power of Oak as an Internet development tool. HotJava is well-known in the industry, and the HotJava project is still active, with new versions under development.

Finally, in 1995, Oak was renamed Java (for marketing purposes) and announced at SunWorld 95. Since then, Java's rise in popularity has been meteoric. Even before the first release of the Java compiler in January of 1996, Java was considered an industry standard for Internet development.

In the first six months of 1996, a number of leading software and hardware companies licensed Java technology from Sun, including Adobe, Asymetrix, Borland, IBM, Macromedia, Metrowerks, Microsoft, Novell, Oracle, Spyglass, and Symantec. These, and other Java licensees, will be incorporating Java into their desktop products, operating systems, and development tools.

There are also several integrated development environments now available for Java developers from Sun, Symantec, Metrowerks, Borland, and Natural Intelligence. At the time of this writing, Java implementations are still a little rough around the edges. Many Java-related products are in alpha and beta phases, and Java's security features are still being validated. Yet the momentum of this technology is so great that few doubt Java's ability to overcome these initial hurdles and utterly transform the computer industry as we know it.

NOTE Perhaps the most common question about Java's history is about the origin of the name *Java*. The answer is that the name *Java* survived the trademark search.

Java and the Web

Today, the most likely place you'll find Java is on the World Wide Web. The Web acts as a convenient transport mechanism for Java programs, and the Web's ubiquity has popularized Java as an Internet development tool.

After a brief introduction to the World Wide Web, you will be presented with a simplified explanation of how Java dynamically extends the capability of Web media.

An Introduction to the World Wide Web

This primer will quickly introduce you to the World Wide Web. If you are already familiar with the Web, you may want to skip this introduction and go on to the next section.

The World Wide Web is a huge collection of interconnected *hypertext* documents on the Internet. A hypertext document is a document which contains *hot links* to other documents. Hypertext links are usually visible as highlighted words in the text, but they can also be graphics, and are frequently used for online help systems. Links are activated by clicking on them with a mouse.

There are many thousands of hypertext authors on the Internet, each of them free to connect their documents to anyone else's. It follows then that the Web has no beginning and no end, though groups of associated pages are usually structured hierarchically. Since organization of the Web is not enforced, finding your way around can be difficult. Thankfully Web search engines, such as Yahoo, Lycos, and Infoseek, have alleviated much of the navigation problem by allowing users to search by keyword, name, or subject. The lack of regulation has gone a long way toward broadening the user base and enriching the content. As things stand, anyone who learns to write hypertext documents can make information available over the Internet.

The World Wide Web is based on two standards: the *HTTP* protocol and the *HTML* language. HTTP stands for HyperText Transfer Protocol, and it describes the way that hypertext documents are fetched over the Internet. HTML is the abbreviation for HyperText Markup Language, and it specifies the layout and linking commands present in the hypertext documents themselves.

TIP

For the purposes of this book, a *protocol* is a procedure followed by all sides of an Internet conversation in order to facilitate the transfer of information. The most popular application protocols on the Internet are HTTP (hypertext transfer protocol), FTP (file transfer protocol), and SMTP (simple mail transfer protocol). Each protocol defines commands sent to the server from a program requesting services and the way the server may respond.

Resources on the Web are specified with a *Uniform Resource Locator* (URL). A URL specifies the protocol used to fetch a document as well as its location. For example, the URL for the Sybex home page for the book *Internet for Kids* is `http://www.sybex.com:80/i4kids/index.html`. The URL can be broken into five pieces, as shown in Figure 1.1:

FIGURE 1.1:

A typical URL, broken down into its components

The `http:` prefix indicates that the document should be fetched via HTTP. The `//www.sybex.com` specifies the machine that is running the Web server. The `:80` refers to the port number—each protocol server on a machine is typically assigned its own port number. The default port number for HTTP is 80, and Web server administrators rarely change it. For this reason, the port number is rarely specified in HTTP URLs. The file itself is called `index.html`, and it is located in the directory `/i4kids`. Actually, `index.html` is the default document name; that is, we could specify the same document by using the URL `http://www.sybex.com:80/i4kids` or by omitting the default port number, `http://www.sybex.com/i4kids`. Java also uses URLs to specify the locations of network resources.

The HTTP protocol is implemented in software on the server and on the user's machine (also known as the client machine, or simply the client). The server software is called a Web server or HTTP server, and the client software is called a Web browser. To open an HTML document, the Web browser sends an HTTP command to the server requesting the document by its URL. The Web server responds by sending the HTML document to the client. The client then displays the document on the user's screen. If the HTML document contains graphics, the Web browser makes additional requests for the graphics files to be sent, and then displays the graphics with the text. Figure 1.2 illustrates this process.

FIGURE 1.2:

How Web documents are fetched with HTTP

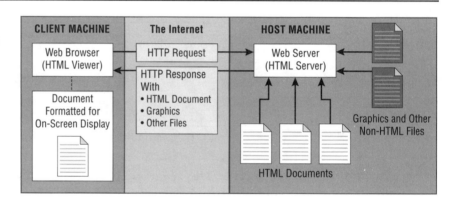

Thus, Web documents are essentially static objects. When the HTML document reaches the browser, it is in its final form.

> **NOTE**
>
> There are protocol extensions that allow an HTML document to be refreshed after reaching the client. These extensions are called *server-push* and *client-pull*, and are written into documents or scripts on the server. These enhancements force the HTML document that was downloaded from the server to be refreshed at regular intervals.

Some servers generate HTML upon request using *Common Gateway Interface* (CGI) programs. With the ability of CGI and HTML to create fill-in-the-blank forms, you can create form-based applications on the Web. Perhaps the most notable application like this was created by Federal Express for package tracking (see Figure 1.3). Users can track their FedEx packages over the Internet at `http://www.fedex.com/track_it.html`.

FIGURE 1.3:

The FedEx tracking form. The user fills in their tracking number, selects a destination, and then clicks a button to send the data to the server. This type of form is usually handled by CGI scripts on the server.

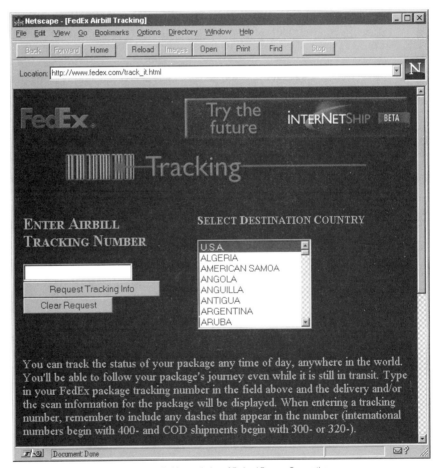

Screen capture and FedEx trademarks used with permission of Federal Express Corporation.

Note that CGI is not suited to real-time display of information. Although CGI programs generate HTML upon request, the document returned to the browser is still a static document.

While CGI programs are very widespread and have generally been successful, they are prone to performance problems. When the Web server runs a CGI program to create an HTML document on the fly, it usually creates a new operating system process for that program on the Web server machine. Creating new processes is time-consuming and inefficient. Nonetheless, CGI is used on the Internet simply because it is compatible with almost every Web browser.

Extending Web Browser Capability

Much of the power of the World Wide Web stems from its platform independence. That is, it presents information in a way that can be viewed on almost every type of machine and operating system. It doesn't matter whether you use a PC, Macintosh, or UNIX workstation—the Web is architecture-neutral, which is why so many people have access to it.

Unfortunately, being so widely accepted also has its drawbacks. It is very difficult to extend the Web protocols without leaving many Web users behind. For instance, Web content developers are constantly trying to extend the capability of the Web by integrating new types of media, like 3-D worlds and animation, but these developers then face the prospect of excluding people without those viewing capabilities, which limits their audience.

The existing Web standards permit seamless integration of graphics with text. Other forms of media—such as sound, video, and animation—are accessible via the Web, but they are not smoothly connected with normal Web content. For example, it is easy to create a link to a sound file in an HTML document; the Web browser will either play the sound or download it to a file when the user clicks on the link. However, there is no browser-independent way to create background music for a document, or give audio feedback when a button is pressed. This is just one of the many creative limitations that has frustrated Web developers over the last few years.

Until now, the solution to this extensibility problem has been to create a proprietary protocol, then try to sell the solution to as many users on as many platforms as possible. This is a hard sell, and has had limited success. As a result, Web pages tend to cater to the lowest common denominator; therefore, the content has not reached its full potential in many instances.

Java as a Universal Protocol

Java has begun to address the protocol problem by using Java *applets*. An applet is a Java program which appears embedded in a Web document, just as graphics would be. The Java applet runs when it is loaded by a Java-enabled Web browser like Netscape 2.0 or 3.0. The running applet then draws itself in the user's browser window according to the programmer's instructions. The applet can create its own network connections and use whatever protocol is required to get information from the server.

Let's say we want to create a stock market ticker applet for use in a Web page (a stock ticker is a horizontally scrolling summary of stock prices and stock price changes). The stock quotes have to be sent to the user's Web browser in real-time so that users can get up-to-the-minute information. Since a continuous stream of stock quotes is needed, HTTP is not a good protocol for this application (HTTP is really a kind of file transfer protocol, not a continuous data stream protocol). Therefore, we need to design a new protocol. Let's call it Simple Stock Quote Protocol (SSQP).

Imagine a conversation between the client and the server:

```
Client:   GET NASDAQ
Server:   OK
Server:   AAA 104 3/8 - 1 1/2 ICP 80 1/4 + 1/4 …
```

(Client displays data continuously as long as user requires.)

```
Client:   STOP
```

This conversation is the blueprint for the stock quote protocol. The server responds to the GET commands by acknowledging the request and then sending back a continuous stream of data. The STOP command terminates the conversation.

We can implement the SSQP server in whichever language is best for the job. This could be C, Java, or another nonportable language, because we know that it will run on our server machine. In Java, we can very easily write a stock ticker Java applet which implements the client side of the conversation and displays the returned data. When executed by the browser, the applet connects to the server using SSQP and displays a stock ticker with live data.

Thus, without any manual intervention from the user, a stock ticker can be made to appear in the browser window. Figure 1.4 shows a Web page using a Java applet to display the latest Major League baseball scores. You will notice that the applet integrates seamlessly with the rest of the page. The browser's functionality has been extended automatically and transparently. In this way, Java acts like a protocol for adding new protocols. It would be impractical for Web browser manufacturers to build in every new protocol that comes along. Instead, browsers can be equipped with Java and can learn new protocols on demand.

FIGURE 1.4:

The image in the center is a Java applet that displays up-to-the-minute sports scores. The underlined text is a hypertext link.

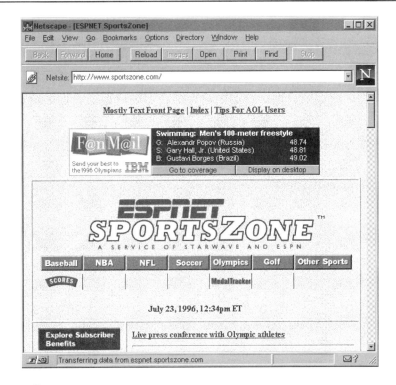

The Java Architecture

Java's strength derives from its unique architecture. The designers of Java needed a language that was, above all, simple for the programmer to use. Yet in order to create reliable network applications, Java needed to be able to run securely over a network, and work on a wide range of platforms. Java fulfills all of these goals and more. The next few sections describe how Java works and the features that make Java a powerful network application development tool.

How Java Works

As with many other programming languages, Java uses a compiler to convert human-readable source code into executable programs.

Traditional compilers produce code that can be executed by specific hardware; for example, a Windows 95 C++ compiler creates executable programs that work with Intel x86 compatible processors. In contrast, the Java compiler generates architecture-independent *bytecodes*. The bytecodes can only be executed by a Java *Virtual Machine* (VM), an idealized Java processor chip usually implemented in software rather than hardware.

NOTE The VM has also been implemented as a hardware chip by Sun Microsystems, and several other electronics companies have announced plans to manufacture Java processors. These processors are expected to have significant performance advantages over VMs written in software. They will also make it easier for Java to be embedded into consumer electronics products such as toasters and TV sets.

The compilation process is illustrated in Figure 1.5. Java bytecode files are called *class files* because they contain a single Java class. Classes will be described in detail in Chapter 3. For now, just think of a class as representing a group of related routines or an extended datatype. The vast majority of Java programs will be composed of more than one class file.

To execute Java bytecodes, the Virtual Machine uses a *class loader* to fetch the bytecodes from a disk or from the network. Each class file is fed to a *bytecode verifier* that ensures that the class is formatted correctly, and the class will not corrupt memory when it is executed. The

FIGURE 1.5:

Java compilers produce Java bytecodes, not traditional executable files.

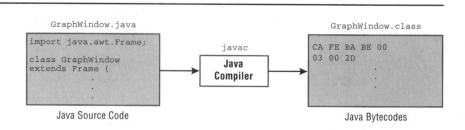

bytecode verification phase adds to the time it takes to load a class, but it actually allows the program to run faster because the class verification is performed only once, not continuously as the program runs.

The execution unit of the VM carries out the instructions specified in the bytecodes. The simplest execution unit is an *interpreter,* a program which reads the bytecodes, interprets their meaning, and then performs the associated function. Interpreters are generally much slower than native code compilers because they continuously need to look up the meaning of each bytecode during execution. Fortunately, there's an elegant alternative to interpreting code—it is called *Just-in-Time* (JIT) compilation (see Chapter 20 for more information on JIT compilers). The JIT compiler converts the bytecodes to native code instructions on the user's machine immediately before execution. Traditional native code compilers run on the developer's machine, are used by programmers, and produce nonportable executables. JIT compilers run on the user's machine and are transparent to the user; the resulting native code instructions do not need to be ported because they are already at their destination. Figure 1.6 illustrates the way JIT compilers work. In the pictured example, identical bytecodes are received by both a Macintosh and a Windows PC, and each client performs a local, JIT compilation.

Java-Enabled Browsers

A Java-enabled Web browser contains its own VM. Web documents that have embedded Java applets must specify the location of the main applet class file. The Web browser then starts up the VM and passes the location of the applet class file to the class loader. Each class file knows the names of any additional class files that it requires. These additional class files may come from the network or the client machine. This may require the class loader to make a number of additional class loading operations before the applet starts. Note that supplemental classes are only fetched if they are actually going to be used.

The JIT compiler in the client system improves performance by compiling bytecodes to platform-specific instructions just before execution. The resulting machine-level instructions are executed directly.

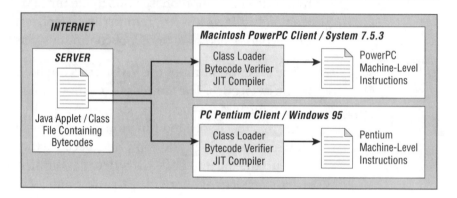

After loading the class file, execution begins, and the applet is asked to draw itself in the browser window. Figure 1.7 shows the Java Virtual Machine fetching classes.

FIGURE 1.7:

The Java Virtual Machine fetches classes from a disk or from the network, and then verifies that the bytecodes are safe to be executed.

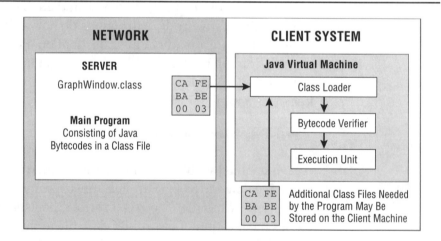

Java Features

In this section, we will look briefly at the seven major characteristics that make Java such a powerful development tool: security, the Core

API, open standards, distributed and dynamic, object-oriented, multithreaded, and memory management. Each of them warrant a separate discussion.

Security

Security is probably the number one problem facing Internet developers. Users are typically afraid of two things: that confidential information will be compromised, and that their computer systems are vulnerable to corruption or destruction by hackers. Java's built-in security addresses both of these concerns.

Java's security model has three primary components: the *class loader*, bytecode verifier, and the *SecurityManager*. You have already learned that the bytecode verifier ensures that the Java programs have been compiled correctly, that they will obey the VM's access restrictions, and that the bytecodes will not access 'private' data when they shouldn't. Without these defenses, the other security constraints within the VM could be bypassed, and there would be no limit to what the applet could do to the system.

The next layer of security is provided by the class loader. When the class loader retrieves classes from the network, it keeps classes from different servers separate from both each other and local classes. Through this separation, the class loader prevents a class that is loaded off the network from pretending to be one of the standard built-in classes, or from interfering with the operation of classes loaded from other servers.

The SecurityManager implements a security policy for the VM. The security policy determines which activities the VM is allowed to perform, and under what circumstances. A key example is file input/output (I/O); for example, saving or loading documents in disk files. Java has the capability to read and write files, but requests to perform such an I/O pass through the SecurityManager first. This allows the SecurityManager to determine if the Java program is trusted to access the disk files without doing malicious damage to the file system.

The SecurityManager is generally written to err on the side of caution. In the most popular Java-enabled browser, Netscape Navigator, the security policy does not even permit file access. However, the SecurityManager is itself written in Java (it is a Java class file), so that it can be overridden if required. Of course, there are safeguards to prevent hostile Java programs from writing their own security policy! These safeguards prevent alternate SecurityManagers from being added to the system while the Web browser is running.

On a private network, file access or arbitrary network access may be necessary to address business requirements. For example, when implementing a client/server database application on a private network, it may be necessary for a Java applet to establish connections with multiple servers. The standard SecurityManager prohibits this because it is a security risk on a public network. The application developers may therefore change the SecurityManager source code and recompile it into the Web browser for each PC on the network. This customizes the security policy for the private network. Custom SecurityManagers are more difficult to write if the private network has any gateways to public networks such as the Internet. Great care must be taken when overriding the SecurityManager, or hostile applets from the public network may take advantage of the relaxed internal security policy.

To summarize, Java's built-in security measures ensure that Java programs will operate within the rules of the VM, and prevent untrustworthy programs from accessing system resources that might contain proprietary information or jeopardize the integrity of the client.

The Core API

API stands for application programming interface. An API is a library of functions designed to be used by application developers to more rapidly construct software. Java's Core API provides a common set of functions on all platforms.

The API is divided into *packages*, which are groups of classes that perform related functions. One of these packages includes some core language functionality such as text handling and error processing; it is almost impossible to write a Java program without using this library. The other packages contain utilities, networking, I/O, graphical user interface tools, and interaction with Web browsers.

Open Standards

Today, Java VMs are available for more than a dozen different hardware-operating system combinations. The most exciting aspect of Java's cross-platform capability is that Java class files do not need to be compiled for each platform in advance. The same compiled Java program will work on the PC, Macintosh, and every other platform that runs a Java VM. You can write a Java application on your system and it should run on every supported platform.

Another key to having a successful cross-platform development tool is having a common core set of functions on every platform. The Core Java API is the same for all implementations of Java, and it is sophisticated enough that native code does not need to be written for desktop applications. Of course, the real world is slightly more complicated: Java is a new language, and most implementations of VM and API have minor problems conforming to the Java specifications, especially with respect to user interface. These problems will dissipate in the coming months. Nonetheless, it would be wise to check the latest bug reports before assuring your boss that your Java application will run perfectly on all of your company's computer systems.

In addition to common desktop operating systems, we can expect to see Java VMs implemented on chip for use in embedded systems. Sun has announced plans to manufacture three Java processors, known as picoJava, microJava, and UltraJava. The first of these processors should be available in mid-1996. LG Semicon, Mitsubishi, and Samsung have also signed letters of intent for the licensing of Java processor technology. Java is on its way toward fulfilling the original goals of the Green project, and will undoubtedly be showing up in household appliances at some point in the near future.

Distributed and Dynamic

In the Windows operating system, parts of programs can be placed into dynamic link libraries (DLLs) so they can be shared and loaded dynamically—that is, when the program is running. The operating system does the final stage of linking at execution time. Using shared DLLs saves memory and improves the modularity of the software.

Java takes dynamic libraries a step further. The VM class loader fetches class files from the network, as well as from the disk, making Java applications distributed as well as dynamic. These features allow a Java-enabled browser to adapt automatically to protocols available at a new Web site. It also means that a Java application need not fetch parts of the program that will not be used.

Java has the potential to change the software distribution model used by the industry. Instead of buying software on disk or CD-ROM, one could "rent" just the pieces (Java classes) of the applications we need directly over the Internet, much like "renting" online time. The software would be the latest version because it came directly from the manufacturer. However, today there are three major obstacles that make this scenario all but impossible: First, the time it takes to download a real-world application is prohibitive for most users. For downloaded software to compete with today's disk-based applications, users will likely need connections that are 100 times faster than today's standard 28.8kbps modems. Second, the standard security policy prevents file I/O that is required to save work on the local machine. Finally, there is no prevailing standard for making secure software rental payments. Without such a standard, it would be as if each software vendor had its own form of currency, requiring you to make a special arrangement with each vendor before renting the software. Though these problems are not insurmountable, it will be some time before the network infrastructure can support this kind of distribution model.

Object-Oriented

Object-oriented programming (OOP) is a way to write software that is reusable, extensible, and maintainable. Java is an object-oriented language; that is, it has facilities for object-oriented programming incorporated into the language. The Java Core API is actually a collection of prefabricated OOP components, known to object-oriented programmers as a *class library*. Class libraries give programmers a big head start when it comes to developing new projects. A detailed explanation of object-oriented technology will be presented in Chapter 3.

Multithreaded

A single-threaded application has one thread of execution running at all times, and such programs can only do one task at a time. If a single-threaded program needs to perform a task that will take several minutes—for example, downloading—its user interface will usually become unresponsive while the task is in progress.

A multithreaded application can have several threads of execution running independently and simultaneously. These threads may communicate and cooperate, and to the user will appear to be a single program. Multithreading is commonly used to perform the following functions:

Maintain user interface responsiveness   If your application needs to perform a time-consuming task, you can use multiple threads to prevent your user interface from becoming unresponsive while the task is in progress. If your program will be downloading information from the Internet (this is very likely), you can create a separate thread for the download routine. This will keep your user interface running at nearly full speed while your download is in progress.

Waiting for a wake-up call   The best way to have a routine wait for a specified time is to place the routine in a sleeping thread. The alternative—continuously watching the time of day clock—is very processor-intensive. For instance, if you wanted an applet to download new data from a server every sixty seconds, you could place the download routine in a thread that sleeps for a minute between transfers.

Multitasking   Multithreading allows you to run multiple instances of a process quite easily. The downloading routine just mentioned can be extended so that the program can transfer multiple files simultaneously and still keep the user interface well-behaved. All you have to do is create another thread for each file to download.

Multiuser applications   Multithreading is often used when building server applications. Server applications wait for requests to arrive, and then they establish conversations with the requester. It is much easier to write a routine that handles a single conversation and spawns multiple copies of that routine than it is to write a piece of code that handles multiple conversations at once.

Multiprocessing   Many operating systems support machines with multiple processors. Most of these systems are unable to break a single thread of execution into multiple pieces for execution on different processors. By breaking an application into different threads, it is possible to make the best utilization of processing power.

Every item in this list has applicability to Internet and embedded-systems applications. Java implements multithreading through a part of its class library, but Java also has language constructs to make programs thread-safe. A thread-safe program guarantees that the different threads will not accidentally harm one another. Java's `synchronized` keyword can be used to prevent two threads from entering the same critical block of code at the same time. This is vital because some program steps need to be made together as one atomic group.

Memory Management and Garbage Collection

Memory management is the bane of all C and C++ programs. During the course of a program's execution, memory will be required for temporary operations, such as sorting lists or displaying images. In C and C++, it is the programmer's responsibility to allocate the required memory, and free that memory after the task has been completed. If the memory allocations do not perfectly match memory deallocations, the program will either crash immediately, or consume system resources until exhausted. In either case, the result is abnormal termination of the program, often bringing down the operating system with it.

Java overcomes this problem by using *garbage collection*. Temporary memory is automatically reclaimed after it is no longer referenced by any active part of the program. This frees the developer from much of the housekeeping that would otherwise be required.

Historically, the problem with garbage collection has been performance. The garbage collector must scan memory for objects that can be eliminated, then sweep the removable objects from memory. Taking out the trash too often is inefficient, but checking too infrequently causes the system to pause while large amounts of garbage are collected. To improve performance, Java's garbage collector runs in its own low-priority thread, providing a good balance of efficiency and real-time responsiveness.

Memory management reinforces the security of the VM. In C and C++, the programmer can access any part of the system available to an application. This can be done by using *pointers*, which are variables that reference specific memory locations. Java does not use pointers in the strict sense of the word. Java's "pointers" are actually references to VM resources, and no arithmetic is permitted with such variables, which prevents programmers from accessing system resources outside the VM.

Using Java with Other Tools

Java is a unique development tool and is already a highly successful product. As an Internet development tool, Java joins several other Internet development tools vying for market acceptance. Recognizing that Java is here to stay, vendors are making their products interoperable with Java.

The following is a brief survey of Java-related Internet technologies.

Native Code

Native code refers to code which is native to a specific processor. On Windows 95, native code refers to code compatible with Intel x86 processors. Java can call native code quite easily, though such calls are not subject to the VM's security measures—this is why most Web browsers do not permit Java applets to make native calls.

Native code access means that Java can call upon millions of lines of existing code, and can be used as a development tool for stand-alone, platform-specific applications.

JavaScript

JavaScript is a subset of the Java language that can be coded directly in an HTML document. That is to say, the JavaScript source code is part of the HTML document itself. JavaScript is less powerful than Java, but it gives the programmer a little more control over the browser, and it is used primarily to create dialog boxes and animation on Web pages. JavaScript does have a limited ability to call Java applet routines and alter Java applet variables; however, Java cannot call JavaScript code or change JavaScript variables.

Netscape Plug-Ins

Netscape Communications has created a standard interface to its Navigator browser product line. Products adhering to the specification are called Netscape Plug-Ins. Netscape provides a Software Development Kit (SDK) so that third parties can implement plug-ins for new types of media, and it allows the new media to integrate seamlessly with the browser. Currently available Plug-Ins support a number of multimedia formats, as well as spreadsheets, AutoCAD drawings, and live news feeds.

Plug-Ins are written with native code—that is, they are platform-specific. The SDK itself changes only slightly from platform to platform, but the implementation details may be totally different between platforms. If you want to use a Plug-In, you will need to download it for your specific platform before being able to utilize the new media. The advantage of this approach is that after downloading a Plug-In to your hard disk, the new media will appear in your browser with no delay.

Netscape has announced an interface, the Java Runtime Interface, which would allow native code (including Plug-Ins) to access Java code and data. A specification of the interface is available from Netscape's Web site.

ActiveX

ActiveX is Microsoft's answer to the Netscape Plug-In. ActiveX (formerly known as OCXs) are controls based on the Component Object Model (COM). COM is used throughout Microsoft's desktop applications for communication and automation, and integrating a Web browser with ActiveX extends the Microsoft desktop across the Internet.

Like Netscape Plug-Ins, ActiveX controls are native code modules, and Microsoft intends to support ActiveX on other platforms, not just on Microsoft Windows. Unlike Plug-Ins, ActiveX controls are designed to be downloaded as needed. A digital signature is used to guarantee that the ActiveX control has not been tampered with. Interestingly, Ncompass Labs has created a Netscape Plug-In that runs ActiveX controls.

Java interfaces and COM interfaces are semantically similar, and Microsoft has designed a VM that allows ActiveX and Java to communicate automatically. Sun has also announced intentions to unite Java with ActiveX through an application programming interface (API) called Java Beans. These bridges will make Java an excellent development tool for creating components that can be used in Windows-based development tools and applications like Word, Excel, Visual C++, Visual Basic, and Delphi.

JDBC

Java Database Connectivity is an API for linking Java programs to databases. JDBC is quite similar to Microsoft's Open Database Connectivity standard (ODBC): JDBC-compliant database applications will not be tied to a specific database vendor. As with ODBC, a vendor-specific driver is used to link JDBC applications to the actual database.

Suppose you write an employee database application using JDBC. There's no need to decide which vendor's database management system (for example, Oracle, Sybase, Informix) you want to use when you write the code because your program will work with any database that has a JDBC driver.

A JDBC-ODBC bridge is slated for release by Sun in the third quarter of 1996, which will give JDBC the ability to interface with the large number of existing ODBC drivers. JDBC is likely to be critical to industry acceptance of Java as a corporate client-server development tool. For more information on JDBC, see Chapter 21.

CHAPTER

TWO

Applets, Applications, and the Java Developers Kit

- Applets versus Applications

- The Java Developers Kit (JDK)

- Building Applications with the JDK

- Building Applets with the JDK

Java programs come in two flavors: *applets* and *Applications*. Simply speaking, a Java applet is a program that appears embedded in a Web document, whereas a Java Application is the term applied to all other kinds of Java programs, such as those found in network servers and consumer electronics. Much of this chapter will be devoted to the differences between these two types of programs, and to the ways these differences affect the Java software development path.

The *Java Developers Kit* (JDK) from JavaSoft, a division of Sun Microsystems, contains the basic tools and libraries necessary for creating and executing both types of Java programs. It also contains a number of useful utilities for debugging and documenting Java source code, and for interfacing C to Java code. You will learn how to download, install, and apply the JDK to the construction of both applets and Applications. Along the way, you will receive a primer on *Hypertext Markup Language (HTML)* for applets, and get your first taste of Java source code.

> **TIP**
> To distinguish Java Applications (the flavor) from generic Java programs, the word *Application* will be capitalized when contrasting with Java applets.

Applets versus Applications

The word *applet* suggests a small application, and in the computer industry, that is traditionally what it has meant. In Java, an applet is any Java program that is launched from a Web document; in other words, from an HTML file, as opposed to a Java Application, which is a program that runs from a command line. As far as Java is concerned, there is no limit to the size or complexity of a Java applet. In fact, Java applets are in some ways more powerful than Java

Applications. However, with the Internet, where communication speed is limited and download times are long, most Java applets are small by necessity.

The technical differences between applets and Applications stem from the context in which they run. A Java Application runs in the simplest possible environment—its only input from the outside world is a list of command line parameters. On the other hand, a Java applet needs a lot of information from the Web browser: It needs to know when it is initialized, when and where to draw itself in the browser window, and when it is activated or deactivated. As a consequence of these two very different execution environments, applets and Applications have different minimum requirements.

The decision to write a program as an applet versus an Application depends on the context of the program and its delivery mechanism. Because Java applets are always presented in the context of a Web browser's graphical user interface, Java Applications are preferred over applets when graphical displays are undesirable. For example, a *Hypertext Transfer Protocol (HTTP)* server written in Java needs no graphical display; it only requires file and network access.

The convenience of Web protocols for applet distribution makes applets the preferred program type for Internet applications, though Applications can easily be used to perform many of the same tasks. Non-networked systems and systems with small amounts of memory are much more likely to be written as Java Applications than as Java applets. However, Applications can easily be Internet based; in fact, some of the better Java programs are.

Table 2.1 summarizes the differences between the two flavors of Java programs.

Table 2.1: The Differences between Java Applets and Java Applications.

	Java Application	Java Applet
Uses Graphics	Optional	Inherently graphical
Memory Requirements	Minimal Java application requirements	Java application requirements plus Web browser requirements
Distribution	Loaded from the file system or by a custom class loading process	Linked via HTML and transported via HTTP
Environmental Inputs	Command line parameters	Browser client location and size; parameters embedded in the host HTML document
Routines Expected by the VM	`main`—startup routine	`init`—initialization routine `start`—startup routine `stop`—pause/deactivate routine `destroy`—termination routine `paint`—drawing routine
Typical Applications	Network server (for example, HTTP); multimedia kiosks; developer tools; appliance and consumer electronics control	Public access order entry systems for the Web; online multimedia presentations; web page animation and navigation

The Java Developers Kit (JDK)

The Java Developers Kit (JDK) was the original Java development environment for many of today's Java professionals. While many programmers have moved on to third-party alternatives, the JDK is still considered to be the reference implementation of Java, so if you can build and test an application with the JDK, it *should* run on any third-party implementations as found in Web browsers, development tools, or device-specific VMs.

NOTE   The latest version of the JDK, version 1.0.2, is available in its entirety on the CD-ROM included with this book. You can also download it for free on the Internet from Javasoft's Web site. For more information on the JDK see *Downloading and Installing the JDK* later in this chapter.

While the JDK can create and display fully graphical applications, the JDK itself has a somewhat primitive command line interface. For instance, the JDK programs are run by typing commands into a command shell window (in Windows, a DOS box). Do not be discouraged by the apparent complexity of the JDK commands—they are all quite easy to use after a bit of practice.

The JDK consists of a library of standard classes and a collection of utilities for building, testing, and documenting Java programs. The core Java *Application Programming Interface (API)* is the aforementioned library of prefabricated classes. You need these classes to access the core functionality of the Java language. The core Java API includes some important language constructs (including String datatypes and exceptions), as well as basic graphics, network, and file I/O. It is generally safe to assume that the non-I/O parts of the core Java API are common to all platforms running Java, including embedded systems. The I/O parts of the API are implemented in general-purpose Java environments. A Java VM in a toaster or other household appliance is unlikely to support the graphics part of the API, but will almost certainly implement Strings and other core API language classes. However, a Web browser running on a general-purpose operating system will likely implement the complete core API.

As for the JDK utilities, there are seven main programs in the kit:

javac   The Java *compiler*. Converts Java source code into bytecodes.

java   The Java *interpreter*. Executes Java Application bytecodes directly from class files.

appletviewer   A Java interpreter that executes Java applet classes hosted by HTML files.

javadoc   Creates HTML documentation based on Java source code and the comments therein.

jdb   The Java *debugger*. Allows you to step through the program one line at a time, set breakpoints, and examine variables.

javah   Generates C header files that can be used to make C routines that can call Java routines, or make C routines that can be called by Java programs.

javap   The Java *disassembler*. Displays the accessible functions and data in a compiled class file. It also displays the meaning of the bytecodes.

Each of the JDK utilities has a companion program for debugging purposes. The companion functions have "_g" at the end of their names: javac_g, java_g, appletviewer_g, and so on.

The way these tools are applied to build and run Applications is illustrated by the flowchart in Figure 2.1. When building applets, the flowchart looks slightly different, as shown in Figure 2.2.

After showing you how to download and install the JDK, we will introduce you to your first Java program—an Application. We will then follow the flowchart in Figure 2.1, illustrating each tool in succession. Finally, we will follow the flowchart for building applets, further explaining the differences between applets and Applications as we go.

FIGURE 2.1:

A flowchart that outlines the process by which Java Applications are built using the JDK.

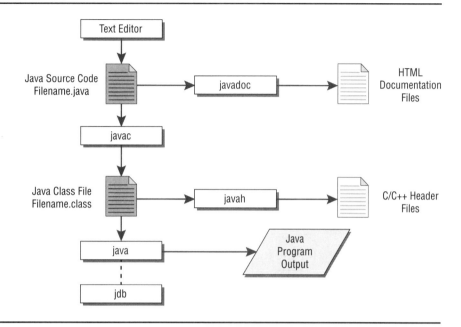

FIGURE 2.2:

A flowchart that outlines the process by which Java applets are built using the JDK.

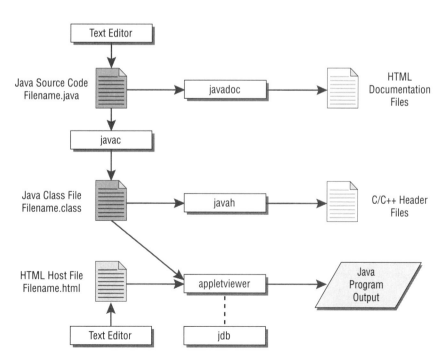

Downloading and Installing the JDK

To help get you started with Java, the following sections summarize the steps you need to follow to install Java on your machine. You need to install it before you can follow any of the exercises covered in the book.

Downloading the JDK

The latest version (1.0.2) of the JDK can be found on the CD-ROM accompanying this book, or it can be downloaded from JavaSoft's Web site at http://java.sun.com. The JDK is a self-extracting compressed executable file. As of this writing, version 1.0.2 is available for the following platforms:

- Solaris 2.4 for both SPARC and x86 architectures

- Windows 95 and Windows NT for x86 architectures

- Macintosh System 7.5 for PowerPC and 68K architectures

Notice that there is no version for Windows 3.1. It takes extra effort to implement Java on Windows 3.1 because Java requires long filenames and some other features that are not present in 16-bit versions of the operating system. Nonetheless, IBM is currently in the process of porting the JDK to Windows 3.1, and is already distributing versions for OS/2 and AIX. IBM is also working on MVS and OS/400 versions of the JDK. Other firms have ported Java to several types of UNIX, including Digital UNIX and Linux.

The first step is to locate the correct binary files at JavaSoft's Web site or at their FTP server, or from the appropriate site if you are using a platform other than those supported by JavaSoft. The complete JDK is distributed as a single file approximately 3–5 megabytes in size. The file will take about 35 minutes to download with a 28.8kbps modem, or about 20 minutes with single-channel ISDN, assuming that the server is not busy. It may help to try downloading the file early in the morning or late in the evening when fewer users will be accessing the site.

Installing the JDK

The installation process is straightforward, but generally takes a little manual setup work to finish off. Be sure to obtain the complete set of instructions from JavaSoft's Web pages, and have them handy during installation. To give you a head start, Table 2.2 summarizes the installation procedure for JDK 1.0.2 for each platform supported by Sun.

Table 2.2: JDK Installation Instructions for the Windows, Solaris, and Macintosh Platforms

	Windows 95 & Windows NT	Sun Solaris *	Macintosh System 7.5
Downloaded file type	Self-extracting executable (`.exe`)	Compressed archive (`.tar.gz`)	Compressed MacBinary HQX (`.sea.bin`)
Where to install the JDK	Usually installed in `c:\java`, by the self-extracting executable.	Can be installed anywhere, preferably a new directory.	The installer will create the folder for you. The default folder name is `JDK-1.0.2-mac`
If you have already installed a previous version of the JDK	Save any files you have changed or created in the original Java directory tree in a separate directory, then delete the original installation.	Rename the old java directory, if there are any files you would like to keep.	Sun provides no specific instructions here, but we recommend that you make a backup folder, if you have files you want to keep.

*Versions 2.3, 2.4, and 2.5 on SPARC-based machines, version 2.5 on x86 based machines

Table 2.2: JDK Installation Instructions for the Windows, Solaris, and Macintosh Platforms (continued)

	Windows 95 & Windows NT	Sun Solaris *	Macintosh System 7.5
Decompression procedure	If this is a new installation, simply run the executable from any directory.	Use `zcat` to decompress the tar archive, and use `tar` to extract the files from the archive.	Use Stuffit to decompress the MacBinary file, then use BinHex4 or DeHQX to decompress the installer.
Additional setup	Add the `java/bin` directory to your path.	Add the `java/bin` directory to your path.	
If you have already installed a previous version of the JDK	Check that the `CLASSPATH` environment variable points to the new version of the JDK.	Check that the `CLASSPATH` environment variable points to the new version of the JDK.	

*Versions 2.3, 2.4, and 2.5 on SPARC-based machines, version 2.5 on x86 based machines

 TIP   Don't forget to obtain the latest documentation and troubleshooting tips for your platform from JavaSoft's Web site (`http://java.sun.com`).

Building Applications with the JDK

Now that you have installed the JDK, it is time to take it for a test drive. To smooth the ride, we will create a small Java Application, and apply each JDK utility to the code. You will see the same code compiled, executed, disassembled, documented, and interfaced to the C language.

Java Source Code

Java source code can be written with a simple text editor. In UNIX, vi or emacs will do, and in Windows or System 7.5 you can use Notepad or EDIT. Many programmers already have a preferred text editor or use the editor shipped with third-party integrated development environments (IDEs). For your convenience, the source code examples are included on the CD-ROM accompanying this book.

The first example is a little Java program that you can use to play with the JDK:

```
public class TestDrive {
    public static void main(String[] argv) {
        System.out.println("JDK Test Drive");
    }
}
```

This is a rework of the classic HelloWorld program. However, this one just prints "JDK Test Drive." It is the simplest Java program you can write, but to the uninitiated it may still look rather cryptic. For the purposes of this chapter, there is no need to understand it all perfectly, so do not worry too much about what each keyword means.

The code defines a Java class called `TestDrive`, which contains a single routine called `main`. When the Java interpreter tries to execute the `TestDrive` class, it will look for a routine called `main`. The `public`, `static`, and `void` keywords will be explained in detail in later chapters; for now, you just need to know that they are required for the `main` routine to behave correctly.

In fact, every Java Application must define a function called `main` as:

```
public static void main(String[] argv)
```

The Virtual Machine will execute this function to run the program. Here, `argv` is an array of `String` (text) variables. When the program is run, the array will be filled with the values of any arguments it was given on the command line.

> **NOTE**
>
> If you know how to program in C, the main function will look familiar. The C equivalent:
>
> ```
> int main(char *argv[], int argc)
> ```
>
> includes `argc`, an integer variable which tells you how many arguments are in the array. In Java, this is unnecessary because, as you will see in a later chapter, arrays know how many elements they contain. Another difference between Java and C is that in C, the first element in the `array`, `argv[0]`, contains the name of the program itself. In Java, `argv[0]` is the first parameter on the command line.

Type the Java source code for the `TestDrive` class into your text editor and save it under the name `TestDrive.java`.

> **TIP**
>
> The name of the Java source file is not arbitrary; it must be the same as the name of the public class defined in the `.java` file. As a consequence of this, there can be only one public class defined in each source file, though there can be additional nonpublic classes defined in each file. If there is no public class defined in the Java source file, the name of the file can be anything you wish.

You are now ready to compile your first Java program.

javac

The javac compiler converts Java source code into Java bytecodes, which can then be executed by the java interpreter, the appletviewer, or any other Java Virtual Machine, such as Netscape.

You can compile your TestDrive program by entering the following at the shell prompt:

```
javac TestDrive.java
```

If the Java code is acceptable to the compiler, no messages will be displayed, and the file `TestDrive.class` will be created. If you are curious to see the details of the compilation, you can use the `verbose` option. The `verbose` option is rarely used, but it is instructive to see it at least once.

The `verbose` option will cause the `javac` compiler to tell you which other Java classes the compiler needs to create the compiled class file, and how long it took to do the compilation. When you enter

```
javac -verbose TestDrive.java
```

it produces

```
[parsed TestDrive.java in 390ms]
[loaded c:\java\lib\classes.zip(java/lang/Object.class) in 110ms]
[checking class TestDrive]
[loaded c:\java\lib\classes.zip(java/lang/String.class) in 160ms]
[loaded c:\java\lib\classes.zip(java/lang/System.class) in 110ms]
[loaded c:\java\lib\classes.zip(java/io/PrintStream.class) in 50ms]
[loaded c:\java\lib\classes.zip(java/io/FilterOutputStream.class) in 60ms]
[loaded c:\java\lib\classes.zip(java/io/OutputStream.class) in 0ms]
[loaded c:\java\lib\classes.zip(java/lang/StringBuffer.class) in 110ms]
[wrote TestDrive.class]
[done in 2250ms]
```

Behind the scenes, the compiler must check that the TestDrive program is consistent with any other classes it uses. `String`, `System`, `PrintStream`, `FilterOutputStream`, `OutputStream`, and `String-Buffer` are all part of Java's standard class library, the Core Java API. The aforementioned classes are all essential to print a string to the standard output.

In version 1.0.2 of the JDK, there are actually about 225 classes in the standard class library, and about 370 supplementary classes provided as a tools and debugging class library. This class library contains a wealth of ready-to-use functionality, and will save you a great deal of development time. These classes are stored in a compressed zip file in the `java/lib` directory. Do not remove the `classes.zip` file because, as you can see from the above, the Java compiler and VM access the library classes from this file directly. If you want to see the source code for the library classes, you can unzip the `src.zip` file, which is stored in the `java` directory.

After running javac to compile `TestDrive.java`, the file `TestDrive.class` contains bytecodes that can be executed by any Java Virtual Machine on any platform. The class file format is an open standard, and a detailed specification for it can be found at JavaSoft's Web site. If you use a binary file viewer to analyze the file, you will notice that there is text as well as binary data in the file. The names of classes and routines used by the class file must be stored in the bytecodes in order to access those classes and routines on the destination system. More information on the class file format can be found in Part Two.

java

After compiling the `TestDrive` class, you can run the program with the Java interpreter by entering the following command:

```
java TestDrive
```

The output will be the words "JDK Test Drive," as shown in Figure 2.3.

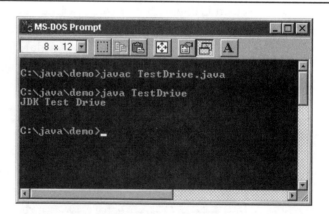

44

The interpreter has 16 command line options, most of which are functions likely to be used by advanced Java programmers. However, there is an especially useful feature built into the interpreter: a *profiler*. A profiler is used to analyze how much time a program spends in each part of the code. You can use this information to determine which parts of a program to optimize. If you use the `prof` option of the interpreter

```
java -prof TestDrive.java
```

a file called `java.prof` will be created that shows how many times each routine was called, and how many milliseconds were spent executing each. An excerpt of the profile for `TestDrive.class` is shown here:

```
count                          callee                          caller          time
   38        java/lang/String.<init>([C)V                <unknown caller>         42
   38  java/lang/System.arraycopy(Ljava/la    java/lang/String.<init>([C)V          0
   38         java/lang/Object.<init>()V     java/lang/String.<init>([C)V          0
   16  java/util/HashtableEntry.<init>()V  java/util/Hashtable.put(Ljava/lang/      0
   16        java/lang/Object.<init>()V  java/util/HashtableEntry.<init>()V        0
   16  java/util/Hashtable.put(Ljava/lang/             <unknown caller>            2
   16     java/lang/String.hashCode()I  java/util/Hashtable.put(Ljava/lang/        2
   15  java/io/BufferedOutputStream.write(    java/io/PrintStream.write(I)V         0
   14    java/io/PrintStream.write(I)V  java/io/PrintStream.print(Ljava/lan        0
   14       java/lang/String.charAt(I)C  java/io/PrintStream.print(Ljava/lan       0
.
.
.
1   java/lang/Thread.currentThread()Lja java/lang/ThreadGroup.<init>(Ljava/       0
        1     java/io/FileDescriptor.<clinit>()V             <unknown caller>      0
# handles-used, handles-free heap-used heap-free
134 78508 8424 2508152
# type count bytes
[C 56 2064
[B 3 384
[J 9 1808
Ljava/lang/Thread; 2 88
[Ljava/lang/Thread; 2 32
Ljava/io/BufferedOutputStream; 2 24
Ljava/io/BufferedInputStream; 1 24
Ljava/util/Properties; 1 20
Ljava/lang/String; 37 444
[Ljava/lang/String; 1 0
Ljava/io/FileInputStream; 1 4
Ljava/io/PrintStream; 2 24
```

```
Ljava/io/FileDescriptor; 1 4
Ljava/util/HashtableEntry; 10 160
[Ljava/util/HashtableEntry; 1 404
Ljava/lang/ThreadGroup; 2 72
[Ljava/lang/ThreadGroup; 1 16
Ljava/io/FileOutputStream; 2 8
```

The first section of the file shows which routines were called in order of decreasing frequency. The next section starts with # handles-used, handles-free heap-used heap-free and tells you how much memory was used. The third section starts with # type count bytes and lists the types of variables that were created, and how many bytes were used to store them. We can use this information to optimize our software. Programs often follow an 80/20 rule: 80 percent of the execution time is spent in 20 percent of the code. The profiler points out which routines are using up the most time, so you can optimize the most time-consuming parts of the code.

javadoc

By adding a few comments to your Java source code, you make it possible for javadoc to automatically generate HTML documentation for your code. Add the following few comments to your TestDrive.java file:

```
/** TestDrive — A test file for demonstration of the JDK. */
public class TestDrive {

    /** This routine is called first by the Java interpreter.
        It prints a message to the console. */
    // javadoc will ignore this comment
public static void main(String[] argv) {

        /* javadoc will also ignore this comment */
        System.out.println("JDK Test Drive");

    }

}
```

> **NOTE**
>
> C and C++ programmers will immediately notice the similarities between Java and C grammars. The curly braces ({}) group code together into blocks. As in C, line indentation is unnecessary, but it helps make the code more readable. Java comment markers are identical to C++ comment markers, though comments between the / * * and the * / markers have special significance for javadoc, the automatic documentation generator.

Java uses the same kind of comments as C, but a comment beginning with multiple asterisks has a special meaning for javadoc. It signifies the start of a *documentation comment* block, which is a comment block which will be used by javadoc to create documentation. Given our newly commented TestDrive.java, javadoc will produce the files `AllNames.html`, `tree.html`, `packages.html`, and `TestDrive.html`, all of which can easily be viewed using a standard Web browser, as shown in Figure 2.4. To run javadoc, simply enter the following command:

```
javadoc TestDrive.java
```

The graphical titles and bullets shown in Figure 2.4 are provided with the HTML documentation for Java API; to see the HTML with the graphics displayed correctly you must copy the image directory to the directory which contains your documentation. The relationship between the graphics and the HTML will be clearer after you have read the HTML primer in the next section.

javah

In order for Java to be applied to platform-specific or performance-critical problems, Java needs the ability to call native code written in C or other languages. Embedded applications are prime examples in which a Java program would need to access platform-specific information such as LED displays, relays, and sensors. Similarly, rendering complex 3-D graphics in real time is an application that demands the raw speed of C. Because Java was originally based on an embedded systems language, Java has built-in support for calling native

FIGURE 2.4:

Source code documentation in HTML format can be automatically produced using javadoc.

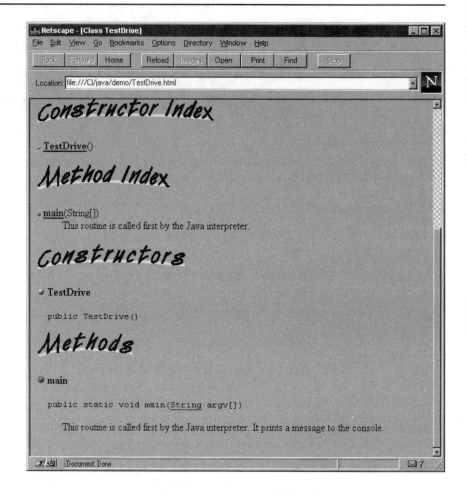

routines. More information on calling native code from Java is provided in Part Three.

To help you write C code that interfaces with Java, the JDK includes javah, a utility that, given a class file, generates the C header files needed by C programs to access the class's data. To fully appreciate how javah works requires a more detailed knowledge of Java as well as knowledge of C, so further discussion of javah will be postponed until Part Three.

jdb

The Java debugger, jdb, is used to monitor and control the execution of a Java program so that bugs can be found. With jdb, a running program can be stopped at any point so that variables and internal operation of the program can be examined. Unfortunately, jdb is difficult to use and is poorly documented, so you would be better off using a third-party debugger, perhaps one that is included with Symantec Café and Borland's Latte development environments. The third-party tools have many of the same features of jdb, but allow you to set breakpoints directly in the code, and view the program internals with separate windows for variables, threads, and function calls.

Before we leave the subject of jdb, we note that this debugger can connect to a running VM which is running in another process, even on a remote machine. This could be especially useful when debugging VMs running on remote servers, or running in appliances or consumer electronics.

javap

It is possible to examine the bytecodes of a compiled class file and identify its accessible variables and functions. The javap utility creates a report showing you not only what functions and variables are available, but what the code actually does, albeit at a very low level. Run javap with no command line arguments:

```
javap TestDrive
```

The output shows you from which file the class was compiled, and the accessible functions and variables:

```
Compiled from TestDrive.java
public class TestDrive extends java.lang.Object {
    public static void main(java.lang.String []);
    public TestDrive();
}
```

In this case, we have no "public" variables, so only the `main` and `TestDrive` functions are displayed. The `TestDrive()` function is a *default constructor*, a special function that is automatically created by the compiler if you do not write one. You will learn more about default constructors in the next chapter.

You can also use the debug version javap_g (with the `-c` option) to display the meaning of the bytecodes in the file:

```
javap_g -c TestDrive
```

The output shows each step that will be taken by the VM to execute the class.

```
Compiled from TestDrive.java
public class TestDrive extends java.lang.Object {
    public static void main(java.lang.String []);
    public TestDrive();

Method void main(java.lang.String [])
   0 getstatic #7 <Field java.lang.System.out Ljava/io/PrintStream;>
   3 ldc #1 <String "JDK Test Drive
">
   5 invokevirtual #8 <Method
java.io.PrintStream.println(Ljava/lang/String;)V>
   8 return

Method TestDrive()
   0 aload_0
   1 invokenonvirtual #6 <Method java.lang.Object.<init>()V>
   4 return

}
```

This is much more complicated than the original `TestDrive.java` file, but it shows each step that the VM will take when executing the program. As you can see, javap is a tool for advanced Java programmers.

Building Applets with the JDK

So far, you have seen the process by which Java Applications are built using the JDK. In this section, you will see Java applets and the HTML documents in which they are hosted.

Using an example Java applet called FilledBox.java, whose only function is to display a filled rectangle in the HTML document, the HTML document will be able to control the color of the rectangle by passing a parameter to the applet, and this will illustrate the relationship of HTML to Java applets.

Before going any further, if necessary, take a minute to understand the following short lesson in HTML. After a brief introduction to HTML, you will be up and running with Java applets in no time.

HTML for Java Applets

HTML files are text files with special character sequences that specify the document formatting characteristics. The special character sequences are called *tags*, and they consist of words placed between left and right angle brackets, as shown in the following excerpt:

```
Here is some normal text. <B>Here is some bold text.</B>
```

The `<B>` tag sets the bold attribute, and the closing `</B>` tag resets it. A Web browser or HTML viewer interprets the HTML file and produces the corresponding output. This excerpt of HTML produces the following output:

Here is some normal text. **Here is some bold text.**

Most HTML tags use the *<tag>* and *</tag>* sequences to set and reset their relevant properties. For example, `<I>` turns on italic, and `</I>` turns it off. Other tags, such as the start new paragraph tag, may not require a closing tag; Web browsers tend to be very forgiving about missing tags, as long as the document can be displayed unambiguously.

A complete HTML file has both formatting and structure tags:

```
<HTML>
 <HEAD>
  <TITLE>Sample HTML Document</TITLE>
 </HEAD>
 <BODY>
  <H1>HTML Demo</H1>
  This document is a sample of HTML.
 </BODY>
</HTML>
```

The HTML tag indicates that the file is an HTML document. The HEAD tag marks the start of an invisible header section that is normally used for recording the title and author of the document; the phrase between the TITLE and /TITLE tags is the name of this document. The BODY of the document contains all the displayed information; in this case, a level one heading and a line of normal text. The output generated by this HTML file is shown in Figure 2.5.

To include an image in an HTML file, use the IMG tag and specify the name and location of the image you wish to load. The full URL of the image may be used, though a simpler relative reference can be used if the graphic is located on the server.

```
<HTML>
 <HEAD>
  <TITLE>Sample HTML Document</TITLE>
 </HEAD>
 <BODY>
  <IMG SRC="sybex.gif">
  <H1>HTML Demo</H1>
  This document is a sample of HTML.
 </BODY>
</HTML>
```

FIGURE 2.5:

A sample HTML file displayed in the Web browser, Netscape Navigator.

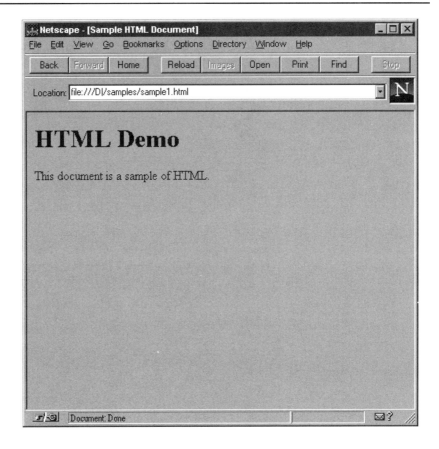

The resulting display is shown in Figure 2.6.

NOTE Web browsers can display image files in *GIF* (CompuServe Graphics Interchange Format) and *JPEG* image formats automatically. Most browsers also support animated and transparent GIF images (also known as GIF89a format). Both of these formats are supported by the core Java API.

If you want to connect this page to another document via a hyper-text link, you must insert an *anchor* tag (<A>). Everything between the anchor tag and the closing anchor tag will be highlighted, so the user

FIGURE 2.6:

An HTML document with an embedded image.

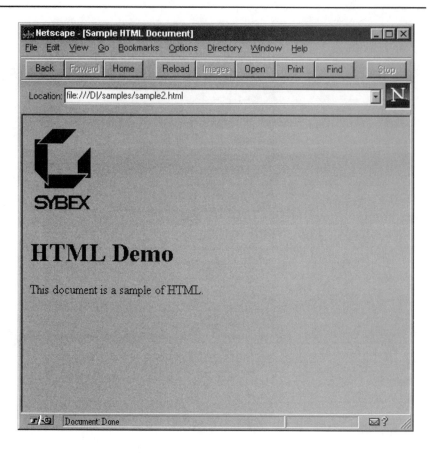

knows that the highlighted text or graphics can be clicked on. The following will build a hypertext link to JavaSoft's home page in our document:

```
<HTML>
 <HEAD>
  <TITLE>Sample HTML Document</TITLE>
 </HEAD>
 <BODY>
  <IMG SRC="sybex.gif">
  <H1>HTML Demo</H1>
  This document is a sample of HTML.
  <P>
```

```
You can get the Java Development Kit from the
<A HREF="http://java.sun.com">JavaSoft Home Page</A>.
</BODY>
</HTML>
```

You have inserted a paragraph tag to make the text easier to read. A Web browser ignores excess spaces and new lines when displaying a document, so if you need to break a line or begin a new paragraph, you must insert <BR> or <P> tags as necessary. Now, your HTML document has text, graphics, and a link, as shown in Figure 2.7.

FIGURE 2.7:

A sample HTML document including text, an image, and a hypertext link.

55

Adding a Java applet to an HTML document is quite straightforward. There is an APPLET tag that specifies the location of the class file and the display area allocated to the applet. Suppose you want to add a clock applet to the document that will display the current time in hours, minutes, and seconds. A compiled clock applet is included on the CD-ROM accompanying this book; it is called Clock.class. Here is a simple example of an applet tag that loads the Clock applet:

```
<APPLET CODE="Clock.class" WIDTH=200 HEIGHT=60> </APPLET>
```

Upon encountering these tags, a browser will start the VM and ask it to load Clock.class. It also tells the VM that the applet may draw in a region that is 200 × 60 pixels. The coordinate of the top left of the applet's display area is determined by the location of the APPLET tag in the document. Add the following lines to your HTML file:

```
<HTML>
 <HEAD>
  <TITLE>Sample HTML Document</TITLE>
 </HEAD>
 <BODY>
  <IMG SRC="sybex.gif">
  <H1>HTML Demo</H1>
  This document is a sample of HTML.
  <P>
  You can get the Java Development Kit from the
  <A HREF="http://java.sun.com">JavaSoft Home Page</A>.
  <P>
  <APPLET CODE="Clock.class" WIDTH=200 HEIGHT=60> </APPLET>
 </BODY>
</HTML>
```

The output should look like the document in Figure 2.8.

As you can see, embedding applets into Web pages is very simple. Java is able to create plug-in components that can be used by novices as well as experts. For this component strategy to work, the HTML author must be able to customize the properties and behavior of the applet via HTML. The Java programmer decides which parameters

FIGURE 2.8:

The Clock applet
embedded in an HTML
document.

will have meaning for the applet, and the HTML author uses
<PARAM> tags to pass initial parameters to the applet.

The Clock applet needs no parameters—telling the time is a universal function. On the other hand, our FilledBox applet needs to know what color to make the box. We can write the FilledBox applet to expect a parameter called "color" to be present in the HTML using the PARAM tag as shown in the following:

```
<APPLET CODE="FilledBox.class" WIDTH=50 HEIGHT=50>
<PARAM NAME=color VALUE="blue">
</APPLET>
```

The PARAM tag accepts two arguments: NAME and VALUE. The NAME argument is used to specify the name of the parameter, and the VALUE argument defines its value. As far as Java is concerned, all parameters are strings, though they can be converted to any other Java datatype quite easily. The output of the FilledBox applet is shown in Figure 2.9.

FIGURE 2.9:

The appletviewer running the FilledBox applet from `FilledBox.html`. Notice that only the applet is displayed.

If the Web browser includes a Java VM, it will display the applet and ignore everything but the PARAM tags, which lie between <APPLET> and </APPLET>. Web browsers that are not Java-enabled will ignore the APPLET and PARAM tags and display any valid HTML between the <APPLET> and </APPLET> tags.

Web Browser Applet Processing

A Java-enabled Web browser follows a specific series of steps when it encounters an APPLET tag in an HTML document:

1. The browser reserves space in the document for displaying the applet. The amount of space used by the applet is determined by the WIDTH and HEIGHT parameters of the APPLET tag.

2. The browser reads the parameters from the PARAM tags.

3. The VM starts and is asked to load and initialize the applet. The applet has access to the names and values in the PARAM tags.

4. The VM creates a running copy of the applet based on the class file.

5. The browser will call the applet's `init` routine so the applet will initialize itself.

6. The VM calls the `start` routine of the applet when it is ready for the applet to start processing. It also calls `paint` to draw the applet in the browser window.

7. Whenever the applet needs to be redrawn (for example, when the user scrolls the applet into view), the browser will call the applet's `paint` routine.

8. The browser will call the `stop` routine when the browser user moves on to another HTML document.

9. The browser calls the `destroy` routine when it clears the applet out of memory.

NOTE For more information on Java-enabled Web browsers, see Appendix A.

Java Source Code

Java applet source code is written in the same way as Java Application source: with a text editor. The difference is that Java applets do not have a `main` routine. Instead, they have several other routines that are called by the VM upon request of the browser. Here is the source code for the simple FilledBox applet:

```
import java.awt.*;
import java.applet.Applet;

/** FilledBox displays a filled, colored box in the browser window.
*/
public class FilledBox extends Applet {

    // This variable stores the color specified in the HTML document
    Color boxColor;
```

```
/** Get the box color from the host HTML file.
 */
        public void init() {

    String s;

    s = getParameter("color");

    // the default color is gray
    boxColor = Color.gray;

// we expect a parameter called color which will have
        // the value red, white or blue. If the parameter
        // is missing, s will be null
        if (s != null) {
    if (s.equals("red")) boxColor = Color.red;
        if (s.equals("white")) boxColor = Color.white;
        if (s.equals("blue")) boxColor = Color.blue;
        }

    }


    /** Paint the box in region assigned to the applet.
        Use the color specified in the HTML document.
     */
    public void paint(Graphics g) {
        g.setColor(boxColor);
        g.fillRect(0, 0, size().width, size().height);
    }

}
```

It is a little more complicated than the Application example, but this is because it does more. You will recall that a `main` routine is required by all Java Applications; it is conspicuously absent in this applet. In fact, Java applets have no required routines at all. However, there are three routines that the VM may request of the Web browser or appletviewer:

public void init()   Initializes the applet. Called only once.

public void start()   Called when the browser is ready to start executing the initialized applet. Can be called multiple times if the user keeps leaving and returning to the Web page.

public void stop()   Called when the browser wishes to stop executing the applet. Called whenever the user leaves the Web page.

public void destroy()   Called when the browser clears the applet out of memory.

public void paint(Graphics g)   Called whenever the browser needs to redraw the applet.

If the applet does not implement any of the functions, the applet will have no functionality at all, as far as the browser is concerned. In our example, we have implemented `init` and `paint`. The `init` function obtains the desired box color from a parameter in the host document (applet parameters are explained in the HTML primer). The paint routine draws the filled box in the browser window.

Save this Java applet as `FilledBox.java`.

javac

The javac compiler works just as well on applets as it does on Applications:

```
javac FilledBox.java
```

If the Java code is acceptable to the compiler, no messages will be displayed, and the file `FilledBox.class` will be created. If there were error messages, you have to go back and fix your code. There are many different types of warning and error messages that the compiler may generate when given a source file. The simplest to fix are syntax errors, such as a missing semicolon or closing brace. Other messages will highlight incorrect use of variable types, invalid expressions, or violation access restrictions. Getting your source code to compile is only the first part of the debugging process: Error-free compilation does not guarantee that your program will do what you want it to.

Before you can run your applet, you must create an HTML document to host it.

HTML

Now that you know a little HTML, it is easy to create a simple HTML file to host your applet:

```
<HTML>
 <HEAD>
  <TITLE>Sample HTML Document With Filled Box</TITLE>
 </HEAD>
 <BODY>
  <H1>FilledBox Demo</H1>
  <P>
  <APPLET CODE="FilledBox.class" WIDTH=200 HEIGHT=60>
  <PARAM NAME=color VALUE="blue">
  </APPLET>
 </BODY>
</HTML>
```

You can create this file by simply typing it into a text editor. Save the file as `FilledBox.html`.

appletviewer

The appletviewer is used to display the applet as it would be seen by the browser without displaying the HTML document itself. In the case of `FilledBox.html`, appletviewer will display a filled box in its own window:

```
appletviewer FilledBox.html
```

Refer back to Figure 2.9 to see the output. For comparison, you can open the file `FilledBox.html` using a Java-enabled Web browser: Figure 2.10 shows the output as it would be seen by Netscape Navigator 2.

FIGURE 2.10:

The Netscape Navigator Web browser displaying the file `FilledBox.html`. Both the applet and the text are displayed.

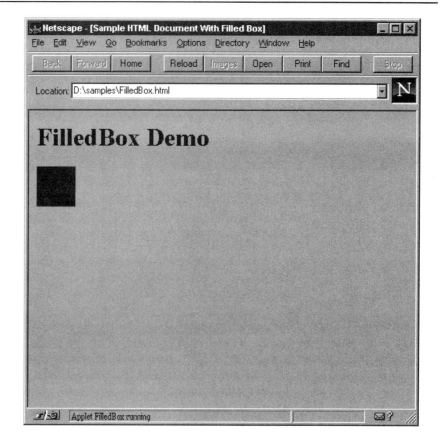

If there is more than one applet in a page, appletviewer will open a separate window for each applet, whereas a Web browser will show them in their respective locations within the same Web page. One rather nice feature of the appletviewer is that it can load classes from across the network, not just from files. Just give appletviewer the URL of the HTML document containing one or more applets, and it will load the applets from across the network. Note, however, that the SecurityManager for the appletviewer may expose your system to greater risks from network-loaded applets than would a Web browser like Netscape Navigator.

The appletviewer allows you to distribute and run Java applets without the aid of a Web browser, so the choice between writing applets versus Applications becomes even more blurred. Most applets are easy to convert into Applications and vice versa. The key to this convertibility is to avoid placing a lot of code directly in the `main`, `init`, `start`, `stop`, `destroy`, and `paint`, and use calls to generic routines instead.

javadoc and javah

As before, javadoc and javah will work on our Java source code. The command lines are just like the Application command lines:

```
javadoc FilledBox.java
```

and

```
javah FilledBox.class
```

Summary

In this chapter, the differences between Java applets and Java Applications were accentuated. Though their initialization processes and context differ, you will find that the nuts and bolts of Java programming do not change. Indeed, it is usually easy to convert an applet into an Application and vice versa (as long as the applet does not require services built into the browser).

After this discussion of the JDK, you should have no problem running demos and examples provided with the JDK and the CD-ROM. Several third-party compilers and development environments are also available—you will find a review of these, and many other products, in Chapter 19.

CHAPTER
THREE

Working with Java Objects

- Object-Oriented Programming

- Constructors and Finalizers

The object-oriented programming paradigm has swept through the software industry over the last decade, bringing with it advances in programmer productivity, software reuse, and maintainability. Object-oriented programming (OOP) is now considered "best practice" in the development business. Java is a fully object-oriented language, and a thorough understanding of object orientation is required to make effective use of the Java programming language. To that end, we will begin this chapter with an introduction to object-oriented programming.

An Introduction to Object-Oriented Programming

Classes of objects closely resemble structures and record types in non-OOP languages, so this section will begin with a review of simple data structures, and a look at the software development problems inherent in structures. To maintain continuity with the sample code as well as provide an illustrative example, the concepts will be applied to the design of an air traffic control system. This example has been chosen because it illustrates most of the aspects of object-oriented programming.

NOTE Though C++ is an object-oriented programming language, it also supports non-object-oriented techniques. Because C++ grammar and Java grammar are so similar, the examples of non-object-oriented code will be in C++.

Data Structures

In almost all programming languages, data is stored in variables that have a specific *datatype*; for example, integer datatypes hold whole numbers, character datatypes hold individual alphanumeric characters, and string datatypes hold strings of alphanumeric characters. Many languages also allow you to create your own datatypes by grouping several simple datatypes together. In C++, these "compound" datatypes are called structures; in Pascal, they are called record types. Here is a sample structure written in C++ that represents an aircraft:

```
struct Flight {
    int    altitude;
    int    heading;
    int    speed;
    float  latitude;
    float  longitude;
}
```

The `Flight` structure is a new datatype made up of built-in C types, namely integers and floating-point numbers. The components of a structure are called *members*. The `Flight` structure could also contain members for the destination of the flight, the type of aircraft, and other pieces of information, but the members here will be sufficient for the purpose of these examples.

The structure itself stores no information—it is only a pattern for creating new `Flight` variables. To declare a new `Flight` variable called `incomingFlight` you would use the following code:

```
struct Flight incomingFlight;
```

You access the members of `incomingFlight` by using the name of the `Flight` variable followed by a period and the name of the member:

```
incomingFlight.altitude = 3000;

if (incomingFlight.heading < 180) {… }
```

In Pascal or Visual Basic, similar code would be used to create the Flight structure and to access member variables.

In non-object-oriented programming, the code that accesses the Flight variables is separate and specific to the datatype. This non-OOP, structure-specific programming will be referred to as *structure-oriented* code. For example, a C++ routine that represents a turn of an aircraft might be declared as follows:

```
void turnFlight(Flight &aFlight, int angle) {

    aFlight.heading = (aFlight.heading + angle) % 360;

    // make sure angle is in the range 0-359 degrees
    if (aFlight.heading < 0) aFlight.heading = aFlight.heading + 360;
}
```

The turnFlight routine expects to be given variables that are Flight and integer datatypes, respectively. Turning an incoming flight 90 degrees to the right is now achieved with the following code:

```
turnFlight(incomingFlight, 90);
```

Similar routines would be written to descend the aircraft and display it on the computer screen. A schematic representation of the code and data structure is shown in Figure 3.1.

Next, you will model commercial flights. A new structure called CommercialFlight is created that includes everything that the Flight structure included, plus the flight number and number of passengers:

```
struct CommercialFlight {

    // extra members in CommercialFlight
    int    flightNumber;
    int    passengers;
```

FIGURE 3.1:

A schematic view of the Flight data structure and the code that references it.

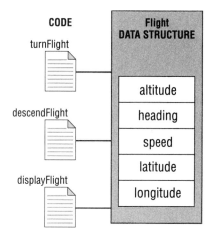

```
// members in Flight
int     altitude;
int     heading;
int     speed;
float   latitude;
float   longitude;
}
```

Again, to create a CommercialFlight variable that is called incomingCommercialFlight, you could simply type

```
struct CommercialFlight incomingCommercialFlight;
```

However, the previous routines for generic flights will not work with CommercialFlight variables. For example, the compiler will not allow you to use the turnFlight routine with a CommercialFlight variable. Therefore, the following call is illegal:

```
turnFlightincoming(CommercialFlight, 90);
```

A schematic representation of the CommercialFlight datatype and its functions is shown in Figure 3.2.

FIGURE 3.2:

The Flight and CommercialFlight data structures and associated routines.

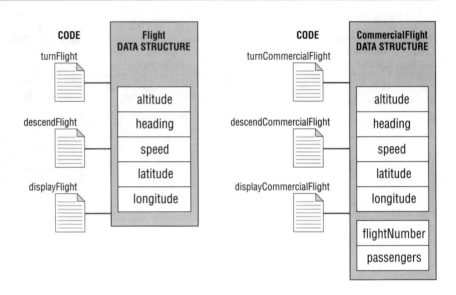

Though there are tricks you can use to circumvent the datatype problem, the tricks make the code harder to read, more complex, and less reliable. The only safe alternative is to create a new routine for commercial flights called turnCommercialFlight:

```
void turnCommercialFlight(CommercialFlight &aFlight, int angle) {

    aFlight.heading = (aFlight.heading + angle) % 360;

    // make sure angle is in the range 0-359 degrees
    if (aFlight.heading < 0) aFlight.heading = aFlight.heading + 360;
}
```

However, this kind of code duplication is a maintenance problem. If changes need to be made for ten different structures, ten different routines need to be modified. Not only is this hard work, but it is also an opportunity to introduce additional defects into the code.

Maintenance is only one of several problems with non-OOP structures. Traditional structures are also difficult to use more than once.

Structures and their associated routines can quickly become entangled, making it difficult for someone to extract the required code for reuse in a new program. In effect, these entanglements force a programmer to look at every detail of the original code in order to use it as part of a new piece of program. To avoid this, the developer must exercise a lot of discipline to keep the interface of a structure and its routines; in other words, the parts which need to be used by future applications, separate from the details of their implementation.

Finally, structure-oriented code has some inherent safety flaws. In the previous examples, you created routines to turn the aircraft by any angle. These routines guaranteed that the angle would always be between 0 and 359 degrees, inclusive. But with structures, there is nothing to stop a programmer who is unfamiliar with the class from bypassing the `turnFlight` routine and entering the following code:

```
//right turn 90 degrees
incomingFlight.heading = incomingFlight.heading + 90;
```

Though the code may be essentially correct, it may lead to headings greater than 359 degrees. This in turn may break some other part of the code that assumes all angles will be in the range 0–359 degrees. This lack of data protection also contributes to the fragility of source code.

NOTE From this point forward, the program code will be Java source code, not C++ source code, though, in many cases, there is very little difference between the two.

From Structures to Classes: Encapsulation

In object-oriented programming, the routines for a structure and the structure itself are combined, or *encapsulated*, into a single entity called a *class*. Here is the Java source code for a `Flight` class, an object-oriented version of the `Flight` structure:

```
class Flight {
    int    altitude;
    int    heading;
    int    speed;
    float  latitude;
    float  longitude;

    // change the flight's heading by angle degrees
    void turnFlight(int angle) {

        heading = (heading + angle) % 360;

        // make sure angle is in the range 0-359 degrees
        if (heading < 0) heading = heading + 360;

    }

    // print information about the flight
    void printFlight() {

        System.out.println(altitude + "/" + heading + "/" + speed);

    }
}
```

The `turnFlight` routine is now a *member function* of the class; that is, the routine is part of the structure itself. You will notice that the code for the function is actually a little cleaner because you no longer need to refer to the heading as a member of a dummy variable—the variable `aFlight` has been eliminated altogether. A member function called `printFlight` also has been added that prints some flight information on the console.

> **NOTE** Member functions are sometimes referred to as *methods*. The terms can be used interchangeably.

Just as with the structure definition, this class definition is just a pattern for variables to be created with the `Flight` class datatype. Variables with the `Flight` class datatype are `Flight` *objects*. In other words, an object is a storage variable that is an instance of a class. Classes define the variables and routines that are members of an object of that class. A look at how to apply the `Flight` class will help you get a feel for using objects.

Based on the `Flight` class, you will create a `Flight` object (this process is sometimes referred to as *instantiation*). An object variable is a reference to an object; creating a reference to an object and creating the object itself are two separate steps. To create the object variable you use

```
Flight incomingFlight;
```

The `Flight` variable can have two possible kinds of value: `null` or a `Flight` object. The default value of `incomingFlight` above is null; it is simply a name and does not yet refer to any object. To create an object referenced by `incomingFlight`, use the `new` operator:

```
incomingFlight = new Flight();
```

Now, `incomingFlight` refers to a new `Flight` object, and you can access its member variables:

```
incomingFlight.altitude = 2500;

if (incomingFlight.heading < 180) {...}
```

Member functions are called in an analogous way:

```
incomingFlight.turnFlight(90);
```

A nice way to think of this is to imagine that `incomingFlight` points to an object that understands how to turn itself, and that you are sending a message to the object, asking it to turn right by 90 degrees. The object-oriented equivalent of Figure 3.1 now looks like Figure 3.3.

Encapsulation also allows us to use *data hiding*, which is a way to prevent direct access to the variables in an object. This forces the programmer to use member functions to alter or read data in member variables. This is a key strength of encapsulation: It separates the interface to the class from its implementation, so you do not need to know the implementation details of the class to safely reuse the code.

FIGURE 3.3:

The `Flight` data structure and associated routines as an encapsulated class.

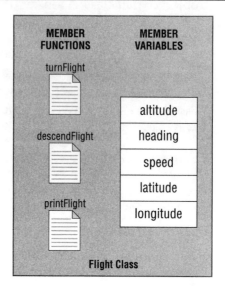

You can modify the `Flight` class to hide the heading member variable by using the `private` keyword:

```
class Flight {
    int     altitude;
    private int     heading;
    int     speed;
    float   latitude;
    float   longitude;

    void turnFlight(int angle) {
        heading = (heading + angle) % 360;

        // make sure angle is in the range 0-359 degrees
        if (heading < 0) heading = heading + 360;
    }

    void setHeading(int angle) {
        heading = angle % 360;

        // make sure angle is in the range 0-359 degrees
        if (heading < 0) heading = heading + 360;
    }
```

```
int getHeading() {
    return heading;
}

void printFlight() {
    System.out.println(altitude + "/" + heading + "/" + speed);
}
```
}

Now that the `heading` variable is private and hidden to code outside the class, you need two additional functions: `setHeading`, in order to set the heading, and `getHeading`, to obtain the current heading.

It is generally good practice to hide as many variables as possible. This separates the implementation of your class from its interface, and makes it harder for another programmer to break your code by bypassing the safety measures in your member functions.

Inheritance

Using classes instead of structures also solves the problem of code duplication. Recall extended structures such as `CommercialFlight`; you needed to create a new copy of each function that acted on the original structure (`Flight`). With classes you can inherit both the data members and member functions when creating a new class:

```
class CommercialFlight extends Flight {

    // extra members in CommercialFlight
    int    flightNumber;
    int    passengers;

}
```

The CommercialFlight class, a *subclass* of Flight, automatically inherits all the data members and member functions of the Flight class, so you can write

```
CommercialFlight incomingCommercialFlight;

incomingCommercialFlight = new CommercialFlight();

incomingCommercialFlight.altitude = 2500;
incomingCommercialFlight.setHeading(45);
incomingCommercialFlight.flightNumber = 101;
incomingCommercialFlight.passengers = 24;
```

As you can see, inheritance makes life much easier. It also makes the code more maintainable because the code to alter the heading of both a Flight and a CommercialFlight is all in one place, namely in the definition of the parent or *base class*. A schematic for the relationship of class and subclass is shown in Figure 3.4.

FIGURE 3.4:

The Commercial-Flight class inherits member variables and functions from Flight, and then adds its own member variables.

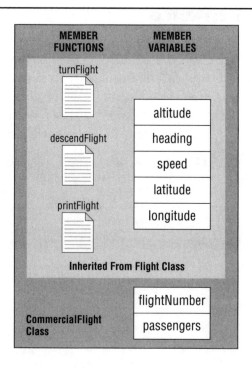

In many cases, you will want a subclass to override one or more member functions of the parent class. Continuing with the example, you may want a commercial flight to print in a special way on the console; for example, to display the flight number. You can easily override the `printFlight` routine of the `Flight` class by re-implementing it in the `CommercialFlight` class:

```
class Flight {
    int     altitude;
    private int    heading;
    int     speed;
    float   latitude;
    float   longitude;

    void turnFlight(int angle) {
        heading = (heading + angle) % 360;

        // make sure angle is in the range 0-359 degrees
        if (heading < 0) heading = heading + 360;
    }

    void setHeading(int angle) {
        heading = angle % 360;

        // make sure angle is in the range 0-359 degrees
        if (heading < 0) heading = heading + 360;
    }

    int getHeading() {
        return heading;
    }

    // print the flight's altitude, heading and speed on the console
    void printFlight() {
        System.out.println(altitude + " ft / " + heading
                            + " degrees/" + speed + " knots");
    }

}

class CommercialFlight extends Flight {

    // extra members in CommercialFlight
    int     flightNumber;
    int     passengers;
```

```
// re-implement the printFlight routine to
// override the previous definition
void printFlight() {
    System.out.print("Flight " + flightNumber + " ");
    super.printFlight();
}

}
```

Notice that the new `printFlight` member function calls `super.printFlight()`. The `super` keyword refers to the superclass of `CommercialFlight`, namely the `Flight` class, and so `super.printFlight()` is a call to the original `printFlight` function as defined in the `Flight` class. You will often see the `super` keyword used when overriding member functions because the overriding function usually implements supplementary processing—it does all its parent class did and more.

If you call a `Flight` object's `printFlight` function:

```
incomingFlight.printFlight();
```

you will get output like the following:

```
2500 ft / 270 degrees / 240 knots
```

If you call a commercial flight's `printFlight` routine:

```
incomingCommercialFlight.printFlight();
```

the output might look like the following:

```
Flight 101 3000 ft / 185 degrees / 350 knots
```

Figure 3.5 shows how the `CommercialFlight` class re-implements the `printFlight` function.

It is sometimes advantageous to use inheritance even when the base class is so generic that it cannot be implemented. This can be done using the concept of abstract classes.

FIGURE 3.5:

The `Commercial-Flight` class inherits member variables and functions from `Flight`, adds its own member variables, and overrides the `printFlight` function.

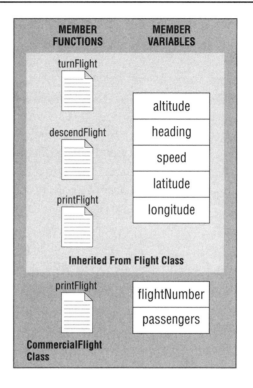

Abstract Classes

In this section, you will incorporate air traffic control facilities into the example by including classes for flight control towers (for aircraft flying, landing, and taking-off) and ground control towers (for taxiing aircraft). To begin, you create `ControlFacility` as a parent class, and then create `FlightControlTower` and `GroundControlTower` as subclasses. Then create a member function called `getClearance`, which is called to see if a facility will clear a flight for landing, take-off, taxiing, and so on. However, you cannot create a generic `Control-Facility` object because you cannot implement `getClearance` without knowing whether you control space on the ground or in the air. On the other hand, you still want to insist that every subclass of `ControlFacility` implements the `getClearance` member function.

The solution to this dilemma is provided by Java's ability to define *abstract classes*. The code for the `ControlFacility` class illustrates how abstract classes work:

```
abstract ControlFacility {

    abstract boolean getClearance(FlightAction request);

}
```

In this piece of code, you declare the new class and the `getClearance` method function that returns a boolean (`true` or `false`) value. The function will accept an object of a class named `FlightAction` (this class will not be defined; it is just part of the illustration). However, the function is defined as `abstract`, and it has no implementation. Any class that has such abstract functions is said to be an *abstract class*, and no objects of such classes can ever be created.

The `FlightControlTower` and `GroundControlTower` subclasses must implement the `getClearance` function, so you can create objects that represent such facilities:

```
class FlightControlTower extends ControlFacility {

    boolean getClearance(FlightAction request) {

        // implementation of the getClearance function for
        // flight control towers
        .
        .
        .


    }

}

class GroundControlTower extends ControlFacility {

    boolean getClearance(FlightAction request) {
```

```
        // implementation of the getClearance function for
        // ground control towers
            .
            .
            .

    }
}
```

Since both these subclasses—`FlightControlTower` and `GroundControlTower`—implement the abstract functions defined in the parent class, they are not abstract classes and can both be instantiated. In addition to formalizing the interface, abstract classes give you other advantages, which will be discussed in the next section.

Polymorphism

Polymorphic functions are functions that do not care which variable types are passed to them. The `PRINT` statement in BASIC and the `writeln` statement in Pascal are examples of polymorphic routines, because you can pass any type of variable to them and they always act appropriately. Standard `BASIC` does not need a `PRINTINTEGER` statement or a `PRINTSTRING` statement, because `PRINT` is smart enough to take care of any datatype. However, the `PRINT` statement has this ability specially coded into the BASIC interpreter, and its ability does not extend to user-defined structures. BASIC also has no provision for creating user-defined polymorphic routines.

Java makes it possible for you to simplify your code with polymorphism in three ways:

Inheritance   Subclasses automatically inherit member functions from their parent classes. Also, any function that accepts a particular class as an argument will also accept any subclass of that class as an argument.

Overloading   Implementing identically named member functions that take different arguments within the same class.

> **Interfacing**   Implementing identically named member functions that take identical arguments in different classes.

Now you will look at these three cases in turn.

Inheritance

Inheritance is the simplest kind of polymorphism, as well as one you have already encountered. In the air traffic control example, you can ask any `Flight` object or `Flight`-subclassed object to turn left by calling the member function `turnFlight(-90)`. This means that instead of requiring a multitude of function names like `turnFlight`, `turnCommercialFlight`, or `turnMilitaryFlight` (for a `MilitaryFlight` class), you can use `turnFlight` consistently:

```
incomingFlight.turnFlight(-90);
incomingCommercialFlight.turnFlight(-90);
incomingMilitaryFlight.turnFlight(-90);
```

Better still, you can easily write code that works with the `Flight` class and all subclasses of the `Flight`. You will create a new class called `Airport` that has a member function called `aircraftInbound`; in turn, this adds a flight to the list of inbound flights:

```
class Airport {
    String airportName;
    Flights[] inboundFlights, outboundFlights;

    void aircraftInbound(Flight aFlight) {

        //implementation of aircraftInbound function
        .
        .
        .

    }
}
```

An `Airport` object will now accept any `Flight` object and any object that is a subclass of `Flight`. For example, you could write

```
Airport CityAirport;

CityAirport = new Airport();

CityAirport.airportName = "City National Airport";
CityAirport.aircraftInbound(incomingFlight);
CityAirport.aircraftInbound(incomingCommercialFlight);
CityAirport.aircraftInbound(incomingMilitaryFlight);
```

Polymorphism by inheritance is also where the advantages of abstract classes come to light. By inheriting from a generic abstract class, you can group together classes that share common functions, but not common implementation. Having created the abstract class `ControlFacility` in the previous section, you can now write code that refers to `ControlFacility` objects and works with all subclasses of `ControlFacility`, even though `ControlFacility` objects themselves can never be created.

Overloading

There is another way to add polymorphic functions, known as *function overloading*. In Java, C++, and other languages that support function overloading, it is possible to define the same function twice while using different parameters for each definition. For example, in the previous listing, the `aircraftInbound` function does the same thing no matter which subclass of `Flight` is passed to it. Suppose you want to add inbound aircraft to the `Airport`'s list of the inbound flights with different priorities according to the type of flight. By overloading the `aircraftInbound` function, you can customize its behavior for each kind of flight object:

```
class Airport {
    String airportName;
    Flight[] inboundFlights, outboundFlights;

    // aircraftInbound function accepting Flight objects
    void aircraftInbound(Flight aFlight) {
```

```
    // implementation of aircraftInbound function for
    // generic flights
    .
    .
    .

}

// aircraftInbound function accepting CommercialFlight objects
void aircraftInbound(CommercialFlight aFlight) {

    // implementation of aircraftInbound function for commercial
    // flights
    .
    .
    .

}

// aircraftInbound function accepting MilitaryFlight objects
void aircraftInbound(MilitaryFlight aFlight) {

    // implementation of aircraftInbound function for
    // military flights
    .
    .
    .

}
}
```

Just as before, you call the function identically no matter which type of flight object is passed to the function:

```
Airport CityAirport;

CityAirport = new Airport();

CityAirport.aircraftInbound(incomingFlight);
CityAirport.aircraftInbound(incomingCommercialFlight);
CityAirport.aircraftInbound(incomingMilitaryFlight);
```

It should be pointed out that overloading is not a feature of object-oriented languages per se, though it is most commonly implemented in object-oriented languages.

Polymorphism can be achieved by implementing the same member functions in different classes, a technique called *interfacing*.

Interfacing

Suppose you need to create a report that lists both airports and all their incoming and outgoing flights. You could do this by writing a `printOnReport` function for both the `Airport` and `Flight` classes:

```
class Airport {
    String airportName;
    Flight[] inboundFlights, outboundFlights;

    // printOnReport function prints an Airport entry on the report
    void printOnReport() {
        System.out.println("Airport: " + airportName);
    }
}

class Flight {
    int     altitude;
    private int     heading;
    int     speed;
    float   latitude;
    float   longitude;

    // print the flight's altitude, heading and speed on the console
    void printOnReport() {
        System.out.println("Flight: " + altitude + " ft / " + heading
                                + " degrees/" + speed + " knots");
    }

}
```

You can call these new functions in the following way:

```
incomingFlight.printOnReport();
CityAirport.printOnReport();
```

Informally speaking, these classes now have a common interface as far as printing reports is concerned. Java allows us to formalize the interface so you guarantee that a class will support all the functions (there may be more than one) that make up an interface. By using formal interfaces, you can write a function that will accept an argument of any class that implements a particular interface.

Let's define a formal interface for the report printing example. Java's `interface` keyword is used just like the `class` keyword:

```
interface ReportPrintable {
    void printOnReport();
}
```

Note that `ReportPrintable` is not a class and cannot be instantiated; essentially, the member functions declared in an interface are abstract. To tell the compiler that the `Airport` and `Flight` classes implement the `ReportPrintable` interface, add an `implements` clause to the class declarations:

```
class Airport implements ReportPrintable {

    .

    .

    .

}

class Flight implements ReportPrintable {

    .

    .

    .

}
```

Next, you can create a `ReportGenerator` class that creates reports from any object that implements the `ReportPrintable` interface:

```
class ReportGenerator {
    void addToReport(ReportPrintable aObject) {
        aObject.printOnReport();
    }
}
```

`ReportGenerator`'s `addToReport` function will accept *any* class that implements the `ReportPrintable` interface.

As you can see, polymorphism greatly simplifies writing code, especially when modeling complex, real-world situations. The programmer need not remember as many function names, and the source code becomes much more readable.

Constructors and Finalizers

There are two special kinds of member functions you can define: *constructors*, member functions that return new instances of the class, and *finalizers*, functions that are called just before an object is garbage collected. If you do not write a constructor, a default constructor can be used to create instances of the class.

Constructors

Going back to the `Airport` class, you will recall that you created and initialized the code with the following code:

```
Airport CityAirport;

CityAirport = new Airport();

CityAirport.airportName = "City National Airport";
```

After the first line, `CityAirport` is defined as an object variable. After the second line, an object is created and `CityAirport` refers to the object. The third line initializes the name of the `Airport` object. The function `Airport()` is the *default constructor* for the `Airport` class. The default constructor is inherited from `Airport`'s parent class, `Object`, and is automatically added to the class by the Java compiler. The `Object`'s constructor allocates storage for any member variables that are declared as one of Java's built-in datatypes. In this case none of the `Airport`'s member variables is allocated because neither the `String` variable nor the `Flight` datatypes are built in (the built-in datatypes will be enumerated in the next chapter). For example, the `airportName` member object variable is `null` until we allocate space for the corresponding `String`, or assign an object to it.

To simplify the object creation process, and to protect yourself from uninitialized object variables, you can create your own constructor for the `Airport` class:

```
class Airport {
    String airportName;
    Flight[] inboundFlights, outboundFlights;

    // a new constructor which takes no arguments
    Airport() {

        super();
        airportName = "Unknown";
    }

    .
    .
    .


}
```

A constructor is defined like an ordinary member function, but it must have the same name as the class, and has no return datatype. In this example, the constructor calls `super()`, which is a reference to the constructor in the parent class, `Object`. Writing the call to `super()` is optional because the compiler will implicitly call the parent class's constructor if you do not call it. You can call the new constructor exactly as you did before:

```
Airport CityAirport = new Airport();

CityAirport.airportName = "City National Airport";
```

Now, after calling the new constructor, `CityAirport.airportName` will default to "Unknown." However, because you will always change the airport name, you can save a step by writing another constructor that creates the `Airport` object and sets the `airportName` to the callers choice as follows:

```
class Airport {
    String airportName;
    Flight[] inboundFlights, outboundFlights;

    // a new constructor which takes no arguments
    Airport() {

        super();
        airportName = "Unknown";
    }

    // a new constructor which takes the new airport's name as an argument
    Airport(String newName) {

        super();
        airportName = newName;
    }

        .
        .
        .


}
```

This is an example of overloading: The two constructors have the same name, but accept different parameters. Now you can write

```
Airport CityAirport = new Airport("City National Airport");
```

to create an `Airport` object with the name "City National Airport."

Constructors can call other constructors. You can rewrite the `Airport()` constructor so that it calls the `Airport(String newName)` constructor by using the `this` keyword:

```
    // a new constructor which takes no arguments
    Airport() {

        this("Unknown");

    }
```

The keyword `this` followed by parentheses (and arguments, if any) refers to a constructor. In this case, the compiler knows that you are referring to the `Airport(String newName)` constructor because it is the only constructor which takes a `String` as an argument. Since the different constructors of a class typically perform common tasks, you will find the ability to call other constructors very useful.

Garbage Collection

Let's examine what happens when an object is no longer needed by the system. The following code and Figures 3.6 and 3.7 illustrate what is meant by "no longer needed":

```
CityAirport = new Airport("City National Airport");
CityAirport = new Airport("Potter's Field");
```

FIGURE 3.6:

The object variable `CityAirport` initially references the object representing City National Airport.

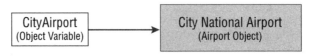

FIGURE 3.7:

The object variable then references a new object representing Potter's Field. Since there are no references to the first object, it will be automatically discarded by the garbage collector.

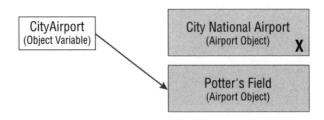

Two objects are created in this code, but there is only one object variable here. After the first statement, `CityAirport` points to the object representing City National Airport. After the second statement

`CityAirport` points to the other object representing Potter's Field, and nothing points to the first object. Just as you would expect, the original object is lost from the system. Java automatically reclaims memory used by an object when no object variables refer to that object, a process known as *garbage collection*. Consider the following assignments and the corresponding Figures 3.8 and 3.9:

```
LocalAirport = new Airport("City National Airport");
CityAirport = LocalAirport;
CityAirport = new Airport("Potter's Field");
```

FIGURE 3.8:

The object variables `LocalAirport` and `CityAirport` initially reference the new object representing City National Airport.

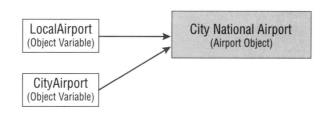

FIGURE 3.9:

Next, the object variable `CityAirport` is used to refer to the new object representing Potter's Field. Since there is still a reference to the first object (`LocalAirport`), the original object will not be discarded by the system.

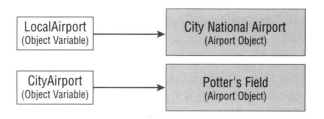

In this instance, the object representing City National Airport is not garbage collected because `LocalAirport` still refers to it.

Finalizers

There are a few situations in which a class needs to clean itself up before garbage collection. It can do this by implementing a finalizer member function. Finalizers are called just before a class is garbage collected. They are typically used to close open files or connections, or to ensure that related tasks get completed before the object is forgotten.

To create a finalizer, simply define a member function called finalize:

```
protected void finalize() {
    System.out.println("This object is about to be garbage collected");
}
```

The `protected` keyword will be explained in the next chapter (it limits the classes that may call the finalizer function).

Finalizers are rather tricky to write because it is impossible to determine exactly when an object will be garbage collected—it could be within microseconds or, if the program is terminated, may never occur. This means that a finalizer should rely as little as possible on the existence of other objects, for there is no guarantee that the other objects were not garbage collected first. It is also possible for an object to avert its own garbage collection by creating a new reference to itself in the finalizer. Therefore, if your class must perform some shutdown or cleanup operation before being garbage collected, you should write a non-finalizer function to take care of the operation, and call that function explicitly before discarding the object. Suppose you write a class called `ComLink` that handles network communications, and write a member function called `close` that closes the network channel. You know you need to close the network channel before discarding any `ComLink` objects, so the simplest solution might appear to be calling `close` from `ComLink`'s finalize method.

However, as pointed out above, it is possible that `close` will not be called for an extended period of time, or perhaps not at all. This could cause the system to run out of network channels because channels have not been freed by discarded `ComLink` objects in a timely manner. The only reliable solution in such cases is to make sure you call the `close` function explicitly, before any objects are discarded.

Summary

Object-oriented programming languages support encapsulation, inheritance, and polymorphism. Encapsulation separates the interface from the implementation by hiding data within the object and making that data accessible via member functions. Subclasses inherit the member functions and variables of their parent classes, making it very easy to reuse the functionality in the parent class. Polymorphism allows you to create generic, reusable code which will work with a wide range of different class datatypes. Because Java supports all these features, Java code is reusable and reliable.

The Core API, Java's core class library, contains about 225 prefabricated classes you can use to do everything from graphics to network programming. You can use Java's object-oriented features to inherit functionality from the class library as you write your own programs. In fact, most interface related classes will inherit much of their capability from the class library.

The next chapter will examine in detail the Java language datatypes, keywords, and expressions, and study the finer points of data hiding.

CHAPTER

FOUR

4

Datatypes, Modifiers, and Expressions

- Java Grammar

- Basic Datatypes

- Java API Datatypes

- Class Definitions

- Datatype and Function Modifiers

Java's program structure and grammar are quite similar to that of C++. The first part of this chapter describes basic Java syntax and Java keywords. You will learn a standard way to choose variable, class, and function names, and how to enter data values into your code.

Java datatypes come in three varieties: basic built-in (or primitive) datatypes, system classes that have been defined in the Java Core API, and user-defined classes. The built-in datatypes hold atomic units of information such as individual characters, numbers, or true-false values. The built-in datatypes themselves are not classes, so they do not have member functions. The API includes a language package (`java.lang`), which has class equivalents of the basic datatypes, and other very commonly used datatypes such as the `String` class for storing strings of characters and the `Thread` class for multithreading. In the last chapter, you learned how to create your own user-defined classes, and in this chapter you will learn how to define your own classes with more advanced data-hiding.

Java Grammar

A language *grammar* defines how and when words can be used, as well as the punctuation required. Java's grammar specifies the way the following are written:

Comments   Remarks added by the programmer for documentation purposes.

Statements   A statement is a single "line" of the program.

Code blocks   A set of statements grouped together as a unit.

File structure   The components of a Java source file, and the order in which they are defined.

Keywords   Words that are predefined in the Java language (not to be used as identifiers).

Identifiers   The names you give to classes, variables, and functions. Identifiers have restrictions on leading characters. There are also some optional, yet widely used, conventions for identifiers.

Literals   Constant values are written differently, depending on the datatype—for example, to distinguish the characters "123" from the number 123.

Expressions   A combination of terms that evaluate to a single data value.

Operators   Operators perform addition, subtraction, multiplication, and other mathematical and non-mathematical operations.

Code blocks   A set of statements grouped together as a unit.

File structure   The components of a Java source file, and the order in which they are defined.

   Each one of these grammatical concepts will be described in the following sections.

Comments

Comments can be added to Java source code in the same two ways as in C++. The first type of comment begins with /* and ends with */, and allows you to add comments that extend across several lines of text:

```
a = b + c;
/* Here is a comment which
   extends across two lines */
```

Generally, you cannot *nest* comments (that is, place comments within comments):

```
a = b + c;
/* Here is a comment which /* a comment within a comment */
   extends across two lines */
```

In this example, the first comment ends at the first */, leaving the second line of text without a starting comment marker. This results in a compile-time error.

As we mentioned in Chapter 2, multiline comments have special meaning for the javadoc utility when the first character inside the comment is an asterisk, that is when the comment begins with /**:

```
a = b + c;
/** This comment has special meaning for the javadoc utility.
    It will be part of documentation automatically generated
    by the javadoc program. */
```

The second type of comment extends from the comment marker // to the end of the line of text:

```
a = b + c;   // this comment extends to the end of this line of text
```

These comments can be embedded within /* */ comments.

Statements

A *statement* is a single "line" of Java code. There is not a one-to-one correspondence between lines of code and lines of text in a Java source file. Java uses the semicolon as punctuation to indicate the end of a line of code. The line

```
a = b + c + d + e + f + g;
```

is the same as

```
a = b + c + d +
    e + f + g;
```

The spaces between terms in a statement can consist of any number of *whitespace* characters. Whitespace characters are spaces, tabs, linefeeds, and carriage returns.

NOTE On UNIX and Macintosh systems, each line of text is usually terminated by a carriage return character (ASCII code 13). In Windows, lines of text are usually delimited by carriage return and linefeed characters (CR/LF, or ASCII code 13 followed by ASCII code 10). Java compilers see all these characters as whitespace, and do not care how lines of text are terminated. For more information on ASCII, see the section on character datatypes, later in this chapter.

Code Blocks

Statements can be grouped together into blocks so that a single statement can easily control the execution of many other statements. Java code blocks are delimited with braces ({ and }). You have already seen code blocks used to group the statements belonging to a class:

```
class Flight {
    int     altitude;
    int     heading;
    int     speed;
    float   latitude;
    float   longitude;

    // change the flight's heading by angle degrees
    void turnFlight(int angle) {
```

```
heading = (heading + angle) % 360;
// make sure angle is in the range 0-359 degrees
if (heading < 0) heading = heading + 360;

    }
}
```

As you can see, code blocks can be nested within other blocks.

The amount of whitespace between braces and statements is arbitrary, but conventionally, a left brace is placed at the end of a line (or the start of the next line), the right brace on its own line, and indentation is used to highlight the grouping of code.

Source File Structure: Packages

Java source files may contain only three types of statements outside of code blocks:

A package statement   This defines the package to which the classes in the file will belong.

Import statements   These establish a shorthand for referring to existing classes (such as those in the API) by class name only, without specifying the full package name.

Class statements   These define your classes.

The package and import statements are both optional. A package is a group of related classes. Classes in the same package have freer access to each other's member variables and functions, and need to be stored in a predefined location on the server or on the client machine. A full description of Java packages appears in the next chapter.

Note that the statements in a source file must appear in the order listed (package, import, then class).

Here is a sample Java source file with all three types of components:

```
package com.sybex.examples;

import java.awt.Panel;
import java.awt.Color;

class ColorPanel extends Panel {

    ColorPanel     .
    .
    .
    .
}
```

This code fragment defines a new class called `ColorPanel` that belongs to a package called `com.sybex.examples`. Another program referring to this class would refer to the class as `com.sybex.examples.ColorPanel`.

The import statements make it easier to refer to classes in an existing package called `java.awt`. The `java.awt` package is the Abstract Windowing Toolkit package, part of the Core API. The first import statement allows you to refer to the class `java.awt.Panel` from class `java.awt` as, simply, `Panel`. Similarly, the second import statement allows you to refer to the `Color` class in the same package by its class name, `Color`, rather the package and class name, `java.awt.Color`.

The last statement in the file is a class definition. It is a compound statement; that is, it is a statement containing a block of other statements. Additional class definitions may follow this one.

Keywords

A *keyword* is a word that has a special meaning for the Java compiler, such as a datatype name or a program construct name. The complete list of keywords is shown in Table 4.1.

Table 4.1: Java Keywords

abstract	boolean	break	byte
case	catch	char	class
const*	continue	default	do
double	else	extends	final
finally	float	for	goto*
if	implements	import	instanceof
int	interface	long	native
new	null	package	private
protected	public	return	short
static	super	switch	synchronized
this	throw	throws	transient*
try	void	volatile	while

* = These keywords are reserved but currently are not used.

Identifiers

An *identifier* is a name given to a variable, class, or function. You can choose identifiers to be anything you wish, as long as the identifier begins with a letter and is not spelled the same as a keyword.

You may have noticed a pattern in the way the identifiers in this book are capitalized. They are capitalized according to the identifier conventions used in the Core API, and it is recommended you follow the same convention to keep your code more readable. Familiarity with these conventions will also make it easier to read the sample code provided. Table 4.2 lists these identifier conventions. The compiler will not complain if you do not follow these conventions.

Identifiers are not restricted to ASCII characters. If your editor supports it, you can have Unicode characters in variable names. Also,

Table 4.2: Conventions for Naming Identifiers

Type of Identifier	Convention	Example
Class names	Capitalize each word within the identifier	`Flight`, `CommercialFlight`
Function names	Capitalize every word within the identifier except the first	`printFlight`, `turnFlight`
Variable names	Capitalize every word within the identifier except the first	`altitude`, `flightNumber`
Constant variable names	Capitalize every letter; underscores between words.	`MAX_INBOUND_FLIGHTS`

Note: There is a special convention for variables that do not change their value.

there is no limit to the number of characters in an identifier. If you have two variables that differ at the 512th position (or beyond), the compiler will detect this and treat them as separate.

Literals

Whereas an identifier is a symbol for a value, a literal is an actual value such as 35, or "Hello". Table 4.3 summarizes the formats for literals for each datatype. As you can see, a datatype may have more than one format for a literal.

By default, integer literals are of type int, but you can override this by adding the letter L to the end of the number to make it a long. Similarly, floating-point literals represent double precision numbers unless the F suffix is used to mark them as floats.

Table 4.3: Formats for Literals of Each Datatype

Datatype	Literal
`byte, short int`	Decimal digits (not starting with 0) `0x` followed by hexadecimal digits; for example, 0xFF 12 0 followed by octal digits, for example, `0726`
`long`	Same as for `int` datatype, but followed by the character 1 or L; for example, `1234L, 0x12FABL, 043543212L, 12341`
`float`	Digits with a decimal point and/or exponent, followed by the character f or F; for example, `1.234f, 1.234E+5F` (1.234x105 = 123400), `.1234F`
`double`	Same as for `float` datatype, but without f or F suffix, and with optional d or D suffix; for example, `1.234D, 1.234, 1.234E-5` (1.234x105 = 0.00001234), `.1234`
`boolean`	`true` or `false`
`char`	An ASCII character within single quotation marks; for example, `'a'` or `'B'`. If your editor supports input of Unicode characters, these can go right into the single quotes. A predefined escape sequence within single quotation marks, for example, `'\t', '\012', '\u000A'` (see Table 4.4)
`String`	A sequence of characters or escape sequences within double quotation marks; for example, `"Hello World\n"`

Expressions and Operators

`Expressions` are combinations of variables, keywords, or symbols that evaluate to a value of some type. The value may be a number, string, or any other class or datatype. You might think of an expression as something that could be written on the right-hand side of an assignment statement.

The simplest expressions are simply variables or literals:

15

or

a

Table 4.4: Character Escape Sequences

Special Escape Sequences	\b	backspace
	\t	horizontal tab
	\n	linefeed
	\f	form feed
	\r	carriage return
	\"	double quote "
	\'	single quote '
	\\	backslash
Octal Escape Sequences	\DDD	Character with ASCII code DDD octal, where DDD is a sequence of three octal digits (0-7); for example, \071 is ASCII character 71 octal, 57 decimal
Unicode Escape Sequences	\uHHHH	Character with Unicode value HHHH hex, where HHHH is a sequence of four hexadecimal digits (0-9, A-F, a-f); for example, \u0041 is Unicode character 41 hex, 65 decimal

or

```
"Hello"
```

These expressions may be found on the right-hand side of an assignment statement such as the following one which assigns the string "Hello" to the variable s:

```
s = "Hello";
```

As in C, an assignment has a value of its own; namely, the value of the assignment is the value of the right-hand side of the assignment itself:

```
b = a = 15;
```

In this example, the value 15 is assigned to a, and the value of the assignment "a = 15" is itself 15, so 15 is also assigned to b.

Member Function Calls

Another type of expression is the member function call. As you have seen, member functions can evaluate to a datatype, so they can appear on the right side of an assignment:

```
a = incomingFlight.getHeading();
b = weatherStation.getCelsius(farenheit);
```

The generic structure of a member function or variable reference is

```
object.membervariable
object.memberfunction( arguments )
```

or in the case of static member functions and variables (see the section "Storage and Lifetime Modifiers" later in this chapter):

```
class.membervariable
class.memberfunction( arguments )
```

Object Allocation

Object allocation is, as you have seen, just a special kind of function call. You can use the new keyword to call the constructor for the class you are instantiating:

```
new classname( arguments )
```

An example is

```
Flight f;
f = new Flight();
```

or

```
Airport f;
f = new Airport("City National Airport");
```

or

```
Airport f = new Airport("City National Airport");
```

If you do not provide a constructor for your class, a default constructor is created that accepts no arguments. However, if you only provide a constructor that requires arguments/parameters, there will be no constructor that accepts no parameters. Note that a class cannot be instantiated if the class is abstract or has only static members.

this and super

There are two special reserved words which can also be used to form expressions. If you want to refer to the current instance of the class in which the code is written, you can use the this keyword. The super keyword refers to the superclass of the class in which the code is written.

Using the this keyword, you can have an object print itself on the console when you call its print method, by adding the following code to any class:

```
public void print() {
    System.out.println(this);
}
```

If, for example, this code were added to the Flight class, you could write:

```
Flight incomingFlight = new Flight();

incomingFlight.setHeading(140);
incomingFlight.print();
```

In the print() method, this points to incomingFlight, so the last line of this listing is equivalent to:

```
System.out.println(incomingFlight);
```

As shown in the last chapter, this is also used when referring to a constructor from within another constructor. In this case, this appears as a function call:

```
public Flight(int heading) {
    setHeading(heading);
```

```
    }

    public Flight(int heading, int newAltitude) {
        this(heading);
        altitude = newAltitude;
    }
```

The call to this(heading) in the second constructor calls the first constructor.

The super keyword is used to refer to the methods or member variables of the superclass. If a subclass defines a member variable with the same name as its parent's member variable, you can use the super keyword to reference the parent's variable from the subclass. super is also used to refer to the methods of the parent class:

```
class Parent {
    String name;

    void print () {
        System.out.println("Parent " + name);
    }
    .
    .
    .
}

class Child extends Parent {
    String name;

    String childName() {
        return name;
    }

    String parentName() {
        // return the name of the parent
        return super.name;
    }

    void print() {
        System.out.println("Child " + name + " is child of");
        super.print();
    }
    .
```

```
.
.
.
}
```

Operator Expressions

The other types of expressions involve combinations of variables, literals, function calls, and operators. An *operator* is a symbol that transforms a variable or combines it in some way with another variable or literal. The multiplication operator, *, combines two numbers to form a third number:

```
a = b * c;
```

The expressions on which an operator acts are called *operands*. The multiplication operator is an example of a *binary operator*—that is, it takes two operands and creates a new result. Other operators act on a single variable to produce a second:

```
a = - b;
```

Here, the negation operator (-) transforms a single variable b into another quantity that is then assigned to a. An operator that creates output from a single operand is called a *unary operator*. Another type of unary operator automatically assigns a new value to the operand; the auto-increment (++) and auto-decrement (--) operators add and subtract one from the operand, respectively:

```
a = 10;
a++; // add one to a (a is now 11)
a--; //subtract one from a (a is now 10)
```

Operator Precedence

When several operators are used in a single expression, it is important to know in which order the operators will be applied. If you use addition and multiplication as shown here:

```
a = 4 + 5 * 6;
```

do you get 34 or 54? The answer depends on *operator precedence* (that is, the order in which the operators will be applied). As with normal math, multiplication (*) has higher precedence than addition (+), so the multiplication is done first, and the answer is 34. If you want to do the addition before the multiplication, you can use parentheses to group parts of the calculation together:

```
a = (4 + 5) * 6; // The number 54 will be assigned to a
```

Java will evaluate expressions in parentheses as a single unit before proceeding with the rest of the calculation, so program defensively. Use parentheses to group parts of the calculation together whenever possible, even when they are not needed:

```
a = 4 + (5 * 6);
```

This is unambiguous and helps you and the reader of your programs know what is going on. It also means you won't have to remember the precedence of the operators.

If two operators have the same precedence, there is a well-defined order in which the computations will be performed—from left to right or right to left. This property of an operator is known as the operator's *associativity*. The multiplication operator is left associative, so when evaluating the product 2 * 3 * 4, the leftmost product will be evaluated first to get 6 * 4, before finally performing the last product and arriving at the result of 24.

Arithmetic Operators

Java's *arithmetic operators* are summarized in Table 4.5. These operators accept integer or floating-point operands and produce integer or floating-point results. We have included the auto-increment and auto-decrement operators in this category.

The remainder operator (%) returns the remainder of dividing the first operand by the second, so 24 % 10 is the remainder left over after dividing 24 by 10, namely 4. This operator also works with floating point operands.

Table 4.5: Arithmetic Operators

Operator	Purpose	Precedence	Associativity
++, ——	Auto-increment, auto-decrement	1 (highest precedence)	Right
+, —	Unary plus, unary minus	2	Right
*	Multiplication	4	Left
/	Division	4	Left
%	Remainder (modulo division)	4	Left
+, —	Addition, subtraction	5	Left

Boolean and Relational Operators

Relational operators compare two quantities to determine if they are equal or if one is greater than the other. The operator which tests for equality is the == operator. If the operands are built-in types (arithmetic, character, or boolean), then the equality operator returns the boolean value `true` if the operands have the same value, and returns `false` otherwise. If the operands are object variables, the equality operator returns `true` if the object variables refer to the same object (or are both null). If the object variables refer to different objects, or if one refers to an object and the other is null, then the equality operator returns `false`. Here are some examples:

When the operands are built-in types, the equality operator works as you would expect:

```
boolean a, b;
a = (2 == 2);  // a will be true
b = (2 == 3);  // b will be false
```

In contrast, if two objects are compared for equality:

```
boolean a, b;
Flight f1, f2;
```

```
// f1 and f2 will be two separate Flight objects
// with the same default values
f1 = new Flight();
f2 = new Flight();

a = (f1 == f2); // a will be false because f1 and f2 refer
                // to different instances, even though they
                // contain exactly the same data

f1 = f2;
b = (f1 == f2); // a will be true because f1 and f2 now refer
                // to the identical instance
```

The inequality operator (!=) does the exact opposite of the equality operator—it returns `true` when the operands are not equal.

Numeric operands can be compared with each other using the greater than (>), less than (<), greater than or equal (>=), and less than or equal (<=) operators:

```
boolean a, b, c, d;

a = (1 > 2); // a is false
b = (1 < 2); // b is true
c = (1 <= 2); // c is true
d = (1 >= 0); // d is true
```

Java has kept C's question mark–colon, or conditional operator, that takes three operands (it is a *ternary operator*). The first operand is boolean, and the two other operands may be of any type. If the boolean operand is true, the result is the second operand; if it is false, the result is the third operand:

```
boolean b;
int c;

b = true;
        c = (b ? 1 : 2); // 1 will be assigned to c because b is true
b = false;
c = (b ? 1 : 2); // now 2 will be assigned to c because b is false.
```

These comparison operators are usually used in conjunction with conditional statements (these are covered in Chapter 6). The relational operators are summarized in Table 4.6.

Table 4.6: Relational Operators

Operator	Purpose	Precedence	Associativity
>, <, >=, <=	Tests relative magnitude	7	Left
==	Tests equality	8	Left
!=	Tests inequality	8	Left
? :	Conditional—returns one of two operands based on a third	14	Right

Boolean operators (Table 4.7) act on boolean operands and return a boolean result. They implement the standard Boolean algebraic operations: AND, OR, NOT, and XOR (eXclusive OR). The AND operator returns `true` if both operands are true. The OR operator returns `true` if either operand is true. Java has two versions of each of these operators. The first version (& for AND, | for OR) forces evaluation of both operands, while the second version (&& for AND, || for OR) will not evaluate the second operand if it can determine the result after evaluating the first.

Here is an example to illustrate the difference between these two versions of the OR operation:

```
boolean b;

// to compute the following, the VM will evaluate both expressions
// and, therefore, will perform both multiplications
b = ( 100 > ( 5 * 6 ) ) | ( 100 > (8 * 8));  // b will be true

// to compute the following, the VM will evaluate only the expression
// on the left, and, therefore, will perform only one
// multiplication (7 * 9)
b = ( 100 > ( 7 * 9 ) ) || ( 100 > (4 * 5));  // b will be true
```

The two AND operators work analogously.

There are occasions when you want the VM to evaluate both sides, whether or not the result of the AND/OR operation can be deduced by evaluating only one operand. In other situations, you do not want the VM to continue because it will result in needless comparisons or exceptions, if you are assuming previous conditions succeeded.

The XOR operator returns true if the operands are not the same—one operand is true, and the other is false. The NOT operator is a unary operator which returns the opposite of its operand.

Table 4.7: Boolean Operators

Operator	Purpose	Precedence	Associativity
!	Not	2 (++/− first)	Right
&	Boolean AND	9	Left
^	XOR	10	Left
|	Boolean OR	11	Left
&&	Conditional AND	12	Left
||	Conditional OR	13	Left

Bitwise Operators

The integral types (`byte`, `short`, `int`, `long`) are represented in the computer's memory as a sequence of bits (binary digits). Just like decimal numbers, binary numbers have their most significant digits to the left. In decimal, the most significant digit in the number 325 is the 3 because it represents 300, and the least significant digit is the 5. Written as a binary number, 325 is 101000101. The leftmost digit represents 100000000 binary (256 decimal) and is the most significant digit.

Java's integers are signed numbers, so Java must use one bit of storage to represent the sign of the integer. For Java's integer datatypes, the high bit is used to represent the sign of the number, as shown in Figure 4.1. If the high bit is 1, the number is negative.

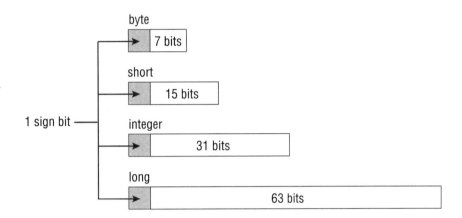

FIGURE 4.1:

Java's integral datatypes use the high bit to indicate the sign of the number. If the high bit is 1, the number is negative.

Java uses the same operators as the C language to manipulate the bits of integers. Because all of Java's integral datatypes are signed, Java supplements the C operators with an additional operator. Bit manipulation operators are referred to as *bitwise* operators, and they are listed in Table 4.8. The bitwise operators perform the same sorts of functions as the boolean operators, as well as bit shifts.

The bitwise AND operator applies the AND operation to the corresponding bits of each operand. The bitwise OR, XOR, and NOT operators work in a similar fashion. The bitwise operators are illustrated in Figure 4.2.

The shift operators shift the bits in an integral type to the left or the right as shown in Figure 4.3. The shift operators are binary operators. The second operand is an integer which determines the number of bits to shift. The standard C shift operators act slightly differently in Java; they preserve the sign of the left operand (they do not shift the sign bit). Java adds the >>> operator which shifts all bits to the right as if the integer was unsigned.

FIGURE 4.2:

Boolean bitwise operators

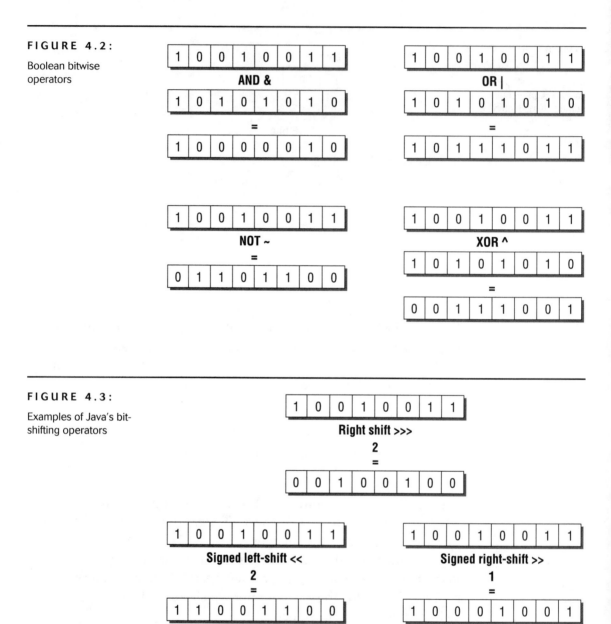

FIGURE 4.3:

Examples of Java's bit-shifting operators

NOTE

For simplicity, we are using signed 8-bit bytes in Figure 4.3. However, you should be aware that Java's shift operators work with `int` and `long` datatypes only. If you shift a negative `short` to the right using the >> operator, you may end up with a larger number than you started with. This is because the left operand is cast to an `int` before being shifted.

Table 4.8: Bitwise Operators

Operator	Purpose	Precedence	Associativity
~	Not (bitwise complement)	2	Right
<<, >>	Left shift, Right shift	6	Left
>>>	Right shift as if unsigned	6	Left
&	Bitwise AND	9	Left
^	Bitwise XOR	10	Left
|	Bitwise OR	11	Left

The concatenation operator (+) is the only operator that applies to strings in particular. It glues two strings together to form a third:

```
String s;

s = "Hello" + " " + "World"; // "Hello World" is assigned to s
```

If only one operand is a string, then the other operand is converted to a string automatically:

```
String s;

s = "5 * 6 =" + (5 * 6); // "5 * 6 = 30" is assigned to s
```

If the nonstring operand is an object, Java uses the `toString()` member function to obtain a string equivalent of the object. The `toString()` function is inherited by all classes, because it is implemented by the `Object` class. The default behavior of `toString()` is to return the name of the class of the object along with an @ and the *hashcode* of the object. The hashcode is a unique number assigned to the class by the class loader. The following code illustrates the implicit use of the `toString()` operator:

```
String s;
SomeObject m;

s = "m is " + m; // "m is a SomeObject@1393870" is assigned to s
```

The concatenation operator has a precedence of 5 and is left-associative.

Assignment Operators

As was mentioned earlier, the assignment operator is an operator that assigns the second operand to the first and returns the second operand as a result.

Other assignment operators are shorthand for combined operation and assignment. If you wanted to add 5 to a number you could write:

```
int i;
i = i + 5;
```

You could also use the assignment operator +=:

```
int i;
i += 5; // this is the same as i = i + 5
```

Assignment operators exist for most of the normal operators already mentioned. They are summarized in Table 4.9.

Special Operators

The *cast* operator converts from one datatype into another. A cast is written as the name of the type into which you are casting the operand within parentheses:

```
int i;
long l;
```

Table 4.9: Assignment Operators

Operator	Purpose	Precedence	Associativity
=	Assignment	15	Right
*=	Assignment with operation	15	Right
/=			
%=			
+=			
-=			
>>=			
<<=			
>>>=			
^=			
|=			
&=			

```
l = 1 << 40; // l is a very large number
l--;
i = (int) l; // l is being cast into an integer
```

If you are assigning a value of lower precision to a variable of higher precision, no cast is necessary. For example, no cast is needed to assign an int to a long, or a float to a double.

Type cast operators have a precedence of 1 and are right-associative.

The instanceof operator is used to test the class of an object:

```
boolean b;
Flight f;
CommercialFlight cf; //CommercialFlight is a subclass of Flight

f = new Flight();
cf = new CommercialFlight();
b = f instanceof Flight; // b will be true
b = f instanceof String; // b will be false
b = cf instanceof Flight; // b will be true because cf is a subclass of Flight
```

The instanceof operator has a precedence of 7 and is left-associative.

Basic Datatypes

Java's built-in datatypes are understood by the compiler itself, without reference to any libraries or the Core API. These types can be classified into numeric, boolean, and character datatypes.

Variable Declarations

Before using any variable, it must first be declared. A variable declaration specifies the datatype, the variable name and, optionally, the default value for the variable. Later in this chapter, we will explain how to limit access to a variable in its declaration. A general variable declaration looks like the following:

```
datatype identifier [ = defaultvalue ] {, identifier [ = defaultvalue ] }  ;
```

Identifiers are just symbols; in this case, they are the names of the variables we are defining. To define integer variables i, j, and k, and initialize them to 1, 2, and 3, respectively, you can enter

```
int i;
int j;
int k;
i = 1;
j = 2;
k = 3;
```

or in an abbreviated form

```
int i = 1, j = 2, k = 3;
```

Variable declarations can be placed anywhere in your code, as long as they precede the first use of the variable. However, it is common practice to place the declarations at the top of each block of code.

Numeric Datatypes

Java has six numeric datatypes that differ in the size and precision of the numbers they can hold. The basic numeric datatypes are listed in Table 4.10.

Table 4.10: Java's Built-in Numeric Datatypes

Type	Description	Size	Minimum Value	Maximum Value
byte	Tiny signed integer	8 bits	−128	127
short	Short signed integer	16 bits	−32768	32767
int	Signed integer	32 bits	−2147483648	2147483647
long	Long signed integer	64 bits	−9223372036854775808	9223372036854775807
float	Floating-point number	32 bits	Positive: $1.40239846 \times 10^{-45}$ Negative: $-3.40282347 \times 10^{38}$	Positive: $3.40282347 \times 10^{38}$ Negative: $-1.40239846 \times 10^{-45}$
double	Double precision floating-point number	64 bits	Positive: $4.9406564584124654 \times 10^{-324}$ Negative: $-1.7976931348623157 \times 10^{308}$	Positive: $1.7976931348623157 \times 10^{308}$ Negative: $-4.9406564584124654 \times 10^{-324}$

Generally, when choosing a datatype for a variable, you will want to use the smallest datatype which holds the largest number you will work with, either now or in the foreseeable future. This saves memory, yet provides room for expansion should your code require modifications. For example, suppose a company carries 6000 items in its catalog, and you need to choose a datatype to represent each item's number. You might select a short integer to save space, but if the company catalog grows to more than 32767 items, the company will have to rewrite the software. Choosing a standard integer datatype will give your code greater longevity.

Choosing the right floating-point datatype is a little trickier, because the decision depends on both the size and precision of the numbers you will be working with. For example, if you are converting Celsius to Fahrenheit, you probably only need four digits of precision, and a range of temperatures between ±150 degrees, so you should use a float. Scientific applications, which involve a large number of computations—for example, orbital trajectories—require higher precision to reduce rounding errors, even if the results themselves will not exceed single precision magnitudes.

The Java VM initializes every numeric variable to zero before it is used. This is in contrast to most other programming languages where uninitialized variables contain random values. This issue generally does not arise because the use of uninitialized variables is detected and prevented by most Java compilers.

Not-a-Number and Infinity

Java's floating-point datatypes have special values for "Not-a-Number," positive infinity, and negative infinity. Not-a-Number, or NaN, is the result of an invalid mathematical operation, such as dividing zero by zero, or multiplying an infinity by zero. Positive infinity is the result of dividing a positive number by zero, and negative infinity is the result of dividing a finite negative number by zero.

Boolean Datatype

Boolean variables hold true or false values. Most languages treat integers as boolean variables, regarding zero as false and nonzero as true. However, like Pascal, Java has its own boolean datatype, separate from any numeric datatype. Although it requires a slightly more verbose programming style, it is considerably safer than using integers as boolean types, because integers will never accidentally be treated as booleans. Uninitialized boolean variables are initialized to false.

Character Datatype

The character datatype, `char`, holds a single character. Each character is a number or character code which refers to a *character set*, an indexed list of symbols. For example, in the ASCII (American Standard Code for Information Interchange, pronounced "as-key") character set, the character code 65 corresponds to the letter *A*, and the character code 49 refers to the digit 1. Most PC character sets use an extended form of the ASCII character set with 256 character codes, so each character can be stored in a byte. The first 127 characters of such character sets are standard across character sets (except for the currency symbol), and the last 128 characters vary from set to set, and are used for special characters, such as foreign alphabetic characters or currency symbols.

Java's creators designed Java with expandability and internationalization in mind. The Java `char` datatype is 16 bits wide and holds a Unicode symbol rather than an ASCII character. Unicode is an extended version of the ASCII character set, designed for handling multiple languages. Fortunately, Unicode corresponds to a standard ASCII character set (ISO-LATIN-1) for the first 127 characters. It is possible to write Java programs and not know you are using Unicode.

NOTE   **For more information on Unicode see** `http://www.stonehand.com/unicode.html`.

String Datatype

A string is a sequence of characters. The `String` datatype is actually a class of the Core API (`java.lang.String`), rather than a built-in type, but it is used so frequently that it is appropriate to cover here. The `String` class has special status in Java, because the compiler recognizes `String` constants; characters within double quotes are recognized by the compiler as `String` literals.

Strings can be as long as you wish—there is no maximum length specified in the Java language specification; however, most implementations will probably limit you to about two billion characters, which is plenty of capacity for almost any application.

Strings are immutable in Java; that is, you cannot change the contents of a string, although you can redefine a `String` object variable. For instance, the string `message` is initially defined as

```
String message = "Hello World";
```

There is no way to change the contents of the object pointed to by `message`, by, say, passing it to another function

```
changeString(s);  // it is impossible to change the object pointed to by s
```

However, you can make the `String` variable `message` refer to a new string object:

```
message = message + "!!";
```

This is a rather subtle point, and the key to understanding it is to keep the concept of object variable and the object itself distinct. There is an additional string-handling class in the API called `String-Buffer`. A `StringBuffer` is like the String datatype, but it has functions for modifying the contents of the `StringBuffer`. When the Java compiler encounters the code in the preceding example, it rewrites it as follows:

```
message = new StringBuffer(message).append("!!").toString();
```

That is, the compiler converts the original `message` into a `String-Buffer`, appends the exclamation points to the `StringBuffer`, and then converts the `StringBuffer` back into a `String`.

Class Declarations

As you have seen in Chapter 3, a class declaration begins with the keyword class, then specifies the name of the class, the name of the superclass (if different from Object), and any interfaces supported by the class:

```
class classname extends parentclassname implements interfacename {

    member-variable-declarations

    member-function-declarations

    class-initializer

}
```

Member variable declarations are just like other variable declarations, but they may have modifier keywords which alter their visibility outside the class:

```
modifier(s) datatype-specifier identifier = initial-value ;
```

(Modifiers are described in the next section.)

Sample member functions were shown in the last chapter. Their general structure is

```
modifier(s) datatype-specifier identifier( argument-list ) {
    code-block
}
```

The *datatype-specifier* can be any datatype or the keyword void. Void means no datatype. Functions can be declared to return void, meaning that they return no value. The *argument-list* specifies the parameters that will be accepted by the function:

```
datatype identifier , datatype identifier, datatype identifier
```

Finally, the code-block consists of one or more statements. Refer back to earlier sample code for examples.

The *class-initializer* contains code that will be executed once when the class is loaded by the VM. The structure of the class initializer is as follows:

```
static { code-block }
```

An example of the use of the class initializer appears later in this chapter in the section on the `static` modifier.

Scope Rules

In early programming languages such as COBOL, all variables are *global* variables. A global variable is a variable that can be accessed from any part of a program, and, consequently, global variables must have unique names. Since all variables in COBOL are global, every variable in a COBOL program had to be unique. This led to the practice of using a single variable for different purposes in different parts of the program. Keeping track of global variables is a difficult task, and makes such programs prone to bugs. In particular, a change in one small part of the code can adversely affect a completely different part of the program.

The solution to the problem of global variables is to use *local* variables, which are variables that have a limited life-span and relate only to a single part of the code. You can use two local variables with identical names as long as they are in different parts of the program. The rules that dictate which parts of the program can see which variables are called *scope rules*.

Variables defined within a member function are local to that member function, so you can use the same variable name in several member functions, as shown in this example:

```
class MyClass {

    int i; // member variable

    int First() {
        int j; // local variable

        // both i and j are accessible from this point

        return 1;

    }

    int Second() {
        int j; // local variable

        // both i and j are accessible from this point

        return 2;
    }

}
```

The variable `j` defined in the function `First()` is created when it is declared as the function is called, and is destroyed when the function exits. The same is true for the local variable `j` in the function `Second()`. With multithreading, it is possible for the interpreter to be in both functions simultaneously, but this causes no conflict, because the two local variables are completely independent of each other. Another way to think of these local variables is to imagine that the compiler renames them uniquely (for example, `j1` and `j2`).

Modifiers

A *modifier* is a keyword that affects either the life time or the accessibility of a class, a variable, or a member function. Table 4.11 shows the applicability of each modifier to classes, functions, member variables, and local variables.

Table 4.11: Applicability of Modifiers to Classes, Member Functions, Member Variables, and Local Variables

Modifier	Classes	Member Functions	Member Variables	Local Variables
abstract	✓	✓	–	–
static	–	✓	✓	–
public	✓	✓	✓	–
protected	✓	✓	✓	–
private	–	✓	✓	–
private protected	–	✓	✓	–
synchronized	–	✓	–	–
native	–	✓	–	–
transient	–	–	✓	–
volatile	–	–	✓	–
final	✓	✓	✓	✓

Storage and Lifetime Modifiers

abstract

When applied to a class, the `abstract` modifier indicates that the class has not been fully implemented and that it should not be instantiated. If applied to a member function declaration, the `abstract` modifier means that the function will be implemented in a subclass. Since the function has no implementation, the class cannot be instantiated, and must be declared as abstract. Interfaces are abstract by default.

static

Ordinarily, each instance of a class has its own copy of any member variables. However, it is possible to designate a member variable as belonging to the class itself, independent of any objects of that class. Such member variables are called *static* members and are declared with the `static` modifier keyword. Static member variables are often used when tracking global information about the instances of a class. The following class tracks the number of instances of itself using a static member variable called `instanceCount`:

```
public class MyClass {
    public static int instanceCount;

    public MyClass() {
        // each time this constructor is called,
        //increment the instance counter
        instanceCount++;
    }

    static {
        instanceCount = 0;
    }
}
```

Notice that we have used a static initializer to initialize the static variable.

Methods can also be declared as static. For example, a static method called `resetCounter()` can reset the instance counter for MyClass:

```
public class MyClass {
    public static int instanceCount;

    public MyClass() {
        // each time this constructor is called,
        //increment the instance counter
        instanceCount++;
    }

    public static void resetCounter() {
```

```
            instanceCount = 0;
    }

    static {
        instanceCount = 0;
    }

}
```

The `resetCounter()` method can be called via the class `MyClass` or via an instance of `MyClass`:

```
MyClass m, n;

m = new MyClass(); // instanceCount will equal 1 after this constructor call
n = new MyClass(); // instanceCount will equal 2 after this constructor call
System.out.println(MyClass.instanceCount + " instances have been created");

m.resetCounter(); // reset the counter
MyClass.resetCounter(); // another way to reset the counter
```

The `System` class that is in the `java.lang` package of the API defines all its public methods and variables as static. All variables and functions are accessed via the class directly, not via an instance of the `System` class. In fact, the constructor for the `System` class is private, so you cannot create a new `System` object with the usual code:

```
System MySystem = new System(); // this is illegal
```

Instead, all variables and functions of the `System` class are accessed via the class itself. Recall from previous examples that you can print information on the console with the following code:

```
System.out.println("Hello World");
```

The member variable `out` is a static member variable of type `PrintStream`. It is defined in the API as

```
public static PrintStream out;
```

Because the `System` class defines its functions as static, you can call the function `currentTimeMillis()` to get the current time, with the following expression:

```
long timeNow = System.currentTimeMillis();
```

`currentTimeMillis()` is defined in the System class as

```
public static long currentTimeMillis()
```

Use totally static classes (classes in which all members are static) when you want to model a unique entity. Use static member variables when you want only a single unique copy of a variable, such as when you want to track the number of times that instances have been created.

synchronized

A synchronized member function allows only one thread to execute the function at a time. This prevents two threads of execution from undoing each other's work.

Suppose you have a function that first checks to see if a network communications channel is in use, and, if it is free, initiates communications on that channel. If two separate threads, here called A and B, execute this function at about the same time, a conflict can occur: Thread A sees that the channel is clear. Thread B sees the channel is clear. Thread A marks the channel for its own use and connects to its desired server. Thread B having already checked that the channel was free, marks the channel for thread B's exclusive use and connects to its own server. The problem is that checking the availability of the channel and actually claiming it are indivisible operations—the steps cannot be executed independently by different threads. By declaring the member function as `synchronized`, you can prevent thread B from entering the function until thread A has completed executing the function. For a more detailed look at threads, see Chapter 8.

Synchronized methods are non-static by default, but may be declared as static.

The synchronized modifier does not apply to classes or member variables.

native

Native methods are implemented in other language, such as C, so they have no code block. Many of the classes in the Core API are native because they need to access operating system specific routines, like drawing graphics on the screen. Here is an excerpt from the API's `Math` class:

```
/**
 * Returns the trigonometric sine of an angle.
 * @param a an assigned angle that is measured in radians
 */
public static native double sin(double a);
```

This declaration calls a function in a native code library that calculates the sine of the angle `a`. On an Intel x86 platform, the native code would call the sine function in the x86 processor's floating-point unit or floating-point coprocessor. On other platforms, the native code function may do the computation with software instead. This function happens to be declared with the `public` and `static` modifiers also.

The `native` modifier applies to functions only.

volatile

A volatile variable is one whose value may change independent of the Java program itself. Typically, volatile variables represent input from the outside world, such as a variable which denotes the time of day. They are also used to flag variables which could be changed by other threads of execution. The `volatile` keyword will prevent the compiler from attempting to track changes to the variable. The variable will always be assumed by the compiler to have a (potentially) new value each time it is accessed by Java code.

transient

The transient modifier currently has no effect in the Java language. It may be used in the future to implement object persistence (a way for objects to persist after the program has terminated).

final

Most languages have a way to declare a variable as constant (that is, unchangeable). Java is no exception. The final keyword indicates that a local variable or member variable cannot be altered. The main use of a final variable is as a symbolic constant. You can refer to a constant by name, and define that name in a single location in your code. If you later have to change the number in your code, you need only make the change at the point your final variable is defined.

Note that if you declare a variable as final, you must also initialize it at the same time:

```
final int MAX_PAGES = 23;
```

(The use of all caps for final variables is in accordance with our naming convention in Table 4.3.)

Member functions and classes can also be declared as final. A final member function cannot be overridden, and a final class cannot be subclassed.

When anything is declared final, the compiler/optimizer can make many assumptions which can dramatically increase performance.

Accessibility Modifiers

Java has other modifiers that are used to change the accessibility of classes and their members to other classes. By default, a class and its member functions and variables are known only to other classes in the same package. For simple applets, this means that a class is only accessible to other classes in the same directory.

The effects of the modifiers are listed here and shown in Figure 4.4. In the figure, there are three bars for each type of member modifier. The first bar represents the ability of a subclass to inherit a member variable or function. The second bar indicates the ability of a subclass to access a member in instances of the original class. The third bar denotes the accessibility of a member by non-subclasses.

For example, the figure shows that member functions or variables that are declared as `private protected`

- Will be inherited by subclasses, whether the subclasses are in the same package or not. This allows a subclass to access these members in instances of the subclass only.

- Can be accessed by subclasses in the same package; that is, subclasses can access these members in instances of the original class.

- Cannot be accessed by non-subclasses at all.

> **NOTE**
> Default is not actually a modifier; that is, there is no keyword for default accessibility. There is a keyword `default` that is used in switch statements (see Chapter 6); however, it is not a modifier. Some people call the default behavior "friendly," but that too is not a modifier.

A public class can be accessed by any other class. When a VM is asked to execute a new applet, the class for the applet must be public.

FIGURE 4.4:

The accessibility of classes and their member functions and variables depends on the modifier used when the class or member was declared public.

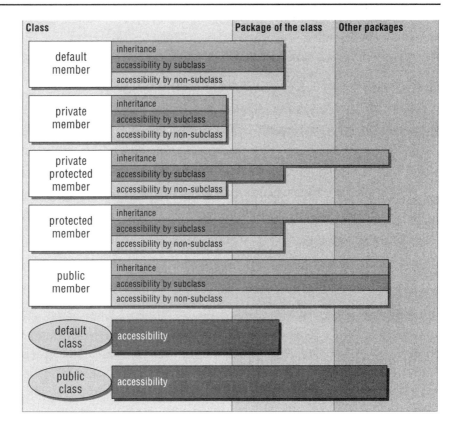

FIGURE 4.4:

The accessibility of classes and their member functions and variables depends on the modifier used when the class or member was declared public.

However, any other classes required by the applet need not be public, as long as they are accessible.

Methods and member variables of public classes that are declared themselves as public can be accessed by code from other classes. Public members can also be accessed by JavaScript, VBScript, and ActiveX controls operating outside the VM. If members of a nonpublic (default) class are declared as public, those members will be accessible to all other classes within the same package. As a guideline, avoid defining functions and variables as public unless it is necessary.

Here is an explanation of each type of modifier and when it would be used:

private

The `private` modifier restricts access to members of a class, so that no other classes can call member functions or directly access member variables.

protected

A `protected` member is like default access, but gives preferred access for subclasses in other packages. Member functions are sometimes created within a class for utility purposes (that is, to be used only within the class itself, and not for general consumption). Declaring utility functions as protected allows them to be used not only by the class itself, but by its subclasses as well.

Suppose you create a class called `Chicken`, which knows how to cross the road. The public member function `crossRoad()` has two steps: (1) check for oncoming traffic, and (2) walk across the road. These steps would be written as two utility member functions called `checkTraffic()` and `walkAcrossRoad()`. The utility functions should not be public because you wouldn't want a programmer who is simply using the class to call `walkAcrossRoad()` without first calling `checkTraffic()`—this could have adverse consequences for the Chicken. However, if you make the utility functions private, you will not be able to reuse these functions yourself when you write the subclass `SmarterChicken`. Ideally, the `SmarterChicken` class can override the `crossRoad()` function to check for a traffic light, then call `checkTraffic()` and `walkAcrossRoad()` as required. By declaring the utility functions as `protected`, they will be available to programmers such as yourself who will be creating subclasses of `Chicken`, and who should, therefore, understand the dangers inherent in crossing roads.

private protected

A `private protected` member is similar to a `protected` member, but it cannot be accessed by any non-subclass, whether in the same package or not.

The choice between private protected and protected depends upon how the classes within the same package will be cooperating. If the `Chicken` class will be part of a `Farm` package, and the `Farmer` class will need to be able to escort a Chicken across the road without the Chicken calling `checkTraffic()`, then the utility functions of `Chicken` class should be declared as `protected`. On the other hand, if the `Chicken` class will always check traffic before crossing the road, there is no need to make the utility functions available to other classes in the `Farm` package, and the functions should be declared as `private protected`.

If no modifier is specified, the default accessibility for the class, variable, or function is assumed.

Summary

The datatypes, modifiers, and expressions described in this chapter make up the essential building blocks of the Java language. Though some of the information in this chapter is reference material, you should now have a feel for how to define your own datatype for best use of storage space, ease of use, and interaction with other classes.

The next chapter describes interfaces and packages and will help you understand the finer points of class design, as well as explain how to use existing Java packages.

CHAPTER

FIVE

More on Classes, Interfaces, and Packages

- Casting

- The Object Memory Model

- Interfaces

- Packages

This chapter continues with the discussion on objects and classes. In particular, you will learn about *casting*, or explicitly converting a value from one datatype to another. And you will learn about using `this` and `super` to refer to the otherwise hidden data members, hidden method members, and constructors of a class and its superclass. This chapter also covers the object memory model, showing you how the memory of an object is handled, and interfaces, Java's solution for multiple inheritance and callback functions. Finally, packages are introduced for grouping classes and interfaces to achieve better organization and minimize naming collisions.

Casting

The general form of a casting operation is

```
(data_type) expression
```

where the datatype can be either a reference type or a primitive one. As a unary operator, casting has the highest operator precedence of the unary operators like ++ and –. For example, casting is used in the following expression to make sure floating point division, rather than integer division, is performed:

```
(float) 5 / 2
```

Since `(float)` has higher operator precedence than the division operator, /, the integer 5 will be converted into a floating number before the division. When one of the operands of a division is a floating number, the other operand will be converted into a floating number and the division will be performed as a floating number operation. If the expression is changed into `(float) 3 + 5 / 2`, an integer division followed by a floating point addition will be performed, because the division operator has higher operator precedence than the addition operator.

Rule number one in casting is that you cannot cast a primitive type to a reference type, nor the other way around. The compiler will check for all violations on casting rules. However, when dealing with object references, there are still cases where the correctness of casting can only be checked at run time. If a casting violation is detected at run time, the exception `ClassCastException` will be thrown. (You will learn more about exception handling in Chapter 7.) The next two sections cover the rules for casting between primitive types and reference types in more detail.

Casting between Primitive Types

As introduced in the previous chapter, the primitive data types can be divided into the boolean type and the numeric type. The boolean type cannot be cast from or to any other data type. Casting from any numeric type—that is, one of `byte`, `char`, `short`, `int`, `long`, `float`, or `double` type—to any other numeric type is allowed. Casting from one numeric type to another may cause loss of information, however. Casting from a wider type (like `int`) to a narrower one (like `byte`) will cause the higher order bits to be discarded. For a signed number, the sign of the number may be changed after the conversion. For example, the result of `(byte) 256` is 0, as the `byte` type can only hold numbers ranging from –128 to 127. If you are going the other way— say from `byte` to `int` or `int` to `float`, or any way that does not present the possibility of information loss—the casting is automatic, and you do not have to manually cast. If the possibility of information loss exists, you must cast yourself.

Assignment of a primitive value to a variable of primitive type is allowed only if the assignment will not cause any loss of information. Otherwise, explicit casting is needed. The same rule applies to arguments of method calls. Automatic widening of the data will be performed if the value of the argument is of a numeric type narrower than the argument type prescribed for the method. For example, in the second statement of the following program fragment, a variable of `float` type is passed into method `sqrt()`, which requires an argument of `double` type. The value of the variable `f` will be converted into `double` type before the method is called.

```
float f = 4;
double d = Math.sqrt(f);
int  i = 1;
byte b = i;
```

> **NOTE**   As you will recall from Chapter 3, a *method* is the same thing as a *member function*.

Also, the last statement is not a legitimate one, because conversion of an `int` type to a `byte` type will possibly lose information. The compiler will give out an error message similar to this one:

```
CastTest.java:6: Incompatible type for declaration. Explicit cast
needed to convert int to byte.
        byte b = i;
             ^
```

To make it pass compiler checking, the statement has to be changed as follows:

```
byte b = (byte) i;
```

Casting between Reference Types

The first rule of casting between reference types is that one of the class types involved must be the same class as or a subclass of the other class type. Assignment to different class type is allowed only if a value of the class type is assigned to a variable of its superclass type. Assignment to a variable of the subclass type needs explicit casting. For example, the second statement of the following program fragment is not a legitimate one, as class `String` is a subclass of class `Object`:

```
Object o = new Object();
String s = o;
```

The compiler will issue an error message similar to this one:

```
CastTest.java:12: Incompatible type for declaration. Explicit cast
needed to convert java.lang.Object to java.lang.String.
        String s = o;
              ^
```

An explicit casting is needed:

```
String s = (String) o;
```

If the casting turns out illegal at run time, a `ClassCastException` will be thrown. This can happen because explicit casting can fool the compiler to allow an object to access the data or method members of its subclass. The attempt at run time to make such a method or data reference will fail, and an exception will be thrown. For example, adding either one of the following two statements to the previous program fragment will incur a runtime exception, because both s and o refer to an object of `Object` type at run time, and the method `length()` is defined in class `String`:

```
int i = s.length();
int j = ((String) o).length();
```

If the exception is not handled, the execution will be terminated, and an error message similar to the following will be displayed:

```
java.lang.ClassCastException: java.lang.Object
        at CastTest.main(CastTest.java:12)
```

this and super

The use of `this` and `super` keywords is twofold: One use is to override the scope rules so that the otherwise hidden data and method members of a class and its superclass can be referred to. The other is to act as method names representing the constructor methods of the current class and its superclass.

this and super for Member References

Local variables in a method can share the same names as instance variables or class variables. Subclasses can define their own instance variables to shadow those defined in the superclasses. Subclasses can also define methods to override the methods defined in their super-classes. Two special references are available inside any instance method to allow for access to the shadowed variables or overridden methods of that instance: `this` and `super`. The former is used to refer to the object the method is called upon, and the latter is used to access the methods or data members defined in the superclass. For example, the constructor of a `Point2D` class to hold the x- and y-coordinates of a two-dimensional point can be defined as follows:

```
public class Point2D {
    int x, y;

    Point2D(int x, int y) {
        this.x = x;
        this.y = y;
    }

    double length() {
        return Math.sqrt(x * x + y * y);
    }

}
```

Here, `this.x` on the left-hand side of the assignment statement refers to the instance variable `x`, whereas the `x` on the right-hand side refers to the argument variable. `sqrt()` is a method defined in class `Math` of package `java.lang` to calculate the square root of the input argument.

You may define a subclass of the `Point2D` class with the same set of instance variables:

```
public class MyPoint extends Point2D {
    int x, y;
```

```
MyPoint(int x, int y) {
    this.x = super.x = x;
    this.y = super.y = y;
}
double length() {
    return Math.sqrt(x * x + y * y);
}

double distance() {
    return Math.abs(this.length() - super.length());
}
}
```

Here, `this.x` refers to the instance variable x defined in class `MyPoint`, and `super.x` refers to the instance variable x defined in class `Point2D`. The `abs()` method is defined in class `Math` of package `java.lang` to calculate the absolute value of its argument. The `this.length()` and `super.length()` methods are defined in classes `MyPoint` and `Point2D`, respectively.

NOTE It is necessary to override the `length()` method defined in class `Point2D`, because the one defined in class `Point2D` can only access data members defined in class `Point2D`, not those defined in its subclass, `MyPoint`.

this and super for Constructor References

In constructors, there is an implied first statement; the superclass constructor with no parameters is automatically called. If you do not like this default behavior, you can override it by using a different `this()` or `super()` method call in the first statement to refer to other constructors of the object and its superclass, respectively. For example, to make the constructor of the `Point2D` class defined earlier more polymorphic, another constructor can be added with only the x-coordinate as the argument:

```
Point2D(int x) {
    this(x, 0);
}
```

Here, the y-coordinate is set to a default value of zero when not specified. Or you can define a constructor with no argument to set the coordinates to default values as follows:

```
Point2D() {
    this(0, 0);
}
```

Also, the constructor of class `MyPoint` can be rewritten as follows:

```
MyPoint(int x, int y) {
    super(x, y);
    this.x = x;
    this.y = y;
}
```

Here, `super` refers to the constructor with two integer arguments defined in class `Point2D`.

Accessing Superclass Members from Outside the Class Definition

Data references are resolved at compile time. If a data member is defined in both a class and its superclass, the data member referred to is decided syntactically by the class type the object is declared to be. Therefore, you can cast an object to its superclass so that you can access the otherwise hidden data member. For example, assume three variables are declared as follows:

```
Point2D p  = new Point2D(11,0);
MyPoint mp = new MyPoint(4,5);
Point2D q  = mp;
```

`p.x`, `mp.x`, and `q.x` refer to the data member defined in classes `Point2D`, `MyPoint`, and `Point2D`, respectively. On the other hand, `((Point2D) mp).x` and `((MyPoint) q).x` refer to the data member defined in classes `Point2D` and `MyPoint`, respectively.

Method references are resolved at run time. The class type an object belongs to when it is first created will determine which method will be called. Casting the object to its superclass, or assigning the object to a variable declared as its superclass type, will not change where the called method is from. For example, both `mp.length()` and `q.length()` refer to the `length()` method defined in class `MyPoint`, whereas `p.length()` refers to the method defined in class `Point2D`.

The following program is added to the definition of classes `Point2D` and `MyPoint` to test out what was just described:

```
class PointTest {
    public static void main(String[] args) {
        MyPoint mp = new MyPoint(4,3);
        Point2D p  = new Point2D(11);
        Point2D q  = mp;

        mp.x = 5; mp.y = 12;

        System.out.println("\n\tData Member Access Test:\n");
        System.out.println("mp = (" + mp.x + ", " + mp.y + ")");
        System.out.println(" p = (" +  p.x + ", " +  p.y + ")");
        System.out.println(" q = (" +  q.x + ", " +  q.y + ")");

        System.out.println("\n\tCasting Test:\n");
        System.out.println("(Point2D) mp = (" + ((Point2D) mp).x + ", " +
        ((Point2D) mp).y + ")");
        System.out.println("(MyPoint) q = (" + ((MyPoint) q).x + ", " +
        ((MyPoint) q).y + ")");

        System.out.println("\n\tMethod Member Access Test:\n");
        System.out.println("mp.length() = " + mp.length());
        System.out.println(" p.length() = " +  p.length());
        System.out.println(" q.length() = " +  q.length());
        System.out.println("mp.difference() = " + mp.difference());

        System.out.println("\n\tCasting Test:\n");
        System.out.println("((Point2D) mp).length() = " + ((Point2D)
        mp).length());
        System.out.println("((Point2D) q).length() = " + ((Point2D)
        q).length());
```

```
        System.out.println("((MyPoint)q).difference() = " + ((MyPoint)
        ➥q).difference());
    }
}
```

The class definition for classes `Point2D` and `MyPoint` is restated as follows:

```
class Point2D {
    int x;
    int y;

    Point2D(int x, int y) {
        this.x = x;
        this.y = y;
    }

    Point2D(int x) {
        this(x, 0);
    }

    Point2D() {
        this(0, 0);
    }

    double length() {
        return Math.sqrt(x * x + y * y);
    }
}

class MyPoint extends Point2D {
    int x;
    int y;

    MyPoint(int x, int y) {
        this.x = super.x = x;
        this.y = super.y = y;
    }

    double length() {
        return Math.sqrt(x * x + y * y);
    }
```

```
    double difference() {
        return Math.abs(length() - super.length());
    }
}
```

The output of the above program is shown here:

```
C:\MasteringJava\Ch05>java PointTest

Data Member Access Test:

mp = (5, 12)
 p = (11, 0)
 q = (4, 3)

        Casting Test:

(Point2D)mp = (4, 3)
(MyPoint) q = (5, 12)

        Method Member Access Test:

mp.length() = 13
 p.length() = 11
 q.length() = 13
mp.difference() = 8

        Casting Test:

((Point2D)mp).length() = 13
((Point2D)q).length() = 13
((MyPoint)q).difference() = 8
```

The Object Memory Model

The dynamically changing part of program memory can be divided into two areas: a *stack* memory area and a *heap* memory area. The stack memory will always grow in one direction and shrink in the opposite direction. This memory area is used to store the local variables declared in methods or blocks. The memory grows as the declaration of local variables (including argument variables in method calls) is encountered. These variables are popped out of the stack upon exit from the enclosing methods or blocks. The heap memory area is used to store the memory for objects. References to the objects can be put in the stack area, but the space for data members of the objects must reside in the heap area. A heap is a huge table of memory cells. Small blocks of memory cells are reserved or allocated from time to time when new objects are created by the new statements. And whenever a block of memory cells is no longer referred to by any existing variables, these unused cells can be freed, or garbage-collected.

NOTE

The term *heap* is also used to mean a complete binary tree where each node is at least as large as the values at its children, as in *heap sort*. These two usages of *heap* represent two totally different concepts and happen to have the same name for historical reasons.

An example might do the explanation one better. Assume you have two methods defined as follows, where class Point2D is defined to hold the x- and y-coordinates of a two-dimensional point (as in the earlier example on this and super):

```
void m1() {
    int    a1 = 1;
    Point2D p1;                // checkpoint #1

    p1 = new Point2D(2,3);// checkpoint #2
    m2(a1, p1);
    a1 = 8;                    // checkpoint #5
}

void m2(int a2, Point p2) {
    int     a3 = 4;
    Point2D p3;               // checkpoint #3

    p3 = new Point2D(5,6);
    a2 = 7;                   // checkpoint #4
}
```

When method `m1()` is called, and its local variable declaration is executed—that is, when `checkpoint #1` is reached—the two local variables, `a1` and `p1`, will be put on the stack memory area with values `1` and `null`, respectively. The memory model at this point is shown in Figure 5.1.

FIGURE 5.1:

The memory model after `checkpoint #1`

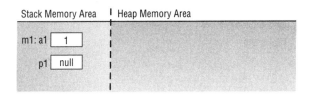

A new object of `Point` type is then created at `checkpoint #2`. The newly created object is put in the heap area whereas a reference to the object is stored in local variable `p1` on the stack. The memory model at this point is shown in Figure 5.2.

FIGURE 5.2:

The memory model after `checkpoint #2`

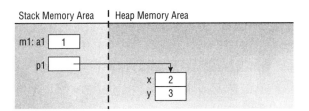

Next, method `m2()` is called with two arguments. Java basically calls by values for arguments of primitive data types; that is, in a method call, the arguments are passed by their values if they are of primitive data types. If the arguments are objects, the values are references to the objects, and the effect is call-by-reference. Therefore, the argument variable `p2` refers to the same object as the local variable `p1` of method `m1()`. At `checkpoint #3`, where the local variables a3 and p3 are declared, the memory model after the declaration looks like Figure 5.3.

FIGURE 5.3:

The memory model after checkpoint #3

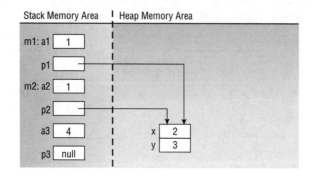

Next, a new object is created by a new statement and assigned to local variable p3. Again, the newly created object is put on the heap area. Then, the argument variable a2 is assigned a new value. Since it is call-by-value, the value of the local variable a1 of method m1() is not affected. The memory model at this point is shown in Figure 5.4.

FIGURE 5.4:

The memory model after checkpoint #4

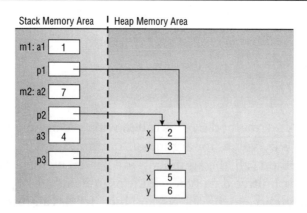

Finally, method m2() is exited, and the memory for the local and argument variables is popped out of the stack area. This leaves the object memory originally allocated for the local variable p3 hanging freely in the heap area with no reference to the block of memory cells. This free-hanging object will be reclaimed later by the garbage collector when needed. At checkpoint #5, an assignment statement is executed; the memory model after the execution is shown in Figure 5.5.

FIGURE 5.5:

The memory model after checkpoint #5

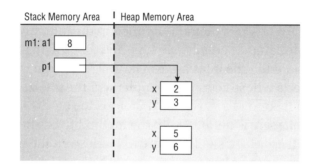

Interfaces

In Java, a class can have only one immediate superclass. Multiple inheritance like C++ uses, where a class has more than one superclass, is not allowed in Java. Problems may arise when you want to have different implementations of a method in different classes and delay the decision on which implementation of a method to execute until run time. In Java, the class where the method is defined must be present at compile time so that the compiler can check the signature of the method to make sure the method call is legitimate. All the classes that could possibly be called for the aforementioned method need to share a common superclass, so that the method can be defined in the superclass and overridden by the individual subclasses. If you want to force every subclass to have its own implementation of the method, the method can be defined as an abstract one. Chances are you will want to move the method definition higher and higher up the inheritance hierarchy so that more and more classes can override the same method. And—guess what—you will find yourself pondering how you can add a few new methods to the `Object` class, the root of all classes, so that these methods can be implemented in many otherwise unrelated classes.

Java's interfaces come to rescue here. An *interface* is a collection of constants and abstract methods. A class can implement an interface by adding the interface to the class's `implements` clause and overriding the abstract methods defined in the interface. A variable can be declared as an *interface* type and all the constants and methods declared in the interface can be accessed from this variable. All objects whose class types implement the interface can then be assigned to this variable. Therefore, to solve our previous problem, an *interface* is defined with the method to be shared among classes. All these classes will declare to implement the interface and create their own implementation of the method. Instances of these classes can then be assigned to a variable of the *interface* type. Reference to this commonly implemented method from the *interface* variable will then be resolved at run time.

Defining an Interface

Defining an interface is just like defining a class except the `class` keyword is replaced with the `interface` keyword, and only constants and abstract methods are allowed in an interface. Every interface is by default abstract. All the methods declared in an interface are by default abstract and public, so you do not need to explicitly put the `abstract` or `public` modifiers before them. Similarly, all the data members declared in an interface are by default public constants, and you do not need to explicitly insert the `final`, `static`, or `public` modifiers before them. For example, `java.lang` package has a `Runnable` interface defined as follows:

```
public interface Runnable {
    void run();
}
```

Interfaces can form hierarchies just like classes. An interface uses the `extends` clause to inherit the methods and constants defined in the superinterface. An interface can never extend a normal class, however.

Additionally, the major difference between extending classes and extending interfaces is that multiple inheritance is allowed in an interface by putting a list of interfaces separated by commas in the `extends` clause. For example, the following program fragment shows that the declaration of an interface, `Operable`, inherits two other interfaces, `Openable` and `Closeable`:

```
interface Operable extends Openable, Closeable {
    . . .
}
```

The implements Clause

A class declares all of the interfaces it is implementing in its `imple-ments` clause of class declaration. The `implements` clause consists of the keyword `implements` followed by a list of interfaces separated by commas, and it must be put after the `extends` clause, if there is one. A class can implement more than one interface. A class implementing an interface will need to override all the methods declared in the interface and all its superinterfaces. Otherwise, the class has to be declared as an abstract one. For example, the following class definition fragment implements the `Runnable` interface declared earlier:

```
class MyClass extends MySuperClass implements Runnable {
    . . .
    public void run() {
        . . .
    }
}
```

Since all the methods defined in an interface are inherently public, the overriding methods implemented in the class have to be declared public, too. In Java, methods cannot be overridden to be more private. If you try to declare an overriding method without the `public` modifier, the compiler will issue an error message similar to this one:

```
InterfaceTest.java:51: Methods can't be overridden to be more pri-
vate. Method void method() is public in interface MyInterface.
   void method() {}
        ^
```

If you forget to override one of the methods in an interface and do not declare your class to be abstract, the compiler will issue an error message as follows:

```
ErrorExample.java:1: class OneError must be declared abstract. It
does not define void run() from interface java.lang.Runnable.
class OneError implements Runnable {
       ^
```

Using an Interface to Implement Callback Functions

A *callback function* in C or C++ is a pointer to a function or function object provided by a service requester for a server to execute when some pre-specified event happens. Callback functions are frequently used in event handling, where event handlers are registered as callback functions to be called when events happen. In Java, references to methods cannot be passed around. Instead, an object is passed to the server, and the method defined for the object is called from the server. If the clients are instantiated from otherwise unrelated classes, an interface needs to be created to define the method the server is calling. And all the classes whose instances are requesting service from the server class have to implement the interface. A client can then pass itself as an argument to the server so that the server can execute the method defined in the client class.

In the next example, a message server is created to call the method, `printMessage()`, to be implemented by the client in regular intervals. The length of the interval and the number of times the method is called is provided by the client when the server instance is created. The server will create a new thread running concurrently with the client when the constructor is called. (See Chapter 8 for more on threads.) The client repeatedly increments a counter after some computation until the counter reaches some preset value. The program listing is as follows:

```java
class CallbackTest {
    public static void main(String[] args) {
        LoopingClient client = new LoopingClient();
        new MessageServer(5, 100, client); // create a new server
        client.run();                       // run the client
    }
}

class LoopingClient implements MessagePrintable {
    int counter = 0;

    void run() {
        while (counter++ < 200000)
            int dummy = counter * counter / (counter + 1);
    }

    public void printMessage() {
        System.out.println("The counter value is now: " + counter);
    }
}

class MessageServer extends Thread {
    int times;
    int interval;
    MessagePrintable object;

    MessageServer(int times, int interval, MessagePrintable object) {
        this.times    = times;
        this.interval = interval;
        this.object   = object;
        this.start();              // start running the new thread
    }

    public void run() {
        // repeat sleep-printMessage several times
```

```
        for (int i = 0; i < times; i++) {
            try { // try-catch is for exception handling
                sleep(interval);
            } catch (InterruptedException e) {}
            object.printMessage();
        }
    }
}

interface MessagePrintable {
    void printMessage();
}
```

The try-catch statement is for exception handling and will be covered in detail in Chapter 7. The output of the above program is as follows:

```
C:\MasteringJava\Ch05>java CallbackTest
The counter value is now: 29750
The counter value is now: 57739
The counter value is now: 87719
The counter value is now: 122998
The counter value is now: 149327
```

Packages

A *package* is a collection of related classes and interfaces. As the first non-comment statement of a file, you can use a package statement to specify which package the classes and interfaces defined in the program file belong to. You can then use import statements to specify the packages whose classes are going to be referred to in the rest of the program. A package is a grouping mechanism with two main purposes. One is to reduce the problems in name collisions. The other is to control the visibility of classes, interfaces, and the methods and data defined within them.

Resolving Class Names

Classes can share the same name only if they belong to different packages. When a class is referred to in a program, the compiler will check all the imported packages to find out where the class is defined. If there is only one imported package in which the named class is defined, the definition of the class in that package will be used. If more than one imported package contains the definition of the named class, the package name has to be used as a prefixing qualifier so that there is no ambiguity regarding the referred class. A period is used as the separator between the class name and the package name. For example, you may define a `Point` class to hold the x-, y-, and z-coordinates of a three-dimensional point in a user-defined `three_d` package, and another `Point` class to hold the x- and y-coordinates of a two-dimensional point in a `two_d` package. If both the `three_d` and `two_d` packages are imported to the program, you will have to use `three_d.Point` and `two_d.Point` to refer to the `Point` class of three- and two-dimensional points respectively.

Packages can be nested to form a nice hierarchy. This nesting capability can help further in grouping classes, just like the hierarchy of directories can help you to organize your files. To refer to a class of a nested package, a fully qualified name with all the containing package names prefixing the class name can be used. For example, to refer to the `Point` class of the `awt` package under the `java` package, the fully qualified class name, `java.awt.Point`, can be used. Or, if `java.awt` is imported and the class name will not clash with the class names of other imported packages, `Point` without any qualifier can be used to refer to the class.

All classes and interfaces in a package are accessible to all other classes and interfaces in that package. All the data and method members of a class can be accessed from any method of any class under the same package, except when the data and method members are declared `private`.

Packages and Directories

Every package must be mapped to a subdirectory of the same name in the file system. Nested packages will be reflected as a hierarchy of directories in the file system. For example, the class files of package `java.awt.image` must be stored under the directory `java/awt/image` in a Unix file system and `java\awt\image` in a Windows file system.

Package directories can be put anywhere in the file system as long as the users have read access to them. The `CLASSPATH` environment variable is used by both the Java compiler and Java run time to locate the packages. The list of directories is separated with semicolons on Windows and colons on Unix. On Windows, for example, a command line similar to the following is placed in the `autoexec.bat` file:

```
SET CLASSPATH=.;C:\java\lib;C:\myprog\classes
```

And on Unix, the following command line might be used under C-shell:

```
setenv CLASSPATH .:/java/lib:/users/hsu/classes
```

When a class reference like `java.util.Date` is encountered, the directory list is searched from start to end, and the `Date` class of the first directory containing `java\util\Date.class` (or `java/util/Date.class` on Unix) will be used. Therefore, if you define your `CLASSPATH` variable as above and there is a subdirectory `.\java\util` (or `./java/util` on Unix) with `Date.java` defined as in the following program fragment, your own `Date` class will be used instead of the one defined under the Java Core API:

```
package java.util;
public class Date {
    . . .

}
```

> **TIP**
>
> You should try to avoid having the fully qualified package name collide with the names of other publicly available packages, such as `java.util`. Other people running your program with the `CLASS-PATH` environment variable set differently may get different behavior or may not run your program at all.

All of the Java built-in classes (that is, the Java Core API) are put under the `java` package. Six subpackages are defined under the `java` package:

Package	Nameclasses
`java.lang`	Essential classes like `String`, `Object`, and `Thread`.
`java.awt`	Graphic user interface components
`java.io`	Input/output streams and files
`java.net`	Networking-related classes
`java.applet`	Applet creation including an audio clip interface
`java.util`	Utility classes for special data structures like vector, hashtable, and date

More details on these packages will be covered in Part Two of the book.

The package Statement

The general form of a `package` statement is

```
package name;
```

where *name* is either a single package name or a list of package names separated by commas. For example, the following two statements are both legitimate package statements:

```
package my_package;
package java.awt.image;
```

Only one `package` statement is allowed in a program file, and it must be the first noncomment statement in the file. If the package statement is omitted from the program file, the classes generated will be put under an unnamed default package that is always imported.

The import Statement

The `import` statement allows classes and interfaces defined in packages to be referred to solely by the class names instead of the fully qualified names. There are two forms of `import` statements:

```
import package_name.class_name;
import package_name.*;
```

where `package_name` is a single package name or a list of nested package names separated by periods.

In the first form, only the specified class of the named package is imported. In the second form, all the classes and interfaces in the named package are directly accessible by simple names. `import` statements must be put in the beginning of a program file. The only noncomment statement allowed before an `import` statement is a `package` statement. In the following program fragment, class `Vector` of `java.util` package is imported, as are all the classes and interfaces of `java.awt` package, but not those defined in the subpackage `java.awt.image`. Therefore, `Vector` can be directly referred to by a simple name, as are the classes (like `Label` and `Button`) defined in `java.awt` package. However, neither the `java.io` package nor the `PrintStream` class defined in the package is imported, and `PrintStream` has to be referred to by its fully qualified name.

```
import java.util.Vector;
import java.awt.*;

class ImportTest {
    Vector v;                   // in java.util package
    Label  label;               // in java.awt package
    Button button;              // in java.awt package
    java.io.PrintStream out; // fully-qualified class name required
}
```

NOTE   Having a class or package imported does not mean the class or classes inside the package will necessarily be loaded at run time. The `import` statement is only used to give the Java compiler hints on resolving class names. The classes or packages mentioned in the import statements may never be referred to in the program body.

Summary

Casting is used to convert a value from one datatype to another type. It can only be done between two primitive types or reference types. If an assignment statement causes loss of information or extension of the datatype, an explicit casting is needed.

`this` and `super` can be used as method names referring to the constructors in the current class and the superclass, respectively. They also can be used to refer to the current object and members in the superclass, respectively.

An interface is a collection of constants and abstract methods. Interfaces are Java's solution to multiple inheritance and callback functions. A class implements an interface by adding the interface to the `implements` clause and overriding the abstract methods defined in the interface and its superinterfaces.

A package is a collection of classes and interfaces. Packages can be nested to form a tree-like hierarchy. A package is reflected as a directory of the same name in the file system. A class defines the package it belongs to with a `package` statement. And `import` statements allow classes and interfaces defined in packages to be referred to by their simple names.

This chapter covered tidbits of information about objects and classes that, together with the information presented in previous chapters, is at the heart of creating Java programs in an object-oriented way. Combine this with arrays, flow-control statements, exceptions, and threading (to be introduced in the following chapters), and you have the core of the Java language. Mastering these basic concepts along with the APIs introduced in the next part of the book will definitely help you utilize the language to its fullest.

CHAPTER
SIX

Arrays and Flow-Control Statements

6

- Using Arrays

- Multidimensional Arrays

- Overview of Flow-Control Statements

- Conditional Statements

- Loop Statements

- Flow-Breaking Statements

Up to this point, you have seen example programs that use variables of a single object type or primitive datatype only. Also in these programs, the line of execution is sequential, from the first line to the last one, with occasional excursions to execute linearly the code segments in methods. The tasks that can be accomplished using these language constructs are very limited, and the need will inevitably arise to execute portions of the code repeatedly or selectively, as will the need to handle a group of similar objects as a whole. In this chapter, you will learn to manipulate groups of objects and to use conditional, loop, and flow-breaking statements—together, these program constructs will allow you to do much more complicated tasks.

What Is an Array?

An *array* is a group of variables of the same type that can be referred to by a common name. The type can be either a primitive datatype like `int`, or an object type like `String`. For example, you can define an array of integers to hold the daily high temperature in a month as:

```
int[] dailyHigh;
```

Or—using the `Point` class defined in package `java.awt`—you can define an array to hold a list of two-dimensional points as

```
Point[] points;
```

An array is an object; that is, it is handled by reference. When you pass an array to a method, only the reference to the array is passed, rather than the whole array of elements. Declaring an array variable only creates a place holder for the reference to the array, not the memory holding the array of elements per se. Also, the actual memory used by the array elements is dynamically allocated either by a `new` statement or an array initializer. The memory referenced by the array variable will be automatically garbage-collected when it is no longer referred to. Every array object has a public instance variable `length` to hold the size of the array.

The following example gives you a close look at the memory model of an array. First, a class to hold a point in two-dimensional graphics is defined as follows:

```
class Point {
    int x;
    int y;
    Point(int x, int y)        // constructor
     {
       this.x = x;
       this.y = y;
     }
}
```

After declaring the array to hold a list of points, the memory model looks like Figure 6.1.

FIGURE 6.1:

The memory model after adding an array declaration: `Point[] points;`

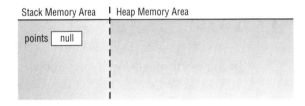

You can then use the following `new` statement to allocate memory space for holding two references to the `Point` object:

```
points = new Point[2];
```

After the allocation, you can access the size of the array as `points.length`. The memory model is shown in Figure 6.2.

FIGURE 6.2:

The memory model after allocating space for array elements: `points = new Point[2];`

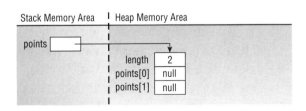

The first element of the array can be filled by

```
points[0] = new Point(1,2);
```

Figure 6.3 shows the memory model after the above statement is added.

FIGURE 6.3:

The memory model after the first element of the array is assigned:
`points[0] = new Point(1,2);`

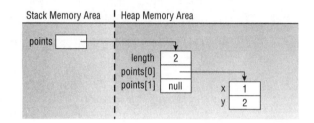

Using Arrays

In this section, you will look at basic array operations, including accessing array elements and declaring, creating, and copying arrays.

Accessing Array Elements

Java follows normal C-style indexing for accessing an array element; that is, you attach an integer-valued expression between square brackets after the name of the array. The array index starts with zero. Therefore, to get the daily high temperature of the second day of the month, you can use the following code fragment:

```
daily_high[1]
```

All subscript accesses will be checked to make sure they are in the legal range—greater than or equal to zero and less than the array length. If the value is out of bounds, the exception `ArrayIndexOut-OfBoundsException` is thrown. See Chapter 7 for details on what exceptions are and how to handle them.

Declaring and Creating an Array

Square brackets are used to declare an array type. There are two formats for declaring an array. One is to put the brackets after the datatype, and the other is to put the brackets after the array name. For example, `int[] a;` is equivalent to `int a[];`. The former format is preferred by the authors of this book, because it shows clearly that an array is an object—a reference to a list of instances of a certain datatype.

A `new` statement is used to allocate the space needed for either holding the actual values of the array elements (if the elements are of primitive datatype) or holding the references to array elements (if they are of object type). For example, to create an array to hold the daily high temperature for the month of January, you can use the following statement:

```
int[] daily_high = new int[31];
```

Or to create an array to hold the coordinates of the three vertices of a triangle, you can declare an array as

```
Point[] triangle = new Point[3];
```

An array created by a `new` statement will have the elements automatically initialized to the default value of the element types. For example, elements of `int` or `double` type will be initialized to zeroes, and elements of object type will be set to `null`.

An array initializer may be used to create an array with preset values. A list of comma-separated expressions that will each be evaluated to the array's element type is enclosed in curly braces. For example, to initialize an array to hold the number of days in each month of a leap year, you can declare the array as

```
int[] month_days = {31, 29, 31, 30, 31, 30, 31, 31, 30, 31, 30, 31};
```

> **TIP**
>
> Array initializers can only be used in array declaration statements, and cannot be used as the right-hand side of normal assignment statements.

Copying an Array

Because an array is an object, assigning the value of an array variable to another array variable will only copy the reference to that array. For example, you can assign the value of the `points` array described in previous examples to the new array variable `points2` as

```
Point[] points2 = points;
```

The memory model for these two variables is sketched out in Figure 6.4.

FIGURE 6.4:

The memory model after assignment: `Point[] points2 = points;`

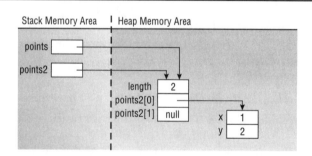

To actually copy the values or a portion of the values stored in an array into another array, the `arraycopy()` method of the `System` class under the `java.lang` package can be used. The synopsis of that method is

```
void arraycopy(Object source_array,
    int source_start_position,
    Object destination_array,
    int destination_start_ position,
    int number_of_elements_to_be_copied);
```

For example, to copy all the values in `points` into `points2`, you can use

```
System.arraycopy(points, 0, points2, 0, points.length);
```

Be aware that the memory space for the destination array must be allocated before calling the `arraycopy()` method. For the above example, `points2` may first need to be created as

```
points2 = new Point[points.length];
```

The memory model after copying the array is shown in Figure 6.5.

FIGURE 6.5:

The memory model after array copy:
```
System.arraycopy(
points, 0,
points2, 0,
points.length);
```

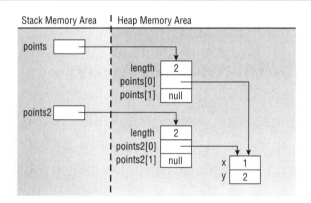

For an array of objects, the values stored in an array are references to the objects. To duplicate an array with its component object elements, you can use the `clone()` method of the `Object` class (the root of all objects) in conjunction with the `arraycopy()` method. Only classes implementing the `Cloneable` interface may be cloned. They include the `Vector`, `Hashtable`, and `BitSet` classes defined in `java.util` package. See Part Two for more details about these classes.

For example, if `val` is already declared and created as an array of `Vector`, the following code fragment can be used to duplicate `val` as `va2`:

```
Vector[] va2 = new Vector[val.length];

System.arraycopy(val, 0, va2, 0, val.length);
for (int i = 0; i < val.length; i++)
  va2[i] = (Vector) val[i].clone();
```

If there is no `clone()` or similar method available, you will need to explicitly create a new copy of each element in the array. For example, the following code segment can be added to the earlier example so that `points2` is a full duplicate of `points`:

```
points2[0] = new Point(points[0].x, points[0].y);
```

Multidimensional Arrays

A *multidimensional array* is implemented as an array of arrays. You can create a nonrectangular multidimensional array by having elements of an array refer to arrays of different sizes. To initialize a multidimensional array, nested curly braces are used. For example, to initialize a two-dimensional array of which the first element has two sub-elements and the second one has three sub-elements, you can declare it as

```
int[][] a = {{1,2}, {3,4,5}};
```

Or to create a three-by-three matrix of integers, you can say

```
int[][] matrix = new int[3][3];
```

The earlier statement for declaring and initializing a can be rewritten as

```
int[]   a0 = {1,2}, a1 = {3,4,5};
int[][] a = {a1, a2};
```

Or even lengthier, as

```
int[]   a0 = {1,2};
```

```
int[]   a1 = {3,4,5};
int[][]  a = new int[2][];
a[0] = a0;
a[1] = a1;
```

The memory model for the previous example is shown in Figure 6.6.

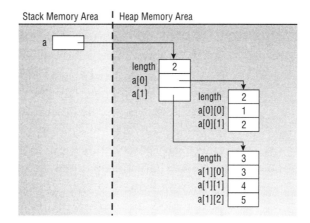

Care should be taken in declaring a list of multidimensional arrays
with different dimensionalities. In the following code fragment, b is
declared as a one-dimensional array, and c as a two-dimensional
array:

```
int[] b, c[];
```

> **TIP**
>
> This can be a little bit confusing to C/C++ programmers. It might
> help if you treat the set of square brackets after the datatype as a
> modifier to the datatype rather than to the array name(s).

The above statement can be legitimately rewritten as

```
int b[], c[][];
```

Overview of Flow-Control Statements

Java's *flow-control statements* are basically modeled after those of C/C++. That is, `if` and `switch` statements are used for selective execution of code segments; `for`, `while`, and `do` statements are used for repeated execution of code segments; and `break`, `continue`, and `return` statements are used for breaking the flow. There are still two major differences in Java, however. First, the conditional expressions used in `if`, `for`, `while`, or `do` statements have to be valid `boolean` expressions that will be evaluated to values of either `true` or `false`. In Java, the values 0 or `null` cannot be a substitute for `false`. Neither can nonzero or non-null values be used in place of `true`. Furthermore, you cannot explicitly cast an `int` type into a `boolean` type. Second, there is no `goto` statement in Java. Labeled `break` and `continue` statements are provided as better solutions where the use of `goto` statements may be justified.

Conditional Statements

Conditional statements allow for the selective execution of portions of the program according to the value of some expressions. Java supports two types of conditional statements: `if` and `switch` statements. In addition, the tertiary `?:` operators can sometimes be used as alternatives to `if-else` statements.

if Statements

The general form of an `if` statement is

```
if (conditional_expression)
      if_statement
else
      else_statement
```

An `if` statement will first test its conditional expression. If it is evaluated to `true`, the statement or block of statements immediately after the conditional expression will be executed. Otherwise, the statement or block of statements after `else` will be executed. The `else` part is optional. For example, the following code fragment will test if a character is a digit, a whitespace, or other type of character and set the appropriate `boolean` variable to `true`:

```
char ch = 'a';
boolean is_digit = false, is_space = false, is_other = false;
if (Character.isDigit(ch))
  is_digit = true;
else if (Character.isSpace(ch))
  is_space = true;
else
  is_other = true;
```

`isDigit()` and `isSpace()` are class methods of the `Character` class defined in `java.lang` package; they are used to determine if the character argument passed in belongs to a certain character type.

Here is another example: The following code fragment will assign a character grade according to the score in a 100-point system:

```
int score = 65;
char grade;
if (score >= 90)
  grade = 'A';
else if (score >= 80)
  grade = 'B';
else if (score >= 70)
  grade = 'C';
else if (score >= 60)
  grade = 'D';
else
  grade = 'F';
```

Using nested `? :` operators, the above example can be succinctly rewritten as

```
int score = 65;
char grade = (score >= 90) ? 'A' :
             (score >= 80) ? 'B' :
             (score >= 70) ? 'C' :
             (score >= 60) ? 'D' : 'F';
```

> **TIP**
>
> Although `if (score = 70)` is valid in C/C++, it will result in a compilation error in Java, since `score = 70` is an assignment operation evaluated to an integer value of `70`, not a conditional expression that will be evaluated to a boolean value of `true` or `false`.

switch Statements

The general form of a `switch` statement is

```
switch (expression) {
    case value1:
        code_segment_1
    case value2:
        code_segment_2
    . . .
    case valueN:
        code_segment_N
    default:
        default_code_segment
}
```

A `switch` statement is used for multiway selection that will branch to different code segments based on the value of a variable or an expression. The optional `default` label is used to specify the code segment to be executed when the value of the variable or expression cannot match any of the `case` values. If there is no `break` statement as the last statement in the code segment for a certain `case`, the execution will continue on into the code segment for the next `case` clause without checking the `case` value. The detailed usage of `break` statements will be introduced later in this chapter.

> **TIP**
>
> It is a common programming error to forget to have a `break` statement as the last statement of a code segment for a `case` clause of a `switch` statement.

The expression used in a `switch` statement must be an integral expression or one whose evaluated result can be implicitly cast into an `int` type without losing information. Datatypes that can be cast into an `int` type without losing information include `byte`, `char`, and `short`. For datatypes like `long`, `float`, and `double`, explicit casting is required. The `case` values must be constant expressions that can be evaluated to or later implicitly cast to a constant value of `int` type at compile time.

As in the earlier example on `if` statements, the following code fragment will set the appropriate boolean variable according to the character type of the character variable `ch` :

```
switch (ch) {
  case '0': case '1': case '2': case '3': case '4':
  case '5': case '6': case '7': case '8': case '9':
    is_digit = true;
    break;
  case ' ':
  case '\t':
  case '\n':
    is_space = true;
    break;
  default:
    is_other = true;
}
```

If the `break` statement after `is_digit` = `true` is missing, both `is_space` and `is_digit` will be set to `true` for characters of digit type.

Loop Statements

Loop statements allow for the repeated execution of blocks of statements. There are three types of loop statements: `for`, `while`, and `do` loops. `for` and `while` loops test the loop condition at the top of the loop, before the loop body is executed, whereas do loops check the condition at the bottom of the loop, after the loop body is executed.

for Statements

The general form of a for statement is

```
for (initialization_statement; conditional_expression;
    increment_statement)
  loop_body
```

To execute a for statement, the initialization statement is first executed. The conditional expression is then evaluated. If it is evaluated to true, the loop body is executed, followed by the increment statement. The evaluation of the conditional expression and the execution of loop body and the increment statement are repeated until the conditional expression is evaluated to false. Multiple initialization or increment statements are allowed if separated by commas. Like C++, local loop variables can be declared in the initialization section of a for loop. The scope of the loop variables is just the loop itself. These loop variables follow the general rules for declaring variables inside a block delimited by curly braces: They cannot have the same names as any variables declared in outer scope and they cannot be referred outside the loop.

For example, the following code fragment can be used to prepare a two-dimensional array for holding a full year's daily high temperatures, grouped by months:

```
int[] month_days = {31, 28, 31, 30, 31, 30, 31, 31, 30, 31, 30, 31};
int[][] daily_high = new int[month_days.length][];
for (int i = 0; i < month_days.length; i++) {
    daily_high[i] = new int[month_days[i]];
 }
```

And the following method can be defined to return the highest temperature in a year:

```
int getYearlyHigh(int[][] daily_high) {
    int yearly_high = Integer.MIN_VALUE;
    for (int i = 0; i < month_days.length; i++)
        for (int j = 0; j < daily_high[i].length; j++)
            if (yearly_high < daily_high[i][j])
                yearly_high = daily_high[i][j];
    return yearly_high;
}
```

MIN_VALUE is a class variable (a constant, in fact) of the Integer class defined in the java.lang package defined as the smallest possible value of type int.

while Statements

The general form of a while statement is

```
while (conditional_expression)
    loop_body
```

To execute a while statement, the conditional expression will first be evaluated. If it is evaluated to true, the loop body is executed. Otherwise, program control passes to the line after the loop body. The testing of conditional expression and the execution of loop body is repeated until the conditional expression is evaluated to false. For example, the following code fragment will print out ten blank lines:

```
int i = 10;
while (i-- > 0)
    System.out.println();
```

do Statements

The general form of a do statement is

```
do
      loop_body
while (conditional_expression);
```

The only difference between a do statement and a while statement is in the order of execution. In a do statement, the loop body will be executed before the conditional expression is evaluated. Therefore, the loop body will be executed at least once in a do statement while the loop body in a while statement may never be executed. For example, the following code fragment will repeatedly prompt the user until *exit* is entered:

```
String buffer;
DataInputStream my_in = new DataInputStream(System.in);

do {
      System.out.print("Enter a command: ");
      System.out.flush();
      buffer = my_in.readLine();
} while (! buffer.equals("exit"));
```

DataInputStream is a class defined in the java.io package with methods allowing you to read text lines and Java primitive datatypes from an underlying input stream, which, in the above example, is the standard input stream, System.in.

Flow-Breaking Statements

Three types of *flow-breaking statements* are supported in Java. The break statements are used to exit from switch statements, loop statements, and labeled blocks. The continue statements are used to jump to the end of the loop body just past the last line of the statement. The return statements are used to exit from a method or a constructor. Statements and blocks of statements delimited by curly braces can be labeled and later referred to by the enclosed break statements. However, only labels of enclosing loop statements can be referred to by `continue` statements.

break Statements

The general form of a `break` statement is

```
break label;
```

where the label is optional. Without a label, the `break` statement will transfer the program control to the statement just after the innermost enclosing loop or `switch` statement. With a label, it will transfer the program control to the statement just after the enclosing statement or block of statements carrying the same label. For example, the following code fragment will print out the third day in a year with a daily high of above 70 degrees:

```
outer_loop:
  for (int i = 0, count = 0; i < daily_high.length; i++)
     for (int j = 0; j < daily_high[i].length; j++)
         if ((daily_high[i][j] > 70) & (++count == 3)) {
             System.out.println("The date is: month = " + (i + 1) +
                                 ", day = " + (j + 1));
             break outer_loop;
         }
// break outer_loop, if executed, will reach here
```

continue Statements

The general form of a `continue` statement is

```
continue label;
```

where the label is optional. Without a label, it behaves exactly the same as in C/C++. The program control is transferred to the point right after the last statement in the enclosing loop body. In `while` and `do` statements, the conditional expressions will now be retested. In `for` loops, the increment statements will be executed next. With a label, the program control will be transferred to the end of the enclosing loop body with the same label, instead of the innermost one. For example, the following code segment defines a method to return the offset position of the first occurrence of one string, str2, in the other string, str1:

```
int indexOf(String str1, String str2)
  {
     int len1 = str1.length();
     int len2 = str2.length();
     char str2_first_char = str2.charAt(0);
  advance_one_char_at_str1:
     for (int i = 0; i + len2 <= len1; i++)
           if (str1.charAt(i) == str2_first_char) {
                for (int j = 1; j < len2; j++)
                      if (str1.charAt(i + j) != str2.charAt(j))
                            continue advance_one_char_at_str1;
                return i;
           }
        return -1;
  }
```

return Statements

The general form of a return statement is

```
return expression;
```

A return statement is used to return control to the caller from within a method or constructor. If the method is defined to return a value, the expression must be evaluated to the return type of that method. Otherwise, only an unlabeled return statement can be used.

An Example: The Daily High

In this section, a complete example demonstrating the use of one- and two-dimensional arrays and various flow-control statements is introduced. Three arrays are used in the example: month_days, a one-dimensional array of `int` type to hold the number of days in each month, `month_names`, a one-dimensional array of `String` type to hold the names of the months, and `daily_high`, a two-dimensional array of `int` type to hold a full year's daily high temperatures, grouped by months. The program first initializes the `daily_high` array with random numbers between 10 and 100. `random()` is a class method defined in the `Math` class of package `java.lang` that will return a random number between 0 and 1 of `double` type. The program then prints out a year's daily high grouped by months. It continues on to print out the third day in the year with a daily high above 76 degrees. At last, it reports the number of months with monthly highs less than or equal to 96 degrees. The whole program is listed here:

```java
class DailyHigh
{
    static int[] month_days={31,28,31,30,31,30,31,31,30,31,30,31};
    static String[] month_names=
        {"Jan", "Feb", "Mar", "Apr", "May", "Jun",
         "Jul", "Aug", "Sep", "Oct", "Nov", "Dec"};
    int[][] daily_high;
    // constructor
    DailyHigh()
      {
        daily_high = new int[12][];
        for (int i = 0; i < 12; i++)
          daily_high[i] = new int[month_days[i]];
      }
    // fill in the 2-d array with random temperatures between 10 and 100
    void init()
      {

        for (int i = 0; i < 12; i++)
            for (int j = 0; j < month_days[i]; j++)
                daily_high[i][j] = (int) ( Math.random() * 90.0
                                     + 10.0);
      }
    // print out the daily_high array
    void print()
      {
        System.out.println("\nDaily High:\n");
        for (int i = 0; i < 12; i++)
          {
            System.out.print(month_names[i] + ":");
            for (int j = 0; j < month_days[i]; j++)
```

```
        {
          if ((j != 0) && (j % 7 == 0))
            System.out.print(j % 14 == 0 ? "\n    " : "  ");
          System.out.print(" " + daily_high[i][j]);
        }
        System.out.println();
      }
  }
  // the number of months with monthly high less than or equal to
  // certain number; a demonstration of usage of labeled continue
  int monthlyHighNotMoreThan(int reference)
  {
      int count = 0;
    outer_loop:
      for (int i = 0; i < daily_high.length; i++) {
          for (int j = 0; j < daily_high[i].length; j++)
              if (daily_high[i][j] > reference)
                  continue outer_loop;
          count++;
      }
      return count;
  }
  public static void main(String[] args)
  {
      DailyHigh t = new DailyHigh();
      t.init();
      t.print();
    // find the third day in the year with daily high above 76
    // a demonstration of use of labeled break
    out:
      {
      System.out.print("\nThe third day with daily high above 76 is: ");
      for (int i = 0, count = 0; i < t.daily_high.length; i++)
          for (int j = 0; j < month_days[i]; j++)
                  if ((t.daily_high[i][j] > 76) && (++count == 3)) {
                      System.out.println(month_names[i] + " " +
  (j + 1));
                      break out;
                  }
      // reach here only when the 3rd date cannot be found
      System.out.println("no such date");
      }
      int reference = 96;
      System.out.println("The number of months with monthly high <= " +
                      reference + " is " +
                      t.monthlyHighNotMoreThan(reference));
  }
}
```

Here is an output of the program, although yours may differ due to random numbers:

```
C:\MasteringJava\Ch06>java DailyHigh

Daily High:

Jan: 81 16 30 35 60 37 38    25 11 59 72 68 23 86
     94 72 85 24 59 95 32    46 37 30 54 29 28 72
     89 56 36
Feb: 90 24 14 44 92 21 66    64 37 71 40 52 40 68
     33 99 10 37 28 26 69    19 74 48 53 63 59 95
Mar: 26 95 64 61 17 62 20    16 68 52 26 62 71 81
     25 25 87 24 26 40 25    45 93 77 77 65 65 48
     14 21 10
Apr: 84 71 74 84 62 55 42    62 84 36 76 70 46 21
     56 10 53 27 58 67 59    76 92 14 18 28 23 36
     70 34
May: 49 22 63 18 34 46 85    65 86 16 38 85 62 58
     35 79 62 28 26 12 82    14 61 80 28 17 98 88
     10 74 62
Jun: 38 21 91 78 81 57 53    99 92 15 59 58 89 56
     17 13 19 33 73 98 43    96 45 83 12 83 58 60
     14 78
Jul: 88 38 36 32 14 54 42    20 53 13 24 37 74 47
     47 43 88 88 27 77 45    61 38 20 70 54 24 43
     51 95 46
Aug: 97 37 67 69 77 59 86    49 70 69 83 87 36 62
     56 82 23 40 46 35 70    82 96 21 81 61 32 47
     72 15 23
Sep: 14 16 85 22 87 24 51    27 97 35 90 78 97 38
     41 16 10 10 74 14 56    96 14 16 57 59 51 13
     51 27
Oct: 80 28 94 55 64 67 29    58 97 96 64 26 82 85
     86 80 55 32 19 58 20    50 94 84 92 61 33 84
     59 26 46
Nov: 51 54 61 52 26 38 85    21 66 66 59 43 81 16
     86 51 95 23 72 13 42    94 43 88 26 43 92 91
     13 40
Dec: 81 27 24 95 75 41 18    76 37 46 42 93 61 68
     86 96 86 88 93 67 32    61 83 58 72 38 19 24
     73 90 90
The third day with daily high above 76 is: Jan 15
The number of months with monthly high <= 96 is 6
```

Summary

This chapter introduced you to arrays and control statements. An array is a group of variables of the same type that can be referred to by a common name. An array is an object. Declaring an array variable only creates a placeholder for the reference to the array. You need to use either a `new` statement or an array initializer to allocate the space for the array. A multidimensional array is implemented as an array of arrays, and therefore can be nonrectangular.

Java has a similar set of flow-control statements as those in C/C++: `if` and `switch` statements are used for selective execution of code segments; `for, while`, and `do` statements are used for repeated execution of code segments; and `break, continue`, and `return` statements are used for breaking the flow. There is no `goto` statement in Java, but labeled `break` and `continue` statements are usually good solutions in places where you would want to use a `goto` statement.

Arrays allow you to handle similar data objects as groups, while flow-control statements allow you to selectively and/or repeatedly execute program fragments. Together with exception handling for handling abnormal conditions and multithreading for concurrent execution of programs, they form the key for writing arbitrarily complicated program control for your application needs.

CHAPTER
SEVEN

7

Exception Handling

As programs become more complicated, making them robust is a much more difficult task. Traditional programming languages like C rely on the heavy use of `if` statements to detect abnormal conditions, `goto` statements to branch to the error handlers, and return codes for propagating the abnormal conditions back to the calling methods. Thus, normal program flow is either buried in the web of exception detection and handling statements, or robustness is sacrificed for the sake of clarity. Using an exception-handling mechanism similar to that of C++, Java provides an elegant way to build programs that are both robust and clear. In this chapter, you will learn to use this cleaner mechanism to handle errors and unusual conditions.

Overview of Exception Handling

An *exception* is an abnormal condition that disrupts normal program flow. There are many cases where abnormal conditions happen during program execution: The file you try to open may not exist; the class file you want to load may be missing or in the wrong format; the other end of your network connection may be nonexistent; or the network connection may be disrupted for some mysterious reason. Also, in order to function normally, all operands must be in the legal range prescribed for operations or methods. For example, an array element index cannot exceed the size of the array, and a divisor in a division operation cannot be zero. Such unusual situations need to be avoided, and if they do occur, they need to be handled properly. If these abnormal conditions are not prevented or at least handled properly, either the program will be aborted abruptly, or the incorrect results or status will be carried on, causing more and more abnormal conditions. Imagine a program that reads from an unopened file and does computations based on those input values!

The Basic Model

Java basically follows C++ syntax for exception handling. First, you `try` to execute a block of statements. If an abnormal condition occurs, something will `throw` an exception that you can `catch` with a handler. And, `finally`, there may be a block of statements you always want executed—no matter whether an exception occurred, and no matter whether the exception is handled if an exception does occur. Throwing an exception is more friendly than terminating the program, as it provides the programmer with the option of writing a handler to deal with the abnormal condition.

For example, the following program fragment causes the program to sleep for ten seconds (10,000 milliseconds) by calling the `sleep()` class method defined in class `Thread` of package `java.lang`. If the sleep is interrupted before the time expires, a message will be printed and the execution continues with the statement following this `try-catch` construct.

```
try {
    Thread.sleep(10000);
} catch (InterruptedException e) {
    System.out.println("Sleeping interrupted.");
}
// will reach here after try-block finished or exception handled
```

The next program, which copies the contents of one file to another, demonstrates exception handling in a more practical setting. Filenames are first taken from the command line arguments. Then, the files are opened, and data is copied in 512-byte block increments. The number of bytes copied is tracked, and the byte count is reported once the operation is completed. The program fragment to carry out these operations is as follows:

```
int     byte_count = 0;
byte[] buffer = new byte[512];
String input_file  = null;
String output_file = null;
```

```
FileInputStream  fin;
FileOutputStream fout;

input_file  = args[0];
output_file = args[1];
fin  = new FileInputStream(input_file);
fout = new FileOutputStream(output_file);
int bytes_in_one_read;

while ((bytes_in_one_read = fin.read(buffer)) != -1) {
    fout.write(buffer, 0, bytes_in_one_read);
    byte_count += bytes_in_one_read;
}

System.out.println(byte_count + " written");
```

The `FileInputStream` and `FileOutputStream` classes are defined in package `java.io`. Their constructors allow you to open files by name, and their methods let you read data from or write data into a single byte or a byte array.

When you look deeper in the program, you may ask yourself: What if the user does not provide the input and output filenames? Or what if the user provides a nonexistent input file? In Java, all these abnormal conditions are system-defined exceptions that will be thrown by the system as they occur. Accessing an array with an index larger than or equal to the array size will cause an `ArrayIndexOutOfBounds-Exception` to be thrown. The constructor of the `FileInputStream` class will throw a `FileNotFoundException` exception if the file cannot be located. The constructor for `FileOutputStream` and the `read()` and `write()` methods will throw an `IOException` exception for an I/O error.

Furthermore, exception handlers can be located together. A `catch` clause is constructed for each exception handler to identify the abnormal condition the handler is attending to. Three handlers are added to the previous program to attend to the three abnormal conditions mentioned above: One handler will print out the usage of the program when the user does not provide both the input and output filenames; the next handler will notify the user when the input file does not exist; and another handler will print out an error message when other I/O exceptions occur. The program to print out the number of bytes copied is moved to the `finally` clause so that it will always be executed—even if some abnormal condition disrupts the normal program flow. Here is the full program:

```java
import java.io.*;

public class MyCopy {

    public static void main (String[] args) {

        int     byte_count = 0;
        byte[] buffer = new byte[512];
        String input_file  = null;
        String output_file = null;
        FileInputStream  fin;
        FileOutputStream fout;

        try {
            input_file  = args[0];
            output_file = args[1];
            fin  = new FileInputStream(input_file);
            fout = new FileOutputStream(output_file);
            int bytes_in_one_read;

            while ((bytes_in_one_read = fin.read(buffer)) != -1) {
                fout.write(buffer, 0, bytes_in_one_read);
                byte_count += bytes_in_one_read;
            }
        }
        catch (ArrayIndexOutOfBoundsException e) {
            System.out.println(
                "Usage: java MyCopy [input_file] [output_file]");
        }
        catch (FileNotFoundException e) {
            System.out.println("Cannot open input file: " + input_file);
        }
        catch (IOException e) {
            System.out.println("I/O exception occurs!");
        }
        finally {
            if (byte_count > 0)
                System.out.println(byte_count + " bytes written");
        }
    }
}
```

Here is a sample output of the previous program run under different conditions:

```
C:\MasteringJava\Ch07>java MyCopy
Usage: java MyCopy [input_file] [output_file]

C:\MasteringJava\Ch07>java MyCopy MyCopy.java temp.java
1273 bytes written

C:\MasteringJava\Ch07>java MyCopy NoSuchFile.java temp.java
Cannot open input file: NoSuchFile.java
```

Why Use Exception Handling?

There are several good reasons why you should use exception handling. One is that error-handling code is separated from normal program flow to increase the readability and maintainability of the program. Imagine how you would rewrite the example from the previous section in C-style when exception handling is not available. You would need an `if` statement after every I/O operation to make sure of the successful completion of the I/O operation. You also need to use an `if` statement to check whether the user provides enough filenames. To handle these abnormal conditions, you would either add more code in place or use `goto` statements to branch to the code fragment that handles common failures. Add a few more I/O calls, and even you, the author of the program, will not be able to easily recognize what the program was originally intended to accomplish. On the contrary, Java allows you to cleanly separate exception-handling code from normal program flow. With Java, there is no need to test if an exception condition happens. Adding more handlers requires adding more `catch` clauses, but the original program flow need not be touched.

Secondly, you can easily say where the exception will be handled. Exceptions propagate up the call stack at run time—first up the enclosing `try` blocks and then back to the calling method—until they are caught by an exception handler. For example, the previous example can be rewritten as a method with input and output filenames as the arguments. The synopsis of this new method is as follows:

```
int copyFile(String input_file, String output_file)
```

The caller of this method may want to handle the abnormal condition by itself. For example, an application with a GUI may want to display a dialog box prompting the user for another filename when the input file does not exist. In this case, the error handler for I/O exception is removed from the method and a throws clause is added to the method declaration. The caller can then have its own error-handling routines for these abnormal conditions. Here is the modified method definition:

```
int copyFile(String input_file, String output_file) throws IOException
{
    int     bytes_in_one_read, byte_count = 0;
    byte[] buffer = new byte[512];
    FileInputStream  fin = new FileInputStream(input_file);
    FileOutputStream fout= new FileOutputStream(output_file);

    while ((bytes_in_one_read = fin.read(buffer)) != -1) {
        fout.write(buffer, 0, bytes_in_one_read);
        byte_count += bytes_in_one_read;
    }

    return byte_count;
}
```

Here is a code fragment to call this method and handle the abnormal conditions by itself:

```
try {
    input_file  = args[0];
    output_file = args[1];
    byte_count = copyFile(input_file, output_file);
}
catch (ArrayIndexOutOfBoundsException e) {
    System.out.println(
        "Usage: java MyCopy [input_file] [output_file]");
}
catch (FileNotFoundException e) {
    System.out.println("Cannot open input file: " + input_file);
```

```
    }
    catch (IOException e) {
        System.out.println("I/O exception occurs!");
    }
    finally {
        if (byte_count > 0)
            System.out.println(byte_count + " bytes written");
    }
```

Finally, as will be explained in the next section, exceptions are objects with hierarchical relationships. You can create a single exception handler to catch all exceptions from a class and its subclasses or a series of exception handlers, each handling exceptions from individual subclasses. The `MyCopy` example demonstrates another option. The second `catch` clause deals with `FileNotFound-Exception`, while the next one catches any other `IOExceptions`. `FileNotFoundException` is a subclass of `IOException`, so you can check for both subclass and superclass exceptions.

Hierarchy of Exception Classes

Just like nearly everything else in Java, exceptions are objects or class instances. Exception classes form their own class hierarchy. The root class of all the exception classes is the `Throwable` class, which is an immediate subclass of the `Object` class. Methods are defined in the `Throwable` class to retrieve the error message associated with the exception and to print out the stack trace showing where the exception occurs (see the next section, "Handling Exceptions," for more details).

There are two immediate subclasses of class `Throwable`: `Error` and class `Exception`. Subclasses of class `Exception` have the suffix `Exception` and subclasses of class `Error` have the suffix `Error` (and then there is `ThreadDeath`, a subclass of `Error`). The subclasses of `Error` are basically used for signaling abnormal system conditions. For example, an `OutOfMemoryError` signals that the Java Virtual Machine has run out of memory and that the garbage collector is unable to claim any more free memory; a `StackOverflowError` signals a stack overflow in the interpreter. These `Error` exceptions are, in general, unrecoverable and should not be handled.

The subclasses of the `Exception` class are, in general, recoverable. For example, an `EOFException` signals that a file you have opened has no more data for reading, and a `FileNotFoundException` signals that a file you want to open does not exist in the file system. You can choose to handle the exceptions by using a `try-catch` block to enclose the statements whose exceptional conditions will be handled.

Figure 7.1 illustrates the hierarchical relationships among some of the more common errors and exceptions.

FIGURE 7.1:

Hierarchy of common exceptions

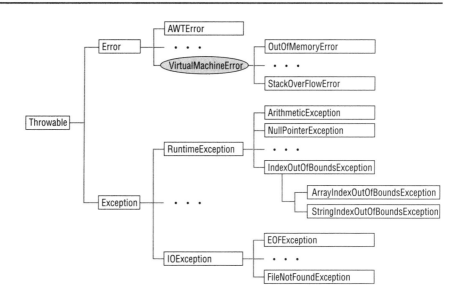

The following example loops through four pathological cases in which the system throws four types of `RunTimeException`:

- `ArithmeticException` for exceptional arithmetic conditions like integer division by zero

- `NullPointerException` for accessing a field or invoking a method of a null object

- `ArrayIndexOutOfBoundsException` for accessing an array element by providing an index value less than zero or greater than or equal to the array size

- `StringIndexOutOfBoundsException` for accessing a character of a `String` or `StringBuffer` with an index less than zero or greater than or equal to the length of the string

Here is the test program:

```
class ExceptionTest
{
    public static void main(String[] args)
    {
        for (int i = 0; i < 4; i++) {
            int k;

            try {
                switch (i) {
                    case 0:     // divided by zero
                        int zero = 0;
                        k = 911 / zero;
                        break;

                    case 1:     // null pointer
                        int[] b = null;
                        k = b[0];
                        break;

                    case 2:     // array index out of bound
                        int[] c = new int[2];
                        k = c[9];
                        break;

                    case 3:     // string index out of bound
                        char ch = "abc".charAt(99);
                        break;
                }
```

```
          }
          catch (Exception e) {
            System.out.println("\nTest case #" + i + "\n");
            System.out.println(e);
          }
        }
      }
    }
```

The output of the previous test program is shown here:

```
C:\MasteringJava\Ch07>java ExceptionTest

Test case #0

java.lang.ArithmeticException: / by zero

Test case #1

java.lang.NullPointerException

Test case #2

java.lang.ArrayIndexOutOfBoundsException: 9

Test case #3

java.lang.StringIndexOutOfBoundsException: String index out of range: 99
```

Handling Exceptions

The general form of an exception-handling construct (the `try` statement) is

```
try {
     normal_program_body
}
catch (exception_class_1 exception_variable_1) {
     exception_handler_program_body_1
}
catch (exception_class_2 exception_variable_2) {
```

```
        exception_handler_program_body_2
    . . .

    }
    finally {
        exit_program_body
    }
```

Early versions of the JDK (before 1.0.2) did not require the use of curly braces in the bodies of a `try-catch-finally` construct, if the program body is consisted of only a single statement. Curly braces are always required, however, in JDK 1.0.2.

The `try` keyword is used to specify a block of statements whose exceptions will be handled by the succeeding `catch` clauses. There can be any number of `catch` clauses. When an exception condition occurs, the body of the first exception handler whose exception class type is the same class as or is a superclass of the thrown exception will be executed. Since exception matching is done sequentially, an exception handler may never be reached if its catch clause is after the catch clause for its superclass exception handler. For example, in an earlier example, the handler for `FileNotFoundException` had to be placed before the handler for `IOException`, the immediate super-class of `FileNotFoundException`. The compiler checks to ensure all exception handlers are reachable. If you exchange the order of the handlers for `FileNotFoundException` and `IOException`, the compiler will issue the following error message:

```
MyCopy.java:33: catch not reached.
        catch (FileNotFoundException e) {
        ^
1 error
```

The exit program block after the `finally` keyword will be executed before the program control is transferred outside the programming construct. This will eventually happen when the execution of the program body or the exception handler is finished, a flow-breaking statement (that is, a `break`, `continue`, or `return` statement) is encountered, or an exception is thrown with no handler inside the construct capable of catching it. The `catch` clause is optional; so is the `finally` clause. However, at least one of the `catch` or `finally` clauses has to exist in a `try-catch-finally` construct. The exit program body comes in handy for freeing resources like the file handles allocated in the normal program body.

The following example demonstrates the effects of `break` and `continue` statements on a `finally` clause. Inside the nested `for` loop, labeled and unlabeled `break` and `continue` statements are executed, and the flow is traced.

```
class FinallyTest {
  public static void main(String[] args) {
    outer_loop:
      for (int i = 0; i < 3; i++)
        for (int j = 0; j < 3; j++)
          try {
            System.out.println("try before if: i=" + i + ", j=" + j);

            if ((i == 0) && (j == 1))
                continue;
            else if ((i == 0) && (j == 2))
                continue outer_loop;
            else if ((i == 1) && (j == 0))
                break;
            else if ((i == 2) && (j == 1))
                break outer_loop;

            System.out.println("try after  if: i=" + i + ", j=" + j);
          }
          finally {
                System.out.println("finally:      i=" + i + ", j=" + j
                                   + "\n");
          }
  }
}
```

The output of the program is shown next. You can see that the `finally` clause is always executed once the `try` block is entered.

```
C:\MasteringJava\Ch07>java FinallyTest
try before if: i=0, j=0
try after  if: i=0, j=0
finally:      i=0, j=0
```

```
try before if:  i=0, j=1
finally:        i=0, j=1

try before if:  i=0, j=2
finally:        i=0, j=2

try before if:  i=1, j=0
finally:        i=1, j=0

try before if:  i=2, j=0
try after  if:  i=2, j=0
finally:        i=2, j=0

try before if:  i=2, j=1
finally:        i=2, j=1
```

If the exception is not caught in the current `try-catch-finally` construct, it will be propagated up the program stack. The same exception-matching process will be repeated for all the enclosing `try-catch-finally` constructs, from the innermost construct to the outermost one, until a matching exception handler can be found. If no match can be found in the current method, the same process will be repeated for all the `try-catch-finally` constructs of the calling method, again from the innermost construct to the outermost one, until a match is found. As the system tries to find a handler for the exception, from innermost to outermost, it executes the `finally` clauses of the `try-catch-finally` construct, from the innermost to the outermost. When the program runs out of `try-catch-finally` constructs and does not find a matching exception handler, it will print out the message associated with the exception and a stack trace showing where the exception occurred; then it will terminate.

Here is a sample output of a program with an uncaught exception:

```
java.lang.ArithmeticException: / by zero
        at NoHandler.inner(NoHandler.java:6)
        at NoHandler.outer(NoHandler.java:11)
        at NoHandler.main(NoHandler.java:15)
```

Even if an exception is caught, the handler can rethrow the exception or throw another exception, and the exception matching process will continue. The next example generates three different exceptions in the `for` loop of the `method()` method. The first exception, `ArithmeticException`, is caught in the inner `try-catch-finally` construct because of an exact match in exception type. The second exception, `ArrayIndexOutOfBoundsException`, is caught in the inner `try-catch-finally` construct, because it is a subclass of `IndexOutOfBoundsException`, but then it is rethrown and caught by the outer `try-catch-finally` construct. The last exception, `StringIndexOutOfBoundsException`, is caught in the inner `try-catch-finally` construct, because it is also a subclass of `IndexOutOfBoundsException`. It is then rethrown, but no handler in the outer `try-catch-finally` construct can catch it. It is thus propagated to the calling method and caught because it is a subclass of `RuntimeException`.

```
class NestedException {

    public static void method()
{
      for (int i = 0; i < 3; i++) {
        int k;

        try {
          System.out.println("\nOuter try block; Test Case #" + i);

          try {
            System.out.println("Inner try block");

            switch (i) {
              case 0:     // divided by zero
                int zero = 0;
                k = 911 / zero;
                break;

              case 1:     // array index out of bound
                int[] c = new int[2];
                k = c[9];
                break;

              case 2:     // string index out of bound
                char ch = "abc".charAt(99);
                break;
            }
          }
          catch (ArithmeticException e) {
            System.out.println("Inner ArithmeticException>" + e);
          }
          catch (IndexOutOfBoundsException e) {
```

```
                  System.out.println("Inner IndexOutOfBoundsException>" + e);
                  throw e;
                }
                finally {
                  System.out.println("Inner finally block");
                }
              }
              catch (ArrayIndexOutOfBoundsException e) {
                System.out.println("Outer ArrayIndexOutOfBound>" + e);
              }
              finally {
                System.out.println("Outer finally block");
              }
            }
          }

          public static void main(String[] args)
          {
            try {
              method();
            } catch (RuntimeException e) {
              System.out.println("main() RuntimeException>" + e);
            } finally {
              System.out.println("\nmain() finally block");
            }
          }
        }
```

Here is the output of the program:

```
C:\MasteringJava\Ch07>java NestedException

Outer try block; Test Case #0
Inner try block
Inner ArithmeticException>java.lang.ArithmeticException: / by zero
Inner finally block
Outer finally block

Outer try block; Test Case #1
Inner try block
Inner IndexOutOfBoundsException>java.lang.ArrayIndexOutOfBoundsException: 9
Inner finally block
Outer ArrayIndexOutOfBound>java.lang.ArrayIndexOutOfBoundsException: 9
Outer finally block

Outer try block; Test Case #2
Inner try block
```

```
Inner IndexOutOfBoundsException>java.lang.StringIndexOutOfBoundsException: String
➡index out of range: 99
Inner finally block
Outer finally block
main() RuntimeException>java.lang.StringIndexOutOfBoundsException: String index out
➡of range: 99

main() finally block
```

Methods Available to Exceptions

All errors and exceptions are subclasses of class `Throwable` and thus can access the methods defined in it. Of them, the most commonly used ones are `getMessage()` to obtain the error message associated with the exception or error, `printStackTrace()` to print a stack trace showing where the exception occurs, and `toString()` to show the exception name along with the message returned by `getMessage()`. Most exception classes have two constructors: one with a `String` argument to set the error message that can later be fetched through the `getMessage()` method; the other with no argument. In the second case, the `getMessage()` method will return `null`. The same error message will be embedded in the return of the `toString()` method or be a part of the stack trace output by the `printStackTrace()` method. An example of output or return from these methods is listed here:

```
*** example of return from getMessage() ***
/ by zero

*** example of return from toString() ***
java.lang.ArithmeticException: / by zero

*** example of output by printStackTrace() ***
java.lang.ArithmeticException: / by zero
        at NoHandler.inner(NoHandler.java:6)
        at NoHandler.outer(NoHandler.java:11)
        at NoHandler.main(NoHandler.java:16)
```

The throw Statement

A `throw` statement causes an exception to be thrown. The synopsis of a `throw` statement is

```
throw expression;
```

where the expression must be evaluated to an instance of class `Throwable` or its many subclasses. In the most common usage, a new statement is used to create an instance in the expression. For example, the following statement will throw an I/O exception with "cannot find the directory" as the error message:

```
throw new IOException("cannot find the directory");
```

The throws Clause

A method that throws an exception within it must catch that exception or have that exception declared in its `throws` clause unless the exception is a subclass of either `Error` class or `RuntimeException` class. When multiple exceptions are to be put in one `throws` clause, use commas to separate them. For example, the following program segment declares a method that propagates out `IOException` and `InterruptedException`:

```
int ReadModel(String filename) throws IOException, InterruptedException
```

There are three reasons why exceptions that are subclasses of `Error` or `RuntimeException` class need not be declared or handled in a method. First, if you need to `catch` or declare a `throws` clause for every such exception that might occur in the method, the program will look very cumbersome. Second, it is also very difficult to check at compile time whether such exceptions will occur. For example, every reference to an object potentially can throw a `NullPointer-Exception`. It is a formidable task for a compiler to make sure that every object referred to will be non-null at run time, especially when the object is passed in as an argument of the method. Finally, most of the errors can occur beyond the programmer's control. It does not make too much sense to ask the programmer to be responsible for handling these errors.

As a matter of fact, the compiler relies on the declaration of `throws` clauses to determine if an exception may occur in an expression, a statement, or a method. The exceptions that may occur in a method are derived as the union of all the exceptions that can be generated by the `throw` statements within the method, and all the exceptions contained in the `throws` clauses of the methods that might be called within the method. The compiler issues an error message for any method that does not declare all (non-error/non-runtime) exceptions in its throws clause. A sample output for such an error message is shown here:

```
DontCompile.java:8: Exception java.io.FileNotFoundException must be
➥caught, or it must be declared in the throws clause of this method.
       FileInputStream fin = new FileInputStream("BasicException.java");
                             ^
```

Creating Your Own Exception Classes

When writing a method, there are two ways to report abnormal conditions to the calling method: One way is to use a predefined error code as the return value and the other is to throw an exception. If an exception is thrown, the calling method is automatically handed the convenience and power of the whole exception-handling mechanism to respond to the abnormal conditions. It will also be possible for the compiler to check if these abnormal conditions are dealt with properly since these abnormal conditions are declared in the `throws` clause of the method.

When throwing an exception, you can create an instance from an exception class already defined in the language or from one you define on your own. It is always difficult to find a predefined exception that is designed for situations like yours. By using an exception already prescribed for other conditions, you may also complicate the exception handler's task. The reason is that the exception handler may need to differentiate your abnormal condition from the ones the exception class is originally prescribed for, if they can both occur in the method.

The common practice in creating a customized exception class is to subclass the `Exception` class. This ensures the compiler checks if it is dealt with properly. However, if you are writing system- or hardware-related utilities, you may be justified in creating subclasses from either `Error` or `RuntimeException` classes. You should not subclass `Error` or `RuntimeException` just so you do not have to create `throws` clauses for your methods.

Exception classes are class objects and therefore can have data members and methods defined within. As an example, `Interrupted-IOException` defined in `java.io` package has a public instance variable, `bytesTransferred`, to hold the number of bytes read or written before the operation is interrupted. You may choose to create customized exception classes in a hierarchy so that the handler has the option to handle the superclass as a whole, the subclasses individually, or both classes simultaneously.

An Example: Age Exceptions

This example demonstrates how to create a hierarchy of user-defined exception classes for abnormal conditions and how to write a program using these user-defined exceptions for abnormal condition handling. In the first part of the example, a hierarchy of exception classes to report age-related anomalies is constructed, as shown in Figure 7.2.

The root of this hierarchy is `AgeException` class. It has a data member, `age`, to hold the age causing the occurrence of the exception. It has two subclasses: class `OutOfAgeLimitException` for cases

FIGURE 7.2:

The class hierarchy for
`AgeException` class

where the age given is too young or too old to perform a certain activity and class `IllegalAgeFormatException` for cases where the age given is out of the legal age range or in the wrong format. The former class has a data member, `age_limit`, to hold the limit being violated. The program for defining these classes is listed here:

```
class AgeException extends Exception
{
    int age;

    AgeException(String message) {
        super(message);
    }
    AgeException() {
        super();
    }
}

class OutOfAgeLimitException extends AgeException
{
    int age_limit;

    OutOfAgeLimitException(int age_limit, String message) {
        super(message);
        this.age_limit = age_limit;
    }
    OutOfAgeLimitException(String message) {
        super(message);
    }
}

class TooYoungException extends OutOfAgeLimitException
{
    TooYoungException(int age, int age_limit, String message) {
        super(age_limit, "You are too young to " + message + ".");
```

```
            this.age = age;
        }
        TooYoungException() {
            super("too young");
        }
    }

class TooOldException extends OutOfAgeLimitException
{
    TooOldException(int age, int age_limit, String message) {
        super(age_limit, "You are too old to " + message + ".");
        this.age = age;
    }
    TooOldException() {
        super("too old");
    }
}

class IllegalAgeFormatException extends AgeException
{
    IllegalAgeFormatException(String message) {
        super(message);
    }
    IllegalAgeFormatException() {
        super("Illegal age format");
    }
}

class NegativeAgeException extends IllegalAgeFormatException
{
    NegativeAgeException(String message) {
        super(message);
    }
    NegativeAgeException(int age) {
        super("Age must be nonnegative.");
        this.age = age;
    }
}
```

The second part of the example is a program to utilize the previous exception hierarchy. The program will loop through different ages to see if people in the age specified can ride a roller coaster. The method `RideRollerCoasterAtAge()` will throw `TooYoungException`, `TooOldException`, or `NegativeAgeException` if it finds an age that is too young, too old, or negative, respectively. The program listing is as follows:

```
class AgeExceptionTest
{
    static void RideRollerCoasterAtAge(int age)
            throws NegativeAgeException, OutOfAgeLimitException
    {
        System.out.println("Trying to ride a roller coaster at age " +
                    age + "...");

        if (age < 0)
            throw new NegativeAgeException(age);
        else if (age < 5)
            throw new TooYoungException(age, 5,
                                    "ride a roller coaster");
        else if (age > 45)
            throw new TooOldException(age, 45,
                                    "ride a roller coaster");

        System.out.println("Riding the roller coaster....");
    }

    public static void main(String[] argc)
    {
        int ages[] = {-3, 2, 10, 35, 65};

        for (int i = 0; i < ages.length; i++)
            try {
                RideRollerCoasterAtAge(ages[i]);
                System.out.println("Wow! What an experience!");
            }
            catch (OutOfAgeLimitException e) {
                System.out.println(e.getMessage());
                if (ages[i] < e.age_limit)
                    System.out.println((e.age_limit - ages[i]) +
                        " more years and you'll be able to try it.");
                else
                    System.out.println((ages[i] - e.age_limit) +
                        " years ago riding it was like a piece of cake.");
            }
            catch (NegativeAgeException e) {
                System.out.println(e.getMessage());
            }
```

```
        finally {
            System.out.println();
        }
    }
}
```

The output of the previous program is listed here:

```
C:\MasteringJava\Ch07>java AgeExceptionTest

Trying to ride a roller coaster at age -3...
Age must be nonnegative.

Trying to ride a roller coaster at age 2...
You are too young to ride a roller coaster.
3 more years and you'll be able to try it.

Trying to ride a roller coaster at age 10...
Riding the roller coaster....
Wow! What an experience!

Trying to ride a roller coaster at age 35...
Riding the roller coaster....
Wow! What an experience!

Trying to ride a roller coaster at age 65...
You are too old to ride a roller coaster.
20 years ago riding it was like a piece of cake.
```

Summary

Java provides a clean and robust mechanism for handling abnormal conditions. First, you try to execute a block of statements. If an abnormal condition occurs, an exception is thrown and you can catch the exception. And, finally, there can be a code fragment you always want to execute, whether or not an exception happens and is handled.

Exceptions are objects, and exception classes form their own hierarchy. The root of all error and exception classes is the `Throwable` class. You can create your own exception classes as subclasses of `Exception` class. The whole exception-handling mechanism is then at your disposal to use for processing them—you can even create a hierarchy of exception classes so that the handler has more flexibility in handling the exceptions.

A method that may cause an exception to be thrown must catch that exception or have that exception defined in its `throws` clause, unless the exception is a subclass of either `Error` or `Runtime-Exception` class. Checking of the above rule is done at compile time.

It is always unpleasant for a user to encounter errors in your application. How you deal with these errors will make a difference to the user, and will be an important factor in your application's success. The clean and robust exception-handling capability provided with Java make writing a friendly program an easier task.

Threads

- Thread Basics

- Advanced Threading

Up to now, all our example programs have been single-threaded; that is, they have had only one line of execution. If the program execution is blocked waiting for the completion of some I/O operation, no other portion of the program can proceed. However, users of today's modern operating systems are accustomed to starting multiple programs and watching them work concurrently, even if there is only a single CPU available to run all the applications. *Multithreading* allows multiple processes to execute concurrently within a single program. The advantage of multithreading is twofold. First, programs with multiple threads will, in general, result in better utilization of system resources, including the CPU, because another line of execution can grab the CPU when one line of execution is blocked. Second, there are a lot of problems better solved by multiple threads. For example, how would you write a single-threaded program to show animation, play music, display documents, and download files from the network at the same time? Java was designed from the beginning with multithreading in mind. Not only does the language itself have multithreading support built in, allowing for easy creation of robust, multithreaded applications, but also the runtime environment relies on multithreading to concurrently provide multiple services—like garbage collection—to the application. In this chapter, you will learn to use these built-in features to utilize multiple threads in your Java programs.

Introduction

A *thread* is a single flow of control within a program. It is sometimes called the *execution context* because each thread must have its own resources—like the program counter and the execution stack—as the context for execution. However, all threads in a program still share a lot of resources like memory space and opened files. Therefore, a thread may also be called a *lightweight process*: It is a single flow of control like a process (or a running program), but it is easier to create and destroy than a process because less resource management is involved.

> The terms *parallel* and *concurrent* occur frequently in computer literature, and the difference between them can be confusing. When two threads run in parallel, they are both being executed at the same time on different CPUs. However, two concurrent threads are both in progress, or trying to get some CPU time for execution, at the same time, but are not necessarily being executed simultaneously on different CPUs.

A program may spend a big portion of its execution time just waiting. For example, it may wait for some resource to become accessible in an I/O operation, or it may wait for some time-out to occur to start drawing the next scene of an animation. To improve CPU utilization, all the tasks with potentially long waits can be run as separate threads. Once a task starts waiting for something to happen, Java run time can choose another runnable task for execution.

The first example demonstrates the difference between a single-threaded program and its multithreaded counterpart. In the first program, a run() method in the NoThreadPseudoIO class is created to simulate a ten-second long I/O operation. The main program will first perform the simulated I/O operation, then start another task. The method showElapsedTime() is defined to print out the elapsed time in seconds since the program started, together with a user-supplied message. The currentTimeMillis() method of the System class in the java.lang package will return a long integer for the time difference, measured in milliseconds, between the current time and 00:00:00 GMT on January 1, 1970. The single-threaded program is listed here:

```
class WithoutThread {
    public static void main(String[] args) {

        //  first task: some pseudo-I/O operation

        NoThreadPseudoIO pseudo = new NoThreadPseudoIO();
```

```
            pseudo.run();

            //  second task: some random task

            showElapsedTime("Another task starts");
        }

        static long base_time = System.currentTimeMillis();

        // show the time elapsed since the program started

        static void showElapsedTime(String message) {
            long elapsed_time = System.currentTimeMillis() - base_time;

            System.out.println(message + " at " +
                               (elapsed_time / 1000.0) + " seconds");
        }
    }

// pseudo-I/O operation run in caller's thread

class NoThreadPseudoIO {
    int data = -1;

    NoThreadPseudoIO() {      // constructor
        WithoutThread.showElapsedTime("NoThreadPseudoIO created");
    }

    public void run() {
        WithoutThread.showElapsedTime("NoThreadPseudoIO starts");

        try {
            Thread.sleep(10000);      // 10 seconds
            data = 999;               // the data is ready

            WithoutThread.showElapsedTime("NoThreadPseudoIO finishes");
        }
        catch (InterruptedException e) {}
    }
}
```

Even if the second task doesn't refer to any data generated or modified by the pseudo-I/O operation, the task cannot be started until the I/O operation is finished. For most real I/O operations, the CPU will just be sitting idle most of the time waiting for a response from the peripheral device, which is really a waste of precious CPU cycles. A sample output of the above program is shown here:

```
C:\MasteringJava\Ch08>java WithoutThread
NoThreadPseudoIO created at 0.06 seconds
NoThreadPseudoIO starts at 0.11 seconds
```

```
NoThreadPseudoIO finishes at 10.11 seconds
Another task starts at 10.11 seconds
```

The multithreaded second program declares the class for the pseudo-I/O operation as a subclass of the `Thread` class:

```
class ThreadedPseudoIO extends Thread {
```

After the thread is created, it uses the `start()` method of the `Thread` class to start the I/O operation:

```
ThreadedPseudoIO pseudo = new ThreadedPseudoIO();
pseudo.start();
```

The thread's `start()` method in turn calls the `run()` method of the subclass.

TIP

Up to Java Developers Kit (JDK) version 1.0.2, there is a bug in the code for running multiple threads under Windows 95 and NT: Programs that start multiple threads will not automatically exit. The workaround is to either have the last running thread call the `System.exit()` method or have a thread monitor other threads by calling the `join()` methods of the monitored threads. `exit()` is a class method defined in the `System` class of the `java.lang` package for terminating Java run time. For security reasons, an applet is not allowed to call `exit()`. Forcibly calling `exit()` from an applet will cause a `SecurityException` to be thrown. (The use of the `join()` method will be explained in a later section.) The workaround is not necessary for other platforms. However, for your program's ultimate portability, you may want to use the workaround all the time before the bug is fixed.

A full listing of this multithreaded program is as follows:

```
class WithThread {
    public static void main(String[] args) {

        // first task: some pseudo-I/O operation

        ThreadedPseudoIO pseudo = new ThreadedPseudoIO();
        pseudo.start();

        // second task: some random task
```

```
        showElapsedTime("Another task starts");

        // the following is the workaround for a bug in JDK 1.0.x
        // implementation on Windows 95 and NT;
        // it is used for the main thread to wait for the pseudo's completion

        try {
            pseudo.join();
        } catch (InterruptedException e) {}
    }

    static long base_time = System.currentTimeMillis();

    // show the time elapsed since the program started

    static void showElapsedTime(String message) {
        long elapsed_time = System.currentTimeMillis() - base_time;

        System.out.println(message + " at " +
                          (elapsed_time / 1000.0) + " seconds");
    }
}

// pseudo-I/O operation run in a separate thread

class ThreadedPseudoIO extends Thread {
    int data = -1;

    ThreadedPseudoIO() {      // constructor
        WithThread.showElapsedTime("ThreadedPseudoIO created");
    }

    public void run() {
        WithThread.showElapsedTime("ThreadedPseudoIO starts");

        try {
            Thread.sleep(10000);      // 10 seconds
            data = 999;               // data ready

            WithThread.showElapsedTime("ThreadedPseudoIO finishes");
        }
        catch (InterruptedException e) {}
    }
}
```

Here is the output of the multithreaded program. You will notice that the second task starts even before the pseudo-I/O operation starts; this is natural when you have only one CPU running two threads. The run() method of the newly created thread will not be executed until the currently running thread relinquishes program control.

```
C:\MasteringJava\Ch08>java WithThread
ThreadedPseudoIO created at 0.05 seconds
Another task starts at 0.05 seconds
ThreadedPseudoIO starts at 0.05 seconds
ThreadedPseudoIO finishes at 10.05 seconds
```

Thread Basics

This section introduces the basic working of a thread: how to create and run a thread, the thread-controlling methods defined in the `Thread` class, the life cycle of a thread, thread groups, and how to get information about threads and thread groups.

Creating and Running a Thread

When you have a task that you want to be run concurrently with other tasks, there are two ways to create the new thread. One is to create a new class as a subclass of the `Thread` class. This subclass should define its own `run()` method to override the `run()` method of the `Thread` class. This `run()` method is where the task is performed. Just as the `main()` method is the first user-defined method the Java run time calls to start an application, the `run()` method is the first user-defined method the Java run time calls to start a thread. An instance of this subclass is then created by a `new` statement, followed by a call to the thread's `start()` method to have the `run()` method executed. This is exactly what has been done with the `Threaded-PseudoIO` class in the previous example.

The other way to create a new thread is to declare a class implementing the `Runnable` interface. The `Runnable` interface requires only one method to be implemented—the `run()` method. You first create an instance of this class with a `new` statement, followed by the creation of a `Thread` instance with another `new` statement, and finally a call to this thread instance's `start()` method to start performing the task defined in the `run()` method. A class instance with the run() method defined within must be passed in as an argument in creating the Thread instance so that when the start() method of this Thread instance is called, Java run time knows which run() method to execute. This alternative way of creating a thread comes in handy when the class defining the run() method needs to be a subclass of other classes: The class can inherit all the data and methods of the superclasses, and the Thread instance just created can be used for thread control. The previous multithreaded example can be re-implemented using the Runnable interface by first changing the class definition to implement the Runnable interface instead of subclassing the Thread class:

```
class RunnablePseudoIO implements Runnable {
```

Then, an instance of the class is created and passed to a newly created Thread instance, followed by a call to the start() method to start the execution of the run() method as follows:

```
RunnablePseudoIO pseudo = new RunnablePseudoIO();
Thread thread = new Thread(pseudo);
thread.start();
```

A full listing of the program is included here:

```
class RunnableThread {
    public static void main(String[] args) {

        //  first task: some pseudo-I/O operation

        RunnablePseudoIO pseudo = new RunnablePseudoIO();
        Thread thread = new Thread(pseudo);
        thread.start();

        //  second task: some random task

        showElapsedTime("Another task starts");

        //  The following is workaround for the bug in JDK 1.0.x
        //  implementation on Windows 95/NT;
        //  it is used for the main thread to wait for the pseudo's completion

        try {
            thread.join();
```

```
        } catch (InterruptedException e) {}
    }

    static long base_time = System.currentTimeMillis();

    // show the time elapsed since the program started

    static void showElapsedTime(String message) {
        long elapsed_time = System.currentTimeMillis() - base_time;

        System.out.println(message + " at " +
                        (elapsed_time / 1000.0) + " seconds");
    }
}

// pseudo I/O operation run in a separate thread

class RunnablePseudoIO implements Runnable {
    int data = -1;

    RunnablePseudoIO() {    // constructor
        RunnableThread.showElapsedTime("RunnablePseudoIO created");
    }

    public void run() {
        RunnableThread.showElapsedTime("RunnablePseudoIO starts");

        try {
            Thread.sleep(10000);    // 10 seconds
            data = 999;             // data ready

            RunnableThread.showElapsedTime("RunnablePseudoIO finishes");
        }
        catch (InterruptedException e) {}

        System.exit(0);
    }
}
```

The output of the program is, as expected, very similar to that of the
earlier program:

```
C:\MasteringJava\Ch08>java RunnableThread
RunnablePseudoIO created at 0 seconds
Another task starts at 0 seconds
RunnablePseudoIO starts at 0.06 seconds
RunnablePseudoIO finishes at 10.05 seconds
```

The Thread-Controlling Methods

There are many methods defined in the Thread class to control the running of a thread. Here is a list of some of the ones most commonly used:

start()   Used to start the execution of the thread body defined in the run() method. Program control will be immediately returned to the caller, and a new thread will be scheduled to execute the run() method concurrently with the caller's thread.

stop()   Used to stop the execution of the thread no matter what the thread is doing. The thread is then considered dead, the internal states of the thread are cleared, and the resources allocated are reclaimed.

suspend()   Used to temporarily stop the execution of the thread. All the states and resources of the thread are retained. The thread can later be restarted by another thread calling the resume() method.

resume()   Used to resume the execution of a suspended thread. The suspended thread will be scheduled to run—if it has a higher priority than the running thread, the running thread will be pre-empted; otherwise, the just-resumed thread will wait in the queue for its turn to run.

sleep(long sleep_time_in_milliseconds)   A class method that causes the Java run time to put the caller thread to sleep for a specified time period. The exception, InterruptedException, may be thrown while a thread is sleeping. Either a try-catch-finally statement needs to be defined to handle this exception, or the enclosing method needs to have this exception in the throws clause.

join()   Used for the caller's thread to wait for this thread to die—for example, by coming to the end of the `run()` method.

yield()   A class method that temporarily stops the caller's thread and puts it at the end of the queue to wait for another turn to be executed. It is used to make sure other threads of the same priority have the chance to run.

> **TIP**
>
> All the class methods defined in `Thread` class, such as `sleep()` and `yield()`, will act on the caller's thread. That is, it is the caller's thread that will sleep for awhile or yield to others. The reason is that a class method can never access an instance's data or method members unless the instance is passed in as an argument, created inside the method, or stored in a class variable visible to the method.

The following example shows how some of the above methods are used. The main thread will create two threads, then wait for the first thread to finish by calling the first thread's `join()` method. The first thread will call the `sleep()` method to be asleep for ten seconds. Meanwhile, the second thread calls its own `suspend()` method to suspend itself until the main thread calls its `resume()` method. After the first thread comes to an end, the main thread will resume its execution, wake up the second thread by calling the second thread's `resume()` method, and wait until the second thread also comes to an end by calling the second thread's `join()` method. The program is as follows:

```
public class MethodTest {

    public static void main(String args[]) {
        FirstThread  first  = new FirstThread();
        SecondThread second = new SecondThread();

        first.start();
        second.start();

        try {
        System.out.println("Waiting for first thread to finish...");
            first.join();
```

```
        System.out.println("It's a long wait!");

        System.out.println("Waking up second thread...");
        second.resume();

        System.out.println("Waiting for second thread to finish...");
        second.join();
        } catch (InterruptedException e) {}

        System.out.println("I'm ready to finish too.");
    }
}

class FirstThread extends Thread
{
    public void run() {
        try {
            System.out.println("First thread starts running.");
            sleep(10000);
            System.out.println("First thread finishes running.");
        }
        catch (InterruptedException e) {}
    }
}

class SecondThread extends Thread
{
  public void run() {
    System.out.println("  Second thread starts running.");
    System.out.println("  Second thread suspends itself.");
    suspend();
    System.out.println("  Second thread runs again and finishes.");
  }
}
```

The output of this program is shown here:

```
C:\MasteringJava\Ch08>java MethodTest
Waiting for 1st thread to finish...
  First thread starts running.
  Second thread starts running.
  Second thread suspends itself.
  First thread finishes running.
It's a long wait!
Waking up second thread...
Waiting for second thread to finish...
  Second thread runs again and finishes.
I'm ready to finish too.
```

The Thread Life Cycle

Every thread, after creation and before destruction, will always be in one of these four states (see Figure 8.1 for the transition diagram):

Newly Created   A thread enters this state immediately after creation; that is, right after the thread-creating `new` statement is executed. In this state, the local data members are allocated and initialized, but execution of the `run()` method will not begin until its `start()` method is called. After the `start()` method is called, the thread will be put into the runnable state.

Runnable   When a thread is in this state, the execution context exists and the thread can be scheduled to run at any time. That is, the thread is not waiting for any event to happen. For the sake of explanation, this state can be subdivided into two sub-states: the running and queued states. When a thread is in the running state, it is assigned CPU cycles and is actually running. When a thread is in the queued state, it is waiting in the queue and competing for its turn to spend CPU cycles. The transition between these two substates is controlled by the runtime scheduler. However, a thread can call the `yield()` method to voluntarily move itself to the queued state from the running state.

Blocked   This state is entered when one of the following events occurs:

- The thread itself or another thread calls the `suspend()` method.

- The thread calls an object's `wait()` method.

- The thread itself calls the `sleep()` method.

- The thread is waiting for some I/O operation to complete.

A thread in a blocked state will not be scheduled for running. It will go back to the runnable state, competing for CPU cycles, when the counter-event for the blocking event occurs:

- If the thread is suspended, another thread calls its `resume()` method.

- If the thread is blocked by calling an object's `wait()` method, the object's `notify()` or `notifyAll()` method is called.

- If the thread is put to sleep, the specified sleeping time elapses.

- If the thread is blocked on I/O, the specified I/O operation completes.

Dead   This state is entered when a thread finishes its execution or is stopped by another thread calling its `stop()` method.

FIGURE 8.1:

The thread life cycle

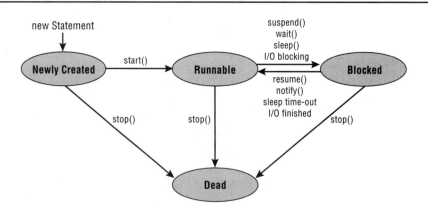

TIP

Under the JDK 1.0.2 and earlier implementations of the Java run time on Windows 95 and Solaris 2, `stop()` will be ignored if a thread is created but not yet started. Also, `stop()` on a blocked thread is remembered but will not take effect until the thread is returned to the runnable state by the occurrence of the proper event. Hopefully, in later releases the behavior of the `stop()` method will be changed to follow the language specification.

To find out whether a thread is alive—that is, currently runnable or blocked—use the thread's `isAlive()` method. It will return `true` if the thread is alive. If a thread is alive, it does not mean it is running, just that it can.

Thread Groups

As its name implies, a `ThreadGroup` is a group of threads. Every thread instance is a member of exactly one thread group. A thread group can have both threads and other thread groups as its members. In fact, every thread group, except the system thread group, is a member of some other thread group. All the threads and thread groups in an application form a tree with the system thread group as the root.

When a Java application is started, the Java run time creates the main thread group as a member of the system thread group. A main thread is created in this main thread group to run the `main()` method of the application. By default, all new user-created threads and thread groups will become the members of this main thread group unless another thread group is passed as the first argument of the `new` statement's constructor method. A new thread group is created by instantiating the `ThreadGroup` class. For example, to create a thread group named `MyThreadGroup` as a member of the default main thread group, and then create a thread named `MyThread` as a member of the newly created thread group, the following two statements can be used:

```
ThreadGroup group = new ThreadGroup("MyThreadGroup");

Thread thread = new Thread(group, "MyThread");
```

Three methods are defined in the `ThreadGroup` class to manipulate all the threads in the thread group and its subthread groups at once: `stop()`, `suspend()`, and `resume()`. They have exactly the same functionality as their thread method counterparts. They come in handy when you need to, say, suspend all your animation or multimedia threads at a time.

Getting Information about Threads and Thread Groups

There are abundant methods defined in `Thread` and `ThreadGroup` for getting information about the thread and thread group. Some of the most commonly used methods for threads are listed here:

currentThread()   A class method returning the caller's thread

getName()   Returns the current name of the thread

getThreadGroup()   Returns the parent thread group of the thread

getPriority()   Returns the current priority of the thread

isAlive()   Returns `true` if the thread is started but not dead yet

isDaemon()   Returns `true` if the thread is a daemon thread

Some commonly used methods for thread groups are listed here:

getName()   Returns the name of the thread group

getParent()   Returns the parent thread group of the thread group

getMaxPriority()   Returns the current maximum priority of the thread group

activeCount()   Returns the number of active threads in the thread group

activeGroupCount()   Returns the number of active thread groups in the thread group

enumerate(Thread[] list, boolean recursive)   Adds all active threads in this thread group into the `list` array. If `recursive` is `true`, all the threads in the subthread groups will be copied over as well. This method will return the number of threads copied. The `activeCount()` method is often used to size the `list` when the space of this thread array is to be allocated.

enumerate(ThreadGroup[] list, boolean recursive)   Adds all the active thread groups in this thread group into the `list` array. If `recursive` is `true`, all the thread groups in the subthread groups will be copied over as well. This method will return the number of thread groups copied. The `activeGroupCount()` method is often used to size the `list` when the space of this thread group array is to be allocated.

Thread priorities and daemon threads will be discussed in later sections.

Here is an example using all the methods described above to show the information on all the threads and thread groups in an application. The program creates a thread group named `MyThreadGroup` and creates four threads in the thread group. It then continues on to print all the information by calling the `printAllThreadInfo()` method. The `printAllThreadInfo()` method first locates the root thread group of all the running threads and thread groups. It then prints out the information of the underlying threads and thread groups recursively from the root. The output is indented to show the depth of individual threads or thread groups in the tree. The full program is as follows:

```
public class ThreadInfo
{
    public static void main(String[] args) {
        Thread[] threads = new Thread[4];
        ThreadGroup group = new ThreadGroup("MyThreadGroup");

        if (args.length > 0) {
            Thread thread = Thread.currentThread();
            thread.setName(args[0]);
        }

        for (int i = 0; i < 4; i++)
            threads[i] = new Thread(group, "MyThread#" + i);

        ThreadInfo.printAllThreadInfo();
    }

    // list information about all the threads and thread groups
    // in the application

    public static void printAllThreadInfo() {
        ThreadGroup parent, root;

        //        find the root of all running threads

        root = parent = Thread.currentThread().getThreadGroup();
        while ((parent = parent.getParent()) != null)
            root = parent;
```

```
        // print information recursively from the root

        System.out.println();
        printThreadGroupInfo("", root);
    }

    // print information about a thread group

    public static void printThreadGroupInfo(
            String indent, ThreadGroup group)
    {
        if (group == null) return;

        System.out.println(indent +
            "THREAD GROUP: " + group.getName() +
            "; Max Priority: " + group.getMaxPriority() +
            (group.isDaemon() ? " [Daemon]" : ""));

        // print information about component threads

        int no_of_threads = group.activeCount();
        Thread[] threads  = new Thread[no_of_threads];

        no_of_threads = group.enumerate(threads, false);
        for (int i = 0; i < no_of_threads; i++)
            printThreadInfo(indent + "    ", threads[i]);

        // print information about component thread groups

        int no_of_groups  = group.activeGroupCount();
        ThreadGroup[] groups = new ThreadGroup[no_of_groups];

        no_of_groups = group.enumerate(groups, false);
        for (int i = 0; i < no_of_groups; i++)
            printThreadGroupInfo(indent + "    ", groups[i]);
    }

    // print information about a single thread

    public static void printThreadInfo(String indent,
                                       Thread thread)
    {
        if (thread == null) return;
```

```
System.out.println(indent +
    "THREAD: " + thread.getName() +
    "; Priority: " + thread.getPriority() +
    (thread.isDaemon() ? " [Daemon]" : "") +
    (thread.isAlive() ? " [Alive]" : " [NotAlive]") +
    ((Thread.currentThread() == thread) ? " <== current" :                "")));
    }
}
```

The output of the previous program run on a PC under Windows 95 is as follows:

```
C:\MasteringJava\Ch08>java ThreadInfo

THREAD GROUP: system; Max Priority: 10
    THREAD: Finalizer thread; Priority: 1 [Daemon] [Alive]
    THREAD GROUP: main; Max Priority: 10
        THREAD: main; Priority: 5 [Alive] <== current
        THREAD GROUP: MyThreadGroup; Max Priority: 10
            THREAD: MyThread#0; Priority: 5 [NotAlive]
            THREAD: MyThread#1; Priority: 5 [NotAlive]
            THREAD: MyThread#2; Priority: 5 [NotAlive]
            THREAD: MyThread#3; Priority: 5 [NotAlive]
```

The same program run under Solaris 2.5 produces similar output, as follows:

```
harpoon:/users/hsu/java/examples/ch8> java ThreadInfo

THREAD GROUP: system; Max Priority: 10
    THREAD: clock handler; Priority: 11 [Daemon] [Alive]
    THREAD: Idle thread; Priority: 0 [Daemon] [Alive]
    THREAD: Async Garbage Collector; Priority: 1 [Daemon] [Alive]
    THREAD: Finalizer thread; Priority: 1 [Daemon] [Alive]
    THREAD GROUP: main; Max Priority: 10
        THREAD: main; Priority: 5 [Alive] <== current
        THREAD GROUP: MyThreadGroup; Max Priority: 10
            THREAD: MyThread#0; Priority: 5 [NotAlive]
            THREAD: MyThread#1; Priority: 5 [NotAlive]
            THREAD: MyThread#2; Priority: 5 [NotAlive]
            THREAD: MyThread#3; Priority: 5 [NotAlive]
```

Advanced Threading

This section introduces some advanced multithreading topics: thread synchronization, interthread communications, thread priorities and scheduling, and daemon threads. *Synchronization* is the way to avoid data corruption caused by simultaneous access to the same data. *Interthread communications* allow threads to talk to or wait on each other. *Priorities* are the way to make sure important or time-critical threads get executed frequently or immediately. *Scheduling* is the means to make sure priorities and fairness are enforced. *Daemon threads* are persisting threads providing services to other threads.

Synchronization

Because all the threads in a program share the same memory space, it is possible for two threads to access the same variable or run the same method of the same object at the same time. Problems may occur when multiple threads are accessing the same data concurrently. Threads may race each other, and one thread may overwrite the data just written by another thread. Or one thread may work on another thread's intermediate result and break the consistency of the data. Some mechanism is needed to block one thread's access to the critical data, if the data, is being worked on by another thread.

For example, assume you have a program to handle a user's bank account. There are three subtasks in making a deposit for the user: The first subtask is to get the current balance from some remote server, which may take as long as five seconds; the second is to add the newly deposited amount into the just-acquired balance; the last is to send back the new balance to the same remote server, which again may take as long as five seconds to complete. If two depositing threads, each making a $1,000 deposit, are started roughly at the same time on a current balance of $1,000, the final balance of these two deposits may reflect the result of only one deposit. A possible scenario is depicted in Table 8.1.

Table 8.1: Two Depositing Threads Running Concurrently

Time	Thread #1	Thread #2	Balance in remote server
a	getting balance		$1,000
b	waiting...	getting balance	$1,000
c	get balance = $1,000	waiting...	$1,000
d	compute new balance = $2,000	waiting...	$1,000
e	setting new balance	waiting...	$1,000
f	waiting...	get balance = $1,000	$1,000
g	waiting...	compute new balance = $2,000	$1,000
h	waiting...	setting new balance	$1,000
i	new balance set	waiting...	$2,000
j		new balance set	$2,000

The balance stored in the remote server only increases by one deposit amount! An example program simulating the above scenario is created. An `Account` class is defined with three methods: `getBalance()`, to fetch current balance from some pseudo server with a simulated five-second delay; `setBalance()`, to write back the new balance to the same pseudo-server with (again) a simulated five-second delay; and `deposit()`, to use the other two methods to complete a deposit transaction. A `DepositThread` class is declared to start the deposit operation on the account passed in. The main program creates an account instance and then starts two threads to make a deposit of $1,000 each to that account. The full program listing is as follows:

```
class Deposit {
    static int balance = 1000;   // simulate the balance kept remotely

    public static void main(String[] args) {
        Account account = new Account();
        DepositThread first, second;
```

```
        first  = new DepositThread(account, 1000, "#1");
        second = new DepositThread(account, 1000, "\t\t\t\t#2");

        // start the transactions

        first.start();
        second.start();

        // wait for both transactions to finish

        try {
            first.join();
            second.join();
        } catch (InterruptedException e) {}

        // print out the final balance

        System.out.println("*** Final balance is " + balance);
    }
}

class Account {
    void deposit(int amount, String name) {
        int balance;

        System.out.println(name + " trying to deposit " + amount);

        System.out.println(name + " getting balance...");
        balance = getBalance();
        System.out.println(name + " balance got is " + balance);

        balance += amount;

        System.out.println(name + " setting balance...");
        setBalance(balance);
        System.out.println(name + " new balance set to " +
                           Deposit.balance);
    }

    int getBalance() {
        try {   // simulate the delay in getting balance remotely
            Thread.sleep(5000);
        } catch (InterruptedException e) {}

        return Deposit.balance;
    }

    void setBalance(int balance) {
        try {   // simulate the delay in setting new balance remotely
            Thread.sleep(5000);
        } catch (InterruptedException e) {}

        Deposit.balance = balance;
    }
}
```

```
class DepositThread extends Thread {

    Account account;
    int      deposit_amount;
    String   message;

    DepositThread(Account account, int amount, String message) {
        this.message  = message;
        this.account  = account;
        this.deposit_amount = amount;
    }

    public void run() {
        account.deposit(deposit_amount, message);
    }
}
```

A possible output of the above program is as follows:

```
C:\MasteringJava\Ch08>java Deposit
#1 trying to deposit 1000
#1 getting balance...
                                #2 trying to deposit 1000
                                #2 getting balance...
#1 balance got is 1000
#1 setting balance...
                                #2 balance got is 1000
                                #2 setting balance...
#1 new balance set to 2000
                                #2 new balance set to 2000
*** Final balance is 2000
```

Java uses the idea of monitors to synchronize access to data. A monitor is like a guarded place where all the protected resources have the same locks on them. There is only a single key to all the locks inside a monitor, and a thread has to get the key to enter the monitor and access these protected resources. If many threads want to enter the monitor at the same time, only one thread is handed the key; the others have to wait outside until the key-holding thread finishes its use of the resources and hands back the key to Java run time. Once a thread gets a monitor's key, the thread can access any of the resources controlled by that monitor countless times as long as the thread still owns the key. However, if this key-holding thread wants to access the resources controlled by another monitor, the thread has to get that particular monitor's key. At any time, a thread can hold many monitors' keys. Different threads can hold keys for different monitors at the same time. Deadlock may occur if threads are waiting for each other's key to proceed.

In Java, the resources protected by monitors are program fragments in the form of methods or blocks of statements enclosed in curly braces. If some data can only be accessed through methods or blocks protected by the same monitor, access to the data is indirectly synchronized. The keyword `synchronized` is used to indicate that the following method or block of statements is to be synchronized by a monitor. When a block of statements is to be synchronized, an object instance enclosed in parentheses immediately following the `synchronized` keyword is required so Java run time knows which monitor to check with.

Figure 8.2 depicts this monitor model of Java. A monitor is sketched here as a guarded parking lot where all the synchronized methods or blocks are just like cars you can drive (or execute, if you are a thread). All the cars share the same key. You need to get this

FIGURE 8.2:

The Java monitor model

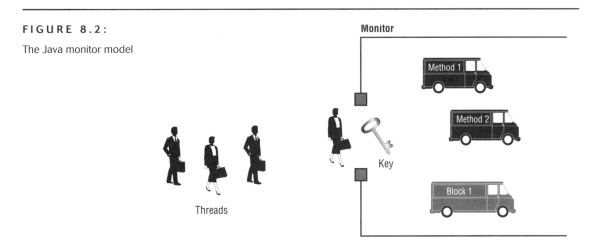

unique key to enter the parking lot and drive any of the cars as you wish until you hand back the key. At that time, one of the persons waiting to get in will get the key and be able to drive the car(s) of his or her choice.

For example, the `deposit()` method in the previous example can be synchronized to allow only one thread to run at a time. The only change needed is a `synchronized` keyword before the method definition as follows:

```
synchronized void deposit(int amount, String name) {
```

A sample output of the modified program is as follows:

```
#1 trying to deposit 1000
#1 getting balance...
#1 balance got is 1000
#1 setting balance...
#1 new balance set to 2000
                              #2 trying to deposit 1000
                              #2 getting balance...
                              #2 balance got is 2000
                              #2 setting balance...
                              #2 new balance set to 3000
*** Final balance is 3000
```

Alternately, a block of statements in the `deposit()` method can be synchronized on the called object as follows:

```
void deposit(int amount, String name) {
    int balance;

    System.out.println(name + " trying to deposit " + amount);

    synchronized (this) {
        System.out.println(name + " getting balance...");
        balance = getBalance();
        System.out.println(name + " gets balance = " + balance);

        balance += amount;
```

```
        System.out.println(name + " setting balance...");
        setBalance(balance);
    }

    System.out.println(name + " set new balance = " + balance);
}
```

The output of the previous program is almost the same as before, except the first message from the second thread will be interleaved in the messages from the first thread, as the first `println()` method is not inside the synchronized block. A possible output is as follows:

```
#1 trying to deposit 1000
#1 getting balance...
                                #2 trying to deposit 1000

#1 balance got is 1000
#1 setting balance...
#1 new balance set to 2000

                                #2 getting balance...
                                #2 balance got is 2000
                                #2 setting balance...
                                #2 new balance set to 3000
*** Final balance is 3000
```

One unique key will be issued to every object containing any synchronized instance method or being referred by any synchronized block. For synchronized class methods, the key is issued to the class because the method may be called before any class instances exist. That is, every object and every class can have a monitor if there are any synchronized methods or blocks of statements associated with it. Furthermore, a class monitor's key is different from any of the keys of its class instance monitors. The next example demonstrates the difference between a synchronized method and a synchronized block and the difference between class-based synchronization and object-based synchronization. Class `SyncToken` contains three methods, all synchronized differently and all calling the `ticker()` method to print out three ticks in random intervals. Class `SyncTestRunner` is a thread class that will choose different methods of class `SyncToken` to run based on the id given. The `main()` method of the `SyncTest` class will generate ten threads running the tickers with different synchronization schemes so the comparison can be made. The program is listed as follows:

```
class SyncTest {

    static public void main(String[] args) {
        SyncToken token = new SyncToken();
        SyncTestRunner[] runners = new SyncTestRunner[10];

        for (int i = 0; i < 10; i++) {
            runners[i] = new SyncTestRunner(token, i);
            runners[i].start();
        }
        // workaround for the bug in the Windows implementation

        for (int i = 0; i < 10; i++)
            try {
                runners[i].join();
            } catch (InterruptedException e) {}

    }
}

class SyncTestRunner extends Thread {

    SyncToken token;
    int       id;

    SyncTestRunner(SyncToken token, int id) {
        this.token = token;
        this.id    = id;
    }

    public void run() {
        switch (id % 3) {
            case 0:
                SyncToken.class_ticker("\t\t\tClass #" + id, token);
                break;
            case 1:
                token.method_ticker("Method #" + id);
                break;
```

```
            case 2:
                    token.block_ticker ("Block  #" + id);
                    break;
            }
        }
    }

    class SyncToken {
//  the ticker method: give three ticks in random interval
        void ticker(String message) {
            for (int i = 0; i < 3; i++) {
                try {
                    Thread.sleep((int) (800 * Math.random()));
                } catch (InterruptedException e) {}
                System.out.println(message + ", tick #" + i);
            }
        }

        // class-based synchronization
        static synchronized void class_ticker(String message,
                                        SyncToken token) {
        token.ticker(message);
        }

        // object-based synchronization: synchronized block
        void block_ticker(String message) {
            synchronized(this) {
                ticker(message);
            }
        }

        // object-based synchronization: synchronized method
        synchronized void method_ticker(String message) {
            ticker(message);
        }
    }
```

An output of the previous program is included. You can see that object-based synchronized methods and synchronized blocks share the same monitor key if they are for the same object. Also, class-based synchronization and object-based synchronization do use different keys, as their output interleaves each other. The output is listed as follows:

```
Method #1, tick #0
                        Class #0, tick #0
Method #1, tick #1
Method #1, tick #2
Block  #2, tick #0
                        Class #0, tick #1
                        Class #0, tick #2
Block  #2, tick #1
                        Class #3, tick #0
Block  #2, tick #2
                        Class #3, tick #1
Method #4, tick #0
                        Class #3, tick #2
Method #4, tick #1
                        Class #6, tick #0
                        Class #6, tick #1
Method #4, tick #2
                        Class #6, tick #2
Block  #5, tick #0
                        Class #9, tick #0
Block  #5, tick #1
Block  #5, tick #2
                        Class #9, tick #1
Block  #8, tick #0
Block  #8, tick #1
                        Class #9, tick #2
Block  #8, tick #2
Method #7, tick #0
Method #7, tick #1
Method #7, tick #2
```

Synchronization is an expensive operation, and the use of it should be kept to a minimum, especially for frequently executed methods or blocks of statements. However, synchronization can help reduce the interference among different threads. Good use of it will definitely improve the stability and robustness of the program.

Interthread Communications

There are three ways for threads to communicate with each other. The first is through commonly shared data. All the threads in the same program share the same memory space. If the reference to an object is visible to different threads by the syntactic rules of scopes, or explicitly passed to different threads, these threads share access to that object's data members. As the previous section showed, synchronization is sometimes needed to enforce exclusive access to the data to avoid racing conditions and data corruption.

The second way for threads to communicate is by using thread-control methods, so threads wait for each other. For example, the `join()` method can be used for the caller thread to wait for the completion of the called thread. Also, a thread can suspend itself and wait at a rendezvous point using the `suspend()` method; another thread can wake it up through the waiting thread's `resume()` method, and both threads can run concurrently thereafter.

Deadlock may occur when a thread holding the key to a monitor is suspended or waiting for another thread's completion. If the other thread it is waiting for needs to get into the same monitor, both threads will be waiting forever. The `wait()`, `notify()`, and `notifyAll()` methods defined in class `Object` of package `java.lang` are introduced to solve this problem. These methods are the third way for threads to communicate. The `wait()` method will make the calling thread wait until either a time-out occurs or another thread calls the same object's `notify()` or `notifyAll()` method. The synopsis of the `wait()` method is

```
wait()
```

or

```
wait(long time_out_period_in_milliseconds)
```

The former will wait until the thread is notified. The latter will wait until either the specified time-out expires or the thread is notified, whichever comes first. When a thread calls the `wait()` method, the key it is holding will be released for another waiting thread to enter the monitor. The `notify()` method will wake up only one waiting thread, if any, whereas `notifyAll()` will wake up all the threads that have been waiting in the monitor. After being notified, the thread will try to reenter the monitor by requesting the key again and may have to wait for another thread to release the key. Note that these methods can only be called within a monitor. The thread calling an object's `notify()` or `notifyAll()` method needs to own the key to that object's monitor. Otherwise, `IllegalMonitorState-Exception`, a type of `RuntimeException`, will be thrown.

The next example demonstrates the classical use of the `wait()` and `notify()` methods to solve the producer and consumer problem. In this problem, the producer will generate data for the consumer to consume. However, if the producer produces data faster than the consumer can consume, the newly created data may get overwritten before it is consumed. On the other hand, if the consumer consumes faster than the producer can produce, the consumer may keep using already processed data. Synchronization alone will not solve the problem, as it only guarantees exclusive access to the data, not availability. The first implementation uses a monitor, an instance of the `NoWaitMonitor` class, to control the access to the data, `token`. The producer and consumer will set and get, respectively, the token value in random intervals with the maximum interval length regulated by the `speed` argument passed to their constructors. The main program accepts up to two command-line arguments for setting the producing and consuming speed, creates an instance of the monitor, creates a producer and a consumer, and watches them run for ten seconds. The program is listed as follows:

```
class NoWaitPandC {

    static int produce_speed = 200;
    static int consume_speed = 200;

    public static void main(String[] args) {
        if (args.length > 0)
            produce_speed = Integer.parseInt(args[0]);
        if (args.length > 1)
            consume_speed = Integer.parseInt(args[1]);

        NoWaitMonitor monitor = new NoWaitMonitor();
        new NoWaitProducer(monitor, produce_speed);
        new NoWaitConsumer(monitor, consume_speed);

        try {
            Thread.sleep(1000);
        } catch (InterruptedException e) { }

        System.exit(0);
    }
}

class NoWaitMonitor
{
    int token = -1;

    //   get token value

    synchronized int get () {
        System.out.println("Got: " + token);

        return token;
    }

    //   put token value

    synchronized void set(int value) {
        token = value;

        System.out.println("Set: " + token);
    }
}
```

```
class NoWaitProducer implements Runnable {

    NoWaitMonitor monitor;
    int   speed;

    NoWaitProducer(NoWaitMonitor monitor, int speed) {
        this.monitor = monitor;
        this.speed = speed;
        new Thread(this, "Producer").start();
    }

    public void run() {
        int i = 0;

        while (true) {
            monitor.set(i++);
            try {
              Thread.sleep((int) (Math.random() * speed));
            } catch (InterruptedException e) {}
        }
    }
}

class NoWaitConsumer implements Runnable {

    NoWaitMonitor monitor;
    int   speed;

    NoWaitConsumer(NoWaitMonitor monitor, int speed) {
        this.monitor = monitor;
        this.speed = speed;
        new Thread(this, "Consumer").start();
    }

    public void run() {
        while (true) {
            monitor.get();
            try {
              Thread.sleep((int) (Math.random() * speed));
            } catch (InterruptedException e) {}
        }
    }
}
```

An output of the program where the producer outpaces the consumer is as follows:

```
C:\MasteringJava\Ch08>java NoWaitPandC 100 400
Set: 0
Got: 0
Set: 1
Set: 2
Set: 3
Set: 4
Got: 4
Set: 5
Set: 6
Set: 7
Set: 8
Set: 9
Set: 10
Got: 10
Set: 11
Set: 12
```

You can see there is a lot of data generated (shown as `Set`) but over-written before it is processed (shown as `Got`).

Another output where the consumer is faster is shown here:

```
C:\MasteringJava\Ch08>java NoWaitPandC 400 100
Set: 0
Got: 0
Got: 0
Got: 0
Got: 0
Got: 0
Got: 0
Set: 1
Set: 2
Got: 2
Set: 3
Got: 3
```

```
Got:  3
Got:  3
Got:  3
Got:  3
Set:  4
Got:  4
Got:  4
Got:  4
Got:  4
Got:  4
```

This time, some of the data is processed multiple times. The second implementation uses the wait() and notify() methods to make sure all data is created and used exactly once. The program is the same as before, except for the implementation of the monitor. A boolean variable, value_set, is added to indicate whether the data is ready for consumption or already used. The get() method will first test if the data is ready for consumption. If not, the calling thread will wait until some other thread sets the data and notifies the current thread. The boolean variable is then set to indicate that the data is consumed. Any thread waiting to produce new data will then be notified to start the production. If there is no thread waiting to produce, the notify() method will just be ignored. The get() method is shown here:

```
synchronized int get() {
    if (! value_set)
        try {
            wait();
        } catch (InterruptedException e) { }

    value_set = false;

    System.out.println("Got: " + token);

    notify();

    return token;
}
```

Symmetrically, the set() method will first test whether the data is already used. If not, the calling thread will wait until some other thread uses the data and notifies the current thread. The boolean variable is then set to indicate that the data is ready for consumption. Any thread waiting to consume the data will then be notified to start the consumption. If there is no thread waiting, the notify() method will just be ignored. The set() method is shown here:

```
synchronized void set(int value) {
    if (value_set)
        try {
            wait();
        } catch (InterruptedException e) { }

    value_set = true;

    token = value;

    System.out.println("Set: " + token);

    notify();
}
```

The full program listing is shown here:

```
class PandC {

    static int produce_speed = 200;
    static int consume_speed = 200;

    public static void main(String[] args) {
        if (args.length > 0)
            produce_speed = Integer.parseInt(args[0]);
        if (args.length > 1)
            consume_speed = Integer.parseInt(args[1]);

        Monitor monitor = new Monitor();
        new Producer(monitor, produce_speed);
        new Consumer(monitor, consume_speed);

        try {
            Thread.sleep(1000);
        } catch (InterruptedException e) { }

        System.exit(0);
```

```
        }
    }

class Monitor
{
    int token;
    boolean value_set = false;

    //    get token value

    synchronized int get () {
        if (! value_set)
            try {
              wait();
            } catch (InterruptedException e) { }

        value_set = false;

        System.out.println("Got: " + token);

        notify();

        return token;
    }

    //    set token value

    synchronized void set(int value) {
        if (value_set)
            try {
              wait();
            } catch (InterruptedException e) { }

        value_set = true;

        token = value;

        System.out.println("Set: " + token);

        notify();
    }
}

class Producer implements Runnable {

    Monitor monitor;
    int   speed;

    Producer(Monitor monitor, int speed) {
```

```
        this.monitor = monitor;
        this.speed = speed;
        new Thread(this, "Producer").start();
    }

    public void run() {
        int i = 0;

        while (true) {
            monitor.set(i++);
            try {
              Thread.sleep((int) (Math.random() * speed));
            } catch (InterruptedException e) {}
        }
    }
}

class Consumer implements Runnable {

    Monitor monitor;
    int    speed;

    Consumer(Monitor monitor, int speed) {
        this.monitor = monitor;
        this.speed = speed;
        new Thread(this, "Consumer").start();
    }

    public void run() {
        while (true) {
            monitor.get();
            try {
              Thread.sleep((int) (Math.random() * speed));
            } catch (InterruptedException e) {}
        }
    }
}
```

An output of the above program is as follows:

```
C:\MasteringJava\Ch08>java PandC 400 100
Set: 0
Got: 0
Set: 1
Got: 1
```

```
Set: 2
Got: 2
Set: 3
Got: 3
Set: 4
Got: 4
```

This time, every piece of data generated is consumed exactly once.

Priorities and Scheduling

If you have only one CPU, all of the runnable threads have to take turns being executed. *Scheduling* is the activity of determining the execution order of multiple threads. Every thread in Java is assigned a priority value. When more than one thread is competing for CPU time, the thread with the highest priority value is given preference. Thread priority values that can be assigned to user-created threads are simple integers ranging between `Thread.MIN_PRIORITY` and `Thread.MAX_PRIORITY`. User applications are normally run with the priority value of `Thread.NORM_PRIORITY`. Up to JDK 1.0.2, these constants—MIN_PRIORITY, MAX_PRIORITY, and NORM_PRIORITY—of the `Thread` class have the values of 1, 10, and 5, respectively. Every thread group has a maximum priority value assigned. This is a cap to the priority values of member threads and thread groups when they are created or want to change their priority values.

When a thread is created, it will inherit the priority value of the creating thread if the priority value doesn't exceed the limit imposed by its parent thread group. The `setPriority()` method of `Thread` class can be used to set the priority value of a thread. If the value to be set is outside the legal range, an `IllegalArgumentException` will be thrown. If the value is larger than the maximum priority value of its parent thread group, the maximum priority value will be used. The `setMaxPrioriy()` method of class `ThreadGroup` can be used to set the maximum priority value of a thread group. For security reasons (so that a user-created thread will not monopolize the CPU), a Web browser may not allow an applet to change its priority.

Java's scheduling is *preemptive*; that is, if a thread with a higher priority than the currently running thread becomes runnable, the higher priority thread will be executed immediately, pushing the currently running thread back to the queue to wait for its next turn. A thread can voluntarily pass the CPU execution privilege to waiting threads of the same priority by calling the `yield()` method.

In some implementations, thread execution is *time-sliced*; that is, threads with equal priority values will have equal opportunities to run in a round-robin manner. Even threads with lower priority will still get a small portion of the execution time slots, roughly proportional to their priority values. Therefore, no threads will be starving in the long run. Other implementations do not have time-slicing. A thread will relinquish its control only when it finishes its execution, is preempted by a higher-priority thread, or is blocked by I/O operations or the `sleep()`, `wait()`, or `suspend()` method calls. For computation-intensive threads, it is a good idea to call the `yield()` method once in a while to give other threads a chance to run. It may improve the overall interactive responsiveness of graphical user interfaces.

> **TIP**
> Up to JDK 1.0.2, Java run time for Windows 95 and NT is time-sliced, whereas Java run time for Solaris 2 is not time-sliced. Hopefully, the behavior of Solaris 2 implementation will become consistent with that of Windows 95 and NT in the next release, JDK 1.1.

The next example demonstrates the effect of scheduling on threads with different priorities. The main program will accept an optional command-line argument to indicate whether the threads created will yield to each other regularly. The main program starts four threads with priority values of 2, 3, 4, and 4, respectively. Each thread will increment its counter 600,001 times and optionally yield to threads with equal priority on every 3000th increment. Because the main thread has a higher priority value, 5, than these computation-intensive threads, the main thread may grab the CPU every 0.6 second to print out the counter values of these four computing threads. The program is listed as follows:

```
class PriorityTest {
    static int     NO_OF_THREADS = 4;
    static boolean yield = true;
    static int[]   counter = new int[NO_OF_THREADS];

    public static void main(String[] args) {
        int no_of_intervals = 10;

        if (args.length > 0)
            yield = false;

        System.out.println("Using yield()? " + (yield ? "YES" : "NO"));

        for (int i = 0; i < NO_OF_THREADS; i++)
            (new PrTestThread((i > 1) ? 4 : (i + 2), i)).start();

        ThreadInfo.printAllThreadInfo();
        System.out.println();

        //   repeatedly print out the counter values

        while (true) {

            try {
                Thread.sleep(600);
            }
            catch (InterruptedException e) {}

            System.out.print("Step " + i + ": COUNTERS:");
            for (int j = 0; j < NO_OF_THREADS; j++) {
                System.out.print(" " + counter[j]);
                if (counter[j] < 600000)
                    all_done = false;
            }
            System.out.println();

            if (all_done)
                break;
        }

        System.exit(0);
    }
}

class PrTestThread extends Thread {

    int  id;

    PrTestThread(int priority, int id) {
        super("PrTestThread#" + id);
```

```
            this.id = id;
            setPriority(priority);
    }

    public void run() {
        for (int i = 0; i < 600001; i++) {
            if (((i % 3000) == 0) && PriorityTest.yield)
                yield();
            PriorityTest.counter[id] = i;
        }
    }
}
```

The program is first run on a time-sliced system with the computing threads frequently yielding to each other. From the output, you can see that threads with lower priority values still get small portions of CPU time, and the two threads with the highest priority get roughly equal portions of CPU time. The output is shown here:

```
C:\MasteringJava\Ch08>java PriorityTest
Using yield()? YES

THREAD GROUP: system; Max Priority: 10
    THREAD: Finalizer thread; Priority: 1 [Daemon] [Alive]
    THREAD GROUP: main; Max Priority: 10
        THREAD: main; Priority: 5 [Alive] <== current
        THREAD: PrTestThread#0; Priority: 2 [Alive]
        THREAD: PrTestThread#1; Priority: 3 [Alive]
        THREAD: PrTestThread#2; Priority: 4 [Alive]
        THREAD: PrTestThread#3; Priority: 4 [Alive]

Step 0: COUNTERS:  0 2999 98999 89999
Step 1: COUNTERS:  2999 8999 224999 221999
Step 2: COUNTERS:  11999 17999 347999 347999
Step 3: COUNTERS:  14999 26999 473999 476999
Step 4: COUNTERS:  20999 43011 600000 600000
Step 5: COUNTERS:  38999 289258 600000 600000
Step 6: COUNTERS:  56999 535929 600000 600000
Step 7: COUNTERS:  256657 600000 600000 600000
Step 8: COUNTERS:  522386 600000 600000 600000
Step 9: COUNTERS:  600000 600000 600000 600000
```

The same program is run on Java run time with no time-slicing and, again, with the threads yielding to each other regularly. From the output, it is obvious that lower-priority threads do not have any chance to run until all the higher-priority threads finish their execution. The output is shown here:

```
harpoon:/users/hsu/java/examples/ch8> java PriorityTest
Using yield()? YES

THREAD GROUP: system; Max Priority: 10
    THREAD: clock handler; Priority: 11 [Daemon] [Alive]
    THREAD: Idle thread; Priority: 0 [Daemon] [Alive]
    THREAD: Async Garbage Collector; Priority: 1 [Daemon] [Alive]
    THREAD: Finalizer thread; Priority: 1 [Daemon] [Alive]
    THREAD GROUP: main; Max Priority: 10
        THREAD: main; Priority: 5 [Alive] <== current
        THREAD: PrTestThread#0; Priority: 2 [Alive]
        THREAD: PrTestThread#1; Priority: 3 [Alive]
        THREAD: PrTestThread#2; Priority: 4 [Alive]
        THREAD: PrTestThread#3; Priority: 4 [Alive]

Step 0: COUNTERS: 0 0 103563 101999
Step 1: COUNTERS: 0 0 206999 208476
Step 2: COUNTERS: 0 0 314999 312189
Step 3: COUNTERS: 0 0 419999 416889
Step 4: COUNTERS: 0 0 527999 520335
Step 5: COUNTERS: 0 67070 600000 600000
Step 6: COUNTERS: 0 295645 600000 600000
Step 7: COUNTERS: 0 521522 600000 600000
Step 8: COUNTERS: 145375 600000 600000 600000
Step 9: COUNTERS: 374097 600000 600000 600000
Step 10: COUNTERS: 515023 600000 600000 600000
Step 11: COUNTERS: 600000 600000 600000 600000
```

Then, the same program is run on a time-sliced system with no yielding. Interestingly, the lower-priority threads get more chances to run than in the previous run with yielding. This is probably because yielding disturbs the scheduler's original plan to execute lower-priority threads by forcing the scheduler to look for threads with equal priority first. With no yielding, all the schedules for lower-priority threads can be smoothly exercised. The output is shown here:

```
C:\MasteringJava\Ch08>java PriorityTest 0
Using yield()? NO

THREAD GROUP: system; Max Priority: 10
    THREAD: Finalizer thread; Priority: 1 [Daemon] [Alive]
    THREAD GROUP: main; Max Priority: 10
        THREAD: main; Priority: 5 [Alive] <== current
        THREAD: PrTestThread#0; Priority: 2 [Alive]
        THREAD: PrTestThread#1; Priority: 3 [Alive]
        THREAD: PrTestThread#2; Priority: 4 [Alive]
        THREAD: PrTestThread#3; Priority: 4 [Alive]

Step 0: COUNTERS: 15236 37419 282994 213847
Step 1: COUNTERS: 26765 54548 375313 299946
Step 2: COUNTERS: 30711 72722 501015 416601
Step 3: COUNTERS: 49419 99759 600000 533904
Step 4: COUNTERS: 74398 267193 600000 600000
Step 5: COUNTERS: 110608 497597 600000 600000
Step 6: COUNTERS: 272488 600000 600000 600000
Step 7: COUNTERS: 539175 600000 600000 600000
Step 8: COUNTERS: 600000 600000 600000 600000
```

Finally, the program is run with no yielding on an implementation with no time-slicing. The lower-priority threads have no chance to run until all the higher-priority threads finish. Even threads with equal priority values do not have the chance to run until the main thread preempts the running thread. When a thread is preempted, it will be put to the end of the waiting queue. When the main thread relinquishes program control after printing out the counter values, the previously waiting thread that is ahead in the queue will get the chance to run. You can see proof of this from the output listing—only one of the highest-priority threads advances its counter between each printing. The output is shown here:

```
harpoon:/users/hsu/java/examples/ch8> java PriorityTest 0
Using yield()? NO

THREAD GROUP: system; Max Priority: 10
    THREAD: clock handler; Priority: 11 [Daemon] [Alive]
```

```
THREAD: Idle thread; Priority: 0 [Daemon] [Alive]
THREAD: Async Garbage Collector; Priority: 1 [Daemon] [Alive]
THREAD: Finalizer thread; Priority: 1 [Daemon] [Alive]
THREAD GROUP: main; Max Priority: 10
    THREAD: main; Priority: 5 [Alive] <== current
    THREAD: PrTestThread#0; Priority: 2 [Alive]
    THREAD: PrTestThread#1; Priority: 3 [Alive]
    THREAD: PrTestThread#2; Priority: 4 [Alive]
    THREAD: PrTestThread#3; Priority: 4 [Alive]
Step 0: COUNTERS: 0 0 203552 0
Step 1: COUNTERS: 0 0 203552 210978
Step 2: COUNTERS: 0 0 413376 210978
Step 3: COUNTERS: 0 0 413376 422790
Step 4: COUNTERS: 0 0 600000 444539
Step 5: COUNTERS: 0 57353 600000 600000
Step 6: COUNTERS: 0 272848 600000 600000
Step 7: COUNTERS: 0 488745 600000 600000
Step 8: COUNTERS: 100596 600000 600000 600000
Step 9: COUNTERS: 314749 600000 600000 600000
Step 10: COUNTERS: 587513 600000 600000 600000
Step 11: COUNTERS: 600000 600000 600000 600000
```

Daemon Threads

Daemon threads are service threads. They exist to provide services to other threads. They normally enter an endless loop waiting for clients requesting services. When all the active threads remaining are daemon threads, Java run time will exit. For example, a timer thread that wakes up in regular intervals is a good candidate for daemon threads. This timer thread can notify other threads regularly about the time-outs. When no other thread is running, there is no need for the timer thread's existence.

To create a daemon thread, call the setDaemon() method right after the thread's creation and before the execution is started. The constructor of the thread is a good candidate for making this method call. By default, all the threads created by a daemon thread are also daemon threads. The synopsis of the setDaemon() method is

```
setDaemon(boolean is_daemon)
```

When *is_daemon* is true, the thread is marked as a daemon thread; otherwise, it is marked as a non-daemon thread.

Summary

A thread is a single line of execution within a program. Multiple threads can run concurrently in a single program. A thread is created by either subclassing the Thread class or implementing the Runnable interface. In either case, a public run() method is defined as the thread body to be run in the newly created execution context when the thread's start() method is called. In addition to the start() method just described, there are stop(), suspend(), resume(), join(), yield(), and sleep() methods defined in the Thread class to control the execution of a thread.

Any thread that has not been destroyed yet is always in one of four states: newly created, runnable, blocked, and dead. When the state of a thread is changed into the blocked state by I/O blocking or a call to the suspend(), wait(), or sleep() method, a counter-event of the event putting the thread into the blocked state will move the thread back to the runnable state. These counter-events are: I/O being finished for I/O blocking, the resume() method being called for a suspend() method call, the notify() or notifyAll() method being called for the wait() method call, and time-out occurring for the sleep() method call.

Every thread is the member of exactly one thread group. Thread groups can be nested. All the threads and thread groups in a program form a tree with the system thread group as the root. The stop(), suspend(), and resume() methods are defined in class ThreadGroup to allow for manipulating all the threads inside a thread group by a single method call. There are abundant methods defined in the Thread and ThreadGroup classes to get the information about a thread or a thread group.

Synchronization is a way of avoiding data corruption caused by simultaneous access to the same data. In Java, synchronization is implemented by the monitor model. A monitor is a guarded place for methods and blocks of statements. Only one thread is allowed in a monitor at a time. Every object can become a monitor if there are synchronized instance methods defined in the class the object is instantiated from, or synchronized blocks of statements that refer to the object. The wait() method is used inside a monitor for a thread to wait for another thread to call the called object's notify() or notifyAll() method.

Every thread has a priority value associated with it. In the event of multiple threads competing for execution, the thread with the highest priority is preferred. Java's scheduling is preemptive; that is, a higher-priority thread will preempt the lower-priority running thread and be executed immediately.

A daemon thread is a service thread. When all the active threads remaining are daemon threads, Java run time will exit. A thread is marked as a daemon thread by calling the setDaemon() method.

Multithreading allows for multiple lines of execution at the same time. Multiple threads running concurrently can not only improve the utilization of resources but also open the door for easier and creative programming of multimedia or animation effects. Having the threading capability defined in the language will definitely encourage the creation of multithreaded programs. We can expect to see more and more multithreaded applets on the Web enriching our Web-surfing experiences.

PART II

Applying Standard
Java Classes

CHAPTER

NINE

9

Standard Java Packages

- **Package** `java.lang`

- **Package** `java.util`

- **Package** `java.io`

- **Package** `java.awt`

- **Package** `java.awt.image`

- **Package** `java.net`

- **Package** `java.applet`

Java has been object oriented from day one. And as befits real object-oriented languages, as opposed to OO-procedural hybrids like C++, it comes with a standard set of support classes. These classes are very different from the familiar libraries which accompanied procedural languages like C or Pascal. Java's support classes transcend simple libraries, because they exploit the full potential of every object-oriented language. Class inheritance is by far the most common and most powerful feature used. (See Chapter 5 for a detailed explanation of the mechanisms of class inheritance.)

The entire Java hierarchy can be viewed from two organizational angles: as an object-oriented *inheritance hierarchy* and as groups of classes in *packages*. The inheritance hierarchy groups classes that share common implementation aspects (that is, code and/or variables), while packages simply collect classes on a more pragmatic basis: Classes with related functionality are bundled together in the same package, whether they share code or data or not. In addition to their obvious structuring benefits, packages use *namespace partitioning*, which means that every class contained in a package has a unique name that cannot conflict (*collide*) with class names defined elsewhere. This namespace partitioning is the main reason packages are used.

The language's strict *single inheritance* scheme determines the way Java's standard classes relate to one another in terms of object-oriented inheritance. The resulting inheritance tree is, therefore, a pure tree, and not a graph, as is the case with multiple inheritance object-oriented hierarchies. Multiple inheritance of sorts is employed within the Java classes by using the language's powerful interface mechanism (discussed in Chapter 5).

Multiple Inheritance

Multiple inheritance is the mechanism of allowing one class to inherit from more than one superclass. This has the net effect of mixing the characteristics of those classes into the new class. Multiple inheritance was introduced to solve single inheritance's straightjacket effect. Here is an example of the type of brick wall single inheritance might confront you with: Say you have a single inheritance hierarchy branching into two fundamental subtrees, `Living` and `InAnimate`. From `Living` grows the successive subclass branch `Plant–FruitTrees–Banana`. The `InAnimate` branch could have a `Valuable–Food` subbranch. Now `Food` might quite understandably want to have `Banana` as its subclass, as well. Single inheritance does not let us have both. Class `Banana` is either a `FruitTree` or a `Food`; it can only inherit from one superclass hierarchy, not two (or more). The single inheritance tree (shown below) illustrates the limitations of pure single inheritance.

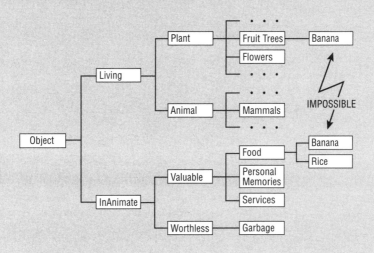

Since packages give you an easy handle on the entire hierarchy, they will now be your guides as you explore the Java class hierarchy.

The hierarchy consists (at the time of this writing) of the following main packages:

java.lang Package `java.lang` contains the main language support classes. Areas dealt with are object wrappers, strings, and multithreading, among others.

java.util Package `java.util` contains language support classes of a more utilitarian nature. These include linked list, stack, and hashtable classes, as well as some useful abstract designs codified by the interfaces `Enumeration` and `Observer`.

java.io Package `java.io` presents you with device independent file and stream input and output services.

java.awt Package `java.awt` hides the bulk of all standard classes. Containing Java's Abstract Windowing Toolkit, the package should really be considered as the heart of the entire hierarchy. The whole hierarchy is there to make the lives of application developers easier, but in particular it was meant to make GUI development quick and painless.

java.awt.image Package `java.awt.image` contains image-processing related classes.

java.net Package `java.net` combines the classes supporting low-level Internet programming plus WWW/HTML support.

java.applet Package `java.applet` contains a single class with support for HTML embedded Java "applets."

In the next section, you will look at each of these packages in turn and survey the major classes they contain.

Package java.lang

The java.lang package inheritance tree is shown in Figure 9.1. As you can judge from the shape of the tree, this collection of classes is very flat and shallow. Apart from the Number subhierarchy, all classes are equals within this hierarchy. The large majority of java.lang classes extend class Object directly, which is the root for the entire Java class hierarchy, not just the root for java.lang.

FIGURE 9.1:

Package java.lang inheritance tree

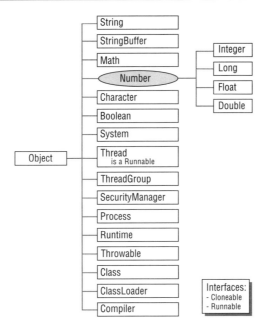

The Number subhierarchy is a good example of how object-oriented inheritance works and when to apply it. Classes Integer, Long, Float, and Double all have "things" in common, so a superclass was created to hold (*encapsulate*) these shared traits. Note that class Number is also declared abstract. You cannot make (*instantiate*) objects directly from an abstract class—you can only do this from concrete classes. Although having a parent class (*superclass*) that is abstract occurs frequently, it is by no means necessary. Concrete classes can be the local roots of entire subhierarchies (class Object being a prime example).

Out of all the packages, package java.lang is an exception, because it is the only package which you never need to explicitly import in your programs. The compiler implicitly does so by adding the following line at the top of all your source files:

```
import java.lang.*;
```

(The asterisk in the above line means that all of the package's classes are imported.)

Package java.lang gets special treatment because some of its classes are so low-level that they are considered part of the language proper. The dividing line between language and external libraries might be important to language designers, but to application programmers the difference is mostly academic. BASIC, for example, has its string manipulation commands defined as part of the language definition. C, on the other hand, relies instead on an external (and internationally recognized) standard library of functions to accomplish those tasks. Since Java adheres more to the C philosophy of keeping a language core as simple as possible, it too relies on an external collection of methods for anything beyond the simplest data processing or algorithmic control.

The type of classes contained in package `java.lang` are

- Type wrapper classes
- String support classes
- A math library class
- Multithreading support classes
- A low-level system access class

The following sections look at these classes in more detail.

The Type Wrapper Classes

Java deals with two different types of entities: primitive types and true objects. Numbers, booleans, and characters behave very much like the familiar equivalents of procedural languages like Pascal, C, or even C++. Other object-oriented languages, like Smalltalk, do not handle these primitive types in the same way. Smalltalk, for example, uses objects for everything—numbers are objects, booleans are objects, characters are objects, and so on.

Although Java is truly object oriented, it does not use objects for the most primitive types for the usual reason—performance. Manipulating primitive types without any object-oriented overhead is quite a bit more efficient. On the other hand, a uniform and consistent playing field, made up only of objects, is simpler and can be significantly more powerful.

Java contains many subsystems which can work only with objects. With many of these subsystems, the need frequently arises to have the system handle numbers or flags (*booleans*) or characters. How does Java get around this dilemma? By wrapping the primitive types up in some object sugar coating. You can easily create a class, for example, for the sole purpose of encapsulating a single integer. The net effect would be to obtain an integer object, giving you the universality and power that comes with dealing only with objects (at the cost of some performance degradation).

Package `java.lang`, contains such "type wrapper" classes for almost every Java primitive type:

- Class `Integer` for primitive type `int`
- Class `Long` for primitive type `long`
- Class `Float` for primitive type `float`
- Class `Double` for primitive type `double`
- Class `Character` for primitive type `char`
- Class `Boolean` for primitive type `boolean`

The primitive types which are left unsupported in this way are `byte` and `short`. This is no great loss since class `Integer` can be used without too much extra runtime overhead or coding overhead.

Among the numeric types, classes `Integer`, `Long`, `Float`, and `Double` are so similar that they all descend from an abstract superclass called `Number`. Essentially, every one of these classes allows you to create an object from the equivalent primitive type, and vice versa.

The String Classes

There are two string support classes in `java.lang`:

- `String`
- `StringBuffer`

Class `String` supports "read-only" strings, while class `StringBuffer` supports modifiable strings. Although both classes obviously have a few things in common, they are unrelated, in that neither inherits from a common "string" superclass.

Class `String` contains the following core functionality:

- String length function
- Substring extraction
- Substring finding and matching
- String comparison
- Upper- and lowercase conversion
- Leading and trailing whitespace elimination
- Conversion to/from char arrays
- Primitive types to `String` conversions

NOTE

The conversion and whitespace stripping methods might seem contradictory in view of the read-only nature of `String` strings. This is true, but class `String` does not break its own rules. What it does during these operations is create brand *new* read-only strings from the old ones, which class `String` unceremoniously discards in the process.

Class `StringBuffer`, on the other hand, concentrates on operations that typically modify the string or change its length:

- Appending strings (converted from any type, including objects)

- Inserting strings (again converted from any type)

The Multithreading Support Classes

Two classes (`Thread` and `ThreadGroup`) are the gateways to adding multithreaded behavior in your applications or applets. Multithreading amounts to having a multitasking operating system within your own application. Several program threads can execute in parallel and at the same time. In a similar way that a multitasking operating system is more powerful and flexible than a single-tasking operating system, users greatly benefit from multithreaded applications: A printing command can be handled in the background; repaginating a long document can be done while the user carries on editing that same document; and so on. Java is one of the rarer languages that provides multithreading from within the language itself (Ada is another example; C, C++, LISP, Pascal, and BASIC all lack built-in multithreading support).

The `java.lang` class `Thread` is the more important class of the two, giving you a collection of methods that allows you to

- Create new threads. This lets your applications spread independent jobs over several internal "subprograms." Overall application performance increases when several of these threads need to do I/O operations.

- Kill a thread. When a thread has completed its job, or when a thread goes crazy due to a bug, you need to kill it. This returns the resources the thread was using back to the system.

- Start and stop threads. When a thread is initially created it does not start running immediately. You need to start it explicitly with a `start()` command. Sometimes it is also necessary to stop a thread (this simply freezes it, permanently).

- Suspend threads or put threads to sleep for a given amount of time. When a thread has no more work to do while sitting in a loop, the thread should put itself to sleep to let other threads use more of the processor's resources.

- Change thread priority, name, or daemon status. Threads have several attributes that can be dynamically altered as the thread runs. The priority attribute in particular will affect the proportion of processing resources the thread receives from the processor. Threads can also be flagged as being daemon threads. (See Chapter 8 for a detailed discussion of Thread attributes.)

- Query thread attributes. Any thread can find out what its priority, name, or daemon status is. This is useful when you launch several thread clones (differentiated only by name, for example) who nevertheless need to act as individuals (like twins in real life).

Class ThreadGroup encapsulates methods similar to those listed above, except that thread groups are just that—a scope for related threads to operate in. They allow a number of related threads to share attributes and be affected in bulk by thread group changes.

Class Math

Class Math groups together a typical and quite conservative collection of mathematical functions. The functions provided can be classified into

- Absolute, min, and max functions. These are suitably overloaded so that you can pass in any numeric type without having your arguments automatically cast to different types, thereby possibly losing accuracy.

- Square root, power, logarithm, and exponential functions. All of these take and return double values only. Double, and not float, is the default floating point accuracy used by Java. You need not use casts when passing other numeric types like int or float, because Java's compiler will automatically convert (compatible) argument types for you.

- Trigonometric functions (sin, cos, tan, asin, acos, atan). These functions all work with angles expressed in radians instead of degrees. A full circle in radians is 2*PI radians (as opposed to 360 degrees). Pi is conveniently defined to double precision as the Math class constant Math.PI.

- Pseudo-random number generator function. One method (random()) is provided as a basis for randomness in applications. Random numbers are very important in simulations, statistical analysis, and, of course, games.

Class System

Class System encapsulates the classic file handles stdin (as System.in), stdout (as System.out), and stderr (as System.err). These allow you to write output to or get input from the console in the usual way. In addition to these class variables, the following method types are located in System:

- Platform optimized array copying

- Catastrophic exit (terminates application and the Java interpreter subsystem!)

- System properties querying

- Security policy related methods

Package java.util

Package java.util contains more abstract data type (ADT) classes plus two interfaces, one of which (Enumeration) is used frequently within the class hierarchy and within user programs. As you can see from Figure 9.2, package `java.util` uses inheritance more than package `java.lang`. The `Properties` class, for example, is an extension (subclass) of class `Hashtable`, which itself is an extension of `Dictionary`. As you look at more packages later, you will see that the hierarchies gradually become deeper and more complex. Note also how a `Stack` is implemented as a subclass of a `Vector`. One class you would expect to see alongside `Stack` is some form of `Queue` class. Surprisingly, there is no explicit `Queue` support in `java.util`. (Luckily, `Vector` provides all the functionality to quickly cook up a `Queue` as a subclass of `Vector`.)

FIGURE 9.2:

Package `java.util` inheritance tree

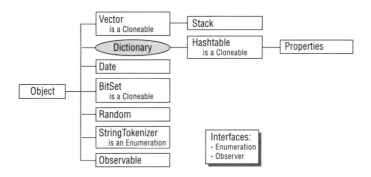

The main classes contained in package `java.util` are

- `Vector`

- `Hashtable`

- `Stack`

- `Date`

- `BitSet`

- interfaces `Enumeration` and `Observer`

Each of them is discussed in more detail on the following page.

Vector

Class `Vector` encapsulates a heterogeneous linked-list and array hybrid. It is heterogeneous because it doesn't insist on its elements being of a certain type—any object types can be mixed within one vector. The core `Vector` methods are

- Appending an element
- Finding an element
- Changing an element
- Indexed element access
- Inserting of elements
- Removing of elements
- `Vector` size and emptiness functions
- Contents enumeration

Hashtable

Class `Hashtable` actually embodies slightly more than simple hash table functionality; it implements a dictionary abstract data type. Dictionaries are data structures which contain key-value pairs (the keys being the handles to the value entries).

The core methods for this class provide for

- Adding a key-value pair
- Retrieving the value of a key-value entry, given its key
- Checking whether a key is already present
- Removing an entire key-value entry

- Counting the number of entries

- Enumerating all key-value pairs

Stack

Class `Stack` implements that old faithful: a simple Last In First Out (LIFO) stack. The available methods do not deviate much from the topic:

- Pushing objects

- Popping objects

- Checking for an object's presence

- Peeking at the top of stack element

- Checking whether stack is empty

As with `Vector` (and `Hashtable` for that matter), object types can be mixed freely on a `Stack`.

Despite the amount of pages invested in stack data structure examples in books, stacks are not often used in real application programs. `Queue` data structures (which are missing in the standard Java package), for example, are much more frequently employed.

The main use for a stack is in systems which need to "remember" things. One application where stacks are common is 2-D or 3-D graphics. Stacks can store nested coordinate system transformations in such a way that the application can easily revert to any previous coordinate system. `Queues`, on the other hand, are universally used to buffer objects (events, data packets, commands) so that an application can process them at its leisure and in the same arrival order. A `Queue` structure also allows the source for these objects (the producer) to be decoupled from the system which processes the items in the `Queue` (the consumer). This `Queue` side effect is probably the most common reason for employing `Queues`.

NOTE

You also may have come across the term *bag*. Other object-oriented frameworks often provide one or more `Bag` classes. The difference between a bag and a set is that bags can contain duplicates (as in real life), whereas a set only contains zero or one instance of any object type. If you wanted your own Java `Bag` class, a good place to start would be with class `Vector` (and subclassing it).

Date

Class `Date` encapsulates the representation and manipulation of dates; this includes finding out the current date and time. Class `Date` supports the following types of methods:

- Constructing of date objects (including current date and time)
- Altering year, month, day, hour, minute, and second components
- Querying year, month, day, hour, minute, and second components
- Converting to and from strings and long integers
- Comparing date and time values (including calendar arithmetic)
- Time-zone support

BitSet

Class `BitSet` implements a set of bits. Unlike many other `BitSet`-type classes or language features in other languages, this bit set has no limits. You can therefore go way beyond the typical 32 or 256 bit limits imposed by other implementations. `BitSet` operations include

- Setting, clearing, and getting single bits
- Anding, oring, and xoring bitsets together
- Comparing bitsets

Interface Enumeration

Interface `Enumeration` is an impressive example of Java's powerful interface feature. It defines the behavior (in terms of methods to be supported) of being able to enumerate every component, element, object, or entry—in short, every *thing* contained by any class having some "container" quality.

Take `Vector` objects—these definitely have some container quality, since they can accumulate and manipulate objects a program hands them at run time. So, a `Vector` should be able to enumerate all the elements it contains. And it can, by implementing the `Enumeration` interface (indirectly, through an intermediary object of type `Enumeration` returned by the `Vector` method `elements( )`). The `Enumeration` interface forces any class to implement the following two methods:

- `public boolean hasMoreElements()`

- `public Object nextElement()`

These two methods mean that any object that supports enumerating its components via this standard (method) interface can be explored using the following standard Java `while` loop:

```
enum = someContainer.someMethodReturningAnEnumeration();
while (enum.hasMoreElements()) {
   containedObj = enum.nextElement();
   // process this object
}
```

This simple, clean, and, more importantly, standardized approach to listing or processing every element of a container class is used repeatedly throughout the class hierarchy.

Interface Observer and Class Observable

Interface `Observer` and class `Observable` together exemplify the way Java's designers have tried to avoid reinventing the wheel, an all too common occurrence in software development. The `Observer`-`Observable` metaphor addresses a design obstacle slightly more abstract than the enumeration problem solved by the previous interface. Sometimes, within an application, it is necessary that a change in an object trigger changes in other objects; these changes may, in turn, trigger changes in yet other objects. In short, you have a number of objects which are in some way dependent on other objects; this is called a *dependency network*. Java's class hierarchy designers developed the `Observer`-`Observable` duo to solve this design obstacle.

The mechanism enforced by this duo is quite simple: Any root object that needs to send some kind of notification to other objects should be subclassed from class `Observable`. Secondly, any objects that need to receive such notifications should implement interface `Observer`. The sole method interface `Observer` requires is

```
public void update(Observable o, Object arg)
```

To establish the dependency, any observer objects (that is, any objects implementing interface `Observer`) are added to the observable object (that is, the object subclassed from class `Observable`). Whenever this observable object changes, it can then call its `Observable` method `notifyObservers( )`.

Package java.io

Package `java.io` contains a whole arsenal of I/O related classes, as shown in Figure 9.3. A top-level classification organizes them into

- Input and output streams

FIGURE 9.3:

Package `java.io` inheritance tree

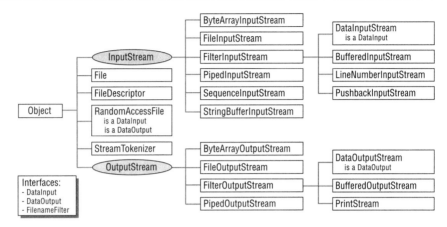

- Stream filtering

- Stream tokenization

- Class `RandomAccessFile`

As you can see from the inheritance tree, the input and output stream branches form the bulk of the tree. A *stream* is an abstract concept used frequently in the context of I/O programming. It represents a linear, sequential flow of input or output data. Streams can be "flowing towards you," in which case you have an input stream, or they can "flow away from you," in which case you talk of an output stream. You read from input streams (that is, you read the data a stream delivers to you) and you write to output streams (that is, you transfer data to a stream). The key thing about streams is that they shield you from the input or output devices you are ultimately talking to. If your code deals with these abstract objects (streams) instead, you can easily switch to different physical I/O devices without changing any of the I/O processing code in your application. This is the main raison d'être of streams.

The stream classes in package `java.io` can be classified into two types according to what their main concern is:

- Classes linking a stream to concrete I/O data sources or destinations

- Classes enhancing stream functionality

InputStreams

Class `InputStream` is an abstract class from which the entire input stream subhierarchy inherits. Its definition is clean and simple:

```
public class InputStream extends Object {
    public InputStream();
    public abstract int read() throws IOException;
    public int read(byte b[]) throws IOException;
    public int read(byte b[], int off, int len) throws IOException;
    public long skip(long n) throws IOException;
    public int available() throws IOException;
    public void close() throws IOException;
    public synchronized void mark(int readlimit);
    public synchronized void reset() throws IOException;
    public boolean markSupported();
}
```

Essentially, any input stream can simply read one or more bytes (and only bytes) of data from whatever data source it supports (the mark/reset related functionality is not supported by default). Five subclasses deal with specific data sources for the input stream:

ByteArrayInputStream   The data source for this input stream is an array of bytes you specify when constructing an instance of the class.

FileInputStream   The data source for this input stream is an external file, again specified as an argument to the class constructors.

PipedInputStream   The data source for this input stream is another pipe stream of type `PipedOutputStream`.

SequenceInputStream   The data source for this input stream is two or more other input streams concatenated together.

StringBufferInputStream   The data source for this input stream is a `String` (and not a `StringBuffer` as you could be forgiven for thinking) passed as the constructor's argument.

Figure 9.4 will help you visualize the relationship between an input stream and its data source. The figure depicts class `ByteArray-InputStream`, an input stream which lets you read from the stream, as usual, a single byte or a block of bytes at a time (as defined by class `InputStream`). In the case of class `ByteArrayInputStream`, the bytes read in this way originated from an array of bytes. Other classes will have other data sources; for example, class `FileInput-Stream` will take its data from a file, and so on.

FIGURE 9.4:

Data source and input stream

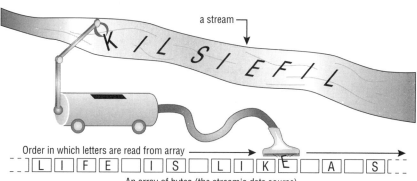

An array of bytes (the stream's data source)

The input stream hierarchy also contains classes whose accents lie less on the source of the stream's data, but rather on behavioral enhancements to `InputStream`'s vanilla functionality. The abstract class `FilterInputStream` is the root for the subtree grouping together these extra classes:

BufferedInputStream This class inserts a performance enhancing input buffering mechanism between `InputStream`'s standard reading functionality and your application.

DataInputStream This class adds support for reading all of Java's primitive types previously saved to a stream.

LineNumberInputStream This class adds the concept of a running line number to any stream being read (useful for line-based text input streams).

PushbackInputStream This class adds the option of undoing the last single byte read operation.

> **TIP**
>
> These `FilterInputStream` subclasses can be powerfully combined with other `InputStream` classes. For example, you could create a `ByteArrayDataInputStream` or a `FilePushback-Input Stream`. To do this, you would pass an instance of a data source-type `InputStream` (`Byte`, `File`, `Pipe`, `Sequence`, or `String`) object as argument to the constructor of the filter-type `InputStream` (`Buffered`, `DataInput`, `LineNumber`, or `Pushback`). Because these `FilterInputStream` subclasses are themselves `InputStreams`, you could even combine several filtering types. You could therefore conceivably create a `BufferingPushbackLine-NumberingStringInput Stream` (although by then you would be breaking every readability rule in the book). This same technique is possible with `OutputStreams`.

OutputStreams

Class `OutputStream` is an abstract class from which the entire output stream subhierarchy inherits. Its definition is even simpler than that of its sister superclass `InputStream`:

```
public class OutputStream extends Object {
    public OutputStream();
    public abstract void write(int b) throws IOException;
    public void write(byte b[]) throws IOException;
    public void write(byte b[], int off, int len) throws IOException;
    public void flush() throws IOException;
    public void close() throws IOException;
}
```

As you can deduce from the class definition, any output stream's sole requirement is to be able to write a single byte or write an array of bytes. (Flushing and closing the stream are peripheral to what an output stream is all about.) As was the case with input streams, output streams cannot exist on their own; they need to be connected to a data destination before they become a useful stream.

`OutputStream`'s subclasses can similarly be classified according to their main concern—choice of data destination (called *sink*) or choice of enhanced stream writing behavior.

There are only three classes which deal with guiding the stream's data to a specific destination:

ByteArrayOutputStream   This class stores all the data written to the stream into a byte array.

FileOutputStream   This class saves all of the stream's data to an external file.

PipedOutputStream   This output stream class pipes all of its data to a receiving input pipe at the other end (an instance of a `PipedInputStream`).

As with the equivalent input stream classes, you specify the destination as an argument to the constructor of the particular class.

Figure 9.5 will help you visualize the relationship between an example output stream and its data sink. The figure depicts the scenario for class `FileOutputStream`. The bytes that were written to the stream all end up stored in an external file; you specify the file when you create the output stream.

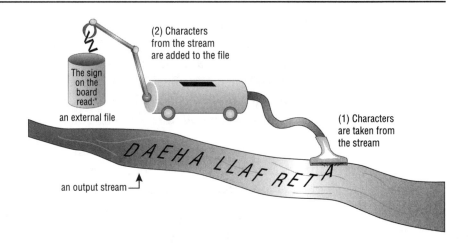

The output stream classes that enhance output stream behavior all descend from the output equivalent of `FilterInputStream`: `FilterOutputStream`. The predefined concrete subclasses you can use in your applications are

BufferedOutputStream   This class inserts a performance-enhancing output buffering mechanism between the standard `OutputStream` functionality and your application. This is the symmetrical equivalent of `BufferedInputStream`.

DataOutputStream   This class supports writing all of Java's primitive types to a stream. This is again the output counterpart of class `DataInputStream`.

PrintStream   This class is similar to `DataOutputStream` except that the values output are not represented in binary but as readable ASCII lines. (There is no input equivalent to this class.) Familiar examples of this type of output stream class are `System.out` and `System.err`. (That's right—you've been using a `PrintStream` all along!)

RandomAccessFile

Class `RandomAccessFile` encapsulates full read and write access to files. This class is rather odd when compared to the other classes in the I/O hierarchy. You would expect the class to be derived from both an abstract input class and an abstract output class (plus some seeking functionality), but since `RandomAccessFile` descends directly from `Object`, a rather conventional (that is, not object-oriented) design approach was used instead.

The methods implemented by `RandomAccessFile` can be summarized into the following groups:

- Reading of primitive types and byte arrays (in binary form)
- Writing of primitive types and byte arrays (in binary form)
- Positioning of the file pointer (seeking)

StreamTokenizer

Class `StreamTokenizer` extracts identifiable substrings and punctuation from an input stream according to user-defined rules. This process is called *tokenizing* because the stream gets reduced to tokens. Tokens typically represent keywords, variable names, numerical constants, string literals, and syntactic punctuation like brackets, equal signs, and so on. The `StreamTokenizer` methods that give you this functionality are, essentially,

- Various methods that affect the rules for parsing the input stream into tokens

- Method `nextToken()` to extract the next token from the input stream

Text tokenizing is a common technique used to reduce the complexity of textual input. The archetypal application that uses text tokenizing is the programming-language compiler. Compilers do not analyze your source file as-is, because that would lead to an onslaught of independent characters. They analyze a stream of tokens representing and extracted from your source file. Keywords, identifiers, punctuation, comments, strings, and so on, all first get compressed into easy-to-manipulate tokens. Only after this *lexical analysis* stage does a compiler start to check the complex grammar of any programming (or other) language. Class `StreamTokenizer` is used by the original Java compiler (`javac`) for exactly this purpose.

Package java.awt

As you can see from Figures 9.6 and 9.7, the package `java.awt` is organized into the following main groups.

The two GUI component branches:

- The `Component` subtree. This subtree, which contains most of the GUI classes supported by the AWT, is the heart of the package. Buried slightly deeper within this subtree is another important subtree: the `Container` subtree.

- The `MenuComponent` subtree

FIGURE 9.6:

Package `java.awt`
main inheritance tree

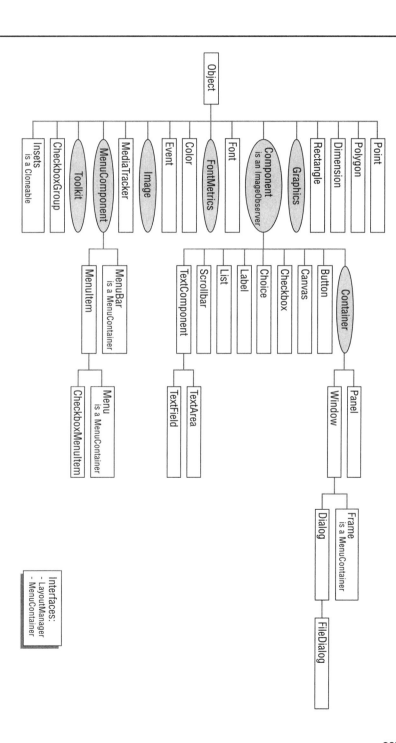

FIGURE 9.7:

Package `java.awt`
`LayoutManager`
classes.

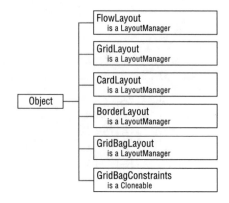

The `LayoutManager` classes:

- `FlowLayout`
- `BorderLayout`
- `CardLayout`
- `GridLayout`
- `GridBagLayout` and `GridBagConstraints`

The graphics classes:

- `Graphics`
- `Image`
- `Color`
- `Font`
- `FontMetrics`

The geometry classes:

- `Point`
- `Polygon`

- `Dimension`

- `Rectangle`

Other miscellaneous classes:

- `MediaTracker`

- `Event`

- `Toolkit`

Java's Abstract Windowing Toolkit (AWT) package is the largest and most important package of the entire hierarchy. This is what you'd expect in an age when the design and implementation of application GUIs can easily consume over a third of software development resources. The AWT aims to significantly reduce this proportion by allowing GUIs to be platform independent in a hassle-free way—a revolutionary step.

All the classes outlined below are 100 percent hardware and software independent. This means your Java GUI-based applications will run happily on every platform that is Java-capable.

GUI Classes

The bulk of the classes within package `java.awt` relates to GUI creation and management. The classes can be classified into the following groups:

- `Widget` classes

- `Container` classes

- `Widget layout` classes

- `Menu` classes

Widget Classes

The fundamental building blocks of GUI designs are called widgets, gadgets, or buttons, depending on the GUI school that invented them. The most common term, and the one used in this book, is *widgets* (window gadgets). Java implements quite a nice variety of them, all of which are easily deployed in your GUI designs, as you will see in later chapters.

Button   Class `Button` implements that bread and butter widget: the button. `AWT Buttons` are very simple to use. Their simplest and by far most common incarnation is the labeled variety. You can also have buttons with iconic identification instead of the rather simplistic string label. (This is not supported by class `Button`, but can be achieved readily by giving a `Canvas` an image and trapping mouse clicks on it.)

Canvas   A `Canvas` component provides a drawable area. As such it is invisible (it has no graphical representation) but can detect mouse click and move events, which can then be used by the application.

Checkbox and CheckboxGroup   Classes `Checkbox` and `CheckboxGroup` implement checkable items. The latter class forces the former into a mutually exclusive grouping—radio buttons.

Choice   Class `Choice` implements a multiple-choice component. The number of choices is typically quite low (use List for long lists of choices or items). The graphical implementation for a `Choice` usually looks like a pop-up menu.

Label   A `Label` is used purely to give GUI zones a title or to label other widgets. It just encapsulates a single line of read-only text.

List   A `List` is a heavy duty list display and item selection widget. It comes with a vertical scroll bar to allow you to scroll and find the item(s) you are after. Multiple items can be selected at the same time.

Scrollbar   This is the Java slider control. You can have either vertical or horizontal incarnations of a `Scrollbar`. If a List object fails to provide you with enough listing functionality, you could design your own custom lister by incorporating a vertical `Scrollbar` object in a `Panel` subclass, for example. This widget represents a continuous range of values that can be "sampled" at any time by the application. Clicks on the `Scrollbar` arrow icons are treated as "line increment" commands that move the scroll bar cursor according to a defined line increment. Similarly, clicking above or below the cursor is interpreted as "page increment" commands with analogous results. `Scrollbar` components are indispensable for inputting values clamped to any min–max numerical range.

TextField   The `TextField` widget is the pillar of GUI form screens. It allows you to enter any text within a short, single-line input window.

TextArea   This is a variant of the `TextField` widget and allows multiple-line entry of text. This could be used for free-form "memo" type fields. Both `TextField` and `TextArea` allow unconstrained data entry, which often isn't what an application needs. To implement entry fields that accept only strict types of data (text only, numbers only, dates only, and so on), you need to subclass either `TextField` or `TextArea` (depending on your requirements) and enhance their behavior by validating the user's input to the type of data allowed.

Container Classes

An application's window typically is not just an unstructured heap of clickable or selectable components. Well-designed GUIs are highly structured to aid you in your navigation of the interface. This structuring can be in part achieved by using component containers. A window can be subdivided into areas or zones, each containing related buttons, choices, lists, and so on. When you use containers to implement these visual and logical areas, you mirror the hierarchy in your code. This is just another example of the key object-oriented principle of projecting the vocabulary and structures of the problem domain into your code. The container classes in Java's AWT are also the entities on which the layout manager classes work (see the following section, "Widget Layout Classes").

WARNING   Do not confuse the term *container*, as used by Java's AWT, with the more general term *container class*, as used by other object-oriented frameworks. AWT Containers are GUI component containers. Generic container classes, on the other hand, are abstract data type classes that can contain other objects (for example, linked lists, stacks, bags, and vectors).

Container   This abstract class is the generic widget container on which layout managers act. All other container classes below are derived from it.

Panel   This is a concrete incarnation of class `Container`. It does not have a graphic representation, not even a simple outline. You typically subclass a `Panel` to define and control a logical grouping of widgets (for example, giving you a KeyPanel, as in the StackCalculator example of Chapter 14).

Frame   Confusingly, class `Frame` is the building block class for producing fully fledged windows. (There's also a `Window` class which produces "windows" without any borders or a menu bar.) Frames have titles, background colors, optional menu bars, and layout managers.

Dialog Class `Dialog` is used for implementing direct application-to-user feedback or questions. Typical uses include pop-up warning dialog windows, quit confirmation dialog boxes, and so on. The `Dialog` class is not a self-contained component like, for example, `Frame`. In fact, it relies on class `Frame` to provide it with a display medium in which to display itself.

FileDialog Class `FileDialog` implements the indispensable file Open/Save/Save As dialog window, complete with filename filtering capability, plus any transparent extras provided by the native operating system. On Windows 95, for example, the Java `FileDialog` allows the user to create new directories on the fly, before saving a file.

Widget Layout Classes

One of Java's innovations in the field of GUI programming is its GUI component placement strategy. With other GUI frameworks you usually have to specify pixel coordinates for all of your components. Even with GUI building tools, you need to position your components absolutely. Java was designed to be platform independent, but since AWT still relies on the host's native windowing system to provide it with its window and button building blocks, it is not possible to specify component dimensions and placement with absolute precision. The AWT uses an automatic layout system based around `LayoutManagers` instead.

Five standard layout managers are currently defined:

FlowLayout This class is the simplest of the `LayoutManager` classes. Every component under its layout control will be positioned and sized in the same way flowing text is in a WYSIWYG word processor: from left to right, and then overflowing to the next line when the first line is filled, and so on.

BorderLayout   This `LayoutManager` class positions and scales components according to the conventional distribution of components around a generic window. It allows components to be laid out along the top, bottom, left, or right edges of a window and leaves one large central area for the remainder of the components. Any unassigned areas will be recovered by the other areas.

GridLayout   As the name suggests, this class enforces a simple grid layout. But unlike what you would expect from a grid layout, you can't specify the positions of your components using two-dimensional coordinates. You are in fact forced to position them using a one-dimensional index. (You can use `GridBagLayout` to avoid this annoying situation.)

GridBagLayout   This `LayoutManager` class extends the approach taken by class `GridLayout`. It basically allows any one component to use up more than one grid cell, in either horizontal or vertical direction. Extra control over the exact layout process is provided by instances of a helper class: class `Grid-BagConstraints`. This is the most powerful layout manager of all the standard ones provided.

CardLayout   Class CardLayout embodies the concept of a number of cards which can be flipped through, with only one card visible at any one time. This layout management style is most commonly used to implement multiple "pages" (or cards) that the user can view by selecting their "tabs." Since class CardLayout's responsibilities don't go beyond laying out the components in a collection of cards, this means that the trendy rendering of the card tabs themselves should be handled by another class. Unfortunately, there is currently no such standard Component class to do this.

Menu Classes

Drop-down or pop-up menus associated with windows are part of any modern application. Java's AWT supports quite complete menu functionality (submenus and checkable menu items are included) using a small and surprisingly easy-to-use set of menu classes:

MenuBar Class `MenuBar` acts as the anchor for the entire collection of menus connected to an application, or to be more precise, connected to a `Frame`. Every Java `Frame` can have its own menu bar with menu items responding to selections private to its context.

Menu The `Menu` class is the logical building block for any menu system. Menus hold logically related menu items and/or submenus. A menu is identified primarily by a simple menu title.

MenuItem and CheckboxMenuItem These two classes are the logical leaves of any menu system. These classes represent the menu items which a user selects on a menu.

WARNING Don't let the class hierarchy confuse you. A `MenuItem` (or `CheckboxMenuItem`) is *logically* the leaf component in a final, concrete menu system. But as far as the object-oriented hierarchy is concerned, a `MenuItem` has to be `Menu`'s parent. This is totally counterintuitive, but can be understood as follows: Wherever you have a menu item, you can in fact substitute an entire submenu for it. So, class `Menu` has to be a subclass of `MenuItem`. In any case, this admittedly chicken-and-egg type situation does not in any way complicate AWT menu programming. The fact is that adding menus to applications is probably the easiest thing you can do within AWT.

The Graphics Classes

For animation or special effects, you need something very different from standard GUI classes. You need to be able to control colors and imagery without any of the window-metaphor constraints imposed by a set of GUI classes. Java, therefore, provides elementary rendering classes, class `Graphics` being the core class in this area.

Class Graphics

This is Java's only real rendering class. It supports a simple 2-D painting model with the usual rendering primitives. Specifically, the following classes of methods are provided:

- Text rendering
- Rectangular area copying (also called *blitting*)
- Filled and outlined
    - rectangles
    - ovals
    - polygons
    - arcs
- Lines
- Coordinate system translation
- Clipping rectangle support
- Changing current drawing color
- Various graphics state querying functions

Class Image

Class Image encapsulates a platform-independent image data structure. This approach shields you from the profusion of hard- or software dependent bitmap "standards" (bitplane, chunky, interleaved, and so on). The methods provided by class Image allow you to

- Query the image's dimensions
- Query the image's properties (for example, source image format, copyright information, and so on)
- Create a graphics context for the image so you can use the Graphics rendering methods on this image

Class Color

Class `Color` encapsulates a platform independent color data structure. As with bitmapped images, a color can be implemented in a variety of ways. The `Color` class shields you from these platform dependencies. The provided methods support

- Conversion between RGB (Red, Green, Blue) and HSB (Hue, Saturation, Brightness) color models

- Accessing the red, green, and blue color components

- Increasing or decreasing the brightness of a color

Classes Font and FontMetrics

These two classes give you a platform-independent way of accessing and querying the platform local fonts. The methods broadly let you do the following:

- Specify a font family, style, and point size

- Query font attributes and metrics (family name, style, point size, character and string widths, ascender and descender lengths)

Geometry classes

Package `java.awt` contains four geometry classes. These encapsulate the mathematical concepts point, polygon, rectangle, and dimension:

Point This class represents a simple (x,y) data structure along with two methods: `move()` and `translate()`. As with all geometry classes, integers are used instead of floating point numbers. This reflects the main use of these classes as helper classes for GUI programming (and not pure math, which assumes numbers and shapes to have infinite precision).

Polygon   This class represents an ordered collection of points treated as the definition of a polygon. Three methods enhance the data structure: `addPoint()` modifies the polygon to include the new point; `getBoundingBox()` calculates the smallest rectangle enclosing all points of the polygon; and `inside()` tests whether a given point lies inside or outside the polygon.

Dimension   This class is a pure data structure holding a width and height variable. No methods enhance the raw data structure (in other words this is really equivalent to a C structure or a Pascal record).

Rectangle   This class represents a rectangle at a certain (x,y) position. The class adds several methods to manipulate rectangles (move, shrink, grow, calculate intersection with other rectangles, and test whether a point is inside a rectangle or not).

Although these classes have nothing to do with rendering or with GUI programming per se, they are used by those higher-level classes to improve code reuse, robustness, and readability. Since GUI programming constantly involves dealing with positions and rectangular component dimensions or outlines, it makes sense to localize (*abstract*) some representation and a set of common operations for those positions and dimensions. This way, you avoid scattering your code with bits of identical functionality with slightly differing implementations.

Package java.awt.image

This package groups together classes that deal with image generation and manipulation, plus the color models associated with bitmap image encoding. To effectively use images, you will also need to use classes `java.awt.Image` and `java.awt.Component`.

WARNING

Do not confuse the package `java.awt.image` with the class `java.awt.Image`, which is a `java.awt` package class. The simple trick to keep them apart is to remember that package names only contain lowercase letters and class names always start with a capital. With this knowledge it is impossible to confuse `java.awt.Image` with a package name, and `java.awt.image` with a class name.

Package `java.awt.image` enforces (for better or worse) a producer/consumer metaphor on all image processing. Producer classes and consumer classes need to be linked together before the image processing can begin. This approach is initially difficult to understand, but as with most of these systems, the payoff justifies the investment.

The inheritance tree for package `java.awt` is illustrated in Figure 9.8.

At the heart of package `java.awt.image` lie these three interfaces:

- `ImageProducer`
- `ImageConsumer`
- `ImageObserver`

FIGURE 9.8:

Package `java.awt.image` inheritance tree

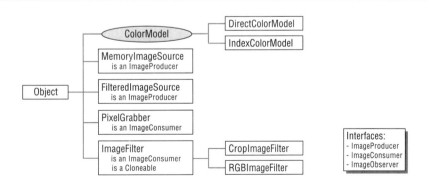

The following two classes implement the `ImageProducer` interface:

MemoryImageSource   This class is an `ImageProducer` which uses a simple array of bytes (for up to 8 bits per pixel) or ints (for up to 32 bits per pixel) as the source image data. `Memory-ImageSource` allows you to easily construct algorithmically generated images. These can be as simple as a color gradient fill or as infinitely complex as the Mandelbrot fractal (see the example in Chapter 13). Since the image data is constructed in a 2-D array of pixels, this class makes any pixel manipulations easy to implement.

FilteredImageSource   This class also is an `ImageProducer`. Its image data source is another `ImageProducer` (for example, an instance of class `MemoryImageSource`) that gets filtered according to the filtering characteristics of an `ImageFilter` compliant filter (described below).

The next four classes implement the `ImageConsumer` interface:

ImageFilter   Unmodified, this class passes through the image data without altering (filtering) it in any way. You need to subclass this class to implement useful filters. Possible useful filters include color-to-gray filters, brightness-altering filters, image noise filters, edge enhancement filters.

CropImageFilter   This class is a subclass of `ImageFilter`. It "filters" a source image by producing a new image which is a rectangular sub-image of the original.

RGBImageFilter   This is another subclass of `ImageFilter`. It allows you to change the color of every pixel of a source image—for example, to produce a grayscale version of the image.

PixelGrabber   This class is used for extracting rectangular areas of another image and storing them into an array of ints for further processing.

ColorModel   Naturally, the concept of a color model is closely associated with image processing. The ubiquitous Red Green Blue (RGB) pixel encoding, for example, can be implemented using a variety of exact bit field assignments. There are also other color models like the Hue Saturation Brightness (HSB) system. All of these can be supported via subclasses of `ColorModel`, the following of which are included as standard:

- `IndexColorModel`
- `DirectColorModel`

The use of all these classes is too complex even to briefly summarize in this chapter; their interrelationships will be explained in Chapter 13.

Package java.net

The `java.net` package is one of the class hierarchy's other main features. It provides very high-level interfaces to the rather less high-level set of data communication protocols (and their associated API) called TCP/IP. The `java.net` classes hide many of the technical quagmires inherent to low-level Internet programming.

Interfaces again feature deep within the package—this time not to lay the framework for the abstract or concrete java.net classes to obey, but as templates for using the Factory design pattern. This design pattern will be explained in more detail in Chapter 17.

The `java.net` classes can be grouped according to the following responsibilities:

- Internet addressing (classes `InetAddress` and `URL`)
- UDP/IP connectionless classes (`DatagramPacket`, `DatagramSocket`)
- TCP/IP connection-oriented classes (various `Socket` classes)

- MIME content type handlers (`ContentHandler`, `URLStreamHandler`)

- WWW related classes (`URLConnection`, `URLStreamHandler`)

The inheritance tree for `java.net` is illustrated in Figure 9.9.

FIGURE 9.9:

Package `java.net` inheritance tree

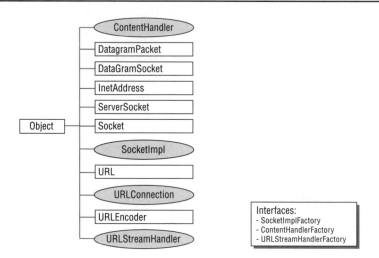

Here's a brief overview of the commonly used `java.net` classes:

InetAddress   This class deals with Internet addresses in their mnemonic (host.domain) form and their 32-bit numeric form (byte.byte.byte.byte).

URL   This class encapsulates a Uniform Resource Locator (URL) specification plus associated methods including opening a connection to the URL resource (a web page, a file, or telnet port), retrieving the URL resource, querying URL fields (protocol, host, filenames, and port number).

ServerSocket and Socket   These two classes together give you complete TCP/IP connectivity support. Each class supports one side of the client/server application model. Class `Socket` is used to implement a client. Class `ServerSocket` is used to implement a server. Class `Socket` provides methods to connect any stream (as input or output) to a socket to communicate through. This way, you can essentially divorce internetworking technicalities (and pitfalls!) from your application by working at the abstract stream level instead. See Chapter 17 for a detailed exploration of these classes.

> **NOTE** Sockets are the software interfaces that connect an application to the network beyond. On the Internet, each machine has 65536 (64K) addressable sockets it can use. All standard Internet services (like e-mail, FTP, and so on) use agreed-upon socket numbers, colloquially termed *well-known port numbers*. Server programs listen to these sockets for any incoming service request. A client program has to open a socket of its own before it can connect to a server socket at the other end.

DatagramPacket and DatagramSocket   These classes together provide User Datagram Protocol (UDP) Internet services. In terms of complexity—and, therefore, ease of use—the UDP protocol lies in between the Transmission Control Protocol (TCP) protocol and the Internet Protocol (IP) protocol of TCP/IP. IP and TCP being, respectively, the low and high level protocols of the protocol stack. As the names of the classes suggest, UDP is a datagram-oriented protocol. This means data packets travel individually (like letters in the postal system), without any guarantees of delivery. This is because, unlike with TCP, UDP does not attempt to detect or correct loss of packets. This lack of protocol overheads is what makes UDP interesting for certain types of applications. The design of a financial server broadcasting currency exchange rates, for example, might choose UDP over TCP to gain speed at the cost of an occasional lost rate update.

Through class `DatagramPacket`, you can specify a packet's Internet host destination (using an `InetAddress` instance), the port (or socket) to connect to on that host, and the binary contents of the packet. You can then send or receive datagrams via an instance of class `DatagramSocket`.

> **NOTE**
>
> Note that most Internet applications do not use the UDP protocol to achieve their functionality, but instead use the TCP protocol, which supports a guaranteed delivery end-to-end link.

Package java.applet

A big reason for Java's runaway success is that it's a highly efficient and easy-to-learn language for *distributed software components*. (Distributed software components? That's what Java applets are. Nothing more or less.) Even so, the standard class framework contains little which explicitly deals with those instrumental applets.

As you can see from Figure 9.10, package `java.applet` looks very barren compared to the other packages. Its sole contents are one class and three interfaces. Class `java.applet.Applet` is the main repository for methods supporting applet functionality. The methods it makes available can be grouped into the following categories:

- Applet initialization, restarting, and freezing

- Embedded HTML applet parameter support

- High-level image loading

FIGURE 9.10:

Package `java.applet` tree hierarchy

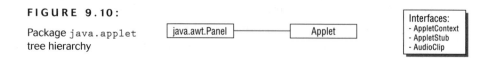

```
java.awt.Panel ——— Applet
```

```
Interfaces:
- AppletContext
- AppletStub
- AudioClip
```

- High-level audio loading and playing
- Origins querying (`getDocumentBase()` and `getCodeBase()`)
- Simple status displaying (`showStatus(String)`)

Summary

Java's standard class hierarchy contains a wide variety of classes which, given some time and effort to learn, should allow you to write applications within realistic time frames. The collection of classes spans a wide spectrum, with no significant gaps to obstruct real-life software development. However, as you will gradually discover, Java's classes are still a bit rough around the edges. Other class frameworks (Borland's Delphi object-oriented framework springs to mind) are significantly more mature and full-bodied. Sun is quite aware of this and will no doubt ensure that in time, Java too will be enveloped by a world-class collection of supporting classes.

AWT: GUI Layout Management in Applets and Applications

- Applets

- Applications

- Designing Java GUIs with Layout Managers

Java's big joker card is its Abstract Windowing Toolkit (AWT). It is an object-oriented Graphical User Interface (GUI) framework that allows you to design modern, mouse-controlled, graphical application interfaces—which isn't a revolutionary step in and of itself. But Java's AWT lets you design and implement GUIs that run unmodified (unported even) on PCs running Windows 95, Windows NT, or OS/2; Macs running MacOS; or even UNIX machines running X-Windows. And *that* is revolutionary.

Ever since Xerox's pioneer work in the seventies and Apple's subsequent mass-market introduction of mouse- and icon-driven user interfaces, developers have had to pick competing GUI "standards" and stick to them religiously. Mastering any given GUI standard is a non-trivial exercise, so it's no wonder that developers don't switch GUI APIs at the drop of a hat. Like computer languages themselves, GUIs have been thoroughly mutually incompatible. This—and the associated lack of a standard terminology—greatly helped to segregate the various GUI schools, a wasteful and divisive state of affairs. Java's GUI approach could abolish the GUI wars by supporting a functional subset of most modern GUI components and presenting them through a new platform-independent API.

NOTE

The jargon wars will rage for a while longer. Java's AWT introduces new terms and concepts and uses some existing terms in incompatible ways (sigh). In Java land, when we talk about a "component," we mean a GUI element, a widget, a gadget, a control, or a button (depending on the GUI background you have).

At this point, you might ask yourself whether the AWT also imposes a new look and feel on our brave new (Java) world. If you are used to, for example, the Macintosh user interface, it is annoying to suddenly have an application that stubbornly thrusts upon you a GEM-style interface instead. Modern machines have personalities that they impose on us through their native and often proprietary GUI. AWT respects these personalities by employing the underlying machine's native GUI API to construct its own universal components. So Java applications built around the AWT reassuringly retain the Mac look and feel on Macs and the Windows look and feel on PCs.

Since the AWT consequently does not specify the exact look and feel—and therefore the dimensions and exact pixel rendering—of your GUI elements, how do you ensure that your GUIs will look great on every platform? The AWT answer is *layout managers*. These fundamental AWT classes are responsible for laying out all the visual components in aesthetically acceptable ways without you having to specify absolute positions. Unfortunately, this process is not yet fully automatic. Java's AWT does not have artificial intelligence or graphic design experts embedded in its layout managers. Instead, your applications give these layout managers hints as to component placement and preferred sizes. These hints vary from quite vague ("north," "center," or "third" placements) to quite specific (grid coordinates).

You'll begin by studying layout managers in great detail, since these are fundamental to any Java GUI implementation and, even more relevant, GUI design.

AWT Environments: Applets and Applications

Before embarking on your exploration of Java's novel layout system and the components it affects so thoroughly, you need to understand the two quite different contexts a Java GUI can be embedded in. Java's AWT can be used in the following two environments:

- In Java applets (mini WWW applications)

- In stand-alone applications

Both have different frameworks to respect. The AWT itself is not aware of the context you choose to deploy it in, but the chosen context means different coding techniques, possibilities, and limitations for your Java programs. The easiest context to start using is Java applets.

Applets

An *applet* is a small program that runs embedded in a Web browser's HTML page. As such, any applet has a drawing or work area equal to an imaginary picture situated in the same spot (see Figure 10.1).

FIGURE 10.1:

Applets as interactive, intelligent pictures

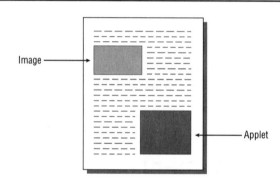

Image

Applet

When applet code starts running, it can immediately use its applet area without any further initializations or checks. For example, the first statement in an applet could be to draw a diagonal line right across its surface. The ease with which you can have an applet up and running is what makes applets easier to write than applications—in the beginning (it gets rather more complex for nontrivial applets). It is quite possible to write simple little applets without knowing much about the underlying AWT mechanisms at all.

Here is an example that draws the diagonal line:

```
import java.awt.Graphics;
public class Appletlet extends java.applet.Applet {

public void paint (Graphics g) {
    g.drawLine(0,0, 100,100);
}}
```

As you can see, the applet has no lengthy initializations whatsoever before it starts using AWT classes. Here you use the `Graphics` class to draw a line with its `drawLine()` method (you will study this class in detail in Chapter 13). To write an applet, you have to begin by extending (or subclassing) class `Applet`. That's because the browser *needs* your applets to be instances of the `Applet` class. Any old Java program won't do. The `paint()` method used in this example is an `Applet` method that we override.

WARNING   Make sure you understand the difference between overriding a method and simply inventing a new one. Overriding a method means you cannot change the name or signature of the method to anything else but the original method signature defined in the superclass you are extending—in our example, `public void paint(Graphics g)`. If the signature differs in any way, then you are creating a brand new method, not overriding an existing one. Sometimes subtle bugs can slip through when you *meant* to override a method but instead failed to use the same signature. The compiler won't generate an error, and your code will invoke the wrong method at run time (the superclass method).

Whenever the browser needs to draw the page containing this applet, it tells the applet to draw itself by calling the `paint()` method. For simplistic applets, this calling protocol between the browser and your applet might be all that you need, but for more complex applets (for example, those using animation) this approach is too limited. In fact, the browser calls many more Applet methods that were not overriden here, so only a small subset of the full browser-applet protocol was used.

For starters, there is the `init()` method that the browser calls to initialize an applet. There was not an `init()` method in the simple example because nothing needed to be initialized, but if your applet has any initialization to do (namely, code it only needs to execute once, at the start of its execution), it should put all this code in an overridden `init()` method. Here is an example that overrides the `init()` method:

```
import java.awt.Graphics;
import java.util.Date;

public class Applet2 extends java.applet.Applet {

String then;

public void init () {
Date now;
    now = new Date();
    then= now.toString();
}

public void paint (Graphics g) {
    g.drawString("I was born on " + then, 10,10);
}}
```

In addition to the `paint()` method responsible for the redrawing of the applet, you now have a customized `init()` method. This method will be called once by the browser before the applet is displayed. In this example, the `init()` method records the date and time at the moment the applet gets initialized, and converts this to a string which the `paint()` method will use to draw this frozen time when the applet needs to be redrawn.

TIP You can obtain the current date and time by making a new `Date` object using the default `java.util.Date` constructor.

Graphically printing a string is done with the Graphics `drawString()` method. It takes a string and the coordinates for the string's position.

There are three more methods that the browser invokes on an applet during an applet's life cycle:

start()   When the applet's HTML page comes into view

stop()   When the applet's HTML page is left

destroy()   When the browser's garbage collector determines the applet is no longer necessary to keep around in memory

To see the full browser-applet protocol in action, type in the following program, compile it, and tell your favorite Web browser to load a Web page with the applet embedded in it. Make sure that your browser shows "Java console output." On Netscape's Navigator browser, you enable this by selecting Show Java Console in the program's Options menu.

```
import java.awt.Graphics;

public class AppletLife extends java.applet.Applet {

public void init () {
    System.out.println("Browser wants me to: initialize myself");
}
public void start () {
    System.out.println("Browser wants me to: start running");
}
public void stop () {
    System.out.println("Browser wants me to: stop running");
}
public void paint (Graphics g) {
    System.out.println("Browser wants me to: redraw myself");
}
public void destroy () {
    System.out.println("Browser wants me to: clean up before being removed.");
}}
```

The first time you load the HTML page, you should see the following output printed to the Java console:

```
Browser wants me to: initialize myself
Browser wants me to: start running
Browser wants me to: redraw myself
```

This means the `init()`, `start()`, and `paint()` Applet methods are always called when an applet is first loaded and run. The sequence can differ from what is listed above: due to asynchronous aspects of the protocol, the `paint()` method can be legally called before the `start()` method. The `init()` method, however, is guaranteed to be called before all others.

Now, whenever the browser window needs to repaint itself—for example, after having been obscured by other windows overlapping it—you should see an additional

```
Browser wants me to: redraw myself
```

This is because the browser had to completely redraw itself to undo the graphically inconsistent picture it was showing.

Remember that the entire GUI desktop metaphor your machine maintains is just a clever, graphical illusion. Any computer has a flat, uniform screen bit map that doesn't enforce or care about these "overlapping" and clipping rectangular areas called "windows." The "natural behavior" of a computer screen is much more like that of a painting canvas in a painting program: The canvas has no restrictions whatsoever. In a GUI environment, then, when windows are depth arranged in this plain bitmap environment, it means that some windows will get partially or entirely overwritten while others will have to redraw themselves. Since your applet is part of a window, it too has to play along to maintain the illusion. If not, your applet will soon become graphically corrupted, or more likely, erased completely. This is why it is important to have an applet repaint itself using the `paint()` method whenever the browser commands it to (and as quickly as possible, as always).

If you load a different Web page in your browser, you should see your applet print out the following line:

```
Browser wants me to: stop running
```

You will probably wonder what this means, since your applet was not executing any code at the time anyway. Think about the kind of applications applets can be used for—animation, real-time updating of information fetched from an Internet server, general entertainment, and so on. All these types of applets are *real* applets, and are very different from what has been demonstrated so far in this book. Real applets usually run constantly.

To illustrate, imagine that the `start()` method in your last applet never ended because it had to animate something all the time. Such an applet would be very wasteful of processor resources if it kept on animating even after the user switched to a different page. Yet that is exactly what it would do if we didn't take any steps to avoid this problem; the way to avoid the problem is by using threads. In Chapter 8, you saw how threads allow you to do several things at the same time, well, imagine all of an applet's core processing and functionality (the animating for example) being run in a separate thread. This way, whenever the applet's page is displaced by a new page, you can simply freeze the thread, and when the applet's page is reloaded, you can let the thread run again—this is the real purpose of the `start()` and `stop()` `Applet` methods. They assume that all your applets are written with multithreading in the first place. In later chapters you will learn how to actually write applets built around a thread, but for now, you are fine knowing that `start()` and `stop()` are really meant to control applet threads so that they do not consume processor resources while not in view.

> **WARNING**
>
> A related use for the `start()` and `stop()` methods is to control sounds produced by your applet. Most sounds keep playing forever because they just loop round. To have a sound stop playing when the user leaves your applet's page, you need to explicitly stop that sound.

If you now click on your browser's Back button to revisit the page with our applet, you will see the console print

```
Browser wants me to: start running
Browser wants me to: redraw myself
```

Because the browser assumed your applet thread had been put to sleep when we switched pages, it now asks your applet to wake up the thread again, immediately followed by an urgent request to repaint the applet. This is because our applet's facade was overwritten a long time ago by the previous page and its applets.

The final method (literally) a browser can invoke on applets is the `destroy()` method. Just quit your browser altogether and carefully watch the console window again. What you should have seen just before the console vanished was

```
Browser wants me to: stop running
Browser wants me to: clean up before being removed
```

The final call to `destroy()` gives your applet an opportunity to release any persistent and/or expensive resources it had locked while in existence. Files, I/O streams, network connections, unwritten buffers, and so on might all need some extra closing bookkeeping operations before the applet gets discarded.

WARNING   Java's garbage collection feature means that ex-Pascal/C/C++ programmers can suddenly ignore clean-up issues with a vengeance. While the language feature itself is to be applauded (buggy clean-up code has been the cause of innumerable bugs in the past), developers shouldn't be lulled into a false sense of comfort. Java's garbage collection works only on objects that have no more parts of your application referencing them. Open files, output buffers, and network connections, for example, are more than just simple objects. You should therefore remain conscious of the (old) issues of correct code termination (the opposite of code initialization). Files should still be closed, output buffers flushed, and network connections disconnected properly.

Before we close this introduction to applets, you should make your life easier whenever you deal with more applet programs in the future. If you find modifying the <APPLET CODE= ...> HTML tag repetitive and a general waste of time, then you should try to automate the process. Here's a shell utility written in Java that takes your applet's class name and generates a minimal HTML file with the applet tag pointing correctly to your applet. The program uses file and stream I/O, so you may wish to ignore its internals until you are ready for the chapter dealing exclusively with the java.io package (Chapter 15).

```
//————————————————————————————————————————————————
// GenAppletHTML utility
// ————————--
// Usage: GenAppletHTML <AppletName>
//
// This Java application generates an HTML file named "page.html" which
// can be passed to the JDK appletviewer utility to test Applets.
//————————————————————————————————————————————————

import java.io.*;

class GenAppletHTML {

public static void main (String[] args) throws IOException {

FileOutputStream file;
PrintStream      html;

    // we need the name of an Applet as argument
    if (args.length == 0) {
       System.out.println("Please specify the name of the applet to view.");
       System.exit(10);
    }

    // give usage summary if user asks for it
    if ( args[0].indexOf("?") != -1 || args[0].equals("-h") ) {
       System.out.println("Usage: GenAppletHTML <AppletName>");
       System.exit(0);
    }

    // guard against illegal class names being passed (GIGO)
    if ( ! (
            Character.isLowerCase( args[0].charAt(0) ) ||
            Character.isUpperCase( args[0].charAt(0) ))
            ) {
```

```
            System.out.println("'" + args[0] + "' Is not a legal class name.");
            System.exit(10);
        }

        // enforce convention of classnames starting with a capital letter
        if (Character.isLowerCase( args[0].charAt(0) )) {
            System.out.println("Class names should (by convention) start with a capital
            ➥letter.");
            System.out.println(args[0]);
            System.out.println('^');
            System.out.println("is lower case.");
            System.exit(10);
        }

        // open file (combining FileOutput and PrintStream to get println() comfort
        file = new FileOutputStream("page.html");
        html = new PrintStream(file);
/* Generate an HTML file with the following structure:

<HTML>
<HEAD></HEAD>
<BODY>
<HR>
<APPLET CODE= ........ WIDTH=400 HEIGHT=300>
<PARAM NAME=arg1 VALUE="val1">
<PARAM NAME=arg2 VALUE="val2">
</APPLET>
<HR>
</BODY>
</HTML>
*/

        html.print("<HTML><HEAD></HEAD><BODY><HR><APPLET CODE=");

        html.print(args[0] + ".class ");

        html.println("WIDTH=400 HEIGHT=300>");
        html.println("<PARAM NAME=arg1 VALUE=\"val1\" >");   // note backslash esc
        html.println("<PARAM NAME=arg2 VALUE=\"val2\" >");
        html.println("</APPLET><HR></BODY></HTML>");
        html.close();
}}
```

To run the program, you invoke it as a stand-alone application, that is, from the command line. For example:

```
C:\> java GenAppletHTML MyApplet
```

The GenAppletHTML utility is useful mainly on non-UNIX machines that lack proper batch-processing command languages. It also nicely illustrates how Java can be used as a powerful and *universal* batch-programming language.

You should now have a clear overview of applet internals. As you can see, the difficulties lie not in any special precautions you need to take when using AWT classes in applets. The precautions to be taken are imposed on you by the browser-applet calling protocol. We will now study how applications are written and what, if any, precautions need to be taken when writing them.

Applications

Since stand-alone applications are by definition responsible for every aspect of themselves, such Java programs

- Are free from any browser protocol

- Do not inherit a window or drawing area to use "straight away"

The first point means that anything goes for applications: They do not need to be subclasses of class `Applet` and do not consequently need any overridden `init()`, `paint()`, `start()` or `stop()` methods. An application can be any class, as long as it has the obligatory static `main()` method as a starting point for the code.

The second point is where the main difference lies when you want to start writing applications instead of applets (if you are used to writing applets). Applications do not have a convenient window in which to draw or add GUI components. Moreover, they do not have a `paint()` method that hands you a Graphics object on a plate. All this needs to be somehow acquired by the application itself, and this is how a minimal application does it:

```
import java.awt.Frame;
import java.awt.Graphics;

class Application {

public static void main (String[] args) {
```

```
Frame myWindow;
Graphics winGr;

    myWindow = new Frame("Window !");
    myWindow.resize(300,300);
    myWindow.show();
    winGr = myWindow.getGraphics();
    winGr.drawLine(0,0, 300,300);
}}
```

The program first creates a window (which initially is not visible) by constructing a new `Frame` object.

WARNING Java `Frames` are other people's normal windows. This unfortunate class nomenclature is only made worse by another AWT class called `Window`. A Java `Window` is a featureless rectangular pane (no title, menu bar, kill, or resize buttons) from which you can construct windows that ignore any and all local GUI style conventions. As such, class `Window` is far less used than class `Frame`. Instead of `Window` and `Frame`, these classes might have been better named `Pane` and `Window`.

The `Frame` constructor takes a string that will be the window's title. Next, the program specifies a size for this window using the `resize()` method (the window still is not visible). And finally, it commands the window to pop open and display itself by invoking the `show()` method. To draw the impressive diagonal again, it now needs to get hold of a `Graphics` object linked to the new window. The Frame method `getGraphics()` allows you to do this. Once you have the graphics context object, drawing the line is done in exactly the same way as with your applet before. For simple applications of the same (trivial) complexity as the first applet in this chapter, this is all that is required to set up a window in which you can then draw and/or build a GUI. In Chapter 12, we will return to the differences between applets and applications.

Now that we had a look at the fundamental difference between the code frameworks required for applets and applications, it is time to attack this chapter's main topic: designing GUIs using the AWT layout manager classes.

Designing Java GUIs with Layout Managers

Layout managers are so important to Java GUI programming that discussion of them should precede talk of Java buttons, menus, sliders, and text fields. To explain how layout managers work, concrete AWT components will be used as the passive subjects of the layout process; in this case, simple deaf-and-dumb buttons that will not respond to any clicks will do the trick. Please indulge this approach and ignore the nagging questions relating to these buttons you will see being manipulated on your screen. Later, you will study buttons (and every other component) in detail, but only in Chapter 11, after you have seen how layout managers manipulate components in general.

Before tackling the easy task of exploring the different preprogrammed layout styles, you need to understand how the layout manager classes interact with their client classes: classes `Container` and `Component`.

Containers, Components, and Layout Managers

You will kick off your exploration of layout management with another simple applet. Type in (or copy from the accompanying CD-ROM) the following program:

```
import java.awt.*;

public class FlowLayoutTest extends java.applet.Applet {

    public void init() {
```

```
        setLayout(new FlowLayout());      // default for Applets

        add(new Button("First"));
        add(new Button("Second"));
        add(new Button("Third"));
        add(new Button("Fourth"));
        add(new Button("Fifth"));
    }
}
```

This class implements a very simple applet with five buttons laid out according to the style enforced by the `FlowLayout` layout manager (see Figure 10.2).

FIGURE 10.2:

An applet using its default layout: `FlowLayout`

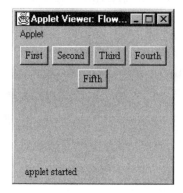

You will by now recognize the familiar hallmarks of applet code. For applets you need:

- A class that extends class `java.applet.Applet` (or simply `Applet` if you explicitly import `java.applet.Applet` at the beginning of your source files)

- An `init()` method that contains all of the code for a minimalist applet (or `init()`, `paint()`, `start()`, and `stop()` methods for real life applets)

NOTE

The example does not include any `paint()` method this time, because it doesn't need one: AWT GUI elements are repainted automatically by the applet.

With the first line of method `init()`, the applet invokes the `setLayout()` method. This lets the applet pick one of the preprogrammed layout styles for the GUI components it will use, in this case the five buttons added immediately after the `setLayout()` statement. Because you are extending class `Applet`, it would seem this `setLayout()` method comes from class `Applet`. But check out this class definition:

```
public class Applet extends Panel {
    public Applet();
    public final void setStub(AppletStub stub);
    public boolean isActive();
    public URL getDocumentBase();
    public URL getCodeBase();
    public String getParameter(String name);
    public AppletContext getAppletContext();
    public void resize(int width, int height);
    public void resize(Dimension d);
    public void showStatus(String msg);
    public Image getImage(URL url);
    public Image getImage(URL url, String name);
    public AudioClip getAudioClip(URL url);
    public AudioClip getAudioClip(URL url, String name);
    public String getAppletInfo();
    public String[][] getParameterInfo();
    public void play(URL url);
    public void play(URL url, String name);
    public void init();
    public void start();
    public void stop();
    public void destroy();
}
```

You can see the `init()` method that is overridden in most applet programs in this chapter. But it appears that `setLayout()` is not a method belonging to `Applet`.

You might want to see if `setLayout()` is defined in `Panel`, since `Applet` is itself a subclass of class `Panel`:

```
public class Panel extends Container {
   public Panel();
   public synchronized void addNotify();
}
```

No luck again. (This class looks very anemic indeed—just a constructor and a mysterious `addNotify()` instance method.) Yet method `setLayout()` has to be defined somewhere! Consider further class `Panel`: It is a subclass of a yet higher-level class, class `Container`. Here is what a `Container` is all about:

```
public class Container extends Component {
   public int countComponents();
   public synchronized Component getComponent(int n) throws Array
   ➥IndexOutOfBoundsException;
   public synchronized Component[] getComponents();
   public Insets insets();
   public Component add(Component comp);
   public synchronized Component add(Component comp, int pos);
   public synchronized Component add(String name, Component comp);
   public synchronized void remove(Component comp);
   public synchronized void removeAll();
   public LayoutManager getLayout();
   public void setLayout(LayoutManager mgr);
   public synchronized void layout();
   public synchronized void validate();
   public synchronized Dimension preferredSize();
   public synchronized Dimension minimumSize();
   public void paintComponents(Graphics g);
   public void printComponents(Graphics g);
   public void deliverEvent(Event e);
   public Component locate(int x, int y);
   public synchronized void addNotify();
   public synchronized void removeNotify();
```

```
    protected String paramString();
    public void list(PrintStream out, int indent);
}
```

Finally, there is the `setLayout()` method. So, in your program you can simply call `setLayout()` without any further qualifiers, because the `Applet` you extend is in fact also a `Container` (and a `Panel` too, in the same way that a dog can be a mammal and an animal at the same time). Normally, invoking a method is always done "on an object": `object.someMethod()`. But the unqualified use of a method implicitly means "on myself": `this.someMethod()`. Our `Applet` subclass therefore invokes `setLayout()` on itself, thus selecting some layout style for itself. The argument for the method is any `LayoutManager` object. (The next section discusses all the possible standard AWT layout managers.)

Having identified the origins of the `setLayout()` method and part of the meaning of the statement it is used in, your next question should be: Why is this method defined in class `Container`? The answer is quite simple and brings us back to this chapter's main topic, layout managers. Every container has associated with it its own, private layout manager. This is because layout managers lay out components contained by a container. Class `Container` is there to allow you to group together related GUI elements. So now you can readily understand what the second core method is for any `Container`: method `add()` (the same `add()` we used in our program to add the five buttons to the applet).

These points are summarized here, because they are key to the understanding of this and virtually all other AWT programs:

- Every container has its own layout manager (that is, layout style).

- Individual components are grouped together in containers.

- Every applet is a container.

So when applet code invokes an `add()` method on itself, it does so in its role as a container.

If you now look back at some of the methods class `Container` defines, they will make a lot more sense:

- `public             Component add(Component comp)`

- `public synchronized Component add(Component comp, int pos)`

- `public synchronized Component add(String name, Component comp)`

These overloaded methods all add a new GUI element to the container (the applet or the application's window). The `Component` type specified in all these methods is the root class for the entire GUI elements branch of the `java.awt package` hierarchy (refer back to Figure 9.6 in Chapter 9). When an AWT method requires a `Component` type parameter, what it really means is that it requires *any* subclass of class `Component`—a `Button`, a `Panel`, a `Container`, a `TextField`, a `Scrollbar`, and so on. This is perfectly analogous to the numerous Java methods that specify argument type `Object` when in fact they mean "any object type." In both cases these methods rely on the fact that subclasses of a particular superclass are considered compatible with that superclass. A `Button`, for example, essentially *is* a `Component`. Similarly a `String` *is* an `Object`.

Whenever you see type `Component` specified in an AWT method's signature, mentally substitute this type with any of these: `Button`, `Canvas`, `Checkbox`, `Choice`, `Container`, `Label`, `List`, `Panel`, `Scrollbar`, `TextArea`, or `TextField`.

Class `Container` is hiding silently in the above list of `Component` subclasses, which means a container can `add()` one or more subcontainers to itself, since `Container` is a subclass of `Component`! It is important that you grasp this nesting capability because it is used frequently and allows your GUI designs to be more modular, and therefore more flexible (in exactly the same way as black-box nesting applied to code makes your programs more modular and flexible). Having nested containers, each with their own layout style, gives you a powerful and flexible way to organize your GUI logically and aesthetically pleasing. When you explore layout managers later, bear in mind that rarely is one layout manager alone used to manage the layout for an entire GUI. Layout managers are almost always used in combination.

Now, take a look back at the three `add()` method variants. Your program used the first one to add some buttons to the applet. The second and third variants allow you to put components in specific spots by passing a position argument. To this end, the second `add()` needs a numerical position argument, the third `add()` takes the position as a string label.

To demonstrate the `add(comp, pos)` method, modify your simple applet so that it reads

```
add(new Button("First"));
add(new Button("Second"));
add(new Button("Third"));
add(new Button("Fourth"));
add(new Button("Fifth",2));    // << change here
```

If you run the applet, you will see that the order of the buttons has been changed to first, second, fifth, third, fourth. The extra 2 argument in the last add() inserted the fifth button in between the second and third buttons already added to the container.

Now that you understand the hows and whys of your applet's init() method, you can focus your attention on the five standard component layout styles the Abstract Windowing Toolkit gives us:

- FlowLayout

- BorderLayout

- CardLayout

- GridLayout

- GridBagLayout

FlowLayout

The FlowLayout layout manager is the simplest layout manager in AWT. As the name suggests, it lays out your GUI elements in a flowing, writing-like fashion, like a word processor arranges words in a paragraph. The exact behavior can be understood more intuitively by running the following program:

```
import java.awt.*;

class FlowingButtons {

public static void main (String[] args) {

Frame win = new Frame();

    win.setLayout( new FlowLayout() );
    win.resize(80,120);
    win.show();

    for (int i = 0; i< 15; i++) {
        win.add( new Button( Integer.toString(i) ) );
```

```
        win.validate();
        try {Thread.sleep(1500); }catch (Exception e) {};
        System.out.println(i);
    }

}} // End of main and class
```

Figure 10.3 shows the program's window when it is two-thirds of the way through its loop:

FIGURE 10.3:

A centering
`FlowLayout`

The program successively adds one button at a time and forces a redisplay of all the buttons so far. This way you can see exactly what effect the layout manager has on the size and location of the buttons.

This program is not an applet this time. It lacks the code hallmarks of an applet, so it must be an application (you can run it without having to use your web browser or the appletviewer utility). Like all applications, the program starts executing with its `main()` static method. Here you create a new window with the `Frame()` constructor. Then, you select the `FlowLayout` layout manager for this window, size the window to some initial dimensions, and order it to display itself.

TIP

The `setLayout()` should not confuse you now: It is still the same `Container setLayout()` method you saw earlier. And a `Frame` (like an `Applet`) is a subclass of `Container`, so it is perfectly entitled to invoke the method on itself, too. But since our example class does not subclass `Frame` (it explicitly creates a `Frame` instance), we have to invoke `setLayout()` on our window using the fully qualified `object.method()` notation.

Once the window is visible, the program enters a short loop which adds and displays increasing numbers of buttons. The `validate()` method indirectly invokes the layout manager for the window (that is, the `Container` for the buttons) and redisplays the result.

Our program used the simplest `FlowLayout` object constructor possible: the one taking no arguments. But FlowLayouts can be customized somewhat by specifying an optional alignment style and the minimum gaps to use between the components.

- `public FlowLayout(int align)`

- `public FlowLayout(int align, int hgap, int vgap)`

The alignment parameter should be one of these three `FlowLayout` class constants:

- `public final static int LEFT`

- `public final static int CENTER`

- `public final static int RIGHT`

The default constructor you have used so far is actually shorthand for `new FlowLayout(FlowLayout.CENTER)`. This is why the example program centered all buttons on each line. You can easily familiarize yourself with the predictable results of the two other alignment styles by substituting the `win.setLayout( new FlowLayout() )` line by `win.setLayout( new FlowLayout (FlowLayout.RIGHT) )` and again with `FlowLayout.LEFT`.

The third `FlowLayout` constructor lets you specify a *pixel* component spacing in both horizontal and vertical direction.

Be careful with any AWT features that let you specify in absolute terms either component positions, dimensions, or spacing. As we said before, AWT's way of positioning components is platform dependent. Using only *relative* positional and dimensional specifications for components and containers allows layout managers to produce acceptable GUI layouts on all platforms. From the moment when you start "descending" into absolutes, you might be improving the look of the GUI on your machine, but it will degrade or even corrupt the layout of the same GUI running on a different platform.

Unlike most classes you will use when writing Java programs, most layout manager classes are not called directly at all (apart from their various constructors). This makes them very simple to use. Using the `setLayout()` method, you just pick one of the existing managers and from then on the container will be managed by that layout manager. If you are curious about the internals of layout managers or think you need to write one yourself to use in your software productions, look at the section on "LayoutManagers Internals: Interface LayoutManager," later in the chapter.

Insets

One layout feature that is not a layout manager and yet affects all layout styles is called *insets*. Every container can define a border to be left clear of any components. This border is called the container's insets. If you look back at the definition for class `Container`, you'll see a method with the following signature:

```
public Insets insets()
```

The method is there to be overridden by your classes, and has to return an instance of an `Insets` object. Class `Insets` is very simple; here is its definition:

```
public class Insets extends Object implements Cloneable {
    public int top;
    public int left;
```

```
    public int bottom;
    public int right;
    public Insets(int top, int left, int bottom, int right);
    public String toString();
    public Object clone();
}
```

Since it doesn't have any instance methods to speak of, it is not much of a class—it is more of a pure data structure. The constructor for the `Insets` class takes four parameters that together specify the border to be left clear of components. This is illustrated in the following example of how insets affect the final layout of a container. Below is a Java application program which creates a window laid out using the `FlowLayout` style and using custom insets. Four different `insets()` methods are listed disabled. You should enable them one at a time (by taking away the double slash comments), compile, and run each version. Each `insets()` method accentuates insetting one edge at a time. Figure 10.4 shows the end results.

```
import java.awt.*;

//——————————————————————————————————————————————————————
class inset {

public static void main (String[] args) {

myFrame win = new myFrame();

    win.setLayout( new FlowLayout() );
    win.add( new Button("One") );
    win.add( new Button("Two") );
    win.add( new Button("Three") );
    win.add( new Button("Four") );
    win.pack();
    win.show();
    System.out.println( win.insets() );
}} // End of main and class

//——————————————————————————————————————————————————————
class myFrame extends Frame {

// public Insets insets() { return new Insets(100, 2,2,2); }
// public Insets insets() { return new Insets(25, 100, 2,2); }
```

```
// public Insets insets() { return new Insets(25,2, 100, 2); }
// public Insets insets() { return new Insets(25,2,2, 100); }

} // End of class
//————————————————————————————————————
```

FIGURE 10.4:

(a) Accentuated top inset; (b) accentuated left inset; (c) accentuated bottom inset; (d) accentuated right inset

(a)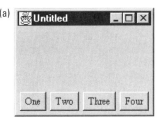

(b)

(c)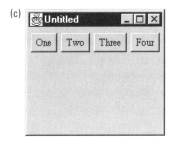

(d)

BorderLayout

The second layout manager is not quite as simple as FlowLayout. Class BorderLayout enforces a five-zone layout as depicted in Figure 10.5. The BorderLayout manager is the default layout manager for Frame and other containers except Panel. The zones reflect the typical distribution of components in and around a window.

The five zones in Figure 10.5 are in fact filled by exactly the same type of buttons as those used by the FlowLayout example.

FIGURE 10.5:

A `BorderLayout`

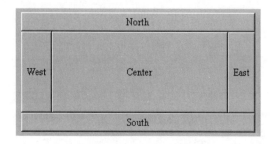

`BorderLayout`, as you can see, sizes its components so that they expand to fill the space available to them. Here is the program which created the output of Figure 10.5:

```java
import java.awt.*;

public class BorderLayoutTest extends java.applet.Applet {

    public void init() {

        setLayout(new BorderLayout());

        add("North",  new Button("North"));
        add("South",  new Button("South"));
        add("West",   new Button("West"));
        add("East",   new Button("East"));
        add("Center", new Button("Center"));

    }
}
```

The coding differences with the `FlowLayout` example lie, for one, with the selection of a `BorderLayout` layout by passing an instance of the `BorderLayout` class to `setLayout()`. Secondly, the `add()` method used when adding components to a container using a `BorderLayout` is not the simple `add(Component)` one. You need to use the labeled `add(String position, Component comp)` overloaded variant. As you can see clearly from the code, the position is indicated by name instead of by number. This makes the code much more readable.

NOTE

The class implementors could have used class constants like `BorderLayout.NORTH` to achieve the same readability without incurring the performance penalty resulting from using strings.

WARNING

`BorderLayout` relies on the position string being case-sensitive. Passing `NORTH` or `north` instead of `North` will not work. Moreover, the compiler has no way of enforcing this, so your code will compile without error messages if you do make case mistakes. The end result will be a very nasty bug which could take a while to track down.

A `BorderLayout` can only deal with five components to be laid out: four components located flush against the four edges of a container and one component located centrally and occupying the bulk of the container's surface area. When using a `BorderLayout` manager, you are not obliged to specify all five components. Figure 10.6 shows what `BorderLayout` does when the "Center" component is left out.

FIGURE 10.6:

A `BorderLayout` with its "Center" component missing

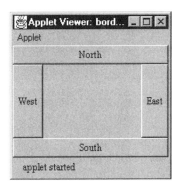

As you can see, the edge components do not grow to fill the void created by the missing center component. Only when one or more of the edge components is left out will the space vacated by those be used by other components. Although there are 32 (2^5) different `BorderLayout` component combinations, the subset shown in Figure 10.7 should suffice to give you an accurate feel for how `BorderLayout` manipulates components when not all five are specified.

FIGURE 10.7:

(a) A `BorderLayout` with its "North" component missing; (b) a `BorderLayout` with its "North" and "West" components missing; (c) a `BorderLayout` with its "East" component missing; (d) a `BorderLayout` with its "North", "South", "East", and "West" components missing; (e) a `BorderLayout` with "Center", "East", and "West" components missing

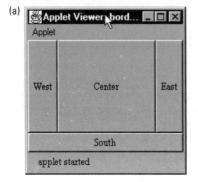

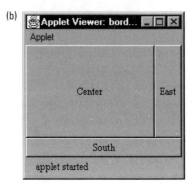

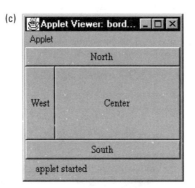

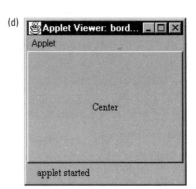

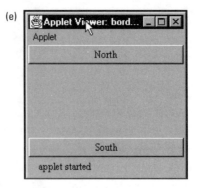

As with the `FlowLayout` layout manager, there is a variant of the `BorderLayout` constructor that allows you to specify additional horizontal and/or vertical spacing when the border layout is applied. Replace the `setLayout()` line with the following line to see which effects you can obtain:

```
setLayout(new BorderLayout(10,40));
```

Figure 10.8 shows the unattractive layout which results from this change. A ten-pixel spacing was inserted between horizontally separated components and a forty-pixel spacing was used to space the components vertically. See our (clearly justified) warning regarding the use of such absolute values in the "FlowLayout" section earlier in the chapter.

FIGURE 10.8:

An ugly `BorderLayout` obtained by specifying absolute spacing

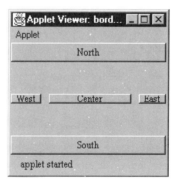

TIP

Problematic layouts like the one in Figure 10.8 can be avoided by not relying on absolute distances or dimensions within your GUI designs. For GUIs that use a `Frame` as container, you normally call `pack()` just before displaying the window. This `pack()` method (defined in class `Window`) does a full layout of the `Frame`, using the components' preferred sizes as guidelines for the layout process.

CardLayout

The CardLayout layout manager is not really a layout manager as such. What it does is let you define any number of "cards" containing, typically, a logically related collection of components. Figure 10.9 shows you a typical card-based configuration window (which wasn't implemented using Java).

FIGURE 10.9:

A typical card-based GUI

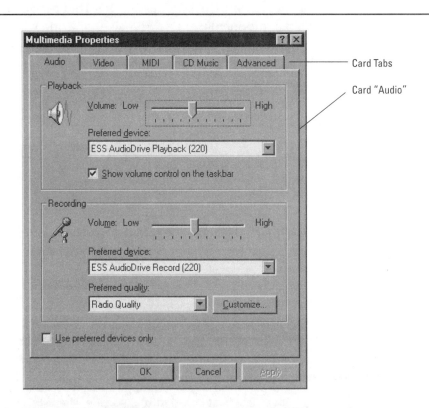

Card Tabs

Card "Audio"

TIP   Other GUI frameworks use the terms *page* or *sheet* instead of card.

The following program demonstrates the use of CardLayout with five cards containing a single button each.

```
import java.awt.*;

public class Cards extends java.applet.Applet {

CardLayout layout;

public void init() {
    layout = new CardLayout();
    setLayout(layout);
    add("1", new Button("Card 1 Button"));
    add("2", new Button("Card 2 Button"));
    add("3", new Button("Card 3 Button"));
    add("4", new Button("Card 4 Button"));
    add("5", new Button("Card 5 Button"));
}

public boolean keyDown(Event e, int key) {
    layout.next(this);
    return true;
}}
```

Notice the add() method used to add cards to a CardLayout. As with border layouts, you have to use the labeled variety to pass a card name (in addition to the card itself) to the layout manager. Later, you can refer to your cards by name, instead of indexed by number, for example. Also note that a CardLayout variable was created. In the previous layout manager examples, you simply had a new X() within the brackets of the setLayout() call. But in this example, you actually need to refer to your CardLayout object after you have created it—this is why you need the variable to keep a reference to it.

To demonstrate the ability to cycle through the cards, this applet was made to listen to the keyboard and select the next card whenever you press a key. Since event handling will be discussed in detail in Chapter 12, no further explanation of the keyDown() method will be given. The only thing that is relevant at this point is the invocation of the next() method on your CardLayout object. This commands it to show the next card under its control. When it reaches the last card and you ask it to show the next() card again, it simply cycles back to the beginning.

> **NOTE**
>
> The cards in this example were defined as being single buttons. In practice, however, you will rarely have single components representing an entire card in a `CardLayout`. You will typically add a group of components which have been prepared as a subclass of `Panel`. You would add the whole `Panel` in one go (since a `Panel` can stand for a `Component`). This way the cards themselves will be little sub-GUIs with their own layouts.

Figure 10.10 shows the applet produced by the program.

FIGURE 10.10:

`CardLayout`'s default layout

Undoubtedly, you expected to see a full-fledged bells-and-whistles-included rendering of our five different cards (as in Figure 10.9), *including* the clickable tabs to select any one of the cards. Unfortunately `CardLayout` does not do this for you. You have to implement the tabs and the card outlines yourself. At this stage, you do not know how `LayoutManager` classes work internally, so you will have to wait before you can implement an enhanced `TabCardLayout` layout manager that will more closely meet your original expectations. At this stage though, you can already implement an interim solution that combines the three layout managers you already know about: `FlowLayout`, `BorderLayout`, and no-bells-or-whistles `CardLayout`. Even though such a program relies on a little bit of button event handling to detect a card tab selection, here is a possible solution to console your frustration with CardLayout's "standard inadequacy":

```java
import java.awt.*;

public class Tabs extends java.applet.Applet {

public void init() {

TabCards cards = new TabCards();

    cards.addCard("Card 1", new Button("Card 1 Button"));
    cards.addCard("Card 2", new Button("Card 2 Button"));
    cards.addCard("Card 3", new Button("Card 3 Button"));
    cards.addCard("Card 4", new Button("Card 4 Button"));
    add(cards);
}}

//———————————————————————————————————————————————————————————————

// Class TabCards implements a "TabControl" using standard buttons
// for the "tabs"

class TabCards extends Panel {

private Panel tabStrip;        // a container Panel to hold the tabs
private Panel cardDeck;        // a container Panel to hold the cards
private CardLayout cardLayout; // the layout manager used by our cardDeck

TabCards() {

    setLayout(new BorderLayout() );        // Panel divided North and Center

    tabStrip = new Panel();
    cardDeck = new Panel();

    tabStrip.setLayout(new FlowLayout() );  // tabs use simple FlowLayout
    cardLayout = new CardLayout();
    cardDeck.setLayout(cardLayout);         // cards use CardLayout of course

    add("North" , tabStrip);                // tabs occupy top area
    add("Center", cardDeck);                // cards can have the rest
}

// addCard() is the method you call to add cards to a TabCards object.
// The comp argument would usually be an entire Panel full of GUI elements

void addCard( String cardname, Component comp) {

    tabStrip.add(new Button(cardname));
    cardDeck.add(cardname, comp);
}
```

```
// The action() method for TabCards captures the tab button selections
// and changes the currently shown card to reflect the chosen tab

public boolean action(Event e, Object arg) {
    cardLayout.show(cardDeck, (String) arg);
    return true;
}} // End of Class TabCards
```

The aesthetically less-than-stunning result of our poor man's TabCards component is shown in Figure 10.11.

FIGURE 10.11:

Class TabCards for tab control component prototyping

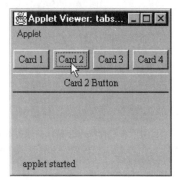

The TabCards class is by no means meant to be used for production quality code. But the class is fine for prototyping applications that need to rely on tab controls. By the time your application nears completion, you can either see if a new release of the Abstract Windowing Toolkit supports fully rendered tab controls, or write a "deluxe" version of class TabCards that renders tabs that look like tabs and card outlines in the de facto 3-D style.

Unlike FlowLayout and BorderLayout, class CardLayout does have some user-callable methods. You have already seen two of its methods: next() and show(). Here is the complete definition of the class:

```
public class CardLayout extends Object implements LayoutManager {

    public CardLayout();
```

```
    public CardLayout(int hgap, int vgap);

    public void addLayoutComponent(String name, Component comp);
    public void removeLayoutComponent(Component comp);
    public Dimension preferredLayoutSize(Container parent);
    public Dimension minimumLayoutSize(Container parent);
    public void layoutContainer(Container parent);
    public void first(Container parent);
    public void next(Container parent);
    public void previous(Container parent);
    public void last(Container parent);
    public void show(Container parent, String name);
    public String toString();
}
```

The methods of interest are `first()`, `last()`, `next()`, `previous()`, and `show()`. All other methods are the internal layout manager methods that you will only look at when you investigate layout manager internals, after having studied two more standard AWT layout managers. The `first()`, `last()`, `next()`, and `previous()` methods simply select the card indicated by the name of the method. The `show()` method is more interesting: It allows you to show any card directly by specifying its name. You had to use this method when receiving a button click within your new `TabCards` component to switch to any card.

GridLayout

The `GridLayout` layout manager enforces a grid-based layout on components.

Here is the program that produced the applet in Figure 10.12 :

```
import java.awt.*;

public class GridLayoutTest extends java.applet.Applet {

    public void init() {

        setLayout(new GridLayout(3,2));
```

FIGURE 10.12:

A GridLayout

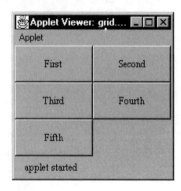

```
            add(new Button("First"));
            add(new Button("Second"));
            add(new Button("Third"));
            add(new Button("Fourth"));
            add(new Button("Fifth"));
        }
    }
```

You specify the number of grid rows and columns to the constructor for class GridLayout. In this example, three rows and two
columns were used. Again, five test buttons were added using the
default add(component) method. Notice in which order the buttons
end up laid out—the linear adding sequence is used to fill the rows
top to bottom. If this implicit ordering is not good enough, you can
use the second Container add() method, which takes an additional
single numerical position argument. If you change the five add()s to
use this explicit positioning as follows:

```
add(new Button("First"), 0);
add(new Button("Second"), 1);
add(new Button("Third"), 2);
add(new Button("Fourth"), 3);
add(new Button("Fifth"), 4);
```

you should see that the resulting layout is exactly the same as in
Figure 10.12. In other words, you have decoupled the adding order
from the positioning.

When Implementation Interferes with Interface

Unfortunately, this decoupling cannot be taken to its logical extreme by, for example, coding a button layout using a jumbled up sequence like this:

```
add(new Button("Fifth"), 4);
add(new Button("Second"), 1);
add(new Button("Third"), 2);
add(new Button("Fourth"), 3);
add(new Button("First"), 0);
```

The first `add()` will throw an `IllegalArgumentException("illegal component position")` exception. This is because the semantics of the `add()` method is to *insert* a component at the given position. Internally, class `Container` uses an array, and as you know, you cannot index array elements beyond the end of the array. So in trying to avoid an `ArrayIndexOutOfBounds` exception, the `Container` code checks to see whether the component can be safely inserted at the given position specified. It would have been much more intuitive for this method to have the semantics of simply *placing* a component at a given position (namely, overwriting the array element) and growing the array automatically if positions are specified beyond the end of the array.

When implementation details like these affect the use of a class in such a counterproductive way, then this is a sure sign of poor design and should prompt a reworking of the semantics. The design of the component management inside class `Container` should allow a jumbled up sequence of `add()`s to add its components without making a fuss at all.

Because grid cells are usually specified using two-dimensional grid coordinates instead of one linear, one-dimensional coordinate, you are probably wondering why you have not seen an `add(component,` x, y) method. The answer is rather subtle: All these add()s are not methods belonging to any layout managers, but instead are defined in class Container. This is because the add()s *primarily* add components to a container. The laying out process is not yet relevant at this stage of adding components—it usually happens much later, right before the GUI is displayed, as a result of a display command. Unfortunately, then, there is no two-dimensional add(component, x, y) method.

The GridLayout manager was no doubt added to AWT quite a bit later than when class Container was designed and specified. So it wasn't anticipated that some future layout manager would like to have a two-dimensional add(). This oversight can be understood if you consider that, as mentioned before, class Container uses a one-dimensional array to hold all the components it manages. In that light, it would indeed have been uncommon for a programmer to think ahead and imagine a future requirement for an add() with two-dimensional position coordinates. This and other limitations of the GridLayout manager become irrelevant if instead you use the more flexible (and more difficult) GridBagLayout manager, explained in the next section.

GridBagLayout and GridBagConstraints

The topic of component dimensions resulting from the layout process has yet to be broached. All of the examples used to show off the different layout managers so far simply used buttons that had not been asked to appear drawn to any set size. Before inspecting the last and most complex standard layout manager, class GridBagLayout, you first should learn a bit about component sizes.

Every Component can give hints to layout managers as to how big or small they would *like* to appear in the GUI. Two sizes can be explicitly specified—a preferred size and a minimum size. To specify these for your components, you need to create a subclass of the generic component class (`Button`, `List`, `TextField`, and so on) and override the following two `Component` methods:

```
public class Component extends Object implements ImageObserver {
    :
    :
   public Dimension preferredSize();
   public Dimension minimumSize();
    :
    :
}
```

NOTE   Class `Component`'s two-page definition is listed in full in Chapter 11.

Because there is no way to specify these size hints for non-subclassed components, the use of these two methods is avoided altogether in the previous examples. Doing otherwise would have meant creating `Button` subclasses in all of the layout manager examples, and that would have detracted your attention from the core layout manager issues. In real-life applets and applications, however, windows and their contents can be resized (unless you take explicit steps to force a window of fixed size). But when a user shrinks your window, there is going to be a point where simply linearly scaling every component accordingly will result in either an ugly or a plainly non-functional GUI. Similarly, when a user stretches your windows, a point may be reached where your components scaled up proportionally will look ridiculous. Methods `preferredSize()` and `minimumSize()` help layout managers size your components so that the end result of any window resizing operation remains acceptable.

If you rerun the `GridLayout` demos using the JDK tool appletviewer and play around with the applet window size, you will see that the five buttons can be stretched or shrunk to very extreme sizes. You can counter this flexibility overkill by creating `Button` subclasses that specify some reasonable sizes using `preferredSize()` and `minimumSize()`, and using a layout manager that honors these hints, like `GridBagLayout` (`GridLayout` does not). The way this is done is by overriding the methods, for example:

```
public Dimension preferredSize() {
      return new Dimension(200,150);
}
```

If this overridden method were included in any `Component` subclass you created, it would tell any layout manager that this component's preferred dimensions are 200×150 pixels.

> **NOTE**
>
> Due to `GridBagLayout`'s extensive flexibility, a full and detailed exposé of this layout manager's functionality would consume a lot of space. Accordingly, the discussion that follows unfortunately gives only an overview of the functionality of the class. Consult online documentation for the full picture—or better still, experiment with every aspect of the layout manager.

`GridBagLayout` is special among the standard layout managers in that it uses a helper class (`GridBagConstraints`) to specify a whole host of layout parameters, normally one class instance per component. `GridBagLayout`'s main (but by no means only) added value above what `GridLayout` provided, is the possibility to have a component use up more than one grid cell. A component's size can be specified as the number of horizontal and/or vertical grid cells the component ought to occupy on the grid. These parameters are controlled by the helper `GridBagConstraints` class, so here is its definition:

```
public class GridBagConstraints extends Object implements Cloneable {
     public final static int RELATIVE;
     public final static int REMAINDER;
     public final static int NONE;
     public final static int BOTH;
     public final static int HORIZONTAL;
     public final static int VERTICAL;
     public final static int CENTER;
     public final static int NORTH;
     public final static int NORTHEAST;
     public final static int EAST;
     public final static int SOUTHEAST;
     public final static int SOUTH;
```

```
public final static int SOUTHWEST;
public final static int WEST;
public final static int NORTHWEST;

public int gridx;
public int gridy;
public int gridwidth;
public int gridheight;
public double weightx;
public double weighty;
public int anchor;
public int fill;
public Insets insets;
public int ipadx;
public int ipady;
public GridBagConstraints();
public Object clone();
}
```

This class consists essentially of instance variables and a collection of class constants (it also has a constructor and an overridden implementation of the `Object clone()` method, the latter of which we shall come back to a bit later).

Enumeration Types and Java

If you look at the list of `GridBagConstraints` class constants, you can really appreciate the problem of Java's unfortunate and remarkable *lack* of enumerated types support. Every constant is typed as a thoroughly nondescriptive `int`, whereas a Pascal type declaration for the same would be infinitely more readable:

```
TYPE
    FillBehavior = {NONE, HORIZONTAL, VERTICAL, BOTH};
    AnchorType   = {CENTER, NORTH, NORTHEAST, EAST, SOUTHEAST,
    ➡SOUTH, SOUTH WEST, WEST, NORTHWEST}
VAR
    fill : FillBehavior;
    anchor : AnchorType;
```

The most important `GridBagConstraints` fields are `gridx`, `gridy`, `gridwidth`, and `gridheight`. These control a component's placement and size on the grid. Unlike with the one-dimensional placement limitations of the `add()` method for components added to a `GridLayout`, the `gridx` and `gridy` fields do allow you to specify `GridBagLayout` components in any order and in two dimensions.

Figure 10.13 shows an example `GridBagLayout` that clearly demonstrates the additional possibilities the class provides over classes `FlowLayout` and `GridLayout`.

FIGURE 10.13:

A `GridBagLayout`

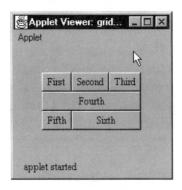

Here is the program that produced the GUI layout in Figure 10.13:

```
import java.awt.*;

public class Gridbag extends java.applet.Applet {

public void init() {

GridBagLayout        gb = new GridBagLayout();
GridBagConstraints gbc = new GridBagConstraints();
Button b;

setLayout(gb);

gbc.gridwidth  = 1;
gbc.gridheight = 1;
gbc.gridx = 0;
gbc.gridy = 0;
```

```
gbc.fill = GridBagConstraints.HORIZONTAL;

b = new Button("First");
gb.setConstraints(b, gbc);
add(b);

b = new Button("Second");
gbc.gridx = 1;
gbc.gridwidth = 2;
gb.setConstraints(b, gbc);
add(b);

b = new Button("Third");
gbc.gridx = 3;
gbc.gridwidth = GridBagConstraints.REMAINDER;
gb.setConstraints(b, gbc);
add(b);

b = new Button("Fourth");
gbc.gridy++;
gbc.gridx = 0;
gb.setConstraints(b, gbc);
add(b);

b = new Button("Fifth");
gbc.gridwidth = 1;
gbc.gridy++;
gb.setConstraints(b, gbc);
add(b);

b = new Button("Sixth");
gbc.gridwidth = GridBagConstraints.REMAINDER;
gbc.gridx = 1;
gb.setConstraints(b, gbc);
add(b);

}}
```

This applet's `init()` method begins by creating one new `GridBagLayout` object and one helper `GridBagConstraints` object. After setting the current layout to `GridBagLayout`, the code initializes initial "constraint" parameters for the first object to be added. This is done by filling in `GridBagConstraints` fields. You set the width and height to 1 cell and start adding components in the top left-hand corner of the grid (grid coordinates 0,0). The next line sets the fill style for the components. This determines how a component will fill the available space if that space allows it to stretch beyond its `preferredSize()`. The legal values for the fill variable are NONE, HORIZONTAL, VERTICAL, and BOTH. You then associate these layout parameters with your component by calling the `setConstraints()` method. You can then `add()` your component as usual.

To summarize, adding a component to a `GridBagLayout`-styled container consists of these three steps:

1. Set any desired `GridBagConstraints` parameters.

2. Invoke the `setConstraints()` method on the layout manager.

3. Invoke the usual `add()` method to add the component to the container.

Regarding the first step, there is an interesting subplot going on in the example code. First, you initialize some of the `GridBagConstraints` object's fields, and then you call the `setConstraints(Component comp, GridBagConstraints gbc)` method for the first button. This lets the `GridBagLayout` manager bind the first button with the `GridBagConstraints` object as defined at that point. You then proceed to modify some of the `GridBagConstraints` values and call `setConstraints()` again to bind the second button with your *same* but modified `GridBagConstraints` object (you only have one instance for the entire program). You just changed its `gridx` and `gridwidth` instance variables, but left the `gridy` and `gridheight` variables alone. This means you have just clobbered half of the `GridBagConstraints` parameters for button one.

Remember that Java objects are passed by reference and not by value (that is, copied). Should you therefore not have had to create a new `GridBagConstraints` object for each button? Normally, yes, but in this exceptional case, no. The reason lies hidden inside the `GridBagLayout` class itself. Method `setConstraints()` uses the `clone()` method to make a *copy* of the `GridBagConstraints` objects given to it. And this is why you can safely use a single `GridBag Constraints` object instance for any number of components.

The `clone()` method is available only on classes that implement the `Cloneable` interface. If you check back at the definition of `GridBagConstraints`, you will see that this class does just that. Since very few classes do implement this interface, this type of object "pass by value" feature is very rare in Java. The norm is that method arguments let your objects have full (shared) access to the passed object, and thus the programming technique used in our example would be quite incorrect. In this instance, however, it has become a Java idiom, so you can improve readability of code sections dealing with `GridBagLayout` managers by exploiting the object cloning behavior.

There is one more `GridBagConstraints` parameter to be introduced. To see its effect, recompile and run the applet with the following line removed:

```
gbc.fill = GridBagConstraints.HORIZONTAL;
```

Figure 10.14 shows the resulting `GridBagLayout`.

FIGURE 10.14:

A `GridBagLayout` with
`fill = NONE`

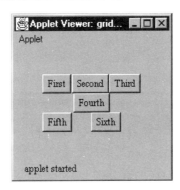

The reason why the layout suddenly looks very un-gridlike (if you look closely, the Fourth and Sixth buttons are not aligned to any grid), is because of that other `GridBagConstraints` parameter—anchor. Without an explicit value for the fill parameter, you simply get its default: NONE. This means that any components will be sized to their `preferredSize()` (if possible). The odd-looking placement of buttons four and six is because the default anchor style is now affecting their position. And the default anchoring style CENTERs components within the grid space they allocated using `gridwidth` and `gridheight`. If you now add the following line (where we used to set the fill style), then you should obtain the result shown in Figure 10.15.

```
gbc.anchor = GridBagConstraints.NORTHWEST;
```

The valid values for the anchor parameter are: CENTER, NORTH, EAST, NORTHEAST, SOUTHEAST, SOUTH, SOUTHWEST, WEST, and NORTHWEST.

WARNING

These class constants, like all class constants, are also case sensitive, like the `BorderLayout` orientations are. Confusingly, the `GridBagConstraints` constants use a different capitalization convention from that used by `BorderLayout`: all uppercase instead of first-letter capitalization only. This is a sure way to mix the two styles up, and if Murphy's Law is indeed a law, mix them up at the most inappropriate times. There is one small facet that reduces the gravity of this constants-naming flaw, and this is that your Java compiler will generate errors when you make any mistakes with `GridBagConstraints` constants (because they are not hidden in Strings).

NOTE

In this example, the NORTH aspect of the NORTHWEST anchoring is effectively unused. Buttons four and six simply got pushed due WEST. This is because none of the components can move up or down within their grid size allocations (they are all one cell tall). If you make some components taller (gridheight is greater than one) and experiment with the anchor parameter, you will clearly see the components move about in their "mooring" spaces according to the anchor style used.

FIGURE 10.15:

A GridBagLayout with
fill set to NONE and
anchor set to NORTHWEST

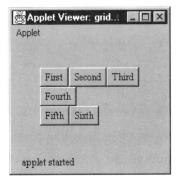

This concludes your look at the standard AWT layout managers. As promised, you will now explore the innards of layout managers by studying what all layout managers have in common.

LayoutManagers Internals: Interface LayoutManager

Layout managers are powerful black boxes to help you design GUIs rapidly. But what if you wanted to write your own? If you look up the (online) class definition for any of FlowLayout, BorderLayout, CardLayout, GridLayout, or GridBagLayout, you will see that these classes all implement the same interface: interface LayoutManager. This interface is the key to understanding layout manager internals. Here is its definition:

```
public interface LayoutManager extends Object {
    public abstract void addLayoutComponent(String name, Component comp);
    public abstract void removeLayoutComponent(Component comp);
    public abstract Dimension preferredLayoutSize(Container parent);
    public abstract Dimension minimumLayoutSize(Container parent);
    public abstract void layoutContainer(Container parent);
}
```

The methods the interface asks you to implement can be grouped into three groups:

- Adding/removing components to a container

- Calculating preferred and minimum container sizes

- Actually doing the layout operation

At first sight, you might think that the addLayoutComponent() method is a direct analog of the add() container methods. This is only partially correct. A layout manager's addLayoutComponent() method is only called by a container's add(String, Component) method and *not* by the simpler add(Component) method. Layout managers FlowLayout, GridLayout, and GridBagLayout implement their addLayoutComponent() methods as follows:

```
public void addLayoutComponent(String name, Component comp) {
}
```

That's right—a void body. These managers don't manage the growing collection of components added to their associated container, because they don't need to. The container object keeps track of all the components it contains (that is its primary function, after all). And when layoutContainer() is called, the layout manager receives a handle to the container it should lay out. Via this handle, the layout manager can access all of the container's components, in sequence, with the Container methods countComponents() and getComponent(). This is how some layout managers can afford to have empty add- and removeLayoutComponent() methods. But this is not universal. Layout managers BorderLayout and CardLayout have non-empty bodies for these methods, because these two layout managers use the second type of Container add: add(String, Component). While the unlabeled add() essentially just adds a component to the container's internal list, the labeled `add()` is very different, as you can judge from its default implementation in class `Container`:

```
public synchronized Component add(String name, Component comp) {
    Component c = add(comp);
    LayoutManager layoutMgr = this.layoutMgr;
    if (layoutMgr != null) {
        layoutMgr.addLayoutComponent(name, comp);
    }
    return c;
}
```

The first line of the method still `add()`s the component to the container, but the remainder of the method then proceeds to *also* add the component to the container's layout manager. Therefore, when designing a custom layout manager, you should start by deciding which "type" of layout manager to use—the simple type that relies on the container's list of components alone, or the more complex type which needs to manage, in parallel, the same list of components on its own. The second approach need not be much harder to implement: keeping track of components might simply mean storing them into a `Vector` for future reference, until the container calls its `layout()` method. What happens behind the scenes at this point can be seen from `layout()`'s default implementation in class `Container`:

```
public synchronized void layout() {
    LayoutManager layoutMgr = this.layoutMgr;
    if (layoutMgr != null) {
        layoutMgr.layoutContainer(this);
    }
}
```

Method `layoutContainer()` is really the heart of any layout manager. No layout manager can afford to have it have a void body because `layoutContainer()` is where all the laying out finally takes place. Here the layout manager will use the container's insets settings and all the components' preferred sizes to determine exactly how to size and position each component.

Here is a concrete example of a `layoutContainer()` method; this is `BorderLayout`'s `layoutContainer()`:

```
public void layoutContainer(Container target) {
    Insets insets = target.insets();
    int top = insets.top;
    int bottom = target.height - insets.bottom;
    int left = insets.left;
    int right = target.width - insets.right;

    if ((north != null) && north.visible) {
        north.resize(right - left, north.height);
        Dimension d = north.preferredSize();
        north.reshape(left, top, right - left, d.height);
        top += d.height + vgap;
    }
    if ((south != null) && south.visible) {
        south.resize(right - left, south.height);
        Dimension d = south.preferredSize();
        south.reshape(left, bottom - d.height, right - left, d.height);
        bottom -= d.height + vgap;
    }
    if ((east != null) && east.visible) {
        east.resize(east.width, bottom - top);
        Dimension d = east.preferredSize();
        east.reshape(right - d.width, top, d.width, bottom - top);
        right -= d.width + hgap;
    }
    if ((west != null) && west.visible) {
        west.resize(west.width, bottom - top);
        Dimension d = west.preferredSize();
        west.reshape(left, top, d.width, bottom - top);
        left += d.width + hgap;
    }
    if ((center != null) && center.visible) {
        center.reshape(left, top, right - left, bottom - top);
    }
}
```

`BorderLayout` starts by determining the available working area by subtracting the insets from the container's dimensions. It then proceeds to lay out its five possible components; `north`, `south`, `east`, `west`, and `center`, in that sequence. Remember that `BorderLayout` components have to be `add()`ed using the labeled add, `add(String, Component)`. `BorderLayout` therefore manages its "list" of components by storing each component directly into its private variables north, south, east, west, and center (this is done by its addLayout-Component() method). The actual layout logic is of course totally manager dependent. What all managers need to have in common, though, is to use the preferred size of components to make their layout decisions. Components are eventually positioned and sized using their reshape() method.

Then there are the other two LayoutManager methods:

```
public abstract Dimension preferredLayoutSize(Container parent)
public abstract Dimension minimumLayoutSize(Container parent)
```

These two are in fact very similar to layoutContainer(), except that they do not actually lay out the components for real. Their goal is to work out what the size of the container *could* be set to if a layout was done honoring all components' preferred, respectively, minimum sizes. The logic for these two methods is virtually identical to that of layoutContainer(), bar the reshape() calls. Additionally, method minimumLayoutSize() calls the minimumSize() method on components instead.

Summary

This chapter taught you the absolute basics of how to use the Abstract Windowing Toolkit (AWT). You saw that there are two fundamentally different contexts in which the AWT can be used: applets and applications. Applets are bound to the applet-browser protocol, while applications need to build their GUIs from scratch, starting with a window to hold the GUI. You then studied Java's solution to platform-independent GUI designing: layout managers.

Layout managers are responsible for laying out your GUI's graphical elements in such a way that the resulting windows or screens look acceptable on all Java platforms. Layout managers interact closely with container classes (all descendants of class Container), for which they perform the layout function, and with component classes (all descendants of class Component), which are the objects being laid out. The AWT currently provides five different preprogrammed layout styles, that, when used in concert, offer enough layout flexibility to create modern, functional, and—last but not least—platform-independent GUIs. The preprogrammed layout managers are, in increasing order of complexity, FlowLayout, GridLayout, BorderLayout, CardLayout, and GridBagLayout, which relies on a helper class called GridBagConstraints.

For those rare occasions when the standard AWT layout managers lack in creative possibilities, you looked at how layout managers themselves are implemented, with a view on designing your own. Essentially, and regardless of layout approach, the sole requirement for any layout manager class is that it implements the LayoutManager interface.

CHAPTER
ELEVEN

11

AWT GUI Components

- About AWT Components

- Superclass Component

- Standard AWT Components

- Menu-Support Components

Modern GUIs are very rich in the type of graphical elements employed to make the human-computer interface (HCI) as productive as possible. Buttons and menus are still the ubiquitous and original classics, but nowadays we have a whole collection of evolutionary descendants. The spectrum of popular buttons and menus ranges from

- Radio buttons

- Pop-up menus

- Slider controls

to the more complex agglomerates like

- Listviews

- Treeviews

- Toolbars

- Install progress status window

Java's Abstract Windowing Toolkit only contains a healthy mix of the simpler components. The complex components, which allow you to produce the professional-looking applications everyone has come to expect these days, were unfortunately not provided at the time this book was written. Bear in mind that Java is a very recent development and that it breaks new ground in several areas, including Graphical User Interface design and implementation. Therefore, the supported components and their encapsulating classes cannot be as mature and complete as, say, the Macintosh GUI toolkit, which has had more than a decade to evolve and perfect itself. With the current speed at which all things Java evolve, AWT's immaturity may have already been addressed by the time you read this—by Sun or by a third party establishing a de facto standard.

In the meantime, the standard AWT components you will examine in this chapter are

- `Button` (shown in Figure 11.1)

- `Canvas` (shown in Figure 11.2)

- `Label` (shown in Figure 11.3)

- `Checkbox` (shown in Figures 11.4 and 11.5)

- `Choice` (shown in Figures 11.6a and 11.6b)

- `List` (shown in Figure 11.7)

- `Scrollbar` (shown in Figure 11.8)

- `TextField` (shown in Figure 11.11)

- `TextArea` (shown in Figures 11.9 and 11.10)

In terms of menu support, these components will also be examined:

- `MenuBar` (shown in Figure 11.12)

- `Menu` (shown in Figure 11.12)

- `MenuItem` (shown in Figure 11.12)

- `CheckboxMenuItem` (shown in Figure 11.12)

All of the above components are accessed and used via corresponding AWT classes, which are the focus of the remainder of this chapter. Before systematically exploring the listed components, you will want to take a close look at the granddad of all components (except menus): class `Component`, itself.

Superclass Component

Do GUI elements have anything in common? You could say that—they actually have *lots* in common. And when classes have things in common you immediately think "abstraction." Object-oriented methodology demands there be a superclass to any group of classes with identifiable, shared characteristics. A *superclass* localizes code and/or data structures that would otherwise be duplicated and scattered around your systems (negatively affecting code robustness and flexibility). The AWT GUI classes have one such superclass: class Component.

Here is what every component is supposed to have in common with every other AWT component:

```
public class Component extends Object implements ImageObserver {

  // event related
  public void deliverEvent(Event e);
  public boolean postEvent(Event e);
  public boolean handleEvent(Event evt);
  public boolean mouseDown(Event evt, int x, int y);
  public boolean mouseDrag(Event evt, int x, int y);
  public boolean mouseUp(Event evt, int x, int y);
  public boolean mouseMove(Event evt, int x, int y);
  public boolean mouseEnter(Event evt, int x, int y);
  public boolean mouseExit(Event evt, int x, int y);
  public boolean keyDown(Event evt, int key);
  public boolean keyUp(Event evt, int key);
  public boolean action(Event evt, Object what);
  public boolean gotFocus(Event evt, Object what);
  public boolean lostFocus(Event evt, Object what);
  public void requestFocus();
  public void nextFocus();

  // moving/sizing related
  public void move(int x, int y);
  public void resize(int width, int height);
  public void resize(Dimension d);
  public synchronized void reshape(int x, int y, int width, int height);
```

```
// position/geometry related
public Point location();
public synchronized boolean inside(int x, int y);
public Dimension size();
public Rectangle bounds();

// graphics/rendering related
public Graphics getGraphics();
public synchronized ColorModel getColorModel();
public Font getFont();
public synchronized void setFont(Font f);
public FontMetrics getFontMetrics(Font font);
public Color getForeground();
public synchronized void setForeground(Color c);
public Color getBackground();
public synchronized void setBackground(Color c);
public Toolkit getToolkit();

// layout manager related
public Dimension preferredSize();
public Dimension minimumSize();
public void layout();

// self painting related
public void paint(Graphics g);
public void update(Graphics g);
public void paintAll(Graphics g);
public void repaint();
public void repaint(long tm);
public void repaint(int x, int y, int width, int height);
public void repaint(long tm, int x, int y, int width, int height);
public void print(Graphics g);
public void printAll(Graphics g);

// parent/sub-components related
public Container getParent();
public Component locate(int x, int y);

// state changing methods
public synchronized void enable();
public void enable(boolean cond);
public synchronized void disable();
public synchronized void show();
public void show(boolean cond);
public synchronized void hide();
public void validate();
public void invalidate();
```

```
// state querying functions
public boolean isValid();
public boolean isVisible();
public boolean isShowing();
public boolean isEnabled();

// Image related methods
public boolean imageUpdate(Image img, int flags, int x, int y, int w, int h);
public Image createImage(ImageProducer producer);
public Image createImage(int width, int height);
public boolean prepareImage(Image image, ImageObserver observer);
public boolean prepareImage(Image image, int width, int height, ImageObserver
    observer);
public int checkImage(Image image, ImageObserver observer);
public int checkImage(Image image, int width, int height, ImageObserver observer);

// component peer related methods
public ComponentPeer getPeer();
public void addNotify();
public synchronized void removeNotify();

protected String paramString();
public String toString();
public void list();
public void list(PrintStream out);
public void list(PrintStream out, int indent);
}
```

Rather a long and intimidating collection of methods, isn't it? This is because AWT components are complex and multifaceted in terms of possible behavior.

> **NOTE**
>
> For every AWT component class described, the complete class definition will be listed "for the record." This is to help you recognize which methods belong to which classes. Unfortunately, space limitations mean that no systematic explanations can be given with these definitions. Even a condensed study of every class method would be well beyond the scope of this book. You may wish to consult an upcoming reference to the Java API, *The Java Class Hierarchy* (Sybex, 1997), for more in-depth coverage once you have mastered the material in this volume.

Although class Component is huge, very few of its methods are actually used frequently by the vast majority of programs. Having said that, class `Component` is so fundamental to Java AWT programming that a study of its method groups is in order. The rest of the section will explore these method groups. The important thing to keep in mind throughout the following discussions is that *any* component (that is, all of the descendant classes of `Component`) will support *all* of these methods.

> **NOTE**
> You might have noticed that class `Component` implements the interface `ImageObserver`. This interface is just a very small facet of the class: It only specifies a single method, `imageUpdate()`, to be implemented. The function of this method and the relevance of all components being `ImageObservers` will be explained in Chapter 13.

Event-Handling Methods

The most important group of Component methods by far are those relating to event handling:

```
public boolean handleEvent(Event evt);
public boolean action(Event evt, Object what);
public boolean mouseDown(Event evt, int x, int y);
public boolean mouseDrag(Event evt, int x, int y);
public boolean mouseUp(Event evt, int x, int y);
public boolean mouseMove(Event evt, int x, int y);
public boolean mouseEnter(Event evt, int x, int y);
public boolean mouseExit(Event evt, int x, int y);
public boolean keyDown(Event evt, int key);
public boolean keyUp(Event evt, int key);
public boolean gotFocus(Event evt, Object what);
public boolean lostFocus(Event evt, Object what);
public void requestFocus();
public void nextFocus();
```

Within this list, the most important methods are the `action()` and `keyUp()` and `keyDown()` methods. The `action()` method is used to trap any GUI events, like button clicks, radio button changes, or

`Choice` selections. The key event methods are used to listen to the user's keyboard or trap `TextComponent` events. The mouse-related methods are used less, since the AWT itself first interprets all mouse events and transforms them into GUI events, when applicable. Any "leftover" mouse activity that does not relate to the GUI gets passed to the mouse event methods, which an application may then process itself (a typical example of this is in painting programs).

NOTE
Aspects of the platform-independent AWT event model have been criticized by the growing Java programmer community. This is mainly because of behavioral discrepancies of Java programs when run on different machines. As a result, it is possible (and desirable) that Sun will have made some minor modifications to this model by the time you read this.

Component Moving and Resizing Methods

```
public void move(int x, int y);
public void resize(int width, int height);
public void resize(Dimension d);
public synchronized void reshape(int x, int y, int width, int height);
```

As you learned earlier, AWT is novel in its way of positioning and sizing an application's GUI elements. With Java, you always rely on a layout manager (class) to give your components their final, absolute positions and dimensions. So the methods listed here are there for the layout managers to use, and not for you to call. This is the general rule, the exception being that you can use these methods on class `Window` and its children. Layout managers have no say on where you put windows or how big or small you make them (their jurisdiction is the contents of windows). The way you position or size your application windows on a given desktop is your business.

Position and Geometry Querying Methods

```
public Point location();
public Dimension size();
public Rectangle bounds();
public synchronized boolean inside(int x, int y);
```

Since layout managers have so much control over the final placement and size of your components, these methods allow you to find out what the layout managers finally decided upon in terms of position and size, once the layout is done.

Graphics/Rendering Methods

```
public Graphics getGraphics();
public synchronized ColorModel getColorModel();
public Font getFont();
public FontMetrics getFontMetrics(Font font);
public Color getForeground();
public Color getBackground();
public synchronized void setFont(Font f);
public synchronized void setForeground(Color c);
public synchronized void setBackground(Color c);
public Toolkit getToolkit();
```

The most important of these methods is `getGraphics()`. When working with entire windows (class `Frame`) or with `Canvas` components, you can draw inside them using any of the rendering methods of class `Graphics` after you have obtained the graphics context for your drawing medium (see Chapter 13 for a detailed account of the `Graphics` class). You use `getGraphics()` to obtain a component's associated graphics context.

> **WARNING** This method is in fact not supported by all components. Only `Frame` and `Canvas` components let you draw in them. `Buttons`, `Choices`, and so on won't let you have their `Graphics` context for you to alter their appearance.

The other methods let you query or set some graphical `Component` attributes (for example, the `Font` used for any text rendering and the foreground and background colors for the component).

Layout Manager Methods

```
public Dimension preferredSize();
public Dimension minimumSize();
public void layout();
```

Methods `preferredSize()` and `minimumSize()` have already been discussed in our study of layout managers. To briefly reiterate, these methods need to be overridden by your `Component` subclasses (`MyButton`, `ZIPCodeTextField`, and so on) to let the layout managers know how to size them under various packing conditions. The `layout()` method itself forces an immediate layout for the component. You should never call this method yourself since it is called by the `validate()` method.

Self-Painting Methods

```
public void paint(Graphics g);
public void update(Graphics g);
public void paintAll(Graphics g);
public void repaint();
public void repaint(long tm);
public void repaint(int x, int y, int width, int height);
public void repaint(long tm, int x, int y, int width, int height);
public void print(Graphics g);
public void printAll(Graphics g);
```

Here, `paint()`, `update()`, and `repaint()` are the important methods. You have already seen `paint()` in action: You need to override it in order to refresh your applet. That's right—the `paint()` method is not an `Applet` method at all but a `Component` method. All components without visible native imagery (`Canvas`, `Panel`, `Applet`) redraw themselves via overridden `paint()` methods. You might have wondered why we never suggested you clear your applet window by filling it to a background color, before starting to redraw it. This is because the `paint()` method starts with a clean slate each time, courtesy of method `update()`.

Here is the default implementation in class `Component` for this method:

```
public void update(Graphics g) {
    g.setColor(getBackground());
    g.fillRect(0, 0, width, height);
    g.setColor(getForeground());
    paint(g);
}
```

There are situations when you want to avoid this window-cleaning action, in which case you can override this method instead of overriding `paint()` (you will use this technique in Chapter 13). The `repaint()` methods are usually called by external entities (the browser, for example) to request a Component redraw. The `repaint()` variant with the empty argument list is a possible exception. You can call it to force an `update()` (and, therefore, a `paint()`, too) to happen as soon as possible.

WARNING The exact mechanism of delayed repainting is too complex to go into detail here. The intricate dynamics will be explained when we talk about asynchronous image loading and updating in Chapter 13.

Parent/Subcomponents Methods

```
public Container getParent();
public Component locate(int x, int y);
```

In practice, a `Component` is almost always part of a nested GUI hierarchy of parent containers, containers, and subcontainers. Any `Component` can find out whether it is part of a container by using the `getparent()` method (a `null` return value means you are the top-most container). If a `Component` is a `Container` itself, it can find out which component is located at its *relative* coordinates (x,y) by calling `locate()` on itself.

State-Changing and Querying Methods

```
public synchronized void enable();
public void enable(boolean cond);
public synchronized void disable();
public synchronized void show();
public void show(boolean cond);
public synchronized void hide();
public void validate();
public void invalidate();
public boolean isValid();
public boolean isVisible();
public boolean isShowing();
public boolean isEnabled();
```

Any component can find itself in the following boolean states:

- enabled/disabled

- showing/hiding

- valid/invalid

You *disable* components to make them unresponsive to user selections; this is sometimes called *graying out* or *ghosting*. Or you can *hide* a component, if it is to be unavailable for prolonged periods. (Disabling a component means it is only temporarily unavailable.) Components can also become invalidated after you have modified them by `add()`ing or `remove()`ing components. You need to call `validate()` to revalidate their state and have the screen updated accordingly.

Image-Related Methods

```
public Image createImage(ImageProducer producer);
public Image createImage(int width, int height);
public boolean imageUpdate(Image img, int flags, int x, int y, int w, int h);
public boolean prepareImage(Image image, ImageObserver observer);
public boolean prepareImage(Image image, int width, int height, ImageObserver observer);
public int checkImage(Image image, ImageObserver observer);
public int checkImage(Image image, int width, int height, ImageObserver observer);
```

Components like `Canvas` and `Frame` can be used to draw images in. These are some of the methods you need in order to add images to components. We will look at image creation and manipulation in detail in Chapter 13.

Component Peer Methods

```
public ComponentPeer getPeer();
public void addNotify();
public synchronized void removeNotify();
```

Lastly, every component has some methods to let it communicate with its peer. Earlier you learned that the AWT relies on native components to retain the native platform's look and feel for GUIs. In reality, however, AWT goes a step further than this: It relies on the native components for event handling, too. When a Java applet uses a Java AWT Button on a Windows 95 machine, a "peer" Windows 95 button is used to incarnate the Java AWT Button. Behind the scenes, therefore, a delicate protocol keeps the two buttons (one abstract, the other concrete) in sync with each other.

> **WARNING**
>
> This approach—keeping two different but equivalent systems in sync—is always a tricky and fragile balancing act: If the entities lose their synchronization for any reason (like a bug), the whole system breaks down. At the time of writing there are several problems of exactly this nature in the Windows NT/95 implementation of the AWT peers. The result is that the visible GUI, managed and presented by the peers, does not always mirror the messages addressed to the AWT components in the code.

The `getPeer()` method allows an AWT component to get a reference to its associated peer component. All peer `Component` classes are defined in a "parallel universe" package called `java.awt.peer`. It contains the same list of components, defined in almost exactly the same way as AWT components. The big difference is that `java.awt.peer` classes are in fact all interfaces. This is because a concrete `java.awt.peer` package by definition has to be machine dependent since it liaises intimately with the native GUI components of a particular machine.

The methods `addNotify()` and `removeNotify()` are used to force the creation and destruction, respectively, of the peer. All three peer-related methods should never be called by application programmers. These are low-level methods used purely by the Components themselves to communicate with their peers. In particular, calling `addNotify()` or `removeNotify()` could disrupt the abstract-component/concrete-component protocol, resulting in serious out-of-sync inconsistency problems.

You now have a general idea of the types of methods all components have to react to. Before we explore the concrete subclasses of class `Component`, there's one more important point to highlight. As you know by now, any subclass inherits all of its parent class(es) methods. So all AWT component classes will inherit the entire list of `Component` methods you just saw. Take class `Canvas` for example:

```
public class Canvas extends Component {
    public Canvas();
    public synchronized void addNotify();
    public void paint(Graphics g);
}
```

This much smaller class seems to consist only of its constructor and two methods, but this is not the case. Class `Canvas` *extends* class `Component`, so it is even larger than class `Component`. This is something to be very conscious of whenever you study a subclass definition: Never forget the functionality inherited from parents and all its parents.

NOTE To be perfectly truthful, class `Canvas` is only one item bigger than `Component`; the two instance methods are actually overridden methods from class `Component`, so they don't really count. Only the constructor is really new. Class `Component` lacks a constructor altogether.

Button

Launch any application on any modern desktop computer and you will see buttons all over the place. Several types of buttons are generally used to manipulate windows on every platform:

- A resizing button

- Minimize (or iconify) and maximize buttons

- A kill button

Toolbars are "bulk" collections of buttons. Scrollbars consist of at least three buttons: two for the up and down arrows and one stretched-out button for the scroll area. Status bars can also contain buttons camouflaged as simple labels. But whatever its exact appearance, a button always boils down to a rectangular window area that has associated with it a unique, individual behavior compared to other similar areas. From this definition, it is just a small step to graphically highlight this rectangular area by drawing its outline and by adding a descriptive label or icon to mnemonically identify it.

Java's idea of a button is just that: an outline and a label. Here is its class definition:

```
public class Button extends Component {
    public Button();
    public Button(String label);

    public synchronized void addNotify();
    public String getLabel();
    public void setLabel(String label);
    protected String paramString();
}
```

To use this class, all you need to understand is how to use the constructors. The most commonly used constructor for a Button takes a string which will be depicted on the button as its label (see Figure 11.1).

FIGURE 11.1:

A Button component

Adding buttons to Java applets or applications is simplicity itself, as proven by the demonstration program that created the button shown in Figure 11.1:

```
import java.awt.*;

public class ButtonTest extends java.applet.Applet {

public void init() {
Button b;

    b = new Button("A Java Button!");
    add(b);
}}
```

This applet just declares a variable b of type Button, creates a new Button object for it and add()s this button to the applet. The button label A Java Button! was specified as the string argument to the Button constructor. As you can see in Figure 11.1, the button is centered automatically. This is because the default layout manager for applets is FlowLayout, which itself uses its own default alignment style: CENTER. Being an applet, the ButtonTest class subclasses Applet. This is specified with its full package name as java.applet.Applet.

The first import statement makes available all java.awt classes to the compilation unit (the source file). In this instance we could have simply used

```
import java.awt.Button;
```

instead, since this is the only AWT class used in the program.

NOTE Contrary to popular Java beliefs, importing whole packages does not increase the size of your executables. Import statements only make class definitions *visible* to other classes at compilation time. The actual linking is done at run time and not at compile time. This explains why the executables do not swell up by importing external classes, as they do with most other compiled languages.

You can change the label of a `Button` at any time using the `setLabel()` method. Similarly, you can find out which `Button` you are manipulating by asking the button what its label is with `getLabel()`.

Canvas

```
public class Canvas extends Component {
    public Canvas();
    public synchronized void addNotify();
    public void paint(Graphics g);
}
```

If class `Component` is abstract (and it is), then one could say that `Canvas` is the simplest concrete incarnation of class `Component`. The only behavior it adds to that of `Component` is of having a default `paint()` method that clears the entire component (canvas) area to the component's background color. You use this class whenever you need a generic, drawable surface area that can respond to mouse and key inputs (see Figure 11.2). Another possible use for class `Canvas` is as a foundation for creating your own components—for example, creating enhanced buttons which can have an icon instead of a textual label.

TIP	Remember that the default `update()` method for `Component` also cleared the component to its background area. A default `Canvas`, then, clears its background twice—first in its `update()`, followed by its `paint()`. Since this is clearly superfluous, you should either override the `update()` or `paint()` methods to avoid this double clear.

Figure 11.2 shows a custom `Canvas` component drawn with an outline to highlight the `Canvas` area. Note that the bottom line of the outline gets overwritten by the "`applet started`" string printed by appletviewer (in other words, the code doesn't have a bug).

FIGURE 11.2:

An outlined `Canvas` component

Here is the demonstration program behind Figure 11.2 :

```
import java.awt.*;

public class CanvasTest extends java.applet.Applet {

    MyCanvas doodle;

    public void init() {
        doodle = new MyCanvas(size().width, size().height);
        add(doodle);
    }
}

class MyCanvas extends Canvas {

    int width;
    int height;

    public MyCanvas() {
        this(100,100);
    }

    public MyCanvas(int width, int height) {
        this.width = width;
        this.height = height;
        resize(width,height);
    }

    public void paint(Graphics g) {
        g.drawRect(0, 0, width-1, height-1);
    }
}
```

In this program, you actually subclass class `Canvas` to create your own variety. Its `paint()` method draws an outline around (or to be precise, just inside) the `Canvas` area. Class `MyCanvas` also contains two constructors: The default constructor takes no parameters but creates a Canvas 100×100 pixels big. The constructor you actually called from within the applet is the generic constructor that takes any dimensions.

Note how the default constructor calls the generic constructor—this is an almost universal technique among class constructors. Classes provide a small collection of overloaded constructors, of which the most flexible is the "true" constructor, while the others are just convenient shorthand forms for common default cases. Since it takes very little effort to provide such collections of overloaded constructors, we encourage you to do likewise with your own classes.

Label

```
public class Label extends Component {
    public final static int LEFT;
    public final static int CENTER;
    public final static int RIGHT;
    public Label();
    public Label(String label);
    public Label(String label, int alignment);
    public synchronized void addNotify();
    public int getAlignment();
    public void setAlignment(int alignment) throws
IllegalArgumentException;
    public String getText();
    public void setText(String label);
    protected String paramString();
}
```

A Label component is simply a passive (that is, completely non-interactive) and graphically unassuming single line of text. Its purpose, for example, is to label areas of your GUI that are grouped together in a Container.

Here is the demonstration program behind Figure 11.3, which illustrates three Label components:

```
import java.awt.*;

public class LabelTest extends java.applet.Applet {

    public void init() {
        setLayout(new GridLayout(3,1));
        add(new Label("Left label"));                  // default left justify
        add(new Label("Center label", Label.CENTER));  // center
        add(new Label("Right label", Label.RIGHT));    // right justify
    }
}
```

FIGURE 11.3:

Three Label
components

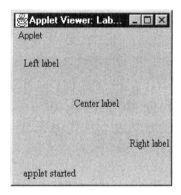

As you can see, the only additional attribute of a Label is its alignment. You can choose between LEFT, CENTER, or RIGHT. The label text and alignment properties can be changed or queried with the methods getAlignment(), setAlignment(int alignment), getText(), and setText(String label).

The alignment of a Label will only have a visual effect if the LayoutManager that controls the Label allows components to appear sized to dimensions other than their minimumSize().

Changing the alignment of labels within a `FlowLayout`, for example, has no effect since `FlowLayout` always sizes components to their most compact dimensions.

Checkbox

```
public class Checkbox extends Component {
    public Checkbox();
    public Checkbox(String label);
    public Checkbox(String label, CheckboxGroup group, boolean state);
    public synchronized void addNotify();
    public String getLabel();
    public void setLabel(String label);
    public boolean getState();
    public void setState(boolean state);
    public CheckboxGroup getCheckboxGroup();
    public void setCheckboxGroup(CheckboxGroup g);
    protected String paramString();
}
```

A `Checkbox` component is a two-state button which is typically used in GUIs containing selectable items (like voting forms or option preference pages).

Here is the demonstration program behind Figure 11.4:

```
import java.awt.*;

public class CheckboxTest extends java.applet.Applet {

    public void init() {
        Checkbox cb = new Checkbox("Black and White");
        add(cb);
    }
}
```

The program declares and constructs a `Checkbox` object that is labeled with the string passed as argument to the `Checkbox` constructor (see Figure 11.4). The `Checkbox` component is then added, as usual, with the `add()` method. If you look at the definition for class `Checkbox`, you'll see that sometimes there is a bit more to building

FIGURE 11.4:

A Checkbox
component

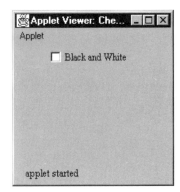

a checkbox than simply constructing one and adding it to your container: If you want simple checkable buttons, then that is all there is to it. But if you want a group of checkboxes to be mutually exclusive, then you need the more complex constructor and the associated methods.

To define a group of checkboxes to be mutually exclusive (called RadioButtons in other GUI frameworks) you need one extra helper class: CheckboxGroup. Here is its definition:

```
public class CheckboxGroup extends Object {
    public CheckboxGroup();
    public Checkbox getCurrent();
    public synchronized void setCurrent(Checkbox box);
    public String toString();
}
```

The purpose of CheckboxGroup is to provide the scope for the mutually exclusive group and to manage the group's state.

Here is a demonstration program which uses a CheckboxGroup instance to define a mutually exclusive collection of checkboxes:

```
import java.awt.*;

public class MutexCheckboxTest extends java.applet.Applet {

public void init() {
```

```
CheckboxGroup checkboxFence = new CheckboxGroup();
Checkbox check1 = new Checkbox("Black and White", checkboxFence, false);
Checkbox check2 = new Checkbox("256 Greyscale" , checkboxFence, false);
Checkbox check3 = new Checkbox("True Color"     , checkboxFence, false);

    add(check1);
    add(check2);
    add(check3);
}}
```

The difference with independent checkboxes is that, as you can see, a different constructor is used to build the Checkbox instances. For mutually exclusive checkboxes, you need to pass in a CheckboxGroup instance that defines the extent of the group. The third constructor argument is the initial state for the checkbox—false for deselected and true for selected. Within any group of mutually exclusive checkboxes, you can only make one of the radio buttons selected. Figure 11.5 shows the result of the above program.

FIGURE 11.5:

Mutually exclusive checkboxes

Note the layout of the buttons in Figure 11.5. This is again a result of the default FlowLayout used by applets.

To change the state of any Checkbox that is part of a mutually exclusive group, you need to use the CheckboxGroup method setCurrent(Checkbox box) to ensure that the mutual exclusiveness is maintained (you should not use the Checkbox method setState()).

Choice

```
public class Choice extends Component {
   public Choice();
   public synchronized void addNotify();
   public int countItems();
   public String getItem(int index);
   public synchronized void addItem(String item) throws
NullPointerException;
   public String getSelectedItem();
   public int getSelectedIndex();
   public synchronized void select(int pos) throws
IllegalArgumentException;
   public void select(String str);
   protected String paramString();
}
```

The Choice class encapsulates a pull-down choice list component. The component allows a user to select one of several options or items in one space-saving place. When GUI real estate becomes crowded you can substitute a collection of mutually exclusive radio buttons with a single, compact Choice component (see Figure 11.6).

FIGURE 11.6:

A Choice component

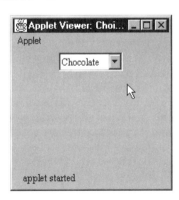 

Here is the demonstration program behind Figure 11.6:

```java
import java.awt.*;

public class ChoiceTest extends java.applet.Applet {

    public void init() {
        IcecreamChoice coolChoices = new IcecreamChoice();
        add(coolChoices);
    }
}

class IcecreamChoice extends Choice {

    public IcecreamChoice() {
        addItem("Chocolate");
        addItem("Vanilla");
        addItem("Strawberry");
    }
}
```

This applet uses a customized Choice class with a default constructor which employs the addItem() method to define its list of choices. To use the IcecreamChoice component we constructed an instance of it and added the object to the applet container via the add() method.

TIP

You may be wondering if it's overkill to define an entire class just for IcecreamChoice—it isn't. Creating compact, self-contained software objects, like IcecreamChoice, significantly improves your software. It reduces the complexity of your application by collapsing algorithms and/or data structures into easily manageable entities (classes, which you can then treat as black boxes). It makes your code more maintainable and improves readability. It also unambiguously draws boundaries for subsystem responsibilities. And it helps you to view your programs as collections of interacting objects. The advantages of properly exploiting the object-oriented class mechanism (by encapsulating chunks of code and data), are so numerous that you should consult a good book on object-oriented software engineering. The investment will repay itself a hundredfold. In the mean time, you might want to rely on the following rule of thumb: "Better a class too many than one too few."

Choice components are great for reasonably small lists of selectable items (say, from three to ten items). But if you only have two choices, it might be better to use mutually exclusive checkboxes instead (unless the list of choices is dynamic and is expected to grow beyond two). If, on the other hand, your list of choices becomes large, then you should consider using the next AWT component: a List. Class Choice gives you a couple of methods that allow you to access and/or set the currently selected item in the list.

getSelectedItem()	Returns the string of the item itself
getSelectedIndex()	Returns the index position of the item
select(int pos)	Selects an item by index position
select(String str)	Selects an item by name

List

```
public class List extends Component {
    public List();
    public List(int rows, boolean multipleSelections);

    public synchronized void addNotify();
    public synchronized void removeNotify();
    public int countItems();
    public String getItem(int index);
    public synchronized void addItem(String item);
    public synchronized void addItem(String item, int index);
    public synchronized void replaceItem(String newValue, int index);
    public synchronized void clear();
    public synchronized void delItem(int position);
    public synchronized void delItems(int start, int end);
    public synchronized int getSelectedIndex();
    public synchronized int[] getSelectedIndexes();
    public synchronized String getSelectedItem();
    public synchronized String[] getSelectedItems();
    public synchronized void select(int index);
    public synchronized void deselect(int index);
    public synchronized boolean isSelected(int index);
    public int getRows();
    public boolean allowsMultipleSelections();
    public void setMultipleSelections(boolean v);
```

```
public int getVisibleIndex();
public void makeVisible(int index);
public Dimension preferredSize(int rows);
public Dimension preferredSize();
public Dimension minimumSize(int rows);
public Dimension minimumSize();
protected String paramString();
}
```

Consider a List component (see Figure 11.7) as a heavyweight analog of a Choice component. The differences between the two components are mainly as follows:

- Lists are used for much longer lists of items.

- Lists are used when multiple selections are needed.

- Lists typically use up a large proportion of a GUI's real estate.

- Class List contains many more methods supporting its functionality.

FIGURE 11.7:

A List component

Here is the demonstration program behind Figure 11.7:

```
import java.awt.*;

public class ListTest extends java.applet.Applet {
```

```
    public void init() {

        String[] colors = { "Red", "Orange", "Yellow",
                            "Green", "Blue","Indigo", "Violet" };
        MyList colorList = new MyList(5, colors);
        add(colorList);
    }
}

class MyList extends List {

    public MyList(int numItemsToDisplayAtOnce, String[] elements) {

        super(numItemsToDisplayAtOnce, false);

        for (int i=0; i<elements.length; i++) {
            addItem(elements[i]);
        }
    }
}
```

If you look at the default constructors provided by a vanilla List, you will notice that the constructors do not let you build a fully initialized List in one step (a Choice did not have that possibility either). You normally need to use the addItem() method to incrementally fill the List before activating it on the screen. Since there is no good reason for not having a higher level constructor, you design a new List constructor in your MyList subclass that is much more programmer friendly. It can take an array of Strings which provides the List with its initial list of items. The numeric argument to the constructor does not specify the number of list items (since the constructor gets this information from the array.length field), but tells the List component how many lines tall it should be. The extra methods provided by class List are analogous to those of class Choice, but they contain some extra support for manipulating multiple item selections and deleting items.

Lists come in two interactive varieties: One allows multiple selections (created using the second constructor and passing true for argument multipleSelections), the other behaves exactly like a Choice in that it only accepts single (mutually exclusive) selections. To process multiple selections, then, the following methods are available:

int[] getSelectedIndexes() This method returns an array of indices specifying the multiple selection.

String[] getSelectedItems() This method is similar to `getSelectedIndexes()`, except it returns an array of selected item names.

boolean allowsMultipleSelections() You can find out whether a `List` currently accepts multiple selections or not via this method.

void setMultipleSelections(boolean v) You can change the multiple select behavior of a `List` by calling `setMultipleSelections()`. This is only advisable before the `List` becomes active; after that point, a `List` should not change its response to multiple selections, as this will surely confuse the user!

Scrollbar

```
public class Scrollbar extends Component {
    public final static int HORIZONTAL;
    public final static int VERTICAL;
    public Scrollbar();
    public Scrollbar(int orientation) throws IllegalArgumentException;
    public Scrollbar(int orientation, int value, int visible, int minimum, int maximum);
    public synchronized void addNotify();
    public int getOrientation();
    public int getValue();
    public void setValue(int value);
    public int getMinimum();
    public int getMaximum();
    public int getVisible();
    public void setLineIncrement(int l);
    public int getLineIncrement();
    public void setPageIncrement(int l);
    public int getPageIncrement();
    public void setValues(int value, int visible, int minimum, int maximum);
    protected String paramString();
}
```

When you want your GUI users to enter numerical values that can range contiguously from one minimum value to another maximum value, you should provide them with slider controls to achieve this efficiently. Java's support for slider controls comes in the form of class `Scrollbar`, listed previously. The most common placement for scrollbars is to the right and bottom of windows, so the natural layout manager to accompany `Scrollbar` components is `BorderLayout`. Scrollbars are used most often when only part of an entity (document, list, picture, directory, and so on) can be displayed by the application (because either the display itself or the window is too small). The value the `Scrollbar` depicts then becomes the starting point for a scrollable "window" on the data set. Figure 11.8 shows vertical and horizontal scrollbars.

FIGURE 11.8:

Vertical and horizontal scrollbars

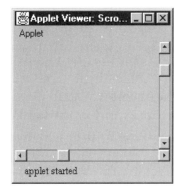

Here is the demonstration program behind Figure 11.8 :

```
import java.awt.*;

public class ScrollbarTest extends java.applet.Applet {

public void init() {
Scrollbar upDown, leftRight;

    setLayout(new BorderLayout() );

    upDown    = new Scrollbar(Scrollbar.VERTICAL  , 30, 1, 0, 120);
    leftRight = new Scrollbar(Scrollbar.HORIZONTAL, 5, 2, 0, 10);

    add("East" , upDown);
    add("South", leftRight);
}}
```

This applet begins by overriding its default layout (`FlowLayout`) and specifying `BorderLayout` instead. It then creates two `Scrollbar` objects: one horizontal (by specifying `Scrollbar` class constant `Scrollbar.HORIZONTAL`), the other vertical (using `Scrollbar.VERTICAL`). The extra numeric arguments passed to the `Scrollbar` constructor are

value   The starting position for the slider knob (some value within the range *minimum…maximum*).

visible   The proportion of the numeric range used. For example, to indicate that your document view shows half of the document, you set this value to half of maximum.

minimum and maximum   The minimum and maximum values this scrollbar can represent; for example, 0–100 (for percentages), 6–120 (for ages), 1–31 (for dates).

A `Scrollbar` defines two speeds at which you can alter the value represented by it. It has a *line increment* and a *page increment* speed. The easiest way to understand these concepts is to think of your favorite word processor: When you click on the vertical scrollbar's up or down arrows, you move up or down one document line at a time. When you click inside the scrollbar's slider area (but not on the slider itself), you will move a whole page up or down at a time. This behavior is supported by class `Scrollbar` through the following methods:

- `setLineIncrement(int lineIncr)`

- `setPageIncrement(int pageIncr)`

NOTE   Chapter 12 will show you how to respond to slider movements and how to retrieve the value the `Scrollbar` slider is indicating.

TextField

```
public class TextField extends TextComponent {
    public TextField();
    public TextField(int cols);
    public TextField(String text);
    public TextField(String text, int cols);
    public synchronized void addNotify();
    public char getEchoChar();
    public boolean echoCharIsSet();
    public int getColumns();
    public void setEchoCharacter(char c);
    public Dimension preferredSize(int cols);
    public Dimension preferredSize();
    public Dimension minimumSize(int cols);
    public Dimension minimumSize();
    protected String paramString();
}
```

A `TextField` implements that old favorite: a single-line text input box. Text fields share behavior with a related class called `TextArea` (discussed as the next component in our list). Both inherit from an intermediate superclass called `TextComponent`. Before looking at `TextField` itself, you should first study the fundamental functionality shared by both text component classes by looking at the `TextComponent` class:

```
public class TextComponent extends Component {
    public synchronized void removeNotify();
    public void setText(String t);
    public String getText();
    public String getSelectedText();
    public boolean isEditable();
    public void setEditable(boolean t);
    public int getSelectionStart();
    public int getSelectionEnd();
    public void select(int selStart, int selEnd);
    public void selectAll();
    protected String paramString();
}
```

Any text component contains some text it manages and renders. This text might be user editable, and the user can always select some part of it by click-dragging the mouse pointer over the required text. This selection ability is used in part to support the general clipboard cut/copy/paste mechanism of the host operating system. The majority of the methods defined by class TextComponent all relate to these text component issues shared by TextFields and TextAreas. The method naming accurately reflects their function and behavior.

You will return now to the first subclass of TextComponent: class TextField. Figure 11.9 shows a simple Java AWT TextField component embedded in an applet:

FIGURE 11.9:

A TextField component with selected text

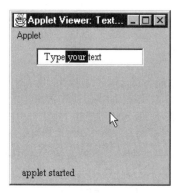

Here is the demonstration program behind Figure 11.9:

```
import java.awt.*;

public class TextFieldTest extends java.applet.Applet {

    public void init() {
        MyTextField text = new MyTextField();
        add(text);
    }
}
```

```
class MyTextField extends TextField {

    public MyTextField() {
        super("Type your text", 20);
    }
}
```

The way you add a `TextField` is very much along the same lines as with all the other simple AWT components: You call its constructor and `add()` the resulting object to your container. In this case, you enhanced the standard `TextField` slightly by creating a subclass that initializes all blank TextFields with the string "`Type your text`". If you refer back to TextField's class listing, you will see that the second numeric parameter specifies the width of the text input box (in characters).

TextFields have one interesting feature that might come in handy on occasion: You can have them accept text that is masked on the screen to prevent bystanders from reading the text. The main application of this feature is for password entry. Figure 11.10 gives you an example of this.

FIGURE 11.10:

A `PasswordField` as a subclass of `TextField`

Here is the program that produced the applet shown in Figure 11.10:

```
import java.awt.*;

public class PasswordTest extends java.applet.Applet {
```

```
     public void init() {
         PasswordField passwordField = new PasswordField(6);
         add(new Label("Enter password:") );
         add(passwordField);
     }
 }

 class PasswordField extends TextField {

 public PasswordField() {
     this(12);
 }
 public PasswordField(int cols) {
     super("x",cols);

     setEchoCharacter('*');
 }

 } // End of Class PasswordField
```

In this program, you created a subclass of `TextField` that by default sets itself in password-entry mode. This is done by setting the "echo" character used to mask the real characters on the screen. A conservative asterisk is used for that purpose. To give the user some early hint that this `TextField` takes passwords (there are no graphical changes compared to a `TextField` in normal entry mode), you forced its initial contents to be a single character (just an "x" in the program), which will therefore appear as an asterisk.

TextArea

```
public class TextArea extends TextComponent {
    public TextArea();
    public TextArea(int rows, int cols);
    public TextArea(String text);
    public TextArea(String text, int rows, int cols);
    public synchronized void addNotify();
    public void insertText(String str, int pos);
    public void appendText(String str);
    public void replaceText(String str, int start, int end);
```

```
    public int getRows();
    public int getColumns();
    public Dimension preferredSize(int rows, int cols);
    public Dimension preferredSize();
    public Dimension minimumSize(int rows, int cols);
    public Dimension minimumSize();
    protected String paramString();
}
```

The `TextArea` component, as its name suggests, is used when larger amounts of text need to be input, or more often, just displayed. Figure 11.11 shows you a typical `TextArea` component.

FIGURE 11.11:

A `TextArea` component

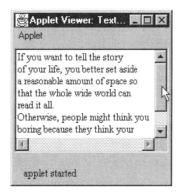

Here is the demonstration program behind Figure 11.11:

```
import java.awt.*;

public class TextAreaTest extends java.applet.Applet {

    TextArea disp;
    String multiLineText =

        "If you want to tell the story\n"
      + "of your life, you better set aside\n"
      + "a reasonable amount of space so\n"
      + "that the whole wide world can \n"
      + "read it all.\n"
      + "Otherwise, people might think you\n"
      + "are boring because they think your \n"
```

```
            + "life can be summarized in such a \n"
            + "tiny amount of text !";
public void init() {
    disp = new TextArea(multiLineText, 7, 30);

    add(disp);
}}
```

The `TextArea` constructor we used in the program lets us specify the initial block of text and the dimensions of the `TextArea` box (in character rows and columns). Note how a single String composed of multiple lines was created. This is achieved by embedding new line characters in a String directly, using the standard control character escape sequence "\n".

Coding Style Tip

Note the formatting for the block of code creating your text `String`. Not only are all the string concatenation operators (the plusses) aligned neatly and vertically to accentuate the fact that you are building a long string, but the plusses are aligned to the left of the `String` constants. This combines two good coding styles in one fell swoop:

a.   The concatenation operators are much more conspicuous there than on the right hand side. This way you can instantly spot whether one is missing or not (not likely with right-side formatting)!

b.   The neat alignment will not be upset the instant you change any text strings. This makes the code cheap to maintain and more robust to the introduction of bugs. Putting the concatenation plusses on the right has no such advantages.

Menu Systems

Java menus are special AWT GUI components because they do not descend from class `Component`. The few menu classes you will look at all descend from their own common menu superclass, called `MenuComponent`. This means that you cannot `add()` menus to applets, since menus are not of the right type for `add(Component comp)`. Menus can only be added to `Frame` (window) objects using a different binding mechanism altogether. But first you should look at the root menu class: `MenuComponent`. Here is its definition:

```
public class MenuComponent extends Object {
    public MenuComponent();
    public MenuContainer getParent();
    public MenuComponentPeer getPeer();
    public Font getFont();
    public void setFont(Font f);
    public void removeNotify();
    public boolean postEvent(Event evt);
    protected String paramString();
    public String toString();
}
```

The main methods of interest are `getFont()` and `setFont()`, which allow you to query and set the font to be used for the rendering of the menu bar and items, respectively. Although this class is not abstract, it is never instantiated directly. Extending this `MenuComponent` class are the four classes that you do instantiate: classes `MenuBar`, `Menu`, `MenuItem` and `CheckboxMenuItem`. Here are their definitions:

```
public class MenuBar extends MenuComponent implements
MenuContainer {
    public MenuBar();
    public synchronized void addNotify();
    public void removeNotify();
    public Menu getHelpMenu();
    public synchronized void setHelpMenu(Menu m);
    public synchronized Menu add(Menu m);
```

```
    public synchronized void remove(int index);
    public synchronized void remove(MenuComponent m);
    public int countMenus();
    public Menu getMenu(int i);
}
```

The MenuBar is there primarily to group together a collection of Menu instances. In this respect, its add() method is its core method (analogous to the add() methods of class Container). The MenuBar class also supports the concept of a "help" menu. A single menu on the menu bar can be designated as being the help menu. Its behavior, position and/or rendering can then reflect this special status (this is done in platform specific ways).

```
public class Menu extends MenuItem implements MenuContainer {
    public Menu(String label);
    public Menu(String label, boolean tearOff);
    public synchronized void addNotify();
    public synchronized void removeNotify();
    public boolean isTearOff();
    public int countItems();
    public MenuItem getItem(int index);
    public synchronized MenuItem add(MenuItem mi);
    public void add(String label);
    public void addSeparator();
    public synchronized void remove(int index);
    public synchronized void remove(MenuComponent item);
}
```

A Menu is there primarily to group together a collection of MenuItems *and* other submenus. The core Menu method is the add() method used to incrementally specify the list of MenuItems (or Menus) contained by the menu. Menus (like MenuBars) also implement a feature not universally supported on all platforms: tear-off menus. Marking a Menu as being a tear-off type menu has no effect on machines which do not have such a menu feature. Menus can also have a separator added at any point in the list using a call to `addSeparator()`. This is handy when your menus become rather long, as adding separators between groups of related items structures the menu and prevents it from becoming a messy, endless list of choices.

```
public class MenuItem extends MenuComponent {
    public MenuItem(String label);
    public synchronized void addNotify();
    public String getLabel();
    public void setLabel(String label);
    public boolean isEnabled();
    public void enable();
    public void enable(boolean cond);
    public void disable();
    public String paramString();
}
```

This class (and its close relative, `CheckboxMenuItem`) embodies the final user-selectable menu item. These can be dynamically enabled or disabled to reflect the state of the application. For example, an Edit menu usually grays out (disables) the Cut and Copy menu items when there is no currently selected aspect of the project (text, picture, waveform, and so on). As soon as the user selects all or part of the project, the menu items become available by `enable()`ing them.

```
public class CheckboxMenuItem extends MenuItem {
    public CheckboxMenuItem(String label);
    public synchronized void addNotify();
    public boolean getState();
    public void setState(boolean t);
    public String paramString();
}
```

This class is a variation on `MenuItem` in that it incorporates an on/off state which is depicted graphically in a menu using a check mark or other glyph to that effect.

The following application program uses all four menu classes to construct a menu strip attached to a simple window:

```
import java.awt.*;

public class MenuTest {
public static void main(String[] args) {
    MainWindow w = new MainWindow();
    w.resize(400, 300);
    w.show();
}}

class MainWindow extends Frame {

public MainWindow() {
    super("MenuTest Window");

    FileMenu fileMenu = new FileMenu();
    HelpMenu helpMenu = new HelpMenu();

    MenuBar mb = new MenuBar();

    mb.setHelpMenu(helpMenu);
    mb.add(helpMenu);

    mb.add(fileMenu);
    setMenuBar(mb);


}}

class FileMenu extends Menu {

public FileMenu() {
    super("File", true);  // tear-off menu
    add(new MenuItem("Open"));
    add(new MenuItem("Close"));
    add(new MenuItem("Exit"));
}}

class HelpMenu extends Menu {

public HelpMenu() {
    super("Help");
    add(new MenuItem("About MenuTest"));
    add(new MenuItem("Class Heirarchy"));
```

```
        addSeparator();
        add(new CheckboxMenuItem("Balloon Help"));

        Menu subMenu = new Menu("Categories");
        subMenu.add(new MenuItem("A Little Help"));
        subMenu.add(new MenuItem("A Lot of Help"));
        add(subMenu);
}}
```

Note how cleanly the program is structured to follow the main
objects of its particular problem domain—the startup class `MenuTest`
relies on a `MainWindow` class to create its application window. The
`MainWindow` class in turn relies on two local classes to implement one
menu each: menus `FileMenu` and `HelpMenu`. The two menu classes
construct themselves, privately as it were, without encumbering the
rest of the program with details of the composition of their menus.
This nesting of abstraction levels is an application of the information-
hiding principle made possible by object-oriented design and implementation. (The `MenuTest` class does not care about the structure of
the menus attached to the window, it just wants to pop up the window—with or without menus.)

In class `MainWindow`, the menu bar is constructed by creating a new
`MenuBar` object and then using the `add()` method to link the two
menus to it. To attach it to the window you call the Frame
`setMenuBar()` method, passing in the `MenuBar` instance. In class
`HelpMenu`, you build this menu by first defining its title (this is done
by calling the standard `Menu` constructor and passing the menu title
label as a `String`). Then, several calls to `add()` create the list of
MenuItems which the menu should contain. An `addSeperator()`
invocation separates the normal items from the two special menu
items at the end of this menu. The first special menu item is the
"`Balloon Help`" `CheckboxMenuItem`, which can be toggled on or
off. The second special item is an entire submenu containing two
more simple menu items. Figure 11.12 shows the menu bar in action.

FIGURE 11.12:

MenuBar with Menus
and MenuItems (and
submenu)

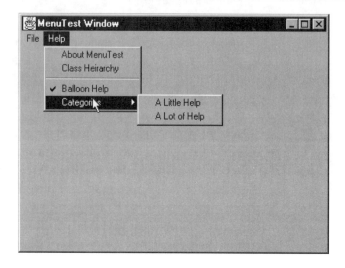

Summary

There are two concrete GUI component branches provided by the Abstract Windowing Toolkit hierarchy: the Component branch and the MenuComponent branch. The bulk of the AWT widgets are subclasses of the large, but abstract, superclass Component. You explored how to use Buttons, Labels, Choices, Lists, TextFields, TextAreas, ScrollBars, plain and mutually exclusive Checkboxes, and the generic Canvas component. You rounded out your tour of AWT building blocks by looking at how menu systems are constructed and attached to application windows.

In combination, all these elements can be used to construct clear, functional, and—last but not least—*portable* graphical user interfaces for the applications of tomorrow.

CHAPTER
TWELVE

12

Event Handling

- Object-Oriented GUI Event Basics

- Component Event Types

An *event* is an unexpected, external happening that imposes itself on you. If a fireman shouts "Fire! Everyone out of the building!" while demolishing your front door, that is an event. If you are asleep early in the morning and your alarm clock goes off, that is another event (less traumatic maybe, but equally annoying). In software systems, events have similar attributes, but programs are less flexible in dealing with the unexpected than humans. Code has to be in place to recognize and handle every possible event, or else your program will be oblivious to unexpected events (it may even crash).

In the context of hardware and systems programming, events are called *interrupts*. When you hit a key, the electronics inside your keyboard interrupt your desktop machine to send it the keycode of the key you pressed. Your machine responds by immediately halting whatever it was doing, receiving the key's identifying code, acknowledging the interrupt, and resuming whatever it was doing before the interrupt occurred. Within the field of GUI design and programming, user events (like a mouse click) have much the same urgency as their lower-level interrupt counterparts. Responsiveness is one of the most important attributes a GUI should have.

Event handling lies at the very heart of GUI programming. Unlike first-generation applications, in which programs imposed a rigid sequence of program-user interaction, modern applications put the user firmly in the driving seat. The user controls the sequence of operations that the application executes via a GUI that passively waits for the user to activate a button or slider or menu. This approach is called *event-driven programming*. An event-driven application typically constructs a GUI at initialization time, displays the GUI, and then enters a tight loop waiting for user events requesting an operation: the application's main *event loop*. When such an event (or *trigger*) occurs, a large `switch` statement determines the generated event type and invokes a corresponding action, as shown in the following pseudocode:

```
 while not quitting
|   wait for a GUI event
|   grab event
|   switch depending on event type
|   |   button click    : handle button clicks
|   |   textfield entry  : handle textfield entries
|   |   slider movement  : handle slider movements
|   |   choice selection : handle choice selections
|   |   eventtype x      : handle events of type x
|   |   eventtype y      : handle events of type y
|   |   eventtype z      : handle events of type z
|   |   default          : beep  (error)
```

In a realistic event-processing situation, the `switch` statement would typically be quite a bit longer. This central switchboard was a common scenario when the implementation language was of the older procedural kind like Pascal or C. In object-oriented languages, the script has been modified slightly.

Object-Oriented GUI Event Basics

Object-oriented GUIs are still very much event-driven, but the way events are caught and processed is more flexible than in non-object-oriented languages. GUI elements happen to be natural candidates for implementation as objects derived from highly structured, object-oriented GUI hierarchies. (The AWT package class hierarchy diagram in Chapter 9 illustrates this.) If the root of this hierarchy is defined as being able to respond to user events itself, as an object, then all of its descendants will likewise be responsible for their own event handling (because of inheritance). For example, if a framework defined a class `RadioButton` as inheriting from such a GUI root class, then a resultant radio button would be able to respond directly to the user activating it. In this way, an individual GUI element can independently deal with events that pertain to itself.

In theory, the object-oriented approach does away with the need to have a main event loop. All of the application's event processing is scattered throughout your GUI code, staying close to the GUI elements responsible for the events themselves. This approach lies at the other extreme of having one single and central event loop which deals with all of the application's events. But neither scenario is perfect. The main loop scenario has the disadvantage of becoming unmanageable for real-life applications with very complex GUIs that can find themselves in a large number of different states or modes. The pure object-oriented scenario where each little component deals with its own events itself becomes unmanageable when components are grouped together as logical groupings. Take a collection of mutually exclusive radio buttons, for example. How does one radio button tell all its other colleagues to switch off when it has been selected as the new button to be "on"? Clearly, a less black-or-white system allowing more pragmatic distribution of responsibilities would provide the solution for both these problematic situations. And that is exactly what Java's AWT gives us with its event-handling architecture.

Java's AWT event handling approach is basically like the object-oriented approach described earlier, but it is modified to allow it to "degenerate," in a fine-grained way, all the way back to the main loop approach of older procedural languages. Somewhere in between lies the perfect, extensible, and easy-to-maintain compromise. A real-life example of a configuration window GUI follows; it explains the mechanism AWT uses to achieve its flexible event-handling approach. Remember that individual GUI elements (`Components`) are almost always organized as logically grouped, nested hierarchies within any given GUI. See Figure 12.1 for an example of such a nested GUI design.

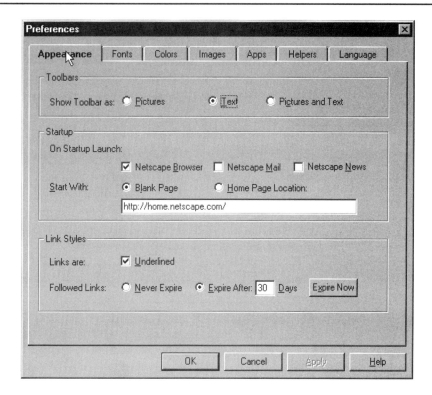

The Preferences window of Netscape's Navigator browser (Figure 12.1) is a good example of the typical nesting employed to clearly and logically organize a GUI. This window is *nested* in that the window is the outermost organizational level. It contains seven *cards* that can be selected by clicking on the appropriate tab, and it has a row of buttons at the bottom of the window: OK, Cancel, Apply (shown disabled), and Help. Each card is organized further into sub-panels. The Appearance card, for example, is divided into three sub-panels, labeled Toolbars, Startup, and Link Styles. The Startup panel is further organized as a collection of three option buttons plus a second collection of two mutually exclusive radio buttons. The second of these has a text entry field associated with it.

Even though the layout and purpose of this GUI is clear to the user, it is not as immediately obvious how, from a programming point of view, to process the numerous types of events this window and its components can generate. Java's AWT lets you decide on a case-by-case basis. Every single component does not have to handle its own events. If it would be more logical for a component's container to handle the event, then the component can "pass the bucket" and let its container handle it instead. This mechanism is generic, meaning that the container itself might decide that this event better be handed to its parent and all the way up to the top of the nesting hierarchy—the window itself. If all components and their containers are implemented to pass their events up to the next level (also called letting the event *bubble up* the container hierarchy), then you effectively obtain the giant main switch scenario.

WARNING Used in this context, the term *hierarchy* has nothing to do with the object-oriented class hierarchy in which the components are organized. It means, instead, the nesting of containers in a GUI, which forms another type of hierarchy.

If you look again at the definition of class Component, you will see the group of methods that manage GUI events:

```
public boolean handleEvent (Event evt);
public boolean mouseDown   (Event evt, int x, int y);
public boolean mouseDrag   (Event evt, int x, int y);
public boolean mouseUp     (Event evt, int x, int y);
public boolean mouseMove   (Event evt, int x, int y);
public boolean mouseEnter  (Event evt, int x, int y);
public boolean mouseExit   (Event evt, int x, int y);
public boolean keyDown     (Event evt, int key);
public boolean keyUp       (Event evt, int key);
public boolean action      (Event evt, Object what);
```

```
public boolean gotFocus   (Event evt, Object what);
public boolean lostFocus  (Event evt, Object what);
```

All these methods have several things in common, but the aspect your attention should be drawn to is the return type: All of them have to return either `true` or `false`. This simple boolean return value is the key to AWT's event-handling mechanism. If a given component or container prefers not to handle an event itself, it should return `false` to indicate to its container that it (the parent container) should handle the event instead. Any component or container anywhere along the event chain can process and consume an event by returning `true`. This will terminate the chain then and there.

The default implementation for all of these methods is to return `false`; in other words, they signal, "Here, you can have my event. I don't want to deal with it." This means all the standard components you saw in the previous chapter do not allow you to trap their events. If, for example, you wrote an application that added a single vanilla (that is, non-subclassed) `Button` to an equally off-the-shelf `Frame` window, you would not be able to trap any events generated by the button or the window. (Within object-oriented GUI frameworks, you cannot poll a GUI element to check if it has accumulated any events.) If you clicked on the vanilla button, the button would receive a button click event, but its default `action()` method (where button clicks "arrive") would simply return `false`, so the event travels up to the buttons container, which in this example is a standard `Frame` object. So the `Frame` gets the event, again through its `action()` method, but it too refuses to handle the event, and the event is thrown out of the window (figuratively and literally —the window is the outermost container level, so it does not have any containers to pass the bucket on to). To trap these events, you have to *subclass* any of the components you want to have trap events.

WARNING You cannot trap GUI events without somehow subclassing component classes.

All the event methods just listed are there to be *overridden* in sub-classes created from the vanilla `Button`, `Choice`, `TextField`, and other classes. Before you are given concrete examples, you need to have a look at what shapes and colors the events can come in.

Class Event

`Event` objects are passed as arguments to each and every event-trapping method. Here is the `Event` class definition:

```
public class Event extends Object {
    public Object target;
    public long when;
    public int id;
    public int x;
    public int y;
    public int key;
    public int modifiers;
    public int clickCount;
    public Object arg;
    public Event evt;

    public Event(Object target, long when, int id, int x, int y, int key,
    ➥int modifiers, Object arg);
    public Event(Object target, long when, int id, int x, int y, int key,
    ➥int modifiers);
    public Event(Object target, int id, Object arg);
    public void translate(int x, int y);
    public boolean shiftDown();
    public boolean controlDown();
    public boolean metaDown();
    protected String paramString();
    public String toString();
}
```

NOTE For brevity's sake, not all of the `Event` class constants are listed here. All of the constants will be listed later in the chapter.

If you look at the overall structure of class `Event`, you will see that it consists of several instance variables, three constructors, and a number of instance methods. In fact, this class is much more data structure than code since the methods are mostly simple state query-ing functions (`shiftDown()`, `controlDown()`, and `metaDown()`). Here are the more important instance variables:

target   This object reference points to the GUI element that caused the event. If the event emanated from a `Button`, this variable would hold a reference to that `Button`.

when   A timestamp value expressed in milliseconds since January 1, 1970. This value can be used to calculate the time between events (see *clickcount*, below).

id   The event type ID code (see list of event types on the next page).

x,y   The coordinates of the mouse pointer at the time of the event.

key   For keyboard events only: the ASCII key code for standard keys or one of the special keys (`HOME`, `RIGHT`, `F2`, and so on…) for `KEY_ACTION` (and release) events.

modifiers   For all events: flags for Ctrl, Alt, Shift, and Meta modifier keys held down at the time of the event.

clickcount   For mouse click events: the number of clicks (sin-gle, double, triple, and so on).

arg   The argument object. This can be anything that helps to further identify the event-causing GUI element (for example, the string label of a `Button`, the value of a `Checkbox`, and so on).

evt   A pointer to the next event in the linked list of events (or `null` if this is the last event).

The event `id` field can hold any of the `Event` types listed in Table 12.1. The table tells you which components can generate which types of events.

Table 12.1: Event Types and Possible Component Sources

Event ID	Button	Canvas	Checkbox	Choice	List	Panel	Scrollbar	TextField	TextArea
ACTION_EVENT	✓		✓	✓	✓				
KEY_PRESS	✓	✓	✓	✓	✓	✓		✓	✓
KEY_RELEASE	✓	✓	✓	✓	✓	✓		✓	✓
KEY_ACTION	✓	✓	✓	✓	✓	✓		✓	✓
KEY_ACTION_RELEASE		✓	✓	✓	✓	✓		✓	✓
MOUSE_DOWN		✓				✓			
MOUSE_UP		✓				✓			
MOUSE_MOVE		✓				✓			
MOUSE_ENTER		✓				✓			
MOUSE_EXIT		✓				✓			
MOUSE_DRAG		✓				✓			
SCROLL_LINE_UP							✓		
SCROLL_LINE_DOWN							✓		
SCROLL_PAGE_UP							✓		
SCROLL_PAGE_DOWN							✓		
SCROLL_ABSOLUTE							✓		
LIST_SELECT					✓				
LIST_DESELECT					not used!				
LOST_FOCUS		✓				✓			
GOT_FOCUS		✓				✓			

> **NOTE**
>
> The concept of a GUI *focus* is as follows: To avoid having to use the mouse exclusively when working with a GUI, the user can use keyboard command equivalents. Particularly, to select a component with the keyboard, you would use the arrow keys to go to the component and then hit enter to "click" it. The mouse pointer doesn't actually move when you use the arrow keys, so another technique is used to show where you are: the focus. The focus is the component cursor used to highlight the currently selected component.

Table 12.1 shows that there is little consistency in the type of events generated by each component. The table was derived by experimentation (on a Windows 95 machine) using the following program:

```java
import java.awt.*;

public class WhatGeneratesWhat extends java.applet.Applet {

public void init() {

    // use two components to test TABing between them and whether they
    // support FOCUS LOST/GOT events

    add(new ComponentToBeTested() );
    add(new ComponentToBeTested() );
}}

//————————————————————————————————————————
// To test a specific components, you just uncomment the line
// with the desired component
//————————————————————————————————————————

//class ComponentToBeTested extends Button {
//class ComponentToBeTested extends Canvas {
//class ComponentToBeTested extends Checkbox {
//class ComponentToBeTested extends Choice {
//class ComponentToBeTested extends List {
//class ComponentToBeTested extends Scrollbar {
//class ComponentToBeTested extends TextField {
//class ComponentToBeTested extends TextArea {
class ComponentToBeTested extends Panel {        // <- this one tested now

ComponentToBeTested() {

// Some code specific for Choice and List components
//    addItem("One");
//    addItem("Two");
//    addItem("Three");
```

```
        // Some code specific to Scrollbars
        //    super(Scrollbar.HORIZONTAL, 0,10,0,100);
        //    super(Scrollbar.VERTICAL, 0,10,0,100);

        // Some code specific to TextAreas
        //    super("Hello mum\nTesting..\nTesting..",5,5);

        // Some code specific to test Panels
            add(new Button("In a Panel"));
        }

        public Dimension preferredSize() {
            return new Dimension(100,50);
        }

        public void paint(Graphics g) {
            // for Canvas and Panel the diagonal indicates where their
            // zones are (otherwise they are completely invisible)
            getGraphics().drawLine(0,0, 100,100);
        }

        public boolean handleEvent(Event evt) {
          switch (evt.id) {
            case Event.MOUSE_ENTER:
                System.out.println("Mouse ENTER");          return true;
            case Event.MOUSE_EXIT:
                System.out.println("Mouse EXIT");           return true;
            case Event.MOUSE_MOVE:
                System.out.println("Mouse MOVE");           return true;
            case Event.MOUSE_DOWN:
                System.out.println("Mouse DOWN");           return true;
            case Event.MOUSE_DRAG:
                System.out.println("Mouse DRAG");           return true;
            case Event.MOUSE_UP:
                System.out.println("Mouse UP");             return true;
            case Event.KEY_PRESS:
                System.out.println("Key PRESS");            return true;
            case Event.KEY_ACTION:
                System.out.println("Key ACTION");           return true;
            case Event.KEY_RELEASE:
                System.out.println("Key PRESS RELEASE");    return true;
            case Event.KEY_ACTION_RELEASE:
                System.out.println("Key ACTION RELEASE");   return true;
            case Event.ACTION_EVENT:
```

```
            System.out.println("ACTION EVENT");        return true;
    case Event.GOT_FOCUS:
            System.out.println("Got FOCUS");            return true;
    case Event.LOST_FOCUS:
            System.out.println("Lost FOCUS");           return true;
    case Event.LIST_SELECT:
            System.out.println("List SELECTION");       return true;
    case Event.LIST_DESELECT:
            System.out.println("List DESELECT");        return true;
    case Event.SCROLL_PAGE_UP:
            System.out.println("Slider PGUP");          return true;
    case Event.SCROLL_PAGE_DOWN:
            System.out.println("Slider PGDN");          return true;
    case Event.SCROLL_LINE_UP:
            System.out.println("Slider LINE UP");       return true;
    case Event.SCROLL_LINE_DOWN:
            System.out.println("Slider LINE DOWN");     return true;
    case Event.SCROLL_ABSOLUTE:
            System.out.println("Slider ABSOLUTE");      return true;
    default:
            System.out.println("Unknown ID! " + evt.id);
  }
  return false;
}}
```

NOTE   The program overrides method `handleEvent()` in each targeted `Component` to trap all possible events it generates. Method `handleEvent()` is explained later in the chapter.

At the time of this writing, there are well-documented platform differences (namely, bugs) as to what component generates what event. It is advisable to use the previous program to ascertain whether your machine handles every Event/Component combination in the same way shown in Table 12.1. Currently, the support for focus switching on Windows 95 platforms is very poor. For example, when you press the Tab key in a TextField, you should receive a LOST_FOCUS event from the field you left and a GOT_FOCUS from the next component in the layout, especially if it is another TextField, but at this time you do not. This problem may be fixed by the time you read this, however.

In addition to normal keys trapped as `KEY_PRESS` and `KEY_RELEASE` events, the keyboard events `KEY_ACTION` and `KEY_ACTION_RELEASE` signal the use of the following nonstandard keys in the key field:

- `HOME` and `END`

- `PGUP` and `PGDN`

- `UP`, `DOWN`, `LEFT`, and `RIGHT`

- `F1` through `F12`

WARNING Not every keyboard has these keys, so do not write an application that relies on them so heavily that the application would be useless if the user cannot press them.

The keyboard and mouse events are also qualified by the presence or absence of modifier keys like Shift, Ctrl, Alt, and a platform-specific *meta* key. These keys are flagged in the `modifiers` field and can be extracted by anding with one or more of the following binary masks.

- `SHIFT_MASK`

- `CTRL_MASK`

- `META_MASK`

- `ALT_MASK`

TIP For Shift, Ctrl, and Meta, you should use the methods `shiftDown()`, `controlDown()`, and `metaDown()`. The absence of such a method for the Alt modifier means you have to use the manual method of anding for Alt.

All the constants listed so far are `Event` class constants, which means you need to specify them with their class name (`Event`) prepended. Here are some examples:

```
if (event.id == Event.LIST_SELECT) …
if (event.key == Event.F10) …
if ((event.modifiers & Event.ALT_MASK) != 0 ) …
```

Now that you have looked closely at the class that lies at the heart of event processing, the next section will look at how applets and applications deal with events generated by AWT components.

Applet Event Trapping

This section provides some concrete examples of event handling, starting with applets. As with using GUI components and layouts, applets initially make it simple to trap and process events, as compared with applications. The reason for this is that the first coding step in building an applet (subclassing `java.applet.Applet`) makes it easy to handle events as well. Subclassing has a very convenient side effect: It allows you to override any of the `Component` event-trapping methods straightaway (an `Applet` is a distant extension of a `Component`, remember). Here is an example:

```
import java.awt.*;

public class EventTest extends java.applet.Applet {

public boolean mouseUp(Event event, int x, int y) {
    dumpEvent(event, "MOUSE_UP");
    return true;
}

public boolean mouseDown(Event event, int x, int y) {
    dumpEvent(event, "MOUSE_DOWN");
    return true;
}
```

```
public boolean mouseDrag(Event event, int x, int y) {
    dumpEvent(event, "MOUSE_DRAG");
    return true;
}

public boolean mouseMove(Event event, int x, int y) {
    dumpEvent(event, "MOUSE_MOVE");
    return true;
}

public boolean mouseEnter(Event event, int x, int y) {
    dumpEvent(event, "MOUSE_ENTER");
    return true;
}

public boolean mouseExit(Event event, int x, int y) {
    dumpEvent(event, "MOUSE_EXIT");
    return true;
}

public void gotFocus() {
    showStatus("GOT_FOCUS event");
    System.out.println("GOT_FOCUS event");
}

public void lostFocus() {
    showStatus("LOST_FOCUS event");
    System.out.println("LOST_FOCUS event");
}

public boolean keyDown(Event event, int key) {
    if (event.id == Event.KEY_PRESS) {
        dumpEvent(event, "KEY_PRESS event  : " + (char) key + " key");
    } else
        if (event.id == Event.KEY_ACTION) {
        dumpEvent(event, "KEY_ACTION event  : " + (char) key + " key");
    }
    return true;
}

public boolean keyUp(Event event, int key) {
    if (event.id == Event.KEY_RELEASE) {
        dumpEvent(event, "KEY_RELEASE event: " + (char) key + " key");
    } else
        if (event.id == Event.KEY_ACTION_RELEASE) {
        dumpEvent(event, "KEY_ACTION_RELEASE event: " + (char) key + " key");
    }
    return true;
}

private void dumpEvent(Event event, String info) {
String shift, ctrl, alt, meta;
int x,y;
```

```
showStatus(info);

x       = event.x;
y       = event.y;

shift = event.shiftDown()                         ? "(SHIFT)" : "";
ctrl  = event.controlDown()                       ? "(CTRL)"  : "";
meta  = event.metaDown()                          ? "(META)"  : "";
alt   = ((event.modifiers & Event.ALT_MASK) != 0) ? "(ALT)"   : "";

System.out.println(info + " @("+ x +","+ y +")" +shift+ctrl+meta+alt);
}}
```

If you run this applet, you should see how the applet responds to mouse clicks, mouse drags, mouse moves, and keyboard input. Try spending a good ten to fifteen minutes familiarizing yourself with the idiosyncrasies of the event-reporting system. For example, a mouse drag can leave the window area, while mouse moves are restricted to stay within the window. Also, AWT always seems to insert a mouse-drag event between a mouse-down and a mouse-up event, whether you move the mouse or not.

The dumpEvent() method prints information on all of these events on both the console (using the usual System.out.println()) and in the status line of the browser you are using to view the applet. This is done with the showStatus() applet method. It also uses the modifier-key checking methods to tell whether one of those keys accompanied the event. Using these methods in your own programs allows you to check for shift+clicks, control+double-clicks, and so on. Also notice that all event methods (except the focus methods) return true to signal to the applet's container (that is, the browser) that the event has been consumed. The browser never hears of the events.

Trapping events within applets is very simple. Before you learn how to add components that respond to various event types to your applets, you should see how applications tackle events. This is a bit more complicated.

Application Event Trapping

You usually start writing an application by creating a brand new class, which is not as cozy as subclassing class `Applet`, a situation in which you can override any event-trapping method right from the word go. With applications, you need to subclass any GUI component that you want to have trap its events. For example, to trap an `ACTION_EVENT` of a `Button` added to a `Frame`, you might do the following:

```
import java.awt.*;

class AppButton {

public static void main (String[] args) {

Frame window;
MyButton myButton;

    window   = new Frame("a vanilla Frame window");
    myButton = new MyButton("I had to be subclassed");

    window.setLayout(new FlowLayout());
    window.add(myButton);
    window.resize(300,100);
    window.show();
}}

class MyButton extends Button {

MyButton(String label) {
    super(label);
}

public boolean action (Event e, Object arg) {
    System.out.println("Pressed button: " + arg);
    return true;
}}
```

Figure 12.2 shows the resulting application window and button.

A whole new `Button` subclass had to be added to override the button's `action()` method, which is where events are sent to for

FIGURE 12.2:

Standard `Frame`
window with a
subclassed `Button`

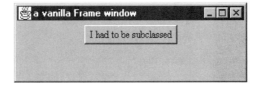

Button, Choice, Checkbox, and List components. Just click the button and you will see that `System.out.println()` is called. The `action()` method has two arguments: the event itself and an extra *event argument*. In the case of buttons, this is the button's label `String` (which is what you are printing out to prove the button got pressed). The `MyButton` class also needed a constructor: Since you would like to keep giving your buttons a label, an analogous constructor had to be written that takes a `String` label argument.

But it is wasteful to add a whole new class simply to trap a simple button click. Imagine a real GUI with dozens of components—you would be creating classes like rabbits make new rabbits! There is another way to catch a button click, but it still means creating a new class. As you learned earlier, all default event handling methods for standard `Component` subclasses refuse to handle their events by passing events to their container. So, to avoid subclassing `Button`, you let a vanilla `Button` give its click event to its container, your `Frame` window object. But this means you need to subclass `Frame` to catch the event, as follows:

```
import java.awt.*;

class AppButton2 {

public static void main (String[] args) {

MyFrame myWindow;
Button button;

    myWindow = new MyFrame("A subclassed Frame window");
    button   = new Button("I'm a vanilla Button");
```

```
        myWindow.setLayout(new FlowLayout());
        myWindow.add(button);
        myWindow.resize(300,100);
        myWindow.show();
}}

class MyFrame extends Frame {

MyFrame(String label) {
        super(label);
}

public boolean action (Event e, Object arg) {
        if (e.target instanceof Button) {
                System.out.println("Buttons are so lazy...");
                System.out.println("Button pressed:" + arg);
        }
        return true;
}}
```

Figure 12.3 shows a `Frame` window with a vanilla `Button`.

The `Frame`'s `action()` method is slightly different from the previous example's `Button action()`. First, you check whether the event you obtained came from your `Button` by making sure the event's target field is of type `Button`. You never know what kind of events might arrive here. The resulting program is almost exactly the same size as in the first example, and there is still an unwanted subclass cluttering your software, so what's the advantage of moving up one level the responsibility for handling the event? The big advantage is that you can now add a whole mixture of dozens of standard components to this single subclassed `Frame` object, and all of their different events will arrive at the same spot, where they can be processed by one method: the `action()` method.

> **TIP**
>
> Minimizing the number of classes in your programs is important for applets or applications dynamically loading classes off the Internet. Each class is loaded using a separate connection (like the parallel loading of images in a Web page). While this mechanism is faster than sequentially loading your program's classes, loading fewer classes is faster still.

There is a simple trick to merging the two classes into one. Look at the class names given to the startup class, `AppButton` and `AppButton2`. Why not have your startup class *be* the `Frame` subclass? This would mean you could immediately override the event-handling methods for your window and simply add standard components which will all hand their events to the window. Here is an example:

```
import java.awt.*;

class AppFrame extends Frame {

public static void main (String[] args) {

AppFrame myWindow;
Button button;

    myWindow = new AppFrame("A subclassed Frame window");
    button   = new Button("I'm a vanilla Button");

    myWindow.setLayout(new FlowLayout());
    myWindow.add(button);
    myWindow.resize(300,100);
    myWindow.show();
}

AppFrame(String label) {
    super(label);
}
```

```
public boolean action (Event e, Object arg) {
    if (e.target instanceof Button) {
        System.out.println("Buttons are so lazy...");
        System.out.println("Button pressed:" + arg);
    }
    return true;
}}
```

Bingo—you have created an application made from a single class using a non-subclassed `Button` which still reacts to button clicks. This is much better than the two previous approaches. And now comes the icing on the cake: Using this technique, you can write applications that are applets too, or vice versa—applets that double as applications. Here's how, starting from the beginning:

- For an applet you *have* to subclass `java.applet.Applet`

- For an application you *have* to have a `public static void main()` method

Consequently, if you just add a `main()` method to an existing applet, you are halfway there. The only other thing needed to make such a chameleon class work is a (browser-imitating) window for the applet to run in and a call to the applet's `init()` method:

```
import java.awt.*;

public class Chameleon extends java.applet.Applet {

public static void main (String[] args) {

Frame window;
Chameleon ourselves = new Chameleon();

    window = new Frame ("A vanilla Frame window");

    window.add("Center", ourselves);
    ourselves.init();
    window.resize(300,100);
    window.show();
}
```

```
public void init() {
Button button;
    button = new Button("A vanilla Button");
    add(button);
}

public boolean action (Event e, Object arg) {
                        if (e.target instanceof Button) {
        System.out.println("Applets always have to do everyting around here.");
        System.out.println("Button pressed:" + arg);
    }
    return true;
}}
```

Viewed as an applet, the program just overrides the init() method to add a Button to itself and overrides its action() method to catch the Button events which the standard Buttons throw away. If viewed as an application, the program is much more interesting: Starting with the main() method, the application creates an instance of itself. Variable ourselves represents the entire applet. The main method proceeds with the creation of a Frame window and adds the applet to this window. Note that, since you did not use a setLayout() on the window, you are stuck with a Frame's standard layout manager: a BorderLayout. To add the applet "component," then, you need to tell it to go in the "Center" BorderLayout zone, where it will actually expand to fill the whole window, since no other BorderLayout components are specified. Next, in exactly the same way as any browser would do, you call the applet's init() method (which adds a Button to itself, laid out using *its* default layout manager: FlowLayout). The next two steps are the usual window sizing and displaying commands. If you compile this program, you can either run it directly from your prompt as an application, or feed it to any browser as an applet.

Method handleEvent()

The convenient event-trapping methods—action(), keyUp(),
mouseDown(), mouseDrag(), and so on—that you need to override in
your classes are actually called themselves by a lower-level
Component method you can also override. Method handleEvent() is
the main events switchboard for components. Studying its default
implementation is instructive:

```
public boolean handleEvent(Event evt) {
    switch (evt.id) {
      case Event.MOUSE_ENTER:
        return mouseEnter(evt, evt.x, evt.y);
      case Event.MOUSE_EXIT:
        return mouseExit(evt, evt.x, evt.y);
      case Event.MOUSE_MOVE:
        return mouseMove(evt, evt.x, evt.y);
      case Event.MOUSE_DOWN:
        return mouseDown(evt, evt.x, evt.y);
      case Event.MOUSE_DRAG:
        return mouseDrag(evt, evt.x, evt.y);

      case Event.MOUSE_UP:
        return mouseUp(evt, evt.x, evt.y);

      case Event.KEY_PRESS:
      case Event.KEY_ACTION:
        return keyDown(evt, evt.key);

      case Event.KEY_RELEASE:
      case Event.KEY_ACTION_RELEASE:
        return keyUp(evt, evt.key);

      case Event.ACTION_EVENT:
        return action(evt, evt.arg);
      case Event.GOT_FOCUS:
        return gotFocus(evt, evt.arg);
      case Event.LOST_FOCUS:
        return lostFocus(evt, evt.arg);
    }
    return false;
}
```

As you can see, mouse, key, and button (action) events arrive first in `handleEvent()`, quickly to be shunted onwards toward the simpler methods like `mouseDown()`. Another interesting point is that the x,y and `key` arguments you get as parameters in `mouseDown()` and `keyDown()`, for example, are available from the `Event` object itself. In other words, these event-handling routines were really designed to make our lives as easy as possible. Realizing what `handleEvent()` does you might be forgiven for thinking that it is best to leave this method well alone. If not, all our convenient event-trapping methods will cease to function. True. But `handleEvent()` is not perfect: It does not support `List` selections and `Scrollbar` manipulations. This is why you will have to override this master event handler too, at some point, if you want to handle `List` or `Scrollbar` interaction at all in your programs. This is demonstrated in the next section.

Component Event Types

This section will show you explicitly how to handle the various events generated by the following AWT components:

- `Button`

- `Canvas`

- `Checkbox`

- `Choice`

- `TextField`

- `List`

- `Scrollbar`

- `Menus`

The example programs are all combined application-applet chameleons and most let the component's events bubble up to the applet, where they are processed.

Button Events

Buttons were already used in all of the introductory programs; since the `Canvas` demonstration adds a `Button` to its demonstration, please see the `Canvas` example in the next section.

Canvas Events

A `Canvas` is a drawable area without any graphical outline or highlight. In other words, it is an invisible component. A very simple little doodling program demonstrates how to trap `Canvas` events and draw in a Canvas. It uses an enhanced (subclassed) `Canvas` component to provide the doodling area, and it includes a button to erase the canvas when your scribbles have become worthless.

Figure 12.4 shows the Doodle demo window with an unhappy doodle about to be wiped.

FIGURE 12.4:

A `Doodle` class based on a `Canvas`

Here is the code behind Figure 12.4:

```
import java.awt.*;

public class DoodleTest extends java.applet.Applet {

Doodle doodle;

public static void main(String[] args) {
    Frame f = new Frame("DoodleTest");
    f.add("Center", new DoodleTest());
    f.resize(300, 150);
    f.show();
}

public DoodleTest() {
Button b = new Button("Clear");

    doodle = new Doodle();
    add(doodle);
    add(b);
}

public boolean action(Event e, Object label) {
    System.out.println("Clear");
    doodle.repaint();
    return true;
}}

class Doodle extends Canvas {

int x = 0;
int y = 0;

public Dimension preferredSize() {
    return new Dimension(90,90);
}

public void paint(Graphics g) {
    g.drawRect(0, 0, this.size().width-1, this.size().height-1);
}

public boolean mouseDown(Event e, int x, int y) {
    this.x = x;
    this.y = y;
    return true;
```

```
    }

    public boolean mouseDrag(Event e, int x, int y) {
        getGraphics().drawLine(this.x, this.y, x, y);
        this.x = x;
        this.y = y;
        return true;
    }}
```

The core of the program is the `Doodle` class. This class extends the `Canvas` class so that it can handle `Canvas` events itself as well as to give it a handy outline, so users can tell where the canvas starts and stops. The overridden `mouseDown()` and `mouseDrag()` methods together implement the free-form doodling capability of class `Doodle`. Method `mouseDown()` is used to remember the starting coordinates of a stroke, and `mouseDrag()` is used to add lines that connect the last position with the new. When moving the mouse slowly, this results in smooth curves being drawn. But if the mouse is dragged in a quick, jerky way, the program gives away its implementation details as the straight lines drawn by `drawLine()` become very clear.

`Doodle` also overrides the `paint()` method in class `Component`, so that whenever the `canvas` needs to redraw itself, it highlights itself by drawing an outline around its drawing surface. This brings us to a very important point: The `Doodle` class does not store your doodles anywhere other than directly on the screen, which means that any windows overlapping your doodle will effectively erase it. A "real" doodle program (if such a beast is ever needed) should draw the user's strokes on the screen *and* in an off-screen buffer that it can then copy to the screen whenever a window refresh is called upon. See Chapter 13 for more about off-screen buffers.

The last point to note about class `Doodle` is the overridden `preferredSize()` method. This tells the layout manager used by the container in which the doodle is placed that it would really like to be sized to 90 × 90 pixels.

The `Doodle` canvas is used alongside a Clear command button in an `Applet` container. As an applet, class `DoodleTest` introduces a new technique for constructing its GUI: Instead of overriding the `init()` method as you have done so far, it simply uses its constructor to `add()` the components to itself. This way you avoid having to call an `init()` on the applet since constructing the object will initialize the applet instead.

The applet's `action()` method is overridden to catch the `Button`'s click event, which commands the program to erase the doodle drawing. This is achieved indirectly by calling method `repaint()`, a `Component` method which calls `paint()`. The advantage of calling `repaint()` is that you do not have to gain access to a `Graphics` object to pass to the `paint()` method; `repaint()` takes no arguments at all.

Checkbox Events

Checkboxes, as you saw in the previous chapter on AWT components, are independent on/off state buttons. A simple program that gives a user two options to alter the appearance of the overused "`Hello World`" string demonstrates their use. One checkbox selects a different font (Courier instead of Times Roman) to render the string, while the other checkbox selects a different color (red instead of black). Figure 12.5 shows how the program looks on the screen.

FIGURE 12.5:

Trapping `Checkbox` events

Here is the code behind Figure 12.5:

```
import java.awt.*;

public class CheckBoxes extends java.applet.Applet {

boolean  bFancyFont   = false;
boolean  bShowColor   = false;
String   strFancyFont = "Fancy Font";
String   strShowColor = "Show Color";

public static void main(String[] args) {
    Frame f = new Frame("CheckBoxes");
    f.add("Center", new CheckBoxes());
    f.resize(300, 150);
    f.show();
}

public CheckBoxes() {
    add(new Checkbox(strFancyFont));
    add(new Checkbox(strShowColor));
}

public boolean action(Event event, Object argument) {

    if (event.target instanceof Checkbox) {
        Checkbox checkbox = (Checkbox) event.target;

        if (checkbox.getLabel().equals(strFancyFont) ) {
            bFancyFont = checkbox.getState();
        }

        if (checkbox.getLabel().equals(strShowColor) ) {
            bShowColor = checkbox.getState();
        }
        repaint();
    }
    return true;
}

public void paint(Graphics g ) {
Font f;

    if (bFancyFont) {
        f = new Font("TimesRoman", Font.BOLD, 36);
    } else {
```

```
        f = new Font("Courier", Font.BOLD, 36);
    }

    if (bShowColor) {
        g.setColor(Color.red);
    } else {
        g.setColor(Color.black);
    }

    g.setFont(f);
    g.drawString("Hello World", 50, 75);
}}
```

The core of the program is (fittingly) the applet's action() method where the code gains access to the Checkbox object that generated the event by casting the event's target field into a Checkbox variable. It then identifies which of the two checkboxes generated the event by comparing their label strings. Finally, to alter the attributes of the "Hello World" string, it obtains the new state of the changed checkbox by using the method getState(). The final repaint() call is again used to indirectly call paint(), which then renders the string using the new attributes.

The paint() method uses the setColor() and setFont() methods to alter the graphics context state before redrawing the text string in its altered appearance (see Chapter 13 for more on graphics methods).

Checkboxes can also be made to act as mutually exclusive radio buttons through the additional use of the CheckboxGroup helper class. Here is a program which uses the two and processes events generated by the radio buttons.

Here is the code behind Figure 12.6:

```
import java.awt.*;

public class RadioButtons extends java.applet.Applet {

final String    str8  = "8";
final String    str14 = "14";
final String    str24 = "24";
```

```
final String   str32 = "32";
Integer  intFontSize;

public static void main(String[] args) {
    Frame f = new Frame("RadioButtons");
    f.add("Center", new RadioButtons());
    f.resize(300, 150);
    f.show();
}

public RadioButtons() {
    CheckboxGroup cbg = new CheckboxGroup();

    add(new Checkbox( str8,  cbg, true ) );
    add(new Checkbox( str14, cbg, false) );
    add(new Checkbox( str24, cbg, false) );
    add(new Checkbox( str32, cbg, false) );

     intFontSize = new Integer( str8 );
}

public boolean action(Event event, Object argument) {
    if (event.target instanceof Checkbox) {
        Checkbox checkbox = (Checkbox) event.target;
        intFontSize = Integer.valueOf(checkbox.getLabel());
        repaint();
    }
    return true;
}

public void paint(Graphics g) {
    Font f = new Font("TimesRoman", Font.BOLD, intFontSize.intValue());
    g.setFont(f);
    g.drawString("Hello World", 50, 75);
}}
```

Figure 12.6 shows how the program looks on screen.

As you can see, the technique to handle the button events remains the same. After checking the type of generating component with the if instanceof idiom, the action() method transforms the label of the radio button into a font size using the Integer.valueOf() class method. The paint() method then creates a new Font object of the

FIGURE 12.6:

Trapping mutually exclu-
sive Checkbox events

FIGURE 12.6:

Trapping mutually exclu-
sive Checkbox events

selected point size and sets it as the current font to be used with
setFont(). Finally, drawString() reflects the change requested by
the user.

Choice Events

As you learned in the previous chapter, Choice components are very
similar in purpose to a collection of mutually exclusive checkboxes in
that they allow you to select one item from a small list of items. The
ease with which you can switch back and forth between using checkboxes and choice lists is only made more apparent when you notice
how alike their event-handling code is. You modified the CheckBoxes
demo to use a Choice list instead. Although the graphical result is
very different (see Figure 12.7), the code did not need many changes
at all:

```
import java.awt.*;

public class ChoiceList extends java.applet.Applet {

    String   str8  = "8";
    String   str14 = "14";
    String   str24 = "24";
    String   str32 = "32";
    Integer  intFontSize;
```

FIGURE 12.7:

Trapping Choice events

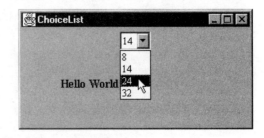

```java
public static void main(String[] args) {
    Frame f = new Frame("ChoiceList");
    f.add("Center", new ChoiceList());
    f.resize(300, 150);
    f.show();
}

public ChoiceList() {
  Choice choice = new Choice();

  choice.addItem(str8);
  choice.addItem(str14);
  choice.addItem(str24);
  choice.addItem(str32);

  choice.select(str14);

  add(choice);

  intFontSize = new Integer(str14);
}

public boolean action(Event event, Object argument) {
  if (event.target instanceof Choice) {
     Choice choice = (Choice) event.target;

     intFontSize   = Integer.valueOf(choice.getSelectedItem());
     repaint();
  }
  return true;
}

public void paint(Graphics g) {
  Font f = new Font("TimesRoman", Font.BOLD, intFontSize.intValue());
  g.setFont(f);
```

```
    g.drawString("Hello World", 50, 75);
}}
```

The main difference between the `action()` method that handles a `Choice` event and the one that deals with `Checkbox` events is that the `Choice action()` method does not have to identify which component generated the event. In the case of the `ChoiceList` example, there is only one component. On the other hand, the `ChoiceList action()` method still has to find out which `Choice` item the user selected. This it does with the `Choice getSelectedItem()`method. Since the items are again just the strings "8", "14", "24", or "32", these can be used directly in a string-to-integer conversion to set the new font size.

TextField Events

Although TextFields channel their events purely through the various keyboard event types (KEY_PRESS, KEY_RELEASE, and so on), and therefore you should normally trap these via the `keyDown()` and `keyUp()` methods, you can stick to overriding an `action()` method as long as you override it in the container for the `TextField`(s). The program below illustrates this. It simply accepts a string which is used to change the string being printed as feedback.

Figure 12.8 shows a screen shot of the program in action.

FIGURE 12.8:

Trapping `TextField` events

Here is the code behind Figure 12.8:

```
import java.awt.*;

public class TextBox extends java.applet.Applet {

String strMessage = "Hello World";
Font    f         =  null;

public static void main(String[] args) {
    Frame f = new Frame("TextBox");
    f.add("Center", new TextBox());
    f.resize(300, 150);
    f.show();
}

public TextBox() {
    f = new Font("TimesRoman", Font.BOLD, 24);
    add(new TextField(strMessage, 15));
}

public boolean action(Event event, Object argument) {
    if (event.target instanceof TextField) {
        strMessage = ((TextField) event.target).getText();
        repaint();
    }
    return true;
}

public void paint(Graphics g) {
    g.setFont(f);
    g.drawString(strMessage, 50, 75);
}}
```

Here, the TextBox applet's action() method catches the event which the vanilla TextField refuses to handle (standard keyDown() and keyUp() methods return false). After checking that the event does emanate from the TextField, the action() method extracts the full string from the TextField using the TextComponent getText() method. Note the on-the-fly casting of the event.target field to avoid having to declare a TextField variable.

List Events

If you look back at Table 12.1 and check which events a List component can generate, you will see that it can generate LIST_*xxx* events
and the usual ACTION_EVENT event. Do not let this confuse you. Since
a List generates an ACTION_EVENT in the same way a Button,
Checkbox, or Choice does, trapping its event is done in exactly the
same way: by overriding the action() method. Here is an example
program that does just that:

```
import java.awt.*;

public class ListTest extends java.applet.Applet {

public void init() {
    String[] items = { "Red", "Orange", "Yellow",
                       "Green", "Blue","Indigo", "Violet" };
    MyList m = new MyList(5, items);
    add(m);
}}

class MyList extends List {

public MyList(int numItemsToDisplayAtOnce, String[] elements) {
    super(numItemsToDisplayAtOnce, false);

    for (int i=0; i<elements.length; i++) {
        addItem(elements[i]);
    }
}

public boolean action(Event e, Object selectedEntry) {
    System.out.println("Selected " + selectedEntry);
    return true;
}}
```

Figure 12.9 shows the resulting applet running.

FIGURE 12.9:

Handling List
selections

Scrollbar Events

Among the subclasses of class Component, class Scrollbar is rather
an oddity. It is not supported by the convenience event-trapping
method action(). The standard handleEvent() method
implemented by components does not even check for Scrollbar's
five events:

- SCROLL_LINE_UP

- SCROLL_LINE_DOWN

- SCROLL_PAGE_UP

- SCROLL_PAGE_DOWN

- SCROLL_ABSOLUTE

You are therefore forced to override the handleEvent() method to
be able to trap these events. As the following program shows, this is
actually not any harder than overriding the usual action() methods, it is just one level "higher" in the calling hierarchy.

The program creates the applet shown in Figure 12.10.

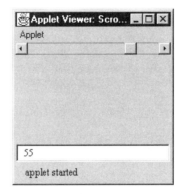

Here is the code behind Figure 12.10:

```java
import java.applet.*;
import java.awt.*;

public class ScrollbarTest extends Applet {

TextField display;

public static void main(String[] args) {
    Frame f = new Frame("ScrollbarTest");
    f.add("Center", new ScrollbarTest());
    f.resize(300, 150);
    f.show();
}

public ScrollbarTest() {
    setLayout(new BorderLayout());
    MyScrollbar sb = new MyScrollbar(this);
    display = new TextField("0", 5);
    add("North", sb);
    add("South", display);
}

public void setValue(int value) {
    display.setText(Integer.toString(value));
}}

class MyScrollbar extends Scrollbar {
```

```
ScrollbarTest applet;

public MyScrollbar(ScrollbarTest app) {
    super(Scrollbar.HORIZONTAL, 0, 10, -100,100);
            // make it a horizontal scrollbar
            // initial value is 0
            // how much to "page" up or down
            // range is [-100,100]
    applet = app;
}

public boolean handleEvent(Event e) {
    int temperature = ((MyScrollbar) e.target).getValue();
    applet.setValue(temperature);
    return true;
}}
```

This program lets the Scrollbar handle its events. The Scrollbar does not pass on its events to its container. This is indicated by the true return value in the overridden handleEvent() Scrollbar method. This method does not need to check where the event came from using an if instanceof statement, because it knows it is the only source for any events. The handleEvent() Scrollbar method also ignores testing for the different SCROLL_*xxx* event types by homing straight in and fetching the Scrollbar's represented value. This it does with a call to getValue(). To communicate this value back to the main program, it uses a method provided by your Scrollbar-Test class: setValue(). To be able to invoke this method on the applet, a reference to the applet object had to be stored for this future use. That is the sole purpose of MyScrollbar's constructor argument: app. In the main class it is passed as the this self reference. This technique of passing a this reference to a client class so that it can "call back" the main class is very common in object-oriented systems.

Menu Events

Menu systems, if you recall from the last chapter, are special entities in your Java GUIs: Menu classes do not inherit from class Component, while all the other GUI elements in Java do. It follows that the menu classes do not have the same `action()`, `mouseDown()`, `keyDown()`, and so on methods to override. How then do you trap menu events? The answer is hidden in the following clue: Menus pass on their events to their container, which can only be of one type—the `Frame` window they are attached to. The way to trap menu events, then, is to use `Frame` subclasses with overridden `action()` methods that test for menu events. The following program enhances the `DoodleTest` program presented in the section on `Canvas` event trapping, by adding some menus to the program. This way, the `Frame`'s `action()` method will have to differentiate between `Button` and `Menu` events, demonstrating the kind of event sorting that a real-life `action()` method must do.

```java
import java.awt.*;
//──────────────────────────────────────────────────────────
public class DoodleMenuTest extends Frame {

private Doodle doodle;      // all instance methods need access to doodle

public static void main(String[] args) {
    new DoodleMenuTest("Super Deluxe Paintbox");
}

// Application constructor does all the hard work

DoodleMenuTest(String windowTitle) {
    super(windowTitle);

    doodle = new Doodle();

    setLayout(new FlowLayout() );      // chuck BorderLayout
    add(doodle);                       // add Canvas and Button
    add(new Button("Clear") );
    setMenuBar(new DoodleMenuBar());   // add Menus

    resize(300, 200);
    show();                            // go !
}

// action() method deals with menu and button events (Canvas manages itself)

public boolean action(Event event, Object label) {
    if (event.target instanceof MenuItem) {

        if ( ((String)label).equals("Pen") ) {
            doodle.setDrawingMode(Doodle.DRAW);
        } else
```

```
            if ( ((String)label).equals("Eraser") ) {
                doodle.setDrawingMode(Doodle.ERASE);
            } else

            if ( ((String)label).equals("Freehand") ) {
                doodle.setDrawingStyle(Doodle.FREEHAND);
            } else

            if ( ((String)label).equals("Single Dots") ) {
                doodle.setDrawingStyle(Doodle.SINGLEDOT);
            } else

            if ( ((String)label).equals("Quit") ) {
                dispose();
                System.exit(0);
            }

        } else if (event.target instanceof Button) {
            doodle.repaint();
        } else {
            System.out.println("Totally unexpected Event type: " + event);
        }
        return true;
}}
//————————————————————————————————————————————————————————————————
class Doodle extends Canvas {

static final int FREEHAND   = 0;
static final int SINGLEDOT  = 1;

static final int DRAW       = 0;
static final int ERASE      = 1;

private int x = 0;
private int y = 0;
private int drawingStyle = FREEHAND;
private int drawingMode  = DRAW;

private Color drawColor = Color.black;

// instance methods to let client classes alter the way Canvas draws

void setDrawingStyle(int drawStyle) {
    drawingStyle = drawStyle;
}

void setDrawingMode(int drawMode) {
Graphics g = getGraphics();

    drawingMode = drawMode;
    drawColor = (drawingMode == DRAW) ? Color.black : getBackground();
    setForeground(drawColor);
}
```

```
public Dimension preferredSize() {
    return new Dimension(120,100);
}

public void paint(Graphics g) {
    g.setColor(Color.black);
    g.drawRect(0, 0, this.size().width-1, this.size().height-1);
}

public boolean mouseDown(Event e, int x, int y) {
    this.x = x;
    this.y = y;
    if (drawingStyle == SINGLEDOT) {
        getGraphics().drawRect(x,y, 1,1);          // a single 1x1 pixel
    }
    return true;
}

public boolean mouseDrag(Event e, int x, int y) {

    if (drawingStyle == SINGLEDOT) {
        getGraphics().drawRect(x,y, 1,1);
    } else
    if (drawingStyle == FREEHAND) {
        getGraphics().drawLine(this.x, this.y, x, y);
    }
    this.x = x;
    this.y = y;
    return true;
}}

//————————————————————————————————————————————————————————————
class DoodleMenuBar extends MenuBar {

DoodleMenuBar() {
    add(new ToolsMenu() );
    add(new StylesMenu() );
}}

//————————————————————————————————————————————————————————————
class ToolsMenu extends Menu {

ToolsMenu() {
    super("Tools");

    add("Pen");
    add("Eraser");
    addSeparator();
    add("Quit");
}}
```

```
//————————————————————————————————————
class StylesMenu extends Menu {

StylesMenu() {
    super("Styles");

    add("Freehand");
    add("Single Dots");
}}
```

Figure 12.11 shows the program in action.

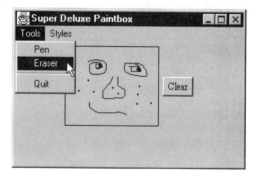

This application consists of five classes:

- The startup and `Frame` subclass, `DoodleTestMenu`

- The modified `Doodle` class

- The three application menu classes: `DoodleMenuBar`, `ToolsMenu`, and `StylesMenu`

First, the `Doodle` class is modified to support new drawing behavior. It now handles drawing and erasing pens, and it also has two drawing styles: freehand (as before) and single dots. To put the `Doodle Canvas` in these modes, clients should call the new `setDrawingMode()` and `setDrawingStyle()` `Doodle` methods. These take mnemonic `Doodle` class constants (declared as static finals).

The menu subclasses together define the menu bar which contains two menus: a Tools menu and a Styles menu. These are linked to the menu bar by the `DoodleMenuBar` constructor. The entire menu bar is itself added to the window using a `setMenuBar()` call in the window's constructor.

The window's `action()` method is where all the events (except those generated by the `Canvas`) congregate: The clear button clicks and the menu item selections all arrive here. The method therefore consists of several `if` statements that, by way of elimination, home in on the source of the event. Once the exact source is known, they call the associated `Doodle` state-changing methods to have the program reflect the user's wishes. One menu item is rather special: the "`Quit`" item in the "`Tools`" menu. To quit itself, the program first closes its window by calling the `Component hide()` method, and then—to ensure that no window or menu resources are left allocated (on the platforms native components side)—it calls the `Frame dispose()` method.

Summary

GUI event-handling is not a black art. Standard approaches have existed for procedural and object-oriented languages ever since the introduction of the GUI. Since both the procedural and object-oriented approaches, if applied strictly, have their advantages and disadvantages, the AWT event-handling architecture allows you to create an optimal hybrid system. At one extreme, you can have one central event-handling method (the old procedural approach), and at the other, you can have every single component handle its own events (the object-oriented approach). In practice, Java programs use code that exploits the strengths of both approaches while avoiding their weaknesses. The strength of having one, central event loop is its highly localized compactness. Paradoxically, the strength of the pure object-oriented approach lies in its distributed event handling: Having individual components handle their own events is more in keeping with the black box nature of object-oriented objects. The best of both worlds is achieved by overriding the `action()` method of containers, and not individual components.

CHAPTER

THIRTEEN

Animation and Images

- Rendering Basics with Class Graphics

- Animation Basics

- Image Processing

Of all our senses, vision is the most high-performance, high-bandwidth input device nature has given us. No wonder there has been serious demand, ever since their earliest use in the 1950s, that computer systems evolve into systems that interact through text and pictures, instead of switches and indicator lights. No other requirement shaped the evolution of computers so dramatically as that of the need for the (bitmapped) graphical user interface. And as proof of the success of the resulting Graphical User Interface, let's not forget that it took us all only a couple of years to master GUIs, before they became second nature.

Graphical programming, animation, and image manipulation has therefore become a skill *sine qua non* for any modern application developer. This chapter will introduce you to some of the basic techniques, set in the context of Java and its standard classes.

Rendering Basics with Class Graphics

Class Graphics in package java.awt encapsulates a small collection of *rendering* (that is, drawing) primitives you can use to dynamically generate images at run time. Here is its definition:

```
public class Graphics extends Object {
    protected Graphics();
    public abstract Graphics create();
    public Graphics create(int x, int y, int width, int height);
    public abstract void translate(int x, int y);
    public abstract Color getColor();
    public abstract void setColor(Color c);
    public abstract void setPaintMode();
    public abstract void setXORMode(Color c1);
    public abstract Font getFont();
    public abstract void setFont(Font font);
    public FontMetrics getFontMetrics();
    public abstract FontMetrics getFontMetrics(Font f);
    public abstract Rectangle getClipRect();
    public abstract void clipRect(int x, int y, int width, int height);
    public abstract void copyArea(int x, int y, int width, int height, int dx, int dy);
```

```
public abstract void drawLine(int x1, int y1, int x2, int y2);
public abstract void fillRect(int x, int y, int width, int height);
public void drawRect(int x, int y, int width, int height);
public abstract void clearRect(int x, int y, int width, int height);
public abstract void drawRoundRect(int x, int y, int width, int height, int
➥arcWidth, int arcHeight);
public abstract void fillRoundRect(int x, int y, int width, int height, int
➥arcWidth, int arcHeight);
public void draw3DRect(int x, int y, int width, int height, boolean raised);
public void fill3DRect(int x, int y, int width, int height, boolean raised);
public abstract void drawOval(int x, int y, int width, int height);
public abstract void fillOval(int x, int y, int width, int height);
public abstract void drawArc(int x, int y, int width, int height, int startAngle,
➥int arcAngle);
public abstract void fillArc(int x, int y, int width, int height, int startAngle,
➥int arcAngle);
public abstract void drawPolygon(int xPoints[], int yPoints[], int nPoints);
public void drawPolygon(Polygon p);
public abstract void fillPolygon(int xPoints[], int yPoints[], int nPoints);
public void fillPolygon(Polygon p);
public abstract void drawString(String str, int x, int y);
public void drawChars(char data[], int offset, int length, int x, int y);
public void drawBytes(byte data[], int offset, int length, int x, int y);
public abstract boolean drawImage(Image img, int x, int y, ImageObserver observer);
public abstract boolean drawImage(Image img, int x, int y, int width, int height,
➥ImageObserver observer);
public abstract boolean drawImage(Image img, int x, int y, Color bgcolor,    `
➥ImageObserver observer);
public abstract boolean drawImage(Image img, int x, int y, int width, int height,
➥Color bgcolor, ImageObserver observer);
public abstract void dispose();
public void finalize();
public String toString();
}
```

Each platform that supports Java, in fact, has its own (subclassed) implementation of Graphics. Class Graphics itself is abstract and cannot be instantiated. (Look at the declaration of its constructor: It is declared protected. Only subclasses can use Graphics's constructor.) So whenever you obtain a Graphics object (called a graphics context or graphics handle), you are actually using some platform-specific subclass of Graphics.

If you browse the methods defined by Graphics, you will quickly get a feel for what it is all about—plain 2-D rendering. The class is nothing fancy and most definitely does not support 3-D (Sun has announced a standard 3-D API for Java that the company will release sometime during the first half of 1997; see Chapter 21). The methods can be classified broadly into the following categories:

Drawing Lines	`drawLine()`
Drawing filled and outlined shapes:	
Rectangles	`drawRect()`, `clearRect()`, `fillrect()`, `drawRoundRect()`, `fillRoundRect()`, `draw3DRect()`, `fill3DRect()`
Polygons	`drawPolygon()`, `fillPolygon()`
Ovals	`drawOval()`, `fillOval()`
Arcs	`drawArc()`, `fillArc()`
Text rendering	`drawString()`, `drawChars()`, and `drawBytes()`
Copying rectangular areas	`copyArea()`
Changing current graphics state	`setColor()`, `setPaintMode()`, `setXORMode()`, `setFont()`
Translating the coordinate system	`translate()`
Clipping rectangle support	`clipRect()`
Various graphics state querying functions	`getColor()`, `getFont()`, `getFontMetrics()`, `getClipRect()`
Image rendering	`drawImage()`

Two notable omissions from this list are some pixel-plotting and flood-fill methods. Although the need for plotting individual pixels occurs less frequently than the need for using higher primitives, not having any pixel routines is annoying. The main work-around for drawing single pixels in AWT is to either call `fillRect()` or `drawLine()` using parameters that define 1×1-pixel rectangles or lines, respectively. It goes without saying that this will be far less efficient than having a native AWT pixel routine. There is one other (not obvious) approach to plotting single pixels: using the

`MemoryImageSource` class. See the Mandelbrot program at the end of the chapter for an example.

The lack of flood-fill methods is far less dramatic since this type of rendering is quite rarely used (and when it is used, it can often lead to graphical corruption if the wrong part of an image is flood filled). Flood filling, as its name suggests, uses an algorithm that fills an enclosed area by letting pixels spread out from an initial location, as a liquid would in reality.

You will now explore most of the listed methods, as they are the basic tools you will use for animation and enhancing your GUIs.

Lines and Rectangles

The following methods support basic rendering of lines and rectangles:

- `public void drawLine(int x1, int y1, int x2, int y2);`

- `public void fillRect(int x, int y, int width, int height);`

- `public void drawRect(int x, int y, int width, int height);`

- `public void clearRect(int x, int y, int width, int height);`

The artistic applet in Figure 13.1 demonstrates the above methods.

Here is the code behind the output of Figure 13.1:

```
import java.awt.*;
public class Picasso extends java.applet.Applet {
public void paint (Graphics g) {
```

```
            g.fillRect(30,10,200,100);
            g.clearRect(50,30,70,50);
            g.drawRect(60,50,40,20);
            g.drawLine(10,55,250,55);
        }}
```

FIGURE 13.1:

Picasso applet

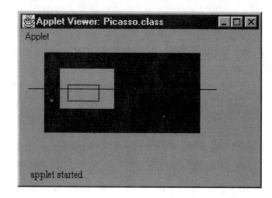

All rectangle methods take the same parameters: the coordinates of the upper-left corner of the rectangle plus the width and height of the rectangle. Note that only single-pixel wide lines and outlines are supported. There is therefore no such method as `setLineWidth()` or something similar. Slightly more complex than the methods above are the following rectangle-drawing methods that support rounded corners or a 3-D lighting effect:

- `public void drawRoundRect(int x, int y, int width, int height, int arcWidth, int arcHeight);`

- `public void fillRoundRect(int x, int y, int width, int height, int arcWidth, int arcHeight);`

- `public void draw3DRect(int x, int y, int width, int height, boolean raised);`

- `public void fill3DRect(int x, int y, int width, int height, boolean raised);`

The rounded corner variants necessitate some extra explanation. In addition to the normal rectangle-defining arguments x, y, width, and height, you need to specify the dimensions of an imaginary rectangle acting as bounding box for the corner. The following program illustrates the control this invisible box has by varying its size for different instances of an identical base rectangle:

```
import java.awt.*;

public class Corner extends java.applet.Applet {
final int RWIDTH = 40;
final int RHEIGHT = 30;

public void paint (Graphics g) {

    for (int i=0; i< 7; i++) {

        int cornerBoxSize = (i+1)*3;

        if (i%2 == 0) {
            g.fillRoundRect(10 + i*(RWIDTH+10), 40, RWIDTH, RHEIGHT,
                                        cornerBoxSize, cornerBoxSize);
        } else {
            g.drawRoundRect(10 + i*(RWIDTH+10), 40, RWIDTH, RHEIGHT,
                    cornerBoxSize, cornerBoxSize);

            g.drawRect(10+ i*(RWIDTH+10)+RWIDTH-cornerBoxSize, 40,
                    cornerBoxSize, cornerBoxSize);
        }
    }
}}
```

When run, the applet produces the output of Figure 13.2.

FIGURE 13.2:

Rounded rectangles with
varying rounding degrees

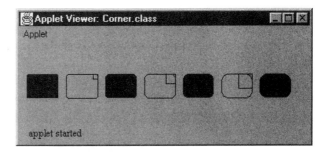

Note how the code alternates between filled and outlined rounded rectangles: It uses a modulo two (%2) function to figure out if the loop's index i is odd or not. Adding 10 to the x-coordinates of all boxes drawn is done simply to move the string of boxes to the right a bit, away from the applet's left-hand window edge.

Polygons

Arbitrary outlined or filled polygons are supported by class Graphics, and there are no limitations on concavity or self-intersection. (Many other toolkits cannot handle self-intersecting or concave polygons.)

TIP

A concave—as opposed to convex—polygon is one whose outline has one or more indentations. (Or put mathematically, a concave polygon has one or more negative angles between successive line segments). An easy mnemonic aid for remembering the difference between concave and convex is to associate the word *cave* with *concave*.

The following Graphics methods deal with polygon rendering:

- public void drawPolygon(int xPoints[], int yPoints[], int nPoints);

- public void drawPolygon(Polygon p);

- public void fillPolygon(int xPoints[], int yPoints[], int nPoints);

- public void fillPolygon(Polygon p);

Both the outline and filled versions come in two flavors. They can either take a low-level (and error-prone) collection of arguments defining a polygon, or they can take an instance of class Polygon. The following demonstration below uses the latter, more readable option. Figure 13.3 shows the kind of polygons that can be produced.

FIGURE 13.3:

Filled convex, outlined concave, and filled self-intersecting polygons

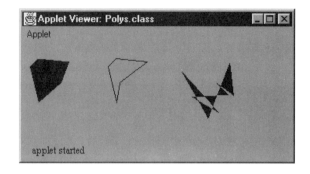

```
import java.awt.*;

public class Polys extends java.applet.Applet {

public void paint (Graphics g) {

Polygon convex, concave, selfintersecting;

    convex = new Polygon();
    convex.addPoint(20,20);
    convex.addPoint(60,24);
    convex.addPoint(50,50);
    convex.addPoint(21,75);
    convex.addPoint(10,30);

    concave = new Polygon();
    concave.addPoint(100+ 20,20);
    concave.addPoint(100+ 60,24);
    concave.addPoint(100+ 25,50);
    concave.addPoint(100+ 21,75);
    concave.addPoint(100+ 10,30);
    concave.addPoint(100+ 20,20);

    selfintersecting = new Polygon();
    for(int i=0; i< 10; i++) {
        selfintersecting.addPoint( 200+ (int) (Math.random()*80),
                                    20 + (int) (Math.random()*80));
    }
    g.fillPolygon(convex);
    g.drawPolygon(concave);
    g.fillPolygon(selfintersecting);
}}
```

This program relies on another AWT class, class `Polygon`, that is useful when working with graphical polygons. The definition of class `Polygon` is very simple:

```
public class Polygon extends Object {
    public int npoints;
    public int xpoints[];
    public int ypoints[];
    public Polygon();
    public Polygon(int xpoints[], int ypoints[], int npoints);
    public void addPoint(int x, int y);
    public Rectangle getBoundingBox();
    public boolean inside(int x, int y);
}
```

This class cannot draw polygons itself; it is only used to define the outline of polygons. This is done with method `addPoint()`, as in the example program.

The position of the polygons is implicitly defined by the list of the polygon's vertices. The polygon rendering methods cannot position the polygon (for example, by taking x,y coordinates as extra arguments) like, say, the `drawLine()` and `drawRect()` methods do for lines and rectangles, respectively. See the discussion of `translate()`, later in the chapter, to learn to tackle this problem.

Ovals

Ovals and circles are supported through the following two methods:

- `public  void drawOval(int x, int y, int width, int height);`

- `public  void fillOval(int x, int y, int width, int height);`

The difference between an oval and the more frequently supported ellipse shape is that the major and minor diameters of ovals are always parallel to the x- and y-axes. Ellipses usually can be rotated at will. Nevertheless, an oval is needed most of the time. Figure 13.4 shows a colorful effect obtained by drawing ever-shrinking, filled ovals. (The same result would be obtained by using outlined ovals, but using the filled variety is far more impressive at run time.)

FIGURE 13.4:

The "Eye of Khan"
(alias drawOvals())

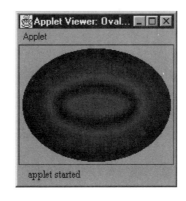

```
import java.applet.*;
import java.awt.*;

public class Ovals extends Applet {

float hue         = 0.0f;
float saturation  = 1.0f;
float brightness  = 1.0f;

public void paint(Graphics g) {
int     w,h;
float   zeroToOne;

    w = bounds().width; h = bounds().height;
    g.setColor(Color.darkGray);
    g.draw3DRect(0, 0, w-1, h-1, false);

    g.translate(5,5);
    w -= 10; h -= 10;

    int squareSide = Math.min(w, h);
    for (int i=0; i < squareSide/2; i++) {
        zeroToOne = ((float) i) / (squareSide/2.0f);
        hue        = zeroToOne;
        brightness = zeroToOne;
```

```
        g.setColor(Color.getHSBColor(hue, saturation, brightness));
        g.fillOval(i,i, w - 2*i, h -2*i);
    }
}}
```

This program is very straightforward. It draws an outline around the applet's available drawing area. It then uses the `min()` function from class `Math` to work out what the largest *square* drawing area is (applet aspect ratios can be very non-square), and proceeds to fill this with the concentric ovals (that are therefore circles). Note that since the oval rendering methods do not take center coordinates and radii (as is most common in other graphics toolboxes) but an enclosing bounding box specification, you "slide" a shrinking bounding box from the top-left corner towards the center of the eye to achieve your result. Using other ellipse APIs, you would normally keep the center fixed and decrease the radii instead.

Arcs

Arcs are elliptical segments (or, more frequently, just circular segments). Two `Graphics` methods let you render arcs:

- `public void drawArc(int x, int y, int width, int height, int startAngle, int arcAngle);`

- `public void fillArc(int x, int y, int width, int height, int startAngle, int arcAngle);`

The Java Development Kit (JDK) contains an interactive `ArcTest` program to demonstrate the arc rendering methods. Unfortunately, this program uses text fields to input starting angles and arc size (again in degrees). But since you learned how to use scrollbar sliders in Chapter 12, this program has been reworked to use more user-friendly scrollbars. Figure 13.5 shows the kind of output you get from the improved `ArcTest` program.

FIGURE 13.5:

JDK `ArcTest` program with improved user interface

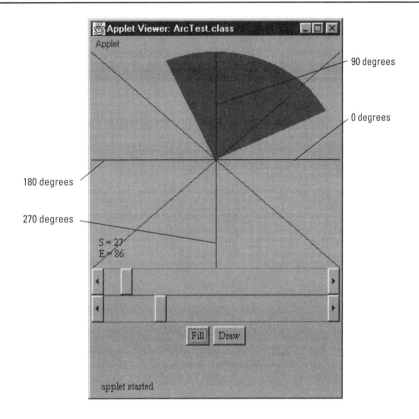

```
/*
 * Copyright (c) 1994-1995 Sun Microsystems, Inc. All Rights Reserved.
 * Copyright (c) 1996 Laurence Vanhelsuwe.
 *
 * Permission to use, copy, modify, and distribute this software
 * and its documentation for NON-COMMERCIAL or COMMERCIAL purposes and
 * without fee is hereby granted.
```

<SEE ACCOMPANYING CD-ROM FOR FULL AND ORIGINAL COPYRIGHT INFORMATION>

```
 */
import java.awt.*;
import java.applet.*;

/**
 * An interactive test of the Graphics.drawArc and Graphics.fillArc
 * routines. Can be run either as a standalone application by
 * typing "java ArcTest" or as an applet in the AppletViewer.
 */
public class ArcTest extends Applet {

ArcControls controls;

public void init() {
    setLayout(new BorderLayout());
    ArcCanvas c = new ArcCanvas();
    add("Center", c);
    add("South", controls = new ArcControls(c));
}

public void start() {
    controls.enable();
}

public void stop() {
    controls.disable();
}

public boolean handleEvent(Event e) {
    if (e.id == Event.WINDOW_DESTROY) {
        System.exit(0);
    }
    return false;
}}

class ArcCanvas extends Canvas {

int     startAngle = 0;
int     endAngle   = 45;
boolean filled     = false;
Font    font;

public Dimension minimumSize() {
    return new Dimension(100,100);
}

public void paint(Graphics g) {
Rectangle r = bounds();

    drawGrid(g);

    g.setColor(Color.red);
    if (filled) {
        g.fillArc(0, 0, r.width - 1, r.height - 1, startAngle, endAngle);
```

```
    } else {
        g.drawArc(0, 0, r.width - 1, r.height - 1, startAngle, endAngle);
    }

    g.setColor(Color.black);
    g.setFont(font);
    g.drawLine(0, r.height / 2, r.width, r.height / 2);
    g.drawLine(r.width / 2, 0, r.width / 2, r.height);
    g.drawLine(0, 0, r.width, r.height);
    g.drawLine(r.width, 0, 0, r.height);
    int sx = 10;
    int sy = r.height - 28;
    g.drawString("S = " + startAngle, sx, sy);
    g.drawString("E = " + endAngle, sx, sy + 14);
}

private void drawGrid(Graphics g) {
Rectangle r = bounds();
int hlines = r.height / 10;
int vlines = r.width / 10;

    g.setColor(Color.pink);
    for (int i = 1; i <= hlines; i++) {
        g.drawLine(0, i * 10, r.width, i * 10);
    }
    for (int i = 1; i <= vlines; i++) {
        g.drawLine(i * 10, 0, i * 10, r.height);
    }
}

public void redraw(boolean filled, int start, int end) {
    this.filled     = filled;
    this.startAngle = start;
    this.endAngle   = end;
    repaint();
}}

class ArcControls extends Panel {
Scrollbar start;
Scrollbar end;
ArcCanvas canvas;
boolean fillMode = false;

public ArcControls(ArcCanvas canvas) {
    this.canvas = canvas;
    setLayout(new GridLayout(4,1));
    add(start = new Scrollbar(Scrollbar.HORIZONTAL, 0 ,1, 0,359));
    add(end   = new Scrollbar(Scrollbar.HORIZONTAL, 45,1, 0,359));

    Panel subPanel = new Panel();          // using FlowLayout now
    subPanel.add(new Button("Fill"));
    subPanel.add(new Button("Draw"));
    add(subPanel);
```

```
      }
public boolean handleEvent(Event ev) {
    if (ev.target instanceof Button) {
        String label = (String) ((Button)ev.target).getLabel();
        fillMode = label.equals("Fill");
        canvas.redraw(fillMode, start.getValue(), end.getValue());
        return true;
    }
    if (ev.target instanceof Scrollbar) {
        canvas.redraw(fillMode, start.getValue(), end.getValue());
        return true;
    }
    return false;
}}
```

This program consists of three classes reflecting the three main components of the applet:

- The applet itself

- The Canvas area to draw the arcs (and the grid backdrop)

- The control panel at the bottom of the window

The heart of the program is the ArcCanvas paint() method that invokes either the drawArc() or fillArc() method using the user-selectable starting and ending arc angles. The exact method is determined by the current drawing mode (fill or outline) used by the program. The angles that both arc methods take need to be in degrees and not radians (with 0 coding for three o'clock). The remainder of the program consists mainly of GUI code (as is so often the case with "real" applications) that applies the type of GUI techniques you learned in the previous two chapters.

Text Rendering

The Graphics class only supports simple left-to-right, horizontal text rendering. Rotated text is not supported. The three methods that support text rendering are

- `public void drawString(String str, int x, int y);`

- public void drawChars(char data[], int offset, int
  length, int x, int y);

- public void drawBytes(byte data[], int offset, int
  length, int x, int y);

Method `drawString()` is the usual method you use for drawing text strings. It just takes a string and the starting (rendering) position for the first letter of your string. The rendering position for text is always the left-most point on the text's baseline. The two other text-rendering methods use arrays of `byte` or `char` as their text source but allow a substring to be rendered. Here is a demonstration program using the latter that produces the output in Figure 13.6:

```
import java.awt.*;

public class Text extends java.applet.Applet {

public void paint (Graphics g) {

String subject = "ZigZagging Text";
char[] text;

    g.setFont(new Font("TimesRoman", Font.PLAIN, 16));
    text = subject.toCharArray();

    for (int i=0; i <= text.length-3; i+=2) {
        if (i==0) {
            g.drawChars(text, 0, text.length, 20, 20);
        } else if (i == text.length-3) {
            g.drawChars(text, 0, text.length, 20, 20 + (i/2)*17);
        } else {
            g.drawChars(text, (text.length-3-i), 4,
                20+ (text.length-3-i)*7, 20+ (i/2)*17);
        }
    }
}
}}
```

The program uses the `setFont()` method to change the currently used rendering font. Method `setFont()` takes a `Font` object that can be constructed on-the-fly using a new `Font("<fontFamilyName>"`, `<fontStyle>`, `pointSize)`. See the discussion of `setFont()`, later in the chapter, for more details.

FIGURE 13.6:

Zigzag text using
`drawChars()`

Moving Rectangular Areas

The `copyArea()` method is the only graphics area moving method available. Since it does not allow any type of masking, it is mostly useful for scrolling areas vertically or horizontally. Here is the method's signature:

- `public void copyArea(int x, int y, int width, int height, int dx, int dy)`

The `x`, `y`, `width`, and `height` arguments specify the area to move, and the `dx` and `dy` arguments specify by how many pixels and in which direction. As you can see from the method's signature, only screen-to-screen copies are supported. You cannot grab a screen area and store it for future use—for example, to copy it back to the screen at a later date. Figure 13.7 shows one of those executive toy-type applets that relies on moving rectangular puzzle pieces horizontally and vertically. The program that follows produced the (animating) output of Figure 13.7.

NOTE You can move an image from an off-screen buffer into the screen using the `drawImage()` method; this is discussed in the "Animation Basics" section later in the chapter.

FIGURE 13.7:

Puzzle applet

```
import java.awt.*;

public class Puzzle extends java.applet.Applet {

Graphics g;
Color bg;
int pieceWidth, pieceHeight;

final int PUZ_WIDTH  = 5;
final int PUZ_HEIGHT = 5;

final int MOVE_UP    = 0;      // these values are designed so that negating
final int MOVE_DOWN  = 3;      // one produces the opposite direction. E.g.
final int MOVE_RIGHT = 1;      // ~MOVE_UP = MOVE_DOWN  (when ANDed with 3)
final int MOVE_LEFT  = 2;

int holeX = 0;                 // starting spot for the puzzle's "hole"
int holeY = 0;

int[] xDirs={0,1,-1,0};        // dxs and dys indexable by one of the MOVE_s
int[] yDirs={-1,0,0,1};
int xDir, yDir;
int x,y;                       // pixel coordinates of a puzzle piece
//————————————————————————————————————————————————————————————————————————
// work out the size of the puzzle pieces from the available applet area
//————————————————————————————————————————————————————————————————————————
public void init() {

    pieceWidth  = (bounds().width-20) /PUZ_WIDTH;
    pieceHeight = (bounds().height-20)/PUZ_HEIGHT;
}
//————————————————————————————————————————————————————————————————————————
// draw a nice background for our puzzle, draw the pieces and start
```

```
// animating the lot.
//──────────────────────────────────────────────────────────
public void paint (Graphics g) {

    this.g = g;
    g.translate(10,10);
    bg = getBackground();

    g.setFont(new Font("TimesRoman", Font.BOLD, 85));
    g.drawString("Hey!",10,70);
    g.setColor(Color.gray);
    g.drawString("Hey!",12,72);

    drawPieces();

    while(true) {
        occupyHole();    // animate the puzzle by moving pieces
    }
}
//──────────────────────────────────────────────────────────
// At init time we draw the piece outlines over the backdrop picture
//──────────────────────────────────────────────────────────
private void drawPieces() {
    for (int row=0; row < PUZ_HEIGHT; row++) {
        for (int col=0; col < PUZ_WIDTH; col++) {
            drawPieceAt(row,col);
        }
    }
}
//──────────────────────────────────────────────────────────
// Pick a valid, random neighbor around the hole.
// then move that neighbor into the hole's spot. The old neighbor's
// cell becomes the new hole.
//──────────────────────────────────────────────────────────
private void occupyHole() {
int neighborDir;      // randomly chosen neighbor cell direction
int moveDir;          // opposite direction (to move into hole cell)
int neighborX;
int neighborY;

    // choose a random neighboring direction 0..3
    do {
        neighborDir = (int) (Math.random()*4);
    } while ( cellisIllegal(neighborDir) ); // but avoid going off the
    ➥grid

    neighborX = holeX + xDirs[neighborDir];
    neighborY = holeY + yDirs[neighborDir];

//    System.out.println("Hole: " + holeX + "," + holeY);
//    System.out.println("Nbor: " + neighborX + "," + neighborY);
```

```
        moveDir = (~neighborDir)&3;      // opposite dir UP<->DOWN, RIGHT<->LEFT

        movePiece (neighborX, neighborY, moveDir);

        holeX = neighborX;
        holeY = neighborY;

        delay(0.5);
    }
    //————————————————————————————————————————————————————————————————————————
    // Check that a tentative neighbor cell is within the puzzle
    //————————————————————————————————————————————————————————————————————————
    private boolean cellisIllegal(int direction) {

        xDir = xDirs[direction];
        yDir = yDirs[direction];

        if (holeX + xDir < 0) return true;
        if (holeY + yDir < 0) return true;
        if (holeX + xDir >= PUZ_WIDTH) return true;
        if (holeY + yDir >= PUZ_HEIGHT) return true;

        return false;
    }
    //————————————————————————————————————————————————————————————————————————
    // Graphically move a piece in one of the four directions
    //————————————————————————————————————————————————————————————————————————
    private void movePiece(int row, int col, int direction) {

        xDir = xDirs[direction];
        yDir = yDirs[direction];

        x = row * pieceWidth;
        y = col * pieceHeight;

        if (xDir != 0) {
            for (int i=0; i < pieceWidth; i++) {
                g.copyArea(x+(i * xDir),y, pieceWidth, pieceHeight, xDir, 0);
                delay(0.004);
            }
        } else {
            for (int i=0; i < pieceHeight; i++) {
                g.copyArea(x,y+(i * yDir), pieceWidth, pieceHeight, 0, yDir);
                delay(0.004);
            }
        }
    }
    //————————————————————————————————————————————————————————————————————————
    // At initialization time we cut up the background into puzzle pieces.
    // Each piece has an outline which is slightly inset so as to avoid
    // smearing when copyArea() slides pieces around
    //————————————————————————————————————————————————————————————————————————
    private void drawPieceAt(int row, int col) {
```

```
        x = row * pieceWidth;
        y = col * pieceHeight;

        g.setColor(bg);
        g.drawRect(x,y, pieceWidth, pieceHeight);
        g.drawRect(x+1,y+1, pieceWidth-2, pieceHeight-2);

        g.setColor(Color.gray);
        g.drawRect(x+1,y+1, pieceWidth-3, pieceHeight-3);
}
//————————————————————————————————————————————————————————
private void delay(double seconds) {
    try {
        Thread.sleep( (int) (seconds*1000));
    catch (Exception ignored) {}
}}
```

As you saw when running the applet, the program does not contain any of the game's logic. Adding this is left as an exercise for the reader. The core of the program is the `movePiece()` method. It takes the puzzle piece coordinates of the square to move and a direction in which to move the piece. The pieces are moved smoothly, one pixel at a time using repeated calls to `copyArea()`. Note that `copyArea()` does not alter the source area at all. Therefore, when sliding a rectangular image one pixel at a time in a given direction, a graphical trace may be left behind depending on the pixel contents of the trailing edge. To avoid this, the program draws the "outlines" for the pieces a couple of pixels on the *inside* of the piece, surrounded by an invisible outline of background color. This way, pieces can be slid around without leaving any traces.

Graphics State

Beyond being a collection of rendering primitives, what other function does a `Graphics` object have? Its crucial function is to allow a multitude of different graphic *contexts* to coexist. When the `paint()` method hands you a `Graphics` object, that object holds all graphical attributes or *state* for your applet's drawing area. Your applet's drawing origin (coordinates 0,0) for example, is situated in the top-left corner of the applet's drawing area, and not in the top-left corner of the browser's window or the top-left corner of the screen. A Graphics controlled drawing area has several more such attributes besides the customized coordinate origin. Graphics objects also keep track of the following:

- The current clipping area

- The current drawing Color

- The current drawing mode

- The current Font to use for any text rendering

These attributes can either be altered and/or queried by the following Graphics methods.

Translating the Coordinate System

If you look back at the source of the Polygon example, you will see that the polygons were "manually" spaced apart by adding 100 to the x-coordinates of the second polygon and 200 to the x-coordinates of the third polygon. Using the translate() method

```
public void translate(int x, int y)
```

this could have been avoided altogether, and the source code would have been much more readable. Here is how the code body could be improved with translate(), achieving the same result as in Figure 13.3.

```
concave = new Polygon();
concave.addPoint( 20,20);
concave.addPoint( 60,24);
concave.addPoint( 25,50);
concave.addPoint( 21,75);
concave.addPoint( 10,30);
concave.addPoint( 20,20);
```

```
selfintersecting = new Polygon();
for(int i=0; i< 10; i++) {
    selfintersecting.addPoint( (int) (Math.random()*80),
                               (int) (Math.random()*80));
}
g.fillPolygon(convex);

g.translate(100,0);
g.drawPolygon(concave);

g.translate(100,20);
g.fillPolygon(selfintersecting);
```

Note that translations are cumulative. Each invocation of `trans-late()` translates the current coordinate system, which might already have been translated. To "undo" the last translation you have to remember the amount of the previous translation and then apply the inverse translation. This is done by translating with the previous translation values negated:

```
translate(tx,ty);
// paint stuff
translate(-tx,-ty);
// back to where we were before
```

Specifying a Clipping Area

When you specify drawing coordinates that lie outside your applet's drawing area, none of the graphics primitives complain. Instead they simply restrict whatever they draw to be within the applet's `bounds()` and *clip* any rendering which would draw outside this area. This clipping rectangle can be changed to any other rectangular area located within the original applet drawing area using method `clipRect()`. You can find out what the current clipping rectangle is set to by calling `getClipRect()`, which returns a `Rectangle` instance. Here are the signatures for these two methods:

- `public void clipRect(int x, int y, int width, int height)`

- `public Rectangle getClipRect()`

The following applet `paint()` method proves that the initial clipping rectangle for an applet is identical to the applet's `bounds()`:

```
public void paint (Graphics g) {
    System.out.println( g.getClipRect() );
    System.out.println( bounds() );
}
```

If you ran this code within a minimal applet class, it would output the following:

```
java.awt.Rectangle[x=0,y=0,width=200,height=150]
java.awt.Rectangle[x=104,y=92,width=200,height=150]
```

Current Drawing Color

Every `Graphics` context has a current (foreground) drawing color. Surprisingly enough, there is no associated current *background* drawing color. Java does have a concept of background color, but only in the context of GUI components (via the `setBackground()` and `getBackground()` methods in class `Component`). You alter the rendering color to be used by calls to `setColor()`. Finding out which color is being used for all current rendering is done via calls to `getColor()`:

- `public void setColor(Color c)`

- `public Color getColor()`

The type of objects handled by both calls are instances of class `Color`. Here is its definition:

```
public final class Color extends Object {
    public Color(int r, int g, int b);
    public Color(int rgb);
    public Color(float r, float g, float b);
    public int getRed();
    public int getGreen();
    public int getBlue();
    public int getRGB();
    public Color brighter();
    public Color darker();
    public int hashCode();
```

```
public boolean equals(Object obj);
public String toString();
public static Color getColor(String nm);
public static Color getColor(String nm, Color v);
public static Color getColor(String nm, int v);
public static int HSBtoRGB(float hue, float saturation, float brightness);
public static float[] RGBtoHSB(int r, int g, int b, float hsbvals[]);
public static Color getHSBColor(float h, float s, float b);
}
```

The `Color` constructors should be your main focus. You can construct a new color by specifying either:

- Red, green, and blue primary components in the integer range 0–255

- Red, green, and blue primary components in the float range 0.0F–1.0F

- A single integer encoding red, green, and blue in the standard 8-bits-per-primary format

- Hue, saturation, and brightness values in the float range 0.0F–1.0F (this is via the `getHSBColor()` static method, and not via a constructor)

If your color requirements can be satisfied by the following basic palette, then the `Color` class defines some class constants of type `Color` (itself): white, gray, lightGray, darkGray, black, red, pink, orange, yellow, green, magenta, cyan, and blue. As with all class constants, you need to prepend the name of the class to use these—for example, `Color.blue`.

Current Drawing Mode

All rendering can be executed in one of two modes, paint or XOR mode, using these two methods:

- `public void setPaintMode()`

- `public void setXORMode(Color c1)`

Paint mode simply overwrites any pixels already there, in the current drawing color, while XOR mode applies a color-swapping function (reminiscent, but not equal to, bitwise exclusive oring). The swapped colors are the color being passed as argument to `setXORMode()` and the current drawing color. The following applet demonstrates the effect:

```java
import java.awt.*;

public class XOR extends java.applet.Applet {

public void paint (Graphics g) {

    g.setFont(new Font("TimesRoman", Font.BOLD, 32) );
    g.drawString("Java", 10, 30);
    g.drawString("Sumatra", 10, 60);

    // draw both strings on top of another in both paint and XOR mode

    g.setPaintMode();
    g.drawString("Java", 10, 100);
    g.drawString("Sumatra (Paint)", 10, 100);

    g.setXORMode(Color.white);
    g.drawString("Java", 10, 130);
    g.drawString("Sumatra (XOR)", 10, 130);
}}
```

Figure 13.8 shows paint and XOR drawing modes.

FIGURE 13.8:

Paint and XOR drawing
modes

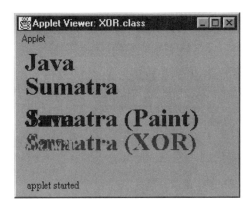

Current Font

Two methods are provided that handle font aspects:

- `public void setFont(Font font)`

- `public Font getFont()`

You specify the current font using the `setFont()` method. The argument it takes is a `Font` object, which is usually constructed in place, within the argument brackets of `setFont()` (see the example code on the next page). The `Font` constructor has the following signature:

`public Font(String name, int style, int size)`

The name argument denotes the font family and can be

- `Courier`

- `Dialog`

- `DialogInput`

- `Helvetica`

- `ZapfDingbats`

- `TimesRoman`

The style argument can be

- `Font.PLAIN`

- `Font.BOLD`

- `Font.ITALIC`

These can be specified either alone or in combination (by oring them together). The size argument is the font scaling in pixels. The following demo program combines `Font` and `FontMetrics`; it finds out what the list of all available fonts (available to Java, that is) is, and it renders samples of each with expanding point sizes.

```
import java.awt.*;

public class FontList extends java.applet.Applet {

String[]     fontList;
Font         theFont;
FontMetrics fm;
int          fontHeight;

public void init() {
    fontList = Toolkit.getDefaultToolkit().getFontList();
}

public void paint(Graphics g) {
    for (int i = 0; i < fontList.length; i++) {
        System.out.println(fontList[i]);
        theFont = new Font(fontList[i], Font.BOLD, 16+i*4);
        g.setFont(theFont);
        fm = getFontMetrics(theFont);
        fontHeight += fm.getHeight();
        g.drawString(fontList[i] + " " + (16+i*4) + " point", 10, fontHeight);
    }
}}
```

Figure 13.9 shows Java AWT standard fonts.

FIGURE 13.9:

Java AWT standard fonts

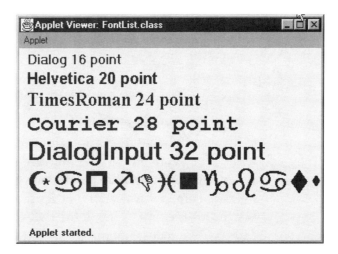

Note how you obtain a list of available fonts. The Toolkit class has a getFontList() method that does the job. The way you get a

Toolkit object in the first instance (to invoke getFontList() on) is by using the Toolkit *class* method getDefaultToolkit().

> **NOTE**
>
> This standard Java idiom for finding the list of fonts should receive the same treatment sleep() got in the context of threads. At first, to put the current thread to sleep for some time, you had to use Thread.currentThread().sleep(). Because no one ever put any other threads to sleep, the sleep() instance method was "promoted" to a class method with the new semantics of always putting the current thread to sleep. Toolkit instance method getFontList() should likewise be promoted to a class method Toolkit.getFontList(); it would then take on the meaning of producing a font list for the current Toolkit. See the JDK online documentation for details on the Toolkit class.

Accessing the Current Font's FontMetrics

Two more font-related methods are provided to access a font's set of metrics:

- public FontMetrics getFontMetrics()

- public FontMetrics getFontMetrics(Font f)

Whenever you render anything around rendered text, you need to know exactly what the various font dimensions are. If not, things will not be symmetrical or centered correctly, or worse—subsequent rendering might "collide" with parts of the text. Modern computer fonts all come with a set of metrics that define various heights and widths for the font. Consult the JDK online documentation on class FontMetrics to learn about these font metrics. The following program shows you how you can get at a font's FontMetrics object and how to use it; in this case, you would use it to highlight the metrics graphically, as shown in Figure 13.10.

FIGURE 13.10:

Font metrics for font
`TimesRoman`

In addition to producing the graphical output shown in Figure 13.10, the program also dumped the following metrics to the console (for a "`TimesRoman`" font requested to be 100 points):

```
ascent   90
descent  24
height   118
leading  4
maxAdv   109
maxAsc   90
maxDes   24
```

The metrics listed were obtained on a Windows 95 host machine, and because font metrics vary across platforms, the program might print different values on your machine. Here is the program behind the console output and Figure 13.10:

```
import java.awt.*;

public class FMetrics extends java.applet.Applet {

Font        theFont;
FontMetrics fm;

public void init() {
    theFont = new Font("TimesRoman", Font.PLAIN, 100);
}
```

```
public void paint(Graphics g) {
int baseline    = 100;
String testStr  = "WIactiyg";

    g.setFont(theFont);
    fm = g.getFontMetrics();

int ascent  = fm.getAscent();     System.out.println("ascent   " + ascent  );
int descent = fm.getDescent();    System.out.println("descent  " + descent );
int height  = fm.getHeight();     System.out.println("height   " + height  );
int leading = fm.getLeading();    System.out.println("leading  " + leading );
int maxAdv  = fm.getMaxAdvance(); System.out.println("maxAdv   " + maxAdv  );
int maxAsc  = fm.getMaxAscent();  System.out.println("maxAsc   " + maxAsc  );
int maxDes  = fm.getMaxDescent(); System.out.println("maxDes   " + maxDes  );

    g.drawString(testStr, 10, baseline);

    drawHLine(baseline);
    drawHLine(baseline-ascent);
    drawHLine(baseline-maxAsc);
    drawHLine(baseline+descent);
    drawHLine(baseline+maxDes);
    drawHLine(baseline+maxDes+leading);

    int charX = 10;
    for (int i=0; i< testStr.length(); i++) {
        drawVLine(charX);
        charX += fm.charWidth(testStr.charAt(i));
    }
}
void drawHLine(int y) {
    getGraphics().drawLine(10,y,500,y);
}
void drawVLine(int x) {
    getGraphics().drawLine(x,10,x,200);
}}
```

Note that the FontMetrics object is not obtained from the Font it relates to. The Graphics object is the entity that gives you a FontMetrics object for the currently selected rendering Font. Note also you can improve readability and keep the code short by writing two simple little utility rendering functions: drawHLine() and drawVLine(). Simple methods like these that are only a couple of lines long can greatly improve the readability of your programs.

Animation Basics

The essence of all animation is moving pictures—a sequence of still images displayed at a fast enough rate to fool the brain into thinking the animation is continuous. Once the animation rate (the *frame rate*) is high enough, the discrete, static pictures merge into a constant flow of movement. Movies use a frame rate of 24 frames per second (fps). In other words, the images are renewed at 24 Hertz (Hz, or cycles per second). Normal televisions use 60Hz (for the United States NTSC broadcasting standard) or 50Hz (for the European PAL standard), although recently, newer (digital) models using 100Hz have invaded the marketplace. Multisync computer monitors can display their frames from "slow" TV rates to approximately 120Hz. Faster update rates mean less image flicker and consequently more solid or realistic-looking animations.

Redrawing an entire screen or even just a sizable window in one-twenty-fourth of a second is no mean feat—especially if its content is complex and needs a lot of computations to redraw it. Luckily, animation effects can be achieved without having to redraw the entire drawing canvas each time. Modifying only those areas that contain the changing parts can be just as effective.

The following applet demonstrates this technique. It only draws one new straight line for each new "frame," but it does so in such a way that the result is fascinating to watch. Figure 13.11 shows a snapshot of the Qix applet in action.

> **NOTE**
>
> Qix was one of the classic arcade games of the early eighties. The object of the game was to gradually restrict the movements of the "Qix"—some sort of energy field—by building a fence around it. If the Qix touched you in the middle of building a fence, you died.

FIGURE 13.11:

Qix animation applet

```
import java.awt.*          ;
import java.util.Random    ;

public class Qix extends java.applet.Applet {

private Random rnd = new Random();

private Rectangle    bounceRect;
private Rectangle    colorBounce;
private BouncyPoint endPoint1,endPoint2;
private BouncyPoint R_Bouncer, G_Bouncer, B_Bouncer;
private int startx1, startx2, starty1, starty2;

public void paint (Graphics g) {

    bounceRect = this.bounds();            // Applet's bbox
    bounceRect.x = 0;
    bounceRect.y = 0;

    startx1 = 4 + ((rnd.nextInt()&1023) % (bounceRect.width - 8) );
    startx2 = 4 + ((rnd.nextInt()&1023) % (bounceRect.width - 8) );
    starty1 = 4 + ((rnd.nextInt()&1023) % (bounceRect.height -8) );
    starty2 = 4 + ((rnd.nextInt()&1023) % (bounceRect.height -8) );

    endPoint1 = new BouncyPoint(bounceRect, startx1, starty1,  -1.0, 1.5);
    endPoint2 = new BouncyPoint(bounceRect, startx2, starty2,   1.0,-2.5);

    colorBounce = new Rectangle(0,0, 255,255);
    R_Bouncer = new BouncyPoint( colorBounce, 200,0, 1.0, 0.0);
    G_Bouncer = new BouncyPoint( colorBounce, 200,0, -1.0, 0.0);
    B_Bouncer = new BouncyPoint( colorBounce, 200,0, -2.0, 0.0);

    for (;;) {
        endPoint1.carryOnBouncing();       // bounce the two line endpoints around
        endPoint2.carryOnBouncing();
        R_Bouncer.carryOnBouncing();       // bounce the colors around too !
```

```
        G_Bouncer.carryOnBouncing();
        B_Bouncer.carryOnBouncing();

        g.setColor(new Color(R_Bouncer.x, G_Bouncer.x, B_Bouncer.x) );
        g.drawLine(endPoint1.x, endPoint1.y,   endPoint2.x, endPoint2.y);

        try { Thread.sleep(10); } catch (Exception ignored) {}
    }
}} // End of Class Qix

//——————————————————————————————————————————————————————————————————
// BouncyPoint class
//
// This implements a (commonly employed) bouncing "endpoint".
// i.e. you could use 2 instances of this to animate a bouncing line
// or use 4 of these to animate a Bezier curve or a stretchy-bouncy rectangle
//——————————————————————————————————————————————————————————————————
class BouncyPoint extends Point {

private Rectangle boundingBox;
private double x_direction;
private double y_direction;

BouncyPoint (Rectangle limits, int startx, int starty, double dx, double dy) {

    super(startx, starty);

    boundingBox = limits;

    x_direction = dx;
    y_direction = dy;
}

public boolean carryOnBouncing () {

boolean boing=false;

        // add velocity to current position
        // if resulting position outside box, undo move and reverse speed

    x += (int) x_direction;
    if ( ! boundingBox.inside(x,y)) {
        x -= (int) x_direction;
        x_direction = - x_direction;
        boing = true;
    }

    y += (int) y_direction;
    if ( ! boundingBox.inside(x,y)) {
        y -= (int) y_direction;
        y_direction = - y_direction;
        boing = true;
    }
```

```
        return boing;
    }

    public String toString() {
        return super.toString() + "-Speed dx=" + x_direction +
                                    " dy=" + y_direction;
    }
} // End of Class BouncyPoint
```

The applet relies on a perfectly reusable class whose sole purpose is to "bounce around" a 2-D point within a rectangular box. The BouncyPoint class extends the `java.awt.Point` class (which consists mainly of an x,y coordinate). Two BouncyPoint instances are used to hold the moving endpoints of the animated line. The gradual color animation is also handled by more BouncyPoint instances. The program uses the numeric ping-pong functionality of a BouncyPoint to modify the red, green, and blue color components independently. Since each color primary is just a one-dimensional scalar, only the x part of a BouncyPoint is used for the colors.

WARNING This Qix applet has a serious shortcoming: It never returns from its `paint()` method. A `for(;;)` loop was used to implement an infinite loop that controls the (infinite) animation. Applets that do this are useless in real-life Web pages, because they soak up CPU resources that should normally be shared among all applets. This flaw is ignored throughout this chapter's applets, because the issue will be addressed in detail in Chapter 14.

Working with Java Images

Animating a straight line—or any other graphics primitive—is fine for screen-saver programs or to relax a stressed-out manager, but sooner or later you will want to animate predrawn cartoons or even a large sequence of (digital) video frames. For this purpose, Java supports an Image class, along with other related classes.

The Java API is rather confusing with regard to image manipulations. Several packages, classes, and methods deal with images in one way or another: The `java.awt.Image` class is abstract, so you cannot create `Image` instances from it (a bit like having a succulent apple pie behind armored glass). The `java.awt.image` package is entirely devoted to image processing. In package `java.applet`, two `getImage()` methods are tucked away in class `Applet`. Class `Component` defines two `createImage()` methods. Finally, class `Graphics` contains several `drawImage()` methods.

Here is an example program which draws an image inside an applet:

```
import java.awt.*;

public class GetImage extends java.applet.Applet {

Image myimg;

public void init() {
        myimg = getImage(getDocumentBase(), "image.gif");
}

public void paint(Graphics g) {
    g.drawImage(myimg, 0, 0, this);
}}
```

This applet, when run, produces a window like that shown in Figure 13.12.

The applet's core consists of two statements: : `getImage()` and `drawImage()`. This, fortunately or unfortunately (depending on your viewpoint), is the simplest aspect of using Java images; the remainder of the material will be uphill all the way.

Class `Image` is abstract and therefore cannot be the source for `Image` instances itself. Other classes have to create instances of `Image` for us. To delegate object instantiation to other classes is called using a *factory class*. In this example, applet method `getImage()` is a *factory*

FIGURE 13.12:

A GIF image displayed
by an applet

method for `Image` objects. It not only creates brand new `Image` objects, it also performs the very handy function of loading an external image file and turning it into a runtime usable `Image` object, ready to be rendered. The image formats that are supported are mainly GIF and JPEG, the two de facto Internet image file formats.

The signature of the `getImage()` method used looks like this:

```
public Image getImage(URL url, String name)
```

The Uniform Resource Locator (URL) parameter allows this method to grab image files from any willing Internet site in the world! Another `Applet` method, `getDocumentBase()`, specifies the URL origin (directory) of the picture as whatever site the applet's HTML document came from. If you run the applet on your own machine, this document base URL will have the form of a file URL, like `file:/C:/JAVA/MASTERING/../../page.html`. If you ran the applet from a Web server, then the document base URL would have the form of an HTTP URL, like `http://www.sybex.com/Java/Mastering/../page.html`. The name parameter is the image file's filename in the specified directory, whether local or halfway around the world.

To actually show the image on screen, you use the `drawImage()` method from class `Graphics`. Throughout Java's scattered image-support classes and methods, you can always count on one thing: You always use `drawImage()` to finally render images. The parameters it takes are the x,y coordinates for the top left-hand corner where the image to be drawn and a `this` parameter:

```
g.drawImage(image, x, y, this);
```

And what about the `this` parameter? Your first clue is embedded in the online documentation description for `getImage()`: "This method returns immediately, even if the image does not exist. The actual image data is loaded when it is first needed." This means the `getImage()` statement actually does not get the image after all. The reason is the Internet: The entire image-processing and image-handling support that Java gives us takes the Internet's daily reality into account. In particular, the design reflects

- The unpredictable delays that occur when accessing remote Internet files

- The length of time it takes to download any sizable files (image files often range between 1K and 100K, depending on complexity, color depth , and so on)

The `Image` subsystem deals with these issues by decoupling the loading of images from their actual use. The example code says "load that image and draw it," not knowing or caring about Internet response times or transfer rates, so the two (loading and using images) are completely decoupled. Another way of putting this is that the image loading is *asynchronous*, meaning the main program does not wait for the load to finish (if it did wait, that would be a *synchronous* approach). What really goes on behind the scenes is rather less simple, but it's all for a good purpose: to make Java applet development easier and improve performance for the user. The exact details of the mechanisms used to fetch the image all the way from a remote site and into the `Image` object are platform dependent. In general, though, the `getImage()` method creates an `Image` object that, when asked to draw itself, will start the download process and render the image bit by bit, as the image data is received. This is the function of the `this` parameter in the `drawImage()` call.

Here is the method's signature:

```
public boolean drawImage(Image img, int x, int y, ImageObserver observer)
```

You can see that the last parameter has to be of type `ImageObserver`. `this` is because it, in this applet's context, is a reference to the applet object itself. And applets are, as distant descendants of class `Component`, `ImageObservers`.

To understand why `drawImage()` needs an `ImageObserver`, you must first understand what an `ImageObserver` is. `ImageObserver` is an interface and not a class. Its definition is very short (which doesn't make it easier to understand its purpose, however):

```
public interface ImageObserver extends Object {
    public final static int WIDTH;
    public final static int HEIGHT;
    public final static int PROPERTIES;
    public final static int SOMEBITS;
    public final static int FRAMEBITS;
    public final static int ALLBITS;
    public final static int ERROR;
    public final static int ABORT;
    public abstract boolean imageUpdate(Image img, int infoflags, int x,
    ➥int y, int width, int height);
}
```

Apart from the collection of constants, it defines a single method to be implemented by `ImageObservers`: `imageUpdate()`.

Here is how all of the various pieces fall into place: `getImage()` does not actually load the image, `drawImage()` does. But since loading images from the Internet can be a lengthy proposition (or even worse, the load can fail), even *it* returns immediately. Method `drawImage()` kicks off the asynchronous loading of the image it wants to render, and returns immediately. Another invisible Java subsystem which runs in a different thread actually does all the hard work of transferring the image over the network. Each time this image loading system has a reasonable chunk of new image data, it tells the `ImageObserver` for the image that some extra data is available. It does this through an invocation of the `imageUpdate()` method.

Again, the `ImageObserver` in this case is the applet. To understand its response to an `imageUpdate()` you will want to sneak a peek at the API source itself. The default `imageUpdate()` method is to be found in class `Component`:

```
 * Repaints the component when the image has changed.
 * @return true if image has changed; false otherwise.
 */
public boolean imageUpdate(Image img, int flags,
               int x, int y, int w, int h) {
int rate = -1;
if ((flags & (FRAMEBITS|ALLBITS)) != 0) {
    rate = 0;
} else if ((flags & SOMEBITS) != 0) {
    String isInc = System.getProperty("awt.image.incrementaldraw");
    if (isInc == null || isInc.equals("true")) {
    String incRate = System.getProperty("awt.image.redrawrate");
    try {
        rate = (incRate != null) ? Integer.parseInt(incRate) : 100;
        if (rate < 0)
        rate = 0;
    } catch (Exception e) {
        rate = 100;
    }
    }
}
if (rate >= 0) {
    repaint(rate, 0, 0, width, height);
}
return (flags & (ALLBITS|ABORT)) == 0;
}
```

What you are looking for is that last `if` statement: `if... repaint()`. Most of the time, a call to `imageUpdate()` will trigger a `repaint()` of the applet, which in turn means the applet's familiar `paint()` method will be called. And what does the applet's `paint()` method do? `drawImage()`! And you are back to where you started. Only this time your `drawImage()` will have a chunk of its image to render, which it does before terminating again. In the meantime, the background image-loading thread continues loading data, which it will again pass on as a stream of image chunks. This cycle continues until the entire image is loaded and displayed.

Although this long chain of cause-and-effect is admittedly arduous, it is a small price to pay for the advantages you gain:

- The logic of your applets does not have to be concerned with multithreaded, asynchronous loading of image data. Everything is taken care of behind the scenes (by daemon Java threads).

- The images are rendered on the screen as the data comes in. This is a very handy form of user feedback, because the user can at any point ascertain the progress of the images being loaded.

- Multiple images can be loaded in parallel by using multiple TCP connections to exploit the bandwidth wasted by and inherent in any burst-pause-burst-pause communication link.

This last point is at least as important as the first. Had image loading been left up to the thousands of applet programmers out there to program, then chances are that the vast majority of applets would have used very inefficient (that is, slow) "brute force" algorithms to load images. Instead, the API designers implemented a complex but high-performance system to be used by all.

Some aspects of this implementation unfortunately could not remain hidden from the application developer. The component `repaint()` methods are a case in point. Two of the overloaded variants take a repaint time-out value. To understand what a time-out parameter has to do with refreshing a graphical display, add a simple

`System.out.prinln()` to your applet and observe the applet's `paint()` dynamics carefully. Add the following line after the `drawImage()` statement in the `paint()` method:

```
System.out.prinln("Had to paint!");
```

If you now rerun the applet, the console should print a number of "Had to paint!" lines:

```
Had to paint!
Had to paint!
Had to paint!
Had to paint!
```

You know why `paint()` gets called several times like this: Each time a new image chunk becomes available, the `imageUpdate()` method causes the applet to repaint itself. In fact, things are a little more subtle still. Suppose you have an applet with a dozen images, all loaded and displayed using the simple `getImage()`/`drawImage()` duo. Since many of the images will be loaded in parallel, new image data will become available in a fairly continuous flow, leading to an onslaught of `imageUpdate()` events. It is clear that calling the applet's `(re)paint()` method each time any of the images has more data available would be inefficient overkill. And that's where the time-out comes in: AWT defines an *incremental draw rate* property that determines how long the system can buffer image data before actually physically updating it on the screen.

NOTE Java system properties are Java-private *environment variables* that the user can usually tune to have different values. See the online documentation for classes `java.util.Properties` and `java.lang.System` for more information on Java properties support.

If you look back at the default implementation for `imageUpdate()`, this is what all the rate (redraw rate) code is about before the `if()`

repaint() at the end. In effect, the imageUpdate() method is saying, "OK, image loader, thanks very much for the new data, but let me see if the user really needs to see this data displayed *right now*." The method determines the refresh rate to be used and passes this on to repaint(). Internally, repaint() determines if this refresh timeout has expired or not. If not, it delays the full repaint, thereby avoiding a potentially expensive call to paint().

As you have seen, a minuscule applet can be a deceptively simple facade hiding some seriously nontrivial software activity. Luckily, you can rely on this complex machinery to do all the hard work for you, all by using two very simple methods: getImage() and drawImage().

Animation's Worse Enemy: Flicker

What if you do not need to load already stored images, but would like to use the Graphics class rendering methods to construct an image from scratch and then render that image instead, in one go? This is possible, but you will not be able to use the applet method getImage() any more, so your Image object will have to come from another factory method in another class: createImage() in class Component.

Here is an example applet that creates an image of a ball and bounces it around the applet over a simple background:

```
import java.awt.*;

public class Ball extends java.applet.Applet {

final static int BALL_RADIUS = 70;

Image ball = null;

public void init() {

    ball = createImage(BALL_RADIUS, BALL_RADIUS);
    Graphics ballG = ball.getGraphics();
```

```
    for (int i=0; i<60; i++) {
        ballG.setColor(new Color((float)Math.random(),
                                 (float)Math.random(),
                                 (float)Math.random() ) );
        int x1 = (int)(Math.random()*BALL_RADIUS);
        int y1 = (int)(Math.random()*BALL_RADIUS);
        int x2 = (int)(Math.random()*BALL_RADIUS);
        int y2 = (int)(Math.random()*BALL_RADIUS);
        ballG.drawLine(x1,y1, x2,y2);
    }

    ballG.setColor(Color.gray);
    for (int i=-20; i<=0; i++) {
        ballG.drawOval(i,i, BALL_RADIUS + ((-i)*2),
                           BALL_RADIUS + ((-i)*2));
    }
}
public void paint(Graphics g) {

    for (int x = 0; x <400; x++) {
        double angle = ((double)x) / 20;
        int y = (int) (Math.abs( Math.sin(angle) )*80);
        g.clearRect(0,0, bounds().width, bounds().height);
        drawBackground(g);
        g.drawImage(ball, x, 80-y, this);
        delay(25);
    }

    System.out.println("paint() done!!");
}
private void drawBackground(Graphics g) {
    for (int i= 0; i<10; i++) {
        g.drawLine(0, i*10, 400, i*10);
    }
}
private void delay (int millis) {
    try { Thread.sleep(millis); } catch (Exception ignored) {}
}}
```

Figure 13.13 shows a snapshot frame of the animation.

FIGURE 13.13:

Bouncing ball animation

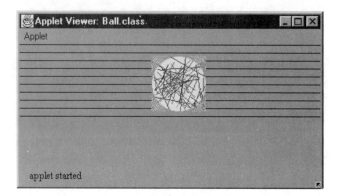

TIP

You don't need to be a latter-day Newton to breath some gravity-like controlled motion into an object. The motion of the ball in this applet follows a sine curve whose negative lobes have been folded up using the `Math.abs()` method. It might not be an accurate modeling of physical reality, but it looks good, and that is what animations are primarily about.

This applet's `init()` method starts by creating a blank ball image by invoking the `createImage()` method on itself. Applets can do this since they are descendants of `Component`. The `createImage(int width, int height)` method is actually an image constructor that creates a special type of off-screen image in which you can draw using the familiar `Graphics` drawing primitives. Images obtained via the `getImage()` applet method cannot be drawn into like this.

To start drawing into your off-screen image, you need to obtain the `Graphics` handle associated with this image. This is done with a call to `getGraphics()`, which returns a `Graphics` object. Once you have such an object in your possession, all graphics-rendering methods can be utilized as usual. The applet draws a ball-like object consisting of random lines of random colors. The `paint()` method then proceeds by repeatedly

- Erasing the entire applet

- Redrawing the background for the animation

- Drawing the ball in its next position

You probably have noticed the problem with this animation already: It flickers like mad. And Walt Disney's animations do not flicker at all, do they? Time for bouncing ball, take two.

Smooth Animation Using Double Buffering

Animation flicker occurs when animation contains sharp and repetitive discontinuities in movement and/or colors within successive frames. In the bounding ball applet's case, the problem is the *on-screen* wiping of the applet area. This causes a repeated and massive color discontinuity that spoils the animation. You need to wipe the whole frame; otherwise, the bouncing ball will leave behind a trace of itself. You can see this by commenting out the `g.clearRect()` statement. After several frames, the applet looks like the one depicted in Figure 13.14.

FIGURE 13.14

Bouncing ball animation
with wipe step removed

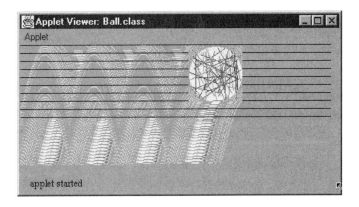

If you could only treat the entire applet drawing area as the same type of *off-screen* image as the ball itself, then maybe you could do all of the animation steps off-screen and display the finished frames in

the applet on-screen. The following program is an enhanced version
of Ball.java that does exactly that:

```java
import java.awt.*;

public class Ball2 extends java.applet.Applet {

final static int BALL_RADIUS = 70;

Image ball   = null;
Image applet = null;

Graphics appG, ballG;

public void paint(Graphics g) {
    if (ball == null) {
        applet = createImage(bounds().width, bounds().height);
        ball   = createImage(BALL_RADIUS, BALL_RADIUS);

        appG  = applet.getGraphics();
        ballG =   ball.getGraphics();

        for (int i=0; i<60; i++) {
            ballG.setColor(new Color((float)Math.random(),
                                     (float)Math.random(),
                                     (float)Math.random() ) );
            int x1 = (int)(Math.random()*BALL_RADIUS);
            int y1 = (int)(Math.random()*BALL_RADIUS);
            int x2 = (int)(Math.random()*BALL_RADIUS);
            int y2 = (int)(Math.random()*BALL_RADIUS);
            ballG.drawLine(x1,y1, x2,y2);
        }

        ballG.setColor(Color.gray);
        for (int i=-20; i<=0; i++) {
            ballG.drawOval(i,i, BALL_RADIUS + ((-i)*2),
                                BALL_RADIUS + ((-i)*2));
        }
    }

    for (int x = 0; x <400; x++) {
        double angle = ((double)x) / 20;
        int y = (int) (Math.abs( Math.sin(angle) )*80);

        appG.clearRect(0,0, bounds().width, bounds().height);
```

```
        drawBackground(appG);
        appG.drawImage(ball, x, 80-y, this);

        g.drawImage(applet, 0,0, this);
        delay(25);
    }
}
private void drawBackground(Graphics g) {
    for (int i= 0; i<10; i++) {
        g.drawLine(0, i*10, 400, i*10);
    }
}
private void delay (int millis) {
    try {
        Thread.sleep(millis);
    } catch (Exception ignored) {}
}}
```

The following changes were made in this newer incarnation of the bouncing ball applet: `creatImage()` was used to obtain a second off-screen image buffer of exactly the same dimensions as the applet. This image will be used to draw everything previously drawn directly into the applet. Therefore, an extra `Graphics` context `appG` is needed to give you drawing access to this new image. The rest of the code is identical except for the use of `appG` instead of the usual `g`. Finally, you still need to use the `Graphics` object for the on-screen applet (g) when you draw the completed frame, in the blink of an eye, into the applet using `g.drawImage()`.

When you run this new applet you will see that all the flicker has magically disappeared. This technique is called *double buffering*, and is one of the most basic computer graphics techniques for smooth animation. The technique can be summarized as follows:

1. Do all your drawing off-screen.

2. Copy the finished product (a single animation frame) to the screen.

3. Repeat the previous two steps as quickly as possible.

Since the frames displayed on-screen never differ beyond the changes intended by the animation itself, flicker is completely eliminated.

Jerkiness

If your animation rate drops below, say, 20 frames per second, your animation will suffer from *jerkiness*. Home computer flight simulators are often a prime example of jerky animations. The scenery frames take so much time to generate (because of the complexity of the scenes and the expensive calculations), that the program simply can't produce a new frame every one-fiftieth of a second.

Once your animations become complex, yours might also suffer from dropping frame rates. It will then be a question of optimizing the animation for speed, a subject that alone could fill an entire volume. Here are some pointers with which you can start:

- Draw as little as possible.

- Reduce the complexity of your animation.

- Use faster rendering algorithms.

- Reduce the dimensions of the animation (shrink the viewport).

- Use tricks like color cycling to animate parts cheaply.

- Use textures to cheaply introduce detail (or complexity).

- Use fixed-point integer math for 3-D calculations.

- Use look-up tables with precalculated results where complex math is involved.

Image Processing

Image processing is a very broad term for a large collection of diverse computer graphics applications. The following list is just a sampling of what image processing is used for:

- Optical character recognition (OCR)

- Image compression and decompression

- DTP-type graphic manipulations (adjusting brightness, color saturation, and so on)

- Movie special effects

- Image interpretation (for factory robots, automated car control, surveillance, and so on)

- Image clean-up (digitally cleaning up old movie classics)

These applications all have something in common: Any real-time aspect of the application is secondary to achieving the primary goal, which is usually very expensive in terms of CPU resources. Modern full-color images easily need over 1Mb of storage alone (an 800 x 600, 24-bit-per-pixel picture requires nearly 1.4Mb). Any algorithm that needs to analyze or process such a picture will almost necessarily fall short of having realtime response characteristics. But this does not mean image processing is used any less for that reason. Java supports image processing in various ways, all of them having one feature in common—platform independence. Colors and bitmaps can be extensively manipulated in hardware-independent ways, using an image pipeline metaphor, before being output to the screen. The pipeline metaphor is analogous to the streams I/O model provided by the `java.io` package (discussed in detail in Chapter 15). Before explaining the pipeline model, as embodied by the `ImageProducer` and `ImageConsumer` interfaces, you need to have a look at how color itself can be represented and manipulated.

Color Models

Color emanating from a radiating source can be decomposed into the three primary *additive* colors—red, green, and blue. All colors used by computers are mixtures of these three colors. The spectrum of a computer's palette will be determined by the number of different red, green, and blue shades that are available. This is in turn determined by the number of bits the hardware uses to encode the red, green, and blue primaries. The number of bits used has evolved historically from 1 bit each to the current norm: 8 bits each. The first systems, which used 1 bit per primary, could display eight different colors. Those eight colors are listed in Table 13.1.

Table 13.1: Minimal Eight-Color Palette

Color	Red Bit	Green Bit	Blue Bit
Black	0	0	0
Red	1	0	0
Green	0	1	0
Blue	0	0	1
Yellow	1	1	0
Cyan	0	1	1
Magenta	1	0	1
White	1	1	1

Modern systems use 8 bits per primary, so they can display 16.7 million colors. In between, there are numerous asymmetrical bit assignment combinations that invariably favor green, allocating, for example, 5 bits for red and blue and 6 bits for green. (This is because the human eye is more discerning when it comes to shades of green.)

The end result is that there are a large number of incompatible color representations out there. Instead of choosing one (the most popular one for example) and enforcing its use on all Java programmers, Java defines a software layer that shields us from these platform dependencies. The abstract class ColorModel is the key to this buffer layer:

```
public class ColorModel extends Object {
    protected int pixel_bits;
    public ColorModel(int bits);
    public static ColorModel getRGBdefault();
    public int getPixelSize();
    public abstract int getRed(int pixel);
    public abstract int getGreen(int pixel);
    public abstract int getBlue(int pixel);
    public abstract int getAlpha(int pixel);
    public int getRGB(int pixel);
}
```

The main feature of any ColorModel is that it allows you to use pixels that are encoded using almost any concrete hardware-encoding scheme (the notable exception is bitplane-based architectures). A customized ColorModel should allow you to extract the universal red, green, and blue (and alpha transparency) components from any pixel encoded using any color-coding scheme. Although Java's image-processing classes support this flexible color model independence, they still define a default *preferred* color architecture—the popular 32-bit ARGB pixel format that uses the following bit assignments:

bits 0–7	blue
bits 8–15	green
bits 16–23	red
bits 24–31	alpha transparency

The `java.awt.image` package has two concrete incarnations of this abstract `ColorModel` class: classes `DirectColorModel` and `IndexColorModel`.

Class `DirectColorModel` encapsulates a `ColorModel` reflecting a True Color–style color architecture. In such a system, pixels hold the color value they represent themselves. This is as opposed to indexed architectures, in which pixels hold an index value used to index a table holding the final color values. And this is what class `Index-ColorModel` models—a `ColorModel` using a Color Look-Up Table (CLUT) color architecture.

This color model independence means your applications have almost limitless flexibility in the way they encode pictures "behind the scenes."

Algorithmic Image Generation

Images are usually external files containing photographs, diagrams, or other art that was produced sometime in the past. There is one other fascinating source for images, and that is the computer itself, or rather algorithms that generate pictures dynamically, using numerical methods. Class `MemoryImageSource` exists just for those types of applications needing per-pixel control over their images. Its constructor takes an array of int (or bytes) representing a two-dimensional pixel map. Therefore, with this class, you can implement rendering algorithms of arbitrary complexity, since you have full and efficient access to every pixel of an image (remember that the `Graphics` class did not have a single pixel plotting method). The program below demonstrates this by generating the classic fractal: the Mandelbrot set. Figure 13.15 shows the applet's output (which on a 100Mhz Pentium PC, using the standard Sun JDK, is generated in a very respectable less than five seconds). The source code for the applet is listed on the following page.

Mandelbrot set
generated via a
`MemoryImageSource`

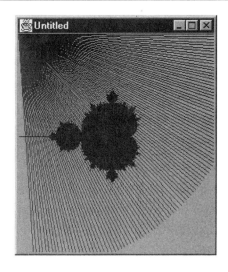

```java
import java.awt.*;
import java.awt.image.*;

class Mandelbrot {

public static void main(String[] args) {
    new MandelWindow();
}}
//————————————————————————————————————
class MandelWindow extends Frame {

Image    img;
int      w = 256;
int      h = 256;
int[]    pix = new int[w * h];

MandelWindow() {

int index = 0;
int iter;
double p,q, psq, qsq, pnew, qnew;
double a,b;                            // real and imaginary axis

    resize(260,300);
    show();
    Graphics g = getGraphics();

    double WIDTH_STEP = 4.0/w;
    double HEIGHT_STEP = 4.0/h;
```

```
for (int y=0; y < h; y++) {          b = ((double)(y-128))/64;
    for (int x=0; x < w; x++) {       a = ((double)(x-128))/64;

        p=q=0;
        iter = 0;
        while (iter < 32) {          // see if point a,b is in the set
            psq = p*p; qsq = q*q;
            if (psq+qsq >= 4.0) break;
            pnew = psq - qsq + a;
            qnew = 2 * p*q + b;
            p = pnew;
            q = qnew;
            iter++;
        }
        if (iter == 32) {
            pix[index] = 255<<24 | 255;
        }
        index++;
    }
}

for (float i=0.0F; i< 1.0F; i+=0.01F) {  // draw a pretty background
    g.setColor(new Color(i,0,0));
    g.drawLine(0,0, (int)(300*Math.cos(i*1.5)),
                    (int)(300*Math.sin(i*1.5)) );
}

img = createImage(new MemoryImageSource(w, h, pix, 0, w));
g.drawImage(img, 0,0, null);
}}
```

The code clearly shows the power of class MemoryImageSource: You simply

1. Declare any old array of ints (pix in this example) to hold the pixels you will "plot" yourself.

2. Generate the image using any rendering algorithm of your choice.

Now you are just a creatImage() and drawImage() away from seeing the result displayed by your Java program. Plotting pixels in such arrays can be done extremely efficiently (more efficiently even than plotting individual pixels directly to the screen using some kind of plotPixel(x,y,color) method). The example program does not even address the array two-dimensionally (although, logically, it is a 2-D array w pixels wide and h pixels high). Instead, it uses a most efficient linear (one-dimensional) sequential addressing (`pix[index]`). The actual plotting of a pixel is done by storing `255<<24 | 255` as its value. This, under the default RGB color model, means alpha equals 255 (completely opaque, bits 24–31) and blue equals 255; in other words, an everyday "pure blue" pixel. Since you are not plotting pixels for the points outside the Mandelbrot set, the set is surrounded by fully transparent (alpha equals 0) pixels, thus letting the background show through in those areas. (You are relying on newly allocated `int` arrays containing only zeroes. This is guaranteed by the language itself.)

NOTE The mathematics behind the Mandelbrot set is beyond the scope of this book. It involves complex numbers and requires some insight of nonlinear equations. Consult any good book on fractals if you want to know the ins and outs of the Mandelbrot (and other) fractals.

Back to the subject of color models: If you look at the definition of class `MemoryImageSource`, you will notice that most of its constructors allow you to specify a `ColorModel` to be used with the memory image:

```
public class MemoryImageSource extends Object implements ImageProducer {
    public MemoryImageSource(int w, int h, ColorModel cm, byte pix[], int off,
    ➥int scan);
    public MemoryImageSource(int w, int h, ColorModel cm, byte pix[], int off,
    ➥int scan, Hashtable props);
    public MemoryImageSource(int w, int h, ColorModel cm, int pix[], int off,
    ➥int scan);
    public MemoryImageSource(int w, int h, ColorModel cm, int pix[], int off,
    ➥int scan, Hashtable props);
    public MemoryImageSource(int w, int h, int pix[], int off, int scan);
    public MemoryImageSource(int w, int h, int pix[], int off, int scan, Hashtable
    ➥props);
    public synchronized void addConsumer(ImageConsumer ic);
    public synchronized boolean isConsumer(ImageConsumer ic);
    public synchronized void removeConsumer(ImageConsumer ic);
    public void startProduction(ImageConsumer ic);
    public void requestTopDownLeftRightResend(ImageConsumer ic);
}
```

In this example, the Mandelbrot class uses the simplest constructor that conveniently avoids ColorModel issues. This means that your memory image actually uses the AWT preferred color model—the default 32-bit ARGB format (defined in the section on color models). But the image-processing flexibility of the java.awt.image package does not force you to use this at all. Therefore, you could ignore what Java prefers and impose a 4-bit VGA color encoding scheme. (This is used purely for illustrative purposes and in no way suggests that VGA schemes—that is, limitations—still have a place in modern graphics applications.) The following code implements the new Mandelbrot class using a VGA color model.

```
import java.awt.*;
import java.awt.image.*;

class MandelIndex {

public static void main(String[] args) {
    new MandelWindow();
}}

//————————————————————--
class MandelWindow extends Frame {

final static byte[] VGAreds   = {-128, -1,  0,   0,   0,   0,-128,  -1,   0,   0,
➡-128, -1,   0,-128,-64,  -1};
final static byte[] VGAgreens = {  0,   0,-128,  -1,   0,   0,-128,  -1,-128,  -1,
➡   0,  0,   0,-128,-64,  -1};
final static byte[] VGAblues  = {  0,   0,  0,   0,-128,  -1,   0,   0,-128,  -1,
➡-128, -1,   0,-128,-64,  -1};

Image   img;
int     w = 512;
int     h = 512;
byte[]  pix = new byte[w * h];

MandelWindow() {

int index = 0;
int iter;
double p,q, psq, qsq, pnew, qnew;
double a,b;                          // real and imaginary axis

    resize(512,400);
    show();
    Graphics g = getGraphics();
```

```
double WIDTH_STEP = 4.0/w;
double HEIGHT_STEP = 4.0/h;

for (int y=0; y < h; y++) {          b = ((double)(y-256))/128;
    for (int x=0; x < w; x++) {      a = ((double)(x-256))/128;

        p=q=0;
        iter = 0;
        while (iter < 32) {          // see if point a,b is in the set
            psq = p*p; qsq = q*q;
            if (psq+qsq >= 4.0) break;
            pnew = psq - qsq + a;
            qnew = 2 * p*q + b;
            p = pnew;
            q = qnew;
            iter++;
        }

        if (iter == 32) {
            pix[index] = 15;     // VGA color 15
        } else {
            pix[index] = 4;      // VGA color 4
        }
        index++;
    }
}
img = createImage(new MemoryImageSource(w, h, new IndexColorModel(8, 16, VGAreds,
➥VGAgreens, VGAblues), pix, 0, w));

g.drawImage(img, 0,0, null);
}}
```

To modify the Mandelbrot class to plot VGA-style pixels instead of expensive 32-bit pixels, you start by declaring an array of bytes instead of ints, and then change the actual plotting . It is now much simpler to do this, of course: You store color index numbers instead of specifying the color value itself. The `if` statement colors a pixel white (VGA color 15), if it is inside the set, and colors all other pixels blue (VGA color 4) for all points outside the Mandelbrot set. Then, to convince `drawImage()` to use the VGA-style coloring scheme, you use an explicitly defined color model that allows Java to map your VGA pixels to its own preferred 32-bit style. (Luckily `drawImage()` doesn't know anything about VGA.) Since VGA uses a color look-up table mechanism, you create an instance of an `IndexColorModel` that defines this mapping, and tell it your pixels are only 8 bits wide and that the look-up table only holds 16 color entries. The look-up table itself is passed as three separate byte look-up arrays, one for each primary color:

```
new IndexColorModel(8, 16, VGAreds, VGAgreens, VGAblues)
```

> **TIP**
>
> Note the color byte arrays are filled with some bytes in the range 128–255 using negative values. The Java range for bytes is −128–+127, because bytes are always signed numbers (like all other numerical types in Java). Literally specifying the unsigned byte value 255, for example, is not possible without using casts. And since using a cast for each item in the arrays would seriously degrade readability, we chose to go negative using the two's complement scheme. The signed byte −128 is equivalent to the unsigned byte 128. Likewise, −1 is equivalent to 255, and so on.

Since `createImage()` binds this custom color model to the image you are creating, any subsequent `drawImage()` calls will use this color model to translate the custom pixel encoding to whatever the native image subsystem implementation uses (one safe bet is that it won't be using VGA).

If you wanted to eliminate the use of the verbose `IndexColorModel` constructor by subclassing `IndexColorModel` into a `VGAColorModel` class, say, to enhance readability, and using the constructor for the new class instead, then something interesting happens to the program. Here is the readability enhancing `VGAColorModel` class:

```
class VGAColorModel extends IndexColorModel {

final static byte[] VGAreds   = {-128, -1,   0,   0,   0,   0,-128,  -1,   0,   0,
➡-128,  -1,   0,-128,-64,  -1};
final static byte[] VGAgreens = {  0,   0,-128,  -1,   0,   0,-128,  -1,-128,  -1,
➡0,   0,   0,-128,-64,  -1};
final static byte[] VGAblues  = {  0,   0,   0,   0,-128,  -1,   0,   0,-128,  -1,
➡-128,  -1,   0,-128,-64,  -1};

public VGAColorModel() {
    super(8, 16, VGAreds, VGAgreens, VGAblues);
}}
```

With this new class, you can now write a much more descriptive

```
new MemoryImageSource(w, h, new VGAColorModel(), pix, 0, w)
```

The unexpected result comes when you run the program again using the new class—it is *much* slower. The drop in performance cannot have anything to do with the Mandelbrot calculations (since nothing changed here), so the slowdown must clearly be attributed to the `drawImage()` method. Without the subclass, our VGA Mandelbrot appears on-screen in less than 1 second. Using the subclass, it takes 7.5 seconds!

Why the discrepancy in times? To begin, the core method of class `ColorModel` is `getRGB()`. This method is used by the image subsystem to construct in-core images in optimized formats that are native to the platform running your Java programs—for example, BMP format on Windows machines or X-Bitmaps on X-Windows machines. So, for every pixel in your images, whatever their encoding is, the image subsystem has to invoke the `getRGB()` method on the associated color model being used for this image. If you now subclass `IndexColorModel` without overriding this `getRGB()` method (which you can't do anyway, because it is declared final in `IndexColor-Model`), then Java's dynamic method look-up mechanism will fail to find this method in the `VGAColorModel` class. Undeterred (this is why it's called dynamic), it will then follow the inheritance chain up to the superclass to see if the method is available there, which, sure enough, it is.

Did one paltry extra level of inheritance cause such a huge performance hit? (If it had, Java would be unusable.) The real cause lies in the declaration of the original `getRGB()` method. It was declared final—that is, you could not override it in subclasses. And final methods are very quick to call (there is no dynamic look-up whatsoever). Your first version did not subclass `IndexColorModel`, so the `getRGB()` method was called statically (that is, quickly). Then, you suddenly forced this method to be accessed *via* a dynamic method lookup, putting into stark contrast the differing performances of static versus dynamic method binding. And that is the cause for the performance hit. Had the original method not been declared final, the difference would have been far less.

The Producer-Consumer Design Pattern

A *design pattern* is a design solution that has been proven to work time and time again. As such, you can use off-the-shelf design patterns in your software (or in construction, electronics, or architecture) with a better than even chance that the design pattern will be a solid foundation to the problem at hand (*if* you pick the right pattern for the type of problem you're dealing with). There are many kinds of design patterns out there, most of which have not yet been identified as such. The realization that the field of software also has its own design patterns is a rather recent development in computer science. Some patterns which have already been identified, and are used by the Java API, are

Iterator   This is embodied by the `Enumeration` interface in package `java.util`.

Observer   This is embodied by the `Observer` interface and the `Observable` class in package `java.util`.

Composite   This is embodied by the AWT classes `Component` and `Container`.

Except for the Composite design pattern example, the Iterator and Observer patterns are made available by Java in their most powerful forms: as interfaces. An `Enumeration` does not care what you are enumerating through it, and the `Observer-Observable` duo does not care what is being observed or who is doing the observing. It is a pity this generality has not been applied within AWT, too: Classes `Component` and `Container` are an implementation of the `Composite` design pattern (which allows a system to handle individual objects or collections of those objects in the same way), but the design pattern itself is not made available to application programmers. It is used within AWT, but not "exported," like the `java.util` design patterns are.

Package `java.awt.image` also relies on a common design pattern (again without making available the guts of the abstraction): the `Producer-Consumer` design pattern. As with so many of these patterns, the accent lies on decoupling systems. Decoupling is a powerful technique used to introduce more flexibility into a system.

> **NOTE**
>
> You saw a strong example of decoupling in this chapter with the `drawImage()` `Graphics` method: it decouples (internally) the drawing of an image from the image's data source.

The image `Producer-Consumer` design pattern is enforced using two interfaces: `ImageProducer` and `ImageConsumer`. Concrete classes that implement these interfaces are symbiotically linked together to form an image-generation pipeline. An `ImageProducer` is nothing without an `ImageConsumer` and vice versa. This bi-directional dependence is defined by the methods each calls on the other.

Here is a definition for both interfaces, since neither can be explained in isolation:

```
public interface ImageProducer extends Object {
   public abstract void addConsumer(ImageConsumer ic);
   public abstract boolean isConsumer(ImageConsumer ic);
   public abstract void removeConsumer(ImageConsumer ic);
   public abstract void startProduction(ImageConsumer ic);
   public abstract void requestTopDownLeftRightResend(ImageConsumer ic);
}
public interface ImageConsumer extends Object {
   public final static int RANDOMPIXELORDER;
   public final static int TOPDOWNLEFTRIGHT;
```

```
public final static int COMPLETESCANLINES;
public final static int SINGLEPASS;
public final static int SINGLEFRAME;
public final static int IMAGEERROR;
public final static int SINGLEFRAMEDONE;
public final static int STATICIMAGEDONE;
public final static int IMAGEABORTED;
public abstract void setDimensions(int width, int height);
public abstract void setProperties(Hashtable props);
public abstract void setColorModel(ColorModel model);
public abstract void setHints(int hintflags);
public abstract void setPixels(int x, int y, int w, int h, ColorModel model, byte
➥pixels[], int off, int scansize);
public abstract void setPixels(int x, int y, int w, int h, ColorModel model, int
➥pixels[], int off, int scansize);
public abstract void imageComplete(int status);
}
```

If you recall the `Observable-Observer` design pattern explained in Chapter 9, then you should have no problem understanding this pair, as there is a strong similarity between the two design patterns. While the loose coupling of the `Observable-Observer` duo consists of a simple notification implemented by an invocation of the `update()` observer method, with image `Producer-Consumer` pairs there is actual (and substantial) data transfer: image data. This is achieved in much the same way as with the `Observable-Observer` pair: the `ImageProducer` calls methods on the `ImageConsumer` to transfer image data and other information. The main method is the `setPixels()` method. Here is this method's signature (the types of all the `int` arguments have been stripped out to fit the whole signature on one line):

```
void setPixels(x,y, w,h, ColorModel model, byte pixels[], off, scansize)
```

When an `ImageProducer` wants to transfer some image data it has produced to an `ImageConsumer`, it invokes the `setPixels()` method on that consumer. The arguments tell the consumer which subrectangle is being transferred (the x,y and w,h arguments) and what that rectangle contains as pixels.

In practice, these subrectangles will almost always be complete, consecutive strips of the picture. An `ImageProducer` that produced its data as a patchwork collage of rectangles would be rather strange. (There is, however, nothing to stop a producer from having such image production dynamics, and it would not be an error.)

This image data proper is specified as a one-dimensional array of pixels (bytes or ints), an offset within that array, and the size of a horizontal (scan)line of the image. The `scansize` argument is required by the consumer in cases when the rectangle being transferred is narrower than the width of the picture. To extract the individual lines from the subrectangle correctly, the consumer *has* to skip bytes in the array to go to the next line of the subrectangle. The amount to skip is calculated as *scansize–w*.

How does an `ImageProducer` know which `ImageConsumer` it should hand image data to, and when? Here, the responsibility lies with the consumer. It creates the producer-consumer connection by announcing itself to an `ImageProducer` as being interested in receiving image data. This it does by calling the `addConsumer()` method on the producer. The consumer also starts the image factory rolling by calling the `startProduction()` `ImageProducer` method.

As you can guess from the other methods in both interfaces, there is quite a bit more to the protocol between these two partners. But here is a concrete example. You have already manipulated an `Image-Producer` in one of the example programs: Class `MemoryImage-Source`, which we used to generate the Mandelbrot image with, is an `ImageProducer` because it implements the `ImageProducer` interface. If you look back at its definition (listed in the previous section), you will see that it has the five required interface methods. So, somewhere in the Mandelbrot program, you should have its inseparable `ImageConsumer`, too. While it is not stated explicitly anywhere, the image created with the `createImage()` method internally uses an

`ImageConsumer` for the image data it represents. This hidden consumer will activate the producer-consumer protocol at some later point, when a `drawImage()` is done on an `Image`.

There are several benefits to having this decoupling between image data and the entities that actually use this data. For one, doing so means that the path between image data and image user (consumer) can be of arbitrary complexity, and therefore highly flexible. If `createImage()` took a pointer to a pixel bitmap in memory, your options would be rather limited. But since it takes a reference to an `ImageProducer` instead, the data can come from anywhere. Another powerful result of this approach is that the image transfer from producer to consumer can be asynchronous. Although the consumer starts the image production process, it does not control the sequence of image subrectangles produced or their timing. This is the producer's province.

Yet another benefit of the abstract producer-consumer approach is that you can create image processing pipelines. This is achieved by having classes that are both producer *and* consumer—consumer of some previous stage's output and producer of the next stage's input. A possible pipeline is depicted in Figure 13.16 .

FIGURE 13.16:

An image-processing pipeline

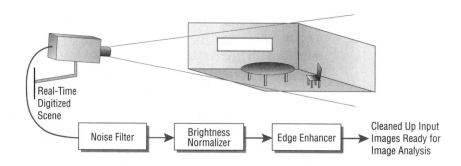

Each stage in an image-processing pipeline is usually called a *filter*. Java's `java.awt.image` package includes explicit support for such filters. The next section explores the classes that deal with image filtering.

Image Filtering

The generic term *image filtering* is almost synonymous with *image processing*. One of the core image-processing techniques is filtering (that is, altering) an image pixel by pixel, although the term is used in the wider sense of image manipulation as well. Pixel-by-pixel processing of images is supported by several classes in `java.awt.image`.

First of all, there is class `FilteredImageSource`, which like `MemoryImageSource` is an `ImageProducer`:

```
public class FilteredImageSource extends Object implements ImageProducer {
    public FilteredImageSource(ImageProducer orig, ImageFilter imgf);
    public synchronized void addConsumer(ImageConsumer ic);
    public synchronized boolean isConsumer(ImageConsumer ic);
    public synchronized void removeConsumer(ImageConsumer ic);
    public void startProduction(ImageConsumer ic);
    public void requestTopDownLeftRightResend(ImageConsumer ic);
}
```

The key to understanding this class is its constructor: Instead of taking an array of pixels (as with `MemoryImageSource`), this class takes *another* `ImageProducer` plus a filter object to combine the two into a new, filtered image. The filter object has to be of type `Image-Filter`, of which two concrete subclasses can be used immediately. These are

- `CropImageFilter`

- `RGBImageFilter`

Using the `CropImageFilter` subclass, you can create sub-images of a bigger image. With `RGBImageFilter`, you can filter the colors of an image either pixel by pixel or—if the image uses a CLUT color model—in bulk by simply modifying the image's palette.

The following program demonstrates the use of both filters on a color image file. The `RGBImageFilter` is used to implement a color-to-gray filter, and the `CropImageFilter` is used to cut a 40×40 pixel sub-image from the original, which we then paste back onto the original magnified to three times its original size. The magnification is achieved simply by specifying a final image size of 120×120 pixels. Figure 13.17 shows the resulting output window.

FIGURE 13.17:

Use of `ImageFilters` on an original color picture

```
import java.awt.*;
import java.awt.image.*;
```
//————————————————————————————————
```
public class Filters extends java.applet.Applet {

Image oldImage, newImage, subImage;
```

```
ImageProducer filtered, cropped;

public void init() {
    oldImage = getImage(getDocumentBase(), "market.gif");
    filtered = new FilteredImageSource(oldImage.getSource(), new GrayFilter());
    cropped  = new FilteredImageSource(oldImage.getSource(), new CropImageFilter
    ➥(300,70,40,40));

    newImage = createImage(filtered);
    subImage = createImage(cropped);
}

public void paint(Graphics g) {
    g.drawImage(newImage, 0, 0, this);
    g.clearRect(20,20,140,140);
    g.drawImage(subImage, 30, 30, 120, 120, this);
    System.out.println(".");
                }}
                //─────────────────────────────────────────────

                class GrayFilter extends RGBImageFilter {

                public GrayFilter() {
                    canFilterIndexColorModel = true;
                }

                public int filterRGB(int x, int y, int rgb) {

                int alpha,r,g,b;
                int gray;

                    alpha   = rgb & (0xFF << 24);
                    r       = (rgb >> 16) & 0xFF;
                    g       = (rgb >>  8) & 0xFF;
                    b       = (rgb >>  0) & 0xFF;
                    gray    = (r+g+b)/3;

                    return alpha | gray<<16 | gray<<8 | gray;
                }}
```

This program loads the image file using a getImage() call and then creates two new images based on the original. Both derived images are obtained using the FilteredImageSource class to combine the picture with a filter. For the grayscale version of the picture, an instance of the GrayFilter that was subclassed from RGBImageFilter is used. For the sub-image, an instance of a CropImageFilter is used (there is no need to subclass it). The two new FilteredImageSource objects are not yet images that can be passed to `drawImage()`. Since `FilteredImageSource` objects are only `ImageProducers`, you have to turn them into images with the two calls to `createImage()`. All of these steps should only be done once, so they are located in the applet's `init()` method. The actual drawing of the applet is done in the `paint()` method, where we draw both processed images using `drawImage()` invocations.

The `GrayFilter` color filter has two aspects to it: the overridden `filterRGB()` method and the constructor. Method `filterRGB()` is called with individual pixels to be processed. The x- and y-parameters method `filterRGB()` receives are the coordinates of the pixel to be processed. Because you do not need to use these coordinates (the color filter is pixel position independent), you signal the outside world that this `RGBImageFilter` can short-circuit the bulk filtering of an image's pixels by simply filtering its palette only. This is several orders of magnitude faster than having to process every single pixel of an `Image`, which makes the simple `canFilterIndexColorModel = true;` assignment well worth the effort of creating the custom constructor.

Although the filtering architecture supported by the classes you have seen so far can be used for many filtering tasks, some image filtering algorithms need to access the image's source pixels to determine the output value of any given pixel. The `ImageFilter` class cannot handle this. One way to solve this problem is to use yet another `java.awt.image` class—`PixelGrabber`. This class is almost the opposite of `MemoryImageSource` in that it takes an `ImageProducer` and extracts the image data from it. You can therefore use full-image image-processing algorithms by

- Converting a source image into a simple (and fast) low-level Java array of ints or bytes, via the `PixelGrabber` class

- Applying the full-image algorithm to the array

- Reconverting the array into an image, via the `MemoryImageSource` class

To demonstrate this approach, you will develop a class that implements the popular *convolve filter*. This filter is defined by a 3×3 matrix of pixel weights to be used when calculating the new value for the pixel at the center of the matrix. Different filtering effects can be obtained depending on the set of values used by the matrix. Among others, smoothing and vertical edge enhancement effects can be achieved. Here is a program that implements this filtering algorithm:

```java
import java.awt.*;
import java.awt.image.*;

//————————————————————————————————————————————————————————————
public class Convolve extends java.applet.Applet {

Image oldImage, newImage;
ImageProducer filtered;
double[] filter = {0.1125, 0.1125, 0.1125,
                   0.1125, 0.0000, 0.1125,
                   0.1125, 0.1125, 0.1125 };

public void init() {

    oldImage = getImage(getDocumentBase(), "hammock.jpg");

    MediaTracker mt = new MediaTracker(this);
    mt.addImage(oldImage, 0);
    try {
        mt.waitForID(0);
    } catch (Exception error) {
        System.out.println("Loading of image failed!");
        System.out.println(error);
        System.exit(10);
    }

    ConvFilter cv = new ConvFilter(filter);
    filtered = cv.filteredImage(oldImage);

    newImage = createImage(filtered);
}

public void paint(Graphics g) {

g.drawImage(oldImage, 0, 0, this);
```

```
        g.clipRect(200,0,1000,500);
            g.drawImage(newImage, 0, 0, this);
    }}
    //——————————————————————————————————————————————————————————
    class ConvFilter implements ImageObserver {

    int[]    oldPixels, newPixels;      // original and result image buffers
    int      w,h;                       // image width and height

    PixelGrabber pg;                    // the way to get at the image's pixels
    MemoryImageSource mis;              // the way to produce an image from result

    // To process the image array we are using 1-dimensional addressing
    // instead of the logical 2-D addressing. index is the main pixel
    // pointer (equivalent to x,y coordinates). The collection of inn
    // indices track index but address the 3x3 matrix neighbors of the
    // center pixel.

    int      index = 0;
    int      i00,i01,i02,i10,i11,i12,i20,i21,i22;   // 3x3 sliding indices
    into image

    int      p00,p01,p02,p10,p11,p12,p20,p21,p22;   // cached pixels
    double   w00,w01,w02,w10,w11,w12,w20,w21,w22;   // cached weights


    //——————————————————————————————————————————————————————————
    // The CONSTRUCTOR for the class just caches (copies) the convolution
    // filter's weights
    //——————————————————————————————————————————————————————————

    public ConvFilter (double[] matrix) {

        w00 = matrix[0]; w01 = matrix[1]; w02 = matrix[2];
        w10 = matrix[3]; w11 = matrix[4]; w12 = matrix[5];
        w20 = matrix[6]; w21 = matrix[7]; w22 = matrix[8];
    }

    public boolean imageUpdate(Image img, int infoflags,
                               int x, int y, int width, int height) {

        System.out.println("ImageObserver update !!!");


        w = width;
        h = height;
        System.out.println("INFO WIDTH = " + (infoflags & ImageObserver.WIDTH));
        System.out.println("INFO HEIGHT = " + (infoflags & ImageObserver.HEIGHT));
        System.out.println("W,H= " + w + " " + h);

        if (w != -1 && h != -1) {
            System.out.println("GOT W & H !!");
```

```
          return false;
      }
      return true;
}

//————————————————————————————————————————————————————————————
// a) find out image width and height
// b) allocate original and result image pixel buffers
// c) extract pixels from image using a PixelGrabber
// d) process image
// e) convert resulting image to ImageProducer using a MemoryImageSource
//————————————————————————————————————————————————————————————

public ImageProducer filteredImage(Image source) {
boolean success;

    w = source.getWidth(null);
    h = source.getHeight(null);

    System.out.println("Image width = " + w + " height = " + h);

    oldPixels = new int[w*h];       // allocate image buffer for original
    newPixels = new int[w*h];       // allocate image buffer for destination

    pg = new PixelGrabber(source.getSource(), 0,0, w, h, oldPixels, 0, w);

    try {
        success = pg.grabPixels(0);       // try to suck entire image into
    } catch (Exception e) {               // our processing buffer
        System.out.println("Duh ! " + e);
    }

    index = w + 1;                    // avoid top and left pixel edges
    for (int y=1; y < h-1; y++) {     // avoid bottom edge too
        calc3x3offsets();             // adjust all tracking offsets
        for (int x=1; x < w-1; x++) {    // and avoid right edge

            p00 = oldPixels[i00];     // cache 3x3 cluster of pixels
            p01 = oldPixels[i01];     // so we don't have to use expensive
            p02 = oldPixels[i02];     // array indexing anymore
            p10 = oldPixels[i10];
            p11 = oldPixels[i11];
            p12 = oldPixels[i12];
            p20 = oldPixels[i20];
            p21 = oldPixels[i21];
            p22 = oldPixels[i22];

                // convolution filter has to be applied to each color
                // primary individually (there's no way to treat a pixel as
                // a whole)

            int newRed  = applyWeights(16);
```

```
                         int newGreen= applyWeights( 8);
                         int newBlue = applyWeights( 0);
                         newPixels[index++] = 255<<24 | newRed | newGreen | newBlue;

                         i00++; i01++; i02++;     // slide all our tracking indices along
                         i10++; i11++; i12++;
                         i20++; i21++; i22++;
                     }
                     index += 2;
                     System.out.println("Y=" + y); // give some feedback of where we're at
                 }

             // we have now done all the image processing on the source image,
             // send the result back to the client as an ImageProducer.

             mis = new MemoryImageSource(w,h,newPixels,0,w);
             return mis;
         }


     //------------------------------------------------------------------
     // Convenience method to keep main loop readable. This just recalculates
     // all neighbor pixel indices from index (this is done once for every
     // image scanline only, within the scanline the indices are just incremented
     // like index).
     //------------------------------------------------------------------
     final void calc3x3offsets() {

         i00 = index-w-1;
         i01 = i00+1;
         i02 = i00+2;
         i10 = index-1;
         i11 = index;
         i12 = index+1;
         i20 = index+w-1;
         i21 = i20+1;
         i22 = i20+2;
     }


     //------------------------------------------------------------------
     // Calculate the new primary for this 3x3 pixel cluster.
     // The primary is specified by the bit shift to apply to a standard 32-bit
     // ARGB pixel so that the primary occupies bits 0..7
     //------------------------------------------------------------------

     final int applyWeights(int shift) {
     double total=0;

         total += ((p00 >> shift) & 0xFF) * w00;
         total += ((p01 >> shift) & 0xFF) * w01;
         total += ((p02 >> shift) & 0xFF) * w02;

         total += ((p10 >> shift) & 0xFF) * w10;
```

```
total += ((p11 >> shift) & 0xFF) * w11;
total += ((p12 >> shift) & 0xFF) * w12;

total += ((p20 >> shift) & 0xFF) * w20;
total += ((p21 >> shift) & 0xFF) * w21;
total += ((p22 >> shift) & 0xFF) * w22;

return ((int)total) << shift;

}} // End of Class
```

The `ConvolveFilter` class takes an array of doubles specifying nine weight values. These nine values correspond to the 3×3 pixel cluster the filter uses to determine the central pixel's new value. The new color of a pixel is calculated by summing the weighted values of all pixels in the 3×3 cluster. This process needs to operate on all three color primaries separately. The actual filtering is done by the `filteredImage()` method. Like we said before, it relies on a `PixelGrabber` object and on a `MemoryImageSource` object to convert the image to and from the internal array representation used by the algorithm to actually do the filtering. Much of the code is concerned with performance issues. It tries to avoid array indexing as much as possible by *caching* (that is, copying) values that need to be used several times. The class also avoids using loops that are considered nonfunctional overhead. Method `applyWeights()` could have been written with a loop to make it shorter and possibly more readable, but doing so would have slowed down the filtering significantly.

On the applet side of the program, there are also a couple of technical points of interest. Our `ConvolveFilter` requires the source image to be fully loaded and available. This is because it relies on the `Image` `getWidth()` and `getHeight()` methods to produce valid results at all times (due to the same asynchronous loading of images, width and height information might not be available until some time *after* the image is created using the `getImage()` method). To guarantee that `getWidth()` and `getHeight()` will not return -1 (which they do when images are not loaded yet), you use a `MediaTracker` object to wait for you until the image is completely ready and loaded. See the code and the online documentation for more information on class `java.awt.MediaTracker`.

The second interesting thing in our applet is the use of clipping to display part of the original image next to the processed image. For this we need to get a second (different!) `Graphics` context. This is because `clipRect()` calls, like `translate()` calls, are cumulative. You cannot just move the clipping rectangle to a new position, so you need to get a second `Graphics` object (which starts off with a `cliprect` as big as the entire applet) and specify the second clipping window in that context. The output of the program, shown in Figure 13.18, shows how a smoothing filter is applied to the original image.

FIGURE 13.18:

Smoothing convolution filter applied to a color image

Summary

This chapter dealt with a lot of graphics-related material, beginning with the basics: graphics-rendering primitives and how to manipulate `Graphics` contexts. Then, you had a look at animation and the key requirements for any good animation: absence of flicker and high frame rates. You learned how double buffering can eliminate all flicker, which led to an exploration of the complex `Image` AWT subsystem. Although easily accessible to application programmers, you saw that the asynchronous background loading of images is not entirely transparent to the application level, and might require the use of `MediaTracker` and other safeguards for robust implementations. You also explored the image-processing aspects of the `java.awt.image` package through the core metaphor of image producer-consumer pairs and the classes—`MemoryImageSource`, `FilteredImageSource`, `PixelGrabber`—that, in one way or other, implement the metaphor.

CHAPTER

FOURTEEN

Advanced Applet Programming

- Purely GUI-Driven Applets

- Selfish Applets

- Multithreaded Applets

- Minimizing Applet Loading Times

So far, the applets you have seen in this book have all been quick demonstrations of some Java class or Java method, although they may not have been pitching for real-life applet status. Real-life applets, however, are usually one or more of the following:

- Seriously cool

- Functional

- Perfectly compatible with all Java browsers

It is a fact of life that the Web is this strange chimera of endless entertainment and serious information broadcasting. On one hand, you have an exploding population of people who use the Web as a vehicle to project their personality (through Web home pages which ooze unrestrained individuality), and on the other hand, you have the world's businesses frantically trying to capture cyberspace market segments, by any means. Both groups are turning to Java to gain the edge over the competition, whether that competition be a multinational's Wall Street–listed arch rival or the guy halfway across the globe whose Web page is nearly as cool as yours. Whichever category you find yourself in, writing real-life applets will test your creative and programming skills to the fullest. But before you start dreaming of having your applet listed in the JARS (Java Applet Rating Service, http://www.jars.com) Top 30 worldwide charts, you will want to work a little bit more on the basics.

Purely GUI-Driven Applets

Using the techniques and knowledge presented so far, you can write some pretty functional applets. As long as you rely purely on a GUI to control your applet's functionality, you already have sufficient knowledge to design and implement programs like simple editors (paint programs, text editors, and so on) or even small games. To demonstrate what can be achieved with just a few buttons and a display area, you will develop a calculator. How about a scientific calculator that allows you to calculate the cosine of the logarithm of your next telephone bill?

Example: A Stack-Based Calculator

Start with some analysis first. What is the most elementary structure of any calculator? Answer: a large number of buttons and a display. These two aspects can form your top-level division of concerns for the applet you are going to write. Although modern calculator displays can plot graphics and even print text, you are going to restrict yourself to supporting simple numbers in scientific notation.

As you know, scientific notation uses a compact notation for huge and very small numbers by expressing numbers as a base number (the mantissa) raised to some power of ten. Since your calculator will have this scientific bias, you might as well make it even more so by designing it as a *stack* calculator. While you may not yet know what stack calculators are, the choice of architecture is appropriate, because of its simplicity compared to normal calculators. Moreover, stacks happen to be very relevant to Java: The Java Virtual Machine is a stack-based architecture with more than a passing resemblance to the calculator presented here.

Stack Calculators

Another name for these types of calculators is *reverse polish notation* (RPN) calculators. These types of calculators were used on the Apollo missions to the moon because the RPN system allows faster entry of complex formulae. On a conventional calculator, you would add 10 and 30 by entering **10**, then hitting the plus key, entering **20**, and then hitting the equal key to get the result calculated and displayed. With an RPN calculator, you would achieve the same by entering **10**, then pressing the Enter key, entering **20**, and finally hitting the plus key. On hitting the

Stack Calculators (continued)

plus key, the result is displayed—there is no need for you to hit an equal key. (So, there is no equal key on an RPN calculator. This confuses and frustrates most people not accustomed to them.)

The advantage of stack calculators really becomes clear when working with complex expressions that involve prioritizing subcalculations using brackets. On RPN calculators (which do not have brackets either) the stack of the machine automatically provides for a prioritizing and remembering mechanism. It is this simple timesaving device (not having to type brackets) that NASA sought after when picking RPN calculators over the conventional type.

The second feature of the calculator applet you will write is its display, or rather the digits displayed by it. Java has a number of fonts that provide you with a couple of digit styles, but none look like real calculator digits. Real calculators have relied (until recently) on seven-segment display elements to construct digits and numbers (first using LEDs, then switching to LCD technology). To give your calculator an authentic feel, you will design your own scalable, seven-segment digit character set from scratch (quite literally).

Figure 14.1 shows the applet's convincing calculator good looks.

The applet's GUI design naturally reflects the functional and structural division of any calculator: There is a display area and a buttons panel. The StackCalculator applet program is subdivided into the following five classes:

StackCalculator   The applet framework

KeyPanel   The customized component holding all the calculator keys and their associated functions

FIGURE 14.1:

A scientific calculator

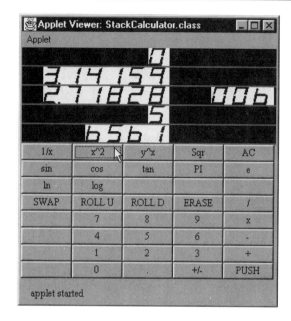

LCDDigitDisplay   The customized component dealing with the numeric display

CalcStack   A class encapsulating the calculator's stack architecture

SevenSegmentDigits   A class encapsulating a scalable character set of calculator-style digits

This is simply an application of the divide and conquer principle: These five classes cleanly subdivide the program, thus simplifying the overall problem of designing and writing a stack-based calculator applet. Although this applet can still be considered fairly trivial in terms of programming difficulty or complexity, it is already much too big to implement as one monolithic chunk of code (that is, in one class). As you have learned, breaking up problems into smaller subproblems that you solve individually, by implementing a class for each one, is good practice. Software problems a couple of times more complex than this calculator challenge are often *so* complex that any attempt that does not break down the problem into smaller subproblems will inevitably run into problems.

Now take a look at each of the calculator software blocks in turn, in a top-down order:

```
import java.applet.*;
import java.awt.*;

public class StackCalculator extends Applet {

final int STACK_DEPTH = 4;        // an N-entry stack calculator

LCDDigitDisplay LCDDisplay;        // the stack display
KeyPanel        calculatorKeys;  // the calculator buttons
//───────────────────────────────────────────────────────────────
public void init() {
    setLayout(new BorderLayout());

    LCDDisplay      = new LCDDigitDisplay( STACK_DEPTH );
    calculatorKeys  = new KeyPanel( LCDDisplay );

    add("North" , LCDDisplay);
    add("Center", calculatorKeys);
}
//───────────────────────────────────────────────────────────────
public String getAppletInfo() {
    StringBuffer s = new StringBuffer();

    s.append("Stack Calculator\n");
    s.append((char) 169);                    // Copyright symbol
    s.append("1996 ORC Incorported & L. Vanhelsuwe, All Rights Reserved\n");
    return s.toString();
}
//───────────────────────────────────────────────────────────────
public String[][] getParameterInfo() {
    String[][] result = {
        { "NONE", "NONE", "This applet takes no HTML parameters" },
    };
    return result;
}
} // End of Applet class
```

Top-level applet code does not come much cleaner than this. It is devoid of almost any application-relevant code and concentrates on its proper, prime concern—being an applet. As such, it only overrides three `Applet` methods: `init()`, `getAppletInfo()`, and `getParameterInfo()`. The latter two are optional but add a touch of polish to the applet. Methods `getAppletInfo()` and `getParameterInfo()` are there for browsers to call when users pick the browser's About Applet or Applet Info menu options (the exact menu titles differ from browser to browser). The first method usually returns a string containing, for example, author, version, and copyright information (plus anything else you care to add to it). `getParameterInfo()` returns an array of `String` triplets describing all the parameters your applet accepts via the *<PARAM NAME= "parameterName" VALUE="parameterValue"* > HTML parameters. Each triplet consists of the parameter's name, its type, and a short description explaining the parameter's function.

The heart of this applet is its `init()` method. It overrides the default `FlowLayout` applet component layout style and selects a `BorderLayout` instead. It then constructs two custom components: one for the calculator display (`LCDDisplay`) and one for the calculator keys panel (`calculatorKeys`). These two components are then positioned in the applet as in any real calculator, with keys below the display.

And that is it. The applet has no more concerns. It does not deal with any of the calculator logic or the display refreshing or the button presses. This means, quite patently, that the objects the applet created manage themselves.

The Calculator Keys Panel

The `KeyPanel` class is the real processing heart of the calculator, so take a look at how it works:

```
import java.awt.*;

//─────────────────────────────────────────────────────────────────
// The KeyPanel class encapsulates the entire calculator buttons "panel"
// and all the mathematical (and other) operations the buttons perform.
//─────────────────────────────────────────────────────────────────
class KeyPanel extends Panel {

final int ROWS     = 8;
final int COLUMNS = 5;
```

```
LCDDigitDisplay display;        // the stack display
CalcStack       stack;          // the stack within the display

// The calculator buttons are arranged as an array of 8 rows of 5 buttons
private String[] keyLabels = {
    "1/x",    "x^2",     "y^x",     "Sqr",     "AC",      // row 0
    "sin",    "cos",     "tan",     "PI",      "e",       // row 1
    "ln",     "log",     "  ",      "  ",      "  ",      // row 2
    "SWAP",   "ROLL U",  "ROLL D",  "ERASE",   "/",       // row 3
    "  ",     "7",       "8",       "9",       "x",       // row 4
    "  ",     "4",       "5",       "6",       "-",       // row 5
    "  ",     "1",       "2",       "3",       "+",       // row 6
    "  ",     "0",       ".",       "+/-",     "PUSH",    // row 7
};

//————————————————————————————————————————————————————————————————————————
public KeyPanel( LCDDigitDisplay display) {

    this.display = display;
    stack = display.getStack();

    setLayout( new GridLayout(ROWS,COLUMNS) );

    Button[] b = new Button[ ROWS*COLUMNS ];
    for (int i=0; i < keyLabels.length; i++) {
        b[i] = new Button( keyLabels[i] );
        add( b[i] );
    }
}
//————————————————————————————————————————————————————————————————————————
public boolean action(Event e, Object arg) {

        // if any of the 0..9 digit keys is pressed
    if (arg.equals( keyLabel(4,1) ) ||
        arg.equals( keyLabel(4,2) ) ||
        arg.equals( keyLabel(4,3) ) ||

        arg.equals( keyLabel(5,1) ) ||
        arg.equals( keyLabel(5,2) ) ||
        arg.equals( keyLabel(5,3) ) ||

        arg.equals( keyLabel(6,1) ) ||
        arg.equals( keyLabel(6,2) ) ||
        arg.equals( keyLabel(6,3) ) ||
        arg.equals( keyLabel(7,1) )    ) {

            enterDigit( Integer.valueOf((String) arg).intValue() );
    }

    if (arg.equals( keyLabel(0,0) )) inverse();    else
    if (arg.equals( keyLabel(0,1) )) square();     else
    if (arg.equals( keyLabel(0,2) )) power();      else
```

```
        if (arg.equals( keyLabel(0,3) )) squareRoot();  else
        if (arg.equals( keyLabel(0,4) )) allClear();    else

        if (arg.equals( keyLabel(1,0) )) sine();        else
        if (arg.equals( keyLabel(1,1) )) cosine();      else
        if (arg.equals( keyLabel(1,2) )) tan();         else
        if (arg.equals( keyLabel(1,3) )) constantPI();  else
        if (arg.equals( keyLabel(1,4) )) constantE();   else

        if (arg.equals( keyLabel(2,0) )) ln();          else
        if (arg.equals( keyLabel(2,1) )) log();         else
//      if (arg.equals( keyLabel(2,2) )) FUTURE();      else
//      if (arg.equals( keyLabel(2,3) )) FUTURE();      else
//      if (arg.equals( keyLabel(2,4) )) FUTURE();      else

        if (arg.equals( keyLabel(3,0) )) swap();        else
        if (arg.equals( keyLabel(3,1) )) rollUp();      else
        if (arg.equals( keyLabel(3,2) )) rollDown();    else
        if (arg.equals( keyLabel(3,3) )) delDigit();    else

        if (arg.equals( keyLabel(3,4) )) divide();      else
        if (arg.equals( keyLabel(4,4) )) times();       else
        if (arg.equals( keyLabel(5,4) )) subtract();    else
        if (arg.equals( keyLabel(6,4) )) add();         else

        if (arg.equals( keyLabel(7,2) )) decimal();     else
        if (arg.equals( keyLabel(7,3) )) changeSign();  else
        if (arg.equals( keyLabel(7,4) )) enter();       else
            ;

        System.out.println("Pressed the " + arg + " key");
        return true;
    }
    //-------------------------------------------------------------
    // A digit got pressed, add it to the number being constructed
    //-------------------------------------------------------------
    void enterDigit(int digit) {
        display.addDigit( digit );
    }
    //-------------------------------------------------------------
    // The ERASE button got pressed, erase the last digit entered
    //-------------------------------------------------------------
    void delDigit() {
        display.removeDigit();
    }
```

```
//—————————————————————————————————————————
// This pushes the accumulator onto the stack
//—————————————————————————————————————————
void enter() {
    stack.pushValue( stack.getAccumulator() );
    display.redrawStack();
}
//—————————————————————————————————————————
void changeSign() {
    stack.setAccumulator( - stack.getAccumulator() );
    display.redrawAccumulator();
}
//—————————————————————————————————————————
void squareRoot() {
    if (stack.getAccumulator() >= 0.0) {
        stack.setAccumulator( Math.sqrt(stack.getAccumulator()) );
        display.redrawAccumulator();
    }
}
//—————————————————————————————————————————
void square() {
    stack.setAccumulator( Math.pow(stack.getAccumulator() , 2) );
    display.redrawAccumulator();
}
//—————————————————————————————————————————
// Sine, cosine and tangents all take an angle in RADIANS
//—————————————————————————————————————————
void sine() {
    stack.setAccumulator( Math.sin(stack.getAccumulator()) );
    display.redrawAccumulator();
}
//—————————————————————————————————————————
void cosine() {
    stack.setAccumulator( Math.cos(stack.getAccumulator()) );
    display.redrawAccumulator();
}
//—————————————————————————————————————————
void tan() {
    stack.setAccumulator( Math.tan(stack.getAccumulator()) );
    display.redrawAccumulator();
}
//—————————————————————————————————————————
void log() {
    if (stack.getAccumulator() > 1.0) {
        stack.setAccumulator( Math.log(stack.getAccumulator()) /
Math.log(10.0) );
        display.redrawAccumulator();
    }
}
//—————————————————————————————————————————
```

```
void ln() {
    if (stack.getAccumulator() > 1.0) {
        stack.setAccumulator( Math.log(stack.getAccumulator()) );
        display.redrawAccumulator();
    }
}
//————————————————————————————————————————————————————————————————
// Raise next-on-stack (NOS) element to the power of top-of-stack (TOS)
//————————————————————————————————————————————————————————————————
void power() {
double pow = Math.pow (stack.getStackElement(1), stack.getAccumulator());
    stack.drop(); stack.setAccumulator(pow); display.redrawStack();
}
//————————————————————————————————————————————————————————————————
void constantE() {
    stack.setAccumulator( Math.E );
    display.redrawAccumulator();
}
//————————————————————————————————————————————————————————————————
void constantPI() {
    stack.setAccumulator( Math.PI );
    display.redrawAccumulator();
}
//————————————————————————————————————————————————————————————————
void inverse() {
    if (stack.getAccumulator() != 0.0) {
        stack.setAccumulator( 1.0/ stack.getAccumulator() );
        display.redrawAccumulator();
    }
}
//————————————————————————————————————————————————————————————————
// The decimal button got pressed. Tell display to go into decimals entry mode
//————————————————————————————————————————————————————————————————
void decimal() {
    display.decimal();
}
//————————————————————————————————————————————————————————————————
// Rotate the stack 1 cell up
//————————————————————————————————————————————————————————————————
void rollUp() {
    stack.rollUp(1);
    display.redrawStack();
}
//————————————————————————————————————————————————————————————————
void rollDown() {
    stack.rollDown(1);
    display.redrawStack();
}
//————————————————————————————————————————————————————————————————
// Swap TOS and NOS
```

```
//─────────────────────────────────────────────────────────────
void swap() {
    stack.swap();
    display.redrawStack(2);
}
//─────────────────────────────────────────────────────────────
// Erase entire stack to zeroes (0.0)
//─────────────────────────────────────────────────────────────
void allClear() {
    stack.clearStack();
    display.redrawStack();
}
//─────────────────────────────────────────────────────────────
// Add TOS & NOS. Consumes NOS.
//─────────────────────────────────────────────────────────────
void add() {
double sum = stack.getAccumulator() + stack.getStackElement(1);
    stack.drop(); stack.setAccumulator(sum); display.redrawStack();
}
//─────────────────────────────────────────────────────────────
void times() {
double prod = stack.getAccumulator() * stack.getStackElement(1);
    stack.drop(); stack.setAccumulator(prod); display.redrawStack();
}
//─────────────────────────────────────────────────────────────
void subtract() {
double diff = stack.getStackElement(1) - stack.getAccumulator();
    stack.drop(); stack.setAccumulator(diff); display.redrawStack();
}
//─────────────────────────────────────────────────────────────
void divide() {
    if (stack.getAccumulator() == 0.0) return;  // avoid div by 0
                                            // .. display error instead

    double div = stack.getStackElement(1) / stack.getAccumulator();
    stack.drop(); stack.setAccumulator(div); display.redrawStack();
}
//─────────────────────────────────────────────────────────────
public String keyLabel (int row, int column) {
    return keyLabels[row*COLUMNS + column];
}
//─────────────────────────────────────────────────────────────
public Dimension preferredSize() {
    return new Dimension(300,200);
}}
```

Before you focus on the application side of this class, you should see what class KeyPanel does on the Java and AWT level. First of all,

`KeyPanel` is subclassed from `Panel`; this is because you need your calculator buttons to be laid out using a different layout manager from what the applet itself uses (`BorderLayout`). And to specify a different layout for an area, you first need to create a new `Container`: the keys `Panel`. Since calculator keys are universally laid out in rows and columns, a natural choice for a layout manager is `GridLayout`. The constructor for the `KeyPanel` class takes a reference (read: a link) to the numeric display component that the applet created. Class `KeyPanel` needs to have this link so that it can call on the display to perform various functions. The design of your calculator means that the key panel is the active, controlling entity among the five classes.

The first thing the `KeyPanel` class does with the reference to the display object is to ask the display to hand it a reference to the numerical calculation stack *embedded* in the display object. As you shall see, the very heart of the calculating machine (the stack) actually "belongs" to the display. This design decision is fairly arbitrary; the core calculator stack could have been created by the key panel object itself, or even by the applet. Whatever approach is taken, the key panel, the display, and the stack objects all have to communicate together one way or the other. The `KeyPanel` constructor then performs its main function, which is to create the panel of calculator buttons from a constant look-up array of button labels.

The next method is the event processing heart of our applet: the `KeyPanel`'s `action()` method. Since the `KeyPanel` constructor used vanilla Buttons to create the array of calculator buttons, this means none of the buttons can respond to user key presses directly. The container component holding them has to handle the key presses, and this is exactly what the `KeyPanel action()` method does. It consists of a large selection of "ifs" that try to determine the origin of the button press event. In fact, the method has only two `if` *statements*, one that tries to determine whether a digit key was pressed and another that tries to match a keypress to any of the other keys. The `keyLabel()` method is used to enhance program readability; it takes two-dimensional (row,column) coordinates and returns the label for the button located at that position. This is much more readable than addressing the *one*-dimensional `String keyLabels` array directly.

If the `action()` method traps a button press on one of the digit keys (0 to 9), it converts the digit `String` label into an equivalent integer, and tells the display to deal with it via the `enterDigit()` method (the key panel does not concern itself with the technicalities of data entry and editing—it is completely stateless). Likewise, with the remaining buttons, it matches each button up with a method that incarnates its function. For example, when the button at position row=0, column=4 is pressed, then the `AC` (All Clear) function is executed.

Note that the large collection of `if`s (after the `if` determining a digit key) is a single if-else statement, with each `else` block again being another if-else, and so on. The code in this (exceptional) instance just does not use consistent indentation to show the increasing depth of the if-else-if nesting (otherwise, you would end up in column 400 in your text editor). Could you have used a switch statement instead? No. Switch statements need cases that evaluate to constants, and the "cases" in the `action()` method boil down to variables (the `String`s the `keyLabel()` method returns).

If you now take a look at some of the methods called to respond to button presses—for example, the `cosine()` method—you will see that you have reached the inner sanctum of your calculator. These methods are where the calculator's main functions are executed. The `cosine()` example shows you the general approach for all these methods: perform the calculator operation and then refresh the numeric display to show the result. Mathematical functions like cosine only take one argument, so the refresh logic is optimized to only redraw the *top-of-stack* (TOS) value, which is shown as the bottom-most element on the display (the TOS value is also called the *accumulator*). Other operations (like `allClear()`) affect the entire stack, so at other times, the stack needs to be redrawn in its entirety. The `redrawAccumulator()` and `redrawStack()` LCDDigitDisplay methods actually do the display refreshing. The math functions our calculator provides are implemented on top of class `Math` methods. The exact implementation of the calculation stack itself though, is hidden from `KeyPanel` by a class that encapsulates all details: `CalcStack`. The cosine function shows how this separation of function and use is nevertheless reunited; the stack object provides the `getAccumulator()` and `setAccumulator()` methods to retrieve and set the current value for the TOS element. Using these two methods, it then becomes trivial to take the cosine of the TOS element and store the result back in the stack. You can now easily figure out how all the other functions are (equally trivially) implemented.

The Calculator Display

The next calculator black box to demand screwdriver, hammer, and X-ray machine is `LCDDigitDisplay`:

```
import java.awt.*;
import java.util.*;

//————————————————————————————————————————————————————————————
//————————————————————————————————————————————————————————————
class LCDDigitDisplay extends Canvas {

CalcStack     stack;                      // the stack of numbers
int           stackDepth;                 // how many items stack holds
Dimension     displaySize, oldSize;       // Canvas drawing area dimension
Dimension     digitSize;
SevenSegmentDigits
              lcd = null;                 // ref to LCD-style 7-segment digits

boolean       freshNumber = true;
int           decimalPosition = 0;
Stack         undoStack;                  // undo system for ERASEing digits

public LCDDigitDisplay(int stackDepth) {

    this.stackDepth = stackDepth;         // note depth
    stack = new CalcStack(stackDepth);    // create calculation stack
    newNumber();                          // reset all entry modes
}
//————————————————————————————————————————————————————————————
// reset all number constructing/editing state
//————————————————————————————————————————————————————————————
```

```
void newNumber() {
    freshNumber      = true;
    decimalPosition = 0;
    undoStack        = new Stack();
}
//————————————————————————————————————————————————————————
// An extra digit is being entered. Depending on which mode we're in,
// this digit should be added before or after the decimal point.
//————————————————————————————————————————————————————————
public void addDigit (int digit) {
int changed = 1;          // how many lines in stack need to be redrawn

    rememberUndo();       // remember current value for possible digit erase

    if (freshNumber) {                      // brand new number ?
        stack.rollUp(1);
        stack.setAccumulator(0.0);          // clear A
        freshNumber = false;                // accumulate digits from now on...
        changed = stackDepth;               // entire stack needs redrawing
    }

        // if we're not entering decimals yet, we can simply shift the
        // number up a digit by x10 and adding the digit in.

    double acu = stack.getAccumulator();
    if (decimalPosition == 0) {
        stack.setAccumulator( acu * 10.0 + digit);
    } else {

        // if we should add a decimal, we've got to add a fraction
        // scaled to the decimal place we've reached so far..

        stack.setAccumulator( acu + ((float)digit)/decimalPosition);
        decimalPosition *= 10;
    }

    refreshStack( changed );    // redraw acu or the entire stack, depending
}
//————————————————————————————————————————————————————————
public void removeDigit () {
    undo();                     // restore number and state to previous
    refreshStack(1);            // only acu needs redrawing
}
//————————————————————————————————————————————————————————
// We're using a stack holding previous values and editing state so that
// we can cheaply revert back to a previous number if user erases a digit.
//————————————————————————————————————————————————————————
public void rememberUndo() {
    undoStack.push(new Double( stack.getAccumulator() ) );
```

```
        undoStack.push(new Boolean( freshNumber )              );
        undoStack.push(new Integer( decimalPosition )          );
    }
    //————————————————————————————————————————————————————————————————
    public void undo() {

        if ( ! undoStack.empty()) {
            decimalPosition  = ((Integer) undoStack.pop()).intValue();
            freshNumber      = ((Boolean) undoStack.pop()).booleanValue();
            stack.setAccumulator( ((Double) undoStack.pop()).doubleValue() );
        } else {
                    newNumber();
                    stack.setAccumulator(0.0);
            }
    }
    //————————————————————————————————————————————————————————————————
    // User pressed '.'. From now on, we have to add decimals
    //————————————————————————————————————————————————————————————————
    public void decimal() {
        if (decimalPosition == 0) {
            decimalPosition = 10;   // tenths, hundredths, etc..
        }
    }
    //————————————————————————————————————————————————————————————————
    public CalcStack getStack() {
        return stack;
    }
    //————————————————————————————————————————————————————————————————
    public void redrawAccumulator() {
        redrawStack(1);
    }
    //————————————————————————————————————————————————————————————————
    public void redrawStack() {
        redrawStack(stackDepth);
    }
    //————————————————————————————————————————————————————————————————
    public void redrawStack(int elements) {
        refreshStack(elements);
        newNumber();
    }
    //————————————————————————————————————————————————————————————————
    // redraw one or more lines of the stack. Starting from TOS
    //————————————————————————————————————————————————————————————————
    public void refreshStack(int elements) {
    int y;
    int LINE_GAP = 2;

            // If we haven't initialized the LCD digits class, or if the
            // size of our drawing Canvas has changed: initialize LCD digits
```

```
    if (lcd == null || displaySize.width != oldSize.width ||
                       displaySize.height != oldSize.height) {

        oldSize = displaySize;      // remember new size

        digitSize = new Dimension(displaySize.width/12,
                            (displaySize.height/stackDepth) - LINE_GAP);

            // create scaled LCD digit "character set"
        lcd = new SevenSegmentDigits(this, digitSize);
    }

    for(int i=0; i < elements; i++) {
        y = (stackDepth-i-1) * (digitSize.height + LINE_GAP);

        getGraphics().fillRect(0,y,displaySize.width, digitSize.height);

        lcd.drawNumber(stack.getStackElement(i), getGraphics(), 0, y);
    }
}
//————————————————————————————————————————————————————————————————
// Re-paint the LCDDisplay
//————————————————————————————————————————————————————————————————
public void paint(Graphics g) {

    displaySize = this.size();

    g.setColor(Color.gray);
    g.fillRect(0, 0, displaySize.width, displaySize.height);
    redrawStack( stackDepth );
}
//————————————————————————————————————————————————————————————————
public Dimension preferredSize() {
    return new Dimension(100, 120);
}}
```

Class `LCDDigitDisplay` is responsible for the look of your calculator's numeric display. It is also a subclass of `Canvas`, so you can draw inside its area to your heart's content. Start with its constructor —all it does is create the numeric stack and reset the data entry mode variables (to which you shall return in a moment). The constructor is obviously not where all the action is hidden, in this case. The action is spread over two parts of the class:

- The `addDigit()` and `removeDigit()` methods

- The `redrawStack()` and related display redrawing methods (including the overridden `Component paint()` method)

If you think about how a humble calculator works, you should first realize that there is more to pressing a digit key and seeing the digit appear in the display than meets the eye. If you use an accumulator to hold the current value being composed, then how do sequentially entered digits translate into a number being formed? Say the display already holds 12, and you enter an additional **7**. The display then holds 127—12 and 7 were transformed into a new number, 127, by multiplying by ten and adding the new digit. But what if the display holds 3.14 and you enter an additional **1**? 3.14 multiplied by 10 is 31.4, plus 1 equals 32.4. Oops. You need to tune your algorithm a bit here. When the decimal point key is pressed, the data entry algorithm should enter a new mode, decimals entry mode. Any digits entered should be first *divided* by some power of ten and then the result should be added to the current accumulator, without multiplying it beforehand by ten. The power of ten is determined by the position of the next decimal. This algorithm is implemented by the `addDigit()` method (the test for `freshNumber` is not part of this algorithm; it is used to start with 0.0 whenever a first digit is being entered).

Real calculators not only let you input numbers as just explained, they are also forgiving when it comes to little errors; they have an erase key to erase the last digits entered. A key was also added to this calculator for this purpose. One possible way to have implemented this would have been to undo the last digit added by somehow reversing the step using the same input data as the `addDigit()` method: the accumulator's value and the decimal entry mode variable (`decimalPos`). But while this is possible, it is overly complex and unnecessary. Instead, you can cheat by remembering the value of the accumulator (and its associated decimal entry state) before you change it, so that you can restore it to its original state if an "erase digit" request arrives. This remember and undo mechanism relies on another stack—a `java.util.Stack` this time—to store each undoable step. Check out `rememberUndo()` and `undo()` for the details.

Both `addDigit()` and `removeDigit()` need to update the display to reflect the change in value of the number being constructed or edited. For this, they rely on `refreshStack()`. This method takes the number of stack slots to redraw. This is an optimization feature which follows from the observation that many calculator operations only change the top of stack, thus allowing a fast (cheaper) redraw of only that value. If you ignore the first `if` statement of `refresh-Stack()` for a moment, you will see that the method consists of a loop that simply redraws the numbers held by the stack. To render the digits of the values, you could have used `drawString()` and some standard Java `Font`. Instead, you had as an initial project requirement that you would use dynamically rendered LCD-style seven-segment digit characters. So the expected `drawString()` has been replaced by `lcd.drawNumber()`. Object `lcd` is an instance of class `SevenSegmentDigits`. This class has the nontrivial responsibility of generating (at run time) a character set of seven-segment style digits. Since it would be highly inefficient to generate these digit images on the fly (that is, as `drawNumber()` required them), the `lcd` object creates and *caches* (stores) them for later use, as part of its own initialization. And that is why the construction of the lcd object is conditional in `refreshStack()`. The `if` statement tests whether the lcd object hasn't been created yet or if the `Canvas` area has changed dimensions. In both cases, the digit character set needs to be (re)generated—scaled to fit the dimensions of the `Canvas`. Later, you will see what goes on when the `lcd` object's constructor is invoked (which is quite a lot).

The Calculator Stack

But first, you should return to code aspects more fundamental to the operation of the calculator. Class `CalcStack` is used as a front end for the calculator's numeric stack data structure. Here is the source for it:

```
//------------------------------------------------------------------
// The CalcStack class encapsulates the numeric stack and all its
// non-mathematical manipulations (i.e. stack manipulations only)
//
// Class java.util.Stack was not used because the stack we need can't
// have an infinite capacity and because we only need doubles on our
// stack, not full-blown objects.
//------------------------------------------------------------------
```

```
class CalcStack {

double[]    stack;                      // the stack at the heart of the machine
int         stackDepth;

//————————————————————————————————————————————————————————————————
// Constructor: build a stack of capacity stackDepth
//————————————————————————————————————————————————————————————————
public CalcStack(int stackDepth) {

    this.stackDepth = stackDepth;
    stack = new double[stackDepth];
    clearStack();
}
//————————————————————————————————————————————————————————————————
public void pushValue(double x) {
    rollUp(1);
    setAccumulator(x);
}
//————————————————————————————————————————————————————————————————
public void rollUp(int times) {
double lastVal;

    for (int r=0; r < times; r++) {
        lastVal = stack[stackDepth-1];
        for (int i = stackDepth-2; i >= 0; i-) {
            stack[i+1] = stack[i];
        }
        stack[0] = lastVal;
    }
}
//————————————————————————————————————————————————————————————————
public void rollDown(int times) {
    rollUp(stackDepth-times);
}
//————————————————————————————————————————————————————————————————
public void swap() {
double temp;
    temp = stack[0];
    stack[0] = stack[1];
    stack[1] = temp;
}
//————————————————————————————————————————————————————————————————
public void clearStack() {
    for (int i=0; i < stackDepth; i++) {
        stack[i] = 0.0;
    }
}
//————————————————————————————————————————————————————————————————
```

```
public void drop() {
    rollDown(1);
    stack[stackDepth-1] = stack[stackDepth-2];
}
//————————————————————————————————————————————————————————————
public void setAccumulator(double x) {
    stack[0] = x;
}
//————————————————————————————————————————————————————————————
public double getAccumulator() {
    return stack[0];
}
//————————————————————————————————————————————————————————————
public double getStackElement(int n) {
    return stack[n];
}
//————————————————————————————————————————————————————————————
} // End of CalcStack class
```

The unassuming statement "double[]   stack;" in the instance variables section at the top of class CalcStack is the core data structure for the entire program. The stack calculator applet relies on this array of doubles to build all of its functionality around. Or rather, it relies on it indirectly, since class CalcStack mediates all access to this stack structure. This mediation is done through the methods provided by the class:

```
class CalcStack {
    public CalcStack(int stackDepth)
    public void pushValue(double x)
    public void rollUp(int times)
    public void rollDown(int times)
    public void swap()
    public void clearStack()
    public void drop()
    public void setAccumulator(double x)
    public double getAccumulator()
    public double getStackElement(int n)
}
```

It is clear, from the absence of a `pop()` method, that this stack has some very un-stacklike properties. This is because the characteristics of a stack have been somewhat modified to be more productive for a calculator application. Foremost is the fact that a `CalcStack` has a fixed size. It has N slots that are always filled with numbers. (Our example uses four number slots, but this can be changed by changing the `STACK_DEPTH` constant in the applet class and recompiling.) Real stacks, on the other hand, can be empty, half-empty (or half-full), or full. Secondly, a `CalcStack` can "roll" its contents "up" or "down." The best way for you to see what this means is to enter a number in the calculator applet and press the ROLL U and ROLL D buttons. The last difference between real stacks and CalcStacks is that when you remove the top of stack value (via a `getAccumulator()` and a `drop()`), the last slot gets to keep its original value (it does not get cleared to 0.0).

Why not provide a `pop()` (which combines a `getAccumulator()` and `drop()`)? You could, but the current design is more efficient. Take adding two numbers together; the brute force solution would be to use the following algorithm (in pseudocode):

a = pop()

b = pop()

sum = a + b

push(sum)

This code requires three full stack shuffles (two for the pops and one for the push), but your code only requires a single stack shuffle. While this is not critical with small stacks of 4 elements, it could make a huge difference if you had a stack with 20 or 50 elements.

The Seven-Segment Digits Subsystem

The only remaining class to be dissected is `SevenSegmentDigits`:

```
//——————————————————————————————————————————————————————————
// Class SevenSegmentDigits encapsulates scalable 7-segment digits which
// can be rendered individually or as full double values
//——————————————————————————————————————————————————————————

import java.awt.*;

//——————————————————————————————————————————————————————————
public class SevenSegmentDigits {

protected Image[] digits;        // holds the computed images for digits 0..9
protected Dimension scale;       // the scale user wanted the digits in
protected Component component;    // any Component so we can createImage()

final int NUM_DIGITS = 10 + 1;   // one extra for minus symbol

final int ox   = 207;
final int oy   =  53;
final int segW = 230;
final int segH = 227;

int           originalWidth;
final double italicPercent = 0.15;   // how much width to use for italicizing
int           italicRange;
int           decimalW, decimalH, decimalXoff, decimalYoff;

    // the vertices making up a 7-seg display cell

final int[] points       = {
    207,53,  385,53,  207,280, 385,280
    ,240,75,  360,75,  240,258, 360,258
    ,207,159,385,159,240,144, 360,144, 240,176,360,176
                        };

    // each segment is a polygon composed of vertices

final int[][] segDefs    = {
    {0,1,5,4},  {0,4,10,8}, {1,5,11,9}, {8,10,11,9,13,12}
    ,{8,12,6,2}, {9,13,7,3}, {6,7,3,2}
                        };

    // each digit is a collection of "ON" segments

final String[] digitDefs= {
    "ABCEFG", "CF", "ACDEG", "ACDFG", "BCDF"
    ,"ABDFG", "BDEFG", "ACF", "ABCDEFG", "ABCDF"
    ,"D"  // minus sign is "digit 10"
                        };
```

```
//------------------------------------------------------------
// Constructor: note the size we've got the scale the digits to and
// dynamically render them (a la Postscript)
//------------------------------------------------------------
public SevenSegmentDigits( Component component, Dimension size ) {

    this.component  = component;
    this.scale      = size;

    originalWidth   = scale.width;
    scale.width = (int) (scale.width * (1.0 - italicPercent));
    italicRange = originalWidth - scale.width;

    digits = new Image[ NUM_DIGITS ];

    for(int digit=0; digit < NUM_DIGITS; digit++) {
        digits[digit] = renderDigit(digit);
    }

        // decimal point image is calculated from digit size only

    decimalW = scale.width/6;
    decimalH = scale.height/10;
    decimalXoff = scale.width - decimalW;
    decimalYoff = scale.height - decimalH;
}
//------------------------------------------------------------
// Render a 7-segment digit from its segment list definition.
// Return as an Image to be stored.
//------------------------------------------------------------
protected Image renderDigit(int number) {

Image digitImage;
Graphics g;
String segments;

    digitImage = component.createImage(originalWidth, scale.height);
    g = digitImage.getGraphics();

    segments = digitDefs[number];

    for(int seg=0; seg < segments.length(); seg++) {
        int segIndex = segments.charAt(seg)-'A';
        renderSegment(g, segIndex);
    }
    return digitImage;
}
//------------------------------------------------------------
// Render a segment polygon in the given Graphics context.
// This is where all the "clever" stuff happens:
```

```
// - we normalize the coordinates of the segment to 0.0 .. 1.0 range
// - we scale them to the sizes required
// - we render the segment as a polygon
//───────────────────────────────────────────────────────────────────
protected void renderSegment (Graphics g, int segment) {

int[] segDef = segDefs[segment];
Polygon p = new Polygon();

    for(int vertex=0; vertex < segDef.length; vertex++) {

        int v = segDef[vertex];

        int x = points[v * 2 + 0] - ox;        // translate to origin
        int y = points[v * 2 + 1] - oy;

        double normX = ((double)x) / segW;     // normalize to 0.0..1.0
        double normY = ((double)y) / segH;

        int polyX = (int) (normX * scale.width); // scale to requested size
        int polyY = (int) (normY * scale.height);

        polyX += (1.0 - normY) * italicRange;    // italicize digits

        p.addPoint(polyX, polyY);
    }
    g.fillPolygon(p);
}
//───────────────────────────────────────────────────────────────────
// digitImage() gives clients access to the rendered digits
//───────────────────────────────────────────────────────────────────
public Image digitImage(int digit) {
    return digits[digit];
}
//───────────────────────────────────────────────────────────────────
// drawNumber() renders a double value in the given gfx context at (x,y)
//───────────────────────────────────────────────────────────────────
public void drawNumber( double number, Graphics g, int x, int y ) {

String doubleStr      = String.valueOf(number);
boolean isNegative    = (doubleStr.charAt(0) == '-');
int exponentPos       = doubleStr.indexOf('e');
int decimalPos        = doubleStr.indexOf('.');
int significantDigits = 6;       // we need valueOf() to gen 6 signif. dig-
its
int digitIndex = 0;
int digitSlot;
int digit;
int digitX = 0 ;

    significantDigits = doubleStr.length();

        // if number is negative, render a minus in left-most slot
```

```
if (isNegative) {
    g.drawImage(digitImage(10), x, y, component);   // draw minus
    significantDigits-;
    digitIndex = 1;
}

if (exponentPos != -1) {
    significantDigits -= 5;     // exponent uses 5 positions, e.g. "+e000"
}
if (decimalPos != -1) {
    significantDigits-;          // a decimal point aint a digit either
}

    // calculate the starting digit slot to align all numbers neatly
digitSlot = 7 - significantDigits;   // slot 1 for max signif. digits
/* SOME DEBUGGING CODE HERE. YOU CAN ENABLE THIS IF YOU ENHANCE THIS CODE

    System.out.println("significantDigits " + significantDigits);
    System.out.println("digitIndex " + digitIndex);
    System.out.println("digitSlot " + digitSlot);
    System.out.println("isNeg " + isNegative);
    System.out.println("Exp " + exponentPos);
*/

    // now the mantissa rendering loop: render all signficant digits
while (significantDigits != 0) {
    if ( (digit = doubleStr.charAt( digitIndex++ )) != '.') {
        digit -= '0';
        digitX = x + digitSlot*originalWidth;
        g.drawImage( digitImage(digit), digitX, y, component);
        significantDigits-;
        digitSlot++;
    } else {                // render decimal point in same slot as last digit
        g.fillRect(digitX + decimalXoff, y + decimalYoff,
                decimalW, decimalH);
    }
}
    // if number contains an exponent, render that too
if (exponentPos != -1) {
    if (doubleStr.charAt(exponentPos + 1) == '-') {  // draw minus
        g.drawImage(digitImage(10), x + 8*originalWidth, y, component);
    }
    digitIndex = exponentPos + 2;      // skip 'e+' or 'e-'
    digitSlot = 9;
    for(int e=0; e < 3; e++) {          // render 'e+nnn'
        digit = doubleStr.charAt( digitIndex++ ) - '0';
        digitX = x + digitSlot*originalWidth;
        g.drawImage(digitImage(digit), digitX, y, component);
        digitSlot++;
    }
}
```

```
}
//—————————————————————————————————————————————————————————
public static void main (String[] args) {

        Frame f = new Myframe();

    f.resize(400,400);
    f.show();
}}

class Myframe extends Frame {

SevenSegmentDigits lcd = null;

public void paint (Graphics g) {
    if (lcd==null) lcd = new SevenSegmentDigits(this, new Dimension(30,35));
    g.translate(10,10);

    int y=0;
    lcd.drawNumber(-10.30        ,g, 0, (y++) *40);
    lcd.drawNumber( 255.9        ,g, 0, (y++) *40);
    lcd.drawNumber(-0.0          ,g, 0, (y++) *40);
    lcd.drawNumber( 0.1          ,g, 0, (y++) *40);
    lcd.drawNumber(-0.12e10      ,g, 0, (y++) *40);
    lcd.drawNumber( 6712.29e-253 ,g, 0, (y++) *40);
    lcd.drawNumber( Math.PI      ,g, 0, (y++) *40);
}}
```

Although this class only provides a more realistic looking alternative to numbers rendered using a standard AWT font and drawString(), class SevenSegmentDigits packs a lot of interesting code. Since your goal for this subsystem is to obtain scalable digits (so the display can be sized according to the applet's dimensions), you have to reject the easy approach of storing every digit as an external GIF (or other) image file. Such inflexible bitmap fonts are not easily scalable, and even when forced, the scaled results are of very poor quality. The approach that therefore imposes itself on you is to use *vector* definitions for your characters. Scalable fonts can be defined in a very compact space, by storing some mathematical (vector) definition of their outline. A magnifying glass held up to any real calculator shows you how digits are usually constructed in the Liquid Crystal Display (LCD). Figure 14.2 shows the structure of the seven-segment display building block used in every calculator.

FIGURE 14.2:

Seven-segment display and an example configuration for digit 3.

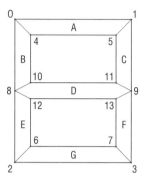
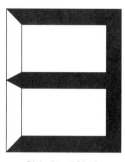

Digit '3' = "ACDFG"

If you now describe every digit as the collection of "on" segments (that is, lit segments) needed to represent it, and every segment as the list of vertices forming a polygon outline for the segment, then you would have a flexible, compact definition for the entire digit character set. The `points[]`, `segDefs[]`, and `digitDefs[]` arrays together define our character set in this way. The points array holds the (x,y) pairs of the nodes (or vertices) from which a seven-segment display is constructed. The exact values of these coordinates were obtained using a simple painting program, and as we shall see later, these values are actually mostly irrelevant to the rest of the code. The `segDefs` array defines each segment as a list of vertices (a vertex is encoded as an index into the `points[]` array). Similarly, the `digitDefs[]` array defines digits themselves as a list of segments. Although for readability, letters were used instead of segment array indices (later, the code simply translates the letters to numeric indices, anyway). The 3 digit, for example, is encoded as the segment list A-C-D-F-G.

> **NOTE**
>
> One thing to note at this stage is that the definitions of the digits are in regular (roman) typeface, and not italicized. If you ran the StackCalculator applet, you noticed that the digits are actually in *italics*. This is achieved algorithmically at the rendering stage. You will see how a bit later.

If you now have a look at the constructor for the `SevenSegment-Digits` class, you will see that it takes two arguments: a `Component` and a `Dimension`. The `Dimension` argument will be used to scale the digits to the requested size. The `Component` argument, on the other hand, is required for a very different reason. We said that we were going to cache the rendered digit images, but what exactly do we mean by this? The mechanism you will use is to render each digit into a separate, off-screen, `Image` object. It is these Images that will simply be stored by the class, so that the `drawNumber()` method can recall them and blast them onto the screen without any further overhead. (This, by the way, is exactly the same technique used by all modern font rendering subsystems, in laser printers, and computer operating systems.) As you learned in Chapter 13, to create off-screen images, you need to use `createImage()`, which is called on a `Component`. Since class `SevenSegmentDigits` is not a `Component` itself (you are not extending any class, except `Object`, implicitly), you cannot just say "createImage()" on its own. You need the client (the class which uses class `SevenSegmentDigits`) to give you some handle to a `Component` so you can ask the `Component` to create a usable `Image` structure.

Once the constructor has taken note of the arguments it received (by making local copies), it performs a one-off calculation which adjusts the digit dimensions to be used for the remainder of the code. The calculation has to do with the algorithmic italicizing of the digits. Figure 14.3 shows you why an adjustment is required.

The constructor adjusts the requested width by -15 percent to make room for the later skewing of the digits, which has to remain entirely within the bounding box dimensions requested. The difference in width between the original digits and the new digits will be the possible skewing range you will vary as a function of the character's height.

Once this initialization step has been taken, the `SevenSegment-Digits` object is ready to render every digit and cache them into an array of Images, called `digits[]` in our program. Note that the `for`

FIGURE 14.3:

Character width adjustment necessary for italicizing digits

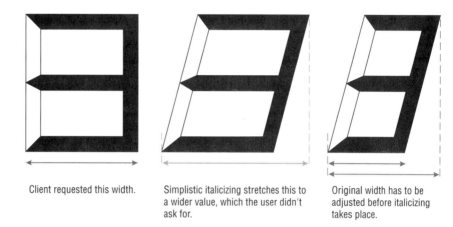

Client requested this width.

Simplistic italicizing stretches this to a wider value, which the user didn't ask for.

Original width has to be adjusted before italicizing takes place.

loop actually renders 11 "digits." The minus sign (segment D on its own) is rendered too, as the eleventh digit. A different approach had to be used for the decimal point. Since the decimal point never occupies a digit slot in the display, but instead is positioned *inside* the slot of the units digit, you actually render a decimal point using a simple `rectFill()` when needed. The alternative—overstriking the previous digit with a decimal point image and relying on transparency—would have been considerably more complicated (although, to be honest, another way of looking at it is that the `rectFill()` solution is a bit of a kludge too).

The `renderDigit()` method called by the constructor is very straightforward. It creates a new `Image` object to draw the digit in, gets the `Graphics` context from the `Image` and proceeds by drawing every segment of the requested digit. It is `renderSegment()`, on which it relies, that contains all the interesting code.

Method `renderSegment()` essentially constructs a polygon which it then renders using `fillPolygon()`. The calculation of the polygon coordinates is the heart of the vector digit scaling and italicizing algorithm. First of all, original vertex coordinates had to be normalized to fit an imaginary bounding box 1.0 units wide by 1.0 units tall.

This step makes it easier to scale the digits to any final, user-requested dimensions; you just multiply by those dimensions. The ox, oy, segW, and segH variables used in this process were defined as constants at the start of our class. Their values were obtained empirically by looking at the arbitrary coordinate system you used to define the digit vertices.

> **NOTE** There is absolutely no significance in the fact that point 0 is located at (207,53). What it does mean however, is that this point acts as the origin for all other points, and that we need to translate all points by those coordinates before we can apply the scaling.

The polyX += (1.0 - normY) * italicRange; statement is where the italic "style" is applied. It skews the points horizontally (by affecting their x-coordinates) as a function of the digit's height. Once all calculated coordinates have been added to the Polygon object used to hold them, the renderDigit() method just uses fillPolygon() to draw the scaled and italicized segment.

Finally, the drawNumber() method has the simple task of drawing the various digits to represent a double passed to it as argument. Its internal workings are left to you, the reader, to discover.

As you can see, you can write a lot of applet code while relying purely on the GUI of your applet to activate various parts of your program. Sooner or later, though, you will write an applet that deviates from this approach, and this will be the source of a lot of problems—and, therefore, experimentation to try and get things right. The following section will short-circuit this (painful) learning experience by highlighting the problem once, and giving you the solution to the problem without further delay.

Selfish Applets

The StackCalculator applet does not have a main loop that needs to "do" something all the time. It can afford to be fully functional by simply relying on the user activating various elements of its user interface, and on related short bursts of processing or graphical activity. But many programs are not so lucky; for example, think of an animation applet. It has a main loop that keeps on updating those animation frames. To illustrate the pitfall awaiting writers of this type of applet, Figure 14.4 shows a screen saver–like StarField applet that might go for the "cool" attribute, but fails miserably in the compatibility department.

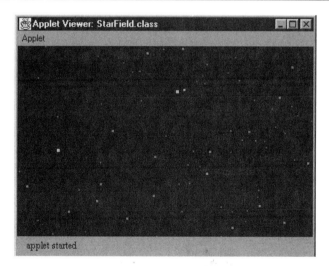

Example: Animating a Star Field

Before the simple mistake committed by this applet is explained, take a look at the things it does right. Animating a star field and creating the illusion of flying through space can be achieved in a variety of ways. This applet actually models real 3-D objects (points, actually) flying toward the observer. The main instance variable of the `Starfield` class is an array holding a large number of `Star` objects. A `Star` object has two attributes: its (x,y,z) position in 3-D space and its star temperature (which determines its color, as in reality). A `Star` has one main instance method, `draw()`, that draws the star in a window viewport. Class `Star` also has a class method `setViewPort()` that allows a client to tell class `Star` what the dimensions are of the viewport to render the stars in.

The core of the program is very simple:

- Move stars toward observer (by adding a `dz` (delta z) speed to their `z` coordinate)

- Project stars from 3-D to 2-D (using a perspective projection formula)

- Render depth-cued stars in 2-D viewport

All these steps are executed sequentially for each star in `Star` method `draw()`. If you refer to the listing, you will see that the code first checks whether the star has moved past (behind) the observer. If so, the star has become invisible, so it better be eliminated from the model. This is done by simply recycling that `Star` object by re-randomizing its 3-D position (in exactly the same way as during `Star` constructor time).

The perspective projection is achieved using these standard formulas:

```
screen x = (D * x)/z

screen y = (D * y)/z
```

The division by z is the key to understanding these equations. Objects located further away from us appear smaller; this is reflected mathematically in that if an object's z coordinate is bigger, then its size will correspondingly shrink. Figure 14.5 illustrates this relationship graphically.

FIGURE 14.5:

Perspective projection

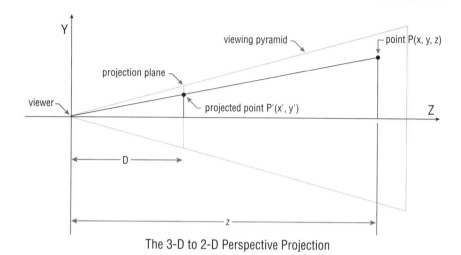

The 3-D to 2-D Perspective Projection

The z coordinate of the stars can also be used for a simple and highly effective 3-D graphics effect—*depth cueing*. This is based on the physical reality that less and less light will reach an observer the further an object is located from the observer. In other words, the object becomes less bright. With modern 256-color (or more) bitmapped displays, you can easily modulate the brightness of anything you draw by multiplying each red, green, and blue primary color component by the same scaling factor. The applet uses one final technique to improve the realism of the effect, and that is to physically scale the infinitely small star point (in this model), depending on its distance from the viewer. To reduce flicker, a simpler technique than double buffering was used: Erase only what changes. Whenever a star draws itself, it first erases its previous position. This way, you completely avoid having to wipe the whole viewport window for every star field redraw. Have a look at the following code to read the remaining nitty-gritty details of the implementation:

```
import java.awt.*;

public class StarField extends java.applet.Applet {

// Instance variables
```

```
private final int NUM_STARS = 70; // the more stars, the slower the animation

private Star[] stars = new Star[NUM_STARS]; // this array holds the StarField

private final int lensFactor = 200;
//—————————————————————————————————————————————————————————————————————
// Applet init()
//
// Create a cloud of random stars. Cloud is housed in an array of Star.
//—————————————————————————————————————————————————————————————————————
public void init() {

    for(int i=0; i< stars.length; i++) {
        stars[i] = new Star(7500);              // argument is depth Z range
    }
    System.out.println("Stars initialized!");
}

//—————————————————————————————————————————————————————————————————————
// Applet (Component) paint()
//
// First time only: wipe background to deep space black.
// Forever:
//   draw starfield
//—————————————————————————————————————————————————————————————————————
public void paint(Graphics g) {

    g.setColor(Color.black);
    g.fillRect(0,0, 10000,10000);
    Star.setViewPort( size() );         // class method !

// Now project and draw every star. Original loop was:
//
//    while(true) {
//        for(int i=0; i< stars.length; i++) {
//            stars[i].draw( g, lensFactor );
//        }
//    }
//
// ... but was changed to the faster unrolled equivalent:

    while(true) {
        int numstars = stars.length / 4;
        for(int i=0; i< numstars; i++) {
            int index = i<<2;
            stars[index++].draw( g, lensFactor );
            stars[index++].draw( g, lensFactor );
            stars[index++].draw( g, lensFactor );
            stars[index  ].draw( g, lensFactor );
```

```
        }
    }
}} // End of class StarField

//—————————————————————————————————————————————————
// Class Star
//
// This class encapsulates the attributes and self-drawing method of
// a star.
//—————————————————————————————————————————————————

class Star {

private static int maxDepth;          //
private static Dimension viewport;    // applet window dimensions

private int x,y,z;                    // star position
private int dz;                       // star speed (parallel to Z axis)

private int sx,sy;                    // projected screen x,y
private int osx,osy;                  // old screen x,y

private int starTemperature;          // 0..100

//—————————————————————————————————————————————————
// CONSTRUCTOR
//
// Randomly position a star in space by generating random (x,y,z) coordinates.
// Assign the star a random Z speed towards the viewer.
// Assign the star a random star color (determined by its temperature).
//—————————————————————————————————————————————————
Star (int depth) {

    maxDepth = depth;       // note the maximum Z distance allowed
    randomizeStar();
}

//—————————————————————————————————————————————————
// Give current star a random position and a random speed
//—————————————————————————————————————————————————
private final void randomizeStar() {

    x = (int) ( (Math.random()-0.5) * 10000);
    y = (int) ( (Math.random()-0.5) * 10000);
    z = (int) (  Math.random() * maxDepth);      // spread throughout volume

    dz = 70 + (int)(Math.random() * 130);        // at random speeds

    starTemperature = (int)(100*Math.random());
}
//—————————————————————————————————————————————————
// draw()
//
```

```
// This method projects and clips a star from 3-D to 2-D and renders
// the depth-cued star in the viewport. To eliminate flicker, the stars
// erase their own old positions before drawing their new position.
// This eliminates the need for a global fillRect() to clear the whole
// viewport, which would create a lot of flicker.
//
final void draw (Graphics g, int D) {

float brightness;        // 0.0 .. 1.0
int starSize;            // 1   .. 5

    z -= dz;                             // move stars towards us

        // recycle stars which have gone past viewer (viewer has z=0)
    if (z <= 0) {
        newStar(g);
    }

    sx = (int) (D*x/z);                  // project (x,y,z) to screen (x',y')
    sy = (int) (D*y/z);

    sx += viewport.width/2;              // center starfield in viewport
    sy += viewport.height/2;

        // clip stars which moved outside of our viewing pyramid
    if (sx < 0 || sx > viewport.width ||
        sy < 0 || sy > viewport.height) {

            newStar(g);
    }

    brightness = (float) (maxDepth - z) / maxDepth;
    starSize   = (int) (brightness * 5);

    g.setColor(Color.black);
    g.fillRect(osx, osy, starSize, starSize);

        // sprinkle sky with small amounts of colored stars
        // 85% are grey-white   (equal amounts of R,G,B)
        // 10% are yellow       (equal amounts of R and G only)
        // 3%  are red          (only R)
    if (starTemperature > 15) {
        g.setColor(new Color(brightness, brightness, brightness) );
    } else if (starTemperature > 5) {
        g.setColor(new Color(brightness, brightness, 0.0F) );
    } else if (starTemperature > 2) {
        g.setColor(new Color(brightness, 0.0F, 0.0F) );
    } else {                         // remaining 2% are blue
        g.setColor(new Color(0.0F, 0.0F, brightness) );
    }
        // draw star
    g.fillRect(sx, sy, starSize, starSize);
```

```
        osx = sx;        // remember star's position to erase it next time
        osy = sy;
    }
    //─────────────────────────────────────────────────────────────
    // newStar()
    //
    // When a star goes past viewer or moves out of view (above, below, left
    // or right), then that star should be eliminated and re-used to make
    // room for a new star which gets "born in the depths of space".
    //─────────────────────────────────────────────────────────────
    private void newStar(Graphics g) {
        randomizeStar();
        z = maxDepth;          // but start them all the way at "the far end"

        g.setColor(Color.black);     // erase old star's twinkle
        g.fillRect(osx, osy, 5,5);
    }

    static void setViewPort(Dimension d) {
        viewport = d;
    }

    // provide a toString() which summarizes a Star's state. This was only
    // used during development.

    public String toString() {

        return "("+ x +","+ y +","+ z +") sx=" + sx +" sy=" + sy;
    }} // End of class Star
```

If you run this applet embedded within any HTML page containing other applets, you will immediately see the problem: This applet uses up all the available CPU resources and consequently prevents other applets from running.

Look at the applet's `paint()` method—it never returns! An infinite loop was used in a method that is called (indirectly) by the browser. Method `paint()` is not meant to hold an applet's main body of code (which *can* legally contain infinite loops). If you run the applet using the appletviewer tool, you will notice that appletviewer itself ceases to function completely, because it relies on the `paint()` method to return before it can continue dealing with other things (like responding to menu selections). Obviously, an applet's body code has to go somewhere else. In fact, you need a different approach altogether to get out of this situation. The next section offers the solution.

Multithreaded Applets

To allow the StarField applet to function in a well-behaved way among other applets located on the same page as our applet, you need to refer back to Chapter 10, where the `start()` and `stop()` applet methods were explained. Remember that applets have a "life cycle" that consists of the following main events:

- Applet initialization (`Applet`'s `init()` method is called)

- Applet gets browser's go ahead to run (`Applet`'s `start()` method is called)

- Applet gets browser order to stop (`Applet`'s `stop()` method is called)

- Applet is told to clean up before being killed (`Applet`'s `destroy()` method is called)

All these methods are imposed on us by the browser framework an applet runs in. And they all assume one important technical detail, which is that your applet is using a *thread* for all its main logic. So far, these applets have not spawned any threads for their functionality to be sidetracked into. However, for the majority of applets, this is a necessary implementation evil we now have to explore.

Chapter 8 taught you all about how to create new threads and how to control these independent program flows. Here is a summary of the basics of threads:

- Any thread has either to be a subclass of `Thread` or to implement the `Runnable` interface.

- A newly created thread has to be started by invoking its `start()` method.

- A thread will stop on the spot if its `stop()` method is called.

- A thread's code starts running with its `run()` method.

The previous applet examples in Part Two of this book have all used the `init()` or `paint()` methods to hold the applet's main code. Neither method is the correct location for this main code. The right place to put the main applet logic is in a thread's `run()` method. This way, any endless loops (like the StarField applet's `while(true)` endless loop) will be controllable by whomever controls the thread. And the applet is the logical choice for the controlling entity. Figure 14.6 illustrates the relationship between the browser, the applet, and its thread.

FIGURE 14.6:

Time sequence diagram between browser, applet, and applet thread

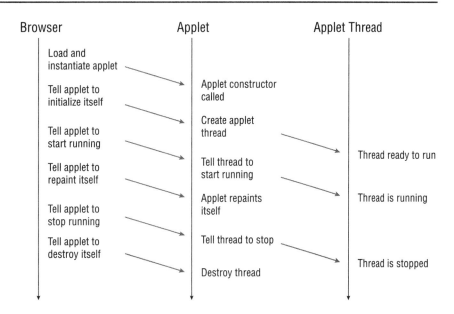

Since this browser/applet/applet thread model is the one *assumed* by all browsers, it is surprising that the basic `java.applet.Applet` class does not reflect this assumption. Luckily, object-oriented subclassing allows us to remedy the situation by enhancing the `Applet`

class to mirror the model. Once you have this new, improved applet class, you can use it instead of the vanilla `Applet` class at very little extra cost, giving you vastly enhanced functionality.

Extending the Applet Base Class to Support Multithreading

To extend class `Applet` to support having the applet logic execute in a thread, it is a simple matter of adding the thread creation, starting and stopping operations in the right places. The `AppletTemplate` class does exactly that:

```
import java.applet.*;
import java.awt.*;

/**
 *  Template for all good Applets
 *
 *  @author Tim Rohaly
 */
public class AppletTemplate extends Applet implements Runnable {

    Thread theThread;

    /**
     * Provides a way for author to associate information with
     * an Applet.  Can be used for copyright, contact information, etc.
     * @return credits
     */
    public String getAppletInfo() {
        StringBuffer s = new StringBuffer();

        s.append("Applet Template\n");
        s.append((char)   169);                 // Copyright symbol
//      s.append((char)0x2122);                 // Trademark symbol
        s.append("1996 ORC Incorported, All Rights Reserved\n");

        return s.toString();
    }

    /**
     * Describes all user parameters for this Applet; their names,
     * types, and default values.
     * @return parameter name, type, description
     */
    public String[][] getParameterInfo() {
        String[][] result = {
```

```
            { "Parameter1", "int",     "Iterations (default 5)" },
            { "Parameter2", "float",   "Variation (default 2.0)" },
            { "Parameter3", "boolean", "Sea (default true)" },
        };
        return result;
}

/**
 * Called once to initialize the Applet.
 * Create Components, lay them out, and perform any
 * initializations here.
 */
public void init() {
}

/**
 * Called to start the Applet initially, and whenever Applet
 * is restarted (re-visiting a page, for instance).
 * Start up threads here.
 */
public void start() {
    if (theThread == null) {
        theThread = new Thread(this);
        theThread.start();
    }
}

/**
 * Called to stop the Applet whenever it is iconified or the
 * user leaves the page.  Guaranteed to be called before destroy().
 * Stop threads here.
 */
public void stop() {
    if (theThread != null) {
        theThread.stop();
        theThread = null;
    }
}

/**
 * Used to clean up system resources.
 */
public void destroy() {
}

/**
 * Used to do any drawing to screen.
 * @param g Graphic to use
 */
public void paint(Graphics g) {
}
```

```
/**
 * All work should be done here.
 */
public void run() {
}

/**
 * Used to handle action events.
 * @param e event which generated this action
 * @param arg data associated with this action
 * @return true if event was handled
 */
public boolean action(Event e, Object arg) {
    return false;
}
}
```

The main additions to `java.applet.Applet` are the `start()` and `stop()` methods. Method `start()` now turns any `AppletTemplate` subclass (that is, your applets) into a thread and starts it. Your applets can be transformed into threads because class `AppletTemplate` implements the `Runnable` interface. Or to be more accurate, you will implement that interface by putting all applet main logic in an overridden `run()` method. When the browser moves to a different page, the `stop()` method will automatically kill the applet thread. This means you have to be very careful that your `run()` method does not contain any initialization code, otherwise this code will be re-executed each time your applet reappears. The right place for true initialization code is the applet's usual `init()` method.

Using the AppletTemplate Class

Now that you have written the `AppletTemplate` class, you can almost forget everything about needing a thread to run your applets in. The class will take care of everything behind your back. You keep using `init()`, `paint()`, and `update()` as usual, and you put your applet's main code inside the `run()` method. The following example applet does this, and as you'll see, it does not concern itself any further with any thread issues whatsoever. Now *that's* information hiding and code reuse at its best!

To prove how easy it is to work with the new `AppletTemplate` class, here is a very short applet which contains a main loop (the analogue of the StarField applet's problematic infinite animation loop), and that behaves properly, respecting the browser-applet protocol in every respect:

```
import java.awt.*;

public class Counter extends AppletTemplate {

int counter;

public void run() {
    while(true) {
        counter++;
        repaint();
    }
}

public void paint(Graphics g) {
    g.drawString(String.valueOf(counter), 10,20);
}
} // End of Class implementation
```

By building on the AppletTemplate class, this Counter applet uses multithreading and obeys the `start()` and `stop()` orders of the browser, and yet, none of these technical details encumber its implementation. Since these technicalities only serve to obstruct your main goal of writing an applet with some required functionality, this is just as well. (The Counter applet, though, has no purpose in life other than to demonstrate that an applet with a main loop can be made to coexist with browsers and other applets.)

A Final Example: An Analog Clock

As an example of a much more functional, well-behaved applet, that uses the `AppletTemplate` class, you will design an analog clock applet.

Digital clocks, in this digital age, are not a challenge to design, because their core can simply consist of the trivial one-liner:

```
g.drawString( (new Date()).toString, 10,10);
```

Analog clocks are a bit harder, because you have to render the time by drawing a clock face and its hour, minute, and second hands. Figure 14.7 shows what you are trying to achieve.

FIGURE 14.7:

GrandmotherClock
applet

First, you should analyze the challenge. You can access the system's local time by constructing a `java.util.Date` object without any arguments. You should somehow convert this time into the graphical representation of Figure 14.7. The first observation is that an analog clock can be viewed as a full 360-degree circle and that the hands can be thought of as indicating angles. Although it is 15:19:38 on this example's clock, you should think of it as that the hour hand is indicating (roughly) -12 degrees, the minute hand -24, and the seconds hand -138 degrees. Shifting your view of analog clocks from indicating times to indicating angles will greatly simplify the design of your program. This is because you can calculate pixel positions within circles easily if we have the following two values: a radius and an angle. This conversion from (radius, angle) to (x,y) coordinates is called converting from polar coordinates to Cartesian (grid) coordinates. The formulas rely on sine and cosine for the transformation:

```
x = radius * cos(angle)
y = radius * sin(angle)
```

This set of equations produces (x,y) points located on the circle centered around the origin and having a radius "radius." Since the clock circle is not located in the origin (0,0) you have to *translate* all the coordinates by adding the coordinate of the new circle origin (ox,oy):

```
x = ox + radius * cos(angle)
y = oy + radius * sin(angle)
```

This is all the math you will need to write any analog clock program. The angle arguments are in radians, but you will only convert your degrees angles into radians at the last minute, just before plugging them in to the formulas.

This clock uses several decreasing radii for the following things:

- The clock face (this is the main radius from which all others are derived)

- The second hand

- The minute hand

- The smallest hand: the hour hand

The main clock-face radius is calculated from the width and height our applet got given by the *<APPLET>* *"WIDTH=.."* and *"HEIGHT=.."* HTML tag parameters.

The core of the program consists of the calculations transforming the current time in the three clock hand angles. This is done in class AnalogClock's draw() method by transforming the 0–59 or 0–23 ranges into the 0–359 range of a full circle. Since zero seconds, minutes, or hours equal +90 degrees on a circle, you simply rotate the derived angles to compensate for this. Once the angles are obtained, all that remains to be done is to draw the hands. Here, an effort was made to eliminate flicker as much as possible while at the same time trying to keep the updating algorithm as simple as possible. This is done by observing that for most of the time (59 seconds out of every minute) the only movement on the clock is the seconds hand indicating the passage of seconds. To animate the seconds, you should not, therefore, erase the whole clock and redraw it every new second. A simple (and frequently employed) technique is to remember the second hand's last position and erase only the second hand next time round, before redrawing it in its new position. This is the same technique employed to control flicker in the StarField applet—remember old positions and erase old graphics before drawing new graphics. Only when the seconds tick over from 59 seconds to 00 seconds does the minute hand (and maybe the hour hand too) need updating. This is when all clock hands are erased before they get repainted in their new positions.

This is the core of the program described. Peripheral to this is the main class structure for the program: The applet template class is being extended to hold all the applet-related aspects of the clock applet. All the analog clock aspects are encapsulated (and ready to be reused) in a separate class called AnalogClock.

Before you dissect the code in detail, look at the following aspects of the source code:

- Every method has a very well-defined function.

- None of the methods are too long.

- The code displays several levels of abstraction.

- The code is well commented.

- The variable identifiers were made as readable as possible.

- Similar code lines were formatted to align features vertically, clearly highlighting their similarities.

Here is the listing for the GrandmotherClock applet:

```
//****************************************************************************
// GrandmotherClock Applet                              (C) L. Vanhelsuwe
// ————————————————————                                 ——————————————————
//
// An analog clock with hour, minute and second hands.
// Uses APPLET PARAMETERS
//   - Timezone : Time Zone from which this clock came
//   - Title    : The clock's title string beneath the clock face
//
// History:
// ———
// 16-JUN-96: first version.
//
//****************************************************************************

import java.awt.*;          // mainly for Graphics
import java.util.*;         // mainly for Date

public class GrandmotherClock extends AppletTemplate {

//————————————————————————————————————————————————————————————————————————————
// GrandmotherClock instance variables. All private
//————————————————————————————————————————————————————————————————————————————

private AnalogClock clock;  // The underlying clock we build on
private Date theTime;

private Font theFont = new Font("TimesRoman",Font.BOLD,16);
private int width;
private int height;
private int radius;

private String title;       // the text printed below the clock
private int strx = -1;
private int stry = -1;

private double hourOffset;  // the time offset for this time zone
private final long hourMillis = 1000*60*60; // no. of milliseconds in 1 hour

//————————————————————————————————————————————————————————————————————————————
// Applet init()
//
// work out clock size from applet dims, grab applet params, calc title
```

```
    // string y coordinate (x coordinate calc needs FontMetrics which we can
    // not access yet from init())
    //————————————————————————————————————————————————————————————————————————
    public void init() {

            // Set clock dimensions
        width  = bounds().width;
        height = bounds().height-20;          // leave room for clock title
        radius = Math.min(width, height)/2;

            // grab applet parameters
            // Timezone can be -12..0..12
            // Title is any reasonable string
        String TZstr = getParameter("Timezone");
        if (TZstr == null) {
            TZstr = "0";
        }
        hourOffset = Double.valueOf(TZstr).doubleValue();

        title = getParameter("Title");
        if (title == null) {
            title = "Local time";
        }
        stry = bounds().height-5;
    }
    //————————————————————————————————————————————————————————————————————————
    // Applet thread body
    //
    // forever:
    //    get local system time, adjust TZ
    //    redraw clock
    //    wait a second
    //————————————————————————————————————————————————————————————————————————
    public void run() {

        while (true) {

            theTime = new Date();
            if (hourOffset != 0.0) {
                theTime.setTime(theTime.getTime() +
    (long)(hourOffset*hourMillis));
            }

            repaint();
            try { Thread.sleep(1000); } catch (InterruptedException ignored)
    {}
        }
    }
    //————————————————————————————————————————————————————————————————————————
    // Applet clock time updating (called indirectly by repaint())
    //
    // if clock has never been drawn yet,
```

```
//      create clock, redraw clock face (the circular hour and minute marks)
// draw the clock hands to reflect the time
//--------------------------------------------------------------------------
public void update(Graphics g) {

    if (clock == null) {
        clock = new AnalogClock(0,0, radius, Color.black,
getBackground());
        paint(g);
    }
    clock.draw(g, theTime);
}
//--------------------------------------------------------------------------
// Applet full clock repaint
//
// if clock already exists (paint() can be called before first update())
//      order clock to redraw itself
//      if title string x coordinate hasn't been calculated yet
//          calc strx to center the title beneath the clockface
//      draw clock title
//--------------------------------------------------------------------------
public void paint(Graphics g) {
    if (clock != null) {
        clock.drawFace(g);
        if (strx == -1) {
            strx = radius - g.getFontMetrics().stringWidth(title)/2;
        }
        g.drawString(title, strx, stry);
    }
}
//--------------------------------------------------------------------------
// getAppletInfo() is called by some browsers when the user requests
// the browser's "About.." or "Applet info" menu options.
// This method should always return some basic information on the
// applet.
//--------------------------------------------------------------------------
public String getAppletInfo() {
    return
        "Author: Laurence Vanhelsuwe\n"
      + "Title : GrandmotherClock v1.0\n"
      + "Copyright 1996 LVA";

}
//--------------------------------------------------------------------------
// getParameterInfo() is also called by some browsers when the user
// requests the browser's "About.." or "Applet info" menu options.
// This method should return an array of String triplets containing
// parameter name/type/description
//--------------------------------------------------------------------------
public String[][] getParameterInfo() {
String[][] paramDescriptions = {
```

```
        {"Timezone", "double", "Which Time Zone this clock comes from."}
        ,{"Title"   , "String", "Simply the title to use for this clock."}};

        return paramDescriptions;

  }} // End of class GrandmotherClock
```

The heart of this applet is its `run()` method. Since the clock needs to run permanently, the method contains a forever loop (a `while-(true)`) that queries the local system time, orders a repainting of the clock (just the hands!), and then goes to sleep for a second. The `repaint()` call will eventually lead to the `update()` method being called, which is overridden to ask the underlying clock object to update its graphically depicted time. The `update()` method is also responsible for the creation of the `AnalogClock` instance. The `if` statement uses the fact of whether the clock object has already been constructed or not as its cue to trigger the first full redraw of the clock (the clock face), via a call to `paint()`. The clock face is only ever drawn when the applet needs to be repainted in full or at initialization time. All of the clock's rendering is the responsibility of class `AnalogClock`, listed here:

```
import java.awt.*;
import java.util.Date;
```

```
//————————————————————————————————————————————
// Class AnalogClock
// This is where all analog clock matters are encapsulated, as opposed to
// applet related things. In particular: time to hand angles calculations
// and clockface and hands rendering.
//————————————————————————————————————————————
class AnalogClock {

private int radius;        // clock radius
private int ox,oy;         // clock center
private Color fg,bg;       // foreground and background colors

private int secondsAngle,secondsAngleOld;   // all angles in degrees
private int minutesAngle,minutesAngleOld;
private int hoursAngle;

private int secondsLength;
private int minutesLength,minutesLength2;
private int hoursLength,hoursLength2;

private final double toRadians = Math.PI/180.0; // to convert degr -> radians
```

```
//————————————————————————————————————————————————————————
// CONSTRUCTOR
//  work out hand lengths as proportions of the given radius
//————————————————————————————————————————————————————————
AnalogClock(int x, int y, int radius, Color fg, Color bg) {

    this.ox     = x + radius;
    this.oy     = y + radius;
    this.radius = radius;
    this.fg     = fg;
    this.bg     = bg;

        // the lengths of the hands are controlled by the percentages here
    secondsLength = (int) (0.88*radius);    // 88% of available radius
    minutesLength = (int) (0.85*radius);
    hoursLength   = (int) (0.75*radius);

        // these secondary lengths determine the diamond shape of the
        // hours and minutes hands.
    minutesLength2 = (int) (0.80*minutesLength);
    hoursLength2   = (int) (0.70*hoursLength);
}
//————————————————————————————————————————————————————————
// draw the circular marks around the clock's edge indicating mins and hours
// every five minutes, render a bigger mark
//————————————————————————————————————————————————————————
void drawFace(Graphics g) {

    for (int angle=0; angle < 360; angle+= 6) {          //   6  = 1 minute
        if ((angle % 30) == 0) {                         //   30 = 5 minutes
            drawRadialLine(g, angle-1, radius-6, radius-2);
            drawRadialLine(g, angle  , radius-8, radius);
            drawRadialLine(g, angle+1, radius-6, radius-2);
        } else {
            drawRadialLine(g, angle, radius-4, radius);
        }
    }
}
//————————————————————————————————————————————————————————
// redraw the clock's hands to reflect the time
// this is done in an intelligent way to avoid flicker:
//    1) calculate angles of all hands
//    2) if minutes haven't changed, erase previous seconds hand cheaply
//       else erase all hands
//    3) draw all hands
//    4) remember position of minute and second hands for next time
//————————————————————————————————————————————————————————
void draw(Graphics g, Date time) {

    secondsAngle = -90 + time.getSeconds()*6 ;   // 0..59 -> 0..360
    minutesAngle = -90 + time.getMinutes()*6 ;   // 0..59 -> 0..360
    hoursAngle   = -90 + time.getHours()  *30;   // 0..11 -> 0..360
```

```
        // let hour hand track minutes in hour smoothly !
    hoursAngle  += (time.getMinutes()*6)/12;

    g.setColor(bg);
    if (minutesAngle != minutesAngleOld) {
            // erase all hands by wiping clock interior (leaving time marks)
        g.fillOval(ox-secondsLength, oy-secondsLength,
                    2*secondsLength, 2*secondsLength);
    } else {
        drawSeconds(g, secondsAngleOld);
    }

    g.setColor(fg);
    drawSeconds(g, secondsAngle);
    drawMinutes(g, minutesAngle);
    drawHours   (g, hoursAngle);

    secondsAngleOld = secondsAngle;
    minutesAngleOld = minutesAngle;
}
//————————————————————————————————————————————————————————————————
// All hand drawing routines rely on lower level methods
//————————————————————————————————————————————————————————————————
void drawSeconds(Graphics g, int angle) {
    drawRadialLine(g, angle, 0, secondsLength);
}
void drawMinutes(Graphics g, int angle) {
    drawHand(g, angle, 3, minutesLength, minutesLength2);
}
void drawHours(Graphics g, int angle) {
    drawHand(g, angle, 6, hoursLength, hoursLength2);
}
//————————————————————————————————————————————————————————————————
// drawRadialLine is used to draw the seconds hand and the time marks
// around the edge of the clock face.
//————————————————————————————————————————————————————————————————
void drawRadialLine(Graphics g, int angle, int innerR, int outerR) {
int x1,y1, x2,y2;

    x1 = ox + (int) (innerR*Math.cos(angle*toRadians) );
    y1 = oy + (int) (innerR*Math.sin(angle*toRadians) );

    x2 = ox + (int) (outerR*Math.cos(angle*toRadians) );
    y2 = oy + (int) (outerR*Math.sin(angle*toRadians) );
    g.drawLine(x1,y1, x2,y2);
}
//————————————————————————————————————————————————————————————————
// drawHand builds a 4-point polygon to represent a clock hand and
```

```
// draws the polygon on the clockface.
//——————————————————————————————————————————————————————————————————————————
void drawHand(Graphics g, int angle, int handThickness,
                         int totalLength, int intermediateLength) {
Polygon hand;
int x,y;

    hand = new Polygon();
    hand.addPoint(ox,oy);

    x = ox + (int) (intermediateLength*Math.cos((angle-handThickness)*toRadians) );
    y = oy + (int) (intermediateLength*Math.sin((angle-handThickness)*toRadians) );
    hand.addPoint(x,y);

    x = ox + (int) (totalLength*Math.cos(angle*toRadians) );
    y = oy + (int) (totalLength*Math.sin(angle*toRadians) );
    hand.addPoint(x,y);

    x = ox + (int) (intermediateLength*Math.cos((angle+handThickness)*toRadians) );
    y = oy + (int) (intermediateLength*Math.sin((angle+handThickness)*toRadians) );
    hand.addPoint(x,y);

    g.fillPolygon(hand);          // this renders the hand on the clock
}} // End of class AnalogClock
```

Class AnalogClock relies heavily on the elementary trigonometry explained at the beginning of the project. As the code is properly commented, its details are left to the reader to discover and, hopefully, enjoy.

Minimizing Applet Loading Times

As you can see, applets do not get any smaller when you try to create a real, functional applet. This means your applet will take longer to load over the Internet. Add to that that applets are very rapidly becoming very popular, so more and more Internet bandwidth is used up to transfer these competing applets from their server machines all the way to your client machine running your favorite Web browser. This can only mean one thing—more bandwidth pressure on the

Internet and a resulting (further) slowing of response times.
Therefore, in this climate of scarce bandwidth, it is very important to

- Minimize the amount of Internet resources your applet uses

- Minimize response times to maintain a swift, interactive feel

These two goals can in turn be achieved by

- Minimizing the size of the applet's executable

- Minimizing the number of classes used

- Minimizing the applet's initialization time

Keeping Executables Small

Large files take longer to travel over the Internet than shorter files,
and applets do not get any special treatment. If you have already had
a look at the sizes of the `*.class` files your Java compiler generates,
you should have been extremely impressed by their compactness.
Compared to compiled C or C++ code, these Java executables are
positively minute. There are two reasons for this:

- Java machine code is very compact (see Chapter 18 for details).

- Every standard class imported by a Java program does not need
  to be a physical part of the program.

Nevertheless, being able to shave off a number of bytes can mean
the difference between a ten-second load and a twelve-second load
(and to a user, waiting always feels like an eternity). This wild discrepancy is a result of a property of Internet file transfers—*packet
segmentation*. You must have noticed the phenomenon when surfing
the Web: The progress indicator fills up burst by burst, and just
before completing the load, it indicates that it is stuck waiting for just
a few dozen more bytes to finish. It is at this stage that you wish your
applet could have been those couple of dozen bytes shorter.

The explanation for this frequent delay, right at the end of a load, has to do with the segmentation of a transmitted file. Although the Internet (the TCP protocol to be correct) accepts data streams of arbitrary length, the networking devices (routers in particular) responsible for getting this data from point A to point B usually have very strict upper limits on the size of packets they can deal with. This limit is frequently one of 256, 512, 1024, or 2048 bytes. Therefore, when an applet is transmitted over the network, it gets segmented into N-1 packets of some fixed size plus one last tail packet containing the remaining few bytes. All these packets travel independently and have to be reassembled into the original applet executable byte stream at the client's end. When the last packet is unfortunate enough to get delayed, you can wait seconds for just a few bytes more to complete the load. And that's pretty annoying at best. So what can you do? Try to round down the size of your applet's classes to multiples of, say, 512 bytes? Unfortunately, it isn't that simple. The Internet is comprised of an incredibly diverse collection of networking hardware, which means that the resulting Maximum Transmission Unit (MTU) used for any end-to-end communication might be almost anything. (The MTU is the largest packet fragment size used by the route chosen by your packets.) So all you can do is to try and keep your class files as small as possible in the hope that, most of the time, those last few bytes will not need to be part of that awkward last fragmented packet. (Having said that, aiming for multiples of 256 bytes might work out well in practice.)

What techniques are available to shrink class sizes without having to waste too much time in the process? You might be able to

- Remove debugging code

- Shrink `String` literals (by editing them to be a bit shorter, reducing verbosity)

- Compile with the javac -O (optimize) option enabled

- Remove methods that are never used

Keeping the Number of Classes Under Control

Few applets consist of only one class that relies exclusively on the standard Java classes for all its building blocks. Rather, the norm is that your applets will rely on more classes you wrote yourself. All these classes will have to be loaded separately by the Java Virtual Machine, and here lies another inefficiency waiting to be optimized. The problem is that, for example, loading 20 small blocks of data separately takes longer than loading one equivalent chunk 20 times the size of the small blocks. This is a result of the overhead incurred by creating network connections for each block (read: class) to be fetched. This means that you should keep a close watch on the number of extra classes your applets rely on.

One area where your project can generate lots of classes is with GUI code. As you learned in Chapter 12, you can approach the event-processing aspect of your GUI by subclassing at various levels of the GUI's container hierarchy. The lower you subclass, the more subclasses you will create. So it pays to design your GUI with this issue in mind. This does not mean you should try to pack everything in one monstrous class either—that would be ignoring every software engineering principle in the book. A compromise solution is always available.

Being Quick on Your Feet

People hate waiting, but once the waiting is over, they themselves need long seconds to process the change that has finally occurred. This means your applets should start doing *something* as soon as possible: Say "Hello" to the user, ask the user their name, show a progress indicator, *keep the user busy*. In the mean time, the applet can frantically continue to initialize itself for real, in the background. This necessitates the use of extra threads to interact with the user, while the time consuming initializations continue as the main thread. This way you can turn an annoyingly slow applet into a lightning quick applet that entertains its viewers to boot!

The saying to remember is, "Time flies when you're having fun." The rate at which time flows can indeed vary tremendously depending on your own perception of it. Waiting for something can stretch time out to a crawl, while when you are enjoying yourself, time zooms along. You can alter your users' perception of your applets' load times by cunningly exploiting this phenomenon. The way you do this can only enhance the applet.

Summary

Applets that rely on a passive GUI to activate aspects of their functionality are the simplest types to implement. The calculator applet is an example of this simpler type, but the majority of real-life applets need to use multithreading. This chapter proved that avoiding the use of threads will get you into trouble sooner or later. There is no way you can write a well-behaved (that is, usable) applet that contains an infinite loop (such as an animation loop) without relying on at least one dynamically created thread. Having accepted this fact, you had a look at how to add this inevitable thread and how to control it the way the browser protocol meant it to be controlled. Since the majority of applets cannot do without this thread for their main code, you proceeded by extending the base `Applet` class into an `AppletTemplate` class that gave you all the thread functionality you need, once and for all, in an easy-to-use, almost transparent way. A small, real-life clock applet was then presented to illustrate how all of the issues seen in previous chapters come together, including the use of our new `AppletTemplate`. We finished off by looking at some techniques to make your applets load quickly and seem fast.

Streams and Input/Output Programming

- **Class** `File`

- **Class** `RandomAccessFile`

- **I/O Streams**

- **Input Streams**

- **Output Streams**

A computer's simplest model consists of the following three-stage pipeline:

- Input

- Processing

- Output

Input and output (I/O) is therefore a fundamental aspect of computing. A computer wouldn't be much good without being able to accept data from the outside world and, as soon after as possible, present its computed results.

Computers are therefore always accompanied by built-in or peripheral I/O interfaces (called ports) like a serial port, parallel port, keyboard port, audio port, video port, SCSI port, and so on. These are used to hook up actual I/O devices like modems, laser printers, keyboards, hi-fi systems, monitors, and hard disks, respectively. Because I/O devices like these are constantly being improved (and eventually become obsolete), their programming would necessitate constant code changes to keep track of the products' evolving features. This is quite obviously an unmanageable situation, which is why the concept of a *device driver* was introduced. A device driver shields the application (to a certain extent) from the ever-changing programming model of a given I/O device. But device drivers themselves aren't immutable over time. At some point, the physical device will have been perfected with such radically new features—or simply have evolved so much—that the driver, too, will need to change its application interface. To address this problem in turn, an extra layer of software is needed to protect the application from this slower, but equally inevitable, evolution in device drivers. This extra *device-independent I/O* layer is provided by the operating system. It is device independent because the services it presents are uniform for all devices. Figure 15.1 illustrates these software layers. A layering (or buffering) approach such as this allows a very slowly evolving (or frozen, in the case of *legacy* systems) application to remain compatible with the very latest hardware, which evolves almost on a monthly basis.

FIGURE 15.1:

Software layers each dealing with different levels of evolution rate

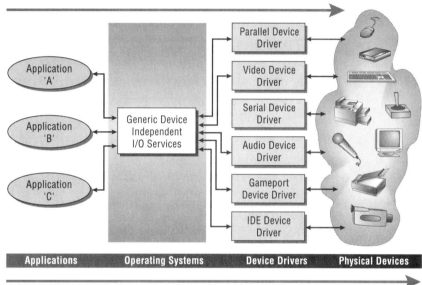

Taking the discussion one step further still, you can view different operating systems as entities that exhibit too many I/O-related differences for any one application to deal with. And that, finally, is why programming languages themselves wrap yet another layer of I/O software around the two layers depicted in Figure 15.1. Java provides this final layer in the form of an entire hierarchy of classes in package `java.io`. The classes it contains shield any application from operating-system-dependent (but nevertheless generic) I/O handling. At the heart of the package lie the concepts of streams and files. Because few applications can do without creating, processing, or managing files, we'll discuss the file classes first and then move on to the bulk of the `java.io` package: the stream classes.

Class File

An operating system's filing system is one of the most basic services it provides to applications. Historically, it was one of the very first services to be developed. During the fifties, the ability of a computer to automatically locate and load a program into its memory was still a luxury for most computer programmers. Nowadays all filing systems allow a hierarchical directory structure of arbitrary complexity to organize files of almost equally arbitrary length (four gigabytes being a common limit per file). These files are identified by filenames limited in length to (usually) 32 to 256 characters. Although all filing systems are essentially identical in terms of these basic services, their exact implementations make them (as usual) mutually incompatible. To shield Java applications from this incompatibility obstacle, class `File` defines platform-independent methods for manipulating a concrete file maintained by a native filing system. The listing below is class `File`'s definition:

```
public class File extends Object {
   public final static String separator;
   public final static char separatorChar;
   public final static String pathSeparator;
   public final static char pathSeparatorChar;
   public File(String path) throws NullPointerException;
   public File(String path, String name);
   public File(File dir, String name);
   public String getName();
   public String getPath();
   public String getAbsolutePath();
   public String getParent();
   public boolean exists();
   public boolean canWrite();
   public boolean canRead();
   public boolean isFile();
```

```
        public boolean isDirectory();
        public boolean isAbsolute();
        public long lastModified();
        public long length();
        public boolean mkdir();
        public boolean renameTo(File dest);
        public boolean mkdirs();
        public String[] list();
        public String[] list(FilenameFilter filter);
        public boolean delete();
        public int hashCode();
        public boolean equals(Object obj);
        public String toString();
}
```

As you can see from the list of supported methods, class `File` does not allow you to access the contents of the file. There are no `read()` or `write()` methods to let you do this. Class `File` is there primarily to name files, query file attributes, and manipulate directories, all in a system-independent way. Following is a description of what you can do with files without opening them.

File Attributes

Class `File` gives you a couple of methods for querying a minimal set of file attributes:

- Whether the file exists

- Whether the file is read protected

- Whether the file is write protected

- Whether the file is, in fact, a directory

Finding out what other common file attributes are, like whether a file is a hidden, a system, or an archived file, is not supported. As with Java's Abstract Windowing Toolkit, the designers of these classes have had to take the least common denominator of all filing systems as their model; otherwise, Java could include features (like a "hidden" attribute) that aren't supported by some systems, thus jeopardizing its universal compatibility across platforms.

> **NOTE** Although the design of the Java machine code (see Part Three for details on the Java Virtual Machine) was heavily influenced (or should that be *crippled*?) by the requirement that Java binaries execute "efficiently" on Intel 80x86-based machines (read: PCs), Java was spared another possible PC anachronism: MS-DOS' pathetic 8+3 filename format. Java requires and relies heavily on the host's ability to handle proper, long filenames. Let us all rejoice if this fact helps to speed the extinction of MS-DOS from this world.

The following program shows how you use a `File` instance to query a file's attributes. The file is specified as a command-line parameter.

```java
import java.io.*;

public class Attr {

public static void main (String args[]) {

File    path;

    path  = new File(args[0]);      // grab command line argument

    String exists   = path.exists()    ? "Yes" : "No";
    String canRead  = path.canRead()   ? "Yes" : "No";
    String canWrite = path.canWrite()  ? "Yes" : "No";
    String isFile   = path.isFile()    ? "Yes" : "No";
    String isDir    = path.isDirectory()? "Yes" : "No";
    String isAbs    = path.isAbsolute()? "Yes" : "No";

    System.out.println("File attributes for '" + args[0] + "'");

    System.out.println("Exists         : " + exists);
    if (path.exists()) {
        System.out.println("Readable       : " + canRead);
        System.out.println("Writable       : " + canWrite);
        System.out.println("Is directory   : " + isDir);
```

```
            System.out.println("Is file        :  " + isFile);
            System.out.println("Absolute path  :  " + isAbs);
        }
    }}
```

You can experiment with this program by passing it various file and directory names, either relative or absolute. Note the use of the *ternary* (?:) operator to select either a "Yes" or "No" string for variables. This approach is more compact than the logical equivalent of using if-else statements.

Directory Manipulations

A handier program would be one that could list the contents of a directory like the dir or ls commands in most operating systems. Class File supports directory-list generation via its list() method. Here's another program that *recursively* (that is, calling upon itself) lists directories and their contents.

```
import java.io.*;

public class Dir {

static int indentLevel = -1;

public static void main (String args[]) {

String  names[] = new String[0];        // list of files in a directory
String  temp[]  = new String[1];        // dummy args[]
String  filename;
File    path, fpath;

    indentLevel++;                      // going down...

    path  = new File(args[0]);
    names = path.list();                // create list of files in this dir

    for (int i=0; i < names.length; i++) {
        for (int indent=0; indent < indentLevel; indent++) {
            System.out.print("    ");
        }

        filename = args[0] + File.separator + names[i];
        System.out.println(filename);

        fpath = new File(filename);
```

```
        if ( fpath.isDirectory() ) {
            temp[0] = fpath.getPath();
            Dir.main(temp);                    // recursively descend dir tree
        }
    }
    indentLevel-;                              // and going up...
}}
```

The program relies on a couple of interesting things. First of all, it calls itself recursively in the statement `Dir.main(temp)`. This repeated re-invocation of the `main()` method restarts the `main()` with new `args[]` arrays, initialized to contain the full name of the deeper directory to list. To highlight the current directory level, the contents of a directory are indented according to its nesting level in the filing hierarchy. This nesting level is in turn determined by the depth of the program's recursion level, which is tracked in the static class variable `indentLevel`. When a method exits, static variables do not get destroyed like simple method variables. The program relies on this behavior to track the recursion level across multiple invocations of `main()`. Static variables have one more interesting attribute: They also do not get allocated anew each time a new instance of a class is made; therefore, they are also called *class* variables. (This aspect of variable `indentLevel` is not relevant in the program because it does not explicitly create instances of class `Dir`, although `Dir` does get instantiated once when the program is loaded.)

The second aspect to note is the program's use of the `File.separator` class constant to display full paths using the same notation your machine uses (that is, the implementation is platform independent). This separator character could be a slash, backslash, or any other reserved character, depending on the native filing system.

Class RandomAccessFile

Because class `File` doesn't let you read or write files, other classes will have to provide this functionality. To read or write files, you can use one of two approaches. You can use the extremely powerful stream classes (which we'll discuss later), or you can use class RandomAccessFile. The latter option is easily mastered but has severe limitations if you want to start writing flexible and/or more complex applications. Class RandomAccessFile only does I/O on *files*, whereas the stream I/O classes can do I/O on almost anything, including files. So bear in mind that there's a much more powerful way to do the same things. In the meantime, the definition of class RandomAccessFile neatly sums up its functionality:

```
public class RandomAccessFile extends Object implements DataInput, DataOutput {
    public RandomAccessFile(String name, String mode) throws IOException;
    public RandomAccessFile(File file, String mode) throws IOException;
        // misc methods
    public final FileDescriptor getFD() throws IOException;
    public long getFilePointer() throws IOException;
    public void seek(long pos) throws IOException;
    public long length() throws IOException;
    public void close() throws IOException;

    public int read() throws IOException;
    public int read(byte b[], int off, int len) throws IOException;
    public int read(byte b[]) throws IOException;
        // DataInput read methods
    public final void readFully(byte b[]) throws IOException;
    public final void readFully(byte b[], int off, int len) throws IOException;
    public int skipBytes(int n) throws IOException;
    public final boolean readBoolean() throws IOException;
    public final byte readByte() throws IOException;
    public final int readUnsignedByte() throws IOException;
    public final short readShort() throws IOException;
    public final int readUnsignedShort() throws IOException;
    public final char readChar() throws IOException;
    public final int readInt() throws IOException;
    public final long readLong() throws IOException;
    public final float readFloat() throws IOException;
    public final double readDouble() throws IOException;
    public final String readLine() throws IOException;
    public final String readUTF() throws IOException;
        // DataOutput write methods
    public void write(int b) throws IOException;
    public void write(byte b[]) throws IOException;
    public void write(byte b[], int off, int len) throws IOException;
    public final void writeBoolean(boolean v) throws IOException;
    public final void writeByte(int v) throws IOException;
    public final void writeShort(int v) throws IOException;
    public final void writeChar(int v) throws IOException;
    public final void writeInt(int v) throws IOException;
```

```
    public final void writeLong(long v) throws IOException;
    public final void writeFloat(float v) throws IOException;
    public final void writeDouble(double v) throws IOException;
    public final void writeBytes(String s) throws IOException;
    public final void writeChars(String s) throws IOException;
    public final void writeUTF(String str) throws IOException;
}
```

In terms of organization, the class can be viewed simply as implementing the two interfaces DataInput and DataOutput. Class RandomAccessFile does not add much functionality beyond the methods defined in these interfaces. Here's the definition for interface DataOutput:

```
public interface DataOutput extends Object {
    public abstract void write(int b) throws IOException;
    public abstract void write(byte b[]) throws IOException;
    public abstract void write(byte b[], int off, int len) throws IOException;
    public abstract void writeBoolean(boolean v) throws IOException;
    public abstract void writeByte(int v) throws IOException;
    public abstract void writeShort(int v) throws IOException;
    public abstract void writeChar(int v) throws IOException;
    public abstract void writeInt(int v) throws IOException;
    public abstract void writeLong(long v) throws IOException;
    public abstract void writeFloat(float v) throws IOException;
    public abstract void writeDouble(double v) throws IOException;
    public abstract void writeBytes(String s) throws IOException;
    public abstract void writeChars(String s) throws IOException;
    public abstract void writeUTF(String str) throws IOException;
}
```

The DataOutput interface specifies a list of output (writing) methods that allow you to write any kind of simple Java type. It also requires all implementing classes to be able to write bytes or blocks of bytes. Outputting objects (apart from strings) is not supported. The exact bitstream produced by these methods should not concern you because a symmetrical interface (DataInput) specifies the equivalent reading methods that allow you to read back any data written out.

Here is the definition for the companion DataInput interface:

```
public interface DataInput extends Object {
    public abstract void readFully(byte b[]) throws IOException;
    public abstract void readFully(byte b[], int off, int len) throws IOException;
```

```
public abstract int skipBytes(int n) throws IOException;
public abstract boolean readBoolean() throws IOException;
public abstract byte readByte() throws IOException;
public abstract int readUnsignedByte() throws IOException;
public abstract short readShort() throws IOException;
public abstract int readUnsignedShort() throws IOException;
public abstract char readChar() throws IOException;
public abstract int readInt() throws IOException;
public abstract long readLong() throws IOException;
public abstract float readFloat() throws IOException;
public abstract double readDouble() throws IOException;
public abstract String readLine() throws IOException;
public abstract String readUTF() throws IOException;
}
```

Some of the asymmetrical differences are the `skipBytes()` method, the unsigned number reading methods and the `readLine()` method instead of the `writeByte()`/`Chars()` methods. Apart from those superficial differences, the two interfaces really are each other's opposites. Class `RandomAccessFile` then, if you look back at its definition, is mainly the implementation of these two interfaces. The main additional methods in `RandomAccessFile` are

- `void seek(long pos) throws IOException`

- `long getFilePointer() throws IOException`

- `long length() throws IOException`

- `void close() throws IOException`

There is no `open()` method because constructing a `RandomAccessFile` object opens the file for you. The `seek()` method is the method that reflects the class' *random access* reading and writing capability. Using `seek()` you can position the file pointer to any position within the file to read or write in any place. You are not limited to sequential reads or writes (although that's what the reading and writing methods default to). Method `getFilePointer()` lets you find out where the next read or write will occur. For a newly opened file, it is always position 0; in other words, the beginning of the file.

By now you have noticed the universal exception type used by class RandomAccessFile (and the DataInput and DataOutput interfaces), which signals a failure within any of its methods: exception IOException. The explicit throws clause at the end of every method's signature means you are required to either:

- Add explicit error-handling code to your methods that use RandomAccessFiles by enclosing any uses with a try-catch pair.

- Let the exception bubble up to your method's caller by declaring your methods to throw IOException in turn.

As an example use of this class, including the explicit handling of possible exceptions, the following program uses two RandomAccess-File objects to compare two files:

```java
import java.io.RandomAccessFile;

class Diff {

//————————————————————————————————————————————————————
// program main()
//
// check command line arg (filename)
// open & load files
// process files
// close files
//————————————————————————————————————————————————————

public static void main (String args[]) {

RandomAccessFile     fh1 = null;
RandomAccessFile     fh2 = null;

int      tail;           // difference in length
int      bufsize;        // size of smallest file
long     filesize1 = -1;
long     filesize2 = -1;
byte[]   buffer1;        // the two file caches
byte[]   buffer2;

         // check what you get as command-line arguments
```

```
if (args.length == 0 || args[0].equals("?") ) {
    System.out.println("File Diff v1.0 (c) 04/96 L. Vanhelsuwe");
    System.out.println("————");
    System.out.println("USAGE: diff <file1> <file2> | ?");
    System.out.println();

    System.exit(0);
}

    // open file ONE for reading

try {
    fh1 = new RandomAccessFile(args[0], "r");
    filesize1 = fh1.length();
        } catch (Exception ioErr) {
    System.out.println("Could not find " + args[0]);
    System.out.println( ioErr );
    System.exit(100);
}
    // open file TWO for reading

try {
    fh2 = new RandomAccessFile(args[1], "r");
    filesize2 = fh2.length();
} catch (Exception ioErr) {
    System.out.println("Could not find " + args[1]);
    System.out.println( ioErr);
    System.exit(100);
}

tail = (int) (filesize2 - filesize1);

if (tail != 0) {
    System.out.println("Files differ in size !");
    System.out.println("'" + args[0] + "' is " + filesize1 + " bytes");
    System.out.println("'" + args[1] + "' is " + filesize2 + " bytes");
}

    // allocate two buffers large enough to hold entire files

bufsize = (int) Math.min(filesize1, filesize2);
buffer1 = new byte [ bufsize ];
buffer2 = new byte [ bufsize ];

try {
    fh1.readFully(buffer1,0,bufsize);
    fh2.readFully(buffer2,0,bufsize);

        // now the HEART of the program...

    for (int i = 0; i < bufsize; i++) {
```

```
            if (buffer1[i] != buffer2[i]) {
                System.out.println ("Files differ at offset " + i);
                break;
            }
        }
    } catch (Exception ioErr) {
        System.out.println("ERROR: An exception occured while processing
        ➥the files");
        System.out.println( ioErr.toString() );
    }

    finally {
        try {
            fh1.close();
            fh2.close();
        } catch (Exception ignored) {}
    }
}}
```

The program uses a performance-enhancing trick that is often useful when processing files. It buffers the entire files in memory by reading them, in one swoop, using `readFully()`. It can be orders of magnitude quicker than reading a file bit by bit in a loop. Once the two files are cached in memory, they can be compared very quickly using simple array accesses (the nearest Java gets to the even more efficient pointer addressing of C and C++). Note how the I/O method invocations had to be surrounded by `try-catch` statements: This is because all `RandomAccessFile` methods can potentially throw an `IOException`. Because Java (quite rightly) insists programs catch potential exceptional circumstances or events, you must explicitly add error-handling code for those occasions. The alternative would be to declare the `main()` method as being able to throw an `IOException` itself. While this strategy would have made the example easier to read, it would not be a good example for you to follow. The `main()` method is the topmost method, and any exceptions it throws will only be thrown straight into the user's face. This is not acceptable, so you should opt to catch the errors explicitly and translate them into more user-friendly error messages (instead of erroneous behavior!). Because exceptions can seriously disturb an algorithm's programmed flow of control (exceptions are essentially `goto`s), you need to ensure that both files get closed under all circumstances: You do this in the `finally` statement at the end of the `main()` method. Regardless of whether exceptions occurred or not, the code within the `finally` statement will always be executed, so that statement is the perfect place to put your file `close()` calls.

I/O Streams

The invention of streams is surprisingly recent, dating back to 1984 when Dennis Ritchie (who codesigned the C language with Brian Kernighan) implemented the first stream I/O system for AT&T's Unix operating system. Software streams are linear flows of data, and, as with real rivers of water, a user can come up to a stream and sequentially fish out (in other words, read) items floating toward her, or she can throw items into the stream (that is, write) in the secure knowledge that the items will be carried to a known destination at the end of a stream. Every stream has either a data *source* (like a spring) in case of input streams or a destination (called a *sink*, like a river's delta) in the case of output streams. Both input and output streams, therefore, have in common the need to be connected to "something" before they will do any useful work. Input streams should be connected to some device producing data, and output streams should be connected to some device that can accept data (see Chapter 9).

Although the exploration of package `java.io` began by looking at classes `File` and `RandomAccessFile`, the package really consists mostly of `stream` I/O classes. It defines two root classes from which most of the package's stream subclasses are derived. Not surprisingly, they are called `InputStream` and `OutputStream`. Study these abstract classes before tackling any of the concrete `stream` classes, as all `stream` classes rely on the fundamental functionality of classes `InputStream` or `OutputStream`.

Input Streams

All input streams have the following in common: They can read bytes of data from some kind of data source. That is their core functionality: reading data in the form of bytes (and only bytes). This reading can be done on a byte-by-byte basis, or it can be done by block of arbitrary length. All other functionality encapsulated in InputStream is peripheral to this elementary reading functionality. The full definition of class InputStream goes as follows:

```
public abstract class InputStream extends Object {
    public InputStream();
    public abstract int read() throws IOException;
    public int read(byte b[]) throws IOException;
    public int read(byte b[], int off, int len) throws IOException;
    public long skip(long n) throws IOException;
    public int available() throws IOException;
    public void close() throws IOException;
    public synchronized void mark(int readlimit);
    public synchronized void reset() throws IOException;
    public boolean markSupported();
}
```

The three mark-related methods mark(), reset(), and markSupported() all deal with an *optional* input stream support for undoing read()s. All input streams should implement markSupported() but are free to return either true or false. Most return false, meaning that mark() and reset() don't do anything (or throw exceptions). Abstract class InputStream itself implements markSupported() to return false, so all classes that inherit from InputStream without overriding this method do not support marks. When the feature is supported, though, the system works as follows: You can mark any position (in an input stream) to come back to later if you want to undo the reading of data that has been read since. The readlimit argument to the mark() method determines how far you can read ahead while still legally being able to reset() the reading position to the marked position. The readlimit is expressed in bytes. It is used to internally allocate a buffer for all the data that potentially needs to be rewound. If you read past the `readlimit` and still do a `reset()`, the results are undefined.

From class `InputStream` descends a whole collection of concrete classes:

- `FileInputStream`

- `ByteArrayInputStream`

- `StringBufferInputStream`

- `SequenceInputStream`

- `PipedInputStream`

- `FilterInputStream`

    - `BufferedInputStream`

    - `DataInputStream`

    - `LineNumberInputStream`

    - `PushbackInputStream`

All these classes have one thing in common (apart from being subclasses of `InputStream`): All their constructors let you specify a data source in one way or other. In the case of the `File-`, `ByteArray-`, `StringBuffer-`, `Sequence-`, and `PipedInputStream` classes, this data source is the attribute that differentiates that class from the others in that list. A `FileInputStream`, for example, is just that because the data stream that flows from it is sourced from a file that is part of your machine's filing system. In the same way, a `PipedInputStream` is just that because the stream that flows from it is sourced from a *pipe* (pipes are explained later in the chapter). And so on...

All the `FilterInputStream` descendants have a very different purpose. Their constructors also allow you to specify a data source, but this is in the form of *another* input stream as the source for the stream. Now, if you think about it, if that was all `FilterInput-Streams` could do, there would be little point in them; they would simply pass on the data unmodified. But the purpose of `Filter-InputStreams` is not to connect to any *specific* data source (like the previous classes) but to *enhance* streams. Streams can be enhanced either by altering the stream's data itself (for example, by compressing it) or by adding handy features to the minimal functionality enshrined in class `InputStream`.

FileInputStream

Class `FileInputStream` is an input stream whose data is sourced from an everyday file. As such, you could consider it as (nearly) half of class `RandomAccessFile`, which allows you to read *and* write files. You could use two `FileInputStream` objects to implement the featured file difference program with equal ease. The constructors for class `FileInputStream` are what the class really adds to the abstract class `InputStream`:

- `public FileInputStream(String name) throws FileNotFoundException`

- `public FileInputStream(File file) throws FileNotFoundException`

These constructors create a new `FileInputStream` object and at the same time open the file, ready for reading. The first constructor takes a filename as a `String`, but you should avoid doing this if the filename has any platform-dependent characters in it. (An example is if you specify a file in a subdirectory of the current directory. This would work on Unix-style filing systems, but not on MS-DOS–based machines.) The second constructor is the one more commonly employed: It takes a platform-independent `File` object describing which file needs to be accessed. Here is a program that uses the `FileInputStream` class to read a text file and calculate its word frequencies:

```
import java.io.*            ;
import java.util.Hashtable  ;
import java.util.Enumeration;

class WC {

public static void main(String args[]) throws IOException {

WordFrequencyCounter wfr;
FileInputStream      longText;
StreamTokenizer      wordStream;
String               word;
int                  tok;

    if (args.length != 1) {
        System.out.println( "Usage: wc <textfile>" );
        System.exit(10);
    }

    wfr        = new WordFrequencyCounter();

    longText   = new FileInputStream( args[0] );
    wordStream = new StreamTokenizer( longText );

        // treat any punctuation as word delimiters

    wordStream.whitespaceChars('!','@');

    while( (tok = wordStream.nextToken()) != StreamTokenizer.TT_EOF ) {
        if (tok == StreamTokenizer.TT_WORD ) {
            word = wordStream.sval;
            wfr.count( word );
        }
    }

    Enumeration e = wfr.keys();
    while ( e.hasMoreElements() ) {
        word = (String) e.nextElement();
        System.out.println( wfr.frequency(word) + " " + word );
    }
}}
//————————————————————————————————————————————————
class WordFrequencyCounter extends Hashtable {

        // no constructor needed, this class is just a fancy Hashtable

        //————————————————————————————————————————
```

```
// first see if this word has already been encountered
// if not then create a fresh counter for it
// otherwise increment its counter
//────────────────────────────────────────────────────────

public synchronized int count (String word) {

Integer counter;

    counter = (Integer) get(word);
    if (counter == null) {
        counter = new Integer(1);
    } else {
        counter = new Integer( counter.intValue() + 1);
    }
    put(word, counter);
    return counter.intValue();
}

//────────────────────────────────────────────────────────
// find out how many times this word has been encountered
//────────────────────────────────────────────────────────

public synchronized int frequency (String word) {

Integer counter;

    counter = (Integer) get(word);
    if (counter == null) {
        return 0;
    } else {
        return counter.intValue();
    }
}} // End of class WordFrequencyCounter
```

The program consists of two classes: the main driver class WC (standing for *Word Counter*, in case you were wondering) and a thoroughly reusable WordFrequencyCounter class. The main class (WC) opens the file specified as a command-line argument by creating a FileInputStream object. It then passes that object straight on to another java.io class: StreamTokenizer (this class is discussed later in the chapter). Class StreamTokenizer takes an input stream as argument to its constructor and then allows you to have the stream tokenized. In this case, *tokenized* simply means chopped up into its constituent words. StreamTokenizer method nextToken() divides the file stream up into words and makes the stream of words available via the StreamTokenizer instance variable sval (String value). The individual words thus extracted from the stream are then passed on to the WordFrequencyCounter object, whose duty it is to keep track of which words have already been encountered and, if so, how many times. It keeps track by relying heavily on the functionality provided by class Hashtable, part of package java.util. A Java Hashtable implements a *dictionary* data structure. Dictionaries consist of paired entries, the first half called the *key*, the second half called the *value*. You use a dictionary to track the number of occurrences of each word, because dictionary keys cannot occur more than once. Therefore, the word itself is the key to the dictionary entry, with the count being the value of the entry. Although the word count need only be a humble integer, Java Hashtables require objects for both keys and values. Primitive datatypes (like boolean, char, int) are not supported. That's the reason you should use a heavyweight Integer object instead, to hold the counter. The main Hashtable methods are put(key, value) and get(key). Because the WordFrequencyCounter class extends Hashtable, it is able to use these methods unqualified, in other words acting on itself (the this object reference is implied).

There's one more interesting aspect to this program: To actually list every encountered word, along with its associated frequency, the program uses the enumerating capability of all Hashtables. The last four lines of class WC's main() method reflect the standard Java idiom for enumerating or listing every element of some collection. The code relies on the Enumeration interface, whose definition is

```
public interface Enumeration extends Object {
    public abstract boolean hasMoreElements();
    public abstract Object nextElement() throws NoSuchElementException;
}
```

Any object of type `Enumeration` will obey the two methods of the definition: `hasMoreElements()` and `nextElement()`. Using these two methods, it then becomes a simple matter to construct a generic list-processing loop of the form

```
Enumeration e = <any Enumeration object>;
while ( e.hasMoreElements() ) {
    <anObject> = (<cast>) e.nextElement();
  <process anObject>
}
```

And if you look back at the `main()` method, that is exactly what `main()` did to list the text file's words and their frequencies.

ByteArrayInputStream and StringBufferInputStream

Both these classes are virtually identical. They both create input streams from strings of bytes. `ByteArrayInputStream` does this literally, from an array of bytes, while `StringBufferInputStream` uses a String (and *not* a `StringBuffer`) as its array of bytes. Because Java Strings are essentially arrays of Java `chars` (in other words, 16-bit wide Unicode characters), you might well wonder how the resulting byte (input) stream is structured: low byte first or high byte first? Well, neither. `StringBufferInputStream` *discards* the high byte of the Unicode characters. While this is fine for Java characters in the range 0 to 255, all other characters that make use of Unicode's vastly expanded encoding space will lose information or be corrupted in the String-to-stream transformation.

The main constructors for the two classes are as follows:

- `public ByteArrayInputStream( byte buf[] )`

- `public StringBufferInputStream( String s )`

> **WARNING**
>
> There is one major but subtle difference between the two classes. Both classes do not copy their respective input data into internal buffers. Therefore, in the case of `ByteArrayInputStream`, the source array might be modified at any time while the stream is being used. This type of conflict can be the source of very hard-to-find bugs. This problem cannot occur for `StringBufferInputStreams` because the source String can never be modified "under the stream's nose." For this reason alone, it is safer to always convert a byte array that will be used as a stream into a String by using the String constructor `String(byte[] array, int hibyte)`.

We'll use both `ByteArrayInputStream` and `StringBufferInput-Stream` objects in the example for the next class: `SequenceInputStream`.

SequenceInputStream

Class `SequenceInputStream` allows you to seamlessly glue together two or more input streams to create one long, concatenated stream. Whenever you read from such a "super" stream and an EOF is encountered by one of the building block streams, class `SequenceInputStream` proceeds to the next stream in the list (*without* letting the EOF reach you). Only when the last input stream is exhausted do you get an EOF (a -1 returned by `read()`). The constructors give you two ways of specifying the sequence of streams:

- `public SequenceInputStream(InputStream s1, Input-Stream s2)`

- `public SequenceInputStream(Enumeration e)`

The first form is convenient when you only need to glue two input streams together. The second form is more general in its ability to take an open-ended list of input streams. The required argument type is rather surprising, though: You would expect a type-safe array of `InputStream` (for example, `InputStream[] list`) to be the ideal way to specify an ordered list of `InputStreams`. Instead, a much fuzzier `Enumeration` object is expected. As you saw earlier, any `Enumeration` object has to implement the `hasMoreElements()` and `nextElement()` methods. You might think this means you need to create a brand-new class that implements interface `Enumeration` simply to specify a list of input streams to this constructor, but there's an easier work-around: Declare a simple Vector in which you `addElement()` the sequence of `InputStreams`, and then use the Vector method `elements()` to get an `Enumeration` object that will do the trick. The following program demonstrates the technique while also gluing together a `ByteArrayInputStream`, a `StringBuffer-InputStream`, and a `FileInputStream` to remind you of the considerable flexibility hiding in any system needing "any `InputStream`," like `SequenceInputStream`:

```java
import java.io.*   ;
import java.util.* ;

class Sequenced {

static final int EOF = -1;

static final String htmlHeader = "<HTML><HEAD></HEAD><BODY><PRE>\n";
static final byte[] array     = {
                    '\n','<','/','P','R','E','>'
                   ,'<','/','B','O','D','Y','>'
                   ,'<','/','H','T','M','L','>'
                };

public static void main(String args[]) throws IOException {

FileInputStream         fis;
StringBufferInputStream sbis;
ByteArrayInputStream    bais;
SequenceInputStream     altogether;
int ch;

    fis  = new FileInputStream( args[0] );
    sbis = new StringBufferInputStream( htmlHeader );
    bais = new ByteArrayInputStream( array );
```

```
Vector inputStreamList = new Vector(3);
inputStreamList.addElement( sbis );
inputStreamList.addElement( fis );
inputStreamList.addElement( bais );

altogether = new SequenceInputStream( inputStreamList.elements() );
do {
    ch = altogether.read();
    if (ch != EOF) {
        System.out.print( (char)ch );
    }
} while (ch != EOF);
System.out.flush();
}}
```

SequenceInputStream's approach of using other input streams as building blocks is a common technique used with the java.io classes. All the filtering streams (descendants of the FilterInputStream and FilterOutputStream classes) rely on exactly this principle to achieve a clean and powerful stream-combination functionality.

Note also how the do-while Java loop was constructed to read all the bytes from the sequenced input stream.

WARNING

Computer science identifies only three fundamental iteration types: the for loop, the while loop, and the repeat-until loop. repeat-until loops (implemented by the Java do-while) are rarely necessary because theoretically any repeat-until can be implemented using the more general while loop. A do-while was used in the previous example only to highlight how easy it is to get confused between the end of a do-while and the beginning of a while. while loops are so frequently used in C, C++, and Java, that do-whiles should be outlawed (at least in C and C++, using their preprocessor, you can quickly create textual substitution macros like #define repeat do and #define until(x) while(!(x))). It's a real shame that Java's designers didn't use their once-in-a-lifetime language architects' prerogative to eliminate that awkward and dangerously named C-style repeat-until: the Java do-while.

PipedInputStream

Pipes are another Unix invention. In fact, the concept is very close to the stream concept, except that the application of pipes is less generic. Pipes are (typically) used when two different processes (or tasks, or threads) need to communicate large(ish) amounts of data in a synchronized fashion. Remember from Chapter 8 that one of the most difficult aspects of using multiple threads is their synchronization. Few multithreaded systems can avoid the need, at one time or other, to have some threads rendezvous for whatever purpose. If that purpose is the exchange of data, then pipes can be used to cleanly solve the problem. A less technical example is the use of the vertical bar character | (pipe) to chain together programs at the Unix or DOS command prompts. For example:

```
C:\> DIR | SORT | MORE
```

would create two pipes, the first connecting the output of the DIR command to the input of the SORT command. The second pipe would similarly connect the output of SORT to the input of MORE. The result would be a directory listing that gets sorted by the MORE utility before being displayed page by page.

Class `PipedInputStream` requires you to connect it with another pipe, an instance of `PipedOutputStream`. The two classes can only be used with each other and are useless without one another. Their respective constructors are as follows:

- `public PipedInputStream(PipedOutputStream src)`
  `throws IOException`

- `public PipedOutputStream(PipedInputStream snk)`
  `throws IOException`

Perfect symmetry! (Don't you just love it when software is this beautiful?) If you analyze these constructors long enough, you will notice that something is in fact missing: How do you create a connection between two pipes if you need to pass the (already constructed) instance of the other type as argument to the constructor? It's a catch-22 situation that you have to bypass using one of the other types of pipe constructor:

- `public PipedInputStream()`

- `public PipedOutputStream()`

These two constructors allow you to create a pipe object that isn't connected yet. To complete the actual connection, you call the respective `PipedInputStream` or `PipedOutputStream` `connect()` method.

The following program demonstrates the use of the piped stream classes in their useful context: interthread communication. The program has a distinct oil industry flavor to it (or should that be smell?); it uses the image of a crude oil tanker that finds an oil refinery, connects itself up to the refinery using pipes (the subject of this section), and transfers its crude to the refinery to be processed and returned back on board as an unspecified refined substance. Here's the program bringing this image to life:

```
import java.io.*;

class PipeTest {

public static void main (String[] args) {

    new OilRefinery();
    new SuperTanker();

}} // End of class PipeTest

//————————————————————————————————————
// This class consists of a Thread that can accept "pipeline" hook-ups
// via the "clickClunk" method. Clients have to find us, though.
//————————————————————————————————————
class OilRefinery extends Thread {

final static int EOF = -1;

static boolean alone = true;

PipedInputStream   inPipe = new PipedInputStream();
PipedOutputStream outPipe = new PipedOutputStream();
```

```
//─────────────────────────────────────────────────────────────
public OilRefinery() {
    start();                    // start the separate Thread
}
//─────────────────────────────────────────────────────────────
public void run() {

int ch;

        // put up the neon sign
    Thread.currentThread().setName("ThePipeTerminal");

    System.out.println("Processing plant operational and on-line.");

    while(alone) {
        try {Thread.sleep(500); } catch (Exception ohLeaveMeAlone) {}
    }
        // at this point a client has connected up to the pipes, so process
        // the flow of oil.

    try {
        while ((ch = inPipe.read()) != EOF) {

            // add some value to raw input..
            outPipe.write( Character.toUpperCase( (char) ch) );
        }
    } catch (IOException pipeMalfunction) {}

    try {
        outPipe.close();    // signal client "the show's over!"
    } catch (IOException ignored) {}

    System.out.println("Processing plant shutting down for maintenance work.");
}
//─────────────────────────────────────────────────────────────
// This is the method clients have to call to connect up to our
// "processing plant."
//─────────────────────────────────────────────────────────────

public boolean clickClunk (PipedOutputStream clientOutputPipe,
                           PipedInputStream  clientInputPipe ) {

    System.out.println("Client arrives to hook up his pipes..");

    try {
        clientOutputPipe.connect(inPipe);
        inPipe.connect(clientOutputPipe);

        clientInputPipe.connect(outPipe);
        outPipe.connect(clientInputPipe);
    } catch (IOException connectionFailed) {
        System.out.println("Hook up failed..");
```

```
        return false;
    }

    System.out.println("Hook-up successful..");
    alone = false;      // signal main loop that you need to go to work.
    return true;        // all systems GO!
}
} // End of class OilRefinery

//────────────────────────────────────────────────────
// This class implements a processing plant client, say a supertanker
// that arrives at the plant to unload its crude oil and load up with
// refined oil.
//────────────────────────────────────────────────────
class SuperTanker {

OilRefinery pipeTerminal = null;
PipedInputStream  returnPipe = new PipedInputStream();
PipedOutputStream crudePipe  = new PipedOutputStream();

//────────────────────────────────────────────────────
public SuperTanker() {

    pipeTerminal = (OilRefinery) findThread("ThePipeTerminal");

    if (pipeTerminal == null) {
        System.out.println(
            "Snow blizzards prevented rendez-vous with processing plant!");
        System.exit(10);
    }

    if ( pipeTerminal.clickClunk( crudePipe, returnPipe)) {
        haveOilProcessed();
    } else {
        System.out.println("Failed to connect pipes to processing plant.");
    }

    try {
        crudePipe.close();
    } catch (IOException brokenValves) {
        System.out.println("Couldn't close valves on output pipe!");
    }
}
//────────────────────────────────────────────────────
// Send data (oil) to processing plant thread, which refines the data
// and sends it back via a second pipe stream.
//────────────────────────────────────────────────────
public void haveOilProcessed() {

byte[] oilToBeRefined = {'C','r','u','d','e',' ','O','i','l'};
int ch;

    try {
```

```
        crudePipe.write(oilToBeRefined);
        crudePipe.close();                // that's all you have today!

        while ((ch = returnPipe.read()) != -1) {
            System.out.print( (char)ch );
        }
        System.out.println();
    } catch (IOException oilFlowFailure) {
        System.out.println("Pipe malfuction.");
    }
}
//————————————————————————————————————————————————————————————
// This generic method hunts down a Thread by its name and returns a
// reference to it. Note that the targeted Thread can die in the
// meantime.
//————————————————————————————————————————————————————————————
public Thread findThread (String targetThread) {

int SAFETY_MARGIN = 10;

ThreadGroup[]    threadGroupList = null;
ThreadGroup      aThreadGroup;
ThreadGroup      rootGroup = Thread.currentThread().getThreadGroup();

Thread[]         threadList      = null;
Thread           aThread;

    // first find the master ThreadGroup from which all others descend

    while (rootGroup.getParent() != null) {
        rootGroup = rootGroup.getParent();
    }
    threadGroupList = new ThreadGroup[ rootGroup.activeGroupCount() + SAFETY_MARGIN ];
    rootGroup.enumerate(threadGroupList, false);

    for(int tg=0; tg < threadGroupList.length; tg++) {
        aThreadGroup = threadGroupList[tg];

        if ( aThreadGroup == null) continue;

        threadList = new Thread[ aThreadGroup.activeCount() + SAFETY_MARGIN ];
        aThreadGroup.enumerate(threadList, false);

        for(int thr=0; thr < threadList.length; thr++) {
            aThread = threadList[thr];

            if ( aThread == null) continue;

            if ( aThread.getName().equals( targetThread )) {
                return aThread;
            }
```

```
        }    // end of for (all threads)
    }        // end of for (all threadGroups)

    return null;
}
} // End of class SuperTanker
```

The program is interesting for more than its use of `PipedInput-` and `PipedOutputStreams`. Have a close look at what goes on in this tongue-in-cheek simulation: First of all, the main program just creates two instances of the main classes in the program: `OilRefinery` and `SuperTanker`. As the `main()` method clearly shows, neither object receives a reference to the other, so initially both objects are completely independent.

If you look at what the `OilRefinery` object does when it is constructed, it just `start()`s itself up as an independent thread (class `OilRefinery` can do this because it is a subclass of Thread). Starting up the thread means that the constructor returns immediately and that the `run()` method of the `OilRefinery` starts executing. The body of the `OilRefinery` thread explicitly labels its own thread so other entities in the same Java Virtual Machine can rendezvous with it. It then goes into a semi-sleep state that waits for a client (a `SuperTanker` ship) to arrive and request its service.

Now switch perspectives and look at what the `SuperTanker` object has been up to until now. If you follow its constructor, you'll see it begins by finding the `OilRefinery` thread by scanning all `Thread-Groups` and all Threads contained by those (we'll discuss the operation of the `findThread()` method later—consider it a black box for the moment). Once found, it hands the `OilRefinery` object two pipe objects: a `PipedOutputStream` for the crude and a `PipedInput-Stream` for the processed oil the `OilRefinery` will return to the supertanker. The `OilRefinery` takes those two pipes (via its `ClickClunk()` method) and connects these pipes up to its own processing input and output pipes. Then a tanker output pipe connects to the plant's input pipe and a plant's output pipe connects back to another tanker input pipe (see Figure 15.2 for a graphic representation of the connections).

FIGURE 15.2:

PipedInputStreams
and PipedOutput-
Streams in a realistic
scenario

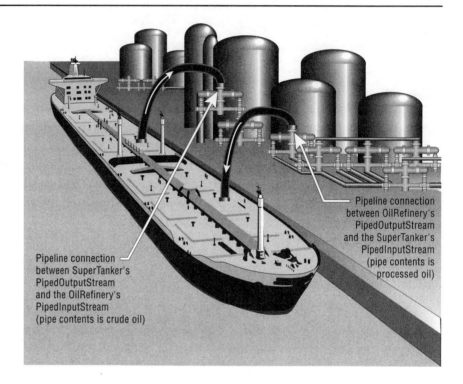

Pipeline connection
between OilRefinery's
PipedOutputStream
and the SuperTanker's
PipedInputStream
(pipe contents is
processed oil)

Pipeline connection
between SuperTanker's
PipedOutputStream
and the OilRefinery's
PipedInputStream
(pipe contents is crude oil)

As part of the clickClunk() method, the OilRefinery wakes up its main thread by changing the state of a boolean. Meanwhile, the SuperTanker object starts its main transfer of crude in the haveOil-Processed() method. The key statement here is the write() invocation on the output PipedOutputStream. This data eventually finds its way to the read() on the OilRefinery's PipedInputStream. To symbolize the oil refinery process, the received data (the string of bytes reading *Crude Oil*) gets changed to all uppercase. These "processed" bytes are then sent out of the refinery and back to the ship via a write() to the OilRefinery's PipedOutputStream. These bytes are then received and printed by the SuperTanker.

A key detail in this interaction is that any writing entity has to signal the other party that there is no more data by *closing* the output stream. The SuperTanker object does this straight after the write()

to its `PipedOutputStream` and the `OilRefinery` similarly does a `close()` after it has detected the end of data on its input stream. This is the only way the receiving end can get an end-of-file indication that allows it to break out of its reading loop.

Now that the two pipe stream classes have been explained, look at how the `SuperTanker` object managed to rendezvous with the `OilRefinery` thread. Any thread running on a Java Virtual Machine is part of a hierarchical collection of `ThreadGroups`. To find a given thread, you therefore have to first find the top of this `ThreadGroup` (tree) hierarchy so you can then *traverse* the entire tree in search of the thread you are after. This is what the `findThread()` method does in class `SuperTanker`. The method relies on two key methods: `getParent()` in class `ThreadGroup` to (stepwise) find the top of the `ThreadGroup` hierarchy, and `enumerate()` in both Thread and `ThreadGroup` to list all instances of Threads and `ThreadGroups`, respectively.

You have now seen all input stream classes characterized by their requirement to connect to specific data sources. Turn now to another branch of input stream classes whose emphasis is very different.

FilterInputStream

Class `FilterInputStream` is a pseudo-abstract class that acts as the superclass for the `java.io` classes `BufferedInputStream`, `DataInputStream`, `LineNumberInputStream`, and `PushbackInputStream`. It is pseudo-abstract because it is neither instantiable nor really abstract in the absolute sense. The class itself is not declared `abstract` and neither are any of its methods, as you can see (therefore it is not *strictly* abstract):

```
public class FilterInputStream extends InputStream {
    protected InputStream in;
    protected FilterInputStream(InputStream in);
    public int read() throws IOException;
    public int read(byte b[]) throws IOException;
```

```
    public int read(byte b[], int off, int len) throws IOException;
    public long skip(long n) throws IOException;
    public int available() throws IOException;
    public void close() throws IOException;
    public synchronized void mark(int readlimit);
    public synchronized void reset() throws IOException;
    public boolean markSupported();
}
```

The key to its pseudo-abstractness is the `protected` constructor. Because of this constructor, normal clients cannot do a `new FilterInputStream()`; only subclasses can invoke the constructor (using the `super()` syntax).

At first sight, you might wonder exactly what this class adds to a vanilla `InputStream`. Its definition looks suspiciously like that of `InputStream`. The answer lies in the *design* of the constructor. `FilterInputStream` descendants all take *another* `InputStream` as their data source (instead of a String or a File or a byte array, as with the previous `InputStream` classes you studied):

```
protected FilterInputStream(InputStream in)
```

As explained in the introduction to input streams, this simple, generic design allows unlimited input stream enhancements to be implemented by various subclasses. Moreover, it allows input stream enhancements to be layered one on top of the other. Before you look at the concrete enhancements encapsulated in package `java.io`'s `FilterInputStream` subclasses, we will subclass `FilterInput-Stream` to create an example of an enhanced input stream class. This demonstration will make it easier to understand the predefined subclasses, which you will study a bit later.

The goal is to create an input stream class that can read data as a *bit* stream instead of a *byte* stream. In keeping with the fairly consistent nomenclature employed in package `java.io`, the new class is named `BitStreamInputStream`. The new, flexible input unit supported in this class will be the *bit field*. Bitfields have a length in bits, and this class will support lengths of 1 to 32 bits.

NOTE The upper limit of 32 bits is determined by the read method requirement of being able to signal an end-of-file using the same −1 as InputStream's `read()` (for consistency's sake). The difference here being that a `long` (and not an `int`) is needed to encode a −1 that is *out of band* from the normal bitfield data stream, which can produce data chunks up to `int` size (out of band means not part of the normal data). This is perfectly analogous with `InputStream`'s `read()` needing to return an integer so that it can encode −1 without confusing this with a 255 ($FF) byte (which is also −1 in two's complement notation).

Note that a length of 8 bits simply boils down to turning the bit stream into a byte stream again. Bitfields can be aligned on arbitrary bit boundaries, and a `BitStreamInputStream` client can alter the current bitfield size at any point while reading the stream. Such a class (and its output counterpart, presented later in the output classes section) can be the foundation for data (de)compression and image-file encoding and decoding algorithms. Both these types of applications need to divorce themselves from the universal byte-oriented storage unit and descend to the more primitive (but more powerful) level of bits and arbitrarily aligned bitfields.

Here's how the API of the `BitStreamInputStream` class looks:

```
public class BitStreamInputStream extends FilterInputStream {
    public BitStreamInputStream(InputStream in);
    public BitStreamInputStream(InputStream in, int bitFieldSize);
    public void setBitFieldSize(int bits) throws IllegalArgumentException;
    public int getBitFieldSize();
    public long readBitField() throws IOException;
    public int read() throws IOException;
}
```

Two constructors are provided; the default constructor simply creates a bit input stream with the bitfield size set to 8. In other words, it defaults to a normal byte input stream. The second constructor allows you to specify the initial bitfield size for the bit stream (you can later alter this at any time using `setBitFieldSize()`). The core method that implements this new stream model is `readBitField()`. Its function is completely analogous to `InputStream`'s vanilla

> read(), except that it will fetch the next n-bit bitfield from the stream. You also override read(), which still reads an 8-bit byte, except that it can now be done on any *bit* boundary. Here is the implementation of the class:

```
//——————————————————————————————————————————————————————————
// Class BitStreamInputStream implements an enhanced InputStream, which
// allows you to read the stream as a stream of bitfields ranging in
// size from 1 bit (a true bit stream) to 32 bits (a stream of integers).
// The size of the current bitfield can be changed at any point while
// reading the stream.
//——————————————————————————————————————————————————————————

import java.io.*;

public class BitStreamInputStream extends FilterInputStream {

final static int EIGHT = 8;      // 8 bits per byte

protected short buffer;          // the BYTE bitstream read-ahead buffer :-)
                                 // declared as short to cope with -1 EOF

protected int bitsInCache;       // how many unread bits left in the byte?

protected int fieldSize;         // current size of bitstream read fields

//——————————————————————————————————————————————————————————
public BitStreamInputStream(InputStream in) {
    this(in, EIGHT);             // default to a normal byte stream
}
//——————————————————————————————————————————————————————————
public BitStreamInputStream(InputStream in, int bitFieldSize) {
    super(in);
    setBitFieldSize(bitFieldSize);
    bitsInCache = 0;             // you haven't got any cached bits
}
//——————————————————————————————————————————————————————————
public void setBitFieldSize(int bits) throws IllegalArgumentException {

    if (bits>32 || bits<1) throw new IllegalArgumentException(
      "BitField size ("+ bits + ") no good. Has to be between 1 and 32.");

    this.fieldSize = bits;
}
//——————————————————————————————————————————————————————————
public int getBitFieldSize() {

    return this.fieldSize;
}
//——————————————————————————————————————————————————————————
// Read a bitfield from the input stream. The number of bits read is the
```

```
// current bitfield length. Bitfield can be on arbitrary bit boundaries.
//————————————————————————————————————————————————————————————————————————
public long readBitField() throws IOException {

int bitField = 0;                    // what we're going to return to caller
int bitsToRead;
int availableNumberOfBits;
int OR_position = 0;
int alignedBFPartial;

    bitsToRead = fieldSize;
    OR_position = fieldSize;

    while (bitsToRead > 0) {

        if (bitsInCache == 0) {
            if ( (buffer = (short) in.read()) == -1) return -1;  // reached EOF
            bitsInCache = EIGHT;   // there's a full byte in there again
        }
        availableNumberOfBits = Math.min( bitsToRead, bitsInCache );
        OR_position -= availableNumberOfBits;
        alignedBFPartial = buffer >> ( EIGHT - availableNumberOfBits);

        buffer <<= availableNumberOfBits;       // keep next partial aligned
        buffer &= 255;                          // and clean

        bitField |= alignedBFPartial << OR_position;     // add bitfield subfield

        bitsInCache -= availableNumberOfBits;   // track # of cached bits
        bitsToRead  -= availableNumberOfBits;   // track how much left to do
    }
    return bitField;
}
//————————————————————————————————————————————————————————————————————————
// Overridden read() still reads a byte, but on any bit boundary!
//————————————————————————————————————————————————————————————————————————
public int read() throws IOException {
int previousBFSize;
int theByte;

    previousBFSize = getBitFieldSize();
    setBitFieldSize( EIGHT );
    try {
        theByte = (int) readBitField();
    }
    finally {
        setBitFieldSize( previousBFSize );
    }
    return theByte;
}
} // End of class BitStreamInputStream
```

The detailed workings of the readBitField() method involves a lot of bit twiddling and shuffling, which is secondary to the purpose of the example (which is to show the principle of subclassing abstract class FilterInputStream to enhance the generic behavior defined by InputStream). Now just add a short test program that puts class BitStreamInputStream through its paces:

```java
import java.io.*;

class BSTest {

public static void main (String[] args) throws IOException {

BitStreamInputStream bsis;

    for (int bfSize = 1; bfSize <= 32; bfSize++) {
        bsis = new BitStreamInputStream(
                    new FileInputStream("test.dat"), bfSize);

        System.out.println("First 5 bitfields of length " + bfSize + ":");

        for (int i=0; i<5; i++) {
            int bits = (int) bsis.readBitField();
            System.out.println( toBinary(bits, bfSize) + "  (" + bits + ")" );
        }
        System.out.println("PRESS return to continue..");
        System.in.read();
    }
}
static String toBinary (int num, int digits) {
StringBuffer bitString = new StringBuffer( Integer.toString(num, 2) );

    while (bitString.length() < digits) {
        bitString.insert(0, '0');
    }
    return bitString.toString();
}
}
}
```

This program reads the external file test.dat with the new BitStreamInputStream class, using the full range of supported bit-field sizes. The test file contains the following test data (listed in hex-dump format):

```
0000: 61 73 6C 64 6B 66 6A 61 91 73 6C 6B 64 9B 61 73    asldkfja.slkd.as
0010: 64 66 61 73 C4 64 66 61 73 64 67 C8 61 73 64 66    dfas.dfasdg.asdf
0020: 68 D2 2C 6E 6D 74 72 65 DC 77 2C 32 33 38 34 E6    h.,nmtre.w,2384.
0030: 35 37 36 37 FF 31 30 32 FF 2D 39 33 34 3D 2D 0D    5767.102.-934=-.
```

```
0040: 0A 61 73 6C 64 6B 66 6A 61 91 73 6C 6B 64 9B 61    .asldkfja.slkd.a
0050: 73 64 66 61 73 C4 64 66 61 73 64 67 C8 61 73 64    sdfas.dfasdg.asd
0060: 66 68 D2 2C 6E 6D 74 72 65 DC 77 2C 32 33 38 34    fh.,nmtre.w,2384
0070: E6 35 37 36 37 FF 31 30 32 FF 2D 39 33 34 3D 2D    .5767.102.-934=-
0080: 0D 0A 0D 0A    ....
```

When you run the test program, you should see the following output:

```
First 5 bitfields of length 1:
0  (0)
1  (1)
1  (1)
0  (0)
0  (0)
PRESS return to continue..

First 5 bitfields of length 2:
01  (1)
10  (2)
00  (0)
01  (1)
01  (1)
PRESS return to continue..

First 5 bitfields of length 3:
011  (3)
000  (0)
010  (2)
111  (7)
001  (1)
PRESS return to continue..

First 5 bitfields of length 4:
0110  (6)
0001  (1)
0111  (7)
0011  (3)
0110  (6)
PRESS return to continue..

       < output for bitfield lengths 5-30 cut for brevity >

First 5 bitfields of length 31:
0110000101110011011011000110010  (817477170)
0011010110110011001101010011000  (450468504)
```

```
0110010001011100110110110001101    (841903501)
0110110010010011011011000010111    (910800407)
0011011001000110011001100001011    (455291659)
PRESS return to continue..

First 5 bitfields of length 32:
01100001011100110110110001100100    (1634954340)
01101011011001100110101001100001    (1801874017)
-1101110100011001001001110010101    (-1854706581)
01100100100110110110000101110011    (1687904627)
01100100011001100110000101110011    (1684431219)
```

It is left as an exercise to convince yourself of the validity of these results.

Note the `toBinary()` method that converts a number to a leading-zeroes–padded string, achieved by building on the basic `toString-(number, base)` Integer class method (which, annoyingly, outputs strings without leading zeroes).

Now that you have seen an example of how easy it is to subclass `FilterInputStream`, look at what package `java.io` provides you in terms of standard, enhanced input stream classes. With the insights gained by creating your own `FilterInputStream` subclass, these predefined classes should now be easy to understand.

BufferedInputStream

Class `BufferedInputStream` enhances bare-bones `InputStream` in such a fundamental way, it should have been incorporated into `InputStream` itself. `BufferedInputStream` simply adds a *read buffer* to `InputStream`, which usually improves reading performance significantly. To demonstrate the speed-up, here's a program that uses a vanilla `FileInputStream` to read in the whole file, byte by byte:

```
import java.io.*;

class Unbuffered {

public static void main (String args[]) {
```

```
InputStream inputStream;
int ch;

    System.out.println("Start !");

    try {
        inputStream = new FileInputStream( args[0] );
        while ( (ch=inputStream.read()) != -1) {
            // read entire file
        }
    } catch (Exception ioErr) {
        System.out.println( ioErr.toString() );
        System.exit(100);
    }

    System.out.println("Stop !");
}}
```

When you run this program on a reasonably large file (for example, Windows 95's COMMAND.COM, 92,870 bytes), it takes 16 seconds to simply read in every byte. Now if you change the InputStream assignment line into the following two lines:

```
FileInputStream fis = new FileInputStream( args[0] );
inputStream = new BufferedInputStream( fis );
```

the time has been reduced to less than 3 seconds! A five-fold improvement. Clearly, taking the trouble to "wrap" nonbuffered input streams up in an instance of a BufferedInputStream pays off handsomely. The exact performance gain is determined by the size of the buffer that is used by the BufferedInputStream object. While the example program uses the default constructor (resulting in a default, but undefined, buffer size being used), you can explicitly set the buffer size, at constructor time, by using the second constructor with the following, predictable signature:

```
public BufferedInputStream(InputStream in, int size)
```

Class BufferedInputStream is also one of the few standard java.io classes that implements the mark and reset mechanism.

DataInputStream

Remember the `DataInput` interface discussed as part of class `RandomAccessFile`? Well, here's the only other class that implements this interface: class `DataInputStream`. This `RandomAccessFile`/`DataInputStream` kinship also exists in the output branch of the `java.io` classes: Class `DataOutputStream` implements interface `DataOutput`, which was also implemented by `RandomAccessFile`. Therefore, there's a data-format compatibility between data written by `RandomAccessFile` and data read back in by `DataInputStream`, or, conversely, data written by `DataOutput-Stream` can be read back via a `RandomAccessFile`. In practice though, this cross-communication does not occur often because data will be written and read back using the naturally corresponding class, most often simply `DataOutputStream` and `DataInputStream`.

Here is the definition of class `DataInputStream`:

```
public class DataInputStream extends FilterInputStream implements DataInput {
    public DataInputStream(InputStream in);
    public final int read(byte b[]) throws IOException;
    public final int read(byte b[], int off, int len) throws IOException;
    public final void readFully(byte b[]) throws IOException;
    public final void readFully(byte b[], int off, int len) throws IOException;
    public final int skipBytes(int n) throws IOException;
    public final boolean readBoolean() throws IOException;
    public final byte readByte() throws IOException;
    public final int readUnsignedByte() throws IOException;
    public final short readShort() throws IOException;
    public final int readUnsignedShort() throws IOException;
    public final char readChar() throws IOException;
    public final int readInt() throws IOException;
    public final long readLong() throws IOException;
    public final float readFloat() throws IOException;
    public final double readDouble() throws IOException;
    public final String readLine() throws IOException;
    public final String readUTF() throws IOException;
    public final static String readUTF(DataInput in) throws IOException;
}
```

The DataInput interface implicitly specifies that implementing classes should handle end-of-file differently than by simply returning -1 (EOF is used to denote end of stream, not just files). Instead, methods should throw an EOFException object (class EOFException is a subclass of IOException; this is why the definition does not talk about EOFException). This means that a different coding template can be used to read streams via a DataInputStream: You can simply implement an endless loop that does not check for EOF, and rely on exception catching code to correctly handle the EOF condition. The following program demonstrates this:

```java
import java.io.*;

class EOF {

public static void main(String[] args) {

DataInputStream is;
byte ch;

    try {

        is = new DataInputStream(new FileInputStream("EOF.java"));

        while (true) {  // no need to check for EOF: exception deals with it

            ch = is.readByte();
            System.out.print( (char) ch );
            System.out.flush();
        }

    } catch (EOFException eof) {
        System.out.println(" —> Normal program termination.");
    } catch (FileNotFoundException noFile) {
        System.out.println("File not found! " + noFile);
    } catch (IOException io) {
        System.out.println("I/O error occurred: " + io);
    } catch (Throwable anything) {
        System.out.println("Abnormal exception caught !: " + anything);
    }
}} // End of Class EOF
```

Aside from this cleaner approach to handling end-of-stream conditions, the most useful feature of class DataInputStream is the following method:

```java
public final String readLine() throws IOException
```

As a lot of real-life input processing is done on ASCII text files, it usually is much easier to approach a text stream as a stream of lines. By wrapping a `DataInputStream` around the data-generating input stream, `readLine()` then allows you to cut up the text stream into single lines of text. See the discussion of `LineNumberInputStream` for an example that uses `DataInputStream` (yet more examples can be found in Chapter 16).

> **WARNING**
>
> The `readLine()` method is an exception to the rule as far as throwing `EOFException` is concerned. This method never throws an `EOFException` object when it encounters the end of the stream; instead, it returns `null` (not the null String "", but the `null` reference).

LineNumberInputStream

Class `LineNumberInputStream` adds line-number tracking for text-input streams. The following two methods are provided to manage the new feature:

- `public void setLineNumber(int lineNumber)`

- `public int getLineNumber()`

The following program uses the class to print out any text file with line numbers starting each line:

```
import java.io.*;

class Lineno {

public static void main (String args[]) {

FileInputStream        fileStream = null;
BufferedInputStream    buffStream = null;
```

```
LineNumberInputStream    lineStream = null;
DataInputStream          dataStream = null;

String line;

    try {
        fileStream = new FileInputStream( args[0] );
        buffStream = new BufferedInputStream( fileStream);
        lineStream = new LineNumberInputStream( buffStream );
        dataStream = new DataInputStream( lineStream );

        while ( (line = dataStream.readLine()) != null) {
            int lineNo = lineStream.getLineNumber();
            System.out.println(lineNo + " " + line);
        }
    } catch (Exception ioErr) {
        System.out.println( ioErr.toString() );
        System.exit(100);
    }

    finally {
        try { dataStream.close(); } catch (Exception ignored) {}
    }
}}
```

The program uses a four-stage input pipeline:

```
fileStream -> buffStream -> lineStream -> dataStream.
```

The data read from dataStream traveled the length of the stream, originating in fileStream and passing through buffStream and lineStream. The BufferedInputStream was used to turbocharge the whole program. A DataInputStream was used to be able to get at the fileStream's text lines. And the LineNumberInputStream was used to give you the line numbers themselves. Note that the order of the different stream types can be important: In this example, it wouldn't make any sense to, say, put the buffered input stream object last in the chain. Buffered input streams always have to be the second link in the chain so that all downstream stages can benefit from the buffering (equivalent BufferedOutputStream objects always have to be last-but-one in any output chain).

> **NOTE**
>
> In this case, you could have easily tracked the line number by trivially using an integer variable that gets incremented for every loop iteration, but it would be reinventing the wheel, which is not what object-oriented programming is about. The Java API classes represents software reuse handed to us on a plate. If you want software reusability to mean something within your software-development cycle, you should make a valiant effort to become familiar with the valuable functionality provided by the different Java packages. This way you can cut your program-development time by simply relying on prewritten (and debugged!) classes.

Remark that the final `dataStream.close()` call will close all other input streams that were part of the pipeline. You therefore only ever need to `close()` the last stream in the chain.

PushbackInputStream

Class `PushBackInputStream` adds a *single* byte pushback (undo) capability to an input stream. It is, in a sense, a minimal form of `mark()`/`reset()` capability with a read limit of 1 byte (although class `PushbackInputStream` does not support `mark/reset`). The sole method that deals with the new feature is

```
public void unread(int ch) throws IOException
```

Note that the method allows you to do slightly more than simply undo the last read: It allows you to cheat and push back a *different* character than the one originally read.

Tokenizing Input Streams

There's one `java.io` input class that does not descend from `InputStream` but really ought to: class `StreamTokenizer`. You already briefly encountered the class in the word-frequency program presented in the discussion of `FileInputStream`. Tokenizing some input means reducing it to a simpler stream of tokens. These tokens represent recurring chunks of data in the stream. Any Java compiler, for example, would check for grammatical correctness of your programs by checking the sequence of tokens representing reserved word strings like `class`, `import`, `public`, `void`, and so on. By not having to actually deal with the exact character sequences themselves, tokenizing as a technique has the following two main advantages:

- It reduces code complexity.

- It allows for flexible, quick changes in input syntax.

If, for instance, the Java designers had at some stage wanted to rename the reserved word *extends* to *subclasses*, they could have done so very easily without it impacting the compiler in any way. The tokenizing stage of the compiler would still deliver the same `TOKEN_EXTENDS` token to the grammar-checking stage, even though Java source codes would now contain the word *subclasses* everywhere. Class `StreamTokenizer` can be used to turn any input stream into a stream of tokens. The programming model for the class is that a stream can contain three types of entities:

- Words (that is, multicharacter tokens)

- Single-character tokens

- Whitespace (including C/C++/Java-style comments)

Before you start processing a stream into tokens, you have to define which ASCII characters should be treated as one of the three possible input types, called *defining the syntax table for the stream*. Once the syntax table is defined, you can proceed by extracting actual tokens. Look at how it is done in practice by first checking out the structure and services of class `StreamTokenizer`:

```
public class StreamTokenizer extends Object {
    public int ttype;
    public final static int TT_EOF;
```

```
    public final static int TT_EOL;
    public final static int TT_NUMBER;
    public final static int TT_WORD;
    public String sval;
    public double nval;
    public StreamTokenizer(InputStream I);
    public void resetSyntax();
    public void wordChars(int low, int hi);
    public void whitespaceChars(int low, int hi);
    public void ordinaryChars(int low, int hi);
    public void ordinaryChar(int ch);
    public void commentChar(int ch);
    public void quoteChar(int ch);
    public void parseNumbers();
    public void eolIsSignificant(boolean flag);
    public void slashStarComments(boolean flag);
    public void slashSlashComments(boolean flag);
    public void lowerCaseMode(boolean fl);
    public int nextToken() throws IOException;
    public void pushBack();
    public int lineno();
    public String toString();
}
```

To begin with, this class has some public instance variables: `ttype`, `sval`, and `nval`. These stand for *token type, string value,* and *number value,* and, contrary to object-oriented rules, the class expects clients to actually access these fields. This you need to do after calling the core method for class `StreamTokenizer`: `nextToken()`. This method is the token-producing conveyor belt. Its return value tells you what type of token it produced: it can either be a multicharacter `TT_WORD` token, or it can be a single-character token, in which case the return value holds the ASCII code for that character. If the stream is exhausted, `nextToken()` returns `TT_EOF`. If you have enabled end-of-line checking by invoking `eolIsSignificant(true)`, then `TT_EOL` will be returned each time the end of a line is reached. If you have enabled number parsing by invoking `parseNumbers()`, `TT_NUMBER` will be returned each time numbers are encountered in the stream (possibly in scientific notation).

When `nextToken()` returns either a `TT_WORD` or `TT_NUMBER` token-type return value, you have to go and dig out the actual string or numeric values out of the `sval` and `nval` instance variables, respectively. This is very un-object-oriented; simple access methods could have been provided—like `getWord()` and `getNumber()`—to accomplish those same tasks.

Before starting to call `nextToken()`, you should set up the syntax table for the input stream. This setup is done via a number of methods that assign different types of significance to different input characters. Method `whitespaceChars()` lets you define a character range with no significance whatsoever: Whitespace can be skipped altogether by the stream tokenizer. Method `wordChars()` lets you define another range of characters that should be treated as building-block characters for "words." In the Java compiler example, all characters that can legally be part of identifiers (like variable names or method names) should be defined as *word* characters. This definition lets the tokenizer treat identifiers, for example, as the atomic wholes they in fact are.

The example program, below, will use class `StreamTokenizer` to tokenize another structured language that is very relevant to the Java developer: HTML. The program consists of a new subclass of `StreamTokenizer` called `HTMLTokenizer` (what else), which can identify a common subset of HTML 2 tags. The driver program (`HTMLtext`) uses the new class to extract all text from a Web page. Here is the listing for the HTMLtext program:

```
import java.io.*;

class HTMLtext {

public static void main(String args[]) throws IOException {
FileInputStream htmlInput;
HTMLTokenizer    htmlTokens;
int tagType;

    if (args.length != 1) {
        System.out.println("Usage: HTMLtext <file.html>");
        System.exit(10);
```

```
            }

            htmlInput = new FileInputStream( args[0] );
            htmlTokens= new HTMLTokenizer( htmlInput );

            while( (tagType = htmlTokens.nextHTML()) != HTMLTokenizer.HTML_EOF ) {

                if (tagType == HTMLTokenizer.HTML_TEXT) {
                    System.out.println("TEXT: " + htmlTokens.sval);
                } else
                if (tagType == HTMLTokenizer.HTML_UNKNOWN) {
                    System.out.println("UNKNOWN TAG: '" + htmlTokens.sval +"'");
                } else
                if (tagType == HTMLTokenizer.TAG_PRE) {
                    if (htmlTokens.nextHTML() == HTMLTokenizer.HTML_TEXT) {
                        System.out.println(htmlTokens.sval);
                        htmlTokens.nextHTML();  // swallow </PRE>
                    }
                }
            }
}}


//————————————————————————————————————————————————————————
// Class HTMLTokenizer is a form of StreamTokenizer that knows about
// HTML tags (but not HTML structure!).
//————————————————————————————————————————————————————————
class HTMLTokenizer extends StreamTokenizer {

static int HTML_TEXT        = -1;
static int HTML_UNKNOWN     = -2;
static int HTML_EOF         = -3;


// The following class constants are used to identify HTML tags.
// Note that each tag type has an odd- and even-numbered ID, depending on
// whether the tag is a start or end tag.
// These constants are returned by nextHTML().

static int TAG_HTML         = 0    , TAG_html     = 1;
static int TAG_HEAD         = 2    , TAG_head     = 3;
static int TAG_BODY         = 4    , TAG_body     = 5;
static int TAG_H1           = 6    , TAG_h1       = 7;
static int TAG_H2           = 8    , TAG_h2       = 9;
static int TAG_H3           = 10   , TAG_h3       = 11;
static int TAG_H4           = 12   , TAG_h4       = 13;
static int TAG_H5           = 14   , TAG_h5       = 15;
static int TAG_H6           = 16   , TAG_h6       = 17;
static int TAG_H7           = 18   , TAG_h7       = 19;
static int TAG_CENTER       = 20   , TAG_center   = 21;
static int TAG_PRE          = 22   , TAG_pre      = 23;
```

```
static int TAG_TITLE       = 24   , TAG_title    = 25;
static int TAG_HORIZONTAL  = 26;
static int TAG_DT          = 28   , TAG_dt       = 29;
static int TAG_DD          = 30   , TAG_dd       = 31;
static int TAG_DL          = 32   , TAG_dl       = 33;
static int TAG_IMAGE       = 34   , TAG_image    = 35;
static int TAG_BOLD        = 36   , TAG_bold     = 37;
static int TAG_APPLET      = 38   , TAG_applet   = 39;
static int TAG_PARAM       = 40   , TAG_param    = 41;
static int TAG_PARAGRAPH   = 42;
static int TAG_ADDRESS     = 44   , TAG_address  = 45;
static int TAG_STRONG      = 46   , TAG_strong   = 47;
static int TAG_LINK        = 48   , TAG_link     = 49;
static int TAG_ORDERED_LIST = 50  , TAG_ordered_list = 51;
static int TAG_LIST        = 52   , TAG_list       = 53;
static int TAG_LIST_ITEM   = 54   , TAG_list_item = 55;
static int TAG_CODE        = 56   , TAG_code     = 57;
static int TAG_EMPHASIZE   = 58   , TAG_emphasize = 59;

// When extending this list, make sure that substring collisions do not
// introduce bugs. For example: tag "A" has to come after "ADDRESS";
// otherwise all "ADDRESS" tags will be seen as "A" tags.

String[] tags = {"HTML", "HEAD", "BODY"
                ,"H1", "H2", "H3", "H4", "H5", "H6", "H7"
                ,"CENTER", "PRE", "TITLE", "HR"
                ,"DT", "DD", "DL", "IMG", "B"
                ,"APPLET", "PARAM"
                ,"P", "ADDRESS", "STRONG"
                ,"A", "OL", "UL", "LI", "CODE", "EM"
                };

boolean outsideTag = true;

//————————————————————————————————————————————————————————————————
// The HTMLTokenizer relies on a two-state state machine: the stream
// can be "inside" a tag (between < and >) or "outside" a tag
// (between > and <).
//————————————————————————————————————————————————————————————————
public HTMLTokenizer (InputStream inputStream) {
    super(inputStream);

    resetSyntax();              // start with a blank character type table
    wordChars(0, 255);          // you want to stumble over < and > only,
    ordinaryChars('<','<');     // all the rest is considered "words"
    ordinaryChars('>','>');

    outsideTag = true;          // you start being outside any HTML tags
}
//————————————————————————————————————————————————————————————————
// grab next HTML tag, text, or EOF
//————————————————————————————————————————————————————————————————
```

```
public int nextHTML() throws IOException {
int tok;

    switch ( tok = nextToken() ) {
        case StreamTokenizer.TT_EOF :    return HTML_EOF;

        case '<'                    :    outsideTag = false; // we're inside
                                         return nextHTML();  // decode type

        case '>'                    :    outsideTag = true;
                                         return nextHTML();

        case StreamTokenizer.TT_WORD:
            if ( ! outsideTag ) {
                return tagType();      // decode tag type
            } else {
                if ( onlyWhiteSpace(sval) ) {
                    return nextHTML();
                } else {
                    return HTML_TEXT;
                }
            }
        default:           System.out.println("ERROR: unknown TT " + tok);
    }
    return HTML_UNKNOWN;
}
//——————————————————————————————————————————————————————————————————
// Inter-tag words that consist only of whitespace are swallowed
// (skipped); this method tests whether a string can be considered
// whitespace.or not.
//——————————————————————————————————————————————————————————————————
protected boolean onlyWhiteSpace( String s ) {

char ch;

    for(int i=0; i < s.length(); i++) {
        ch = s.charAt(i);
        if ( ! (ch==' ' || ch=='\t' || ch=='\n' || ch=='\r') ) {
            return false;
        }
    }
    return true;
}
//——————————————————————————————————————————————————————————————————
// You've just hit a '<' tag start character; now identify the type of tag
// you're dealing with.
//——————————————————————————————————————————————————————————————————
protected int tagType () {

boolean endTag = false;
String input;
```

```
        int start = 0;
int tagID;

    input = sval.substring(1);      // skip leading space (bug in StreamTok)

    if (input.charAt(0) == '/') {   // is this an end tag (like </HTML>) ?
        start++;                    // skip slash
        endTag = true;
    }
        // go through the list of known tags, try to match one
    for (int tag=0; tag < tags.length; tag++) {
        if (input.regionMatches(true, start, tags[tag], 0, tags[tag].length() )) {
            tagID = tag*2 + (endTag ? 1 : 0);
            return tagID;
        }
    }
    return HTML_UNKNOWN;
}} // End of class HTMLTokenizer
```

Because the HTMLTokenizer class extends StreamTokenizer, it is
no surprise that the example stuck to StreamTokenizer's programming model, even if it is less than perfect. The new class needs no
syntax table initialization, though, nor does it provide any methods
in this respect. Its key method is nextHTML(), which is modeled after
nextToken(). Method nextHTML() returns token IDs of the form
TAG_XXX where XXX is some HTML tag type. To help remember all
the different HTML token constants, the convention of using a lower-
cased equivalent, TAG_xxx, is used to denote end tags. For example,
if <HEAD> is a start tag, then </HEAD> is its corresponding end tag.
Their respective token constants are TAG_HEAD and TAG_head.

The parsing approach embodied by HTMLTokenizer is to treat the
opening and closing angle brackets (< and >) as the only special characters in the HTML input stream. All other characters are regarded as
"word" characters, even whitespace. This unconventional syntax
table approach greatly simplifies the remaining logic of the class and
is implemented in the constructor for HTMLTokenizer. The
nextHTML() method can rely on always either being inside or outside a tag. If it switches from out to in, it is a simple matter of identifying the tag while noting whether this is a start or an end tag (end
tags have a slash character before the tag label). Because inter-tag

whitespace should not be taken into account when parsing HTML files, it is filtered out manually (StreamTokenizer's whitespace-filtering capability is not relied on). All other inter-tag data is the raw text for the Web page, stripped of any HTML markups.

Because this program does not implement support for DEL (or future) tags, you may wish to enhance the program yourself. The program is very easily enhanced by adding new tag strings to the tags array and adding the corresponding TAG_xxx ID constant for the new tag.

Output Streams

Package java.io's second main hierarchy branch consists of all stream classes concerned with output. The root for this branch is called OutputStream:

```
public class OutputStream extends Object {
    public OutputStream();
    public abstract void write(int b) throws IOException;
    public void write(byte b[]) throws IOException;
    public void write(byte b[], int off, int len) throws IOException;
    public void flush() throws IOException;
    public void close() throws IOException;
}
```

Output streams are even simpler than input streams in that they do not support the mark/reset mechanism (it simply does not make sense in output streams). The core functionality of output streams, analogous to input streams, is to be able to write data a byte at a time or a whole block of bytes at a time. The destination for this written data can be anything, in theory, although in practice the concrete destinations of files, byte arrays, and network connections are supported (the latter via java.net classes; see Chapter 16). Because there is very little difference between output and input (apart from the direction of information flow), what follows is a condensed overview of the output stream classes.

ByteArrayOutputStream

Class `ByteArrayOutputStream` is the exact opposite of
`ByteArrayInputStream`. Contrary to its input counterpart, the class
provides for some extra methods above the minimal `write()` methods defined by `OutputStream`. Here's the full definition of
`ByteArrayOutputStream`:

```
public class ByteArrayOutputStream extends OutputStream {
   protected byte buf[];
   protected int count;
   public ByteArrayOutputStream();
   public ByteArrayOutputStream(int size);
   public synchronized void write(int b);
   public synchronized void write(byte b[], int off, int len);
   public synchronized void writeTo(OutputStream out) throws IOException;
   public synchronized void reset();
   public synchronized byte[] toByteArray();
   public int size();
   public String toString();
   public String toString(int hibyte);
}
```

Because the constructors do not take an argument specifying an
array to write the stream to, another mechanism is needed to obtain
the resulting byte array: method `toByteArray()`. Four additional
methods are defined:

- `public synchronized void writeTo(OutputStream out)`
  `throws IOException`

- `public int size()`

- `public String toString()`

- `public String toString(int hibyte)`

Method `writeTo()` takes another `OutputStream` and copies the
current contents of the `ByteArrayOutputStream` to it. Method
`size()` determines how many bytes are currently stored in the
stream, and the two `toString()` variants return a String holding the
contents of the stream.

<table>
<tr><td>NOTE</td><td>Within the output stream hierarchy, there is no output equivalent for <code>StringBufferInputStream</code>. This is quite logical if you think about the unmodifiable character of Java Strings. As the stream is written, the String would have to change correspondingly, which is not in keeping with Java String nature.</td></tr>
</table>

FileOutputStream

Class `FileOutputStream` is the exact analog of `FileInputStream`. The constructors have exactly the same signature:

- `public FileOutputStream(String name) throws IOException`

- `public FileOutputStream(File file) throws IOException`

See the example program in the section on `BufferedOutput-Stream` (later) for a sample use of this class.

FilterOutputStream

Class `FilterOutputStream` is the exact analog of `FilterInput-Stream`. It is used as the analog foundation class for the same kind of stream-enhancing and chaining techniques explained in the `InputStream` section, only here it is used for combining output streams.

Because it would be rather unfair to provide you with a `BitStreamInputStream` class (see the section on `Filter-InputStream`) without its partner `BitStreamOutputStream` class, here's the promised implementation for that class, too:

```
//
// Class BitStreamOutputStream implements an enhanced OutputStream, which
// allows you to write a stream of bitfields ranging in size from 1 bit
```

```
// (a true bit stream) to 32 bits (a stream of integers).
// The size of the current bitfield can be changed at any point while
// writing the stream.
//———————————————————————————————————————————————————————————————————

import java.io.*;

public class BitStreamOutputStream extends FilterOutputStream {

final static int EIGHT = 8;        // 8 bits per byte

protected short buffer;            // the BYTE bitstream write buffer :-)
protected int bitsInCache;         // how many cached bits in the byte?
protected int fieldSize;           // current size of bitstream fields

//———————————————————————————————————————————————————————————————————
public BitStreamOutputStream(OutputStream out) {
    this(out, EIGHT);              // default to a normal byte stream
}
//———————————————————————————————————————————————————————————————————
public BitStreamOutputStream(OutputStream out, int bitFieldSize) {
    super(out);                    // call FilterOutputStream constructor
    setBitFieldSize(bitFieldSize);
    bitsInCache = 0;               // you haven't got any cached bits
    buffer      = 0;               // start with clean buffer (for ORs!)
}
//———————————————————————————————————————————————————————————————————
public void setBitFieldSize(int bits) throws IllegalArgumentException {

    if (bits>32 || bits<1) throw new IllegalArgumentException(
      "BitField size ("+ bits + ") no good. Has to be between 1 and 32.");

    this.fieldSize = bits;
}
//———————————————————————————————————————————————————————————————————
public int getBitFieldSize() {

    return this.fieldSize;
}
//———————————————————————————————————————————————————————————————————
// Write a bitfield to the output stream. The number of bits written is the
// current bitfield length. Bitfield can be on arbitrary bit boundaries.
//———————————————————————————————————————————————————————————————————
public void writeBitField(int bf) throws IOException {

int bitsToWrite;           // how many bits left to write
int capacity;              // how many bits fit in write buffer
int partial, partialSize;  // partial bitfield and its size in bits
int bfExtractPos;          // bitfield extract position (bit number)

        // check that bitfield fits in current bitfield size
    if (bf >= ( 1L << fieldSize) ) {
        throw new IllegalArgumentException(
```

```
                    "Can not pack bitfield " + bf + " in " + fieldSize + " bits.");
        }

    bitsToWrite  = fieldSize;
    bfExtractPos = fieldSize;

        // a single bitfield might have to be written out in several passes
        // because the lot has to pass through the single byte write buffer.
        // This inefficient situation is a result of the complex aligning
        // required to append any bitfield to the currently written stream

    while (bitsToWrite > 0) {

        if (bitsInCache != EIGHT) {            // if there's capacity left
            capacity = EIGHT - bitsInCache;    // in write buffer...

            partialSize = Math.min( bitsToWrite, capacity);

            bfExtractPos -= partialSize;

            partial = extract (bf, partialSize, bfExtractPos);

            buffer |= partial << (capacity - partialSize);

            bitsToWrite -= partialSize;
            bitsInCache += partialSize;
        }

        if (bitsInCache == EIGHT) {            // if write buffer is full,
            out.write((int) buffer);           // flush it out
            bitsInCache = 0;                   // and continue with clean
            buffer      = 0;                   // buffer
        }
    }
}
//─────────────────────────────────────────────────────────────────
// extract a bitfield of length 'bits' from an integer source.
// bitfield starts at bit 'pos' and is returned right-aligned to bitpos 0
//─────────────────────────────────────────────────────────────────
private int extract (int source, int bits, int pos) {

    source = source >> pos;          // align bitfield to bit 0
    int mask = ~( (-1) << bits);     // create a mask to get clean bitfield
    return source & mask;            // return bitfield (0 bits padded)
}
//─────────────────────────────────────────────────────────────────
// Override close() method to correctly flush any remaining bitfields in
// write buffer.
//─────────────────────────────────────────────────────────────────
public void close() throws IOException {
    if (bitsInCache != 0) {
        out.write((int) buffer);
    }
```

```
        out.close();
    }
} // End of class BitStreamOutputStream
```

Note that, although both classes `BitStreamInputStream` and `BitStreamOutputStream` contain identical methods (`getBitField-Size()`, for example), there is no way to avoid this distinctly non-object-oriented duplication of code. The duplication could only be eliminated if you could have a common superclass for both classes that holds the shared elements. But because each class has to be subclassed from the respective input or output filter stream class in the first place, a common superclass is impossible. In this case, even the interface mechanism of Java does not offer a solution. It is one of the rare instances when only true multiple inheritance, like that provided by C++, would give you the perfect solution.

BufferedOutputStream

Buffering output can enhance writing performance in exactly the same way as buffering input enhances reading performance. This class is exactly the same as `BufferedInputStream`, except while dealing with output. The following program highlights the difference a write buffer makes by writing a file without buffering and then writing a file with buffering:

```
import java.io.*;
import java.util.*;

class BufferDiff {

public static void main (String args[]) throws IOException {

FileOutputStream        unbufStream;
BufferedOutputStream    bufStream;

    unbufStream = /* a raw file stream */  new FileOutputStream("test.one");
    bufStream   = new BufferedOutputStream(new FileOutputStream("test.two"));

    System.out.println("Write file unbuffered: " + time( unbufStream ) + "ms");
    System.out.println("Write file  buffered: " + time( bufStream   ) + "ms");
}

static int time (OutputStream os) throws IOException {
```

```
Date then = new Date();

    for (int i=0; i<50000; i++) {
        os.write(1);
    }
    os.close();
    return (int)  ((new Date()).getTime() - then.getTime());
}
}
```

When run, the program produced the following statistics on my machine:

```
Write file unbuffered: 8190ms
Write file   buffered: 1370ms
```

The same conclusion as with the findings for BufferedInput-Stream forces itself on us: The simple wrapping of a Buffered-OutputStream object around the final destination stream (that is, the last stage in a chain of output streams) substantially improves write performance.

DataOutputStream

Class DataOutputStream implements the DataOutput interface, which you saw when you looked at class RandomAccessFile. Basically, interface DataOutput specifies methods for saving (writing) every type of Java primitive type plus Strings. Although the exact representation of the types output this way is irrelevant, the reality is that DataOutputStream generates a *binary* stream. That is, output not interpretable by people. When you need to keep external databases whose sizes are an issue, binary is usually the most efficient representation. Say your application manipulates large 3-D models. The definition for those models consists of large amounts of (x,y,z) triplets of doubles, plus extra data of various data types. Such models would probably best be saved in binary to conserve storage resources.

The Endian Wars Are Over

Whenever binary files containing numbers are moved from one architecture to another, the issue of "endianness" crops up. Different CPUs order the bytes in a multibyte number (say a four-byte int) according to *little-endian* (least significant byte at lowest address) or *big-endian* (most significant byte at lowest address) schemes. The Intel 80x86 family of processors is the last major architecture which still insists on being little endian. All other main CPU architectures (Motorola 680x0 and all RISC chips) are either pure big endian or can accommodate both modes (big endian is considered the more logical approach). When a number is written to a file by a little-endian processor, and then subsequently read back by a big-endian processor (or vice versa), the number will have been corrupted (unless it is 0 or −1). Java's `DataOutputStream` and `DataInputStream` classes protect you from this pitfall because, although Java data files are exchanged between very different physical machines, the exchange actually takes place between two (identical) Java Virtual Machines (which, by the way, both use the big-endian scheme).

For smaller entities, say configuration files, binary is not your best choice. Representing data in readable ASCII format is much more attractive. The next output stream class, class `PrintStream`, can be used instead to create a readable stream of data, but `PrintStream` is not as useful as it seems because of a major flaw in the `java.io` hierarchy: There is no corresponding input class to read the data back in. If you need to design a file format for a configuration file, then a completely different class might be the best solution: class `Properties` from package `java.util`.

Properties

Although the `Properties` class is not part of the `java.io` package (it is part of `java.util`), it is so closely related to I/O issues that it will be discussed here. Its definition is

```
public class Properties extends Hashtable {
    protected Properties defaults;
    public Properties();
    public Properties(Properties defaults);
    public synchronized void load(InputStream in) throws IOException;
    public synchronized void save(OutputStream out, String header);
    public String getProperty(String key);
    public String getProperty(String key, String defaultValue);
    public Enumeration propertyNames();
    public void list(PrintStream out);
}
```

Class `Properties` is basically a `Hashtable` with `load()` and `save()` methods added. These take input and output streams, respectively, as arguments, so you can in fact send or receive your `Properties` objects to or from more than just an external file. If you can view a configuration file as a form of dictionary, pairing configuration variables with their values, you should use this class to support program-configuration files. The following program demonstrates how a set of configuration variables can be saved as a `Properties` configuration file.

```
import java.io.*;
import java.util.*;

class Config {

public static void main (String args[]) {

Properties      config;
FileOutputStream fos;

// some dummy configuration variables to be saved in a config file

Double proficiencyScore = new Double(Math.PI);
Boolean hasCDROM = Boolean.FALSE;
String userName = "Peewee";
```

```
try {
    fos = new FileOutputStream("myprogram.cfg");

    config = new Properties();

    config.put("proficiency", proficiencyScore.toString() );
    config.put("hasCDROM"   , hasCDROM.toString() );
    config.put("name"       , userName.toString() );

    config.save( fos, "My Program's very own config file" );
} catch (Exception io) {
    System.out.println("Failed to save configuration file... what now ?");
    System.out.println(io);
}
}}
```

The imaginary configuration variables `proficiencyScore`, `hasCDROM`, and `userName` are saved in an ASCII file of the following format:

```
#My Program's very own config file
#Thu Jun 27 20:30:38  1996
hasCDROM=false
proficiency=3.14159
name=Peewee
```

As you can see, the `Properties` class time- and datestamps these files internally and adds the String you passed to the `save()` method to the top of the file (as a comment). This allows you to store copyright or other information in the file. Note that all configuration variables saved via a `Properties` object have to be objects (primitive types are not supported) and additionally have to be converted to Strings before being put into the `Properties` dictionary using the `put()` `Hashtable` method. To read back the configuration file and initialize your variables from it, you need to `load()` the `Properties` object back (via an input stream) and then extract and convert the variables stored as Strings. Here's the other half of the above program:

```
import java.io.*;
import java.util.*;
```

```
class LoadConfig {

public static void main (String args[]) {

Properties        config;
FileInputStream   fis;

Double proficiencyScore;
Boolean hasCDROM;
String userName;

    try {
        fis = new FileInputStream("myprogram.cfg");

        config = new Properties();
        config.load( fis );

        proficiencyScore = Double.valueOf(config.getProperty("proficiency"));
        hasCDROM         = Boolean.valueOf(config.getProperty("hasCDROM"));
        userName         = config.getProperty("name");

        System.out.println("proficiency = " + proficiencyScore );
        System.out.println("hasCDROM    = " + hasCDROM );
        System.out.println("name        = " + userName );

    } catch (Exception io) {
        System.out.println("Failed to load configuration file... what now ?");
        System.out.println(io);
    }
}}
```

PrintStream

Class `PrintStream` resembles class `DataOutputStream` a lot: The methods it defines mirror the type of `write()` methods provided by `DataOutputStream`. The difference is that they come in two flavors: `print(..)` and `println(..)`. Here's class `PrintStream`'s definition:

```
public class PrintStream extends FilterOutputStream {
    public PrintStream(OutputStream out);
    public PrintStream(OutputStream out, boolean autoflush);
    public void write(int b) throws IOException;
    public void write(byte b[], int off, int len) throws IOException;
    public void flush();
    public void close();
    public boolean checkError();
    public void print(Object obj);
    public synchronized void print(String s);
```

```
    public synchronized void print(char s[]);
    public void print(char c);
    public void print(int i);
    public void print(long l);
    public void print(float f);
    public void print(double d);
    public void print(boolean b);
    public void println();
    public synchronized void println(Object obj);
    public synchronized void println(String s);
    public synchronized void println(char s[]);
    public synchronized void println(char c);
    public synchronized void println(int i);
    public synchronized void println(long l);
    public synchronized void println(float f);
    public synchronized void println(double d);
    public synchronized void println(boolean b);
}
```

Though both sets of methods are superficially identical, there is a difference between this class' `print()` methods and `DataOutput-Stream`'s `write()` methods. Class `PrintStream` converts all of its arguments to ASCII (readable) representations. You have actually been using a `PrintStream` object ever since your first encounter with Java:

```
System.out.println("Hello World!");
```

Object `out` is a static `PrintStream` variable in class `system`. Various instances of the overloaded `print()` and `println()` `PrintStream` methods have been used in most of the programs. The difference between the two is that `print()` does not force the immediate writing of the data (called flushing). It can remain buffered in the stream until a newline character is written or until an explicit `flush()` is done on the `PrintStream`.

There's one additional (and major) difference between `Data-OutputStream` and `PrintStream`: Class `PrintStream` allows you to pass *any* object as argument. The mechanism it uses to convert any object into a sensible ASCII (in other words, string) representation is to call the object's `toString()` method. If you create a new class that doesn't override class `Object`'s `toString()`, you will inherit its default implementation, which is to output the class name along with the object's hashcode, produced by the `hashCode()` `Object` method. The following program demonstrates a `println()` on an instance of a brand new class:

```
class Print {

public static void main (String args[]) {
BrandNew anObject = new BrandNew();

    System.out.println( anObject );
}}

class BrandNew {

}
```

The new class `BrandNew` (which is empty and doesn't even have a custom constructor) is no problem for `PrintStream`'s `println` (`Object obj`) method because it can still invoke the parent `Object` `toString()` method, which in this case produced the following output for object `anObject`:

```
BrandNew@1393758
```

The consistent overloading of both `print()` and `println()` methods means you can literally throw any (single) argument at these methods, without having to cast, and they will perform what you intuitively would expect them to: convert the argument to a string representation and write this string to the output stream.

Although class `PrintStream` is immediately associated with console output because of its use in the `System.out` standard output handle, you shouldn't ignore its true potential: As a subclass of `FilterOutputStream` it can be chained into a more complex composite output stream leading to final destinations other than a mere system console. Using a `FileOutputStream` for the last stage of the pipeline, you can send ASCII data to an external file. And via an

OutputStream obtained from getOutputStream() methods in java.net classes, you can even send ASCII data to other computers on the Internet. We'll show you examples of this possibility in Chapter 16.

Summary

Computers need to interact with the outside world for them to be useful. They need to input external information, process it, and output results. Almost every computer language includes a generic I/O support layer that shields applications, written in those languages, from the more turbulent world of rapidly changing and very different I/O devices "out there." Java's answer to (or rather, its arsenal to cope with) the I/O issue is the java.io package, which in turn presents us with device- and platform-independent classes for file and stream manipulation. The way Java supports streams is especially powerful and flexible. The stream classes support an unlimited chaining mechanism that allows you to mix and match stream classes to achieve any desired I/O functionality. Creating your own enhanced stream classes, to be inserted anywhere along an input or output chain, is straightforward. The type of power and flexibility that the java.io hierarchy puts in developers' hands is only possible because of the application of pure object-oriented techniques, and, it has to be said, clever design.

CHAPTER

SIXTEEN

16

Network Programming

- Internet Addressing Using `InetAddress`

- Low-Level Communication Using UDP

- Connecting to Servers Using TCP

- WWW Support via Classes `URL` and `URLConnection`

- Writing Servers Using `Server Socket`

- Factories and the Factory Design Pattern

Java developed during a period when the GUI had already become commonplace, so Java is accompanied by its Abstract Windowing Toolkit. But Java is also a child of the Internet era, and so it comes with an entire package of classes devoted to Internet and WWW support. No mainstream programming language has ever provided built-in support for high-level Internet programming, until Java. Using other languages, the only way to write applications for the Internet was to descend into the technical depths of operating system dependent networking APIs. With Java, writing a program that accesses a computer on the other side of the planet is easier than ever, and there is no need to grind through your machine's reference volumes for OS networking support.

Java's view of networking means TCP/IP, and only TCP/IP. Novell, IBM, and DEC proprietary networking protocols do not make the grade—and quite rightly so, since TCP/IP is the only true "open" networking standard that links together the four corners of our globe, via the Internet. TCP/IP stands for Transmission Control Protocol/Internet Protocol, the two data communication protocols acting as pillars on which the Internet relies for all its functionality. In practice though, TCP/IP stands for a whole collection of related protocols (a *suite*, in communications jargon) all based around TCP and IP. Simple Mail Transfer Protocol (SMTP) and Network News Transfer Protocol (NNTP) are examples of some older (but still ubiquitous) protocols that are considered part of the TCP/IP suite. The new kid on the block, HyperText Transfer Protocol (HTTP), has become so much a part of the Internet (and therefore TCP/IP) that many people even confuse the Web with the Internet.

Whatever application protocol is used to implement some Internet service, IP lies at the heart of all Internet data communications. You should therefore briefly review what IP's role is and what its limitations are.

IP is a *datagram* protocol, which means that transmitted packets of information (*packets*, for short) are not guaranteed to be delivered. IP packets also do not form part of a stream of related packets; IP is a connectionless protocol. Each IP packet travels on its own, like an individual letter in a postal network (or a guru looking for enlightenment).

Figure 16.1 shows the structure of an IP packet.

FIGURE 16.1:

Internet Protocol datagram packet format

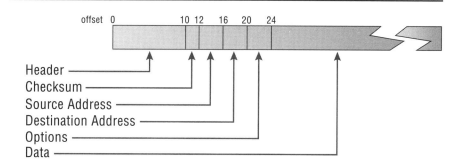

The various fields at the beginning of the *frame* (another word for packet) are collectively known as the *frame header*. The IP packet header determines the IP protocol's functionality and its limitations. Foremost in this respect is the addressing structure employed to encode the source (sender) and destination addresses. There have been 32 bits allocated for each of these address fields, which means the Internet can have a maximum of 2^{32} = 4Gb (4,294,967,296) different machines connected to its global network. (This may sound sufficient, but in reality this address space is already close to being exhausted. The Internet Architecture Board [IAB] is working hard to introduce a less restrictive upgrade to IP, IP Next Generation [IPng].) Instead of writing down 32-digit long bitstrings, like 11001110110000110001011111010000, Internet addresses are almost always expressed in their human-readable, textual form (for example, `www.sybex.com`). On the rarer occasions when the address needs to be expressed numerically, these 32 bit IP addresses are written down as four decimal bytes (for example, 192.31.32.255). The remainder of the header portion of the packet encodes a collection of fields, including the total packet length in bytes. Sixteen bits are allocated for this field, so an IP packet can be a maximum of 64K long.

Since IP packets are never guaranteed to arrive at their destination, a higher-level protocol (TCP) is used to provide a basic service that does guarantee delivery. TCP Manages this by using IP as a building block. The structure of a TCP packet is shown in Figure 16.2.

FIGURE 16.2:

Transmission Control Protocol packet format

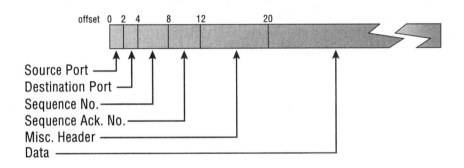

Source Port
Destination Port
Sequence No.
Sequence Ack. No.
Misc. Header
Data

Whereas IP is a datagram service, TCP presents a connection-oriented data *stream* service (like the telephone network). Before sending data via TCP, a computer has to *connect* with the computer at the other end; only then can data be exchanged. Another difference is that the TCP protocol allows you to send or receive arbitrary amounts of data as one big stream of byte data. IP is theoretically limited to sending a 65536-byte packet, which would be insufficient for sending many files or even many large GIF images embedded in Web pages. TCP solves this problem by breaking up the user's data stream into separate IP packets, numbering them, and then reassembling them on arrival. This is the function of the sequence number and sequence acknowledge number fields.

The most important TCP header fields, from a user's standpoint, are the source and destination *port* fields. While IP allows you to send an IP packet to an individual machine on the Net, TCP forces you to refine this addressing by adding some destination port address. Every machine that talks TCP/IP has 65536 different TCP ports (or *sockets*) it can talk through, as shown in Figure 16.3.

FIGURE 16.3:

TCP ports and well-known port numbers

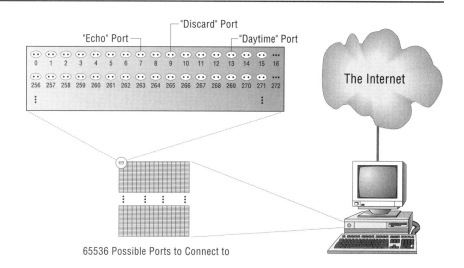

65536 Possible Ports to Connect to

A large collection of standard port numbers have been defined; a small subset of these is listed in Table 16.1 on the following page.

TIP

You might be able to find out more about standard port numbers if you have access to the TCP/IP configuration files on your machine. The file that lists many port numbers is called services. On Windows 95 machines, the file is called C:\WINDOWS\SERVICES. On UNIX systems, the file is located in the /etc directory. If you can access it, be sure not to modify it in any way lest you risk losing part or all of your Internet connectivity.

Table 16.1: Standard TCP Port Numbers

Port name	Port number	Service description
echo	7	Echoes whatever you send to it
discard	9	Discards whatever you send to it
daytime	13	Produces the destination machine's local time
qotd	17	Produces the "quote of the day" for that machine
chargen	19	Produces a test stream of characters (character generator)
ftp	21	File Transfer Protocol port
telnet	23	Telnet protocol port
smtp	25	Simple Mail Transfer Protocol port
finger	79	Finger protocol port
http	80	WWW server port
pop3	110	Post Office Protocol version 3 port
nntp	119	Network News Transfer Protocol port

Table 16.1 shows some port addresses for familiar Internet services; for example, port 21 is universally used for file transfers using the File Transfer Protocol, and port 80 is used for all communications with World Wide Web HTML servers. In later examples, you will talk to port 25 on your Internet provider's machine to send e-mail, and to port 80 of any Web server in the world to request a Web page to be transmitted to you.

The majority of application-level TCP/IP protocols (like SMTP for e-mail transfer) rely on TCP, and not IP, to achieve their functionality. This is because they invariably need guaranteed or error-free transmission of unlimited amounts of data. There is one more low-level TCP/IP protocol which builds on IP to achieve its functionality: User Datagram Protocol (UDP). UDP is like a cross between IP and

TCP—it is a datagram protocol with the same 64K packet size limit of IP, but it also allows port addresses to be specified. In fact, every machine has two sets of 65536 ports to communicate through, one for TCP and one for UDP.

Now that you have had your TCP/IP basics refreshed, you are ready to explore the core `java.net` classes.

Internet Addressing Using InetAddress

There is a `java.net` class that allows you to manipulate a 32-bit IP address (that is, Internet host address) in a more high-level fashion than just using a single 32-bit `int`. Class `InetAddress` essentially lets you convert a textual Internet address of the form `host.subdomain.domain` into an object representing that address.

Here is the definition for class `InetAddress`:

```
public final class InetAddress extends Object {
    public String getHostName();
    public byte[] getAddress();
    public int hashCode();
    public boolean equals(Object obj);
    public String toString();
    public static synchronized InetAddress getByName(String host) throws
    ➡UnknownHostException;
    public static synchronized InetAddress[] getAllByName(String host)
    ➡throws UnknownHostException;
    public static InetAddress getLocalHost() throws UnknownHostException;
}
```

The class thoroughly deviates from the object-oriented norm by not providing a constructor and relying instead on a static class method, `getByName()`, to create instances of InetAddresses. Method `getByName()` takes as its argument the textual address of any host on the Internet, in the form of a String. You can also turn the Internet address of your own machine (localhost) into an `InetAddress` by calling

`InetAddress.getLocalHost()`. To experiment with these two methods, and most other `java.net` methods and classes, you need to have your machine *online*—that is, connected to a live TCP/IP network, if not the Internet itself. One of the reasons for this is that the `java.net` classes need to be able to do full *domain name* lookups via the Domain Name System (DNS). You already learned that Internet addresses are encoded as 32-bit integers within the IP packets exchanged on the Internet. Mnemonic addresses like `www.microsoft.com` or `www.mit.edu` are only used for our benefit, and have to be translated to 32-bit addresses as soon as any real Internet communication needs to be initiated, based on those addresses.

The Domain Name System

How does this translation from textual address to numeric address take place? Does your machine contain a huge file listing every Internet machine in the world, along with its numeric address? Not nowadays. This was the situation during the earlier years of the Internet when there were a couple of hundred machines worldwide. With the exponential growth in hosts connecting to the Internet, this approach became unsustainable (it did not *scale* well). Today, every machine configured to talk TCP/IP needs to know at least one *numeric* address of another, very special, machine it can talk to directly, without needing to translate any textual address to the real 32-bit address—the address of a DNS server. This DNS server is responsible for translating the cozy textual Internet addresses into hard (but efficient) numeric Internet addresses. The Internet's DNS system is like a global (distributed) telephone book for all of the Internet's host machines; given a mnemonic address, the DNS system will return the IP address (the telephone number) of a host.

Method `getByName()` in class `InetAddress` is the transparent interface to the DNS service. When you invoke `getByName()`, the DNS server will be contacted "directly" (using its numeric address) and asked to look up and return the numeric address for the textual address you passed to `getByName()`. If your machine is not online, this look-up mechanism will fail, and an `UnknownHostException` will be thrown (which is why you generally have to be online when working with `java.net` classes). One exception to this occurs if you try to look up your own machine's IP address via `getLocalHost()` or via `getByName()`, passing your machine's name as a string. The program below demonstrates these address look-up possibilities of class `InetAddress`:

```
import java.net.*;

class DNSLookup {

public static void main (String[] args) throws UnknownHostException {
InetAddress someHost;
byte[] bytes;
int[] fourBytes = new int[4];

    if (args.length == 0) {
        someHost = InetAddress.getLocalHost();
    } else {
        someHost = InetAddress.getByName( args[0] );
    }

    System.out.print( "Host '"+ someHost.getHostName() +"' has address: ");

    bytes = someHost.getAddress();
    for(int i=0; i<4; i++) {
        fourBytes[i] = bytes[i] & 255;
    }

    System.out.println( fourBytes[0] +"."+
                            fourBytes[1] +"."+
                                fourBytes[2] +"."+
                                    fourBytes[3] );
}
}
```

The program takes a hostname string as a command line argument. If no hostname is specified, the lookup will be performed for your own machine's address. On this author's machine (which needs to dial in to become part of the Internet, but nevertheless has a fixed, allocated IP address), the program outputs the following when omitting any arguments:

```
Host 'telework.demon.co.uk' has address: 194.222.15.21
```

To get at the numeric address, you use `getAddress()`, which returns an array of four bytes. To print these bytes out, interpreted as unsigned values, you cannot just cast to an `int`; negative byte values will be sign extended to equally negative ints, so the bytes had to be copied into an array of integers while anding with 255 to undo the sign extending. Note that class `InetAddress` overrides `toString()` (like all good classes), which in this context outputs a `String` containing much the same information like that which we constructed manually. Again on this author's machine, using `System.out.println(InetAddress.getLocalHost())`, the following `String` is produced:

```
telework.demon.co.uk/194.222.15.21
```

Low-Level Communication Using UDP

Now that you know how to specify an Internet destination using instances of class `InetAddress`, how do you actually communicate with a remote system? Package `java.net` provides several ways, starting with the most primitive possibility using UDP datagrams. A UDP datagram is embodied in an instance of class `DatagramPacket`:

```
public final class DatagramPacket extends Object {
    public DatagramPacket(byte ibuf[], int ilength);
    public DatagramPacket(byte ibuf[], int ilength, InetAddress iaddr, int iport);
    public InetAddress getAddress();
    public int getPort();
```

```
    public byte[] getData();
    public int getLength();
}
```

Class `DatagramPacket` provides two constructors; the first is used for receive datagrams, while the second is used for transmit datagrams. With both constructors, you need to specify a byte buffer and its length (the `ibuf` array can be bigger than `ilength`, but not smaller). The second constructor additionally needs the destination machine and port number for the datagram (in this constructor's case, the byte buffer contains the message). As you can see, the class does not actually give you the means for sending or receiving any datagrams; this functionality is the responsibility of a companion class, class `DatagramSocket`:

```
public class DatagramSocket extends Object {
    public DatagramSocket() throws SocketException;
    public DatagramSocket(int port) throws SocketException;
    public void send(DatagramPacket p) throws IOException;
    public synchronized void receive(DatagramPacket p) throws
IOException;
    public int getLocalPort();
    public synchronized void close();
    protected synchronized void finalize();
}
```

The methods of interest here are the `send()` and `receive()` methods. The `send()` method simply takes a `DatagramPacket` instance and sends the datagram's data to the previously defined host and port address. The `receive()` method also takes a `DatagramPacket` instance, but this time as a recipient for a datagram to be received. You can extract the data from a received datagram using the `getData()` method in class `DatagramPacket`. To demonstrate the use of both classes in their transmit and receive capacities, here is a short example that addresses Sybex's WWW server and asks it what the local time is (at Sybex headquarters, this is Pacific time).

```
import java.net.*;

class GetDate {

final static int PORT_DAYTIME = 13;      // well-known daytime port

public static void main(String[] args) throws Exception {
DatagramSocket   dgSocket;
DatagramPacket   datagram;
InetAddress      destination;
byte[]  msg = new byte[256];

    dgSocket     = new DatagramSocket();
    destination = InetAddress.getByName("www.sybex.com");

    datagram    = new DatagramPacket(msg, msg.length, destination, PORT_DAYTIME);
    dgSocket.send(datagram);

    datagram    = new DatagramPacket(msg, msg.length);
    dgSocket.receive(datagram);

    String received = new String(datagram.getData(), 0);
    System.out.println("The time in sunny California is now: " + received);

    dgSocket.close();

}} // End of Class GetDate
```

The program first creates a datagram socket that it will use for both transmit and receive. It then proceeds by creating an instance of a transmit datagram packet, to be sent to the daytime port service on Sybex's server. The server's mechanical response is always to return a timestamped datagram (in ASCII). This datagram has to be caught in a brand new `DatagramPacket` instance. (The program does not reuse the transmit packet for receive purposes; the only reuse that occurs is the reuse of the variable name `datagram`.) Once the response datagram is received, the time is extracted from the datagram as an ASCII byte array and converted to a `String` that is printed to the console.

The simplicity of this example program hides a serious problem: Neither the sent or the received datagrams are ever guaranteed to arrive at their destinations. This means the server might never receive your initial datagram, or if it does, its response might never reach your machine. UDP is useful mainly whenever low-value information needs to be broadcast or when information needs to be transmitted on a frequent basis, so that losing a communication now and again does not affect the service. For most communication needs, however, you need guaranteed delivery of your data—and that is TCP's domain.

Connecting to Servers Using TCP

The programming model for TCP communication is similar to that of UDP, except that it does not rely on a class to encapsulate TCP packets. This is to be expected because TCP is a *stream* protocol: It allows you to send arbitrary amounts of data. The core class therefore is simply called Socket:

```
public final class Socket extends Object {
    public Socket(String host, int port) throws UnknownHostException, IOException;
    public Socket(String host, int port, boolean stream) throws IOException;
    public Socket(InetAddress address, int port) throws IOException;
    public Socket(InetAddress address, int port, boolean stream) throws IOException;
    public InetAddress getInetAddress();
    public int getPort();
    public int getLocalPort();
    public InputStream getInputStream() throws IOException;
    public OutputStream getOutputStream() throws IOException;
    public synchronized void close() throws IOException;
    public String toString();
    public static synchronized void setSocketImplFactory(SocketImplFactory fac) throws
    ➡IOException;
}
```

To use the class, you'll need to understand the Socket constructors and the two stream access methods. Look at the second pair of constructors, and you will recognize that the constructor needs to have an instance of an InetAddress object to specify the destination machine you want to connect to. If this were an IP protocol support class, this would be all that is required, but this is a TCP support class, so the constructor also needs a port address for the remote machine. Since using this class puts you in the shoes of a client (within the *client/server* [C/S] application model), you cannot just specify any old number for this port address; you have to stick to one of the *well-known* port numbers, of which the most important ones are listed in Table 16.1. All TCP connections actually involve two ports: the port on the remote machine *and* a port on the local machine, through which the client communicates. You don't specify the local port number, because you don't have to. The TCP/IP software allocates these *ephemeral* ports dynamically. They are called ephemeral ports, because unlike server ports, they exist only for the duration of a volatile client/server transaction, while server ports remain in use as long as the server software (also called a *daemon*) is "up" (that is, running).

NOTE   On UNIX, the server programs that manage the different ports are all implemented as background daemon tasks. That is why their names all end with *d*—*smtpd* for the SMTP service, *ftpd* for the FTP service, *telnetd* for the Telnet service, and so on.

Now you will work out some examples that rely on the `Socket` class to reach out into that cyberspace called Internet.

Example 1: Connecting to an SMTP Mail Server

If you want to deliver e-mail to a machine, you need to knock on that machine's port number 25. Once invited in, you also have to talk to the entity behind that port using a very strict, but simple, data communications protocol called Simple Mail Transfer Protocol (SMTP). This protocol can be summarized in the following steps:

1. The SMTP server sends an initial identification string.

2. You reply by telling it which machine you are sending from.

3. If OK, the server replies with an acknowledge.

4. You reply by giving it the "From:" e-mail address (the sender's address).

5. If OK, the server replies with an acknowledge.

6. You reply by giving it the "To:" e-mail address (the address of the person you want the message to travel to).

7. If OK, the server replies with an acknowledge.

8. You then send the entire e-mail message, line by line, and end the message with a single line containing a full stop ('.').

9. The server should again acknowledge receipt of the message.

10. You sign off by sending QUIT.

If these steps weren't easy enough, the protocol really deserves its name by the fact that the entire exchange is done in readable ASCII—no binary flags or cryptic fields are used within this protocol. If you delve into the fascinating world of Internet protocols, you will see that this is in fact very common among Internet protocols. (Data communications protocols outside the UNIX-derived sphere of the Internet usually rely on complex packet structures encoded in binary.) Few of the Internet's application protocols employ the much more complex (but more efficient) binary representation for their *protocol data units* (PDUs; these are all the packet types used to manage a communications protocol between two peers).

Online Availability of Internet Standards

You can easily obtain the full and authoritative specifications for every Internet protocol (IP, UDP, TCP, SMTP, FTP, HTTP, and so on) by retrieving the standards documents themselves. These are called Request For Comments (RFCs) and are available by anonymous FTP from various sites, including `mit.edu`. There is also an even more convenient e-mail

---

Online Availability of Internet Standards (continued)

service; just send an e-mail message to `rfc-info@isi.edu` with a body containing two lines like

Retrieve: RFC

Doc-ID: RFC0821

The server will then send you the document (ASCII of course) by e-mail within the next 24 hours. What a service!

The next program demonstrates how easy it is to talk TCP with any (willing) port on a remote machine. It actually allows you to send an e-mail message from the command line by specifying the filename of the message to send, the "From" and "To" e-mail addresses, and the address of a mail host that will accept (and possibly forward) the mail message. You should use your usual mail drop-off point.

```
import java.io.*;
import java.net.*;

class SMTPDemo {

public static void main(String[] args) throws IOException UnknownHost
➥Exception {
String msgFile;
String from, to, mailHost;

    if (args.length != 4) {
        System.out.println("Usage: SMTP msgFile from to mailHost");
        System.exit(10);
    }

    msgFile    = args[0];
    from       = args[1];
    to         = args[2];
    mailHost   = args[3];

    checkEmailAddress(from);
    checkEmailAddress(to);
```

```
    SMTP mail = new SMTP(mailHost);
    if (mail != null) {
        if (mail.send(new FileInputStream(msgFile), from, to) ) {
            System.out.println("Mail sent.");
        } else {
            System.out.println("Connect to SMTP server failed!");
        }
    }
    System.out.println("Done.");
}

static void checkEmailAddress(String address) {
    if (address.indexOf('@') == -1) {
        System.out.println("Invalid e-mail address '" + address + "'");
        System.exit(10);
    }
}
}
}
```

//——

```
class SMTP {

public final static int SMTP_PORT = 25;

InetAddress mailHost;
InetAddress ourselves;
DataInputStream in;
PrintStream out;

public SMTP (String host) throws UnknownHostException {

            mailHost = InetAddress.getByName(host);
    ourselves= InetAddress.getLocalHost();

    System.out.println("mailhost = " + mailHost);
    System.out.println("localhost= " + ourselves);
    System.out.println("SMTP constructor done\n");
}

public boolean send (InputStream msgg, String from, String to) throws IOException {
Socket smtpPipe;
InputStream inn;
OutputStream outt;
DataInputStream msg;

    msg = new DataInputStream(msgg);

    smtpPipe = new Socket(mailHost, SMTP_PORT);
    if (smtpPipe == null) {
        return false;
    }
```

```
inn  = smtpPipe.getInputStream();      // get raw streams
outt = smtpPipe.getOutputStream();

in   = new DataInputStream(inn);       // turn into usable ones
out  = new PrintStream(outt);

if (inn==null || outt==null) {
    System.out.println("Failed to open streams to socket.");
    return false;
}

String initialID = in.readLine();
System.out.println(initialID);

System.out.println("HELO " + ourselves);
      out.println("HELO " + ourselves);

String welcome = in.readLine(); System.out.println(welcome);

System.out.println("MAIL From:<" + from + ">");
      out.println("MAIL From:<" + from + ">");

String senderOK = in.readLine(); System.out.println(senderOK);

System.out.println("RCPT TO:<" + to + ">");
      out.println("RCPT TO:<" + to + ">");

String recipientOK = in.readLine(); System.out.println(recipientOK);

System.out.println("DATA");
      out.println("DATA");

String line;
while( (line = msg.readLine()) != null) {
    System.out.println(line);
          out.println(line);
}
System.out.println(".");
      out.println(".");

String acceptedOK = in.readLine(); System.out.println(acceptedOK);

System.out.println("QUIT");
      out.println("QUIT");
return true;
}


}
```

The SMTP demonstration program defines a new class called SMTP that provides a single method, send(). This method allows clients to send some e-mail message to an e-mail recipient. The exact details of the SMTP protocol are beyond the scope of this book, so we refer you to RFCs 821 and 822, which together contain all the information you will need. In particular, the shown implementation of send() simply swallows the responses from the server without checking for errors. This is patently not robust enough to be used in the real world, so RFC 821 explains the possible error codes you would need to check for in a watertight implementation of send(). However, the main program does do a simple check on the e-mail addresses to see if they at least contain the @ character, something all fully qualified addresses require.

If you survey the program's source, you might wonder where all the low-level, technical data communications code is hiding. The bulk of the program simply uses stream input and output methods. That is exactly where the protocol logic is hiding: class Socket lets clients communicate not via some additional send or receive methods (like with DatagramSocket), but via everyday input and output streams that happen to connect all the way to the machine and its socket at the other end. These streams are obtained via the getInputStream() and getOutputStream() methods. It is therefore possible (and desirable, as was done in the send() method) to upgrade the raw InputStream and OutputStream streams by encapsulating them in more high-level streams like a DataInputStream to read, and a PrintStream to write. (See Chapter 15 for a detailed study of the I/O stream classes.) Using these two stream enhancers we can treat both incoming and outgoing data as lines of ASCII text, which, in the case of the SMTP protocol, is most appropriate.

Having demystified the sending of e-mail with such a small Java program, see if you can repeat the exercise by dissolving a whole lot of black magic out of the World Wide Web itself.

Example 2: Connecting to an HTTP Web Server

Another protocol that operates in this transparent, ASCII line-based format is the HyperText Transfer Protocol, on which the WWW relies. The HTTP protocol is quite a bit more complex than the SMTP protocol, so it won't be discussed in any detail here. The following brief summary will suffice; then, you will be given a second, easy to understand example that downloads a Web page (exactly like your browser does).

The HTTP protocol is based on an exchange of multiline *request and response headers*. As always in a client/server situation, it is the client (that is, the browser) that initiates the communication by sending the server a request header. The server then replies to this request by sending a response header, which usually includes any requested resources (Web page, image file, audio clip, and so on) as appended data. Although there are several different request header formats, the most common type, appropriately called a "GET" request, will be employed here to ask the Web server to give you an HTML file you are after. The format of the GET header is as follows:

```
"GET" <URL> "HTTP/1.0"
```

This client request header has three components:

- The request method (GET)

- The resource URL

- The version of the HTTP protocol used for the exchange (HTTP/1.0)

If the request can be satisfied by the server, it replies with a response header of the following (example) format:

```
HTTP/1.0 200 OK
Server:Apache/1.0.2
Content-type: text/html
```

```
Last-Modified: Mon, 04 Sep 1995 12:34:51 PST

<HTML><HEAD>..
..
..
```

The important aspects to note about the HTTP response header are that

- It starts with a status reply (the "200 OK").

- It contains the *type* of resource returned (in the Content-type field).

- It contains an empty line that separates the header from the actual data.

In the example response header, you can see the beginning of a requested HTML file stream in (right after the blank line). Other non-ASCII resources would similarly start just past the empty line. In the case of an audio clip, for example, this data would possibly be encoded in nonreadable binary.

The example program below allows you to grab any Web page off the Internet from the command line. Here is the program's source code:

```
import java.io.*;
import java.net.*;

class GetWebPage {

public static void main(String[] args) throws IOException, UnknownHostException {
String resource, host, file;
int slashPos;

    if (args.length != 1) {
        System.out.println("Usage: GetWebPage <URL>");
        System.exit(10);
    }

    if ( ! args[0].startsWith("http://")) {
        System.out.println("Please specify a legal http URL.");
        System.exit(10);
    }
```

```
        resource = args[0].substring(7);        // skip HTTP://

        slashPos = resource.indexOf('/');        // find host/file separator
        file = resource.substring(slashPos);     // isolate host and file parts
        host = resource.substring(0,slashPos);

        System.out.println("Host to contact: '" + host +"'");
        System.out.println("File to fetch  : '" + file +"'");

        HTTP webConnection = new HTTP(host);
        if (webConnection != null) {
            InputStream page = webConnection.get(file);
            DataInputStream in = new DataInputStream(page);

            String line;
            while( (line = in.readLine()) != null) {        // read until EOF
                System.out.println( line );
            }
        }
        System.out.println("\nDone.");
}}
//————————————————————————————————————————————————————————————————————
class HTTP {

public final static int HTTP_PORT = 80;

InetAddress WWWhost;
DataInputStream in;
PrintStream out;

public HTTP (String host) throws UnknownHostException {

    WWWhost = InetAddress.getByName(host);

    System.out.println("WWW host = " + WWWhost);
}

public InputStream get (String file) throws IOException {
Socket httpPipe;
InputStream inn;
OutputStream outt;

    httpPipe = new Socket(WWWhost, HTTP_PORT);
    if (httpPipe == null) {
        return null;
    }

    inn  = httpPipe.getInputStream();   // get raw streams
    outt = httpPipe.getOutputStream();

    in  = new DataInputStream(inn);     // turn into usable ones
    out = new PrintStream(outt);
```

```
if (inn==null || outt==null) {
    System.out.println("Failed to open streams to socket.");
    return null;
}

    // send GET request
System.out.println("GET " + file + " HTTP/1.0\n");
    out.println("GET " + file + " HTTP/1.0\n");

    // read response until blank separator line
String response;
while ( (response = in.readLine()).length() > 0 ) {
    System.out.println(response);
}

return in;      // return InputStream to allow client to read resource
}
}
```

As with the SMTP demonstration program, a separate class (here HTTP) is created to encapsulate the details about the protocol. Instead of a send() method, a get() method is implemented. This get() method creates a new Socket in exactly the same way the SMTP class did. It then proceeds to get the input and output streams associated with the socket, so it can send and receive data over the HTTP link. The heart of the get() method is the sending of the GET HTTP header followed by the "parsing" of the response header returned by the Web server. The minimalistic implementation given here restricts itself to simply reading and echoing the response header lines until the separator line is encountered. From that point on, all remaining data is part of the resource requested by the main program, so the InputStream itself is returned to the caller, who can then proceed with reading the resource stream (oblivious of the fact that an ASCII header preceded it).

Here is a transcript of a session with the GetWebPage program:

```
C:\>java GetWebPage http://www.ping.be/~ping3100/index.html
Host to contact: 'www.ping.be'
File to fetch  : '/~ping3100/index.html'
WWW host = www.ping.be/193.74.114.17
GET /~ping3100/index.html HTTP/1.0

HTTP/1.0 200 OK
```

```
Server: Netscape-Communications/1.1
Date: Sunday, 07-Jul-96 18:55:39 GMT
Content-type: text/html

<HTML>
<HEAD>
<TITLE>
Home Page for Laurence Vanhelsuwe
</TITLE>
</HEAD>
————— Bulk of HTML file cut —————
</HTML>

Done.
```

If you specified a nonexistent file on a Web server you would get the familiar browser error "404: Not Found." Here is what the GetWebPage program prints when we ask it to get a nonexistent file:

```
HTTP/1.0 404 Not Found
Server: Netscape-Communications/1.1
Date: Sunday, 07-Jul-96 18:55:39 GMT
Content-type: text/html

<HEAD><TITLE>File Not Found</TITLE>
</HEAD>
<BODY> Error 404: Not Found <P> The file or resource you requested
➥could not be found anywhere on this server.
</BODY>
```

Note that the content type field returned by all Web servers uses a standard format called the Multipurpose Internet Mail Extensions (MIME) type. Table 16.2 shows some common MIME types and their meanings.

To fetch other Web resources like images or audio files, you could use the same technique as demonstrated in the GetWebPage program, except that you would need to have different methods or classes to deal with the different types of *content* returned by the server. Before you start implementing mammoth amounts of effort to

Table 16.2 Standard MIME Types and Their Meanings

MIME type	Origin
application/octet-stream	Generic binary byte stream emanating from unspecified application
application/postscript	Postscript language file
application/rtf	Rich Text Format word-processor file
application/x-tex	TeX Typesetter file
audio/basic	`.snd` or `.au` sound clip file
audio/x-aiff	Audio IFF file
audio/x-wav	`.wav` file
image/gif	`.gif` image file
image/jpeg	`.jpg` image file
image/tiff	`.tif` image file
image/x-xbitmap	`.xbm` image file
text/html	`.html` or .htm file
text/plain	`.txt`, .c, .cpp, .h, .pl, .java files
video/mpeg	`.mpg` file
video/quicktime	`.mov` or `.qt` Apple QuickTime file
video/x-sgi-movie	`.movie` Silicon Graphics file

deal with each of these content types, you should know that Java already has a general solution in store:

```
import java.net.*;
import java.io.*;

class GetContent {

public static void main (String[] args)
                throws MalformedURLException, IOException {
Object obj;
```

```
obj = (new URL("http://www.ping.be/~ping3100/gif/ball.gif")).getContent();
System.out.println( obj.getClass().getName() );
}
}
```

This two line program (if you ignore the necessary skeleton code) essentially does the same as the 90-odd line GetWebPage program! The only difference is that the GetContent program retrieves an image file from a Web server instead of an HTML file. No more sockets, no more input or output streams, and no more protocol specific concerns. Great, but how does it work? And does it work for all the MIME types listed in Table 16.2? The answer to these questions lies in the new class silently introduced in the program: class URL discussed next.

WWW Support via Classes URL and URLConnection

Class URL defines a WWW Uniform Resource Locator (URL) plus some operations you can perform on URLs. In its most primitive capacity, this class is similar to InetAddress in that it just lets you create an object which addresses, or points to, something. In the case of class InetAddress, its instances point to Internet hosts, and in the case of class URL instances, these objects point to WWW resources (Web pages, text files, image files, sound clips, and so on). Here is the definition of class URL:

```
public final class URL extends Object {
    public URL(String protocol, String host, int port, String file) throws
    ⮕MalformedURLException;
    public URL(String protocol, String host, String file) throws
    ⮕MalformedURLException;
    public URL(String spec) throws MalformedURLException;
    public URL(URL context, String spec) throws MalformedURLException;
    protected void set(String protocol, String host, int port, String file, String ref);
    public int getPort();
    public String getProtocol();
```

```
    public String getHost();
    public String getFile();
    public String getRef();
    public boolean equals(Object obj);
    public int hashCode();
    public boolean sameFile(URL other);
    public String toString();
    public String toExternalForm();
    public URLConnection openConnection() throws IOException;
    public final InputStream openStream() throws IOException;
    public final Object getContent() throws IOException;
    public static synchronized void setURLStreamHandlerFactory(URLStreamHandler
    ➥Factory fac) throws Error;
}
```

The arguments for the first constructor reflect the basic structure of all well-formed URL addresses:

⟨*protocol*⟩ ⟨*host address*⟩ *[⟨:port number⟩]* ⟨*resource spec*⟩

The protocol field can be `http:`, `ftp:`, `gopher:`, `news:`, `telnet:`, or `mailto:`

The host address is any legal host address like `www.apple.com`. The next field is optional and denotes the port number to connect to, if the default port for this protocol is to be overridden. The resource specification field is usually the full path of a file on the remote machine's file system, although this can be anything which the protocol requires—for example, the name of a news group for the `news:` protocol.

Here are some legal URL examples:

```
http://www.who.org:8080/index.htm
http://java.sun.com/Developers/welcome.html#footer
ftp://ftp.uni-paderborn.de/pub/Aminet/README
news:comp.sys.amiga.*
gopher:gopher.ucdavis.edu
mailto:president@whitehouse.gov
```

Note the first URL, which overrides the standard Web server port (80) to a less common alternative: port 8080. Note also the second

URL, which specifies a *reference* (that is, a location) within the welcome.html document by appending a #, followed by the name of the reference in the document.

To return to the class URL constructors, the first URL object constructor mirrors these URL components in its list of arguments. The second constructor is very similar, except that it omits the need to specify a port number explicitly; it uses the default for the given protocol (port 21 for FTP, port 80 for HTTP, and so on). The GetContent demonstration program used the third constructor (the most compact) to create a class URL instance. It just takes a URL string as you would type it into any Web browser's URL text entry field.

Once you have constructed a class URL instance, you can extract any of the URL component fields using the getPort(), getProtocol(), getHost(), getFile(), and getRef() methods. The core URL method, though, is getContent(), which was used in the demonstration program. Without you having to explicitly specify the *type* of resource addressed, it will fetch the resource and return it in an appropriate form. (An Image object, for example, would be returned for a GIF or JPEG image resource). What class URL hides is that it relies heavily on a closely related class, class URLConnection, to do all its dirty work:

```
public class URLConnection extends Object {
    protected URL url;
    protected boolean doInput;
    protected boolean doOutput;
    protected boolean allowUserInteraction;
    protected boolean useCaches;
    protected long ifModifiedSince;
    protected boolean connected;
    protected URLConnection(URL url);
    public abstract void connect() throws IOException;
    public URL getURL();
    public int getContentLength();
    public String getContentType();
    public String getContentEncoding();
    public long getExpiration();
    public long getDate();
    public long getLastModified();
    public String getHeaderField(String name);
```

```
public int getHeaderFieldInt(String name, int Default);
public long getHeaderFieldDate(String name, long Default);
public String getHeaderFieldKey(int n);
public String getHeaderField(int n);
public Object getContent() throws IOException;
public InputStream getInputStream() throws IOException;
public OutputStream getOutputStream() throws IOException;
public String toString();
public void setDoInput(boolean doinput);
public boolean getDoInput();
public void setDoOutput(boolean dooutput);
public boolean getDoOutput();
public void setAllowUserInteraction(boolean allowuserinteraction);
public boolean getAllowUserInteraction();
public static void setDefaultAllowUserInteraction(boolean defaultal
➡lowuserinteraction);
public static boolean getDefaultAllowUserInteraction();
public void setUseCaches(boolean usecaches);
public boolean getUseCaches();
public void setIfModifiedSince(long ifmodifiedsince);
public long getIfModifiedSince();
public boolean getDefaultUseCaches();
public void setDefaultUseCaches(boolean defaultusecaches);
public void setRequestProperty(String key, String value);
public String getRequestProperty(String key);
public static void setDefaultRequestProperty(String key, String value);
public static String getDefaultRequestProperty(String key);
public static synchronized void setContentHandlerFactory
➡(ContentHandlerFactory fac) throws Error;
protected static String guessContentTypeFromName(String fname);
protected static String guessContentTypeFromStream(InputStream is)
➡throws IOException;
}
```

As the size of class URLConnection suggests, it gives you much more control over the HTTP link created when activating (opening) a URL connection. For example, the following methods are all convenience methods that let you query the values of the HTTP response header fields the Web server sends back:

String getContentType()	Returns the MIME type of this resource
int getContentLength()	Returns the size in bytes of this resource

`String getContentEncoding()`	Returns the encoding used to transmit the resource
`long getDate()`	Gets the date and time stamp for this response header
`long getExpiration()`	Gets the date and time when this resource becomes stale (and should be reloaded to get an up to date version)
`long getLastModified()`	Gets the date and time stamp for the moment the resource was last altered

Only the content type field is mandatory, so all other methods can return `null`s (for `String` return types) or `0` for numeric return types, if the server does not volunteer the information. Note that *content type* and *content encoding* are two different things. Content encoding tells you in which encoding scheme the resource is returned. Common encodings are straight 8-bit binary, UUencoded, and base64 encodings. The last two are used when the entire HTTP response needs to be "seven-bit clean"—that is, the most significant bit of every byte needs to be zero.

Two `URLConnection` methods are very similar to the two key `Socket` methods you saw earlier: `getInputStream()` and `getOutputStream()`. Indeed, these are equally important within the context of class `URLConnection`. Class `URL` also made available a `getInputStream()` method (but no corresponding output stream method); this it does, of course, by calling the underlying `URLConnection`'s `getInputStream()`.

Several methods within class `URLConnection` deal with resource *caching* issues. It is common for Web browsers to cache in-line images, and even entire source Web pages, for future, accelerated loading and display. The downside of this caching is that the original Web pages and/or pictures may undergo important changes that would pass you by if the browser's caching kept all cached resources indefinitely.

The following methods all deal with this resource caching:

`void setDefaultUseCaches` `(boolean defaultusecaches)`	Sets the default caching behavior (on or off) for future instances of the class
`boolean getDefaultUseCaches()`	Queries whether future instances will use caching or not
`void setUseCaches` `(boolean usecaches)`	Allows you to change the caching behavior of a URLConnection object on the fly
`boolean getUseCaches()`	Queries whether a URLConnection object caches resources or not

Finally, two utility functions are provided to guess the content of a file (judging by its name alone) or of a stream (by peeking at its actual content, relying on `mark()`/`reset()` to avoid consuming any data):

- `protected static String guessContentType FromName(String fname)`

- `protected static String guessContentType FromStream(InputStream is)`

Unfortunately, these methods are declared `protected`, which means you need to subclass `URLConnection` before you can use them.

Writing Servers Using ServerSocket

So far, the concentration has been on the client aspect of client/server computing, since the majority of Java developers will view the world from that perspective. If you are part of that minority that needs to write server (not client) software, then this section is for you. The java.net package contains all you need to write any server system, using class ServerSocket:

```
public final class ServerSocket extends Object {
    public ServerSocket(int port) throws IOException;
    public ServerSocket(int port, int count) throws IOException;
    public InetAddress getInetAddress();
    public int getLocalPort();
    public Socket accept() throws IOException;
    public void close() throws IOException;
    public String toString();
    public static synchronized void setSocketFactory(SocketImplFactory fac) throws
    ➥IOException;
}
```

The first constructor is all you need to get going; it creates a new *listening* socket on your machine that can accept incoming connections from clients across the network. The port number argument specifies on which server port your server will be available to the world. If you want to write standard servers like an SMTP or FTP server, then you have to use their respective well-known port addresses. On the other hand, if you want to create a brand new Internet service, then you will need to use a port number no one else is using. Since the full port number range is 0–65535, there is plenty of choice, provided you stay clear of certain ranges. The range 0–1023 is reserved for "standard" Internet protocols (these ranges are controlled by the Internet Assigned Numbers Authority [IANA]). The region from 1024 onward is used for client ephemeral ports. Some systems use the range starting at 32768 for ephemeral ports too, so it is best to avoid these numbers as well. For testing purposes, port number 8001 is quite commonly used, although anything within the 8–16K or 48–64K ranges is fine.

Once a new `ServerSocket` object is created, it does not listen yet on its port for client requests to arrive. This only starts when you call the `accept()` method on the `ServerSocket` object. To illustrate this, you will develop a simplistic server that actually behaves like a real server—when a client connects to its port, it sends an initial welcome identification string, then waits for a client command (the server protocol is modeled on the SMTP protocol seen earlier). The only commands you are going to implement are "HELP" and "QUIT"—not very functional, but these two commands should be implemented by all line-based protocols (and SMTP, NNTP, and FTP all support HELP and QUIT).

As you can see from the list of methods class `ServerSocket` provides, there are no reading or writing methods, nor does `Server-Socket` let you have the input and output streams to the socket. This is because a `ServerSocket` is not used for the actual communication: A `ServerSocket` produces a new `Socket` instance for the server software to talk to the connecting client. This `Socket` instance is created (and returned) when a connection is accepted by the `accept()` method. This means the server programming model is almost identical to that of the client programming model; you just use the input and output streams connected to a socket to implement the required protocol. The following demonstration program shows how all the pieces fit together:

```
import java.util.*;
import java.io.*;
import java.net.*;

public class ServerTest {

final static int SERVER_PORT = 8001;        // our server's very own port

public static void main(String[] args) {
Server server;
String clientRequest;
boolean quit = false;

    server = new Server(SERVER_PORT);
    while ( ! quit ) {
        try {
                // what does client have to say to us?
```

```
            clientRequest = server.in.readLine();

            if (clientRequest.startsWith("HELP")) {
                server.out.println("Vocabulary: HELP QUIT");
            } else

            if (clientRequest.startsWith("QUIT")) {
                quit = true;
            } else {
                server.out.println("ERR: Command '" + clientRequest +"' not
                ➥understood.");
            }

            System.out.println("Client says: " + clientRequest);

                } catch (IOException e) {
            System.out.println("IOEx in server.in.readLine() " + e);
        }
    }
}
}
//————————————————————————————————————————————————————————————
class Server {

private ServerSocket server;
private Socket socket;

public DataInputStream in;
public PrintStream  out;

public Server(int port) {

    try {
        server = new ServerSocket(port);
        System.out.println("ServerSocket before accept: " + server);
        System.out.println("Java Test server v0.01, on-line!" );

            // wait for a client to connect to our port
        socket = server.accept();
        System.out.println("ServerSocket after accept: " + server);

        in  = new DataInputStream(socket.getInputStream());
        out = new PrintStream     (socket.getOutputStream());

            // send initial server ID line
        out.println("Java Test server v0.01, " + new Date() );

    } catch (IOException e) {
        System.out.println("Server constructor IOEx: " + e);
    }
}
}
```

If you run this program, this is what your console should print:

```
C:\LANG\JAVA\SRC\NET> java ServerTest
ServerSocket before accept:
ServerSocket[addr=0.0.0.0,port=0,localport=8001]
Java Test server v0.01, on-line!
```

The server seems to work, but of course you do not have any client that knows about the protocol just invented, and the server expects clients to talk only to this protocol. You can quickly redress the situation by writing a client program customized to talk to our new server. The fact that both client and server will be tested on the same machine does not matter; the client program will simply connect to machine "localhost" at port 8001 (our server's port). Here is the client:

```java
import java.io.*;
import java.net.*;

public class ClientTest {

public static void main(String[] args) {
String welcome, response;
Client client;

    client = new Client("localhost", 8001);

    try {
        welcome = client.in.readLine();
        System.out.println("Server says: '"+ welcome +"'");

        System.out.println("HELLO");
        client.out.println("HELLO");
        response = client.in.readLine();
        System.out.println("Server responds: '"+ response +"'");

        System.out.println("HELP");
        client.out.println("HELP");
        response = client.in.readLine();
        System.out.println("Server responds: '"+ response +"'");

        System.out.println("QUIT");
        client.out.println("QUIT");
    }
    catch (IOException e) {
```

```
                    System.out.println("IOException in client.in.readln()");
                    System.out.println(e);
                }
            try {Thread.sleep(2000);} catch (Exception ignored) {}
    }}
    //————————————————————————————————————————————————————————
    class Client {

        // make input and output streams available to user classes
        public DataInputStream in;
        public PrintStream out;

        // the socket itself remains ours though...
        private Socket client;

        public Client(String host, int port) {

            try {
                client = new Socket(host, port);
                System.out.println("Client socket: " + client);

                out= new PrintStream      ( client.getOutputStream() );
                in = new DataInputStream ( client.getInputStream()   );
            }
            catch (IOException e) {
                System.out.println("IOExc : " + e);
            }
        }
    }
```

If you run this client program in a new console window, while the server is still online and waiting for client connections, then you should see the client go through its paces as follows:

```
C:\LANG\JAVA\SRC\NET> java ClientTest
Client socket: Socket[addr=localhost/127.0.0.1,port=8001,localport=1034]
Server says: 'Java Test server v0.01, Mon Jul 08 10:12:37  1996'
HELLO
Server responds: 'ERR: Command 'HELLO' not understood.'
HELP
Server responds: 'Vocabulary: HELP QUIT'
QUIT

C:\LANG\JAVA\SRC\NET>
```

While the client printed these lines, your server printed the following lines, reflecting its perspective on the exchanges:

```
ServerSocket after accept: ServerSocket[addr=0.0.0.0,port=0,localport=8001]
Client says: HELLO
Client says: HELP
Client says: QUIT

C:\LANG\JAVA\SRC\NET>
```

As you can see, both parties communicate together without a hitch. Of course, this is because the protocol used here is trivial (it is stateless to start with, which always keeps things very simple indeed), and no real network was involved (real TCP packets were created, but they didn't travel far, they just *looped back* internally within the TCP/IP *stack*). Real protocols usually rely heavily on a number of states the protocol can find itself in—for example, idle, connecting, connected, resyncing, disconnecting. These different states require you to implement *state machines* to manage the protocol. State machines that have more than just a few states and accept more than just a few possible events quickly become very complex, necessitating formal mathematical methods to prove their correctness. Unfortunately, protocol state machines usually are nontrivial because real networks can be the cause of so many different types of events and situations. Packets can become corrupted due to line noise; packets can fail to arrive altogether if networking equipment suddenly fails. Packets can even be delayed for so long that the receiver thinks the packet got lost and then suddenly—"pop!"—the original packet arrives, throwing the receiver out of synchronization with the sender. All these factors need to be taken into account when designing a protocol, unless you build your application protocol on a protocol that already takes care of these issues, and that is exactly the function of TCP, the *Transmission Control* Protocol, on which most (but not all) Internet protocols are based.

> **TIP**
>
> Before we leave the topic of clients, servers, and the protocols they use to talk together, here is a tip to help you in developing and debugging client/server protocols easily: Always use a line-based ASCII protocol and use Telnet to exercise the server. You can even test the ServerTest program by using Telnet to connect to it instead of using the ClientTest program. Try it yourself with "telnet localhost 8001" after starting up the server again. With this insight, you will now also realize that writing your own Telnet utility (in Java) is very easy indeed.

Java.net Factories and the Factory Design Pattern

While browsing the classes in `java.net`, you might have come across the term *factory* here and there. Package `java.net` contains three interfaces that all contain the word *factory* in their names. Before the purpose of these interfaces is explained, you should understand what, in the context of object-oriented software, factory classes are. You know what factories are in real life—organizations that produce a variety of related products. In object-oriented software, this factory metaphor can be used to mean classes that can construct objects with diverging (but related) characteristics without invoking the constructors for the objects' concrete classes. The factory design pattern can be used whenever a class needs to instantiate objects from classes it doesn't yet know about. To put this in a concrete context, take a Web browser as an example application that needs the factory design pattern to solve an awkward problem.

Most Web resources are transferred by browsers using the HTTP protocol, but you might have noticed that this is not always the case. At some point, your browser's address input field might start with the characters `ftp://` instead of `http://`. What's going on? Your browser was instructed to fetch a resource using a different protocol than the usual HTTP. It switched to FTP to fetch a file or a directory, but without informing you of the quite dramatic change in internal operation. If a resource's URL specified a brand new protocol, other than the currently supported HTTP, FTP, NNTP, and so on, then your browser would have a problem—it wouldn't know how to handle this foreign protocol.

An analogous obstacle can occur within Web pages themselves. Most browsers can deal with in-lined images in GIF or JPEG format, but not some future popular image format. In the cases of both new protocols and new image file formats, the browser software is stuck because of its lack of dynamic extensibility (addressed by *plug-ins* in Netscape's browser). If it could only load or call upon classes which can deal with either new protocols or new image or file formats, then there would be no problem. And that is exactly what Sun's HotJava browser, which is written in Java of course, *can* do, by relying on the factory design pattern to get around these problems *transparently*. Factory classes can construct new protocol or content *handlers* whenever a new standard starts emerging that needs to be supported by the browser without changing the browser itself.

These factory classes obviously cannot suddenly manufacture new objects to deal with these new developments *in situ*. (For this to be possible, a *lot* more effort on the part of our artificial intelligence colleagues would be needed.) The way the factory classes are able to produce the goods is by loading new protocol or file format handler classes off the Internet, of course. They can do this the very first time; subsequently, they just load them off the client's local disk, as with all other classes. In a very similar vein as the design of Java's image processing and I/O classes, the factory design pattern essentially decouples systems from each other, thereby introducing a whole new level of flexibility that was sought after in the first place.

Now that you have some insight into the factory design pattern, the three mysterious `java.net` interfaces can now be listed:

`ContentHandlerFactory objects`	Builds ContentHandler
`URLStreamHandlerFactory`	Builds URLStreamHandler objects
`SocketImplFactory`	Builds SocketImpl objects

Note that these are all interfaces and not classes. None of the existing `java.net` classes implement any of these interfaces, but several `java.net` classes rely on external classes to be of one or other above factory type. (These classes are external and unknown, by definition, because that is the mechanism that allows future browser extensions without needing to alter the browser any further.) Class `URL`, for example, requires a `URLStreamHandlerFactory` (-typed) object for its `setURLStreamHandlerFactory()` method. Similarly, class `URLConnection` requires a `ContentHandlerFactory` object for its `setContentHandlerFactory()` method. These user classes (and similarly with `Socket` and `ServerSocket` for interface `SocketImplFactory`) lean heavily on their respective factories to off-load nitty-gritty functionality to objects created by those factories.

Here is a very concrete example of how these classes and interfaces cooperate to achieve the sought-after future-proofing. You may want to follow the text while referring to Figure 16.4: When you invoke `getContent()` on a plain `URL` instance (as you did earlier in the example for the `URL` class), what exactly goes on behind the scenes? First of all, a connection is created to the resource, giving you a `URLConnection` object. Then, `getContent()` is called on the new `URLConnection` object instead (`getContent()` is also a method for class `URLConnection`). The `URLConnection` object has associated with it a `ContentHandlerFactory` object that can produce appropriate content handlers via its sole `createContentHandler()` method. The argument this factory method takes is a String specifying a MIME type. Now the HTTP protocol dictates that Web servers always respond to GET HTTP requests using an HTTP response header which specifies the type of data it replies, like the following header for a GIF picture:

```
Server:Apache/1.0.2
Content-type: image/gif
Content-length: 23746
Last-Modified: Mon, 04 Sep 1995 12:34:51 PST
```

Without "touching" the resource itself (say, to read the first ten bytes to figure out what type of resource it is), the `URLConnection` object can already determine the exact MIME type for the resource. And given the MIME type, the factory can then produce a subclass of `ContentHandler` that can deal with this type of content.

If you look at the simple definition of the `ContentHandler` superclass, you will see that there is one very relevant method waiting in hiding:

```
public class ContentHandler extends Object {
   public ContentHandler();
   public abstract Object getContent(URLConnection urlc) throws
IOException;
}
```

Yet another `getContent()`! Only this one (or, rather, the one implemented by the subclass produced by the factory method), does the real content fetching and produces an object of the appropriate type for the resource. For example, if a GIF image was fetched, the `getContent()` method would return an `Image`, and not a (useless) simple `Object`, as hinted at by the method signature for `getContent()`. The previous "logic" is graphically depicted in the object interaction diagram in Figure 16.4.

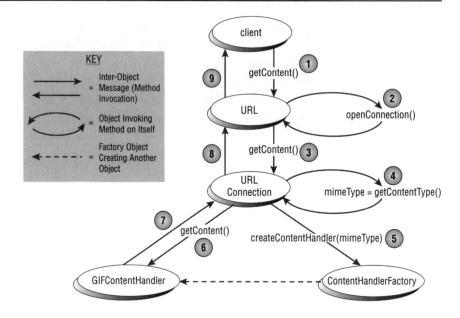

FIGURE 16.4:

The relation between a `ContentHandler Factory` class and class `URL`

The steps depicted in the figure are listed again here.

1. A client class wants to get the content for a resource defined by a URL.

2. The URL opens an HTTP connection to the Web server, creating a `URLConnection` object.

3. The URL object calls `getContent()` on the `URLConnection` object.

4. The `URLConnection` determines which type of resource this is from the HTTP response header (the Content-type field).

5. The `URLConnection` calls its `ContentHandlerFactory` to (please) provide it with an appropriate `ContentHandler` subclass.

6. Upon instantiation of this content handler, the `URLConnection` calls it to deal with the specific resource (a GIF image in this example).

7. The prefabricated content handler returns the resource in a form best suited to it (`Image` for GIF images, `String` for `.txt` files, and so on).

8. The `URLConnection` passes the resource object back to the URL.

The URL passes the resource object back to the client (who now is very happy).

> **NOTE**
>
> There are even more steps involved than those shown in Figure 16.4. The extra steps are an attempt to reduce the poor performance resulting from having to create a new `ContentHandler` object for every client `getContent()` invocation. What class `URL-Connection` adds to the picture is a caching step (involving a `Hashtable`, between steps 4 and 5), which often means that a suitable `ContentHandler` is already available without having to be fabricated by the factory (at, more or less, great expense).

Summary

Java supports network programming through various classes dealing with the TCP/IP suite of data communication protocols. The core `java.net` class is class `Socket` that, together with class `InetAddress` to address hosts, allows you to write client software that connects itself to any server on the Internet. These connections are brought about via specific ports—called well-known ports on the server side, and ephemeral ports on the client side. You also learned how most of the Internet's application-level protocols (SMTP, FTP, HTTP, NNTP, and so on) are ASCII, line-based protocols. This greatly facilitates development, debugging, and day-to-day protocol problem-solving, because the communication link can be intercepted and deciphered easily by any person familiar with the protocol. For example, the HTTP World Wide Web protocol was shown to use a simple system of request and response headers that can be generated and viewed using a simple, standard tool like Telnet. Finally, you learned about the nontrivial workings of the factory classes and their relationship to Java's key, dynamic extensibility in the field of yet-to-be-developed protocols and future Web resource types.

PART III

Advanced Topics

CHAPTER

SEVENTEEN

17

Native Methods

- Uses for Native Methods

- A Native Method—Step-by-Step

Usually, in a Java program, all of the methods are implemented in the Java language. But sometimes there are situations in which you need to look beyond the Java language to do things like interface with specialized hardware or a database driver. In these cases, you declare a Java method and implement the function using the C language and a C compiler/linker specific to a platform (for example, the Visual C++ for Windows platform) to produce a *dynamic loadable library* (DLL). In the Windows platform, the dynamic library will be written as a `.dll` file. (On the Unix side, it will be as a shared library written as a `.so` file.)

> **NOTE**
> At the time of publication, Java required that native methods be written in the C language. (You can do native methods in C++, but this requires a couple of extra steps to ensure the compiler does not mangle names.)

This native object code library is loaded when the class containing the Java native method is instantiated. When a call is made to a Java native method, control is passed to the function in the native object code library that corresponds to this method. The native object function takes over, performs the function, and passes the control back to the Java program.

> **NOTE**
> The current security model—like the one in Netscape Navigator—allows only applications to call the native methods. The security manager prevents applets from making a native method call. This makes sense, because native methods bypass the bytecode verifier and the security manager of the JVM. Technically speaking, applets can call native methods. But no class that comes across the Internet can call a native method. So, if an applet needs a button, it will eventually call native code to create the button.

Native methods make a Java program nonportable and platform dependent, thus negating the two most important advantages of the

Java platform. Because of this, native methods should be used only when absolutely necessary.

Uses for Native Methods

One of the most prevalent uses of the native methods is for implementing a common Java feature for a specific platform. For example, the JDBC-ODBC bridge for interfacing Java Database Connectivity to Microsoft's ODBC database independent driver, is a DLL in the Windows environment; in other environments, it is implemented as a dynamic library suitable for the environment it is in. The JDBC-ODBC bridge methods need to interface with ODBC drivers native to each platform, and this cannot be done with Java alone. Remember, if the JDBC-ODBC bridge needs to be used in an OS/hardware platform, a dynamic library is needed for that platform.

Another scenario that lends itself to the use of native methods is prototyping, especially for Intranet systems that interface with legacy programs. Because of time and effort constraints, you cannot wait until a Java interface is available to develop these systems. In this case, the alternative is to write the interface software components in the C language and implement them as native methods to communicate with the rest of the Java system. This practice, when used judiciously, will aid in prototyping Java systems—especially at this early stage of the Java platform. As the platform matures, the use of native methods in prototyping will not be required.

WARNING Make sure that the native methods interface to legacy systems in prototypes is documented and clearly described in the assumptions/limitations section in the project plan. If the native method relationship is not properly documented, other system personnel can make decisions to move the system to a different platform based on the fact that the prototype was developed using Java!

Native methods are used by system vendors to develop platform-specific optimized function modules like the Just-In-Time (JIT) compiler, extended security managers, faster class loaders, and so on. Symantec's JIT compiler, Borland's AppAccelerator (which is a part of Netscape Navigator), and Microsoft's security manager are all native methods implemented on specific platforms. Symantec has the JIT compiler for different platforms, including the Intel and Motorola processors. Presumably, they have native method implementations of their JIT in all the supported platforms.

Even though these can be categorized as specific implementations of the Java Virtual Machine components, in the future, they will be plug-in modules you can use in your own Java systems. For example, the methods in a common security manager module can be called, to apply uniform authentication and validation policies, from many different Java programs.

> **WARNING** When extending a common Java class with native methods, be careful about different versions of the superclass. Native methods do not have the functionality of the bytecode verifier for matching call interfaces, parameter type checking, and so on.

Native methods are definitely required for supporting the Java platform in new hardware, such as intelligent cellular phones and network appliances. These devices have their own microcontrollers and peripherals that need to be interfaced with the Java platform. The specific device drivers can be written as objects in the Java language, with the device interfaces implemented as native methods in the microcontroller's C language.

In the next section, the development of an object with a native method call will be explored step-by-step, and the implementation will be tested. For this example, Symantec's Java development environment, Café, was used for writing Java programs. Microsoft's

Visual C++ version 4.1 was used to write the C program and create the dynamic loadable library (DLL).

A Native Method—Step-by-Step

This section lays down the steps required to develop an object with a native method.

Step 1 : Design Classes and Methods

As in any development, you should start with a system design. Figure 17.1 shows the objects in the example.

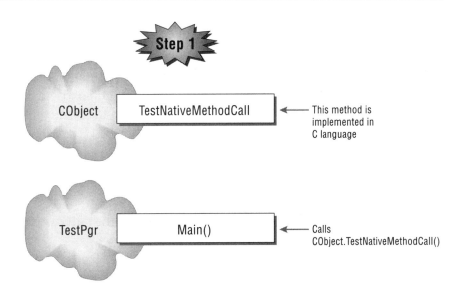

FIGURE 17.1 :

Software design for the native method example

In this example, the CObject class will be developed with one method, TestNativeMethodCall, which will display the message "Inside the Native Method Visual C Program!" This method will be a C function compiled into a DLL.

To test the native method, you will develop an application class TestPgr. In this application, the main method will make a call to the CObject; it will also display suitable messages before and after the call to make sure that the call works properly.

Step 2 : Write the Java Program

The Java program (CObject.java) that defines and implements the CObject is as follows:

```
class CObject{
    public native void TestNativeMethodCall();
    static {
        System.loadLibrary("Test");
    }
}
```

The program is deceptively simple. It declares a class CObject with the method TestNativeMethodCall, a public native method. The keyword native is what tells the Java system that this is a method whose implementation is outside the Java language. When instantiated, the object CObject will load the library "Test" (Test.dll in this case). It is up to the library Test.dll to contain the method TestNativeMethodCall.

Step 3 : Compile the Java Program

To compile the Java program for the native method object, the command is as follows:

```
javac CObject.java
```

The Java compiler (javac) is invoked with the file CObject.java as the argument; it will compile the Java program and will create the CObject.class file.

Step 4 : Using javah to Generate the Header File

Now you have come to the steps specific to the native method. Because the method is going to be implemented in C, you need a scheme to pass information about the environment—as well as any parameters—between the two languages. This is done by a set of .h and .c files. The javah program creates these files. Figure 17.2 shows the relationship and system flow for the various programs and files.

FIGURE 17.2:

Native method .class and .dll generation system flow

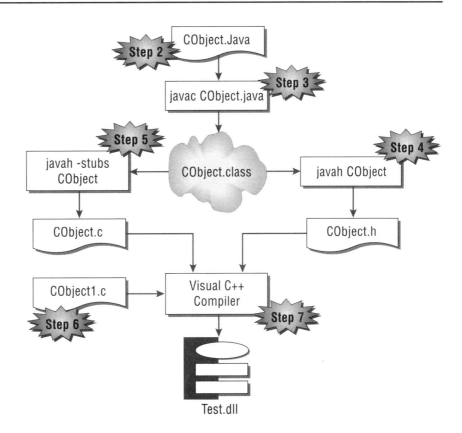

The javah is a header and stub file generator program that is a part of the Java Developers Kit. Essentially, it generates definitions of Java data structures and layouts that can be understood by a program written in the C language. The javah program takes a class name as a parameter. To generate a header file, you invoke the javah program as follows:

```
javah CObject
```

The output is the CObject.h file shown here:

```
/* DO NOT EDIT THIS FILE - it is machine generated */
#include <native.h>
/* Header for class CObject */

#ifndef _Included_CObject
#define _Included_CObject

typedef struct ClassCObject {
    char PAD; /* ANSI C requires structures to have a + least one member */
} ClassCObject;
HandleTo(CObject);

#ifdef __cplusplus
extern "C" {
#endif
__declspec(dllexport) void CObject_TestNativeMethodCall(struct HCObject *);
#ifdef __cplusplus
}
#endif
#endif
```

Step 5 : Using javah to Generate the Stubs File

In this step, the javah program is used to generate a .c file that will have the signature of the method. You invoke the javah program with the -stubs switch and the name of the class as follows:

```
javah -stubs CObject
```

Here is the generated CObject.c program:

```
/* DO NOT EDIT THIS FILE - it is machine generated */
#include <StubPreamble.h>

/* Stubs for class CObject */
/* SYMBOL: "CObject/TestNativeMethodCall()V", Java_CObject_TestNativeMethodCall_stub
➥*/
__declspec(dllexport) stack_item *Java_CObject_TestNativeMethodCall_stub(stack_item
➥*_P_,struct execenv *_EE_) {
        extern void CObject_TestNativeMethodCall(void *);
        (void) CObject_TestNativeMethodCall(_P_[0].p);
        return _P_;
}
```

Step 6 : Write the C Function (Native Code)

In the previous steps, the scene was set up for doing the actual work. The time has come, finally, to write the method in the C language. In steps 4 and 5, the javah program created .h and .c files with the data structure, layout, and the signatures of all the methods declared in the CObject class. In the C program, you will implement the functions denoted by the signature in the CObject.c program.

Our C program is in the file CObject1.c, as shown here:

```
#include <e:\cafe\java\include\StubPreamble.h>
#include "CObject.h"
#include <stdio.h>

void CObject_TestNativeMethodCall(struct HCObject *this) {
    printf("Inside the Native Method Visual C Program !\n");
    return;
}
```

The first line is the include statement to include the StubPreamble.h file, which comes with the JDK and contains various definitions and additional include files.

The second line is the `include` statement to include the `CObject.h` file generated by the javah program in step 4.

The method signature `CObject_TestNativeMethodCall` becomes a function. As per the program design, this function prints a message.

Step 7 : Create the DLL Library

In this step, you compile the CObject.c program generated by the javah program in step 5 and the CObject1.c program written in step 6 to generate the `Test.dll` library.

Visual C++ 4.1 was used to develop this example. A project named `Test` was created to generate a dynamic link library file named `Test.dll`; both the `CObject.c` and `CObject1.c` files were included in the project.

NOTE The DLL filename should be the same as the one loaded using the `System.loadLibrary()` function in step 2.

NOTE When using Visual C++ Microsoft Developer Studio, make sure the directory for the Java-related `include` files is added to the Directories list box (found in Tools▶Options▶Directories▶Show Directories for Include Files). In this example, the directories are `e:\café\java\include` and `e:\café\java\include\win32`. If the compiler cannot find these `include` directories, it will display the error message "Cannot open include file: StubPreamble.h."

Step 8 : Write the Test Program

Now you will create the `TestPgr` class to test this example. The `TestPgr` system flow is described in Figure 17.3.

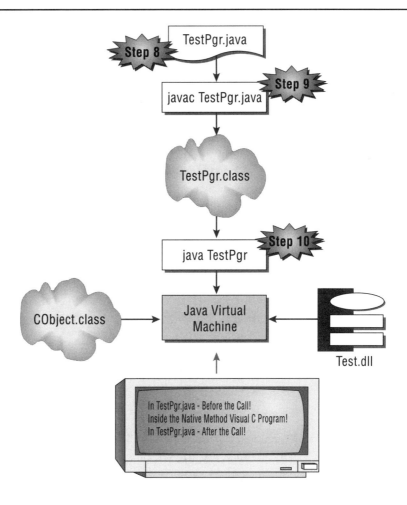

The `TestPgr` Java class is as follows:

```
class TestPgr {
    public static void main(String args[]) {
        System.out.println ("In TestPgr.java - Before the Call!");
        CObject NativeMethodObject = new CObject();
        NativeMethodObject.TestNativeMethodCall();
```

```
System.out.println ("In TestPgr.java - After the Call!");
    }
}
```

The program has the method `main`, which declares the `Native-MethodObject` variable of type `CObject`, and then calls the `Test-NativeMethodCall()` method. It also prints suitable messages before and after the call.

Step 9 : Compile the Test Program

To compile the Java program, the command is as follows:

```
javac TestPgr.java
```

This command will create the `TestPgr` class.

Step 10 : Run the Test Program

To run the TestPgr program, the command is as follows:

```
java TestPgr
```

This command will start the Java Virtual Machine and run the `TestPgr.class` file. The following lines will be displayed on the screen showing the successful execution of the program:

In TestPgr.Java—Before the Call!

Inside the Native Method Visual C Program!

In TestPgr.Java—After the Call!

TIP   For the native method program to find the `Test.dll` file, it should be somewhere in the directories pointed to by the `CLASS_PATH` or `PATH` environment variable, or the file should be in the current directory.

As you can see, the `TestPgr.main()` method first prints the "Before..." message and then calls the `TestNativeMethodCall()` method. The `CObject` passes the control to the `Test.dll` (which it already loaded when the class was instantiated) and calls the C function as denoted by the signature. The `Test.dll` then invokes the `CObject_TestNativeMethodCall` function, which displays the "Inside..." message. After the call, control is returned to the TestPgr, which prints the "After..." message to indicate successful execution.

The above ten steps represent the activities required to successfully develop and test a native method call. Hopefully you will find it easy and fun to try this out in your system!

Summary

In a traditional sense, there is nothing wrong with implementing a function or procedure in lower-level languages (such as the assembly language). In fact, Borland pioneered the technique of inline assembly code that allowed a programmer to include assembly language code directly in Turbo Pascal code! A great feature, this was used by many programmers for speeding up graphics display, faster sort routines, hardware level control (input and output to ports, video routines), and just for fun, among other things. In theory, a native method in Java is no different from inline assembly code in a Pascal program—but the reasons for using native methods in a Java program are not the same reasons that justified the use of inline assembly code in Pascal.

In Turbo Pascal, the main reason inline assembly was used was for speed. Since the system was being developed for one processor and operating system, this close tie to the underlying system through the assembler was not seen as a problem. Since Java is designed to be platfrom-independent, native methods specific to one platform cannot readily be used.

Another reason people used inline assembly in Turbo Pascal was for specialized hardware control. Again, if the hardware device is specialized to a specific processor or operating system, it is acceptable to develop interfaces using native methods, since the device is not going to be easily moved. But remember, if you want to support the hardware device on a different platform, you would need to reimplement the device interface (native methods) for that platform also.

In short, native methods could be employed by system and hardware vendors for implementing device-, hardware-, or OS-dependent modules to the Java platform. Application developers should not use native methods unless absolutely necessary, and then they should be used with caution. And if you are using native methods in a Java system, make sure the native methods are explained clearly in the design documents to avoid future misunderstanding.

CHAPTER

EIGHTEEN

18

Java Virtual Machine

What Is a Java Virtual Machine?

This chapter introduces the Java Virtual Machine from a Java developer's perspective. This knowledge is important to developers because the Java platform differs from traditional systems and follows the new paradigm "network is the computer." The Java platform extends the object-oriented systems to networked computers for encapsulated programs and data. The Java Virtual Machine is central to the Java platform. Many of the attributes that make Java a universal development platform stem from the Java Virtual Machine concept and implementation.

At the most elementary level, the Java Virtual Machine is a software CPU (central processing unit) with the Java bytecode as the instruction set. Figure 18.1 shows a Java system flow diagram, including the Java Virtual Machine. Refering to the figure, follow the bytecodes from the beginning. A developer writes a java program and stores the program in a .java file. The Java compiler converts this Java program in the .java file into a .class file consisting of bytecodes. The bytecodes are the instruction set (like the microcode for a CPU) for the Java Virtual Machine. The bytecodes are of the form <*opcode*> <*... Parameters*>— the instruction code, or *opcode*, is one byte long (hence, the name bytecodes) and can have many parameters. Currently, there about 220 bytecode instructions defined in the Java Virtual Machine specification.

Like normal program loaders, the Java Virtual Machine starts the execution of a program by loading the .class files from either the network or local storage. Since Java does not trust anything that comes across the network, the Java Virtual Machine only verifies the bytecodes of .class files that are passed across a network. If the .class file does not pass the verification, the execution stops there with an error message. If the program successfully passes the verifier phase, the Java Virtual Machine runtime interpreter reads the byte-codes, translates them to the specific OS/hardware instructions, and executes them in the target CPU.

To run the Java bytecodes, a hardware manufacturer or operating system vendor implements the Java Virtual Machine on their hardware-operating system combination. The Java Virtual Machine program modules are usually written in C, C++, or assembly for an OS/CPU. The Java Virtual Machine uses the host operating system facilities for memory functions, file system, display, mouse, keyboard, network, and other device drivers, processing of threads, and so on. Most of the current Java Virtual Machines available now interpret the Java bytecodes versus the normal compilation process of C/C++ programs. As you can see in Figure 18.1, a Java Virtual Machine executable unit is the `.class` file.

FIGURE 18.1:

The Java system flow diagram

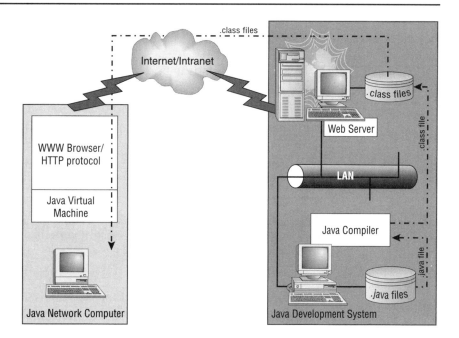

On a conceptual level, each `.class` file corresponds to one object. Unlike traditional applications, in the Java Virtual Machine architecture there is no monolithic executable that gets loaded with all of the program code. One `.class` file could refer to many other `.class` files. (In the Java language, this is done using the the `import`, `implements`, or `extends` clauses.) The Java Virtual Machine loads the `.class` files (called *classes*) from the network or local file system as they are needed by the currently running class. Extending this concept further, the different classes/objects can be developed by different developers, exist in separate servers, and the Java Virtual Machine will dynamically load and bind the class files as required.

> **NOTE** Currently, the security scheme implemented by Netscape Navigator allows applets to load classes only from the servers from which the applets themselves are loaded. This will change when Java supports the concept of *signed classes*.

This dynamic loading and binding architecture enables you to update the `.class` files on the servers providing clients with the latest version of the software. These updates can be bug fixes or new versions of software with additional features. It is precisely the zero administration client, versionless software, and Just-In-Time software delivery architecture that make the Java platform so successful.

> **NOTE** The Just-In-Time (JIT) compiler concept, which is now being offered as a product by many vendors, is an important development for Java Virtual Machine performance enhancement.

Additionally, with the Java Virtual Machine architecture, the `.class` files are cross-platform and architecture-neutral. The same `.class` files can be run on any computer that has a Java Virtual Machine implementation. This is the "compile once, run anywhere" paradigm, revered by software professionals all over the world, and one more compelling reason for the popularity of the Java platform.

The platform-neutral, portable `.class` file architecture means that the Java Virtual Machine's universe starts with a `.class` file. It knows how a `.class` file should look and what it can contain, but is not concerned with what language the source was in.

> **NOTE** In the future, the Java Virtual Machine will need to perform verification of signed classes, and as a result, the origin of the `.class` file will be relevant to the Java Virtual Machine.

As it currently stands, any compiler can output the Java bytecodes in a `.class` file, and the Java Virtual Machine will run the program as long as it conforms to the Java Virtual Machine specification. If the output was not in the appropriate format, the Java Virtual Machine would be unable to load, verify, and execute the classes.

> **NOTE** Because the compiler does not matter to the Java Virtual Machine, you can actually write for the Java Virtual Machine without knowing the Java language. Extending this idea a bit further (and people are doing just that), you could write programs in a language like Ada, Visual Basic, or C, and if a compiler can generate Java bytecodes out of those source files, it is effectively writing applications that will run on any Java Virtual Machine. By the same token, if a manufacturer wants to bring a new intelligent appliance to the market, they can take advantage of the existing talent by incorporating the Java Virtual Machine into the appliance with software like Java OS, or on a chip like the picoJava.

Performance

One important issue on everybody's mind is performance. Because of the additional Java Virtual Machine layer over the host operating system (compared to traditional compiled languages like C and C++), the current Java Virtual Machines are considered to be 10–20 times slower than native compiled code. One can expect that there will undoubtedly be faster Java Virtual Machine implementations coming along very soon (probably by the time you finish this chapter!), but for now, performance is still a legitimate concern for developers. In this section, you will see some of the reasons for the reduction in performance and the ways in which the software vendors are trying to narrow the performance gap between the Java Virtual Machine and the native compiled code.

There are many reasons that the Java Virtual Machine is relatively slower than traditional executables: First, the verification process takes time. As a class is read in, it is verified during run time, whereas traditional compilers perform verification processes during the compilation of the program. Also, as part of the class is executed, the Java bytecodes are converted to native machine instructions. If the same section is executed multiple times, it is converted to native instructions multiple times. It does not cache previously converted bytecodes. Additionally, as each instruction is executed, there are multiple safety checks being performed. For instance, when accessing an array element, the Java Virtual Machine ensures that you are not reading past the end of it.

Another reason for decreased performance is that Java instructions are all byte-sized codes. Since most operations require objects that are larger than a byte (an integer is 32 bits), multiple bytecodes would have to be read to get the various operators and their parameters.

Furthermore, Java is implemented as a stack machine, which means that the instructions take the parameters from the operand stack and return the results to the stack. This is due to the fact that the Java Virtual Machine does not assume any particular CPU architecture, including the word size and register combinations. Many of the intended applications might run on systems with only a few registers, or none at all. Normally compiled programs use very fast register operations and the parameters needed for an operation are available in the CPU registers most, if not all, of the time. Because registers are in the CPU while a stack is in the main memory, register operations are many times faster than stack operations. Also, traditional compilers perform many types of code optimization during compilation, including operation optimization where the results of operations are kept in registers and subsequent operations access the results of previous operations from the registers.

Lastly, the system performs automatic garbage collection for you, which inevitably impacts performance since everything must stop when the garbage collector runs. Automatic garbage collection will be covered in much more detail later in the chapter.

As you can see, many factors conspire to slow things down. However, there is a lot of work being done to address the issues raised here, some of which will be touched upon shortly.

NOTE

The Java Virtual Machine implementor has the freedom and latitude to optimize the system for the target hardware and operating system. The implementation can be fine-tuned to exploit the target system's strengths and compensate for the target system's weaknesses or limited resources. For example, the stack machine can be implemented with the stack caching technique (which emulates a stack with CPU registers) for a CPU that has registers like the Pentium or the UltraSparc chip.

The Java Virtual Machine Architecture

The Java Virtual Machine specification describes all of the required elements needed for a Java Virtual Machine architecture using the following elements:

- Datatypes

- Instruction Set

- Class File Format

- Registers

- Method Area

- Operand Stack

- Garbage Collected Heap

Figure 18.2 shows the major modules of a Java Virtual Machine and how they fit in with the host operating system and hardware.

NOTE   Sun is the keeper of the Java Virtual Machine specification which is maintained publicly at: `http://java.sun.com/doc/vmspec/html/vmspec-1.html`. As the Java Virtual Machine matures, Sun promises any changes will not break past implementations. To ensure compliance with the specification, Sun maintains a compatibility suite. If a vendor implements their own Java Virtual Machine and it passes the compatibility suite, it gets Sun's blessing, is deemed compatible, and boasts that it is "Java Compatible." (The licensing details are discussed later in "Java Licensing.") After reviewing the website, if you have any additional comments or concerns regarding the Java Virtual Machine, you can send them to `jvm@javasoft.com`.

Java Virtual Machine
block diagram

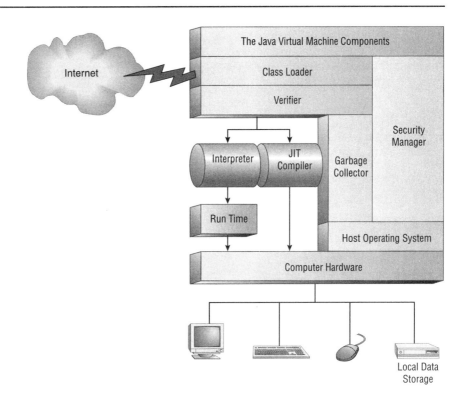

Datatypes

Table 18.1 lists the datatypes supported by the Java Virtual Machine. Integers are implemented as 32-bit sized and floating points in the IEEE 754 format. The sizes of all data types are the same across all operating systems and hardware. The implementor does not have the latitude to change the datatypes.

Arrays of all the datatypes, including objects, are possible. In fact, the arrays themselves are implemented as objects.

Table 18.1: Java Virtual Machine Datatypes

Type	Size	Description
byte	1 byte	Signed 2's complement integer
short	2 bytes	Signed 2's complement integer
int	4 bytes	Signed 2's complement integer
long	8 bytes	Signed 2's complement integer
float	4 bytes	IEEE 754 single-precision float
double	8 bytes	IEEE 754 double-precision float
char	2 bytes	Unsigned Unicode character
object	4 bytes	Reference to a Java object; called a handle
returnAddress	4 bytes	Used with jsr/ret/jsr_w/ret_w (jump subroutine and return from subroutine) instructions

Instruction Set

The Java Virtual Machine has roughly 220 instructions. These instructions are normal machine code types of instructions for loading variables, branching, arithmetic operations, stack manipulation, and so on. Each instruction consists of an instruction code called the opcode, which is 8 bits, and a variable set of operands, which are operated out of the stack. This means that the operations pull their operands from the operand stack and push the results back into the stack. Even though Java Virtual Machine assumes a 32-bit platform, the implementor has the choice to optimize for a larger word size machine/OS, like a 64-bit Windows NT. All operands are stored as one byte long in the class file, so to make a 16- or 32-bit operand, multiple operands are combined in *big-endian* (memory) or network order.

> **NOTE**
>
> Big-endian ordering is also called network ordering. In the big-endian ordering, high bytes of a word are stored first in memory; for example, 0x1234 will be stored in memory as 0x12 0x34 (the big end comes first). RISC and Motorola processors use the big-endian byte ordering, while the Intel 80x86 processors use the little-endian byte ordering. In the little-endian ordering, the word will be stored as 0x34 0x12 in memory (the little end comes first).

As an opcode example, take a look at the most fundamental operation that computers are good at: addition.

The addition of two numbers is achieved in the Java Virtual Machine by the opcodes `iadd` (96) for the `integer` type, `ladd` (97) for adding two `long` integers, `fadd` (98) for adding two numbers of `float` type and `dadd` (99) for adding two numbers of `double` type.

> **NOTE**
>
> In the example `iadd` (96), `iadd` is the mnemonic used for the description in the Java Virtual Machine specification and 96 is the actual opcode stored in the `.class` file representing the `iadd` operation.

Looking at the `iadd` opcode and how it works with the operand stack, we can see that the stack contains the first and second (32-bit) numbers to be added. The Java Virtual Machine will add the two numbers at the top of the stack and at the end of the operation, the result will be pushed onto the stack. Figure 18.3 shows a schematic of the `iadd` operation.

Opcodes 96 through 131 perform the addition (`.add`), subtraction (`.sub`), multiplication (`.mul`), division (`.div`), modulo (`.mod`), negation (`.neg`), and other operations in a similar manner. Another example is the opcodes for array manipulation. To create an array the `new array` (188) opcode is used. This opcode requires array type as a parameter and the array size in the operand stack. The Java Virtual

Schematic diagram for
iadd operation

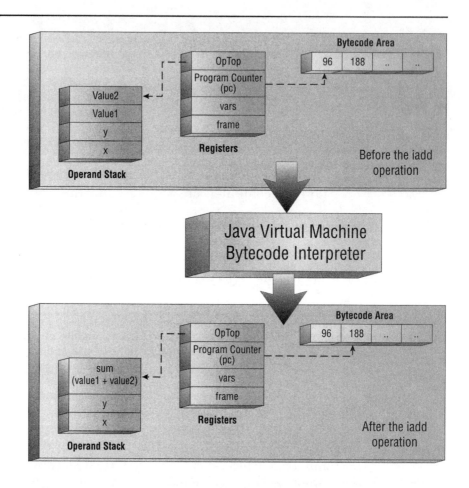

Machine then allocates enough space for the array, initializes all elements to zero and returns the reference handle at the top of the stack.

Class File Format

As you saw earlier, the Java compiler converts the Java source code into the .class file. Each source file will have one corresponding .class file. This file is a stream of bytes, and each byte is 8 bits long.

Bigger entities of 16 or 32 bits are constructed by reading in two or four bytes in the network or *big-endian* format. Table 18.2 lists the major elements in a `.class` file. For a detailed explanation and the underlying data structures, please refer to the Java Virtual Machine specification.

Table 18.2: Class File Format

Size	Name	Default/Value/Description
4 bytes	magic	0xCAFEBABE
2 bytes	minor_version	Minor version of the Java compiler
2 bytes	major_version	Major version of the Java compiler
2 bytes	constant_pool_count	Number of constant pool info variables in following field
variable	Constant pool info	Constant pool information (constant_pool_count-1)
2 bytes	access_flags	Various information flag bits. For example, 0x0100 means it is a native method or 0x0010 means it is a final class, method, variable
2 bytes	this_class	Constant pool index to this class
2 bytes	super_class	Constant pool index to the superclass if one exists
2 bytes	interface_count	Number of interface variables in following field
2 * interface_count	interfaces	Index to constant pool for each interface
2 bytes	fields_count	Number of fields variables in following field

Table 18.2: Class File Format (continued)

Size	Name	Default/Value/Description
variable	fields	Information on all fields including index to constant pool
2 bytes	method_count	Number of methods
variable	methods	Information on each method
2 bytes	attributes_count	Number of additional attributes about this class
variable	attributes	Extra attributes about this class

NOTE   The current Java Virtual Machine specification supports only the source file attribute. The attributes_count field will contain the number 1. The attributes data structure contains a two-byte constant pool index, which is "SourceFile," and a four byte attribute length, which is 2. The "SourceFile" constant pool index points to the constant, where the name of the source file, from which this class file was compiled, is kept.

Registers

The Java Virtual Machine requires four 32-bit *registers*. They are as shown in Table 18.3.

Method Area

The Java Virtual Machine specification gives each method invocation its own space for local variables, symbol tables, and so on. The detailed information about each method is found in the `.class` file

Table 18.3: Java Virtual Machine registers

Register Name	Description
pc	Program counter register which contains the address of the next bytecode instruction
frame	Points to the method area of the method which is being executed
vars	Local variables pointer
optop	Top of the operand stack pointer

on the methods structure (with the name "CODE"). This information includes the maximum stack size, local variable size, the byte code length, the actual byte codes, and exception details. Also, this area has the LineNumberTable and LocalVariable table for debugging. The Java Virtual Machine creates an area to store the transient data and execute the method.

Operand Stack

As we have seen, the instructions need an operand stack to pop parameters and push the operation results. The operand stack is 32-bits wide. The instructions can perform only the specified operations on the stack. For example, the `iadd` instruction can pop two 32-bit numbers from the stack and should push a 32-bit number back after the operation. It cannot, for example, join two 32-bit numbers and form a 64-bit number or push two numbers into the stack. The bytecode verifier will catch such misbehaved operations and will raise an error.

Garbage-Collected Heap

This is where the objects are created during the program execution. Each object in a Java program has a 32-bit pointer to the heap. This limits the maximum heap size to 4GB of memory. As we had discussed earlier, arrays are also implemented as objects, and the space for arrays is allocated in this heap. This heap is garbage collected automatically by the Java Virtual Machine.

Garbage Collection

The Java Virtual Machine automatically performs garbage collection to free up resources. The Java Virtual Machine specification does not specify any garbage-collection schemes or algorithms. Instead, it relies on the implementor to research and develop an efficient and appropriate garbage-collection algorithm.

Because the Java language has no constructs for freeing up memory, deleting objects, and other similar tasks, it is the responsibility of the garbage collector to reclaim discarded memory.

The Java Virtual Machine specification does not guarantee any timing on the garbage collection, so a Java programmer cannot assume that unused memory will be available immediately after an object ceases to exist in the program. The implication is that you should be careful when developing memory-hungry programs that declare and use objects with large data structures. Even though memory used by a huge data structure will be reclaimed when the structure is discarded, you should not use that knowledge to declare another huge structure immediately, especially when there is not enough memory space for both the structures (and you need huge arrays for multimedia types of data). Similarly, when you pack linked lists and other structures, you should not assume that the memory freed by the packing routines will be available immediately.

> **NOTE**
>
> Runtime automatic garbage collection is not a new concept. During the creation and runtime redimensioning of arrays, the Microsoft Visual Basic memory management is one very efficient runtime implementation of garbage collection. The Microsoft implementation of garbage collection in their Basic run time was a point of discussion for many years by programmers, particularly among beta testers. Usually a bug in the memory management and garbage collection will manifest itself as the dreaded general protection faults (GPFs) in the Windows environment. Their memory allocation and deallocation techniques have matured over the years through many versions of the product.

Security

The compiled Java bytecode does not contain any absolute memory references or addresses. Gone are the days of Poke and Peek, or defining arrays at absolute memory references like &H800 (which is the memory reference for the display buffer in IBM PC-compatible display cards). The Java Virtual Machine handles the memory allocation and referencing.

As mentioned earlier, you can create bytecodes directly, without a compiler, or you can write a compiler to generate bytecodes that could possibly snoop around the system, causing security risks. This is guarded by the bytecode verifier. Before the code is run for the first time, the bytecode verifier checks the bytecodes fully for things like mismatched parameters, bypassing access restrictions, and so on.

To prevent valid bytecode programs from causing damage—like deleting all files, corrupting hard disks, or sending local information across the net without the permission from the user—the Java Virtual Machine can have user-configurable access restrictions, such as deny local write, deny network access to other sites, and a host of others.

Most of the security measures rely upon a virus-free Java Virtual Machine. Obviously the security measures cannot prevent a faulty or

Trojan horse–type Java Virtual Machine from causing damage. If you download a Java Virtual Machine that has viruses built into it, there is no safeguard. So, if you glean only one thing from this section, let it be that the Java Virtual Machine should be acquired very carefully. Be extremely careful when you are downloading a Java Virtual Machine environment. Established vendors like Sun, Symantec, and Microsoft check their Java Virtual Machines thoroughly and are usually safe to download and operate. (There are known instances of major software companies having released viruses on their commercial releases.) The Java Virtual Machine is similar to an operating system and should be given the same considerations. Obtaining a secure Java Virtual Machine from an established vendor is the first line of defense against virus-ridden Java programs.

We are entering an era of encrypted, authenticated, and secure Java Virtual Machines and Java applets. All companies, including Microsoft and Sun, are working on public-key/certificate-encrypted delivery systems and signed classes. With signed applets, another level of trust is added.

Among the many levels of security, the two major mechanisms are the security manager and the Java class file verifier. Let's examine them next.

Security Manager

The security manager acts as the enforcer of security. It is an extensible class, thus providing application or system-specific added security implementations. It implements the security envelope and policies configured in the Java Virtual Machine/browser setup. The security manager establishes a namespace for the Java program which can restrict access to network, local file system, and other parts of the program. (A namespace is the boundary for a program established by the operating system or here by the Java Virtual Machine. A program cannot access resources beyond its own namespace.)

Applet Security

The security manager policies are configurable for an applet loaded through a Web browser. In the most common security scheme (used by Netscape Navigator), an applet downloaded from the network can load class files *only* from the same source as the code requesting the class. These are called *untrusted applets,* and if these applets try to access local storage or to communicate with some other server in the Internet, the security manager will generate a security exception. An applet loaded from the local hard disk can be allowed full access to all resources, at which point the security manager will allow the applets loaded locally to access local resources and connect to remote servers.

Application Security

In the case of Java applications, there are no security restrictions—all local and remote resource accesses are open to Java applications.

The use of digitally signed applets, called *signed classes*, is an important development in the area of security. There will be a security system where the user can configure a table of trusted entities. The table will contain certificates, digital signatures, and other related material for identifying the entity, and all entities will sign the Java applets/ classes that they develop. Once implemented, the security manager can allow more privileges to classes developed by trusted entities. If it is verified that the applet is signed by Microsoft, it can be given wider namespace than an untrusted applet downloaded from `http://www.virus.com`. The signed class architecture can be applied to applets as well as Java applications, which ensures that security policies will be uniform across Web browsers and applications.

Java Verifier

The Java verifier runs on a `.class` file and performs the security function to make sure that the Java bytecodes comply with the Java Virtual Machine specification. The bytecode verifier is one of the many levels of security assurance by the Java platform to check that viruses and other malicious programs will not wreak havoc on the local system. The verifier looks for syntax and semantic correctness of the class files, version checking, API conformance checking, and so on. Obviously, this is done before executing the Java program. Among other things, the verifier protects against compiler bugs and the intentional addition of malicious bytecodes. Overflow and underflow of values during arithmetic operations are identified during the verifier check run. Also many other runtime checks are done by the verifier, thus making the Java Interpreter run faster.

> **NOTE**
>
> As mentioned earlier, you really do not need the Java language for the Java Virtual Machine—a C++ or a BASIC compiler can generate Java bytecodes; however, it is the function of the verifier to make sure the generated bytecodes are executable safely and securely.

The verifier is implemented as a four pass operation: class file verification, type system verification, bytecode verification, and (runtime) type and access checking. Let's look at each in a bit more detail:

- Pass 1: Class File Verification—This pass verifies the class file structure. The first four bytes should be 0xCAFEBABE. It also checks that the file does not contain any extra bytes at the end, and runs the class file structure verification.

- Pass 2: Type System Verification—This pass, as the name indicates, does system level verifications like valid subclassing, valid constant, and pool pointers.

- Pass 3: Bytecode Verification—This pass does an exhaustive analysis of the actual bytecodes for each method, including operand stack analysis, method argument validation, and variable initialization.

- Pass 4: Runtime Type and Access Checking—The final pass is where many runtime checks and associations are done. By the time this pass is invoked, the system knows the methods, parameters, and return values. During this pass, it checks their validity and does runtime optimization, like replacing indirect references with direct references. Also, in this pass the access levels for the variables and methods are verified. For example, it verifies that the bytecodes weren't tweaked to provide access to private/protected variables/methods, etc. This pass can be optimized by the Java Virtual Machine implementor.

The verifier is the target of many virus attacks, so this process should be very thorough and fully tested. If a bug or a malicious operation passes the verifier, it could damage the system by deleting files or compromising the security.

Just-In-Time (JIT) Compilers

It is no secret that the Java Virtual Machine is slower in performance than traditional compiled languages. The Just-In-Time (JIT) compiler is a technique currently being developed by Symantec, Borland, and Microsoft, among others, that will greatly improve performance. The JIT compiler translates the bytecode to native machine code just before execution, so we get a bytecode compiler instead of an interpreter. It provides portability without sacrificing speed.

For example, Symantec Café has a JIT for the Apple Mac and 68K platform. Symantec claims that their JIT provides significant performance improvements when running Java-powered applets on the

Macintosh. Applets run up to three times faster when compared to Sun's current Java Virtual Machine for the Macintosh. Symantec's JIT compiler for Windows is also many times faster than Sun's current Java Virtual Machine.

The Microsoft JIT compiler (comes with Microsoft's Visual J++ Java development system now available in beta) reads and compiles the bytecodes to machine code and then keeps a pointer to the compiled code with the bytecode in the method area. This means that when the bytecode is to be executed again (which happens most of the time as programs consist of `do` and `for` loops), it need not go through the JIT. It is rumored that Microsoft might even develop an executable generator for Java programs on Microsoft platforms.

This discussion on JIT will not be complete without mentioning Borland's JIT Java AppAccelerator. Netscape has licensed this JIT for Netscape Navigator. The AppAccelerator is supposed to make Java applications run five to fifteen times faster than the native interpreted code.

Most probably, a JIT compiler will become an integral part of the Java Virtual Machine in the future, thus alleviating any performance concerns.

Java Licensing

Every day there is more news about companies licensing Java. Almost all of the major companies, including Apple, IBM, Microsoft, Novell, and Hewlett-Packard have licensed Java. What are they getting for their license? More importantly, as a developer, what is its significance?

The standard JavaSoft license covers the Java class libraries and the Java Virtual Machine. Each vendor will then become the custodian of Java on its platform, optimizing the engine for system performance and ensuring that Java applets, which are intended to be platform-independent, run just as well on their systems as they do on others. The contracts also require licensees to add all future Java APIs into their implementations.

Microsoft's Java Virtual Machine implementation is as a 32-bit operating system DLL on NT and Windows 95. This is called the *Windows Virtual Machine for Java*. As a DLL, it acts as an operating system extension so Java is available from all Windows applications. Microsoft has licensed the Windows Virtual Machine for Java back to Sun as a reference implementation for the Windows platform.

Apple will get its Java Virtual Machine from a third-party vendor and possibly build one later. Apple's Newton and Pippin are covered under the Java License. Novell has licensed to embed the Java Virtual Machine into the Novell Netware, which will add Java capabilities to Netware servers and clients, while providing capabilities for the distributed network services to create distributed applications for the Smart Global Network.

NOTE It is rumored that the current license fees range from $125,000 for the first platform (annual upgrade $50,000) and $25,000 per additional platform (annual upgrade $5,000) and a $5/unit royalty.

There are two types of licensable logos from Sun related to Java (although one can assume that there will be more coming later): The "Java Powered" Logo (no license fees) for applets and programs, which are developed using the Java Language and unmodified Java binaries; and the "Java Compatible" Logo for OEMs who integrate the Java Virtual Machine. A clean room Java Virtual Machine implementation would successfully complete the Java Test Suits and should maintain Applet API compatibility on all platforms. There is no logo for this compliance.

Summary

You can see how the Java Virtual Machine concept and the design of its elements, like the verifier and security manager, have aided the advancement of the current Internet/Intranet frenzy. The Java Virtual Machine has truly marshalled us into the next era of computing. As the technology matures, there will be more efficient implementations to better address the performance and security issues.

CHAPTER

NINETEEN

Third-Party Tools for Java

- Symantec Café 1.2

- Sun's Java Workshop dev5

- Soft As It Gets' Ed for Windows 3.55

- Penumbra Software's Mojo 1.2

- AimTech/IBM's Jamba Beta

- And many others...

When Java was first released, software companies started scrambling to get *something* on the market for hungry Java programmers who were looking for something more than simple command-line compilers and Notepad or vi editors. Now that the first wave of makeshift programs has passed, a new group of sophisticated tools for Java programming has emerged, and the results are quite impressive for such a new field. Commercial, shareware, freeware, and other products are now available to suit most any level of programmer, from first-time *newbie* to the hardened veteran.

> **NOTE**   Many of the third-party Java tools reviewed in this chapter are available on the CD-ROM accompanying this book. See each vendor's section for more information.

This chapter will help you decide which tools, if any, are appropriate for your Java needs. Many tools were not available at the time this was written, but Internet sites have been included that provide more information on future products.

The list of products included in this chapter is by no means exhaustive, and is not meant to be. Being aware of what some of the major products are—and their relative merits and features—will aid you in making an informed decision when it comes time to purchase third-party tools of your own.

> **NOTE**   Because of the constantly fluctuating nature of this industry and the cutting-edge nature of this information, you are advised to investigate the products covered in this chapter on your own before making a purchasing decision of any kind.

Symantec Café 1.2

The first company to get a full-featured *Integrated Development and Debugging Environment* (IDDE) to the market was Symantec with their Café product. This program, based upon Symantec's previous C++ offerings, is targeted at professional developers and programmers. Currently, Café is the de facto standard for Java development on Windows NT/95. No other major company has as full-featured a product on the market yet, but Symantec's early lead is sure to be shortened as a whole suite of products from Sun, Borland, and Microsoft seek to overtake Café's advantage. Smaller companies, too, have created products that will fill the needs of those not needing all of Café's features. Nevertheless, Café is a very strong package, so anyone doing serious Java development should probably take a long, hard look at it.

Installation

Café's installation is straightforward for both the CD-ROM and the online versions. See Table 19.1 for a list of features.

> **NOTE**
>
> There is one installation problem: In some cases, if you upgrade to Café 1.2, and then attempt to load an old project, Café flashes a "not a text file" dialog box error. The only way to exit Café is to End Task using the Windows 95 task manager. Once the offending file is replaced with a fresh copy, the error goes away, but it is a disconcerting way to enter a new programming environment. Luckily, this error is not reported on every copy of Café 1.2.

Table 19.1: Symantec Café's List of Features

Feature	Description
Graphical management of source files, compiled binaries, and HTML files into projects	Café allows you to easily manage your files by arranging them into projects.
Just-In-Time (JIT) Compiler	This is one of Café's features that is not yet equaled in any other product. With the JIT compiler, applets compiled under Café run as much as ten times faster than under Sun's compiler.
Café Studio	Café Studio provides a graphical environment for managing project resources and building Java GUIs.
Class editor	Café includes a professional-strength editor for writing code; includes color syntax highlighting.
ProjectExpress and AppExpress	These are "wizards" that help you start new projects and applets quickly.
Fully integrated debugger	Café's debugger is one of the most advanced on the market.
Online technical and product support	Café has a section on Symantec's Web page for getting the latest news and updates, as well as technical support.

Café requires 25–60MB of hard drive space, depending on whether you want all of the tutorial and sample files on your hard drive. They are well worth the space, although you can access them directly from the CD-ROM. You will also need a few more megabytes for the 1.2 update and the Just-In-Time compiler. You'll also need *at least* 8MB of RAM; 16 MB is recommended.

Documentation

Café comes with a small booklet of installation and support instructions. However, one of Café's perks is a one-year subscription to Symantec's members-only *Java Central* on the World Wide Web. Here, registered users of Café can download product upgrades and get the latest news about Café and Java. Using this online forum, upgrading from version 1.0 to 1.2 of Café is a snap.

Café also comes with a full array of help files. A Café tutorial, Java API reference, and numerous sample files are all included. The tutorial, shown in Figure 19.1, is adequate, but it is a bit terse and lacks a "big picture" view. It serves mainly to get you familiar with some of Café's basic features, but does not explain all of the features it introduces. It also assumes you have prior experience with Java and the Symantec-style IDDE.

FIGURE 19.1:

The Café tutorial

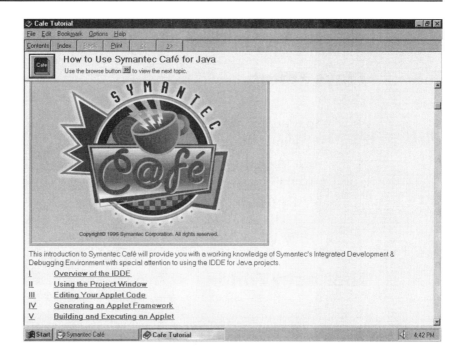

One minor flaw, which Symantec will surely fix, is that the tutorial does not reflect the latest changes to the Café GUI. For instance, the tutorial makes reference to a "project" tab in the Café environment that is simply not there. Despite these minor flaws, Café is well documented. One positive feature is that you can select a Java method and hit F1 and Café will display the online reference for that method. The rest of the online documentation, although somewhat difficult to understand, is thorough and accurate.

Ease of Use

Café's GUI is not the most user-friendly, especially when compared to products like Mojo and Jamba. Café is designed for developers and programmers who have experience with Java and similar environments—to the uninitiated, it can be quite intimidating. Luckily, everything in Café is well-documented so, if you know where to look, you can figure it out relatively easily.

Class Editor

In order to write and edit source code, Café comes with a class editor. Like most other programming editors, the class editor, shown in Figure 19.2, color-codes different parts of the Java language for easy reference. This helps eliminate common mistakes and makes your code easier to read. However, Café is not perfect; it does not color-code Strings. This is only a minor inconvenience—overall, Café's editor is standard.

Hierarchy Editor

Café's Hierarchy Editor, like its class editor, is a useful feature, although hardly unique. The Hierarchy Editor lets you view the relationships between classes in your project, as well as the methods and parameters contained in each class. This makes it easy to see the overview of your application.

FIGURE 19.2:

Café's class editor

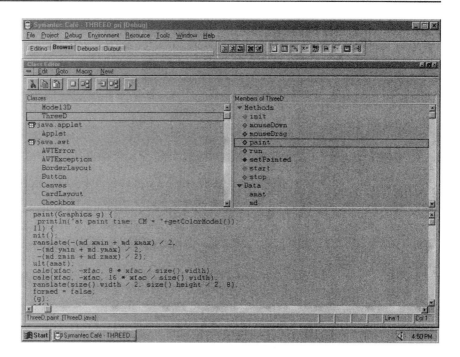

GUI Builder: Café Studio

One of Café's most interesting, but least refined, tools is the Café Studio (pictured in Figure 19.3), which is used to manage *resources* in Café projects. The term resource is a holdover from older languages like C++; this is not a common term shared by most Java development packages. Resources are things like the AWT components that make up the GUI, as well as external components like sounds and graphics. Although this tool is a good one, it is far from finished, and is the only part of Café that really lags behind the competition. Similar features in other products, such as Sun's Visual Java or Mojo's GUI Designer, are more elegant and easy to use, although Café Studio is also very strong.

Although Café does generate accurate code from the resource files created, the end result does not always look the same as displayed in

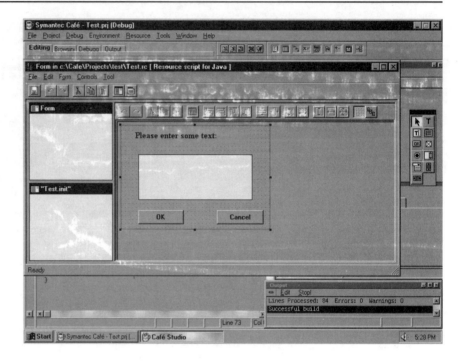

the Studio. Additionally, the Studio's GUI is itself a little buggy, although this consists of mainly cosmetic bugs. In addition, Café's code is not entirely portable across platforms, because it does not make use of Java LayoutManagers; instead, it uses absolute screen positioning. This is a problem unfortunately shared by most GUI builders.

Although the GUI shown in Figure 19.4 still looks a bit messy, it is certainly possible to make better-looking ones in the Studio with a little practice. Like the rest of Café, Studio is very powerful, but has a sharp learning curve.

ProjectExpress and AppExpress

These two "wizards" make starting a new applet in Café simple. They simply guide you through a series of questions and then generate the requisite code for you. Although these tools, along with

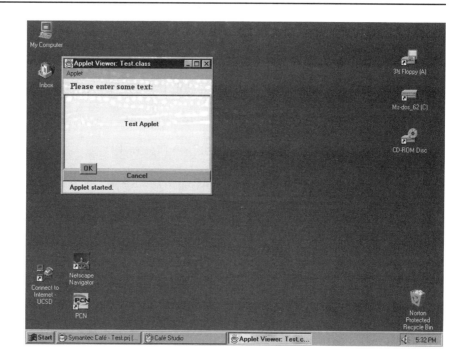

Café Studio, do manage to take some of the "manual labor" out of writing Java programs, they are no substitute for writing code, which Café is designed to let you do. Unlike some other tools, they do not attempt to replace the most difficult coding tasks you will encounter. Nevertheless, they do make creating Java projects in Café much easier.

Graphical Debugger

This is the most unique feature, not only of Café, but of all of the tools available today. Other companies have promised an integrated debugger like Café's, but Symantec is the first to deliver such a product. Using Symantec's custom-created compiler and debugger in concert makes building your project, and finding errors, easy. No longer will you have to use the `println` method of debugging. Café represents a quantum leap forward from using Sun's javac and jdb.

Like its other features, Café's debugger is not as intuitive as it could be, so it takes a little getting used to.

The debugger comes armed with the following features:

- Easily set breakpoints (see Figure 19.5)

- Animated code executions

- Thread control (see Figure 19.6)

- Call chains and variable inspections

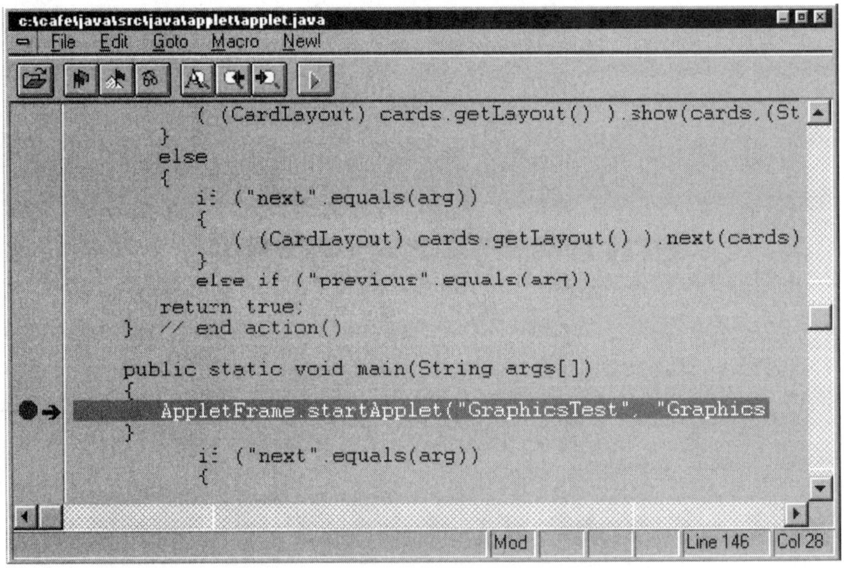

FIGURE 19.5:

Café's graphical debugger's code breakpoint

Conclusion

Café is clearly the top choice for Java developers who want to get their hands dirty writing code *right now*. Its interface and design are solid, if a bit stiff, and the program runs almost entirely error-free

FIGURE 19.6:

Café's Thread control

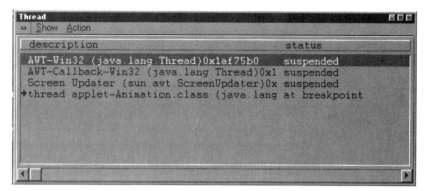

and is very responsive (unlike, for example, Sun's Java Workshop). Its promotional price also makes it a good choice for entry-level programmers who do not want to sacrifice any features and do not mind giving up the glitz of other, more expensive products.

Pricing and Availability: Symantec Café

Latest Version:	1.2
Platforms:	Windows NT/95 only
Pricing:	Standard: $299
	Promotion: $129
	Upgrade from Symantec C++: FREE
For More Information:	*e-mail*: javainfo@symantec.com
	URL: http://cafe.symantec.com/
Customer Service:	Symantec Corporation
	175 W. Broadway
	Eugene, OR 97401
	(800) 441-7234

Sun's Java WorkShop dev5

It stands to reason that the most robust development environment for Java would come from the people who created it. Sun's JavaSoft group has been working overtime on what is destined to be the most dazzling and sophisticated IDE to date. (All of this is still on the horizon, however.) Java WorkShop (JWS) looks to be especially interesting because it is written in Java. While this means it takes advantage of Java's strengths (platform independence, expandability), it also means that JWS suffers from Java's shortcomings (most notably, slow execution speed and bugs). JWS is the IDE of the future, but for now it is slow and crash-prone. Nevertheless, it does boast the coolest set of tools and most useful set of utilities to *almost* hit the market. And since it is free until October 1996, it is well worth the download; just do not try to do anything serious with it unless you have got plenty of time, memory, patience, and CPU to spare. Table 19.2 has a list of Sun's JWS features, and shows how it stands up against Café.

Installation

Be aware that, on any system, *recommended* system requirements for JWS are a Pentium or SPARC-based machine with 24 MB of RAM (32 MB for Solaris). You can run it with 16 MB, but you better have a good book to read. Installation is straightforward, but once you start developing applets, you will notice a few quirks. First of all, JWS cannot create directories for your projects, so you have to either use existing ones, or leave the program and create them yourself. This and other minor bugs will undoubtedly be fixed in time for the release version.

Documentation

The dev5 release of JWS came with no documentation save what you can get on Sun's Web pages. While adequate, it most likely left out many of JWS's powerful features. The only sample code included is a hideous game of checkers that is too slow and too inane to play.

Table 19.2: Key Features of Sun's Java Workshop

Feature	Description	Café?
Project manager	Like most other similar products, JWS lets you organize your work into projects that keep related files together.	YES
"Webcentric" design	JWS is laid out like a Web browser/editor, so integrating your applets with Web pages is simple.	NO
Visual Java GUI builder	Lets you lay out your applets' user interface easily. Similar to Café's resource manager.	YES
Integrated Toolset	Tight integration of JWS's different tools makes work easier and faster.	similar
Build Manager	Helps you build your code and find errors fast.	YES
Portfolios	Allows you to group together related projects. Aids in Web publishing and group programming.	NO
Integrated Applet viewer	"Smart" applet viewer automatically loads necessary resources, including external applications, if necessary.	NO
Source editor/browser	Not as good as other packages; lacks color syntax highlighting, but does allow you to place hyperlinks within source.	YES
Class Browser	Allows you to easily navigate Java classes.	YES
Integrated debugger	Works basically as well as Café's, except it is written in Java. Allows manipulation of Threads, breakpoints, and is integrated with the applet viewer.	YES
Written in Java	Makes JWS (eventually) platform-independent and allows integration of project and environment.	NO

However, since importing your own code can be tricky, it is nice to have something with which to experiment.

Ease of Use

As shown in Figure 19.7, the JWS sports a very nice user interface—when it works. The Java AWT implementation on Win32 machines is shaky at best; at times it can be downright awful. However, the cute buttons and limited online help do make editing projects pretty easy. Most disappointingly, creating a new project is an obtuse and confusing procedure that can be both frustrating and time-consuming. This can only improve in the final release, but currently it is dismal. The Visual Java tool is extremely cool, but it is not clear how to get it to compile into usable source code. And beware of crashes: JWS will crash your computer more often than a beta version of Netscape Navigator!

FIGURE 19.7:

The JWS User Interface, with quirks

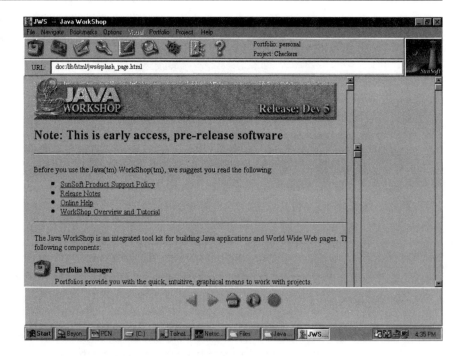

Source and Class Browsers

This is one of the best developed parts of the Java WorkShop. JWS can generate the cool javadoc files used on Sun's Web pages for your own applets, if you document your code well and in a format it can understand. These browsers make it very easy to see the relationship between various methods, variables, and classes (see Figure 19.8).

FIGURE 19.8:

The JWS class browser

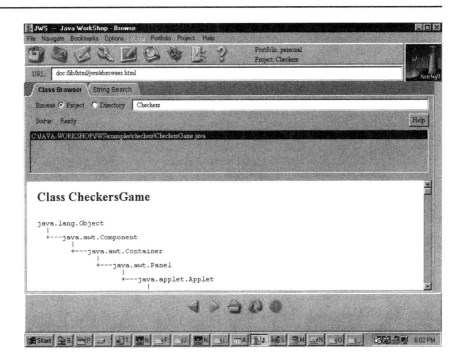

Build Manager and Debugger

These two tools work hand-in-hand. The Build Manager only recompiles those source files that have changed since the last compilation, and then lets you view them in the applet viewer. If a problem arises during execution (or if you select the proper option), the debugger is launched (see Figure 19.9), and you can view everything your applet is doing as it happens. This includes sophisticated Thread control (really nice) and code stepping features.

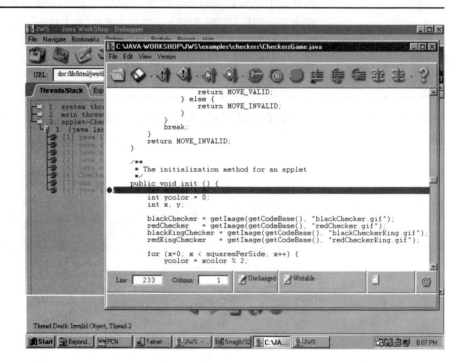

Visual Java

The newest addition to the JWS package is the GUI builder, known as *Visual Java*. This tool makes it easy to add AWT Components to your applet, although getting them to integrate with your source code is a bit tricky. Despite its ease-of-use problems, Visual Java is extremely powerful and will one day be one of the coolest tools in its class. It is also one of the most technically competent GUI builders in its class—it can even support LayoutManagers.

Conclusion

Java WorkShop is the product of choice for professional programmers, Web designers, and anyone else who wants top-of-the-line Java development. Despite its drawbacks, JWS has the most potential of any other package. But beware—when JWS premieres it will carry a pretty steep price tag. Sun says its Slim Kit will retail at about $295, and it is not clear what that will include. The bottom line, then, would seem to be this: If you want the best, you want Java WorkShop. Just be sure you have plenty of patience—and a thick wallet.

Pricing and Availability: Java WorkShop (from Sun's JavaSoft group)

Latest Version:	dev5 prerelease
Final Release Date:	October, 1996
Platforms:	Solaris, Win32 (NT/95); eventually should run on all platforms
Pricing:	FREE as part of Sun's Try and Buy program until October, 1996
	Slim Kit: $295 (this price is not certain)
	Ten-user Slim Kit: $2950 (this price is not certain)
For More Information:	*phone*: (800) SUNSOFT or (512) 434-1511
	e-mail: sunsoft@selectnet.com
	URL: http://java.sun.com
	online information request form: http://www.harte-hanks.com/sun/sunform.cgi

Soft As It Gets' Ed for Windows

Although many companies promised to have an Integrated Development Environment (IDE) for Java immediately following its release, the first company to actually produce one was not one of the major players. In fact, it was a small Australian company, known as Soft As It Gets that has a product known as Ed for Windows. This is a Windows-only IDE for more than 30 programming languages, of which Java is the most recent addition. Although Ed does not have all of the features of a visual Java package, it makes using Sun's tools extremely easy, and provides one of the most powerful source code editors on the planet. For those who use multiple programming languages, or those who want a top-notch editor, Ed is the perfect tool. Look at Table 19.3 to determine how Ed compares to Café.

NOTE   Ed for Windows is available on the CD-ROM accompanying this book. This version is good for 45 days from the time you install it. Please visit their Web site for updates.

Installation

Ed for Windows installs easily, but takes a little configuration to get it started. Because almost every feature is customizable, it may take a few tries to get a look and feel you like. Luckily, Ed comes with a nice default set of options, as well as the ability to emulate many popular editing programs.

Table 19.3: Key Features of Soft As It Gets' Ed for Windows 3.55

Feature	Description	Café?
Multilanguage support	Ed is designed for use with over 30 programming languages, such as C++ and Ada, as well as Java.	NO
Color syntax highlighting	Ed has one of the best syntax highlighting editors on the market. It is fully customizable.	YES
Code templates	Ed has special templates that help you start new projects quickly.	YES—wizards
Autocorrection	This is one of Ed's most unique features. Can be programmed to fix typos and mistakes on-the-fly.	NO
Totally customizable	Every aspect of Ed is user-customizable. From colors to actions to a full-featured macro programming language, Ed is designed to work how you want it to.	NO
Integrates with Sun's JDK	Ed allows you to compile and debug straight from the editor, and can even link references in the output with the source code.	NO—has its own JDK
Class browser	Ed includes a browser for visually stepping through your Java classes.	YES

Documentation

Ed comes with a user manual that provides excellent documentation. Additional documentation is also available from help menus within the program. Ed even displays a "tip of the day" every time you start it up—although, like all of Ed's features, you can turn it off, too. One of Ed's best features is an intuitive interface that makes most documentation unnecessary. Once you have it installed, you can be writing code (even working on your old code) in a matter of minutes. Although this approach will get you started, it is worth checking out the documentation simply to see all of Ed's great features, of which there are literally hundreds.

Ease of Use

Ed is very user friendly. The IDE is easy to use and its syntax coloring is superb (see Figure 19.10).

FIGURE 19.10:

Ed's user interface

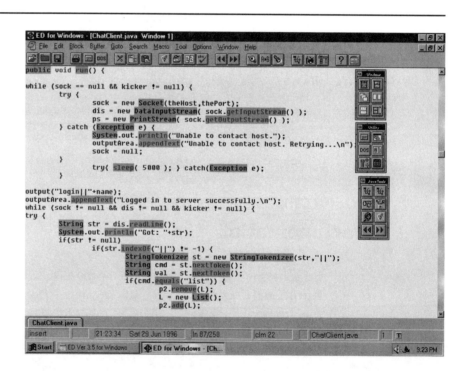

Ed also includes many other features that make it easy to use. It has a sophisticated search-and-replace function and a whole host of spelling options that help reduce tedious tasks. Ed keeps track of the files you have been working on, and automatically opens them as necessary, even after you have quit the program and started again. If you are sharing a computer with multiple people, Ed will keep separate settings for each person.

Java Hierarchy Browser

Ed's hierarchy browser is easy to use and not terribly feature-packed (see Figure 19.11). Although lacking in some of the exotic features of some other Java editors, Ed gets the job done here, too. Using the hierarchy browser, you can easily maneuver through the various classes that make up your Java program. You can also browse through the Java package classes that your project imports. All of these files can easily be loaded into the editor.

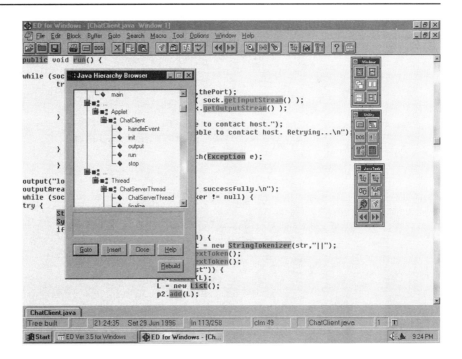

Compiling and Debugging

Getting Ed to compile with your installation of the JDK may take a few minutes of configuring, but is for the most part self-explanatory and well documented. Ed certainly lacks the advantage of an integrated debugger—which both Café and JWS can boast of—but it integrates Sun's command-line compiler (javac) into its graphical environment quite well. With one click of the mouse button, Ed will compile your Java source with user-definable CLASSPATH settings, and then display the compiler's output in a window. If the compiler reports any errors, Ed will immediately highlight them and help you find them in your source code (see Figure 19.12). While not as full-featured a debugging method as some other packages, this method is quite an improvement over the JDK alone.

FIGURE 19.12:

Ed showing errors in source code

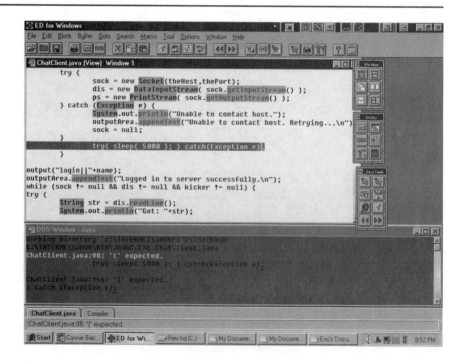

Conclusion

If you use languages other than Java on a Windows computer, Ed is a surefire bet. Its easy-to-use, customizable, and powerful editing environment makes it the perfect choice for most individual programmers. It does lack many of the fancy features of some Java IDE packages; if you are the type of programmer who can live without them, you will be very happy with Ed. It is also one of the only choices for those programmers who use Windows 3.1; although Ed works fine with the Win32 platforms (NT and 95—a 32-bit native version is promised by the fall), it was designed initially for Windows 3.1. Unfortunately, Windows 3.1 users will be unable to compile their source code until someone creates a 16-bit Java compiler.

Pricing and Availability: Ed for Windows (from Soft As It Gets Pty. Ltd.)

Latest Version:	3.55g
Platforms:	Windows 3.1/NT/95 only
Pricing:	Full version: $299
	45-day trial: FREE
For More Information:	Soft As It Gets Pty. Ltd.
	12 Fairview Grove
	Glen Iris, Vic. 3146
	Australia
	phone: +61 3 9885 4445
	fax: +61 3 9885 4444
	Compuserve: 100032,522
	URL: http://www.ozemail.com.au/~saig/

Penumbra Software's Mojo 1.2

Mojo is one of the best visual environments for creating Java applets. Its primary goal is to allow rapid generation of Java applets without writing code. However, unlike some other visual programming environments, Mojo does not isolate the programmer from the code. Although Mojo can do many things for you, it never hides the underlying processes; you can always change methods or properties directly in the source code. Like Ed for Windows, Mojo is an "underdog" product fighting for recognition in a field dominated by giants. It occupies a niche, but unlike Ed, this niche is at the opposite end of the programming spectrum. Ed is a powerful tool for editing source code, but Mojo is for those who prefer a more visual experience. Mojo makes creating applets easy and quick, without sacrificing the powerful advantages of writing code. In general, Mojo is the fun way to write Java applets. Table 19.4 breaks down its features for you.

> **NOTE** A full-featured version of Penumbra's Mojo 1.2 is provided on the CD-ROM accompanying this book. This is a timed-out version of the product, good for 30 days from the time you install it.

Installation

Mojo's installation is straightforward, and configuration is not a problem at all. Once the software is installed, getting it to run requires no additional configuration.

Documentation

Documentation for Mojo is still scarce, although the final release version will undoubtedly ship with extensive documentation. There are

Table 19.4: Key Features of Penumbra Software's Mojo

Feature	Description	Café?
Rapid Java development	Allows you to quickly begin creating applets with no prior programming knowledge.	NO
Zero learning curve	Using Mojo, you can learn Java as you go; there is no need to know the language before using Mojo.	NO
Java Designer	Mojo's intuitive and easy to use GUI builder. Unlike other similar products, Mojo's Designer lets you easily associate actions with Components and gives you simple access to Component variables.	YES
Java Coder	Mojo's Coder is the perfect compliment to the Designer. It combines the features of a class browser and a source code editor to allow you to easily customize components to do just about anything.	YES
Expandable, Component-based system	Mojo revolves entirely around Components, which can be easily plugged in to any application. This means Mojo always grows with you and never limits you.	NO
Open programming	Allows multiple programmers to share components thus adding to the overall Component pool.	NO
Interface with the Java debugger	Not as good as other products that include an integrated debugger, but still allows basic debugging functionality, which is more than most users of this type of system are likely to need.	YES

plenty of demo applets on Mojo's Web site. The online help is decent but not extraordinary, and is largely superfluous. Mojo is intuitive and makes documentation almost unnecessary—odds are, most Mojo manuals will double as paper weights. The only possible source of confusion is in some of Mojo's terminology. Mojo's programming model revolves around *actions* and *events* that are a bit different from the standard Java definition of these words. Veteran

Java programmers may be thrown for a while, but can adapt quickly; novice programmers may never even notice the difference.

Ease of Use

Mojo is a snap to use (see Figure 19.13). Although you can get started creating applets very quickly, adding some specific functions to Components can be difficult if you are used to doing it a different way. For instance, there is no apparent way to add items to a `List` component from the Java Designer. Luckily, flaws like this are few and far between. For most Components, changing attributes and adding actions is simple. For those times when this does not work, you can always write the code by hand.

FIGURE 19.13:

Mojo GUI

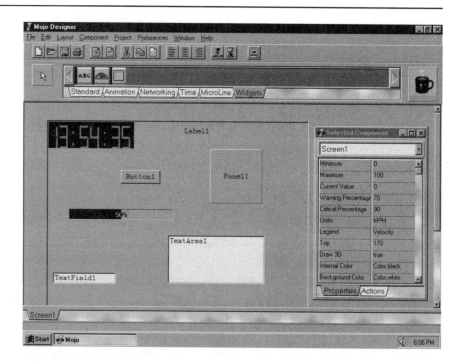

The 1.2 version of Mojo is very stable, and things will probably improve further in future versions. Because parts of Mojo are written in Java (this is not totally apparent from the documentation), it tends to have some slow execution moments, especially when it uses Sun's compiler and debugger, but overall execution speed is more than adequate.

Java Designer

This is so cool, you will never get enough of it. Like Café Studio and Visual Java, Mojo's Designer lets you drag-and-drop Java Components onto *screens* that you then build into an applet. The main difference between Mojo and other GUI builders is (1) it actually works right; and (2) it is easy to use. Another great feature of Mojo is that it comes with many nifty new Components and Widgets, including a LED Clock and a very functional Ticker Tape. Other Components include various Gauges, Trees, Tabs, and Networking Components. When you want to change a Components properties or add an Action, simply double-click and an appropriate tabbed dialog box pops up. Most changes (but not all) are displayed right in the editor. You can also choose to preview the applet within Mojo (see Figure 19.14), or use your Netscape browser to see what it really looks like.

Java Coder

Mojo's Coder is almost as easy to use as its Designer. It comes with a *dual hierarchy* view that allows you to browse both source and class files simultaneously. Its editor, although not the fanciest, gets the job done with very nice color syntax highlighting and cross-referencing. It also allows you to easily override methods as well as add new Components, Actions, Events, and methods instantly. It even generates accurate code from the Designer. Best of all, anything you can do in the Designer, you can do in the Coder—and changes get updated

FIGURE 19.14:

Applet preview

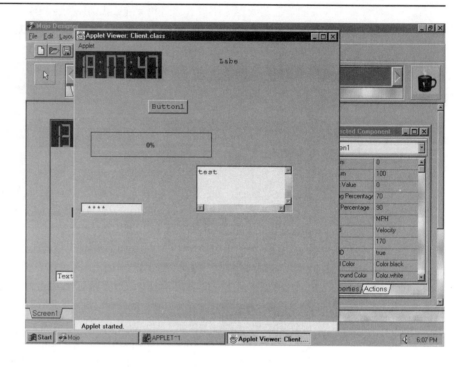

FIGURE 19.14:

Applet preview

in both places. All-in-all, it's a very nice compromise between GUI and code.

Conclusion

If you are the type of person who actually enjoys using UNIX utilities like awk and vi, Mojo is probably not for you. If Perl scripting and Assembly are things you enjoy, perhaps you should look into something like Ed for Windows. However, for the rest of the world, Mojo is a wonderful tool. Even veteran programmers will enjoy not having to write tedious code over and over again, and novice programmers will marvel at how quickly they start programming useful applets. For a delightfully robust alternative to the commercial Java blend, try sipping Penumbra Software's Mojo.

Pricing and Availability: Mojo (from Penumbra Software)

Latest Version: 1.2

Platforms: Windows 95/NT only

Pricing: Full Edition: $149
Student Edition: $49 (requires student ID—for educational purposes only)
Enterprise Edition: $495 (contains JDBC and ODBC support)

For More Information: Penumbra Software
4015 Holcomb Bridge Rd., Suite 350
Norcross, GA 30092

phone: (770) 352-0100
fax: (770) 390-0636
URL: http://www.PenumbraSoftware.com

AimTech and IBM's Jamba Beta

Jamba is a graphical applet builder that has quite a flair for multimedia. Jamba hides most of Java's inner workings by abstracting the flow of your applet into easy to understand steps. Jamba allows you to painlessly create Web pages that are active and interesting. Jamba is not good at more traditional programming tasks, but it does not seek to be all things to all people. With Jamba, writing code is totally unnecessary, so it lacks some of the sophisticated editing and debugging tools of other products. Jamba refuses to apologize for its nonprogramming approach to Java, however. Using Jamba, your Web pages come alive with interactive sights and sounds that blow away any previously available medium. Jamba is a snazzy, easy-to-use environment for creating applets that are just downright cool. Table 19.5 shows some of Jamba's features and how they stack up against Café.

NOTE You can find the Jamba beta on the CD-ROM. It is a full version of the beta, but be sure to see the AimTech Web site for any updated product information at `http://www.aimtech.com/prodjahome.html`.

Table 19.5: Key Features of Jamba Beta

Feature	Description	Café?
Multimedia-oriented development	Far more than any other product, Jamba is designed with the intent to create multimedia Web content.	NO
Built-in support for multimedia formats	Jamba comes ready to incorporate diverse multimedia content without extensions to the user's browser (plug-ins) or operating system. Numerous audio, video, and animation formats are supported.	NO
Non-coding approach	Jamba allows you to create interesting and complex applications without writing a single line of code.	NO
Drag-and-drop GUI builder	Allows you to create your GUI by simply dragging Components into position	YES
ImageLab	Aimtech's extremely advanced image manipulation software makes creating and managing images with Jamba a snap.	NO

Documentation

Jamba's documentation is outstanding. Even though they are offering only a beta-version product, Jamba is one of the best documented tools for creating applets with Java. Their manual is concise, straightforward, and comes with plenty of figures and examples. The HTML tutorial includes examples of what Jamba can do, as well as detailed instructions on how you can use Jamba to create what you want. Jamba also comes with a slew of demo applets that help you understand the way Jamba works (see Figures 19.15 and 9.16), and a "tip of the day," which, thankfully, you can turn off.

Jamba demo applet

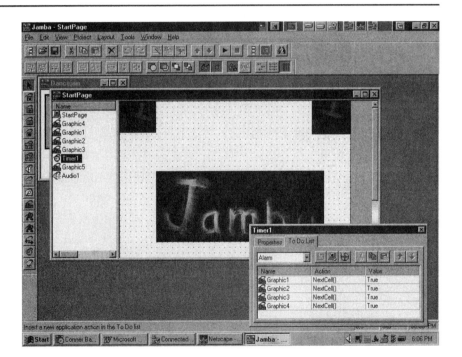

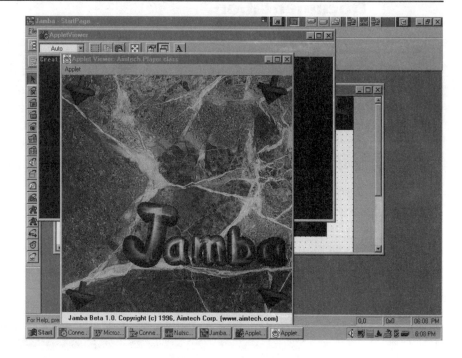

Ease of Use

Jamba is also one of the easiest products to use of those listed here. Although Jamba strays from the standard Java terminology, even veteran programmers will catch on quickly. Applets are composed of one or more *screens* that contain various components. Adding and arranging components is a cinch, as is modifying their properties: To add functionality to a component, you simply add tasks to its To Do List.

GUI Builder

Jamba has no separate facilities for the GUI and underlying code—all programming is done in the GUI builder. However, those used to traditional programming will not find any here. Jamba is made up of screens that contain various components. Each of these components has properties and a To Do List that control how it behaves. To create a program, you simply use Jamba's many toolbars to select what components you want and how you want them to interact with each other and the user.

Figure 19.17 shows the basic Jamba GUI.

FIGURE 19.17:

Using Jamba to create an applet

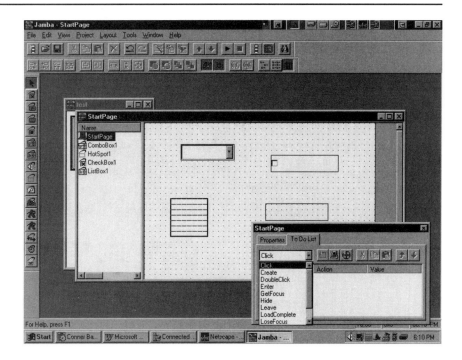

Creating new screens from scratch is easy, as is adding components. Jamba creates special JMB files that control how a Jamba project works—you don't even have to write the HTML code yourself. The only real drawback to this transparent functionality is that it is sometimes hard to troubleshoot if things do not look precisely how you intended. Jamba hides all the underlying tasks from you, so you can't mess with them even if you want to.

ImageLab

Another unique feature of Jamba is its accompanying ImageLab. This piece of software makes creating and manipulating images easy. ImageLab can handle a variety of image formats and can even take screen shots of your desktop. Because Jamba is so multimedia-oriented, having top-notch software like this is a must. Hopefully, future versions of Jamba will come with tools for editing other media like video and sound.

Pricing and Availability: Jamba (from AimTech and IBM)

Latest Version:	Beta
Platforms:	Windows 95/NT (support for Mac/UNIX coming soon)
Pricing:	Final release: $495
For More Information:	*URL*: http://www.aimtech.com/prodjahome .html

Other Tools

Space constraints prevent a full review of every major Java development tool, so the next sections provide you with brief summaries of some intriguing Java-related tools, along with places to go for more information about each one.

SourceCraft's NetCraft

NetCraft, a part of SourceCraft's ObjectCraft professional development package, is a somewhat unstable freeware visual Java builder. Because it is developed as part of a commercial package, it has many of the advantages of an expensive package without the hefty price tag. However, it is still in its preliminary stages and is pretty buggy.

Pricing and Availability: NetCraft (from SourceCraft)

Latest Version:	N/A
Platforms:	Windows NT/95 (others planned)
Pricing:	NetCraft is distributed as freeware
For More Information:	Ed Chuang, Director of Corporate Marketing SourceCraft, Inc. *phone*: 617-221-5665 *fax*: 617-221-5668 *e-mail*: edc@sourcecraft.com *URL*: http://www.sourcecraft.com

Allen Systems Group's WebGalaxy 1.0

WebGalaxy is a very different tool from all of the others. With WebGalaxy, you do not write any code; you ask and then answer a series of questions. These questions are used as a guide to create an interactive problem-solver for your user. WebGalaxy is suitable mainly for commercial purposes. For more information, see their Web page at http://www.webgalaxy.net.

Alladin Software's HOPE Beta

The Human Oriented Programming Environment (HOPE) is a program designed for a team of programmers. HOPE breaks tasks and files up into *particles* for easy team management. HOPE also has support for C and C++, in addition to Java, which makes it great for projects that span those languages. HOPE also sports a full-featured IDE and source browser. For more information, see their Web page at `http://www.hasp.com/hope/hope.htm`.

Innovative Software's OEW for Java 1.0

The Object Engineering Workbench for Java is the product of Innovative Software, a German company that produces industrial-strength OOP projects. OEW is a repository-based class editor that is cross platform and heavy on menus. It comes with professional tools, including a class browser and debugger. Although a bit difficult to use, and in its preliminary stages, OEW promises to be an excellent software engineering tool.

Pricing and Availability: Object Engineering Workbench (from Innovative Software)

Availability:	Version 0.9 available for download
	1.01 available for purchase
Pricing:	Beta: FREE
	Version 1.01: $149 (for Windows 95/NT),
	$349 (for UNIX)
For More Information:	*URL*: `http://www.isg.de/OEW/Java/`

StepAhead's Javelin 4.49

Javelin is another easy-to-use graphical environment for Java. Javelin comes in several different varieties and has many really neat features, including some automatic code generation routines that blow the competition away, so their free evaluation copy is definitely worth a look.

Pricing and Availability: Javelin (from StepAhead)

Availability:	Now (Windows 95/NT only)
Pricing:	10C and 25C limited versions: $39 and $69 Professional version: $199
For More Information:	*URL*: http://www.ozemail.com.au/ ~stepsoft/javidx.html

RadJa 2.1

RadJa is a *Rapid Application Development* tool for creating Java applets quickly, using a visual interface similar to Mojo's. RadJa is distributed as shareware, but a registered commercial version is available for a registration fee. RadJa is multiplatform and requires no coding experience. To code in RadJa, you manipulate a series of *controls*, which provides an intuitive object-oriented approach to Java design.

Pricing: RadJa

Pricing:	Mini RadJa: $39
	RadJa: $190
	RadJa Pro: $390
For More Information:	*URL*: http://www.radja.com

Metrowerk's CodeWarrior 9

The only major affordable Macintosh development tool on the market, Metrowerk's CodeWarrior provides an excellent and robust programming environment. Accessible and well-documented, it is available in the full multilanguage version or as a Java-only "discover" package, and has a discount for academic use. If you have a Macintosh, this is a must-see product.

Pricing: CodeWarrior (from Metrowerk)

Pricing:	Discover: $99
	Gold: $399
	Academic Pro: $119
	Academic 96/97: $79
For More Information:	*URLs*:
	http://www.metrowerks.com/products/ discover/java.html
	http://www.metrowerks.com/products/ announce/cw9.html

For More Information...

Table 19.6 lists some places on the Web where you can find more information about third-party tools for Java.

Table 19.6: Where to Find More Java-Related Information

Name/URL	Description

The Java IDE Page
`http://www.cybercom.net/~frog/`
`javaide.html`
	Possibly the most exhaustive list of Java tools and IDEs, this has been called the *Consumer Reports* of Java third-party tools.

Gamelan `http://www.gamelan.com`	EarthWeb's comprehensive and searchable repository of all things Java.

Usenet Newsgroups
`comp.lang.java.programmer`
`comp.lang.java.tech`
`comp.lang.java.announce`
	Always a good source of information, here you can ask questions and browse comments by thousands of Java enthusiasts worldwide.

TeamJava `http://www.teamjava.com`	Resource for Java programmers, developers, and employers.
JavaWorld Magazine `http://www.javaworld.com`	Excellent online magazine devoted to Java news, and products. Has product reviews and features for developers.
Symantec's Java Central `http://café.symantec.com`	News and links for Java developers; slightly biased towards one particular company.

Java WebIDE
`http://www.chamisplace.com/prog/`
`javaide/`
	The IDE of the future! Truly platform-independent because it runs on the WWW. No extra software required.

The Java Developer
`http://www.digitalfocus.com/`
`digitalfocus/faq/`
	Online resource for Java developers.

Microsoft's Visual J++ `http://www.microsoft.com`	Although Microsoft is notorious for vaporware—advanced programs promised but never, or belatedly, delivered—this has the potential to become a major player in the Java market. Just don't bet any money on it.

CHAPTER

TWENTY

Java and Databases

- Java Enterprise APIs

- Vendor/Third-Party Solutions

An Introduction to Java Database Access

After the initial enthusiasm and the first wave of applets, Java architects at JavaSoft started thinking about extending Java as a client/server platform. The corporate IT and consultants started developing Intranet concepts and realized that Java has a lot of advantages in the client/server market, including zero administration clients, central software update and administration, versionless software, and a Webcentric paradigm. One of the most important sets of Java *Application Programming Interfaces* (APIs) needed was an interface to databases so that data could be created, accessed, shared, updated, and referred across the Internet and Intranet as seamlessly as the current network databases.

> **NOTE**
>
> Java APIs are classes and methods that allow Java programs to interact with the real-world systems. For example, the `java.net` API enables a Java program to communicate using the TCP/IP protocol, and the `java.awt` gives Java programs the ability to display menus, buttons, and list boxes. There are core APIs (like `java.lang`, `java.net`, `java.awt` and `java.applet` classes), which are part of any Java system. Then there are standard extensions like the Java Server API and the Java Management API. Over time, many of these standard APIs will become an indispensable part of the Java language and will move into the core APIs. Chapter 21 discusses the Java APIs in detail.

At the same time, the database vendors, like Oracle and Informix, wanted Java applets to access their databases through the Internet and Intranet, so they went off to start developing Java classes and methods to access data in their databases. This has resulted in many different approaches to database access from Java.

At the JavaOne conference (in May 1996), Sun announced a set of new APIs directed towards client/server, Intranet/Internet applications. There are many APIs including Java Enterprise APIs, Java

Commerce APIs, Java Security APIs, and Java Servlet/Jeeves APIs, all of which elevate the Java language to a platform level and are aimed at developing multitier client/server applications that are Internet enabled.

This chapter focuses primarily on the Enterprise APIs: JDBC API, Java Remote Method Invocation (RMI), Object Serialization, and the IDL system. Of these, the main API is the JDBC (Java Database Connectivity) API, which will soon be widely used in many programs. Currently, database access from Java can be achieved in three major ways: JDBC of the Java Enterprise APIs; database vendor-specific access methods; and the third-party classes, which are applicable to many databases. The following sections will provide you with an overview of vendor-specific and third-party strategies, as well as an in-depth look at JDBC.

Java Enterprise APIs

The Java Enterprise APIs are quickly becoming one of the prized parts of the Java language and the Java Virtual Machine. All the Java licensees will implement these APIs as part of their system. Hence, the Java Enterprise APIs are universal *and* cross-platform.

As stated above, the Java Enterprise APIs consist of the JDBC, RMI, Object Serialization, and the IDL. The JDBC is a set of the database access classes; the Remote Method Invocation (RMI) APIs give Java programs the ability to call methods of objects in a different name-space; Object Serialization API objects and methods enable one to store and retrieve objects directly, rather than storing and retrieving the underlying data; the Interface Definition Language (IDL) system enables Java programs to interface with Object Management Group (OMG) implementations.

This set of APIs make possible the development of enterprise-level multitier client/server applications using Java Objects, applets, and servlets. The term *Enterprise-level applications* refers to utility billing systems, airline reservation systems, catalog systems, marketing systems, Bill of Material and other manufacturing systems, banking systems (from ATM machines to online banking to sophisticated reconciliation systems that span across nations), brokerage systems, and so on.

All these systems employ a three-tier architecture logic (back-end database, middle business rules layer, and a front-end Graphical User Interface [GUI] layer). Extending this architecture, many organizations are employing an *n-tier logic structure*.

What Is N-Tier Logic?

A bit of history may be in order here. Client/server applications started out as a database server and a client with a presentation layer (menus, data screens, and so on). These traditional systems have a fat client program that includes all application logic. This architecture was then refined to the three-tier architecture, where the business logic was separated from the client into a separate layer. This layer was originally either in the server or in the clients.

Later, application servers were added to house this business logic layer. With the Internet and Java applets, the strict layers of application are again reshaping. The business logic, database access, and the presentation layers can be in many applets and are downloaded as needed. The "distributed business functions using objects" concept is the n-tier logic, where each applet can be theoretically looked upon as an application layer.

With the rapid growth of the Internet and platforms like Java, these systems are undergoing a metamorphosis, or a paradigm shift. With

Java applets, objects, and servlets, developers can create Java programs that encapsulate function and data. These applets travel across the network (Internet/Intranet) on a Just-In-Time basis, when invoked by a client, and perform their functions.

To get a perspective on the Java Enterprise APIs, you can look at JDBC as the component that makes database access possible, while RMI and IDL can be seen as the object communication vehicle across heterogeneous platforms and systems. Enough buzz words and strategies, it is time to look at how these lofty ideas are achieved in the APIs.

JDBC

JDBC is the relational database API classes for Java applets and applications. The JDBC was developed by JavaSoft and is a part of Java 1.1. JDBC, like the Java language, is platform- and database-independent. To run JDBC on a platform, the Java Virtual Machine should have the native driver manager; for specific databases, the database driver is needed. The JDBC specification 1.0 can be found at the JavaSoft-JDBC site `http://splash.javasoft.com/jdbc/index.html`. The JDBC went through a three month public review from March to May 1996, and has since been released as version 1.0.

> **NOTE**
> The JDBC design was influenced by XOPEN SQL Call Level Interface (CLI) and Microsoft's Open Database Connectivity (ODBC). ODBC is based on the SQL Access Group (SAG) CLI. Thus, JDBC and ODBC have common roots. The point here is that for those who know ODBC or have implemented ODBC, JDBC will be easier to understand and apply.

The designers of JDBC employed a design and abstraction philosophy to leverage on the ODBC concepts. The two main reasons for modeling JDBC after ODBC are

- ODBC is widely used, which helps shorten the developer's learning curve.

- There are efficient ODBC implementations on all platforms for almost all databases. This means that there is no need to develop new drivers and interfaces for Java; Sun can simply partner with vendors who have mature ODBC products to instantly establish a critical mass of drivers, tools, and implementations.

NOTE One significant difference between the JDBC and the ODBC is that the latter uses many hard-core C language facilities, like pointers and recasting results returning a "void*"—which is not available in Java. In the C world, you could declare functions as returning "void*" to tell the compiler and run time that you want a return pointer with an unknown type. After you get the pointer back from the function, the pointer can be typecast to a particular type. The designers of Java wanted to avoid this and other kinds of pointer manipulation, so they made Java a strictly typed language. Methods return objects that are known in advance. Java has no pointers at all.

The folks at JavaSoft implemented JDBC with key abstractions from ODBC, like connection and ResultSet.

NOTE The most common operations on a database are queries that return rows and rows of data, which consist of many columns, or fields, called a *ResultSet*.

Looking at the JDBC specifications, they have succeeded very well in providing a Java-like solution to SQL database access. In JDBC, simple database tasks, like basic query, create, and update, can be done using simple and straightforward methods. For more complex tasks, like multiple ResultSets and *stored procedures* with IN and OUT parameters, the JDBC has separate statements. For automation programs and designer tools, JDBC has MetaData classes and methods, which provide information about the various features supported in the database, table structure, and other characteristics.

NOTE *Stored procedures* are functions and procedures consisting of database statements stored in the database server. When client programs want to perform a function, instead of using database statements, they call the stored procedure. The advantage is that the stored procedure is in the server, thus providing uniformity, security, and efficiency. Like normal procedures, stored procedures take parameters. IN parameters are passed into the stored procedures and they are not returned; OUT parameters are values returned from a stored procedure. When dealing with stored procedures, the system has to deal with these parameters along with any ResultSets.

The following sections discuss the details of the JDBC—classes and methods—using a mini-project of a sample database access that uses JDBC.

JDBC Implementation

JDBC is implemented as the `java.sql` package. You would use this package using the `import java.sql.*` statement in a Java program. Figure 21.1 shows the JDBC implementation strategy. Underneath the API layer is the JDBC DriverManager for various databases written for the operating system/hardware combination, which is a part of the Java Virtual Machine. The JDBC DriverManager can be written for a specific database, or it can be a generic driver for a variety of databases. Sun's reference implementation includes a generic JDBC DriverManager and a driver for ODBC.

FIGURE 20.1:

JDBC Implementation
components

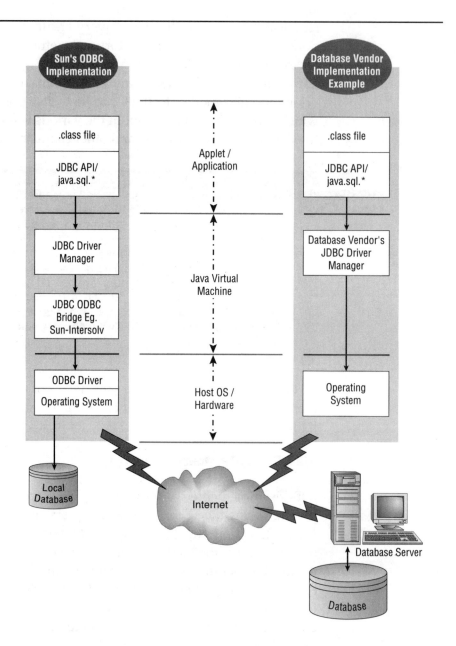

The JDBC/ODBC Bridge is a thin veneer over JDBC to map the JDBC calls to ODBC calls. This bridge is distributed free with JDBC, and was developed by Intersolv. The JDBC/ODBC Bridge is a very thin layer because JDBC follows ODBC very closely in the design of classes and methods, and it enables data access to all the major databases through ODBC drivers. By closely following ODBC and this reference implementation, Sun has made it easy for developers and Independent Software Vendors (ISVs) to start developing database applications in Java. If they had developed a completely different database interface specification, it would have taken much more time and effort to interface Java with major databases.

Vendors like Oracle and Borland have JDBC drivers to directly access their database implementation like the Oracle 7 database and Borland's Interbase. These drivers are equally effective in developing database applications using Java. Please see "Vendor/Third-Party Solutions" later in the chapter for more information on vendor databases.

Looking more closely at the JDBC features, we find that JDBC has dynamic driver selection and loading, interfaces for connection, statements, and ResultSets. JDBC is implemented as *Tubular Data* in the sense that the ResultSet includes datastream as well as a description about the datastream. The datastream description is called the *ResultSet MetaData*. Using `java.sql` methods, one can query the shape of the ResultSets like column names and datatypes. JDBC has prepared statement and callable statement objects for native database processing using compiled and stored procedures.

JDBC Classes in Detail

When you look at the JDBC class hierarchy, as shown in Figure 21.2, you will find the objects in a progressively hierarchical structure. The DriverManager connects to the database and returns a connection object. You use the statement-related methods in the connection object to execute SQL statements, which in turn return ResultSet

objects wherever appropriate. You then take data out of the
ResultSets column by column, and row by row.

JDBC Class hierarchy

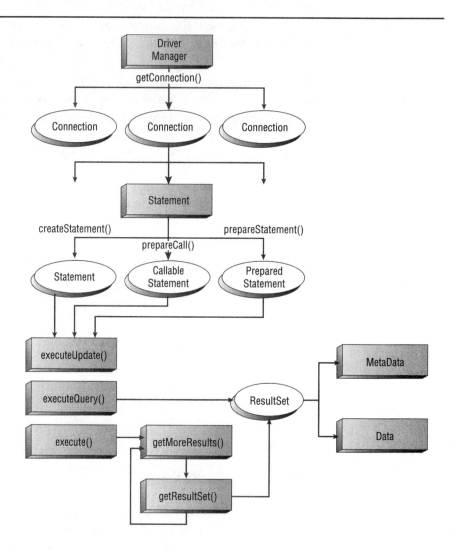

The major class types are implementation, database connection, statements, data, and errors. Table 21.1 shows the types and the JDBC classes for the types, each of which will be covered in detail shortly.

Table 20.1: Major Class Types and Associated Classes

Type	JDBC Class

Implementation	`java.sql.Driver`
	`java.sql.DriverManager`
	`java.sql.DriverPropertyInfo`

Database Connection	`java.sql.Connection`

SQL Statements	`java.sql.Statement`
	`java.sql.PreparedStatement`
	`java.sql.CallableStatement`

Data	`java.sql.ResultSet`
Errors	`java.sql.SQLException` `java.sql.SQLWarning`

NOTE
The JDBC specification describes interfaces. The implementation of these interfaces are the JDBC classes. Since in a Java program we deal with classes, this chapter also uses the term *classes*.

As you go through each class, you will undertake a mini-project. The mini-project is to access a few of the fields in the ORDERS.MDB database that come as an example with Microsoft Access Database. Figure 21.3 shows a schema of four tables for the order entry system.

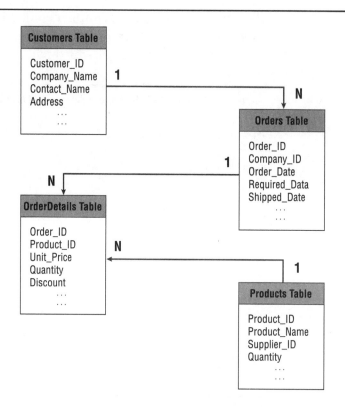

The customers table has customer details. One customer can have many order entries in the Orders Table. Each Order can be many lines long; the lines are stored in the OrderDetails table. Each OrderDetail can have, at most, one product from the Products table, but a product will be associated with many order lines. The Access ODBC driver comes standard with the Access product, as well as many other products like Visual Basic. You can also freely download the 32-bit ODBC driver from Microsoft's Web site.

The first order of business is to create an ODBC entry using the ODBC configuration manager. Figures 20.4 and 20.5 show the ODBC setup on Windows 95. Choose JDBCTest as the Data Source Name, then type **sa** as the user name and **pw** as the password. You will use these parameters to open a connection to this database. (Other platforms have similar setup requirements/steps.)

FIGURE 20.4:

ODBC Setup Screen 1

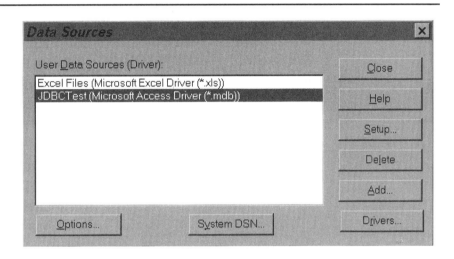

FIGURE 20.5:

ODBC Setup Screen 2

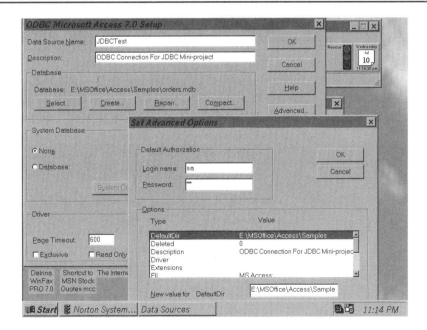

java.sql.DriverManager   The DriverManager layer tracks the available JDBC drivers. It is possible that there are multiple drivers in a system—remote or local. During initialization, the DriverManager loads all of the classes in the sql.drivers system property. The drivers can be implemented using native methods in C/C++, or as a Java program that communicates to a database by Remote Procedure Call (RPC) interface or to a database server that is listening for connections. The implementation and communication details are left to the driver developer. Each driver, sometime during the loading, should register itself using the `DriverManager.registerDriver` method. A good time to do this is in the static class initialization code.

JDBC uses the URL syntax (of the form `jdbc:<subprotocol>:`
`<parameters>`) to identify the JDBC connections. The subprotocol `odbc` is reserved for ODBC-style Data Source Names. As a JDBC URL example, an ODBC source TestDb, with a user name Tester1, and password TestPW, would have the URL `jdbc:odbc:TestDB:`
`UID=Tester1;PWD=TestPW`. The DriverManager maps the drivers to JDBC URLs; in other words, it keeps track of the class loader-driver relationship so that that class loader can access only the driverloaded by itself. When a connection needs to be opened, the DriverManager, by an internal table lookup, selects the associated DriverManager and opens the connection. The drivers must conform to the Java security model. The most common model used by browsers (mainly Netscape Navigator) is that applets can only connect back to their server, while applications have full connection freedom. This model will change very soon to a signed-class, trusted-applets model with variable security settings. The DriverManager provides the connection object, which will be discussed in more detail in the following sections.

java.sql.Driver   The `java.sql.Driver` class implements the general database driver information and setup. It will be loaded during the database initialization, and will be queried for driver information throughout the Java program. This means this class will reside in memory throughout the program's execution. It follows, then, that this class should be as small as possible. The `java.sql.Driver` methods include `connect` (to connect to a database) and `getPropertyInfo` (to get information required for a database connection). As already mentioned, this driver should call the `DriverManager.registerDriver` to register itself. The DriverManager will keep information about the `Driver` class, including the loading source for security and access checks.

As was discussed earlier, the DriverManager will load all known drivers in the sql.drivers system property. An alternate method is to explicitly load a specific driver using the `forName` method in the `Class` object. The usage is

```
java.sql.Driver dbDriver =
Class.forName("SomeCompany.SomeDatabase.Driver").newInstance().
```

This statement will load the driver from `$CLASSPATH\ SomeCompany\Database\Driver.class` and return the resultant `Driver` object.

For your mini-project, you could load the driver using the following program line:

```
Java.sql.Driver dbDriver = class.forName("jdbc:odbc").newInstance();
```

java.sql.Connection   The `Connection` object is a pointer to a database. In other words, this object is a window into a database providing a context for the `Statement` and `ResultSet` objects. The `Connection` object supports transaction properties like begin, commit, and abort, and provides methods to create the `Statement` objects.

The program sequence

```
connection.createStatement()
```

creates a normal `Statement` object.

The program sequence

```
connection.createStatement()
connection.prepareStatement(<SQL String>)
```

makes a `PreparedStatement` object, which is a compiled SQL statement. This type of statement is used if the call is being made more than once in the program. The `PreparedStatement` compiles the SQL string the first time and then uses the compiled statement for the rest of the calls.

The program sequence

```
connection.createStatement()
connection.prepareCall(<SQL String>)
```

makes a `CallableStatement` object, which calls a *stored procedure*. A stored procedure is a procedure in the SQL database in the server. As described earlier, this type of procedure implements business rules consistently across programs as the procedure is stored in the server. The clients invoke the procedure using the {call <procedure-name> [arguments]} syntax.

The Connection's `setAutoCommit` method can turn on or off the *autocommit* of transactions, which allows you to do *transaction processing*. If the autocommit is off, one can use the `commit()` method to commit changes or use the `rollback()` method to discard changes since the last commit.

Transaction Processing

Transaction processing is a general term used in the context of databases to denote, among other things, consistency, recoverability, and data integrity of relational databases. A transaction consists of multiple SQL commands that read and update databases. To assure that all transactions are performed as a single unit of work, the commit and rollback methods are used.

The most common example is the automatic payment transaction in a banking system. The two command sets would be used to debit your checking account and credit your creditor. If both SQL commands are successfully completed, the transaction can be *committed*. But if the system cannot perform either of the commands, the transaction should not be allowed to go through. Not only that, all of the data affected by partial transactions should be reset to their original value, otherwise either the creditor will mysteriously get money, or the customer will lose money from the checking account without paying the bill. This is called a *rollback*.

In short, the commit/rollback control is needed when one is doing simultaneous changes to data in many tables or across multiple data-bases. For data consistency, one should `commit()` all changes if all the updates can be made. If only partial updates are possible, one should `rollback()` and try again later.

For our mini-project, we will create the connection object as follows:

```
Connection testConn = DriverManager.getConnection( "jdbc:odbc:JDBCTest;UID=sa;PW=pw");
```

Now we can create a simple statement object using:

```
Statement simpleStmt = testConn.createStatement();
```

java.sql.Statement   The `Statement` class has the `executeQuery` method for normal SQL statements, which returns data (in the form of a `ResultSet` object), or the execute method for SQL statements, with more than one `ResultSet` (in rare cases). The `executeUpdate` method can be used for statements like UPDATE, DELETE, INSERT, and so on. This method does not return a ResultSet.

java.sql.PreparedStatement   The `PreparedStatement` class extends the `Statement` class to add the precompiled SQL statement capability, and it supports parameters of `IN` type. Precompiling is done for efficiency if the same SQL statement will be executed multiple times. The parameters are set using the `setInt`, `setFloat`, `setLong` (and other) methods.

java.sql.CallableStatement   The `CallableStatement` object extends the `PreparedStatement` to support the stored procedures. It will return parameters of `OUT` type. But they need to be explicitly registered using the `registerOutParameter` method. After the `CallableStatement` object is executed, the `OUT parameter` results can be read using the `getInt`, `getLong`, `getFloat`, and other methods.

java.sql.ResultSet   The `ResultSet` object contains the relational data that is the result of a SQL statement. The data is retrieved as sequential rows. In a row, the data in the columns can be accessed in any sequence by using a positional index or by name. For example, `java.sql.ResultSet.getFloat(5)` will get the number in column five of the current `ResultSet` row. The same data can be retrieved by using the `java.sql.ResultSet.getFloat("AuthorRoyalty")` if the fifth column is the AuthorRoyalty field. The `java.sql` `.ResultSet.next()` method navigates to the next row.

> **NOTE**   The JDBC 1.0 specification does not provide scrollable cursors or ODBC-style cursor bookmarks.

In the case of your mini-project, to get all the orders for a customer "SYBEX Computer Books" the program lines will be as follows:

```
ResultSet rsOrders = simpleStmt.executeQuery( "SELECT Order_ID, Order_Date
➡FROM Orders WHERE Customer_ID='SYBEX'");
while (rsOrders.next())
{
String OrderID = rsOrders.getString("Order_ID");
```

```
java.sql.Date OrderDate = rsOrders.getDate("Order_Date");
.. // Print and other GUI statements to display the ID and Date
}
```

Here the `Statement` object created in the earlier section is used to get two columns (Order ID and Order Date) of all orders with the customer ID "SYBEX." The `next()` method moves to the next row in the `ResultSet`. When there are no more data, this will return a FALSE value and thus end the while loop. The `getString()` and `getDate()` methods are used to get the data from a row of data.

Now, to get details in each order you need to pass the `Order_ID` to the database in the `Statement` object. Refer to the database schema in Figure 20.3 for table relationships. In this case, we use a `PreparedStatement` object with a parameter.

```
PreparedStatement prepStmt = testConn.prepareStatement( "SELECT * FROM OrderDetails
➥WHERE Order_ID = ?);
prepStmt.setString(1, OrderID);// sets the value of the parameter
                // Order_ID (in the prepStmt) as equal to the variable OrderID
                ➥ResultSet rsOrdDet = prepStmt.execute();
while(rsOrdDet.next())
                {
                // Process each row.
                // get column data from the current row
                // using the getXXX() methods, display etc.
    }
```

Here a `PreparedStatement` object is created with one parameter denoted by the `?` in the SQL. Then the first parameter is set (denoted by the `?` in the SQL statement) equal to the `OrderID` we got from the previous statement. Next the query is executed. The above program lines will create a `ResultSet` with all the order details of one order denoted by the `OrderID` variable. The row will contain all columns in the OrderDetails table, since the SELECT * SQL statement was used.

As another example, if you want to update a product in the Products table, you will program as follows:

```
PreparedStatement prepStmt = testConn.prepareStatement( "UPDATE Products SET
➥Product_Name = ? WHERE Product_ID = ?");
PrepStmt.setString(1, "Mastering Java");
```

```
PrepStmt.setString(2, "1935-2");
int updRows = PrepStmt.executeUpdate();
```

Here a `PreparedStatement` with two parameters is created: one for the Product name, and the other for the Product ID. In the next two statements, the first parameter is set with a book name and the second one with the book's ISBN. The `executeUpdate()` does not return a `ResultSet`, but an integer telling you how many rows are updated. As you can see, this is the concept of *simple* methods for *simple* tasks.

MetaData   *MetaData* is information about the underlying object, and is needed by programs to find out about supported features from a database driver, or to find out about column names, sizes, and so on. As already mentioned, the `ResultSet` is a Tubular Data Stream. That means it has description information about the `ResultSet` in addition to actual data. This extra information can be read using the `getMetaData()` method. The `ResultSetMetaData` object returned has a rich set of methods like `getColumnCount()`, `getColumnDisplaySize()`, `getColumnLabel()`, and `getColumnName()`. These functions can be used to get information about the data columns.

In addition to `ResultSetMetaData`, JDBC supports the `DatabaseMetaData` object, which gives information about the database. The `DatabaseMetaData` object has about 100 methods including, `getDatabaseProductName()`, `getDatabaseProductVersion()`, and ranges from implemented features, to schema details, to stored procedure names. There are methods for querying about implementation, specific details, and limitations like `getDatabaseProductName()`, `getDatabaseProductVersion()`, `getMaxConnections()`, `getTables()`, `getTableTypes()`, `getMaxColumnLength()`, `getMaxCharLiteralLength()`, `getProcedures()`, and so on.

As mentioned earlier, the JDBC API turned out 1.0 in June 1996. Sun and Intersolv have released the beta JDBC-ODBC bridge. Other vendors are working hard to implement their own JDBC drivers and extensions. In examining the JDBC implementation, you can see that combined forces of the designers at JavaSoft and the reviewers of JDBC specification have come up with a simple, elegant, and powerful API for database access from Java programs. Figure 20.6 shows a general system flow for an Internet/Intranet database application system.

FIGURE 20.6:

System Flow—Applets, Servlets, and Data

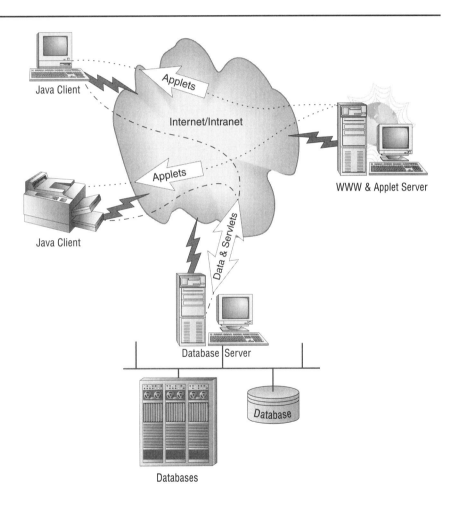

The departmental or organizational applet server has all of the applets required for the system, and the database server has the data. Java clients' PCs, or other Java driven peripherals, download applets, run them, and connect to the Database server using the JDBC.

For example, a printer applet might update printer usage statistics on the server, or get configuration or user information from the database server using JDBC connections. In the case of a Java client PC, the applet might be an expense account form filler that uses the JDBC connection to get information (like categories and expense limits) from the database server and to post the completed expense account into the expense table in the database server. For these types of systems to work, you would either need signed applets so that they can connect securely to another server in the Internet/Intranet, or the applet server and the database server should be the same computer. The currently popular security scheme allows applets to write only to the server from where they are loaded.

Java RMI and Object Serialization

Java Remote Method Invocation (or simply RMI) enables objects to exist over multiple namespaces, distributed across Java Virtual Machines. Each namespace can be in the same computer or in different computers across the network. Since the method calls span over the Java Virtual Machine boundary to a different namespace, there are no global variables that can be shared between the objects. This is where the Object Serialization APIs come in. They enable the objects to exist over time, to be persistent. The Object Serialization is specifically designed for Java objects. That means the objects in a Java program can be stored and retrieved as objects. Combining RMI and Object Serialization, you get objects that can travel across boundaries with data that exists over time. The RMI calls enable you to invoke remote methods, and the object serialization enables you to pass objects to those methods.

NOTE

Look at the home banking system for an example of the concept just described. A client using the home PC invokes a balance inquiry procedure at the bank account server to get their balance in the checking account before paying a huge telephone bill. The client PC might be running windows while the bank server might be an HP-UNIX machine. In this case, the client PC would use the RMI to identify and call the balance inquiry procedure. The account number would be passed to the remote procedure by the Object Serialization classes and methods. The remote balance inquiry would run the SQL commands and pass the result back to the home PC using the object serialization classes and methods.

In abstract terms, the RMI and Object Serialization (collectively called RMI from now on) aid in developing systems with distributed objects. What does this mean? Usually, when you run a program, all the required functions and data are available locally, so the program calls the procedures or functions with parameters to execute them. But in a multitier client/server world, all procedures cannot reside in the local machine for many reasons, including security, proximity to data, and centralized logic store.

If you allow remote procedures to update/add/delete data on a central database, malicious or error-ridden programs can cause data corruption. If you need to do some data summary, it is practical to do the processing locally at the database server rather than transporting the voluminous data to the client. If you have service type of logic, like ID generation or validation of credit limit, it would logically be on a centralized layer. In all these cases, when you need a service, you would use the RMI to invoke the call with the required object parameters.

The actual applets or function modules performing the function can be anywhere on the Internet. After processing the logic, the applets will send the results back to the client through RMI. The packaging and unpackaging of parameters across remote processes is called *marshalling*.

The RMI API adds the `Remote` interface and `RemoteObject`, `RemoteServer`, `RemoteException`, and `UnicastRemoteServer` classes among others. The Java program extends and implements these interfaces to develop object-centric applications that work across namespaces.

The Object Serialization APIs add `ObjectOutput` and `ObjectInput` interfaces and `ObjectInputStream` and `ObjectOutputStream` classes to give the application program capability to store and read objects. The methods available include `readObject` and `writeObject`.

Java IDL

The Java *Interface Definition Language* (IDL) system is conceptually similar to the Java RMI API. The difference is that Java RMI is for object and method invocation only for Java objects, as opposed to IDL, which is independent of OS and language. Java IDL complies with the Common Object Request Broker Architecture (CORBA) standard by the Object Management Group (OMG) and maps Java objects to the CORBA standard.

The CORBA implementation from the OMG standard is widely used in many banking, merchandising, brokerage, and other systems. These systems are well-established and highly functional. The IDL system provides a way for Java programs to interface with these systems and make use of the business logic functions and methods available now. For example, a new Java applet can act as a balance query agent for a CORBA-based brokerage system. The Java applet can encapsulate the client-side security and GUI functionalities. The interaction with the back-end brokerage system will be done by the IDL classes. It is a way to get the best of both worlds.

The IDL system is now in the alpha 2 stage and consists of client runtime modules, server runtime modules, and the IDLGEN development tool. The client run times enable the Java programs to communicate with CORBA servers, the server run times enable the Java programs to act as network servers for IDL clients, and the IDL-GEN program generates Java interface definitions as well as templates for server and client tasks.

Although the IDL system extends the Java platform to CORBA systems and thus enables the Java developers to implement systems that make use of the systems that already exist, the Java IDL is still in the alpha stage. It will surely acquire many more useful features and tools before it reaches version 1 release.

Vendor/Third-Party Solutions

Each vendor has its own strategy to interact with the Web. Almost all of the databases support ODBC; hence, you can use the JDBC to talk to databases. If you want to exploit the features of a particular database or features specific to an architecture like Oracle's Web server or OpenChannel by Visigenic, you need to apply the solutions developed by that vendor. A good approach is to use generic drivers and APIs for programs and applets widely used across the Internet. For corporate Intranet applications, you can apply the architecture and drivers specific to a database or vendor solution.

As an example of database vendor-specific implementation, this section covers the Java strategy from the market leader, Oracle, as well as solutions from Visigenic, as an example of third-party interface software suited for many database systems. Visigenic is known for their cross-platform, cross-database ODBC drivers.

Oracle

Oracle's Web strategy is based on their Web Server 2 product and its integration with the Oracle 7 database system. The data access language PL/SQL is Oracle's SQL implementation. This SQL language conforms to American National Standards Institute (ANSI) standards and also has extensions for the Oracle 7 database. In this section, you'll be introduced to the Java-PL/SQL connection.

Oracle Web Server Architecture

The Web Server 2 is a component architecture-based system. The components are called *cartridges*, which are encapsulated functions and utilities. Examples of cartridges include PL/SQL, credit card processing, business rules, catalog management, and connection to legacy systems.

The Web-request broker component is the front end to the Internet/Intranet. You can encapsulate business modules into cartridges and plug them into the system. The cartridges run on their own namespace/URL and are cross-functional so they can interact with each other using the internal intercartridge exchange API.

The Java Cartridge   One of the cartridges is Oracle's implementation of the Java Virtual Machine on the server side, called Java server. This Java server cartridge can interact with all the other available cartridges as well as any new ones, like connectivity to legacy systems. This means the Java applications can interact with the Oracle PL/SQL to manipulate the Oracle 7 database, which is similar to the ODBC capability available to Java programs from the JDBC API. Here the Java cartridge provides the Oracle's PL/SQL capability for Java programs.

You could develop cartridge applets and servlets using Java that perform a set of well-defined functions, like a database query, update a transaction, or qualify a credit card holder. Oracle is implementing cartridge management APIs so that these cartridge components can be distributed on many servers across the organization or, in the case of credit card and other commerce applications, around the globe.

Oracle-Specific Java Classes   Oracle has added the following packages to Java:

> **oracle.plsql** Java class `Wrapper` to Oracle's PL/SQL language. This gives the Java language all the power to natively manipulate data in the Oracle databases.

> **oracle.rdbms** The database access classes. These classes provide abstraction for database management, including security and database management.

> **oracle.html** Classes for the generation of HTML pages. The Oracle implementation stresses dynamic generation of the pages to ensure that the Web pages reflect the current data. The Web pages are generated from query results and are interactive. You can create secured applications to add/modify/delete information in Oracle databases using any Web browser.

Oracle also supports generic JDBC API, so you can develop generic applications that access Oracle databases. For large-scale Oracle database applications that deal with a lot of data, business rules and functionalities, Java Cartridge APIs, and PL/SQL and related classes are more suitable. In these cases, since the programs deal with only Oracle databases, the Oracle's implementation, which is optimized for Oracle database access, can boost the performance. Here, open architecture does not offer us any advantage.

The Oracle strategy gives you a glimpse of how Java can be extended to support client/server application development for mission-critical database systems like theirs.

Visigenic

Visigenic Software Inc. is a company specializing in developing cross-platform, cross-database drivers. Their product line includes ODBC drivers, ODBC cross-platform development kits and test suites, the OpenChannel products, and object broker products for Java and for CORBA systems. They also support object-based Java applications with the Black Widow product.

With respect to our current topic, database access, they have two approaches to support distributed data access for the Java platform: Visigenic OpenChannel Client for Java, and the Visigenic JDBC to ODBC driver. These products provide remote access to databases via the Internet and corporate Internet/Intranet by using a true client/server architecture supporting full ODBC functionality. Referring back to Figure 20.1, their JDBC/ODBC driver architecture is similar to Sun's JDBC/ODBC implementation, and the OpenChannel architecture is like the database vendor implementation example.

Visigenic OpenChannel Client for Java

Visigenic's OpenChannel is a layer of client and server software that enables applications to transparently access many types of databases, such as Oracle, Sybase, and Microsoft SQL Server. Visigenic is currently extending the capabilities of OpenChannel architecture to support the Java environment. OpenChannel for Java enables interactive applications across the Internet, allowing users to work interactively with remote data. The OpenChannel Client will allow both Java applications and applets to access ODBC-compliant data sources.

The OpenChannel architecture eliminates the need for communication through a Web server using CGI and other server APIs. The OpenChannel Client for Java passes the request *directly* to the OpenChannel Server that resides on the platform on which the database is located. There is no platform-specific layer between the Java driver program and the host operating system. OpenChannel Client for Java is written completely in Java, making it cross-platform, architecture-neutral, secure, and network-aware. Additionally, the client can be downloaded from an applet server when needed for database processing. This is especially advantageous for thin-client systems that have limited storage resources. Referring again to Figure 20.1, the database vendor implementation example, OpenChannel DriverManager is written in Java, which communicates over the Internet to the OpenChannel Server. The server then communicates with the database for data access.

Visigenic JDBC to ODBC Interface

This driver is similar to the JDBC-ODBC Bridge from Sun/Intersolv. It has the advantage of being a layer for any database vendor's ODBC driver. Given that Visigenic has drivers for many platforms (Windows NT/95, ATT GIS, IBM AIX, HP-UX, SCO, Solaris, Sun OS, Macintosh and Power Macintosh, and OS/2), that they site license, in a corporate environment with heterogeneous systems, Visigenic is a good idea. This cross-platform, cross-database capability makes Visigenic better than Sun's JDBC/ODBC layer in heterogeneous corporate environments.

The Future

As you can see, the JDBC and other solutions for database connectivity for Java is still in its infancy. Within a couple of Web-years, more Webcentric paradigms are sure to appear, which will greatly enhance this scenario. One such concept is the interface to object databases. The Object Database Management Group (ODMG) is already working on accessing object databases from Java. As you just learned, JDBC is a relational scheme suited for relational databases. The ODMG plans to implement an object-centric approach. This means Java programs can directly relate (read, write, get information about) with objects, ignoring the database implementations. Java programs, then, can directly write and read objects from any databases that support the ODMG approach. The databases will then act as *persistent object stores*, where one can store and access many types of objects like video, sound, and graphics. This, for example, would pave the way for accessing video via a network on your TV, instead of needing to go to a video store!

Java Futures: New APIs

- Core APIs

- Media APIs

- Java Enterprise APIs

- Java Commerce API

- Java Management API

- Java Server API

- Java Security API

- JavaBeans API

- Java Embedded API

At the JavaOne conference in May of 1996, Sun unveiled a series of strategic alliances and grandiose plans for the expansion of the Java language. As the oft-quoted JavaSoft president Alan Baratz put it:

"The Java industry has asked us for a road map that shows Java's smooth, open evolution from a new object-oriented programming language to a complete programming and operating environment. We've defined new core APIs that will be basic to the highly compact Java platform that will be embedded in the industry's leading operating systems.

"In addition, we've defined Java Standard Extension APIs—standard because they are fully specified and documented to promote consistent, universal usage, extensions because they're additions to the core Java platform. Each of the Java Standard Extension APIs will maintain full compatibility with the Java platform as it moves forward."

As you know, API stands for *Application Programming Interface*. Software companies like JavaSoft release APIs to allow programmers to develop software with particular capabilities. In order to write applications for a particular environment, you need to write code that conforms to the applicable API. For instance, to write programs for Microsoft Windows, you must get the Windows API *Software Development Kit* (SDK) from Microsoft. To write plug-ins for Netscape's Navigator software, you need the Netscape Plug-in API SDK. For writing programs in Java, Sun currently has the Java Development Kit (JDK), which implements the core Java APIs. Each of these future APIs will need to have their own development kits, or be incorporated into the currently existing one.

What does all of this mean for the Java developer and consumer? Will these new extensions bring Java into the mainstream or clog its arteries? How will this affect the nature of the Internet? The truth is that nobody knows. These developments are all so new that there has not been time to evaluate many of them. The major players, like Sun and Netscape, have done a lot of talking, but so far relatively little has happened. Nevertheless, it is important to stay informed of the latest news and to plan for the future. Java is a dynamic language and the Internet is a chaotic place, so you can expect things to change drastically without much notice. Such is life on the bleeding edge of technology.

And Then There Were Nine...

Leading up to and during the JavaOne conference, Sun unveiled nine major additions to the Java language—some of these have already been implemented, some are years away; some have corporate sponsorship, while others are being created in-house by Sun's JavaSoft division. As companies both large and small jump on the Java bandwagon, millions of dollars and many PR opportunities are at stake, so be wary of hidden agendas as you marvel at the future of computing.

Most of the new APIs are being cosponsored by companies other than Sun, and most of these are going to make use of preexisting technologies and be incorporated into the Java language. Alan Baratz made reference to two different kinds of APIs: Core and Extension. The Core APIs will be part of the mainstream Java language that is distributed to every Java-compatible platform. The Extension APIs will be optionally available for developers to use. It is unclear how licensing and distribution of these APIs will work—you may have to pay a fee to JavaSoft or someone else for their use. Notably, even though many of these are being developed by companies who specialize in only one platform, all companies have pledged to support Java's platform independence. This means that every company will provide libraries to provide functionality on all Java-enabled platforms.

This chapter will give you a brief introduction to each of the nine new APIs. Note that none of the APIs is completely finished, so information listed herein is likely to change. The Web is a good place to look for further information on the new APIs. There, you'll be able to find general information and demo versions of certain products, as well as online documentation and vendor support. Table 21.1 at the end of the chapter lists online resources available for each of the APIs discussed in this chapter, as well as other related sites.

Core APIs

You are already familiar with the main part of the Core APIs, formerly known as the JavaApplet API. From this foundation, Sun plans to build an elaborate programming language and operating system that will run on everything from hand-held systems based on picoJava chips to the latest desktop and workstation computers. The Core API was introduced with the 1.0.2 release of the JDK, but will not be fully implemented—or (maybe) bug-free—until version 1.1 (due out in the fall of 1996). This is the only API that has reached that level and has printed and electronic documentation to go along with it. Do not let the terminology trip you up; the Core API has been expanded to include many of the APIs listed in this chapter. For instance, the Java 2D API, although one of the Media APIs, has also been designated a Core API. This simply means that it will be distributed with the Core API, not as a separate package.

Availability

The 1.0.2 version of the JDK is available right now for download on JavaSoft's web pages (see Table 21.1). The JDK implements the latest version of the Java Core API. Full online documentation is also available from the same source.

> **NOTE** You can also find the JDK 1.0.2 on the CD-ROM accompanying this book, in the `JDK` folder.

> **NOTE** A note on terminology: APIs go through a development cycle prior to their final release. First, there is the API overview, usually accompanied by a white paper that describes the API's objectives. Next comes a prerelease *alpha* version of the actual software, sometimes preceded by simple documentation. After several alpha (and even beta) releases, the developer will usually release version 1.0, which will be a mostly bug-free full implementation of the API.

Media APIs

The Media API is definitely one of the most exciting APIs for developers and users alike. It has been the topic of the most talk, but, unfortunately, little action: Most Media APIs are still months away. Many companies are working on getting their names associated with this API, and some are even surreptitiously trying to lock programmers and end-users into their own proprietary platforms.

Key features of the Media API include

- Support for numerous multimedia formats with platform-independent implementations

- Audio support, including MIDI and telephony features

- Video and animation support, including 2-D and 3-D standards

- Special standards for time and clock synchronization

- Java classes for "Collaboration"

Java 2D and 3D

Java 2D and 3D are additions to the Java language (Java 2D is considered a Core API, while 3D is a Standard Extension) that will give Java advanced graphics capabilities. In addition to simple drawing methods, which are available now, Java 2D will provide imaging and font manipulation tools. The 2D API is being written by Adobe, and is based on their Bravo technology, which is already used in their Illustrator and Photoshop products. Although no official specs are available, it looks similar to the Postscript model of 2-D graphics pioneered several years ago. The Java 3D API, on the other hand, is being tackled by Intel and Silicon Graphics (SGI). SGI is basing the 3-D specification on their existing Cosmo 3-D product, which is a format similar to VRML (the Virtual Reality Modeling Language). Unfortunately, this format is not compatible with the 2-D Postscript-style model used in the 2D API.

What does all this mean from a developer's perspective? If things continue like this, functionality that is common to both the Java 2D and 3D APIs will require separate code. For instance, the mathematics required to rotate a square in two dimensions and a cube in three dimensions is extremely similar. However, unless the two APIs are somehow standardized, these tasks will require different methods and techniques. How different is currently not clear, but it could be substantial.

Another factor that may threaten the future platform independence of Java is that both Adobe and SGI have promised special low-level programming access to the underlying hardware in order to boost performance. Although this will make for faster drawing code, it will make affected Java programs (especially those designed to run on extremely high-end workstations) platform dependent. Of course, companies like SGI have a vested interest in making sure that their workstations are the best at running Java. Likewise, Adobe would like their software packages to be the best for creating Java programs. Although both companies have proclaimed their support for Java's platform independence, the early specifications on their respective APIs suggest there may be other motives at work.

What does all this mean for the end consumer? In the long run, probably only good things. Everyone seems to be supporting Sun's effort to expand the Java language, and these graphics APIs will only increase the number of fun and exciting applets in existence down the line.

Availability

Of these APIs, Java 3D is apparently the furthest along. Although both Java 2D and 3D are promised—at least in prerelease form—by the end of the year, the Java 3D mailing list has been recently very active, with Sun engineers promising something public this fall. The Java 2D and 3D APIs may well be the first publicly available Media APIs; they are certainly the most talked about in the developer community. See Table 21.1 for ways to get more information.

Animation, Audio, Video

Most of these efforts are based upon Intel's forays into the multimedia field. No longer content with its hardware exploits, Intel has begun experimenting with providing multimedia software content. These Java APIs are based upon several Intel technologies: For *streaming* (transmitting data across the Web in real time instead of downloading it first) audio and video, there are the H.263 video and G.723 audio standards pioneered by Intel. Other Intel technologies that will be incorporated into the Java API are the Indeo video compression scheme, RSX and RDX systems, WAV, MIDI, MPEG, and animation.

The animation API is still extremely fuzzy. Although Intel has promised something, no details are available. There is also some speculation that Macromedia may contribute to the API using concepts created in its Director software. This approach to 2-D animation is incompatible with both the Postcript-style Java 2D and Java 3D APIs. Intel has also promised their Realistic Display miXer (RDX), which uses Microsoft's DirectX technology to provide ultraquick graphics on the Windows platform. However, if Intel is to meet its cross-platform pledge, RDX will have to be implemented on other platforms. It is conceivable, unfortunately, that Intel wants to lock developers and users into the "Wintel" platform, but hopefully they will not attempt this.

Intel's sound technologies will include support for some standard audio formats as well as compression schemes developed by other companies. At the forefront, however, will be Intel's Realistic Sound eXperience (RSX) which allows for 3-D audio, similar to Dolby's Surround Sound. It is not clear whether this technology will be available on non-Windows platforms.

All of these Media API efforts will help Java transcend its currently limited graphics and audio implementations (support for only AU/GIF/JPEG) and allow it to support a wide variety of exciting new technologies.

Availability

Intel's Indeo, RSX, and RDX technologies are all currently available for Microsoft Windows, although no Java implementation has yet been produced. Microsoft's DirectX and ActiveMovie drivers are also available for Windows, but not yet with Java support. None of these companies has given any indication that these technologies will be available for other platforms, although it seems they would have to be in order to provide a true Java API.

Collaboration, Time, and Telephony

These three APIs are still in the planning stages. Lucent Technologies is slated to provide the telephony features of the Media API, which could include such features as an Internet phone as well as local machine telephone operations. Telephony refers to the relatively new technology of merging computer and telephone operation. Lucent has promised support for existing telephony standards by Microsoft, Apple, and others, as well as a new all-Java telephony standard.

Lucent has already shown a demo of a Java conference calling application. The collaboration API, officially called the Java Share API, will allow multiple computers to use a single application simultaneously. This could be used for Internet conferencing, complete with a Java white board.

Another unrelated API that is not yet sponsored by any company is the Java Media Framework, which will be used for Clock and time synchronization features. More information will be posted on the Web as it becomes available.

Availability

All three of these APIs are supposed to have preliminary specifications ready by the end of 1996, but no progress has been shown to the public. Sun is either keeping these under wraps, or they will not be available for some time. Either way, they will certainly not be ready before the fourth quarter of 1996.

Potential Problems

For companies trying to grab ahold of the Java market, the topic of Java Media APIs is a vehicle for maneuvering. While Sun's willingness to collaborate has many advantages, some players have been left out. Some examples: Dimension X has had a fully-working 3-D Java class set for almost a year, yet they were not included in the Java 3-D API discussions. Netscape's Live3D and LiveConnect, while indirectly supported via JavaBeans (see the section on JavaBeans later in the chapter), will probably compete with Java 3D and Intel's audiovisual APIs. Progressive Networks' RealAudio is the most popular Internet streaming audio protocol, yet they were not invited to be a part of the streaming audio API. Microsoft's ActiveX and DirectX technologies, while used somewhat by Intel, are not included in the API discussions. In fact, at the JavaOne conference, Sun seemed to be preparing to directly compete with Microsoft and Netscape. Thus, neither company, although each a major Internet player, was invited to work on the Media APIs.

How will all of this politicking work out? JavaSoft's HotJava is well behind both Netscape's Navigator and Microsoft Internet Explorer, and although it could conceivably overtake Microsoft in the next year, Netscape is well beyond its grasp. So long as this is true we will see plenty of dueling APIs—if Sun and Netscape do not collaborate. This *vying* process has already begun, with the introduction of Netscape's new *Open Networking Environment* (ONE). Netscape's ambitious new platform has support for Java, but could someday conceivably overtake Java's dominance as the best cross-platform development environment.

Java Enterprise APIs

The Java Enterprise APIs will allow Java applications to work together across the Internet, as well as provide connectivity to existing database and application structures. The Enterprise API is made up of three components: *Java Database Connectivity* (JDBC), *Interface Definition Language* (IDL), and *Remote Method Invocation* (RMI). Unlike the Media APIs, these APIs have generated little talk but much progress. Apart from the Core API, they are the furthest along the development path, probably due to the fact that they are being developed in-house by Sun's JavaSoft.

Key features of Java Enterprise APIs include

- Cross-platform database connectivity

- Platform-independent remote application communication

- Remote Java connectivity

Java Database Connectivity (JDBC)

The Java Database Connectivity API is used to give Java programs easy access to any SQL-compatible database. Previously, the only way to connect an existing database to the Web was through a lengthy CGI process or via some third-party proprietary program. JDBC is a fully-functional *Standard Query Language* (SQL) environment that can be connected to almost any relational database. It uses Java classes to represent SQL queries and connections, and allows Java programs to directly access compatible databases.

NOTE　For a more in-depth coverage of Java, databases, and the JDBC, see Chapter 20.

A JDBC application connects to a database using a special piece of *bridge* software that must be provided by the database's creator. This bridge allows Java SQL calls to be mapped to logical SQL calls on the actual data. This works in a similar way as Windows or Macintosh printer drivers work. The OS defines a standard for printers, and each vendor creates a driver that allows its hardware to implement the software OS standard. JDBC is the same, except it only deals with software. Each vendor must find a way to make its database conform to the JDBC standard. Luckily, the JDBC API is written to conform to the SQL specification, which is the current standard for relational database access and is supported by all major database companies.

Immediately following the release of JDBC, many database vendors jumped on the Java bandwagon. Each has promised to provide a bridge for its software and to ensure that its software is totally compatible with JDBC. While the promises have been many, the results have been few. So far, the only bridge available is for Microsoft's ODBC (Open Database Connectivity) standard, which is used to connect Windows applications to relational databases. Other companies, like Trifox, have also come up with interim products that allow SQL access to databases that do not yet support JDBC. Major vendors, like Informix, were *supposed* to have bridges available by July, 1996—so far, none have materialized.

Availability

JDBC 1.0 was released in June of 1996. This is one of the only APIs that is actually ready to be tested by the public. However, if you have a specific relational database that you want to connect to, you will have to wait for the applicable vendor to construct a bridge before you can use the JDBC software provided by JavaSoft. However, if that database supports ODBC, you can access it using the currently existing JDBC-ODBC bridge. But be careful, Microsoft has some pretty hefty licensing fees associated with ODBC. With any luck, most vendors will have native JDBC bridges ready by the end of 1996.

Java Remote Objects APIs— IDL and RMI

The remote objects APIs are designed to allow a Java program to communicate with an object that is not within the same applet/ application space. With these, an object could be a Java class object, or it could be an object written in another language. For instance, say you want to write a client/server program in Java. Currently, the only way to communicate between the two parts of the program (the client and the server) is to open a network connection and send primitive data types or Strings across. While this works pretty well for most applications, it is very inefficient. With IDL or RMI, a Java program can directly access methods in another program. This makes it very easy for programs to communicate over the Internet.

The first of these APIs is used to communicate with objects that conform to the *Interface Definition Language* (IDL) standard. IDL is a standard maintained by the *Object Management Group* (OMG) that encompasses many programs and many languages. The motivation behind creating a Java IDL API is to allow Java programs to communicate with programs already written in other languages without forcing the programmer to rewrite a program to conform to Java's strict native methods declaration. With Java IDL, any program that conforms to the IDL standard is automatically compatible with Java. This will make it easy for many companies to integrate older legacy applications with new Java applications.

Java IDL works by mapping Java calls to IDL modules, similar to the way that JDBC maps Java calls to database functions. To demonstrate this concept, JavaSoft created a voter applet demo that you can view on their web page. The voter applet uses Java IDL to connect a Java applet to an IDL-compatible server written in C++. The server maintains a question, which is displayed to the user by the client applet. When the user votes, the client uses Java IDL to report back that vote to the server, which keeps a running tally of the vote totals for that question. There is also a tabulator applet that uses Java IDL to get the results from the server and display them to the user. Although, in this instance, the server could have been written in Java—which would eliminate the need for IDL—it does illustrate the concept nicely. What if the server was a commercial application written in C++ many years ago? Java IDL allows the programmer to use that legacy application without rewriting it in Java.

To do true client/server networking entirely in Java, you need *Remote Method Invocation* (RMI). The Java RMI API provides Java programs with the capacity to communicate with other Java programs across the Internet. The RMI API also provides for *object serialization*, which allows Java objects to be converted into something called a *byte stream* (a fancy name for data that represents the object it is created for). Once you create a byte stream for a Java object, you can then recreate the identical object on another machine using Java RMI. This is an exciting new development for Java, because it means that not only can you call methods in other programs across the Internet, you can also send objects across intact.

When are these APIs useful? In the above IDL demo, the voting server was written in C++, and could only accept simple input. However, using RMI and object serialization, the server could be written in Java and could accept more complex input from the client. Say, for instance, you want to have each person's "vote" consist of multiple pieces of data, like a survey. Using these APIs, all of this data could then be encapsulated into an object, the object converted into a byte stream, and the stream sent across the Internet to the server. The server could reconstruct the object from the byte stream, and store it, or operate upon it as necessary. Perhaps the object could contain a Date object that would allow the server to know the exact day and time the data was acquired from the user. All of this complex functionality could be created with tremendous ease using Java RMI.

Availability

As of July, 1996, IDL and RMI are both available in alpha2 form direct from Sun. Both APIs have already undergone a public review and are being revised based on public input. Both APIs should be available, at least on some platforms, in final release (1.0) form by the end of 1996.

Java Commerce API

An exciting new part of the World Wide Web is the ability to conduct business over the Internet. Java is at the forefront of this commercial revolution with the Java Commerce API. Also called the *Java Electronic Commerce Framework* (JECF), the Commerce API will bring online commerce to a new level, providing interactive, secure, and easy-to-use applications for consumers. The encryption-style security for the JECF will be provided by the Java Security API (see the section on this API later in the chapter). The JECF will also include support for the new Secure Electronic Transactions (SET) standards being created by Visa, MasterCard, Netscape, and others. The white papers, API overview, and specification are currently available for viewing (see Table 21.1).

Key features of the Java Commerce API include

- Platform independence

- Secure control, storage, and transfer of user information

- Versatility to use multiple transaction protocols

- Seamless integration with existing commerce structures

The Java Commerce API is inordinately complicated. Because of security concerns, the JECF contains many different objects that must interact and authenticate each other to ensure that everything is valid. To the end user, all of this underlying complexity will not be apparent; he or she need merely point and click to engage in secure transactions. For a thorough and complete (if somewhat convoluted) explanation of every last detail of a JECF transaction, see the JavaSoft JECF web pages.

End-User Perspective

When a consumer using a Java-enabled browser chooses to purchase something online using the JECF, they will have to go through several steps. The first is to add the desired items to the user's *shopping cart*. This is the applet that implements the Java Commerce API and is used to gather a list of the items the user wishes to buy. When the user's purchasing selections are complete, the applet loads an appropriate cassette.

A *cassette* is a Java class that implements a specific transaction protocol. Think of each cassette as a specific type of credit card. When you use, say, a Visa card, the transaction must be processed in a certain way and sent to the correct bank. If you try to use American Express at a store that only accepts Visa, you will not be able to buy anything. The same is true of cassettes—each cassette is used to implement a specific payment protocol. A typical user will have many cassettes, probably one for each of his or her credit cards. Cassettes can also be used to access a checking account or even frequent flier mileage.

Next, the user is presented with a *tally applet* that displays all of the goods and services requested. This applet has the task of authenticating the identity of the seller, as well as allowing the user to choose the method of payment (credit card, check, coupon, and so forth). Once the user approves of the purchases, another confirmation page is displayed. However, this page is generated by the JECF itself, and not by the seller; it displays the actual information that the JECF has collected from the seller. If there is any discrepancy between the information displayed previously and the information displayed by the JECF, the user can abort the sale (and probably write a letter of complaint!).

Once the user has confirmed the transaction, it is posted to the pending transaction list, which records information about the transaction while it is happening. If there is any problem with the transaction, this information can be used to abort the transaction and refund any moneys that have changed hands. Once the transaction is completed, it is added to the user's private *registry*, a database of past transactions. This information is kept secure and encrypted, but the user may choose to make the information available to a *service cassette*. These cassettes differ from payment cassettes, though they are also part of the JECF. Service cassettes use the user's registry information to provide other useful services, such as accounting or advertising. The cassette must go through a very lengthy authentication process, and the user may always choose to keep his or her information private. At no point during the transaction is the seller able to see the complete credit card information of the consumer. The seller is only informed of whether the transaction was successful or not.

Developer's Perspective

With the JECF, the numerous stages of authentication and validation that go on behind the scenes are complex, but important. One of the nice features of the JECF, however, is that developers need not know about all of the security layers, because they are implemented automatically by the JECF. All a developer must do is write code that adheres to the Commerce API's standards.

The core component of the JECF is something called the *Java Wallet*. The Wallet is the Java object that holds all of a user's cassettes: payment, service, and others. Each cassette must be *signed* by some authority that vouches for its safety and reliability. Signed cassettes are encrypted and cannot be tampered with without disrupting the digital signature. This assures users that the cassette has no hidden or unexpected behavior.

The next security measure in place for cassettes is its *identity*. Each cassette has a special Identity object assigned to it by the same organization that signed the cassette. The Identity object contains information about what the cassette does and where it came from; this information is presented to the user when appropriate. To prevent another object from "stealing" a cassette's Identity, the JECF makes use of *tickets*. A ticket is the only object allowed to directly access an Identity object, and it can only be used once. When another object wants to learn about a cassette (the shopping cart applet, for example), it must request a ticket from the cassette. The applet can then ask the ticket to retrieve information about the cassette. The important thing to remember is that while a ticket can be created from an Identity, the reverse is not true. Only a certified signing agent can create a bona fide Identity object.

This security measure is extremely important. It prevents scenarios like the following: Say a malicious hacker writes a shopping cart applet that pretends it is selling a real product. The user authorizes his or her MasterCard to be charged with the expenses incurred.

When a cassette implementing a MasterCard protocol is loaded, the shopping applet asks it for its Identity. If the cassette naively passed along the whole Identity object, the applet could clandestinely make an extra copy. In addition to carrying out the user's desired transaction, this malevolent applet could create another cassette based upon the user's MasterCard cassette, and make unauthorized transactions. However, with the ticket scheme, the applet only has indirect access to the information contained in the Identity object, not direct access to the object itself. Furthermore, while the applet can check the validity of the cassette's digital signature, it cannot access a copy of it.

Another layer of security is provided by the *Permit* system. When cassettes want to access protected data, such as the user's registry, they must apply for a Permit from the controlling object. A Permit is dynamically generated by the Wallet for cassettes that must act in a certain *role*. For instance, a cassette with an administration role will be given a Permit to access the registry data once it presents its "credentials," in the form of an encrypted digital signature.

The JECF is actually much more complicated than this, but now you have an understanding of the basics. If you want to know more, you can read documentation for the entire API on the web (see Table 21.1).

Availability

The JECF white paper, API overview, and specification are all available for public viewing now. An early alpha release implementation will be ready by the end of 1996, with full implementation expected in 1997. With any luck, the JECF's long list of corporate sponsors will expedite its completion.

JavaManagement API

The JavaManagement API is designed to allow developers to write software in Java for doing various network management tasks. It also includes tools that make writing network management software easier, and makes the software more efficient. In fact, the majority of the API is not concerned with network management directly. The reason for this is that an API does not actually "do" anything; the programs that implement it accomplish the tasks. Therefore, the JavaManagement API is mainly concerned with giving developers the tools they need to create network management programs.

The API is currently in its very early implementation stages and so detailed information is not available. According to JavaSoft, the JavaManagement API has the following goals:

- Create consistent user interfaces

- Promote code reusability

- Decrease developer learning curve

- Provide secure systems management and software distribution

- Support heterogeneous network environments

The Admin View Module (AVM)

The *Admin View Module* (AVM) is at the core of the JavaManagement API's GUI enhancements. The AVM is an extension of the Java Abstract Windowing Toolkit that adds some pretty impressive looking components designed to aid network management. The first group of base components simply improves upon existing AWT components, and includes such things as the Image Button and Multicolumn Lists. In addition, there are a series of so-called *power* components that add functionality absent from the AWT. Some examples from this group are a Table component, a help subsystem, and a hierarchy viewer. JavaSoft also promises a set of specialized components that are built especially for the JavaManagement User Interface Style Guide. The Style Guide is a not-yet-released part of the API that will help to standardize the user interfaces of network management programs.

JavaManagement Interfaces

Another key part of the JavaManagement API is the collection of interfaces it will add to the Java language. It mainly consists of interfaces designed to implement the JavaManagement model of network management. For instance, the Base Object Interface is used to give developers an abstract way to represent distributed resources on a network. Because of this feature, it seems that the JavaManagement API and the Enterprise APIs will be closely linked. The next set of interfaces, known as the Managed Interfaces, allow for advanced event, protocol, and database handling across a network. The Managed Notification Interface handles network management events, while the Managed Protocol Interface handles secure communications within a network (undoubtedly linked to the Java Security API). The Managed Data Interface will allow the JavaManagement API to link up with the JDBC API.

Another interface that is equally important is the Simple Network Management Protocol (SNMP) Interface. This is actually a series of interfaces that allows for easy integration with existing resources that implement the SNMP, which is currently the standard for network management. This Interface will give Java applications the advantage of being backwards-compatible with existing management structures, and will help the JavaManagement API achieve its goal of supporting heterogeneous networks.

Last, but certainly not least, come the Applet Integration Interfaces. Although details are not yet available, these interfaces will make it possible for developers to incorporate existing and future Java applets (which implement the Core API, but not necessarily the

JavaManagement API) into their management structures. How exactly this is to be accomplished is somewhat vague at this point, but look for it to become a key part of the JavaManagement API once it debuts in the alpha and final stages.

Availability

The only information currently publicly available about the JavaManagement API is an overview of the API. Public availability of the full API has been promised in the third quarter of 1996. Although little public progress has been made, clues that the API may be farther along than anyone is admitting come from several demonstration applets that have been put together by other vendors. Sponsors like 3Com (maker of networking hardware and software) have not only endorsed the JavaManagement API, but have also produced online demonstration applets, worth looking at if you are interested (see Table 21.1).

Java Server API

Code-named "Jeeves," the Java Server API is the server-side counterpart to the Core API. Not only does Jeeves provide for the creation of full-fledged secure Java servers, it also includes a special API for *servlets*, the server-side incarnation of applets. Unfortunately, very little information is yet available on Jeeves. Apart from the Servlet API, no Jeeves material is open for public consumption. Although an alpha version of Jeeves was promised by July of 1996, none has materialized thus far.

Key features of the Java Server API include

- Provision for tiny applet-like programs running on a server

- Easy creation of Java applications that can act as network servers

- Special classes for server administration and installation

- Security integration with Java Security API

Servlet API

Servlets are being billed as the first step towards true Internet agents—programs that roam the Internet in search of specific information and then return to their host to deliver their find. Servlets are like applets that lack a user interface; they are not designed to interact directly with a user. Instead, servlets run on the server machine and process requests delivered by client applets or applications. Although they can act in a similar way as CGI processes, they are in fact far more advanced and complex. They also represent a more efficient way of implementing CGI-like processes.

Servlets work by integrating themselves into a server similar to the way applets integrate themselves into a WWW browser. Although servlets are going to initially be designed to integrate with HTTP Web servers, they can, in theory, be integrated into any server that implements the Java Server API. On HTTP servers, it seems likely that, at first, servlets will be used to replace currently existing CGI processes. The advantage of using a servlet over a CGI script/program is that only one instance of a servlet need be created to handle multiple client requests. In CGI, every time a client makes a request, a new process has to be created and executed. Servlets are also more permanent than CGI scripts, and are thus more versatile. In fact, when a client makes a request that is handled by a servlet, the servlet is not limited to just passing back an HTML page, as a CGI script does.

The key advantage to using a servlet instead of a CGI process is that a servlet can actually communicate with the client over a socket with a custom protocol. This will eliminate much of the inefficiency involved in client/server programs that are not very complicated, such as most multiplayer networked games. Currently, the only way to write such a game is to have a full-fledged Java application running as the server, which is very inefficient. However, if the HTTP server is a Java Server API server, the game server could be written as a simple servlet that would not use up as many resources.

It seems that Netscape was left out of the discussions regarding the Server API. This is unfortunate, because Netscape already has an API for creating server plug-ins that extend a server's capabilities much the same way Java servlets do. In fact, Netscape even has a series of Java classes that can plug in to its Fastrack server to create CGI-like functionality. While this is not as sophisticated as the servlet API, it seems certain to ensure that there will be dueling APIs once both companies start competing for market share. However, it is possible that Netscape and Sun will cooperate and combine their efforts, but, to date, no such announcement has been made regarding servlets.

Availability

Unfortunately, it seems like there will be a substantial wait before anyone gets to see the full Server API. However, preliminary specs on the Servlet API are available and specifications for the entire API should be ready by Autumn of 1996. As for a final implementation, that will take a while longer, probably until the beginning of 1997. JavaSoft should have a working alpha Jeeves release out by the end of 1996.

Java Security API

Very little is available about the security API other than its desired functionality, which is to provide cryptography and authentication services for Java applications. However, since its inception, Java has raised many concerns about security and the potential for malicious applets. Each of the Java APIs, especially those related to business and corporate programs, will have to rely upon security provided by the Java Security API. This has led to much speculation in the Java community as to what sort of protection the Security API can provide. First, a brief history of the Java security discussion...

Java Security Issues

The first serious security flaw in Java's implementation was initially postulated by several members of the Internet community. Almost immediately, a group of researchers working at Princeton University managed to prove the existence of the bug and exploit it. The bug was a hole in both Sun and Netscape's implementation of the Java SecurityManager that allowed applets to make arbitrary socket connections, even across a firewall. This meant that applets could access and act maliciously upon supposedly secure resources. Luckily, once this particular bug was found, both Sun and Netscape provided patches to eliminate it. However, the incident raised serious questions about the safety of using Java.

The solution used to eliminate the arbitrary socket connection vulnerability in Java was to simply forbid an applet from making socket connections to any computer other than the one it originated from. However, this seriously limits the effectiveness of many Java applets. It also makes it nearly impossible to run applets behind a firewall, because most applets must open a socket back to their host to retrieve the necessary class files to run. The new, stricter, SecurityManager will not allow this behind a firewall because it would mean allowing the applet access to the entire Internet (via the proxy server).

Future Solutions

The real solution that is needed will presumably be provided by the Java Security API. Soon, applets will have the capacity to be "signed" by some authority (usually, whoever created them, or some authority such as Veritas or CERT). This digital signature can then be used by the user to decide whether the applet in question is a trusted applet or not. Trusted applets will be allowed to have controlled access to resources (such as arbitrary socket connections) that distrusted applets may not utilize. Of course, it is assumed that users will have ultimate control over what resources any given applet may access.

Digital signatures are accomplished using the public-key/private-key scheme pioneered by Philip Zimmerman's Pretty Good Privacy (PGP) program. The method is the first unbreakable encryption system. Of course, no system can be totally secure, but PGP is the only one that generated a US Government lawsuit (which, although recently dropped, proves that PGP got the attention of *somebody* important). The idea is remarkably simple, yet the implementation is enormously complex. Luckily, you will never have to worry about the implementation and, if the Security API is done right, you will not even have to worry about the idea either. Nevertheless, you ought to know at least a little bit about public-key encryption. If you want to know more, there are plenty of sites on the Internet you can look at.

When you create a PGP key, you actually generate two keys. One key is said to be your *public key*. This key you distribute to other people so they can send messages to you. The catch is that, while people can encrypt messages with your public key, they cannot decrypt those same messages. Only your *private key* can be used to do that. The two keys are mathematically derived based on some very complex random number generators, so one cannot be used to figure out the other. Messages encrypted for "your eyes only" cannot be viewed by anybody else.

How does all this relate to the Java Security API? Well, you probably will not have to know. The Security API will probably make use of Netscape's Secure Sockets Layer (SSL) 3.0, which uses something similar to PGP to create secure socket connections. When you open a secure socket with Java, the Security API will handle all the encryption and decryption for you. However, all of this is still speculation. It is possible that JavaSoft will require developers to keep track of their own digital signatures for use as public keys, or some similar scheme. Only time will tell.

Availability

JavaSoft has promised an API specification by the third quarter of 1996, with prerelease implementation due by the end of 1996, and final implementation due sometime in 1997. If the other APIs are any indication, delays will probably push these dates back a few months. Also, because the cryptography issue is so sensitive, there will probably be at least one conflict with the United States Department of Defense, Justice Department, or National Security Council, all of whom take an active interest in controlling the development and export of cryptographic software.

JavaBeans API

JavaBeans is the code name for an exciting new project at JavaSoft. Its goal is to make it possible to link Java components (such as applets and AWT widgets) to other component-based architectures, such as Microsoft's ActiveX and Netscape's LiveConnect. This will allow Java programs to integrate themselves into non-Java applications, thus extending Java's usefulness. JavaBeans also seeks to make application development easier by allowing components to be linked together in new and interesting ways without having to be rewritten, thus promoting code reusability.

Key features of the JavaBeans API include

- Cross-platform compatibility

- Easy integration with existing platforms

- "Write-once, use anywhere" program development

- Easy intercomponent communication

- Simplified application development

GUI Merging

One of JavaBeans's, objectives is to provide a way to combine GUI elements across platforms. This way, Java programs that are JavaBeans components can integrate themselves seamlessly into existing GUI structures. A good example would be an add-on for an existing program such as Microsoft Word. Using a JavaBeans to ActiveX bridge, a Java program could become a part of Word, actually merging its GUI components with the host program. Similar things could be accomplished with Netscape Navigator or Sun's HotJava, all without rewriting any code.

Component Reuse

Component reuse is an important aspect of JavaBeans. When writing a program using the JavaBeans model, applications are made up of smaller, independent components that interact. When new functionality is to be added, you simply add another component that interacts with the existing ones. Thus, you can reuse the existing application with only minor adjustments. This rescues you from having to rewrite the entire application.

Cross-Platform Compatibility

JavaBeans will be usable on a number of platforms. JavaBeans will support not only operating systems that currently have Java support, but also a number of programs within those operating systems. With JavaBeans, any program can become a container for JavaBeans components by simply conforming to the JavaBeans API. Thus, Java-Beans components will run as well—and will look, feel, and act the same—in Netscape Navigator on a UNIX machine as they will in Claris Works for the Macintosh.

Component Communication

JavaBeans will be able to send and receive Events in any compatible architecture. This will allow JavaBeans components to invoke actions in other non-Java components, as well as be invoked by them. This allows such things as a button-press in a Netscape JavaScript triggering a graph display in a Java applet.

Java Integration

Every aspect of the Java language will be compatible with JavaBeans. Applets, AWT components, and even RMI and IDL objects will all be considered valid "beans" by this API, and thus will allow Java programs to be integrated into other platforms with no additional effort. JavaBeans represents the culmination of all of JavaSoft's API efforts, and will be the glue that keeps the Java language's various pieces together. It will also enable Java to be easily ported to new platforms and environments.

Availability

JavaBeans has been endorsed by dozens of companies. However, due to the complex nature of integrating all of the disparate architectures involved, do not expect any kind of implementation until at least 1997. JavaSoft has promised an API specification by September 1996. The API is currently being developed and reviewed by a group of interested companies. Little is known about this process, but it seems like Sun wants to be sure it has an industry consensus before taking any action on this API. It is unlikely that the full API will be released until they are all satisfied with it. Also, be aware that JavaBeans will probably be renamed once it becomes "official."

Java Embedded API

Another line of products announced at the JavaOne conference was Sun's new chips based on the Java language. These chips will have the advantage of being able to run Java code natively, so they will not need an interpreter. The first chips of this nature will be produced by Sun, although other companies will probably follow with chips of their own (some have even made product announcements already). And to handle this new level of Java hardware, JavaSoft has promised the Java Embedded API, the only API that is actually a subset of the Core API. The Embedded API will contain only the most essential portions of the java.lang, java.util, and java.io packages to run Java programs. GUI, I/O, and networking will be customizable depending on the application the chip will be used for.

Unfortunately, Sun has not yet released any of its picoJava chips, and will not do so until the beginning of 1997. The picoJava line is targeted at applications that currently use microcontrollers and very low-end processors. Later in 1997, Sun will follow with its microJava line, targeted at devices ranging from printers to cellular phones, as well as its ultraJava line, targeted at network computers and advanced

3-D systems. Until Sun and other companies release chips capable of running Java natively, or other chip manufacturers adapt their chips to emulate the Java Virtual Machine, the Java Embedded API will have to wait.

Availability

JavaSoft has promised an API proposal for August 1996. Since there is minimal demand for sub-Core API Java applications, it seems unlikely that JavaSoft will try and make an API available until at least 1997, when Sun's picoJava chip will premier. Final implementation could come much later, depending on how the chips sell and what applications they are used for. Also, other chip makers have promised faster-than-native speeds with emulated Java chips; these may produce tiny chips capable of the whole Core API, or even third-party versions of the Embedded API. Stay tuned.

For More Information...

You can find plenty of information on the new APIs online. Table 21.1 lists Web resources for the nine APIs introduced in this chapter. The table also includes a wide variety of other resources that you may find helpful online. Of course, because of the fluctuating nature of the Internet, many links may be changed or removed without notice. Should you find a needed resource unavailable, head for a search program like Yahoo or Excite; they will help you find another site. They will also help you find sites that are not listed here.

Table 21.1: Online Resources for the Nine New APIs

Core APIs

JavaSoft home page	`http://java.sun.com` `http://www.javasoft.com`
JavaSoft API home page—source for information about all nine APIs	`http://www.javasoft.com/products/apiOverview.html`
JavaOne conference abstracts	`http://www.javasoft.com/javaone/abstracts.html`
Java platform white paper	`http://www.javasoft.com/doc/whitePaper.Platform/` `CreditsPage.doc.html`
Core API documentation	`http://www.javasoft.com/doc/index.html`
Java Developers Kit (JDK)	`http://www.javasoft.com/java.sun.com/products/JDK/` `index.html`

Media APIs

JavaSoft's Java Media API overview	`http://www.javasoft.com/products/` `apiOverview.html#media`
Intel's Media for Java page	`http://www.intel.com/ial/jmedia/`
Lucent Technologies Java telephony support	`http://www.lucent.com/press/0596/` `960528.gba.html`
Netscape's ONE	`http://developer.netscape.com/library/one/` `index.html`
Adobe	`http://www.adobe.com`
Macromedia	`http://www.macromedia.com`
Progressive Networks	`http://www.realaudio.com`
Microsoft's Java pages	`http://www.microsoft.com`
Silicon Graphics	`http://www.sgi.com`

Table 21.1: Online Resources for the Nine New APIs (continued)

Enterprise APIs

JavaSoft's JDBC home page	`http://splash.javasoft.com/jdbc/`
More information about Trifox and its VORTEX for Java product	`http://www.trifox.com`
JavaSoft's demo JDBC applet	`ftp://splash.javasoft.com/pub/DBDiagram.tar.Z`
JDBC API documentation pages	`http://splash.javasoft.com/jdbc/html/Package-java.sql.html`
List of vendors who support JDBC	`http://splash.javasoft.com/jdbc/jdbc.vendors.html`
JavaSoft's Java Remote Objects page	`http://splash.javasoft.com/pages/intro.html`
JavaSoft's RMI and object serialization page	`http://chatsubo.javasoft.com/current`
JavaSoft's IDL page	`http://splash.javasoft.com/JavaIDL/pages/index.html`
JavaSoft's voting IDL demo	`http://splash.javasoft.com/JavaIDL/pages/idl-demo-voting.html`
Other IDL demos	`http://splash.javasoft.com/JavaIDL/pages/demos.html`
The Object Management Group (OMG)	`http://www.omg.org`
Object Serialization	`http://chatsubo.javasoft.com/current/serial/index.html`
Remote Method Invocation	`http://chatsubo.javasoft.com/current/rmi/index.html`
Java RMI Frequently Asked Questions	`http://chatsubo.javasoft.com/current/faq.html`

Table 21.1: Online Resources for the Nine New APIs (continued)

Commerce API

Main JECF page	`http://www.javasoft.com/products/commerce/`
JECF inquiry e-mail address	`commerce@java.sun.com`
JECF white paper	`http://www.javasoft.com/products/commerce/` `doc.white_paper.html`
Postscript slides presented at JavaOne	`http://www.javasoft.com/products/commerce/` `doc.javaone_slides.ps`
Netscape SET pages	`http://home.netscape.com/newsref/pr/` `newsrelease91.html`

Java Management APIs

JavaSoft's JavaManagement API page	`http://java.sun.com/products/JavaManagement/`
JavaManagement API overview	`http://java.sun.com/products/JavaManagement/` `profile.html`
3Com's demo pages	`http://www.3com.com/0files/mktg/ads/sun/` `index.html`
JavaSoft's demo pages	`http://java.sun.com/products/JavaManagement/` `predemo.html`
Cisco Systems Management Over Java Objects (MOJO—not related to Penumbra Software's product) demo	`http://www.cisco.com/warp/public/734/General/` `java.html`

Java Server API

Jeeves home page	`http://java.sun.com/products/jeeves/`
Java Servlet API specs	`http://java.sun.com/products/jeeves/api/index.html`
JavaSoft's Jeeves contact e-mail	`jeeves@goa.eng.sun.com`
Mail to developer community interested in Jeeves	`jeeves-interest@java.sun.com`

Table 21.1: Online Resources for the Nine New APIs (continued)

Java Server API

Jeeves mailing list	To subscribe, send mail to `listserv@java.sun.com` and put `subscribe jeeves-announce your real name` `subscribe jeeves-interest your real name` in the body
Mailing list with announce-ments about Jeeves	`jeeves-announce`
Mailing list for Jeeves discussion	`jeeves-interest`
Netscape's Fastrack Java API	`http://home.netscape.com/comprod/server_central/support/fasttrack_man/programs.htm#1007954`
The rest of Netscape's Fastrack documentation	`http://home.netscape.com/comprod/server_central/support/fasttrack_man/index.html`

Java Security API

JavaSoft's Java Security API overview	`http://www.javasoft.com/products/apiOverview.html#security`
Steve Gibbons' Java security page	`http://www.aztech.net/~steve/java/`
Computer Emergency Response Team (CERT) coor-dination center home page	`http://www.cert.org`
CERT security advisory on Java (advisory CA-96.05)	`ftp://info.cert.org/pub/cert_advisories/CA-96.05.java_applet_security_mgr`
Princeton researchers who discovered Java security breach and their demonstrated exploit	`http://www.cs.princeton.edu/sip` `http://www.cs.princeton.edu/sip/java-faq.html`
Eric Williams' Java security page	`http://www.sky.net/~williams/java/javasec.html`
Good index of Java security info	`http://ferret.lmh.ox.ac.uk/~david/java/bugs/index.html`
JavaSoft Security FAQ	`http://java.sun.com/sfaq/`

Table 21.1: Online Resources for the Nine New APIs (continued)

JavaBeans API

JavaSoft's JavaBeans page	`http://splash.javasoft.com/beans/`
JavaBeans press release	`http://splash.javasoft.com/beans/press-release.html`
JavaBeans White Paper	`http://splash.javasoft.com/beans/WhitePaper.html`
JavaBeans Overview Talk from JavaOne	`http://splash.javasoft.com/beans/talk.pdf`
Borland's BAJA Event Model for JavaBeans Announcement	`http://www.borland.com/internet/press/1996/bajabe.html`

Java Embedded API

Embedded section of JavaSoft's API page	`http://www.javasoft.com/products/apiOverview.html#embedded`
Sun's Java processors introduction page	`http://www.eu.sun.com/sparc/java/`
Java processing white paper	`http://www.eu.sun.com/sparc/whitepapers/wp96-043.html`

APPENDIX

A

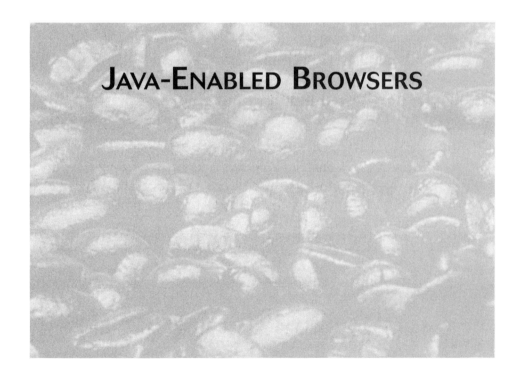

JAVA-ENABLED BROWSERS

This appendix shows you how to use a Java-enabled browser and introduces you to three of the most important Java-enabled browsers in the industry.

Java support is becoming a must-have feature in the Web browser marketplace, and competition is fierce among companies that develop browsers to deliver the fastest, most reliable virtual machine. Unfortunately, this has prompted software companies to release browsers as public beta tests, before they have been completely debugged. Now that the race to add Java JIT support to the latest browsers is winding down, expect browser vendors to concentrate on resolving the quality and compliance problems.

Most browser development companies are releasing their browser software for free in order to take market share. You can download the browsers discussed in this appendix from the respective manufacturer's Web site.

Using a Java-Enabled Browser

Currently, Java-enabled browsers run on every popular hardware/software platform with the noticeable exception of Windows 3.1. Table A.1 lists the Java-enabled browsers and indicates which platforms are supported by each.

Table A.1: Browser Support for Java by Platform

Browser	Win 95	Win NT	Win 3.1	MacOS PowerMac	MacOS 68K	Unix	Other
IBM WebExplorer	✔		Planned				✔ OS/2
Microsoft Internet Explorer 3.0 Beta 2	✔	✔					
Netscape Navigator 3.0 Beta 5	✔	✔	Planned	✔	✔	✔ AIX, Digital Unix, HP/UX, IRIX, Linux, Solaris 1 & 2	✔ OSF/1
Oracle Power Browser 1.5	✔						
Sun HotJava Pre-Beta 1	✔	✔				✔ Solaris 2	✔ JavaOS*

Information current as of July 1996

*As yet, JavaOS has not been released.

Once a Java-enabled browser has been correctly configured, you do not need to do anything special to view Java applets. They simply appear in the browser window as part of the Web page. However, Java applets can create their own floating applet windows, and may send output to a Java console.

Applet Windows

Applets always use part of the browser client area, but they can also create floating windows. These windows often appear with a note or warning at the bottom indicating that the window was created by an applet, as shown in Figure A.1.

A floating applet window

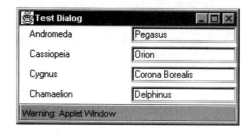

Despite the warning, such windows can be part of the normal behavior of a Java applet. The warning keeps the applet from pretending to be a non-applet window, such as an operating system dialog box or username/password request.

The Java Console

Java-enabled browsers typically provide a console window to display standard output from the applet or applets running in the browser. When you call `System.out.println()` to print to standard output, the resulting text appears in the console window.

The console's primary function is to determine why an applet fails to execute properly. If an exception is thrown that is not caught by the applet, a stack trace is usually printed to the Java console. One of the most common exceptions that you will see on the console is the `SecurityException`, thrown when an applet violates the security policy of the browser. Some applets also use the console to print copyright or version information.

Figure A.2 shows Netscape Navigator's Java console window. To illustrate console use, a "hostile applet" was created that deliberately tries to connect to a network server in violation of the standard security policy. The standard policy allows the browser to connect only with the server from which the applet was loaded. This applet immediately generates a security exception and generates a stack trace in Navigator's console window.

WARNING   Netscape Navigator's console window does not pop up automatically to tell you that an error has occurred. Also, any hostile applet can catch security exceptions, thereby preventing you from seeing any attempts to bypass security. The reason for this is that even trustworthy applets can generate security exceptions in certain situations.

FIGURE A.2:

Netscape Navigator's Java console window

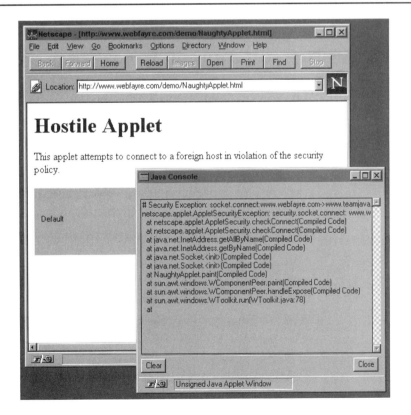

Internet Explorer does not have a console, but instead keeps a log file.

Configuring Java

In today's browser market, competition is fierce, and companies rush their Java implementations to market before the software is bug-free. Performance is a big selling point, but the biggest problem with current browsers is compliance with Java standards, not speed. The Java Core API as specified by Sun Microsystems is supposed to be implemented correctly in every browser. Weaker implementations of the virtual machine and the Core API may cause the browser to crash, or may have security holes that put data at risk, and for this reason, not all users see Java support as an enhancement. This has prompted browser developers to put switches into the browser configuration options that enable and disable Java features.

In some environments, it is desirable to eliminate every possible security risk, and this means deactivating the Java capability of the Web browser. Java-enabled browsers incorporate a switch to enable and disable Java support. Since it is virtually impossible to prove that a virtual machine is totally secure, enabling Java is a gamble that the browser's developer will find any security flaws before the hackers or malfeasants do. These risks are probably extremely small, but when the stakes are high, it's best to disable Java and play it safe. The Java-enabling dialog box in Microsoft Internet Explorer is shown in Figure A.3.

Some of the newest Web browsers have JIT compilers built into them. These JIT compilers can also be turned on and off. In some cases, the JIT compiler may be less reliable than the standard interpreter or cause something to run slower, and the JIT may need to be disabled to run certain applets.

FIGURE A.3:

The Java-enabling dialog box in Microsoft Internet Explorer

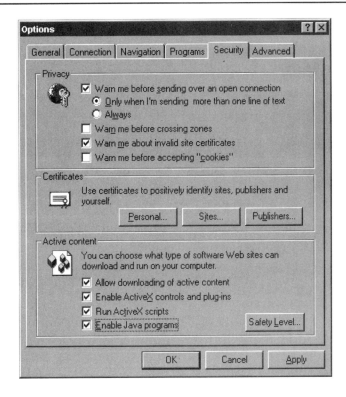

Browser Case Studies

We have selected three of the most popular Java-enabled browsers to examine in more detail: Sun's HotJava, Netscape's Navigator, and Microsoft's Internet Explorer.

The browsers reviewed here include prerelease versions that are still a little rough around the edges. Only Netscape Navigator 2.02 has been solidly tested to conform to Java standards, so Navigator 2.02 will run almost all Java applets securely.

The browser industry is moving so fast that by the time you read this, some of the details may have changed. Use these case studies to get a feel for the differences you may find across browsers, and for a preview of upcoming features.

HotJava

Sun Microsystems's HotJava was the first Java-enabled browser. In fact, HotJava is written entirely in Java, and is testimony to Java's performance and flexibility. The current release of HotJava is pre-Beta 1, so the software has a long way to go before it is ready for prime time. Not surprisingly, this pre-beta release supports only primitive HTML tags, has a rather rudimentary setup program, and renders HTML documents somewhat poorly. However, HotJava incorporates some excellent innovations in terms of browser control; for example, to set browser options, HotJava displays what appear to be Web pages instead of dialog boxes. Sun is positioning HotJava as a new development tool for networked applications, rather than a conventional browser. This means Sun will supply the browser with additional APIs to create an easier way to create Java-based applications. These libraries will include the classes necessary to handle HTML content just as a Web browser would. HotJava will also run on Sun's new JavaOS operating system. HotJava pre-Beta 1 is shown in Figure A.4.

HotJava runs Java applets very quickly for an interpreter, although at this writing, HotJava does not have a JIT compiler.

HotJava can be found at JavaSoft's Web site, `http://java.sun.com`.

Netscape Navigator

Netscape Communications's Navigator browsers lead in market share, and as shown in Table A.1, are implemented on more platforms than any other Java-enabled browser. For some time, Navigator 2.0 was the only Java-enabled browser, and it has been

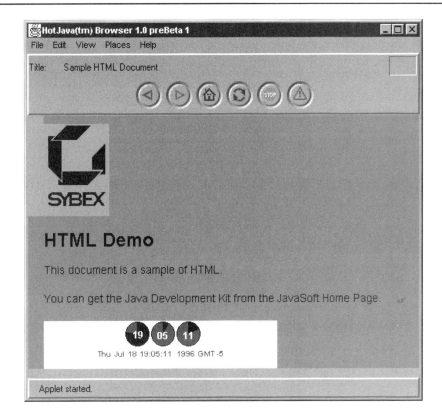

quite thoroughly tested. Most of the bugs and security flaws were fixed (or at least cataloged), making Netscape 2.02 the most compliant Java-enabled browser. Netscape's latest version, 3.0 Beta 5 (see Figure A.5), includes a JIT compiler for speedier calculations, but the overall stability of its Java support is significantly weaker than 2.02. This is to be expected with a beta release, and users who rely on Java will probably stick with version 2.02 until the final version of Navigator 3.0 is released.

FIGURE A.5:

Netscape Navigator 3.0
Beta 5

Navigator can be found at Netscape's home page,
http://home.netscape.com.

Microsoft Internet Explorer

Microsoft's Web browser has only very recently caught up with
Netscape's Navigator in terms of features. In terms of Java performance, Internet Explorer 3.0 Beta 2 (see Figure A.6) is slightly faster,

but its Java support is new and unproven. As in the case of Netscape Navigator's latest beta, expect Java support to be more firm when the release version becomes available.

FIGURE A.6:

Microsoft Internet Explorer 3.0 Beta 2

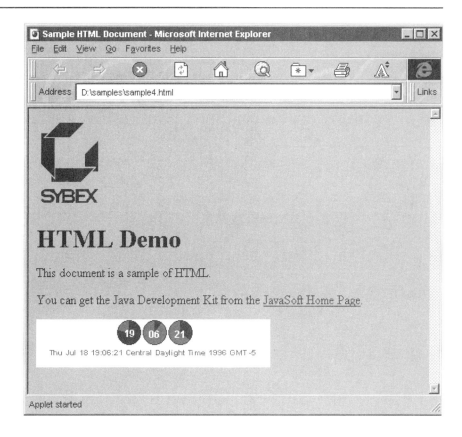

FIGURE A.6:

Microsoft Internet Explorer 3.0 Beta 2

Instead of a Java console, Microsoft Internet Explorer 3.0 Beta 2 sends standard output to a log file named `c:\windows\msjava.log`. Both logging and JIT compilation can be switched on and off via the Advanced Options dialog box (Figure A.7).

Internet Explorer can be downloaded freely from Microsoft's Web page, http://www.microsoft.com.

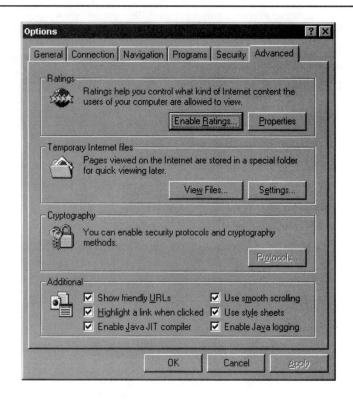

APPENDIX

B

ABOUT THE CD-ROM

The *Mastering Java* CD-ROM is designed for easy access to all source code and executable files from the book; it also contains versions of many of the most popular Java Integrated Development Environments (IDEs) and other third-party tools to use with Java Versions 1.0 and 1.1.

To view the HTML files located on the disk, you will need to use a Java-enabled Web browser, such as Netscape 3.0, Microsoft Internet Explorer, or HotJava. If you do not have an HTML browser, the CD-ROM is set up for you to easily find the directories you need with Windows Explorer or a similiar file management program.

Using an HTML Browser with the CD-ROM

If you have an HTML browser, click the `readme.htm` file to find all the code and examples from the book, which are arranged by chapter. You can also get to the chapter files by going into the `MasteringJava` folder and clicking the `Index.htm` file. Additionally, you will find a full list of products and vendors, along with links to their Web sites.

Installing CD-ROM Files onto Your Hard Drive

To install the *Mastering Java* source code and executable files from the CD-ROM, click on the `install.bat` file in the `MasteringJava` folder. This program will automatically copy the files onto your c: drive. Use your file management program to copy the files to any other drive.

The Chapter folders int he `MasteringJava` folder contain three types of files: `.java`, `.class`, and `.html`.

The `.java` files are the source code from the book.

The `.class` files are the javac-compiled code. These can only be run from an HTML browser or from a Java command line.

The `.html` files run the Java applets via a Web browser.

Installing the Tools

The CD-ROM accompanying *Mastering Java* contains versions of many of the cutting-edge Java tools available on the market today. Each IDE and third-party tool is located in its own folder; for example, Penumbra's Visual IDE, Mojo, is located in the `Mojo` folder, which contains the executable file to install the program. Most vendors have also provided their own `readme.txt` files for additional product information.

The installation instructions may vary slightly, depending on the product. The following sections list the installation proceduresby product. These instructions also appear on the CD-ROM itself, and can be found in the `INSTALLINFO.TXT` files contained in each vendor's folder; for more information visit any of the following Web sites, which are also accessible directly from the `readme.html` file.

JDK

The CD-ROM contains a full version of Sun's JDK version 1.0.2, which lets you write applets that conform to the 1.0 Java applet API and contains

- Java Applet Upgrade Utility

- Java Applet Viewer

- Java Debugger API and Prototype Debugger

- Java Compiler

- Java Interpreter

- Applets

To install the JDK version 1.0.2 onto your hard drive, go to the `jdk` folder and click on `install.bat`. For more information, visit Sun's Web site at `http://www.java.sun.com`.

Jamba

Jamba is a new authoring software tool that enables Internet developers, creative professionals, and Webmasters to create interactive, media-rich Java applets and applications without programming or scripting. Built on industry-standard object-oriented software technology and Sun's Java, Jamba meets the growing demand for easy-to-use tools that enhance the interactivity of a company's Internet efforts.

To install Jamba's beta trial version from the CD-ROM, go to the `Jamba` folder and click on `jambatrl.exe`. Once installed, the trial version is valid for 30 days or 100 uses, whichever comes first. For more information, visit the Jamba Web site at `http://www.aimtech.com`.

Mojo

Penumbra's Mojo is a complete development environment for programmers using the Java language to create networking applets. Mojo consists of two primary components: a GUI Designer that provides a visual means for building Java applets, and a Coder that organizes Java objects and gives the user direct access to all aspects of code. The Mojo Designer is designed for non-programmers who wish to enter the domain of Java programming with the smallest possible learning curve. Although the emphasis is on non-programmers, experienced programmers will benefit from use of Mojo in its reuse of components and easy extensibility.

The CD-ROM contains the release version 1.2 evaluation copy of Mojo. This version will expire in 30 days from installation, after which certain features will be disabled, such as saving. To install the evaluation copy of Mojo, go to the `Mojo` folder and click on `setup.exe`. For more information, visit the Mojo Web site at `http://www.penumbrasoftware.com`.

Hyperwire

Kinetix's Hyperwire, from Autodesk, offers a powerful visual authoring environment to designers and programmers who want to create Java-based titles for the World Wide Web. Hyperwire gives users an intuitive, icon-based environment for building titles that can be distributed over the Web and company Intranets, or viewed in Java-enabled browsers. With Hyperwire, you can create interactive marketing sites, product or workflow simulations, training applications, online games, books, and financial applications. You can design titles that change over time, or update in real time as information streams from the Web.

The CD-ROM contains the Sneak Peek 2 version of the software; to install, click on `Hyperwire.exe`. This is a timed-out version, that will expire on March 15, 1997. You'll need Microsoft's WinG to run Hyperwire, so if you don't already have it installed on your computer, go to the Hyperwire Web site to download it: `http://www.ktx.com/products/hyperwire`.

ED for Windows

ED for Windows, from Soft As It Gets, was one of the first complete and comprehensive Java development environments to hit the market. ED's powerful editing capabilities will make writing code a snap. Templates, smartype, autocorrection, and code completion will write code for you. The Java browser lets you see your complete class and method hierarchy at a glance. With ED's code navigation features, you can move around your classes and methods at the touch of key.

To install the trial version of ED for Windows 3.55 available on the CD-ROM, go to the `SoftAsItGets` folder and click on `edw355g9.exe`. This timed-out version will expire 45 days after it is installed onto your system. For more information, visit the Soft As It Gets Web site at `http://www.getsoft.com`.

JDesignerPro

JDesignerPro, from BulletProof Corp., is a system for building simple, intuitive, yet powerful Java database front ends. JDP gives you a way to quickly make active database applications in Java.

To install JDesignerPro from the CD-ROM, go to the `JDP` folder and click on `jdp090.exe`. Since JDesignerPro is a database design tool used to create Intranet and Web server front ends, the installation information required is unique to your particular Internet/Intranet environment.

For successful installation of JDesignerPro, make sure you do the following:

- Your Web server IP number is required. Get this number from your Internet Service Provider and enter it at the IP number prompt.

- Enter the name of the directory where your Web server stores its main HTML and CGI files at the prompt.

- Enter the name of the directory containing the Sun's JDK Version 1.0.2 and its `.class` files. This will vary depending on the installation procedure you used for the JDK.

Because JDesignerPro requires information specific to your particular setup, SYBEX Inc. will not be able to direct you in matters related to this installation. For more information, we suggest you consult your system administrator and/or the JDesignerPro Web site at `http://www.bulletproof.com`.

Widgets

Widgets™, from Connect! Quick, is a library of sophisticated, pre-built components for assembling commercial-quality Java applications. The product is written entirely in Java and has the same look, feel, and behavior on all Java-enabled environments, including Windows, Mac, and Unix.

To install Widgets, go to the `Connect! Quick` folder and click on `Widgets.exe`. For more information, visit the Connect! Quick Web site at `http://www.connectcorp.com`.

WebXpresso

The WebXpresso plug-in, from DataViews Corporation, marks a major technological advancement for graphics on the Internet. The plug-in makes it possible for Internet and Intranet users to view interactive object-oriented 3-D graphics online, as opposed to the traditional static raster formats currently associated with Internet use.

To install WebXpresso demonstration program from the CD-ROM, go to the `WebXpresso` folder and click on `setup.exe`. For more information, visit the WebXpresso Web site at `http://www.dvcorp.com/webxpresso/index.html`.

CyberAgent

FTP Software's CyberAgents™ are autonomous, agile, and adaptive mobile Java applications that are pushed into networked systems to perform delegated tasks on behalf of the sender. Traveling from desktop to desktop, they execute remotely, gather data, make decisions, take corrective actions, and report results. Moreover, they can work collaboratively and initiate or terminate other processes.

To install the 30-day evaluation version of CyberAgent 2.0, go to the `CyberAgent` folder and click on `setup.exe`. For more information, visit the CyberAgent Web site at `http://www.ftp.com`.

FutureTense Texture

FutureTense Texture™ is a revolutionary system that brings unprecedented control over page layout and functionality to Web page designers. For publishers, Texture provides a truly efficient way to create enticing content for the Web, while faithfully retaining the unique graphic character that defines a publication.

To install the 30-day trial version, go to the `FutureTense` folder and click on `Designer.exe`. For more information, visit the FutureTense Web site at `http://www.futuretense.com`.

A P P E N D I X

C

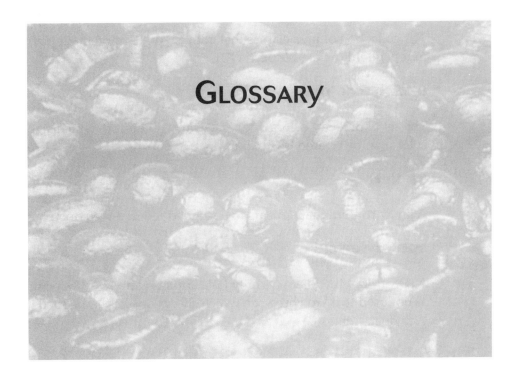

GLOSSARY

abstract

Retaining the essential features of some thing, process, or structure. The opposite of *concrete*.

abstract class

A class that contains abstract methods. Abstract classes cannot be instantiated.

abstract function

A function that is declared but not implemented. Abstract functions are used to ensure that subclasses implement the function.

Abstract Windowing Toolkit (AWT)

The collection of Java classes that allows you to implement platform-independent (hence, *abstract*) GUIs.

additive colors

The set of primary colors (red, green, and blue) from which all other colors can be created by mixing.

applet

A Java program that appears to be embedded in a Web document.

appletviewer

A JDK utility that displays only Java applets from HTML documents, as opposed to a Web browser, which shows applets embedded in Web documents.

Application Programming Interface (API)

A set of methods, functions, classes, or libraries provided by a language or operating system to help application developers write applications without having to reinvent low-level functions. All of the standard Java packages combined form the Java Core API.

array

A group of variables of the same type that can be referenced by a common name. An array is an object with length as its public data member holding the size of the array. It can be initialized by a list of comma-separated expressions surrounded by curly braces.

atomic

Indivisable or uninterruptable. In the context of multithreading, an operation (statement, code block, or even an entire method) that cannot be interrupted. Code that accesses composite data structures shared with other threads usually has to protect its critical sections by making them atomic.

autocommit

A method to turn off and on transaction processing. When autocommit is off, transactions can be undone using the `rollback()` method, or the database can be updated using the `commit()` method. When autocommit is on, transactions are automatically committed after each statement.

base class

The base class for a set of classes is the superclass from which each class in the set inherits members.

big-endian

An internal ordering of data bytes in memory. Big-endian ordering is also called *network ordering*. In the big-endian ordering, high bytes of a word are stored first in memory; for example, 0x1234 will be stored in memory as 0x12 0x34 (the big end comes first). RISC and Motorola processors use the big-endian byte ordering, while the Intel 80x86 processors use the little-endian byte ordering. In the little-endian ordering, the word will be stored as 0x34 0x12 in memory (the little end comes first).

black box

The concept of a functional entity whose internals are wholly irrelevant. A black box is characterized by the type of inputs it takes, the type of outputs produced, and the circumstances under which these outputs are generated (that is, the black box function).

blitting

To BLIT (BLock Image Transfer). In graphical systems, the high-speed, rectangular copy operations often performed by dedicated accelerator hardware. Moving a window, scrolling a window's contents, and rendering text are some typical examples that rely heavily on blitting.

booleans

Variables that can only assume the values `true` or `false`. Booleans can be used to represent things that have a binary state; for example, alive/dead, connected/disconnected, same/not the same, open/closed, and so forth.

break statement

One of the flow-breaking statements. Without a label, control will be transferred to the statement just after the innermost enclosing loop or switch statement. With a label, control will be transferred to the enclosing statement or block of statements carrying the same label.

buffer

In the narrow sense, an amount of storage set aside to temporarily hold and/or accumulate some information (write and read [disk] buffers, frame buffers). In the wider sense, any decoupling system that desynchronizes two entities—that is, lets them run at their own speed or frequency.

bytecode verifier

Part of Java's security precautions, the bytecode verifier checks that the bytecodes can be executed safely by the virtual machine.

bytecodes

Compiled Java code. Bytecodes are portable instructions that can be executed by any Java Virtual Machine.

Call Level Interface (CLI)

An interface to perform SQL calls to databases. A CLI consists of method calls to the database that return values and ResultSets. The SQL statement is embedded in the calls. For example, the call `execute` takes the SQL string as a string parameter.

cartridges

Oracle's name for software modules encapsulating business logic to be added to Oracle's Web Server system. Intercartridge APIs enable communication between different cartridge modules.

case clause

A part of a switch statement. It consists of the case keyword, followed by a constant expression, a colon, and one or more statements. See *switch statement*.

class

A description of a specific kind of Java object, including the instructions that are particular to it.

class file

A binary file containing Java bytecodes. The Java compiler generates a class file from source code for each Java class.

class library

A collection of prefabricated classes which the programmer can use to build applications more rapidly. Java's class library is the Core API. In Java, these are also called *packages*.

class loader

The part of the virtual machine that fetches classes from the client file system or from across the network.

class variable

A variable within a class that is available for use by the class itself. Only one copy of the variable exists, and the class variable is unique to all instances of the class within the program.

client

An entity that relies on another (*server*) entity to accomplish some goal. Clients can be as simple as classes calling on other classes or (more frequently) client programs calling on server programs across a network.

client/server application model

An application model commonly employed in networked environments. The monolithic application program is split into two halves; one half running on the server machine, the other running on the client machines. The client/server model is used as a solution in multiuser systems where central resources have to be shared/changed/consulted by many.

Common Gateway Interface (CGI)

Common Gateway Interface is a standard interface between Web servers and other server programs. The server programs are usually used to process database requests and generate HTML documents on the fly.

compiler

A utility that reads the commands in a source file, interprets each command, and creates a new file containing equivalent bytecodes (or, in the case of a C compiler, creates a file with native machine code instructions).

concrete

Opposite of *abstract*.

conditional statement

A statement for selective execution of program segments, such as the `if` and `switch` statements.

constructor

A *method* that creates an instance of the class to which it belongs.

continue statement

One of the flow-breaking statements. Without a label, control will be transferred to the point right after the last statement in the enclosing loop body. With a label, control will be transferred to the end of the enclosing loop body carrying the same label.

convolve filter

Type of image-processing filter that combines the pixels located around a central pixel to form the new central pixel. Different weights are assigned to each neighbor in a 3×3 matrix. The resulting pixel is the weighted average of all pixels.

critical section

In the context of multithreaded systems, any section of code that needs to take precautions to avoid corrupting data structures shared with other threads.

data hiding

The ability to hide data within a class. Any changes to the hidden data from outside the class, if permitted at all, must be via *methods*.

datagram

A type of packet that represents an entire communication. No connection or disconnection stages are needed to communicate by datagrams. It is analogous to sending a telegram.

debugger

A utility that can monitor and suspend execution of a program so that the state of the running program can be examined.

decoupling

The avoidance of a direct link between two entities by inserting a third entity (an interface, a buffer, or a whole subsystem). Decoupling introduces an extra level of flexibility for the price of a slight reduction in performance. A hallmark of a well-designed software system is the loose coupling between its subsystems (achieved by a multitude of decoupling techniques).

default clause

An optional part of a switch statement. It consists of the default keyword, followed by a colon, and one or more statements. See *switch statement*.

default constructor

A constructor that is automatically available to a class that does not define its own constructor.

design

A reusable, standard approach to a design problem. This is different from algorithms in that design patterns address higher-level issues and usually describe solutions in structural/relational terms.

destructor

A method that is called to delete an object from memory. Java does not directly support destructors.

dial-up connection

An Internet connection that needs to be established by having a leaf machine dial a modem connected to a host that is connected to the Internet 24 hours a day.

disassembler

A utility that displays the meaning of instructions in a compiled file. The Java disassembler (javap) shows you what the Java Virtual Machine will do when it runs a class file of bytecodes.

do statements

One of the loop statements. The loop body is executed once, and then the conditional expression is evaluated. If it evaluates to `true`, the loop body is reexecuted and the conditional expression retested. It will be repeated until the conditional expression evaluates to `false`.

documentation comment

A comment block that will be used by javadoc to create documentation.

Domain Name System (DNS)

A distributed Internet database that can resolve textual Internet addresses to their real numeric forms. The DNS is organized as a hierarchy with each node responsible for a subset of the Internet host address namespace.

double buffering

In general, the use of two buffers to allow one buffer to be constructed while the other is being used. Double buffering is used in animation to display one animation frame while the next is being drawn off-screen.

Double buffering can also be used in the context of I/O logic to decouple the algorithm's performance from the performance limits of the I/O device (called being *I/O-bound*).

dynamic loadable library

An executable library module, usually in binary form as an external file, that will be loaded during the run time of a program on an as-needed basis. In the Windows platform, this is called a *DLL*.

else clause

An optional clause for an `if` statement. If the conditional expression of an `if` statement is evaluated to `false`, the statement or block of statements of the `else` clause will be executed.

encapsulation

Embedding both data and code into a single entity.

finalizer

A method that is called immediately before a class is garbage collected.

flow-breaking statement

A statement for breaking sequential program flow. These include break, continue, and return statements.

flow-control statement

A statement for flow control. These include conditional, loop, and flow-breaking statements.

flushing

Final writing of any output data left in a write buffer. Closing files or streams flush their data buffers automatically (this is one of the reasons to close files or streams).

for statement

One of the loop statements. The initialization part is executed, followed by the evaluation of the conditional expression. If the expression evaluates to `true`, the loop body is executed, followed by the execution of the increment part. This cycle is repeated until the conditional expression evaluates to `false`.

fractal

In graphics, a recursively self-similar structure of infinite complexity. Contradictory to their definition, fractals can often be generated by very simple, finite equations or algorithms.

frame

In the context of GUIs, the graphical outline of a window. In the context of data communications, another word for *packet*.

frame header

The collection of fields at the start of a frame that contain nonuser data necessary for the fluent and efficient operation of the protocol. A typical frame header field is the checksum field that allows a receiver to check whether received data arrived as sent.

frame rate

Frequency at which new images are displayed in animation sequences or film. Typical rates range from 24Hz to 60Hz.

File Transfer Protocol (FTP)

The Internet protocol that allows you to download publicly accessible files from any Internet machine that accepts FTP connections. FTP also allows you to transfer files from your machine to another machine on the Internet.

Gamelan

The most comprehensive online source for Java tools and applets. Its URL is http://www.gamelan.com.

garbage collection

A feature of automatic memory management that discards unused blocks of memory, freeing the memory for new storage.

Graphics Interchange Format (GIF)

A standard format for storing compressed images.

Graphical User Interface (GUI)

The mouse-driven, iconic interface for modern computer operating systems. Also called *Windows Icons Menus and Pointer (WIMP)* interface.

Human-Computer Interface (HCI)

A broad concept comprising the physical and nonphysical interaction between people and computers. Ergonomics is a physical facet of HCI. GUI design is a (mainly) nonphysical aspect of HCI.

Hypertext Markup Language (HTML)

The language in which Web documents are written. Java applets appear embedded in HTML documents.

Hypertext Transfer Protocol (HTTP)

The application protocol used by the World Wide Web for requesting, transmitting, and receiving Web documents.

if statement

One of the two types of conditional statements. It consists of the `if` keyword, followed by a conditional expression enclosed in a pair of parenthesis and a statement (or block of statements) to be executed when the conditional expression evaluates to `true`. It may be followed by an optional `else` clause consisting of the `else` keyword and a statement (or block of statements) to be executed when the conditional expression evaluates to `false`.

image filtering

The process of altering (generally improving) a digital image. This can be as simple as changing a picture's overall brightness or as complicated as applying an optical correction to minimize a flaw in the physical optics of the device that made the picture (as was done with the Hubble telescope, for instance).

inheritance

The ability to write a class that inherits the member variables and member functions (or *methods*) of another class.

instance

An instance of a class; in other words, an *object*.

instance variable

A variable within a class, a new copy of which is available for storage in each instance of that class. Each object of that class has its own copy of the instance variable. (This is as opposed to a *class variable*.)

instantiation

The process of creating an object instance of a class.

Integrated Development and Debugging Environment (IDDE)

The same as an *Integrated Development Environment* (*IDE*) but with built-in debugging features; IDDE programs include Sun's Java WorkShop and Symantec's Café.

Integrated Development Environment (IDE)

A program that aids in application development by providing a graphical environment that combines all tools required to write code.

interface

A formal set of method and constant declarations. The methods must be defined by classes that implement it.

Interface Definition Language (IDL)

A system that enables Java programs to communicate with CORBA systems.

Internet Architecture Board (IAB)

One of the Internet standards bodies that applies the final technical review to any new proposed Internet standard (in the form of Request For Comments [RFCs]).

Internet Protocol (IP)

The core Internet protocol on which all other application-level Internet protocols build. Some of the counterintuitive characteristics of IP are that it does not guarantee delivery of data and that it can only transfer data in maximum 64K chunks.

Internet Service Provider (ISP)

An organization (commercial or not) that allows you to hook your machine up to the Internet via a permanent or dial-up connection.

interpreter

A utility that reads the commands in a file, then interprets and executes each command one at a time.

Java Core API

Java's built-in class library. It contains core language features and functions for such things as networking, I/O, and graphics.

Java Database Connectivity (JDBC)

Defines a set of Java classes and methods to interface with databases.

Java Developers Kit (JDK)

The set of Java development tools distributed (for free) by Sun Microsystems. The JDK consists mainly of the Core API classes (including their source), a Java compiler (written in Java), and the Java Virtual Machine (JVM) interpreter.

Java Virtual Machine (JVM)

The system that loads, verifies, and executes Java bytecodes.

JPEG

A compressed graphics file format. JPEG images may be compressed in a "lossy" fashion that sacrifices image detail for smaller image size, or a "lossless" method, where information about the image is retained, but the file size increases accordingly.

Just-In-Time (JIT) Compiler

Converts verified bytecodes to native processor instructions before execution and can significantly improve Java application performance.

loop statement

A statement for the repeated execution of program segments. These include `for`, `while`, and `do` statements.

marshalling

The process of assembling and disassembling parameters to and from remote objects and methods is collectively called *marshalling* and *unmarshalling* the parameters.

member

The generic term for data or code entities within a class.

member function

See *method*.

member variable

A variable that is part of a class.

message

A method call.

MetaData

A JDBC object that contains a description of the underlying database-related object.

method

A function or routine which is part of a class. Also called a *member function*.

microJava

A medium-end Sun microchip that runs Java natively.

multidimensional array

An array of arrays. It can be nonrectangular. A multidimensional array can be initialized by grouping comma-separated expressions with nested curly braces.

multiple inheritance

The ability to write a class that inherits the member variables and methods (member functions) of more than one class. See *inheritance*.

Multipurpose Internet Mail Extensions (MIME)

Extension to the standard Internet e-mail format to allow the inclusion (as file attachments) of content other than plain text. It is typically used for the newer multimedia types like audio/video clips, but is generally capable of handling any binary file format.

multithreading

The means to perform multiple tasks independent of each other.

namespace

A set of rules allowing the generation of valid names or labels. The e-mail address syntax, US state number license plate format, and global telephone numbering systems all define namespaces. *Namespace* also means the boundaries that can be accessed by a program. The operating system (or the Java Virtual Machine) defines the namespace for a program.

namespace partitioning

A set of rules to structure a *namespace*. The Java package namespace partitioning rules structure the namespace into a collection of non-overlapping trees.

nesting

The Russian doll–effect of repeatedly wrapping or layering entities around other entities. In GUI design, widgets are often nested in container widgets that are themselves nested in bigger containers, and so on.

Network News Transfer Protocol (NNTP)

The Internet protocol behind the newsgroup reading programs. NNTP manages daily threads of discussion in some 15,000 "news" groups, such as `comp.lang.java`.

null

A value that can be held by an object variable that means *no object*.

object

A software "thing" that has characteristics (*state*) and behavior (*methods*).

object pointer

In C++ and Delphi, an object variable that points to a specific memory location.

object variable

A name for an object. It may refer to an object or be null.

octet

Another word for the eight-bit byte. Used only in the data communications world.

opcode

Short name for *operation code*. It is an integer representing the code for an operation.

overloaded functions

Functions defined multiple times, each definition having the same name, but accepting different parameters, either in number or type. The compiler knows which function to call based on the parameters it is passed.

package

A collection of related classes.

packet

A unit of communication. A packet can contain mostly user data, or it can be a pure protocol management packet (that is, containing no user data whatsoever).

packet-switched

A type of Web-structured (as opposed to star- or ring-structured) data communications network that uses datagram packets as its building block packet type. Examples are the global X.25 packet-switching network and the Internet.

parent class

See *superclass*.

persistent object stores

Database-independent, object-oriented storage systems for storing various types of objects, such as video, audio, and graphics.

picoJava

Low-end Sun microchip that runs the Java language.

pipes

Abstract data connections between (typically) two processes or threads. Process A writes data to process B via a pipe. Process B needs to read the data from the pipe to receive any data.

polymorphism

The ability of a single function name to be used to operate on many different types.

Post Office Protocol (POP)

The Internet protocol that handles e-mail collection.

protocol

The set of rules and the structures of legal packets that are used to provide some communication service between two computers. Common examples are TCP/IP, Z-Modem, Kermit, SLIP, PPP, X.25, and IBM SNA.

Rapid Application Development (RAD)

A kind of development tool that enables programmers to create sophisticated programs quickly.

recursive

Self-calling. A recursive method calls itself repeatedly, either directly or indirectly. See *recursive*.

registers

Known areas in a microprocessor for keeping small pieces of information like a pointer to the next instruction, the results of an addition, and so forth. Usually registers are in the microprocessor and can be accessed much faster than memory.

Remote Method Invocation (RMI)

The set of APIs for a Java program to call objects and methods that reside outside the current runtime environment or namespace.

rendering

Computer graphics jargon for drawing (used as both a verb and a noun).

request and response headers

Terms used to denote the ASCII-readable multiline headers of the HTTP protocol. The HTTP protocol consists of client (browser) requests followed by Web server (site) responses.

ResultSet

The most common operations on a database are queries that return data. This data, which consists of many rows and columns, is called a ResultSet.

return statement

One of the flow-breaking statements. It is used to return control to the caller from within a method or constructor. Before the control is passed back to the caller, all of the `finally` clauses of the enclosing `try` statements are executed, from the innermost `finally` clause to the outermost one.

root class

In general, any class that acts as the superclass for a subhierarchy. An entire inheritance hierarchy, like Java's, has a single absolute root class: class `Object`.

router

A device in a packet-switched network that can accept packets and decide to which of its many output ports it should forward the packet to bring the packet a step closer to its final destination.

schema

A description of data elements in a database and their relationships. Primarily used by database designers, developers, and administrators.

SecurityManager

A Java class that restricts access to files, the network, or other parts of the system for security purposes.

server

An entity whose sole purpose is to serve clients (either sequentially or in parallel) by providing them with some kind of well-defined service (for example, searching a database, accepting mail messages, manipulating rectangles).

servlet

Mini server-side programs, similar to applets, defined in the Java Server API.

signature

A method's unique profile, consisting of its name, argument list, and return type. If two methods with the same name have the slightest difference in argument list, they are considered totally unrelated as far as the compiler is concerned.

signed classes

Classes and applets that can be traced to the company who developed them. This is achieved by keeping a tamperproof electronic signature in the `.class` file. The technology for this scheme is in development.

Simple Mail Transfer Protocol (SMTP)

The Internet protocol behind e-mail delivery. See also *Post Office Protocol (POP)*.

sink

The final destination for data moving through a stream. See also *source*.

source

The origin of data moving through a stream. See also *sink*.

source file

A text file containing human-readable instructions. A Java source file is a text file written in the Java programming language.

state

An unambiguous, non-overlapping mode of "being"; for example, the binary states *on* and *off*.

streaming

Term used to denote audio, video, and other Internet content that is distributed in real time and does not have to be downloaded.

subclass

A class that descends or inherits (extends in Java terminology) from a given class. Subclasses are always more specialized than the classes they inherit from.

superclass

A class from which a given class inherits. This can be its immediate parent class, or can be more levels away. Superclasses become more and more generic as you travel up the inheritance hierarchy, and for this reason, can often be abstract.

switch statement

A multiway selection statement. The integer expression is evaluated, and the first case clause whose constant expression evaluated to the same value is executed. The optional default clause is executed if there is no case clause matching the value. The `break` statement is usually used as the last statement of a case clause so that the control will not continue on to statements of the next case clause.

Telephony

Applications that combine telecommunications and multimedia computer technologies.

transaction processing

A general term used in the context of databases to denote, among other things, consistency, recoverability, and data integrity of relational databases. A transaction consists of multiple SQL commands that read and update databases.

Transmission Control Protocol (TCP)

The connection-oriented protocol built on top of the Internet Protocol. TCP guarantees delivery of data and can handle arbitrary amounts of data.

Tubular Data Stream (TDS)

A type of data set from a database, usually relational, that has rows and columns of data.

Uniform Resource Locator (URL)

A string that identifies the location of a resource and the protocol used to access it.

unmarshalling

See *marshalling*.

untrusted applets

Applets downloaded from a network whose source cannot be traced or trusted. They have restricted access control and do not have unrestricted system access.These applets have to be verified before they are executed, as they could contain malicious virus programs.

User Datagram Protocol (UDP)

Protocol between Internet Protocol and Transmission Control Protocol. Allows IP-style datagrams to be sent to a port on a machine (instead of just a machine).

Virtual Machine

See *Java Virtual Machine (JVM)*.

Web browser

A viewer program used by the client machine to display Web documents.

Web server

A network server that, upon request, transmits Web documents via HTTP.

Web site

A set of Web documents belonging to a particular organization. A Web site may share a server machine with other sites, or may extend across several machines.

while statements

One of the loop statements. The conditional expression is first evaluated. If it evaluates to `true`, the loop body is executed, and the conditional expression is reevaluated. It will cycle through the testing of the conditional expression and the execution of the loop body until the conditional expression evaluates to `false`.

widgets

Window Gadgets. This is the generic term for GUI elements like buttons, scrollbars, radio buttons, text input fields, and so on.

Windows Icons Menus and Pointer (WIMP)

See *Graphical User Interface (GUI)*.

World Wide Web (WWW)

A huge collection of interconnected hypertext documents on the Internet.

INDEX

Note to the Reader: Throughout this index **boldface** page numbers indicate primary discussions of a topic. *Italic* page numbers indicate illustrations.

B

(

D

E

F

G

I

K

M

N

U

V

Java™ Binary Code License

Sun grants to you ("Licensee") a non-exclusive, non-transferable license to use the Java binary code versions (hereafter, "Binary Software") without fee. Licensee may distribute the Binary Software to third parties provided that the copyright notice and this statement appear on all copies. Licensee agrees that the copyright notice and this statement will appear on all copies of the software, packaging, and documentation or portions thereof.

In the event Licensee creates additional classes or otherwise extends the Applet Application Programming Interface (AAPI), Licensee will publish the specifications for such extensions to the AAPI for use by third-party developers of Java-based software, in connection with Licensee's commercial distribution of the Binary Software.

Licensee may not distribute the Binary Software in any tangible media distribution that lacks substantial added value, or by using any Sun Microsystems trademarks, logos, or other brand identity, except as provided in the Java Trademark Guidelines at `http://java.sun.com/trademarks.html`. Licensee may distribute the Binary Software online via descriptive FTP downloading links or instruction headlines, e.g., "Download Sun's Java™ Developers Kit."

Licensee acknowledges that Sun owns all Java-related trademarks, logos, and icons ("Java Marks") and agrees to: (1) not use Java Marks in the names of Internet domains or businesses, or of applets, applications, implementations, ports, or other products developed with or from the Binary Software ("Apps"); (2) not use Java-related logos or icons in Apps, Web pages, or marketing materials, except as may be authorized separately in the form of the Java Compatible or Java Powered logos; (3) follow the Java Trademark Guidelines; (4) not do anything harmful to or inconsistent with Sun's rights in the Java Marks; and (5) assist Sun in protecting those rights, including assigning to Sun any rights acquired by Licensee in any Java Mark.

RESTRICTED RIGHTS: Use, duplication, or disclosure by the government is subject to the restrictions as set forth in subparagraph (c) (1) (ii) of the Rights in Technical Data and Computer Software Clause as DFARS 252.227-7013 and FAR 52.227-19.

SUN MAKES NO REPRESENTATIONS OR WARRANTIES ABOUT THE SUITABILITY OF THE BINARY SOFTWARE, EITHER EXPRESS OR IMPLIED, INCLUDING BUT NOT LIMITED TO THE IMPLIED WARRANTIES OF MERCHANTABILITY, FITNESS FOR A PARTICULAR PURPOSE, OR NON-INFRINGEMENT. SUN SHALL NOT BE LIABLE FOR ANY DAMAGES SUFFERED BY LICENSEE AS A RESULT OF USING, MODIFYING, OR DISTRIBUTING THE BINARY SOFTWARE OR ITS DERIVATIVES.

By using or copying this Binary Software, Licensee agrees to abide by the intellectual property laws, and all other applicable laws of the U.S., and the terms of this license. Ownership of the software shall remain solely in Sun Microsystems, Inc.

Sun shall have the right to terminate this license immediately by written notice upon Licensee's breach of, or non-compliance with, any of its terms. Licensee shall be liable for any infringement or damages resulting from Licensee's failure to abide by the terms of this license.

WHAT'S ON THE CD-ROM

This companion CD-ROM contains all the source code and executable files from the book, plus numerous cutting-edge Java Integrated Development Environments (IDEs) and third-party tools to use with Java versions 1.0 and 1.1.

Products you will find on this CD include

- **JDK Version 1.0.2**, the full development package from Sun Microsystems, Inc. for creating Java applications and applets.

- **Jamba**, a new authoring tool from Aimtech, enables Internet developers and Webmasters to create interactive, media-rich Java applets and applications without programming or scripting.

- **Mojo**, from Penumbra Software, is a complete development environment for creating networking applets. Mojo consists of a GUI Designer and a Coder.

- **Hyperwire**, from Autodesk, is a powerful visual authoring tool that gives designers and programmers an intuitive, icon-based environment for building titles for distribution on the Web and Intranets.

- **ED for Windows**, from Soft As It Gets, is a complete Java development environment that offers powerful editing capabilities and code navigation features.

- **JDesignerPro**, from BulletProof Corp., is a system for building simple, intuitive, yet powerful Java database front ends.

- **Widgets**™, from Connect! Quick, is a library of sophisticated, prebuilt components for assembling commercial-quality Java applications.

- **WebXpresso**, a plug-in from DataViews Corporation, allows Internet and Intranet users to view interactive object-oriented 3-D graphics online, as opposed to the traditional static raster formats.

- **CyberAgents**™ are autonomous, agile, and adaptive mobile Java applications from FTP Software, which are pushed into networked systems to perform delegated tasks.

- **FutureTense Texture**™ brings unprecedented control over page layout and functionality to Web designers and provides an efficient way to create enticing content.

The JDK Version 1.0.2 on this CD is the complete product from Sun Microsystems, Inc. The other products are fully functioning trial versions or demos that will time out after 30–45 days of use. Details about each product's capabilities, along with specific installation instructions, are located in Appendix B.